Language and Literacy

Content and Teaching Strategies

SEVENTH CANADIAN EDITION

Pearson

Tompkins | Bright | Winsor

EDITORIAL DIRECTOR: Claudine O'Donnell	**PERMISSIONS PROJECT MANAGER:** Shruti Jamadagni
ACQUISITIONS EDITOR: Kimberley Veevers	**PHOTO PERMISSIONS RESEARCH:** Integra Publishing Services
MARKETING MANAGER: Michelle Bish	**TEXT PERMISSIONS RESEARCH:** Integra Publishing Services
PROGRAM MANAGER: John Polanszky	**INTERIOR DESIGNER:** Alex Li
PROJECT MANAGER: Susan Johnson	**COVER DESIGNER:** Alex Li
MANAGER OF CONTENT DEVELOPMENT: Suzanne Schaan	**COVER IMAGE:** Abstract/Shutterstock
DEVELOPMENTAL EDITOR: Cheryl Finch	**VICE-PRESIDENT, CROSS MEDIA AND PUBLISHING SERVICES:**
PRODUCTION SERVICES: Cenveo® Publisher Services	Gary Bennett

Pearson Canada Inc., 26 Prince Andrew Place, Don Mills, Ontario M3C 2T8.

978-0-13-409589-9

3 2020

Library and Archives Canada Cataloguing in Publication

Tompkins, Gail E.,
[Language arts]
   Language and literacy : content and teaching strategies/Gail E. Tompkins
(California State University, Fresno), Robin M. Bright (University of Lethbridge),
Pamela J.T. Winsor (University of Lethbridge). -- 7th Canadian edition.

Revision of: Language arts : content and teaching strategies/Gail E. Tompkins,
   California State University, Fresno, Robin M. Bright, University of Lethbridge,
   Pamela J.T. Winsor, University of Lethbridge. -- Sixth Canadian edition. -- Toronto:
   Pearson, 2013.

Includes bibliographical references and index.
ISBN 978-0-13-409589-9 (paperback)

   1. Language arts (Elementary). I. Bright, Robin, 1957-, author II. Winsor, Pamela
J. T., author III. Title. IV. Title: Language arts.

LB1576.T64 2016   **372.6'044**   **C2016-904492-0**

To Linda and John Cooke, who are always there for me
—Gail E. Tompkins

To the children in classrooms, the teachers, and the student teachers
who inspire and challenge us to write, research, and teach
—Robin M. Bright, Pamela J. T. Winsor

Brief Contents

Contents

Preface

Teachers who help students grow into literacy and learn to communicate effectively are cognizant of the complexities of those processes. They are also very aware of the cultural and linguistic diversity the students present in their classrooms. Further, technological advances both enhance and transform the nature of language learning and teaching.

It is our intent with this seventh Canadian edition of *Language and Literacy: Content and Teaching Strategies* to provide a useful resource for teachers as they meet the challenges of literacy instruction in today's classrooms. Both pre-service and in-service teachers will find this text a valuable addition to their professional libraries. For pre-service teachers who will work with students in kindergarten through grade 8, the text offers a consistent model of instruction that will help them become knowledgeable about language learning and guide the many instructional decisions they will make. For experienced in-service teachers, the text provides a rich array of strategies and ideas that they can adapt to suit their personal instructional styles. For all, it offers extensive suggestions of high quality literature for children and young adults, among them, many Canadian titles.

The seventh Canadian edition of *Language and Literacy* is a significant revision of a popular core text designed for elementary and middle-school language and literacy courses.

Philosophy of the Text

The philosophy of *Language and Literacy* reflects a constructivist approach to teaching and learning. The processes of reading and writing provide the foundation for the instructional approaches presented: resource-based units, theme study units, inquiry-based units, and readers and writers workshops. Such timeless, research-based approaches to teaching share these important features:

- Establishing a community of learners
- Using exemplary children's and young adult literature
- Involving students in meaningful, functional, and genuine activities and decision making
- Engaging students with new literacies through digital technologies
- Teaching skills and strategies in context
- Integrating instruction and assessment

Goal of the Text

The goal of *Language and Literacy* is to present the nature of language and language learning together with the most effective strategies for teaching the language arts. The text is organized into three parts. The first two chapters present an overview of learning and teaching the language arts. The middle chapters describe the content and teaching strategies that represent research-based best practices for learning and assessment. The final chapter demonstrates how to create a variety of field-tested literacy instructional plans.

Throughout the text, five features are presented to enhance readers' understanding. At the beginning of each chapter, *To Guide Your Reading* sets out goals for reading. The points listed give readers an overview of essential information and guide them in assessing their mastery of chapter content after reading. *Step by Step* informational textboxes show readers the sequential steps in applying teaching strategies that have been described within the preceding text. Collectively, the panels provide a syllabus of the teaching strategies included in the text. *Minilessons* draw attention to specific information concerning broad topics such as reading and writing stories. They list relevant procedures, concepts, strategies, and skills. *Teachers Notebook* textboxes enrich selected topics presented more generally within the chapter text. They expand upon salient aspects of topics by offering detailed information and in many instances offer examples of instructional applications of the information. Finally, the fourth feature, *Differentiating to Meet the Needs of Every Student,* offers readers possible ways to adjust instruction to address the ever-present variations among classroom learners. Suggestions included in this feature show both how to enrich and how to simplify instructional practices. Although each type of textbox is distinctive one from the other, together they guide, elaborate, and extend the topical information of each chapter.

The seventh Canadian edition continues to recognize the importance of the Canadian context for teaching language and literacy in schools, in addition to the valuable role that teachers play in offering effective literacy instruction. This edition also acknowledges the availability of digital technologies in students' lives and provides literacy practices that help learners access, analyze, evaluate, and make use of those expanded technologies.

Highlights and Features of the Seventh Canadian Edition

- New "Literacy in Action" teacher stories before each chapter highlight effective literacy practice in Canadian classrooms.

- New literacies and critical literacy are included in Chapter 1 with reference to literacy practices, such as digital storytelling, blogging, and other online activities.

- New content on viewing and visually representing strengthens the visual literacy component of the book. Teaching and learning activities relating to these specific paired skills have also been added.

- New Canadian research and new culturally diverse Canadian literature and resources have been added, with specific attention to a new genre of literature referred to as *narrative nonfiction* or *creative nonfiction*.

- New resources have been added in the area of integrating the fine arts into literacy programs.

- Content is drawn from across Canada. The work of Canadian researchers is noted and examples are drawn from Canadian classrooms.

- New and extended ideas are offered for differentiating instruction to meet the needs of every student, especially English language learners.

- Lists of exemplary literature have been updated, including a vast array of Canadian children's and young adult literature.

- More information on integrating communication technology into language and literacy classroom programs has been incorporated throughout the book. Specifically, attention is paid to the important relationship between the *foundational literacies* we have always taught in schools (reading, writing, listening, speaking, viewing, and visually representing) and the *new literacies* (navigating websites, using multimedia for communication, synthesizing information, and critically evaluating online resources) required to take advantage of communicating online.

- To Guide Your Reading helps instructors and student teachers set learning goals for the reading of each chapter.

- Step by Step makes clear the sequential steps in employing each of the many instructional strategies described throughout the text.

- Minilessons show readers the procedures, concepts, strategies, and skills encompassed in topics critical to comprehensive language arts instruction.

- Teacher's Notebook offers readers essential background and examples of classroom applications of concepts salient to research-based instruction.

- Differentiating to Meet the Needs of Every Student guides readers to understand how classroom instruction can be varied to meet the instructional needs of diverse learners.

- The Glossary is extensive and provides useful definitions of terms throughout the book.

Instructor Resources

The following instructor supplements are available for downloading from a password-protected section of Pearson Canada's online catalogue (catalogue.pearsoned.ca). Navigate to your book's catalogue page to view a list of those supplements that are available. See your local sales representative for details and access.

- **Instructor's Manual**

  The Instructor's Manual contains a wealth of resources for instructors, including chapter overviews, outlines, teaching suggestions, and further readings. A very practical resource, the Instructor's Manual will help teachers create engaging lesson plans and an environment of literacy for their students.

- **Test Item File**

  This test bank in Microsoft Word format contains a complete series of fill-in-the-blank, true/false, multiple choice, short-answer, and application questions, which will enable teachers to create interesting and meaningful student assessments.

- **Learning Solutions Managers**

  Pearson's Learning Solutions Managers work with faculty and campus course designers to ensure that Pearson technology products, assessment tools, and online course materials are tailored to meet your specific needs. This highly qualified team is dedicated to helping schools take full advantage of a wide range of educational resources, by assisting in the integration of a variety of instructional materials and media formats. Your local Pearson Education sales representative can provide you with more details on this service program.

Acknowledgments

First, we would like to thank the experienced staff from the University of Lethbridge Curriculum Laboratory and Bookstore, whose knowledge of children's and teachers' resources continues to amaze and delight us. They were instrumental in helping us identify high-quality literature to include in this text.

Second, we would like to thank the instructors who have provided invaluable reviewer feedback over the years.

Furthermore, we want to thank the teachers who shared their practices presented in the chapter-opening Literacy in Action vignettes:

Daniel Buchanan, Calgary, Alberta

Jessica Currie, Ottawa, Ontario

Linda Pierce Picciotto, Vancouver, British Columbia

Samantha Wishewan, Sherwood Park, Alberta

Lisa Jensen, Lethbridge, Alberta

Grace Chan, Toronto, Ontario

Dawn King-Hunter, Lethbridge, Alberta

Janice Beland, Yellowknife, Northwest Territories

Kati Devlin, Winnipeg, Manitoba

Heidi Jardine-Stoddart, Quispamsis, New Brunswick

Cheryl Miller, Picture Butte, Alberta

Our appreciation is also extended to the children who provided writing samples, pictures, and photographs that appear in this edition of the text. Finally, thanks go to Kimberley Veevers, Michelle Bish, and John Polanszky from Pearson Canada, and to developmental editor Cheryl Finch, production editor Dipika Rungta and copy editor Joel Gladstone. They have worked diligently with us to make this seventh Canadian edition of *Language and Literacy: Content and Teaching Strategies* a reality.

About the Authors

Gail E. Tompkins I'm a teacher, first and foremost. I began my career as a first-grade teacher in Virginia in the 1970s. I remember one first grader who cried as the first day of school was ending. When I tried to comfort him, he sobbed accusingly, "I came to first grade to learn to read and write and you forgot to teach me." I've never forgotten that child's comment and what it taught me: teachers must understand their students and meet their expectations.

My first few years of teaching left me with more questions than answers, and I wanted to become a more effective teacher, so I started taking graduate courses. In time I earned a master's degree and then a doctorate in reading/language arts, both from Virginia Tech. Through my graduate studies, I learned a lot of answers, but more important, I learned to keep asking questions.

Then I began teaching at the university level. First I taught at Miami University in Ohio, then at the University of Oklahoma, and finally at California State University, Fresno. I've taught pre-service teachers and practising teachers working on master's degrees, and I've directed doctoral dissertations. I've received awards for my teaching, including the Provost's Award for Excellence in Teaching at California State University, Fresno, and I was inducted into the California Reading Association's Reading Hall of Fame. Throughout the years, my students have taught me as much as I taught them. I'm grateful to all of them for what I've learned.

I've been writing college textbooks for more than twenty years, and I think of the books I write as teaching, too. I'll be teaching you as you read this text.

When I'm not teaching, I like to make quilts, and piecing together a quilt is a lot like planning effective language arts instruction. Instead of cloth, teachers use the patterns of practice and other instructional procedures to design instruction for the diverse students in today's classrooms.

Robin M. Bright is a professor in the Faculty of Education at the University of Lethbridge. She teaches courses to undergraduate and graduate students in the areas of language and literacy, children's and young adult literature, reading, writing, and gender. Previously, Robin taught elementary school for ten years. Robin has long been committed to teaching wherever literacy and teaching education are relevant. Unique in her approach as an educator, Robin models for preservice teachers sound pedagogy, curriculum knowledge, and collaborative research; her leadership extends beyond the classroom and the University into school communities, across the province, and the country. She received both the Excellence in Teaching Award from the Alberta Ministry of Education and the Distinguished Teaching Award from the University of Lethbridge. She also served as Board of Governor's Teaching Chair for the University of Lethbridge.

Robin is the author of several books including *Writing Instruction in the Intermediate Grades: What Is Said, What Is Done, What Is Understood* (International Reading Association, 1995); *Write from the Start: Writers Workshop in the Primary Grades* (Portage & Main, 2001); *Write Through the Grades: Teaching Writing in the Secondary School* (Portage & Main, 2007); the co-author of *From Your Child's Teacher: Helping a*

Child Learn to Read, Write and Speak (FP Hendriks, 1998); and has written numerous articles on learning to read and write. Her work has appeared in the *Journal of Reading Education, Canadian Children, the Canadian Journal of English Language Arts, Alberta English, The Writing Teacher, English Quarterly,* and the *Journal of Teacher Education,* and she twice received the *Journal Article of the Year* for research that appeared in International Reading Association-refereed journals. Robin values the opportunity to work with student teachers and teachers through professional development activities related to meeting the varied literacy needs and interests of Canadian children.

Pamela J. T. Winsor is professor emerita from the Faculty of Education at the University of Lethbridge. She taught graduate and undergraduate courses in language education with a focus on early literacy, literacy in elementary classrooms, and literacy across curriculum. She was a supervisor and mentor of student teachers at both beginning and advanced levels of their field experiences.

Pamela regularly presented at local, national, and international conferences on topics related to early literacy development and associated classroom practices. She also shared with teachers and students her enthusiasm for making global children's literature a dynamic part of young readers' experiences with literature. Her work concerning literacy, literature, and teacher education extends internationally. She is currently a volunteer consultant to Reading Kenya, a teacher education project sponsored by CODE that focuses on helping teachers increase their capacity to offer effective early literacy instruction. Kenyan teachers have given her the Masai name, Naisola, meaning the best. In the past, she has participated in educational development projects in Belize, South Africa, Kosovo, Sierra Leone, and Ghana.

A strong believer in a symbiotic relationship between research and teaching practice, she recently developed a global micro-library as a teaching resource and a way of bringing the world to classrooms through multicultural literature. She is the author of Language Experience Approach to Literacy for Children Learning English (Portage & Main, 2009) as well as several articles. Her work has appeared in The Reading Teacher, Journal of Reading, Alberta English, Teaching Exceptional Children, and the Journal of Teacher Education.

Literacy in Action

Chapter 1: Integrating Digital Photography and Life Writing in a Multi-modal Literacy Project

Procedure

The Hope Project has been a favourite for a few years, although it changes from year to year. A major component of the humanities curriculum is constructing and sharing multi-modal life writing texts. By providing space for students to write and share their personal narratives we build a community based on empathy and understanding. Each year, the students' widely differing cultural and linguistic backgrounds, family origins, interests, talents, and ambitions enrich our learning community.

Through the integration of photography, writing, design, and frame construction, the Hope Project's multiple layers of meaning provide students with opportunities to be successful.

I begin the project by showing students a video entitled, *What if Money Were No Object*, a recorded speech by Alan Watts. The central message urges attending to what gives passion in life; what inspires and gives hope. After viewing the video, I ask students the question: "What is hope?" As students give their suggestions, one student records them on the interactive whiteboard. Students offer multiple definitions such as, "It's what gets you up in the morning".

We come to a general understanding that Hope means something different to each person. We then brainstorm ideas from our own lives that give us hope. I present my ideas. I include sports I love playing, the names of my daughters and wife, and ways of being, such as selflessness. When students have a list of ideas, I ask them to circle their top choices to write about. This year, I circled my daughter's name, Holly. I asked the class to watch while I wrote a first draft of my Hope Writing, noting that I was limiting myself to five minutes because this was the first draft. Students watched and read as I wrote about how Holly gives me Hope. When I finished writing, I read it aloud being sure not to correct any mistakes. In draft writing, I want students to focus on their thoughts and feelings, not how to spell or organize a paragraph. I then ask students to write for five minutes about their circled ideas. I collected first drafts and read through each one carefully, circling strong ideas and posing questions that might provoke more insight.

The following day, I returned the first drafts, asked students to read my comments and questions, then gave students 15 minutes to construct second drafts. Limited time helps students attend to the most necessary specifics. On subsequent days, they strive to polish their writing.

On the third day, I asked our school's digital photography teacher to give a lesson on specific "rules" of photography, including leading lines, the rule of thirds, and focal points. To hone their photography skills, the students completed a photography scavenger hunt. In 60 minutes, they were to take photos, upload, and share them on Google Drive. We viewed each class member's portfolio, highlighted strong photos, and made suggestions to enhance others.

Later, I asked students to take a photo related to their Hope writing. The photo had to pair with, and enhance, the meaning of their written text.

In Industrial Arts, the students were creating wooden frames and matting for their Hope photos. They were asked to select key thematic words and phrases from their writing to decorate the edges of their frames. The photos, in their frames, were showcased next to the students' writing in our school's foyer. Each year, we come to value each other and the ways that multi-modal communication helps us learn together.

Assessment

To ensure success, we begin by breaking the assignment into individual components: the writing, the photo, and the frame. After looking at exemplars of past students' work, we brainstorm the indicators of success and develop a draft rubric. I then complete the rubric. From the rubric, we create a checklist of hints to follow when writing, taking photos, and building frames.

Each draft students write gives me an opportunity for assessment and students room for revision. We also spend time looking at and assessing each other's photos and frames. Students use the rubric to make suggestions to their peers.

Adaptation

Students learn quickly that no writing is ever truly completed and that different media can change the writing greatly. When I have asked students "How can we enhance this writing even more?" or "What can we do next?", students often suggest digitizing their stories using available recording devices to create a different experiences for their audience. Some of the digital stories they create are quite breathtaking.

For lower grades, I use the same overall strategies, but focus on a less abstract concept than hope. I read *The Best Part of Me* by Wendy Ewald (2002), and invite students to create works similar to the black and white photos and writing in the book.

Reflection

My goal in Humanities is to design learning tasks through which students understand themselves and their peers more deeply; that they come to consider others in relation to themselves; and contemplate their understanding can ultimately bring about progressive change. By pairing a traditional literacy—writing—with the crafting of a frame and the capturing of a meaningful photo, students come to see themselves as capable of constructing multi-modal complex projects.

From the classroom of Daniel Buchanan, Grades 5 and 6 Humanities Teacher
Simon Fraser Middle School
Calgary, AB

Learning and the Language Arts

Marmaduke St. John/Alamy Stock Photo

LEARNING OUTCOMES

After you read this chapter you should be able to:

1. Explain how children learn

2. Explain the roles of language, culture, and technology in learning

3. Describe how critical literacy affects learning language and learning through language

4. Describe how multiliteracies are important to using technology effectively

5. List and define the six language arts

During their class "Family Literacy Evening" students proudly share their writing about the exemplary books they have been reading. Their writing includes titles, authors, opinions, reflections, and recommendations. This strategy encourages the students to share their reading with each other.

Teachers face new challenges and opportunities every day. The students who come to Canadian classrooms bring with them widely variant cultural and linguistic backgrounds and life experiences. Teachers are teaching and students are learning in diverse environments, rich in possibilities. In these environments, teachers are decision makers. They are empowered with both the obligation and the responsibility to make curricular decisions to meet student needs. In the language and literacy program, these curricular decisions have an impact on the content (information being taught), the teaching strategies (techniques), and the resources (literature, print, digital, and other materials). To make such decisions effectively, teachers draw upon foundational research and understandings concerning how children learn, as well as current insights about instruction and appropriate, high quality resources. When teachers embrace the challenges and opportunities presented in diverse classrooms, everyone benefits.

How Children Learn

Language acquisition theorists emphasize the importance of language in learning and view learning as a reflection of the culture and community in which students live (Heath, 1983b; Vygotsky, 1978, 1986). According to Russian psychologist Lev Vygotsky (1896–1934), language helps organize thought, and children use language to learn as well as to communicate and share experiences with others. Understanding that children use language for social purposes, teachers plan instructional activities that incorporate a social component, such as having students share their writing and discuss their reading with classmates. And because children's language and concepts of literacy reflect their cultures and home communities, teachers must respect students' language and appreciate cultural differences in their attitudes toward learning—and toward learning the language arts in particular.

Swiss psychologist Jean Piaget (1896–1980) developed a theory of learning that radically changed our conceptions of child development. His **constructivist framework** differs substantially from behavioural theories that had influenced education for decades. Piaget described learning as the modification of students' cognitive structures as they interact with and adapt to their environment. He believed that children construct their own knowledge from their experiences. This view of learning requires a close examination of the teacher's role. Instead of being primarily dispensers of knowledge, teachers provide students with reading and writing experiences and opportunities to construct their own knowledge through problem-solving, web-based inquiries, and other dynamic interactive activities.

The Process of Learning

Children's knowledge is not just a collection of isolated bits of information; it is organized in the brain, and this organization becomes increasingly integrated and interrelated as children's knowledge grows. The organization of knowledge is the cognitive structure, and knowledge is arranged in category systems called **schemata** (a single category is called a *schema*). Within the schemata are three components: categories of knowledge, the features or rules for determining what constitutes a category and what will be included in each category, and a network of interrelationships among the categories.

These schemata may be likened to a conceptual filing system in which children and adults organize and store the information derived from their past experiences. Taking this analogy further, information is filed in the brain in "file folders." As children learn, they add file folders to their filing system, and as they study a topic, that file folder becomes thicker.

As children learn, they invent new categories, and while different people have many similar categories, schemata are personalized according to individual experiences and interests. Some people, for example, may have only one general category, *bugs*, into which they lump their knowledge of ants, butterflies, spiders, and bees, while other people distinguish between insects and spiders and develop a category for each. Those who distinguish between insects and spiders also develop a set of rules based on the distinctive characteristics of these animals for classifying them into one category or the other. In addition to *insect* or *spider* categories, a network of interrelationships connects these categories to other categories. Networks, too, are individualized, depending on each person's unique knowledge and experiences. The category of *spiders* might be networked as a subcategory of *arachnids*, and the class relationship between scorpions and spiders might be made. Other networks, such as a connection to a *poisonous animals* category or a *webs and nests* category, could have been made. The networks that link categories, characteristics, and examples with other categories, characteristics, and examples are extremely complex. As children adapt to their environment, they add new information about their experiences that requires them to enlarge existing categories or to construct new ones.

Two processes make this change possible. **Assimilation** is the cognitive process by which new information in the environment is integrated into existing schemata. In contrast, **accommodation** is the cognitive process by which existing schemata are modified or new schemata are restructured to adapt to the environment. Through assimilation, children add new information to their picture of the world; through accommodation, they change that picture on the basis of new information.

Learning occurs through the process of equilibration (Piaget, 1975). When a child encounters something he or she does not understand or cannot assimilate, *disequilibrium*, or cognitive conflict, results. This disequilibrium typically produces confusion and agitation, feelings that impel children to seek *equilibrium*, or a comfortable balance with the environment. In other words, when confronted with new or discrepant information, children (as well as adults) are intrinsically motivated to try to make sense of it. If the child's schemata can accommodate the new information, then the disequilibrium caused by the new experience will motivate the child to learn. Equilibrium is thus regained at a higher developmental level. These are the steps of this process:

1. Equilibrium is disrupted by the introduction of new or discrepant information.
2. Disequilibrium occurs, and the dual processes of assimilation and accommodation function.
3. Equilibrium is attained at a higher developmental level.

The process of equilibration happens to us again and again during the course of a day. In fact, it is occurring right now as you are reading this chapter. If you are already familiar with the constructivist learning theory and have learned about Piaget in other education courses, your mental filing cabinet has been activated and you are assimilating the information you are reading into the folder on "Piaget" or "learning theories" already in your files. If, however, you're not familiar with constructivist learning theories, your mind is actively creating a new file folder in which to put the information you are reading.

Learning Strategies

We all have skills that we use automatically, as well as self-regulating strategies for things that we do well—driving defensively, playing volleyball, training a new pet, or maintaining classroom discipline. We apply skills we have learned unconsciously and choose among skills as we think strategically. The strategies we use in these activities are problem-solving mechanisms that involve complex thinking processes. When we are first learning how to drive a car, for example, we learn both skills and strategies. Some of the first skills we learn are how to start the engine, make left turns, and parallel park. With practice, these skills become automatic. Some of the first strategies we learn are how to pass another car and how to stay a safe distance behind the vehicles ahead of us. At first we have only a small repertoire of strategies, and we don't always use them effectively. That's one reason why we take lessons from a driving instructor and have a learner's permit that requires a more experienced driver to ride along with us. A seasoned driver teaches us defensive driving strategies. We learn strategies for driving on superhighways, on slippery roads, and at night. With practice and guidance, we become more successful drivers, able to anticipate driving problems and take defensive actions.

Children develop a number of learning strategies or methods for learning. Rehearsal—repeating information over and over—is one learning strategy or cognitive process that children can use to remember something. Other learning strategies include:

- **P**redicting: anticipating what will happen
- **O**rganizing: grouping information into categories
- **E**laborating: expanding on the information presented
- **M**onitoring: regulating or keeping track of progress

Reciprocal teaching theory suggests that as children grow older, their use of learning strategies improves (Oczkus, 2003; Palincsar & Brown, 1986).

As they acquire more effective methods for learning and remembering information, children also become more aware of their own cognitive processes and better able to regulate them. Elementary and middle-school students can reflect on their literacy processes and talk about themselves as readers and writers. For example, grade 2 student Trisha describes her writing: "That's the writing we do for 'Kids in the News.' 'Kids in the News' is where we write to somebody. We can write to anybody … and then they have to write back to us something about what we did. I like to write to my mom, my dad, my auntie, my cousin, my brother, my sister, or Miss W. [her classroom teacher], or Janie" (McKay & Kendrick, 2001, p. 14). Fifth grader Hobbes reports that "the pictures in my head help me when I write stuff down 'cause then I can get ideas from my pictures" (Cleary, 1993, p. 142). Eighth grader Chandra talks about poetry: "Poetry is a fine activity, and it can get you in tune with yourself. . . . I think that my favourite person who does poetry is Maya Angelou" (Steinbergh, 1993, p. 212).

Students become more realistic about the limitations of their memories and more knowledgeable about which learning strategies are most effective in particular situations. They also become increasingly aware of what they know and don't know. The term **metacognition** refers to this knowledge children acquire about their own cognitive processes and to children's regulation of their cognitive processes to maximize learning.

Teachers play an important role in developing children's metacognitive abilities. During large-group activities, teachers introduce and *model* learning strategies. In small-group lessons, teachers provide *guided practice*, talk with children about learning strategies, and ask students to *reflect* on their own use of these cognitive processes. Teachers also guide students about when to use particular strategies and which strategies are more effective with various activities.

Social Contexts of Learning

Children's cognitive development is enhanced through social interaction. In his social development theory, known as *sociolinguistics*, Lev Vygotsky asserted that children learn through socially meaningful interactions, and that language is both social and an important facilitator of learning. Children's experiences are organized and shaped by society, but rather than merely absorbing these experiences, children negotiate and transform them as a dynamic part of culture. They learn to talk through social interactions and to read and write through interactions with literate children and adults. Community is important for both readers and writers. Students talk about books they are reading with classmates, and they turn to classmates for feedback about their writing.

Through interactions with adults and collaboration with other children, children learn things they could not learn on their own. Teachers guide and support children as they move from their current level of knowledge toward a more advanced level. Vygotsky described these two levels as, first, the *actual developmental level*, at which children can perform a task independently; and, second, the *level of proximal development*, at which children can perform a task with assistance. Children can typically do more difficult things in collaboration than they can on their own, and this is why teachers are important models for their students and why children often work with partners and in small groups.

A child's **zone of proximal development** is the range of tasks that the child can perform with guidance from others but cannot yet perform independently. Vygotsky believed that children learn best when what they are attempting to learn is within this zone. He felt that children learn little by performing tasks they can already do independently—tasks at their actual developmental level—or by attempting tasks that are too difficult or beyond their zone of proximal development.

Vygotsky and Jerome Bruner (2004) both used the term **scaffolding** as a metaphor to describe adults' contributions to children's learning. Scaffolds are support mechanisms that teachers, parents, or other more competent individuals provide to help children successfully perform a task within their zone of proximal development. Teachers serve as scaffolds when they model or demonstrate a procedure, guide children through a task, ask questions, break complex tasks into smaller steps, and supply pieces of information. As children gain knowledge and experience about how to perform a task, teachers gradually withdraw their support so that children make the transition from social interaction to internalized, independent functioning.

Implications for Learning the Language Arts

Students interact with their environment and actively construct knowledge using the processes of assimilation and accommodation. Students learn when their existing schemata are enlarged because of assimilated information and when their schemata are restructured to account for new experiences being acted on and accommodated.

In the lessons they prepare for their students, teachers can create optimal conditions for learning. When students do not have the schemata for predicting and interpreting the new information, teachers must help students relate what they know to what they do not know. Therefore, the new information must appear in a situation that makes sense and must be moderately novel; it must not be too difficult for students to accommodate it.

How children learn has important implications for how students learn the language arts in school and how teachers teach the language arts. Contributions from the constructivist and sociolinguistic learning theories include the following:

- Students are active participants in learning.
- Students learn by relating the new information to prior knowledge.
- Students organize their knowledge in schemata.
- Students use skills automatically and strategies consciously as they learn.

- Students learn through social interactions with classmates and the teacher.
- Teachers provide scaffolds for students.

Think about these implications and how they will affect your teaching.

Language Learning and Culture

Psychology has largely defined our views on language arts learning and instruction. Behaviourists have focused on the language arts as skill development, while cognitive psychologists have focused on language learning processes, and more recently we've begun to recognize the importance of the social aspects of the process (Bainbridge & Malicky, 2004).

A skill acquisition orientation to the language arts suggests that language is learned from part to whole and that the learning of lower-level skills, such as letter and word identification in learning to read, must precede the learning of higher-level skills, such as comprehension. In this approach, lower-level skills are taught and mastered before moving on to more complex, higher-level skills. In learning to read, for example, children are taught letter- and then word-identification skills as a prerequisite to combining words into sentences, paragraphs, and whole texts, leading eventually to comprehension.

An interactive approach to language arts views the learner as a maker of meaning, who, when reading, discovers the meaning of text through a complex process, and as a creator of meaning through a similarly complex process when writing. The focus is on understanding, and skills are used to the extent that they help clarify meaning. In reading, the language and thought process of the reader interacts with that of the writer. Understanding is achieved when the two come together in what Goodman (1969) called "a psycholinguistic guessing game." The more the reader is familiar with the language and thought of the writer, the easier it will be to achieve understanding. In this sense, meaning is the interaction between the reader and the text, and the language arts are seen as a cognitive process of discovery.

Language is a complex system for creating meaning through socially shared conventions (Halliday, 2006). Before children enter elementary school, they learn the language of their community. They understand what community members say to them, and they share their ideas with others through that language. In an amazingly short period of three or four years, children master the exceedingly complex system of their native language, allowing them to understand sentences they have never heard before and to create sentences they have never said before. Young children are not "taught" how to talk; this knowledge about language develops tacitly, or unconsciously.

The Four Language Systems

Language involves four systems, and together these systems make oral and written communication possible. The four **cueing systems** are:

- the phonological, or sound, system of language
- the syntactic, or structural, system of language
- the semantic, or meaning, system of language
- the pragmatic, or social and cultural use, system of language

For more information on phonics, see Chapter 3, "Emergent Literacy," pages 77–79.

Children develop an implicit understanding of the systems, and they apply their knowledge of the four systems whenever they communicate. No one system is more important than any other one, although at different stages of literacy development, one system may require more attention than another. As children begin learning to read, their attention will necessarily gravitate to the phonological system as they associate written symbols with their familiar oral language counterparts.

THE PHONOLOGICAL SYSTEM

There are approximately forty-four speech sounds in English. Children learn to pronounce these sounds as they learn to talk, and they learn to associate the sounds with letters as they learn to read and write. Sounds are called *phonemes*, and they are presented in print between slashes to differentiate them from *graphemes*, or letter combinations that represent sounds. Thus, the first letter in *mother* is written *m*, while the phoneme is written /m/; the phoneme in *soap* represented by the grapheme *oa* is written /ō/.

The **phonological system** is important in both oral and written language. Regional and cultural differences exist in the way people pronounce phonemes. For instance, the English spoken in different regions of Canada varies. It is common to hear differences in the pronunciation of words like *out* and *about* or *Newfoundland* and *Quebec* across Canada. Children who are **English language learners (ELL)** must learn to pronounce English sounds, and new sounds not found in their native language are particularly difficult for children to learn. Younger children usually learn to pronounce the difficult sounds more easily than older children and adults.

Children use their knowledge of the phonological system as they learn to read and write. In a phonetically regular language, with a one-to-one correspondence between letters and sounds, teaching students to sound out words would be a simple process. But English is not a phonetically regular language, since there are twenty-six letters and forty-four sounds and many ways to combine the letters to spell some of the sounds, especially vowels. Consider these ways to spell long *e*: *sea, green, Pete, me,* and *people*. And sometimes the patterns used to spell long *e* don't work, as in *head* and *great*. **Phonics**, which describes the phoneme–grapheme correspondences and related spelling rules, is an important part of reading instruction. Students use phonics information to decode words. However, because not all words can easily be decoded, and because good readers do much more than just decode words when they read, phonics instruction alone is not sufficient for beginning readers. While they must learn the phoneme–grapheme relationships, they must also learn the various ways phonemes are spelled (the ways their familiar and known speech sounds are represented in print) as well as learn to use cues available to them from the other language systems to aid their word recognition.

For more information on invented spelling, see Chapter 8, Words, Their Meanings, and the Tools to Use Them: Grammar, Spelling, Handwriting, and Word Processing pages 310, 311.

Students in the primary grades also use their understanding of the phonological system to create temporary or **invented spellings**. Grade 1 students might, for example, spell *home* as *hm* or *hom*, and grade 2 students might spell *school* as *skule*, based on their knowledge of phoneme–grapheme relationships and spelling patterns. As students learn more phonics and gain more experience in reading and writing, their spellings become more sophisticated and finally conventional. The spellings of students who are learning English as an additional language often reflect their pronunciations of words.

THE SYNTACTIC SYSTEM

For more information on teaching grammar in the elementary grades, see Chapter 8, "Words, Their Meanings, and the Tools to Use Them: Grammar, Spelling, Handwriting, and Word Processing," pages 302–308.

The **syntactic system** is the structural organization of a language. This system, which describes how words go together to form meaning and how we add affixes to words to change meaning, is the grammar that regulates how words are combined into sentences. Children use the syntactic system as they combine words to form sentences. Word order is important in English, and speakers of the language must arrange words into a sequence that makes sense. Young Spanish-speaking English language learners begin to say, "This is my red sweater," not "This is my sweater red," the literal translation from Spanish.

Students use their knowledge of the syntactic system as they read. They anticipate that the words they are reading have been strung together into sentences. When they come to an unfamiliar word, they recognize its role in the sentence even if they don't know the terms for parts of speech. In the sentence "The horses galloped through the gate and out into the field," students may not be able to decode the word *through*, but they can easily substitute a reasonable word or phrase, such as *out of* or *past*. Many of the capitalization and punctuation rules that elementary students learn reflect the syntactic system of language. Similarly, when students study simple, compound, and complex sentences, they are learning about the syntactic system.

For more information on teaching grammar in the elementary grades, see Chapter 8, "Words, Their Meanings, and the Tools to Use Them: Grammar, Spelling, Handwriting, and Word Processing," pages 302–308.

Another component of syntax is word forms. Words such as *dog* and *play* are **morphemes**, the smallest meaningful units of language. Word parts that change the meaning of a word are also morphemes. When the plural marker *-s* is added to *dog* to make *dogs*, for instance, or the past-tense marker *-ed* is added to *play* to make *played*, these words are now composed of two morphemes because the inflectional endings change the meaning of the words. The words *dog* and *play* are *free morphemes* because they convey meaning while standing alone. The endings *-s* and *-ed* are *bound morphemes* because they must be attached to a free morpheme to convey meaning. As they learn to talk, children quickly become adept at learning to combine words and word parts, such as adding *-s* to *cookie* to create a plural and adding *-er* to *big* to indicate a comparison. They also learn to combine two or more free morphemes to form compound words. *Birthday*, for example, is a compound word created by combining two free morphemes.

Children also learn to add affixes to words. Affixes added at the beginning of a word are *prefixes*, and affixes added at the end are *suffixes*. Both kinds of affixes are bound morphemes. For example, the prefix *un-* in *unhappy* is a bound morpheme, whereas *happy* is a free morpheme because it can stand alone as a word.

THE SEMANTIC SYSTEM

The third language system is the **semantic system**, or meaning system; it focuses on vocabulary. As children learn to talk, they acquire a vocabulary that is continually increasing through the preschool years and the elementary grades. Researchers estimate that children have a vocabulary of 5000 words by the time they enter school and that they continue to acquire 3000 words each year during the elementary grades. Considering how many words students learn each year, it is unreasonable to assume that they learn words only through formal instruction. Students learn many, many words informally via reading and through social studies, science, and other curricular areas. Students probably learn eight to ten words a day—a remarkable achievement!

For more information on vocabulary, see Chapter 8, "Words, Their Meanings, and the Tools to Use Them: Grammar, Spelling, Handwriting, and Word Processing," pages 285–303.

At the same time that children are learning new words, they are also learning that many words have more than one meaning. Words with more than one meaning are referred to as polysemic words. Meaning is usually based on the context, or the surrounding words. The word *run*, for instance, has more than thirty meanings. Read these sentences to see how the meaning of the word *run* is tied to the context in which it is used.

Will the mayor run for re-election?

The bus runs between Montreal and Ottawa.

The advertisement will run for three days.

Did you run in the 50-metre dash?

The plane made a crop-dusting run.

Will you run to the store and get a loaf of bread for me?

The dogs are out in the run.

Children often don't have the full, adult meaning of many words; rather, they learn meanings through a process of refinement.

Children learn other sophisticated concepts about words as well. They learn about shades of meaning—for example, the differences among these *sad* words: *unhappy*, *crushed*, *desolate*, *miserable*, *disappointed*, *cheerless*, *down*, and *grief-stricken*. They also learn about synonyms and antonyms, wordplay, and figurative language, including idioms.

For more information on wordplay, see Chapter 6, "Reading and Writing Narrative Text," pages 224–228.

THE PRAGMATIC SYSTEM

The fourth language system is the **pragmatic system**, which deals with the social and cultural aspects of language use. People use language for many different purposes, and how they talk or write varies according to purpose and audience.

Language use varies among social classes, cultural and ethnic groups, and geographic regions. These varieties are known as **dialects**. School is one cultural community, and the language of school is Standard English. This register, or style, is formal—the one used in textbooks, newspapers, and magazines, and by television newscasters. Other forms of English are alternatives in which the phonology, syntax, and semantics differ from those of Standard English, but they are neither inferior nor substandard. They reflect the communities of the speakers, and the speakers communicate as effectively as those who use Standard English in their communities. The goal is for students to add Standard English to their repertoire of language registers, not to replace their home dialect with Standard English.

The four language systems and their terminology are reviewed in Figure 1-1. Both children and adults use the four systems as they communicate through oral and written language. Their knowledge of and dependence upon the language systems vary with age and experience, with greater emphasis needed at appropriate times.

Culturally and Linguistically Diverse Students

North America is a culturally pluralistic society, and the ethnic, racial, and socioeconomic diversity is being reflected increasingly in elementary school classrooms. According to the 2011 Statistics Canada Household Survey (Statistics Canada, 2012), English and French (Canada's official languages) have retained their positions as the two predominant languages in Canada. However, the number of Canadians reporting a non-official language as their mother tongue has grown. Such languages include Italian, German, Polish, and Spanish, with the Chinese languages representing the third-largest mother tongue group in Canada.

These changing demographic realities will have a significant impact on elementary classrooms as more and more students come from linguistically and culturally diverse backgrounds. More than ever before, today's students live in a global society, and they need the skills and knowledge to live harmoniously as members of a multicultural community.

FIGURE 1-1 OVERVIEW OF THE FOUR LANGUAGE SYSTEMS

System	Description	Terms	Uses in Classroom and Other Communication
Phonological System	The sound system of English with approximately forty-four sounds	• Phoneme (the smallest identifiable unit of sound) • Grapheme (the written representation of a phoneme using one or more letters)	• Pronouncing words • Detecting regional and other dialects • Decoding words when reading • Using invented spelling • Reading and writing alliterations and onomatopoeia
Syntactic System	The structural system of English that governs how words are combined into sentences	• Syntax (the structure, or grammar, of a sentence) • Morpheme (the smallest meaningful unit of language) • Free morpheme (a morpheme that can stand alone as a word) • Bound morpheme (a morpheme that must be attached to a free morpheme to convey meaning)	• Adding inflectional endings to words • Combining words to form compound words • Adding prefixes and suffixes to root words • Using capitalization and punctuation to indicate beginnings and ends of sentences • Writing simple, compound, and complex sentences • Combining sentences
Semantic System	The meaning system of English that focuses on vocabulary	• Semantics (meaning)	• Learning the meanings of words • Discovering that some words have multiple meanings • Studying synonyms, antonyms, and homonyms • Using a dictionary and thesaurus • Reading and writing comparisons (metaphors and similes)
Pragmatic System	The system of English that varies language according to social and cultural uses	• Function (the purpose for which a person uses language) • Standard English (the form of English used in textbooks and by television newscasters) • Nonstandard English (other forms of English)	• Varying language to fit specific purposes • Reading and writing dialogue in dialects • Comparing standard and nonstandard forms of English

Children of diverse cultures come to school with a broad range of language and literacy experiences, many with experiences not the same as those of the majority in their school community. Linguistically diverse children have already learned to communicate in at least one language, and if they don't speak English, they want to learn English in order to make friends, learn, and communicate with their English-speaking classmates. Teachers of culturally and linguistically diverse students must implement a language and literacy program that is sensitive to and reflective of all students' backgrounds and needs. Many teachers take one step toward fulfilling their students' diverse needs by providing multicultural literature.

When the classroom environment, the curriculum, and resource materials are culturally meaningful and relevant for all students, they all have a better chance of succeeding academically and socially (Holloway, 2010).

All teachers must be prepared to incorporate a multicultural perspective in their curriculum in order to prepare their students to interact effectively in Canada's increasingly multicultural society. We take the perspective that cultural and linguistic diversity is not a problem for teachers to overcome; instead, it provides an opportunity to enhance and enrich the learning of all students.

Bilingual Students and English Language Learners (ELL)

Students whose first language is not English are referred to as *English language learners* (ELL). The first language spoken as a child and still understood is often referred to as the *mother tongue*, or *native language*. Children who converse in their native language at home but also speak English fluently at school are *bilingual speakers*.

Students learning English as another language are a diverse group. Some are fluent in both English and their native language, while others know little or no English. Some learn to speak English quickly, and others learn more slowly. It often takes four to seven years to become a proficient speaker of English, and the more similar the first language is to English, the easier it will be to learn English.

VALUING STUDENTS' FIRST LANGUAGE

Until recently, most non-English-speaking students were submerged into English-speaking classrooms and left to "sink or swim." Unfortunately, many students sank and dropped out before graduating from high school. To better meet the needs of linguistically diverse students, teachers now value students' first languages and recognize the potential for their first language to support their learning of English as a second or other language.

A list of suggestions for supporting and valuing students' first language is presented in the accompanying Teacher's Notebook. Even teachers who do not speak or write students' first languages themselves can follow most of these guidelines. For example, they can post signs in the classroom and encourage students to read and write books in their first language. Such activities may help students expand their first-language proficiency, develop greater self-confidence, and value their own language.

LEARNING A SECOND LANGUAGE

Learning a second language is a constructive process, just as learning a first language is, and children develop language in a predictable way through interactions with children and adults. Urzua (1980) lists three principles culled from the research:

1. People use many similar language-learning strategies, whether they are small children learning their first language or older children or adults learning a second language.
2. Just as children learning to speak their first language move through a series of developmental stages, second-language learners move through several stages as they learn a new language.
3. First- or second-language learning takes place only when learners have the opportunity to use language for meaningful, functional, and genuine purposes.

When linguistically diverse children and adults first join English speaking communities, they generally go through a silent period (Krashen, 1982) of several months during which they observe others communicating prior to talking or writing in English themselves. Then they begin tentatively to use language to communicate, and through listening, talking, reading, and writing, their language use becomes more cognitively and linguistically complex. The English spoken by new speakers is often syntactically less complex; in addition, new speakers typically enunciate words clearly, speak more slowly, and avoid using idiomatic expressions.

Guidelines for Supporting and Valuing Students' First Language

1. Use Environmental Print in the Students' First Language

Teachers can post signs and other environmental print written in the students' first languages in the classroom. *Environmental print* refers to words and images students frequently encounter in their environment, such as signs and names of restaurants and stores. In a primary-grade classroom, posters with colour words, numbers, and the days of the week can be written both in English and in the students' first languages. Bulletin board titles and captions in posters can also be translated into the students' first languages. Many language scholars recommend making text in each language distinctive such as using one colour for each language posted.

2. Include Reading Materials in the Students' First Languages in the Classroom Library

Teachers can include books, magazines, digital texts, and other reading materials written in the students' first languages in the classroom library. High-quality books for children written in a variety of languages are becoming increasingly available in Canada. Also, award-winning books of children's literature are being translated into other languages and made available through the International Children's Digital Library (http://en.childrenslibrary.org). Sometimes parents and other members of the community are willing to lend books written in a child's first language for the child to use in school.

3. Encourage Students to Write Books in Their First Language

Linguistically diverse students can write and publish books in their first language. They use the writing process just as English-speaking students do. They can share their published books with others who speakers of their language and place them in the classroom or school library.

4. Use Bilingual Tutors

Linguistically diverse students can read and write with tutors, older students, classmates, and family members who speak their first language. Some classrooms have first-language aides who read and write with students in their first language. Other times community volunteers come into the classroom to work with students as they strive to develop their English language competencies.

5. View Videos in the Students' First Language

Teachers can find videos on the Internet of students reading and dramatizing stories in their first language. In addition, students can dramatize events in history or demonstrate how to do something in their first language. Creating and viewing these videos is useful for both building students' proficiency in their first language and demonstrating their knowledge of the content dramatized.

Source: Adapted from Freeman, D. E., & Freeman, Y. S. (1993). Strategies for promoting the primary languages of all students. The Reading Teacher, 46 , 552–558. © Gail E. Tompkins

New English speakers use very short sentences, often with two or three key-words, much like the telegraphic speech of young children. For example, a new speaker might say "no pencil" for "I don't have a pencil," or "book table" for "the book is on the table." They may also overgeneralize and call all adults in the school "teachers." As English language learners acquire labels for more concepts and more sophisticated syntactic structures, they progressively use longer and more complex sentences. They move out of here-and-now, present-tense verb constructions to past and future constructions; however, many ELL students have difficulty adding the *-ed* past-tense marker to verbs, as in "yesterday I play ball."

After approximately two years, many English language learners are fluent enough to carry on everyday conversations, but it can take these students as many as five, six, or seven years to achieve the same level of fluency in English as their English speaking classmates. For many students joining Canadian classrooms, school may be the only place where they speak English!

Teaching Culturally and Linguistically Diverse Students

Children from each cultural group bring their unique backgrounds of experience to the process of learning. Some may have difficulty understanding concepts outside their backgrounds of experience. This difficulty is greater for students who are learning

English as another language. Think, for example, of the different experiences and language knowledge that Afghan refugee children, Aboriginal children, and children of Hispanic immigrants bring to school. No matter what ethnic group they belong to or what language they speak, all students use the same cognitive and linguistic processes to learn.

Children of diverse ethnic groups have met with varying degrees of success in schools, depending on their previous cultural experiences, the support system available, the expectations students and their parents have, and the expectations teachers have for them. Often a discrepancy exists between the way Canadian classrooms operate and the ways students from various ethnic groups interact. Four examples of cultural behaviours that illustrate discrepancies are

1. *Eye contact.* In some Asian and Aboriginal cultures, avoiding eye contact is polite and respectful behaviour. Teachers sometimes mistakenly assume that when students avoid eye contact, they are not paying attention or are sullen and uncooperative.

2. *Cooperation.* Students from many Southeast Asian, Polynesian, and Aboriginal cultures are taught to cooperate and help each other, and in school they often assist classmates with their work. In contrast, some students have learned to value competition over cooperation, and sometimes teachers view cooperating on assignments as cheating.

3. *Fear of making mistakes.* Teachers encourage students to take risks and view making mistakes as a natural part of the learning process. In some cultures, correctness is valued above all else, and students are taught not to guess or take risks.

4. *Informal classroom environment.* In some cultures the school environment is much more formal than it is in North America. Students from Asia, for example, often view North American schools as chaotic, and they may misinterpret the informality as permission for inattentive behaviour.

Further to these particular behaviours, many students have been taught to keep a social distance between the teacher and themselves. For example, out of respect for the teacher, they look down when they are spoken to, and they feel more comfortable remaining in their assigned seats. Literature discussions, called **grand conversations**, and other informal activities can make these students feel uncomfortable because the informal structure appears to indicate disrespect for the teacher.

For more information on grand conversations, see Chapter 4, "Listening and Speaking in the Classroom," pages 123–126.

McGrath (1991) suggests that "it is impossible to . . . introduce all of our country's children of different cultural backgrounds to one another, but the next best alternative is to introduce them to each other through their own popular literature" (p. 153). Sharing multicultural literature through read-alouds is one of the most beneficial ways teachers can help students experience cultural diversity. "When teachers take a linguistically and culturally informed approach to read-alouds, learners are challenged to use and practice new language by making meaningful text-to-self and text-to-world connections, allow for deeper processing of the new language and deeper understanding of the ideas connected to that language" (Giroir, Grimaldo, Vaughn, & Roberts, 2015, p. 640). Through shared stories, children take pride in their own heritage and develop understanding of other cultures.

Aboriginal students also have unique needs. For too long, schools have neglected and failed these students. Teachers must understand and build on students' abilities, appreciate their varied backgrounds, and nurture their potential for learning. Teachers must also take into account historical, economic, psychological, and linguistic barriers that have led to oppression and low expectations. One way to help raise children's self-esteem and build pride in their cultural groups is to incorporate literature about, for example, Aboriginal and Japanese-Canadian cultures in their instructional programs. Two powerful titles, *Fatty Legs: A True Story* (2010) and *Not My Girl* (2014), by Canadian authors Christy Jordan-Fenton & Margaret Pokiak-Fenton, are beautifully written accounts of a young girl named Margaret, who travels to Aklavik from her village in the Arctic to attend a residential school. She learns to read, but suffers tremendously while there. She emerges strong in spirit, determined, and hopeful. Suki, another determined little girl, joyfully introduces readers to her Japanese culture in *Suki's Kimono* (Uegaki, 2005), when she tells of her grandmother's summer visit. Through sharing stories like these, students and teachers gain appreciation for their diverse classroom communities.

Language and culture have important implications for the ways in which children learn, and teachers teach the language arts. Some of these implications are:

- Children from each cultural group bring their unique backgrounds of experience to the process of learning.
- Children's cultural and linguistic diversity provides an opportunity to enhance and enrich the learning of all students.
- Literature offers a rich selection of well-written and illustrated books to enhance children's critical understanding of the world.

Guidelines for teaching linguistically diverse students are presented in the Teacher's Notebook.

What Is Literacy?

Our views of literacy have been changing for some time. A group of researchers known as the New London Group (1996) raised the important question "What counts as literacy?" In today's society, **literacy** continues to encompass reading a novel and writing an essay, but also includes composing an email, posting or reading a blog entry, and viewing a film.

Literacy, in its traditional sense, is characterized by "the ability to create written text and then to decode and comprehend this text according to certain internalized linguistic rules" (Cammack, 2002, p. 51). Today, technology and the social, economic, political, and cultural contexts surrounding it are challenging this view of literacy, encouraging researchers and teachers to develop a more thorough and complete understanding of what it means to be literate. According to Chandler-Olcott and Mahar (2003), part of being a literate member of society is understanding how information and communications technologies change peoples' lives. Bruce (2002) points out that new technologies challenge the educational system by throwing into question traditional ways of teaching and learning. However, these same technologies support an expanded view of learning, and this has caused researchers to declare that there is already a "fundamental transformation visible in the literacy practices of young people" (Alvermann, 2002, p. 3).

Moreover, the rapid changes in technology and society are both the cause and a result of our changing views of literacy (Knobel & Lankshear, 2007; Leu, 2000). In order to broaden the definitions of literacy, a new emphasis is placed on teaching students to engage in reading and writing, not only in traditional print media such as books and newspapers, but also in multiple formats such as software, music, video, dance, and art. Kist (2005) and Watts Pailliotet (2000) indicate that "new literacies"—sometimes referred to as *critical media literacy*, *multiple ways of knowing*, and *multiliteracies*—involve visual, auditory, and print information and allow us to understand literacy contexts in and out of school. Kist further suggests that new literacy

Guidelines for Teaching Linguistically Diverse Students

1. Provide a Comprehensible Environment
- Use language that is neither too hard nor too easy for students.
- Embed language in context-rich activities.
- Speak clearly, and explain use of unfamiliar idioms.
- Highlight keywords.
- Expand the two- and three-word sentences that students produce.

2. Create an Environment with Minimal Stress
- Show genuine interest in students, their language, and their culture.
- Allow students to speak and write their own language.
- Avoid forcing students to speak.
- Encourage risk-taking.
- Don't correct grammatical errors. Simply model correct usage.
- Understand that diverse students are experiencing two cultures.

3. Provide Opportunities to Use English
- Provide many opportunities for students to speak and listen to English.
- Create opportunities to read and write English in low-risk contexts.
- Have students work together with buddies and in cooperative groups.
- Promote friendships among students.

4. Examine Your Attitude
- Recognize how your personal biases can affect instruction.
- Avoid stereotyping any linguistic or cultural group.
- Hold high expectations of all students.
- Encourage bilingualism.
- Consider your tolerance for non-Standard English and code-switching.

5. Alleviate Home–School Mismatches
- Consider the contrast between how children use language in home communities and at school.
- Smooth the transition between home and school.
- Anticipate students to be uncomfortable in unfamiliar activities.

6. Involve Linguistically Diverse Families
- Establish strategies for communication with families.
- Encourage families to participate in school activities.
- Provide letters, information sheets, and memos in home languages.
- Provide interpreters when needed for school meetings and conferences.
- Plan culturally appropriate parent–child and home–school activities.
- Learn cultural protocols from elders or community leaders.

Sources: Based on Gibbons, 1991; Faltis, 1993; Law & Eckes, 1990; Scarcella, 1990; Alberta Teachers Association, 2010. © Gail E. Tompkins

classrooms are characterized by specific features such as student choice and collaboration; work centred around projects; ongoing, continuous use of multiple forms of representation (e.g., art, sculpture, and drama); and the breaking down of traditional teacher and student roles.

Pahl and Rowsell (2005) assert that the literacy students facing the teacher today are "intelligent, imaginative, and linguistically talented." As such, their use of technology is best understood as social and cultural practice. Using multiliteracies more accurately describes what children, preteens, and teenagers do as literate beings when they play computer games, text-message, use email and instant messaging, surf the Internet, and create and consume webpages and blogs. Accordingly, these activities are seen to be sophisticated literacy practices.

For students today, being literate is much more than reading traditional school-based texts, books, and periodicals. Literacy encompasses "the multiple ways that people use language" (Rowsell, 2005). "Students today must learn to read traditional pages as well as digital text that present multiple reading paths" (Luce-Kapler & Dobson, 2005). Therefore, technology's role helps teachers redefine literacy beyond developing skills in using email and word processing. It points to the need for educators to understand the social and cultural impact of technology use in today's society.

Integrating Technology

There has always been a relationship between literacy and technology. Our conceptions of literacy have continuously evolved since the development of book technologies in the 16th century. Today, this is evident through the advent of many new technologies, including word processors, email, podcasts, digital video, cell phones, and the Internet (Teale, Leu, Labbo, & Kinzer, 2002). *New media* is the term we use to refer to the many types of technology that make it possible to use online environments. The current climate demands that teachers respond by acknowledging the emergence of new or multiliteracies needed to effectively understand, manage, and evaluate available technology. Preparing students to use multiliteracies means helping them learn to use word processors and spell- and grammar-check tools, manage email and communications technology, and choose search engines to locate and evaluate information from the Internet (Watts-Taffe, Gwinn, Johnson, & Horn, 2003). Learning these types of skills is important for both scholastic and workforce/lifestyle technology use.

In school, students are encouraged to use word processing, PowerPoint™, electronic reference tools, visual media, and the Internet. Out of school, students are texting and using social networking sites, email, instant messaging, electronic games, chat rooms, and blogs. In an instant, students are able to log on to the Internet and engage in near-synchronous conversation with another person virtually anywhere in the world. They can also access a wealth of information on virtually any topic. It is up to teachers and parents to ensure that students engage in a variety of ways to learn about the world, express themselves in new ways, and communicate well with others. As students are exposed to multiple technologies, they require thoughtful education about selecting, using, and evaluating these tools.

Wepner, Valmont, and Thurlow point out that "learning should drive the technology, not vice versa" (2000, p. 620). In other words, technology is a tool that facilitates learning. There are many classroom examples of teachers and students using technology to develop literacy skills. These include using alphabet-related websites and early reading software to teach letter recognition for beginners' reading (Duffelmeyer, 2002); finding publishing programs and websites that incorporate text and pictures to write a book review and make a recommendation for reading (Maslin & Nelson, 2002); and writing with technological applications such as brainstorming software, databases and spreadsheets, and the Internet (S. Roberts, 2002). In addition, teachers use assistive technology and well-researched websites to help students with special learning needs to better meet curriculum objectives. Educators have much to learn about literacy and learning at all levels as research into technology use in the classroom continues.

Many new literacy skills are needed for obtaining and comprehending information on the Internet. Students need to be taught to narrow the focus of their search, use the words or phrase that they hope to find, search for one focus at a time (and not repeat their focus), eliminate unnecessary words, and select words for a search in a careful and mindful manner.

Technology can also be a motivation factor for some students. Hagood, Stevens, and Reinking (2002) present one student's comments about the role of the computer in reading. Although Tee, a thirteen-year-old, says, "I don't really like reading," he adds that it's "because I can never find a good book. But computers are good because I like to create cards and other things on the computer" (p. 72). In the educational milieu, it is paramount that the term *literacy* encompass a wide range of experiences and interpretations; otherwise, as Buckingham and Sefton-Green indicated many years ago and before many now commonplace technologies were known, "schools run the risk of becoming anti-educational sites" (1998, p. 81).

Changes in writing technology have also affected literacy in important ways. For instance, word processing software with built-in editing tools has changed the ways in which students write. As students create more and more digital texts, they learn how to organize, store, index, and retrieve their writing.

Another important way in which writing has changed is in its convergence with other activities such as web browsing, instant messaging, finding and listening to music, adding images and video, and using electronic reference tools. These activities are divergent from the conventional image of the solitary writer.

Student writing, once shared only with the teacher and perhaps classmates, can now be posted for a global community and promote feelings of connection among fledgling writers. Also, new technologies make it easier to access, use, and modify photographs and visual images to accompany writing or to demonstrate understanding through visual representation.

Writing processes and products have evolved in at least these three ways. Students manage their writing in new ways, use new forms including multi-media, and reach wide audiences. These new skills in technological literacy not only extend communication possibilities, they call on teachers to focus on a new area of instruction called *digital citizenship*. Digital citizenship is the ability to use technology and communicate online thoughtfully and ethically.

Teaching and Using Multiliteracies

To become fully literate in today's world, students must become proficient in the new literacies of the 21st-century technologies. As a result, literacy educators have a responsibility to effectively integrate these new technologies into the curriculum, preparing students for the literacy future they deserve. In response to a growing need, the International Reading Association (2009) provided a position statement concerning new literacies and 21st century technologies. The statement says students have the right to have:

- Teachers who use ICTs skilfully for teaching and learning effectively;
- Peers who use ICTs responsibly and actively share effective strategies applied to a range of literacy purposes and settings;
- A literacy curriculum that offers opportunities to collaboratively read, share, and created content with peers from around the world;
- Literacy instruction that embeds critical and culturally sensitive thinking into print and digital literacy practices;
- Provincial reading and writing standards that include new literacies;
- Provincial reading and writing assessments that include new literacies;
- School leaders and policymakers committed to advocating the use of ICTs for teaching and learning; and
- Equal access to ICTs for all classrooms and all students.

These principles help guide teachers and school leaders as they provide effective integration of computer technologies into the curriculum. Today's teachers are prepared to embrace an expanded view of literacy in a number of ways.

- They explore instructional strategies and resources developed by other teachers on technology use.
- They stay up to date on technology research to improve students' literacy skills.
- They ensure that students stay safe as they use a variety of technological tools.
- They join professional groups to exchange insights about effective instructional strategies.

As noted above, technology continues to have a substantial impact on our views of literacy. We believe we are on the cusp of a new era in literacy theory, research, and practice, one in which the nature of reading, writing, and communication is being fundamentally transformed by the Internet (Leu, Kinzer, Coiro, Castek, & Henry, 2013). Part of being literate in the Internet age entails understanding how information and communications technologies can change people's lives. As teachers, our goal is to recognize these changes and develop a strong background in effective literacy instruction in order to make sound decisions about selecting, using, and critically understanding them to prepare students for the new literacies of the Internet and other ICTs that define their future.

Critical Literacy

Critical literacy is a reader's ability to "become aware of the messages that texts communicate about power, race, and gender; who should receive privileges; and who has been or continues to be oppressed" (L. Hall & Piazza, 2008, p. 32). It is in this context that critical literacy is important for the teacher and the student. Critical literacy is not an "add-on" activity; it is a deeper, active approach to understanding language and making meaning.

Critical literacy goes beyond the informative *what* of language to its *how*, *why*, and *so what?* It goes beyond the reader's competency and comprehension to require a capacity for reflective insight. It asks the reader to "read" a text's symbolism in a philosophical and political context and discern its cultural influences and the writer's craft. Critical literacy enables not only the comprehension of text, but also its implications for our own lives (Shor, 1999, p. 1).

This understanding of critical literacy is based on Paulo Freire's pedagogy. Freire's (1970) premise is that oppression occurs wherever the powerless are excluded from economic and political life. They can more easily be kept powerless if they are also kept uninformed and unaware. Literacy is, therefore, a political act that serves to challenge the status quo (Comber & Simpson, 2001). Freire sees literacy as an emancipatory process of self-awareness and self-determination that ultimately makes social transformation possible. "Reading the world always precedes reading the word, and reading the word implies continually reading the world" (Freire & Macedo, 1987, p. 25). Freire views critical literacy as one of the ways in which teachers and students learn to read the world.

The Teacher's Role

Children who are encouraged to focus on the craft of a text (how it is produced) and reflect on their responses to it (how it has affected them) develop active, critical, and metacognitive reading strategies.

The teacher's knowledge of how and why children learn the language arts directs how the curriculum unfolds. This means that the teacher's familiarity with and commitment to critical literacy determines the degree to which students learn critical literacy skills. For example, a teacher brings attention to the place of language in relations of power. She examines how these relations are shaped by the social and cultural contexts of the text and of the student. The teacher understands that her own language comes from a particular social and cultural location. She realizes that no language-learning process is neutral and understands that teaching style and instructional choices and decisions influence how students understand themselves.

Teachers who provide learning opportunities that invite students to develop as reflective citizens will help to critique the status quo, and aid students in imagining and planning for an alternative world. Activities such as writing (e.g., journal writing, blogging, and collaborative writing) and portfolio assessment across the curriculum encourage critical thinking. Also, exposure to techniques of parody and comparison, such as those in Robert Munsch's *The Paper Bag Princess* (1980), can lead to an understanding of stereotyped roles and questioning of the dominant, or popular, culture. Studying how advertisements, music videos, packaging, fashion magazines, and history texts are produced also provides tools that enable students to critique the existing social culture and to envision a different kind of society.

Teachers may find this approach daunting, and unpredictable. For example, a critical reading of *Anne of Green Gables* (Montgomery, 1908/1999) shows a setting that rests on the exploitation of child labour. Matthew and Marilla were initially acquiring an orphan as a source of free labour, a common practice of the times. Critically literate teachers may read *Little House on the Prairie* (Wilder, 1953) and its sequels by pointing out the racism and colonization on which the Wilder family's migrations depended. And when Laura is whipped, it is almost always because of disobedience to her father's authority.

A critical reading of the classic *The Secret Garden* (Burnett, 1911) highlights that era's assumptions about class and gender. In the book's fairytale ending, the "invalid" boy Colin is healed by the garden's magic and reunited with his father. He returns to the world of privilege to which he is heir. The women and servants who have helped him fade away.

The introduction to the contemporary Canadian novel *Looking for X* (2002), by Deborah Ellis, contains the unforgettable sentence "Mom used to be a stripper," and might be used to examine and critique stereotypes of the welfare family in literature

For more information on critical viewing and listening, see "Media Literacy" in Chapter 9, pages 341–345.

and the media. Khyber and her mother strive for meaning and dignity in a culture of urban poverty. Khyber is not, at first glance, an appealing child. She is stringy-haired, dressed in welfare hand-me-downs, and abrasive at school. Sleep-deprived, she nods off in class. She has an "attitude." But Khyber is also imaginative, creative, resourceful, loving, and loyal. None of these qualities is recognized by her teachers, who are unresponsive, judgmental, and punitive. Khyber does receive nurturing and inspiration from her struggling mother and from her mother's tough waitress friend. Friendship and acceptance come from X, a schizophrenic street person. As well, Khyber's creative imagination is fed by the public library. Critical literacy is practised in classrooms when teachers and students examine the increasing social and cultural inequities and injustices in society. Literature provides the vehicle for this instruction.

Culture, Gender, and Social Contexts

Each child's family demonstrates the nature of culture, gender, and social roles for that child. In choosing literature for children, teachers should keep in mind that children need to find validation and reflection of their own lives, and they also need to expand their understanding of culture and gender roles beyond their own experience. Literature that satisfies these needs helps children assimilate and accommodate new information. In Vygotsky's terms, well-chosen and challenging literature puts students in a zone of proximal development (see page 7 of this text), and their learning is maximized in a way they might not have managed independently.

Contemporary Canadian literature offers a rich selection of finely written and illustrated books whose images, phrases, and experiences are sufficiently novel, as Piaget would put it, to construct scaffolding that enhances students' critical reading of the world. Here are a few examples:

Caribou Song (Highway, 2001), the first of a trilogy of northern Aboriginal tales of childhood, presents two small brothers who live a close family life with their nomadic parents. They travel by dogsled across the North, moving with the seasons.

SkySisters (Waboose & Deines, 2000) presents a vast and varied northern landscape that dictates the patterns of life and experience. The Ojibway children of this luminous picture book are intimately linked to the beauty of seasonal rhythms, which they learn to read in the context of their rich Aboriginal traditions.

In the Tree House (Larsen, 2013) is the story of an urban-dwelling boy who dreams of building a tree house and gazing up at the stars in the night sky. The city lights, however, make it difficult to see the stars. The little boy shares the tree house, built with the help of his dad, with his older brother. All is well until older brother chooses to spend less time with his younger brother. The story focuses on relationships and reinforces family values.

Me & Mr. Bell (Roy, 2013) is a historical story of young Eddie's remarkable relationship with Alexander Graham Bell with whom he shares a passion for solving problems and from whom he gains courage and confidence. Eddie has a talent for math, but struggles to read and write. From Bell, Eddie learns to take pride in practical skills and his imagination. The novel emphasizes multiple types of intelligence and offers a clear message to trust in your own abilities.

The Breadwinner (Ellis, 2000), set in contemporary Afghanistan, centres on a young girl who *disguises* herself as a boy in order to support her family when her father is imprisoned by the Taliban. This novel was written prior to September 11, 2001, but a sequel, *Parvana's Journey* (2002), follows her odyssey across a bomb-strewn landscape of violence and danger to search for scattered family members. On her way, she constructs an alternate "family" of other orphaned and traumatized children. *Mud City* (2003), the third book of this trilogy, follows the children through refugee camps and across the Pakistan border. This is a book by a writer who has lived in that culture, and offers a description of family life that is difficult, dangerous, and unpredictable. A sequel to the Breadwinner trilogy is entitled *My Name Is Parvana* (Ellis, 2012), and provides a much-anticipated ending to these books.

Through books as varied as those discussed above, students come to understand their worlds, communities, and families are diverse and can be read from many perspectives. They discover that daily lives, activities, and values are structured by geographical location, family relationships, and cultural inheritance. Diverse environments offer students a stimulating mix of the familiar and the new, traditional, and dynamic factors.

Teachers nervous about presenting "difficult" subject matter to children can be reassured that beautifully produced texts written for young readers offer them enriched worlds. Many children already live with the encumbrances of poverty, discrimination, disability, or bereavement. They find their lives and experiences validated through storylines they recognize. At the same time, other children have the opportunity to empathize and expand their horizons of understanding.

As students develop a repertoire of experiences from literature and from life, they develop more schemata and a deeper understanding of themselves and the world. The experiences of family, friendship, and death are universal ones, but the cultural contexts in which they occur demand critical awareness from the reader. Critical literacy helps students understand a diverse and increasingly complex world.

Critical literacy is an important part of language learning. Through a critical literacy approach, teachers and students develop an understanding of how the language arts—listening, speaking, reading, writing, viewing, visually representing—can be used to understand and change our world. Students learn to critique the existing social culture and work toward a new and perhaps better kind of society.

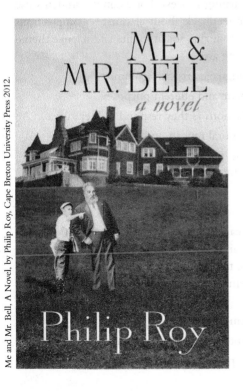

Me and Mr. Bell, A Novel, by Philip Roy, Cape Breton University Press 2012.

Cover from Mud City. Reproduced with permission from Groundwood Books, Toronto. www.houseofanansi.com

The Six Language Arts

Traditionally, language arts educators defined the language arts as the study of the four modes of language—listening, speaking, reading, and writing—but more than a decade ago, the National Council of Teachers of English and the International Reading Association (now International Literacy Association) proposed two additional language arts: viewing and visually representing. These newer language arts quickly became a part of language and literacy curriculum in Canadian schools. They reflect the growing importance of **visual literacy**. Also, *thinking* is sometimes referred to as an additional language art, but, more accurately, it permeates all of the language arts.

LISTENING

For more information on strategies for teaching listening, see Chapter 4, "Listening and Speaking in the Classroom," pages 103, 104.

Beginning at birth, a child's first contact with language is through listening. Listening instruction is often neglected in elementary classrooms because teachers feel that students have already learned how to listen, and that instructional time should be devoted to reading and writing. We present an alternative view of listening and its instruction, and focus on these key concepts:

- Listening is a process of which hearing is only one part.
- Students learn and use effective listening strategies to monitor their comprehension.
- Students listen differently according to their purpose.
- Students listen aesthetically to stories, efferently to information that is to be remembered, and critically to persuasive appeals.

SPEAKING

For more information on speaking activities, see Chapter 4, "Listening and Speaking in the Classroom," pages 118–122 and 126–137.

As with listening, teachers often neglect instruction in speaking during the elementary grades because they feel students already know how to speak. Research emphasizes the importance of speaking in the learning process. For example, students use speech to respond to literature, to provide feedback about classmates' compositions in writing groups, and to present oral reports during social studies and science theme study units. The key concepts about speaking are:

- Speaking is an essential part of the language arts curriculum.
- Students use speaking for both aesthetic and efferent purposes.
- Students participate in grand conversations as they respond to literature.
- Students give presentations, including oral reports and debates.
- Drama, including storytelling and role-playing, provides a valuable approach to learning and a powerful way of communicating.

READING

For more information on the reading process, see Chapter 5, "The Reading and Writing Processes," pages 142–160.

Reading is a meaning-making process. Readers use skills and strategies in order to decode words automatically and fluently and comprehend what they are reading. Students vary the way they read according to their purpose. They read for pleasure differently than they read to locate and remember information (Rosenblatt, 1991). The key concepts about reading are:

- Reading is a strategic, meaning-making process.
- The goals of reading instruction are automaticity, fluency, and comprehension.
- Students read differently for different purposes.

- Students participate in five types of reading: independent reading, shared reading, guided reading, buddy reading, and reading aloud to other students.

For more information on writing stories, journals, and poetry, see Chapter 6, "Reading and Writing Narrative Text," pages 214–225 and 235–245.

WRITING

Like reading, writing is a meaning-making strategic process. Students use the writing process as they write stories, reports, poems, scripts, essays, and other types of writing. Students also do informal writing, such as writing in reading response blogs, text messages, and labelling diagrams. Key concepts about writing are:

- Writing is a process in which students cycle recursively through prewriting, drafting, revising, editing, and publishing stages.
- Students experiment with many written language forms.
- Informal writing is used to develop writing fluency and as a learning tool.
- Spelling, handwriting, and word-processing are tools for writers.

VIEWING

Visual media include film and videos, print and online advertisements, television commercials, photographs and book illustrations, video games, images, PowerPoint™ presentations, and multimedia presentations. Because visual media are commonplace in Canadian life today, children need to learn how to comprehend them and to integrate visual knowledge with other literacy knowledge. The key concepts about viewing are:

- Viewing is an important component of literacy (visual literacy).
- Viewing is much like reading, and students use comprehension strategies in both reading and viewing.
- Students learn to appreciate the illustrations in picture books for their contribution to meaning and as examples of art.
- Students view visual media for a variety of purposes.
- Students learn about propaganda techniques in order to critically analyze commercials and advertisements.

VISUALLY REPRESENTING

Students create meaning through multiple sign systems such as video and music productions; multimedia presentations; hypertext and other computer programs; improvisation role-playing; readers theatre; story quilts; multi-dimensional models; and illustrations for charts, posters, and books they are writing. Projects involving visual texts are often completed as part of resource-based and theme study units and incorporate the use of multiliteracies. Three key concepts about visually representing are presented in this book:

- Students create and interpret visual texts.
- Students consider audience, purpose, and form as they create visual texts.
- Visual texts, like writing, can be created to share responses to literature read and information learned during resource-based units and theme study units.

RELATIONSHIPS AMONG THE LANGUAGE ARTS

Discussing the language arts one by one suggests a division among them, as though they could be used separately. In reality, they are used simultaneously and reciprocally. Almost any activity in this area involves more than one of the language arts.

Resource-based units, readers and writers workshops, across-the-curriculum theme study units and inquiry-based units are four ways to make language arts instruction meaningful. These ways of organizing instruction are fully described in Chapter 11. Students use all six language arts as they engage in all types of units. For example, as grade 5 students read and respond to *Hana's Suitcase* (Levine, 2002), a story set in a small Czech town during the World War II about a found suitcase belonging to a Jewish girl, they use listening, speaking, reading, writing, viewing, and visual representing in some of the ways shown in Figure 1–2. Across–the–curriculum connections are also possible given the historical setting of the story.

Similarly, students use the six language arts as they learn and share their learning in social studies and science theme study units. As second graders learn about dinosaurs in a theme study unit, they use the six arts to explore the concepts they are learning as well as to share what they have learned. See Figure 1–3 for some of these across–the–curriculum connections for a theme study unit on dinosaurs.

FIGURE 1-2 WAYS GRADE 5 STUDENTS USE THE SIX LANGUAGE ARTS IN A RESOURCE-BASED UNIT ON HANA'S SUITCASE

1. Listening
Students listen to Hana's Suitcase by Karen Levine as it is read aloud, and they listen to classmates' comments during literature discussions. They listen and watch as classmates dramatize events from the story and as classmates share reports of information or projects.

2. Speaking
Students speak as they make predictions about what will happen in upcoming chapters and as they share their responses to the story during literature discussions. They may share the results of their research into World War II, or report on the geography of what was Czechoslovakia and locate the town of Nove Mesto, a place the Brady family called home. Students also speak as they dramatize story events and share projects they create after reading the story.

3. Reading
Students read aloud from Hana's Suitcase, with a buddy, or independently. They may reread brief excerpts from the story during discussions or read-arounds. Many students read other books about World War II and the Holocaust such as Kathy Kacer's, (2006), Hiding Edith.. Students read aloud to share their journal entries and quickwrites with classmates. During writing groups, they read aloud, the stories, poems, reports, or other projects they are writing.

4. Writing
Students write their predictions about and reactions to each chapter in reading logs or keep simulated journals written from the viewpoint of one of the characters. Students write quick-writes to help them focus their attention on topics related to the story. They also make notes during presentations by the teacher about World War II and the Holocaust. Students use the writing process as they write letters to the author, poems, reports, and other compositions.

5. Viewing
Students observe as classmates dramatize scenes from the story. They examine large black-and-white photos of war scenes that the teacher has collected, and talk about the impact of the black-and-white photos. They consider how the impact would differ if the photos were in colour. They also watch videos about World War II, make notes after viewing, and talk about the videos in grand conversations.

6. Visually Representing
Students make setting maps of Europe, North America, and Japan and include sites mentioned in the story, and they make a story quilt to celebrate students' favourite quotations from the story. They also make open-mind portraits of the main characters. For these portraits, students draw a large picture of the character's face and cut it out. Then they cut a second piece of paper the same size and glue it on a piece of construction paper. They draw pictures and write words on this piece of paper to represent the character's thoughts. Then they staple the character's face paper on top so that it flips open to reveal the character's thoughts.

FIGURE 1-3 WAYS GRADE 2 STUDENTS USE THE SIX LANGUAGE ARTS IN A THEME STUDY UNIT ON DINOSAURS

1. Listening
Students listen to books about dinosaurs. They listen to their teacher read from Dinosaurs: The Most Complete Up to Date Encyclopedia for Dinosaur Lovers of All Ages (Holtz, 2007), an informational text offering fascinating facts. They look at other informational and picture books such as Creatures of Long Ago (National Geographic, 1996). Students also listen and laugh as they attend to a recorded reading of the humorous rhyming text of Drumheller Dinosaur Dance (Heidbreder, 2006),

2. Speaking
Students talk about dinosaurs and about what they are learning in the theme study unit. After reading or listening to the teacher read a book, they participate in grand conversations in which they share their responses to the book. They also create their own riddles after listening to the teacher read the riddles in Two Dozen Dinosaurs: A First Book of Dinosaurs Facts, Mysteries, Games and Fun (Ripley, 1991). Later, students will reach a wide audience when they pose some of their riddles to the whole school following the morning announcements on the public address system.

3. Reading
In small groups, students read and review informational books such as Where Did Dinosaurs Come From? (Zoehfeld, 2010), then make a timeline in their learning logs of the dinosaurs' time on earth. Students record interesting facts in their learning logs. Also, using books from the classroom library, students read and reread more stories, informational books, and poems about dinosaurs.

4. Writing
Students write in learning logs and make clusters, diagrams, and other charts in the logs, too. Then they use the writing process to research and write reports about dinosaurs. They post their finished reports next to the large papier-mâché mountain they create. Some students work together to write an alphabet book about dinosaurs. Each student chooses a letter and writes and illustrates one page, and then they compile the pages to create a digital text they share with their classmates and families.

5. Viewing
Together as a class, students view videos and examine posters about dinosaurs with their teacher. Working in partners and individually, they search several websites and record their observations from the photos they view and the additional videos they watch.

6. Visually Representing
As they learn about dinosaurs, students take notes and draw pictures and diagrams to help them remember important information. Some students make Plasticine models of dinosaurs and place these on or next to a large papier-mâché display of the dinosaurs' habitat. Others work collaboratively to create a mural that depicts their learning about prehistoric habitat and dinosaur size, shapes, and colours.

Review

Language arts instruction should be based on theories and research about how children learn. Language, culture, and technology also have an impact on how students learn the language arts. Being literate involves the use of multiliteracies to show all the various ways students can communicate—through print, video and other digital texts, images, music, drama, and speech. It is equally important that students learn to read critically and analyze the many texts they encounter. The goal of language arts instruction is for students to develop communicative competence in the six language arts—listening, speaking, reading, writing, viewing, and visually representing.

The following key concepts are presented in this chapter:

1. Language arts instruction should be based on how children learn.
2. Students learn through active involvement in listening, speaking, reading, writing, viewing, and visually representing activities.
3. Teachers should provide instruction within children's zone of proximal development.
4. Teachers scaffold or support children's learning.
5. Students use all four language systems: phonological, syntactic, semantic, and pragmatic.
6. Developing students' abilities to critically analyze texts is an important aspect of literacy instruction.
7. Technology is challenging our view of literacy, and new technologies demand that teachers respond by acknowledging the emergence of multiliteracies needed to effectively understand, manage, and evaluate online reference tools, visual media, and the Internet.
8. Students need opportunities to participate in language arts activities that are meaningful, functional, and genuine.
9. Teachers create a community of learners in their classrooms.
10. Students learn and use language arts strategies and skills.

Theory to Practice

1. Observe a language arts lesson being taught in an elementary or middle-school classroom. Choose one student to observe and try to determine if he or she is working in his or her zone of proximal development described in this chapter. What conclusions can you draw about this student's learning?
2. Observe and record several students' talk. Analyze their phonological, syntactic, semantic, and pragmatic language systems. If possible, compare primary-grade students' language with that of middle- and upper-grade students.
3. Interview a language arts teacher and ask how he or she teaches the six language arts—listening, speaking, reading, writing, viewing, and visually representing. Compare the teacher's comments with the information in this chapter.
4. Observe a student participating in language arts activities. What multiliteracies are being demonstrated by this student's use of technology in the classroom?
5. Examine a popular piece of children's literature and consider it in the context of critical literacy. Imagine how you might teach children about how the text has been produced, by whom, and for what purposes.
6. Talk to an experienced teacher and ask how his or her approach to teaching English language arts has changed over the years because of the introduction of new technologies. What changes does he or she anticipate in the next five years?

Chapter 2: Critical Thinking about Characters

One of my most successful critical thinking units ties in with our focus on character traits. Each month we identify and learn about a different character trait, such as responsibility, fairness, empathy, or integrity. This particular unit focuses on one of my favourite traits, perseverance.

Procedure

To start the unit, I access students' prior knowledge by recording all they think they know about what perseverance is on a piece of chart paper. We then move on to our first read-aloud, which allows us to broaden our definition of perseverance and leads us to create "criteria" for characters who persevere. The guiding question is phrased as "What do characters who persevere do?" After reading *Martin's Big Words* (Rappaport, 2001), an account of the life of Martin Luther King, Jr., the students come up with their criteria. Criteria take an argument from an opinion to a judgment. My students came up with these criteria: characters who persevere never give up, demonstrate patience, set and meet goals, develop a plan and stick to it, and overcome obstacles.

I choose five stories for grade 3 and four for grade 2. Here are the books we read: *Jeremiah Learns to Read* (Bogart, 1999), *The Three Ninja Pigs* (C. R. Schwartz, 2012), *How to Catch a Star* (Jeffers, 2004), *The Story of Ruby Bridges* (Coles, 1995), and *The Story of Jumping Mouse* (Steptoe, 1989). As we read through the stories—usually one or two per week, depending on what else we are working on during our literacy block—students are prompted to listen for all the examples of perseverance they hear. After each read-aloud, I gather the students' thoughts using a variety of strategies. Strategies I use often include think–pair–share; drama in small groups, acting out the scenes showing perseverance; placing the criteria on sticky notes around the room and having students move to the criteria for which they have an example; and illustrating scenes that show perseverance.

As the students are sharing, I record their thoughts on a chart. The chart includes the story titles and characters' names along the left-hand side and the criteria across the top. Students are then asked to choose the character they think persevered the most.

The chart we create through all the read-alouds is a major source of information and is posted during all working periods. Modelling the creation of a good argument is also important, and keeping that model visible for students really helps. This year I asked my grade 3 students to develop four strong arguments, and asked my grade 2 students to create two. Here are some sample arguments from my students.

> "I chose the boy in *How to Catch a Star*. He did not get any help to overcome his obstacles, like when he asked the seagull for help, it said NO. Jumping Mouse got help, like from Magic Frog, the bison, and the wolf."
>
> Mia, grade 2

> "I think Ruby Bridges persevered the most. In *Jeremiah Learns to Read*, Jeremiah was just walking to school. Ruby Bridges had to go through a big, enormous crowd of mad and angry adults. People were saying mean things to her. Jeremiah had nice people by his side."
>
> Eleni, grade 3

> "Jumping Mouse got to the far-off land helping other animals along the way, giving them better sight and the ability to smell. I think he saved some of the animals' lives. None of the other characters helped and persevered."
>
> Jack, grade 3

Assessment

I keep a chart posted in clear view listing all the "look fors" I would like to see. I then turn the expectations or "look fors" into a rubric. Throughout the unit, I regularly take anecdotal notes recording the strengths and needs of all students.

Another form of feedback I like to use is two stars and a wish. The wish is the students' next step or area they could improve upon. Students with modified expectations dictate their arguments so they can be scribed or recorded, or they draw pictures with short captions to represent their arguments. After an assignment like this, I also have a group discussion about the things I saw most students doing really well and the areas that I think all could improve upon. Students also share what they felt they did well, what they thought was challenging, and where they would like to improve.

Adaptation

This particular activity allows for integration within language arts and with other subjects as well. A natural next step for this unit is to stage a debate in which students argue and defend their choices orally. Students can be grouped on the basis of their choices of characters and asked to create a dramatic performance, perhaps a tableau or skit, demonstrating their characters' perseverance. Visual arts and media literacy can be combined as students create a poster promoting the movie version of their storybook starring their persevering character.

Reflection

All children, regardless of their ability to read, write, or draw, can think critically. I have known students who struggle with writing and reading but who absolutely shine in critical thinking activities. Critical thinking adds depth to the curriculum and helps students recognize the power of their own thoughts and ideas. In the beginning, some students may struggle and the results of the activities may not be what teachers expect. But after more discussions, questions, and practice, students start to see and believe in what they can think and do!

From the classroom of Jessica Currie, Primary ETFI Teacher
Rockcliffe Park Public School
Ottawa, Ontario

Teaching the Language Arts

Jules Selmes/Pearson Education

The teacher reads a big book to her students linking their reading to the theme study and inquiry based units of their program.

Language arts instruction should be based on how children learn. Teachers are encouraged to build a literate environment that facilitates the development of lifelong readers and writers (Graves & Kittle, 2005). An effective paradigm for language arts instruction will engage teachers in creating a learning community in the classroom to facilitate student development in language arts, supporting students as they learn skills and strategies related to the language arts, and teaching lessons that allow students to apply what they are learning in listening, speaking, reading, writing, viewing, and visually representing activities. Certainly, the classroom environment reflects teachers' goals for their students. Classrooms filled with books, laptop computers, iPads, and other digital devices equipped for writing and multimedia production and projection reflect teachers' expectations for their students to use all six language arts flexibly and effectively.

Three popular organizational structures involve students in meaningful, functional, and genuine language-learning activities in a balanced way. These three structures are *resource-based units*, *theme-study units*, and *inquiry-based units*. Within these organizational structures, many teachers use readers and writers workshops as ways of organizing a large part of their instruction. Although teachers may use prescribed anthologies as a foundation for their programs, effective language arts instruction, regardless of organizational structure, involves engagement with a variety of texts both narrative and expository—print and other media—and multiple opportunities to explore language and communicate with others. Teachers use a variety of children's and young adult literature as an integral part of their teaching resources and are knowledgeable about effective ways of teaching using this literature.

A Paradigm for Language Arts Instruction

Language arts instruction should be based on how children learn, the impact of language and culture on learning, and society's goals for its children's literacy development. Teachers create a community of learners in their classrooms in order to facilitate students' learning; they support students as they learn skills and strategies related to the language arts; and they teach lessons that encourage students to apply what they are learning about listening, speaking, reading, writing, viewing, and visually representing across all subject areas of the curriculum.

A Community of Learners

Language arts classrooms are social settings. Together, students and their teacher create the classroom community, and the type of community they create strongly influences the students' learning. Effective teachers establish a community of learners in which students are motivated to learn and are actively involved in language arts activities. Teachers and students work collaboratively and purposefully. Perhaps the most striking quality of classroom communities is the partnership that the teacher and students create. Within the community, all the members respect one another and support each other's learning.

Students and the teacher work together for the common good of the community. In a classroom community, students and the teacher are joint owners of the classroom. Students assume responsibility for their own learning and behaviour, work collaboratively with classmates, complete assignments, and care for the classroom. In contrast, when a sense of learning community is not established, the classroom is perceived as the teacher's alone. This doesn't mean that in a classroom community teachers abdicate their responsibility to students. Teachers retain their roles of organizer, facilitator, participant, instructor, model, manager, diagnostician, evaluator, coordinator, and communicator. These roles are often shared with students, but the ultimate responsibility remains with teachers.

Curricula for Canadian schools acknowledge the place of learning communities to foster language learning and offer teachers guidance for their development. As stated in the kindergarten English language arts curriculum guide for Newfoundland and Labrador (Newfoundland and Labrador Department of Education, 2011),

> "To create a community of learners, teachers must ensure that all students feel respected and valued. Diversity in the classroom is celebrated, emphasizing the point that it enhances the learning for all. It is important that students feel comfortable knowing they are supported and cared for by their teacher, and each other.

This type of classroom community improves both the level of student engagement and their level of academic achievement" (p. 15).

Setting up a classroom community requires the teacher take an active role to help students discover that their behaviors make a difference to others in the classroom. According to Bielaczyc, Kapur, and Collins (2013), "Describing teachers as 'facilitators' or 'a guide on the side,' while accurate, does not address the necessary level of detail for helping teachers to shift the ways in which they support students in their learning" (p. 242). The goal is for students to be active in learning which impacts motivation.

Motivation for Learning

Motivation is intrinsic and internal—a driving force within us. Motivation to read can be defined as the likelihood of engaging in reading or choosing to read (Gambrell, 2009). In her recent consideration of what is most important for teachers to know about reading motivation, Linda Gambrell (2011) delineates what she refers to as seven "rules of engagement," or seven observations of motivated readers of significance to teachers. Gambrell notes that students are more motivated to read when:

- reading tasks and activities are relevant to their lives
- students have access to a wide range of reading materials
- students have ample opportunities to engage in sustained reading
- students have opportunities to make choices about what they read and how they engage in and complete literary tasks
- students have opportunities to socially interact with others about the texts they are reading
- students have opportunities to be successful with challenging texts
- classroom incentives reflect the value and importance of reading

Although Gambrell's work speaks specifically to reading, many of her observations apply to students' engagement with all of the language arts. Motivation for the task is key to student learning and success, whether the task is simply reading or engaging in other literate activities as well.

Language Arts Strategies and Skills

Students learn both strategies and skills through language arts instruction. **Strategies** are problem-solving methods or behaviours. Students develop and use both general learning strategies and specific strategies related to the language arts. While there is no definitive list of language arts strategies, researchers have identified a number of strategies that capable readers and writers use (Paris & Jacobs, 1984; Schmitt, 1990). We will focus on twelve of these strategies in this text:

tapping into prior knowledge	applying fix-up strategies
predicting	revising meaning
organizing ideas	monitoring meaning
figuring out unknown words	playing with language
visualizing	generalizing
making connections	evaluating

These strategies are described in Figure 2-1. Students often use more than one of these strategies for a language arts activity, but they rarely, if ever, use all them for a single activity. Students choose the appropriate strategies to accomplish the activities in which they are engaged.

FIGURE 2-1 LANGUAGE ARTS STRATEGIES

1. Tapping into Prior Knowledge
Students think about what they already know about the topic as they listen, read, view, or write. This knowledge includes information and vocabulary about content-area topics such as whales or the solar system, as well as language arts information about authors, types of literature, and literal and figurative meanings.

2. Predicting
Students make predictions about what will happen as they read or view. These guesses are based on students' knowledge about the topic and the type of literature, or what they have read or viewed thus far. Students also make predictions as they speak, write, and visually represent. They make plans and set purposes.

3. Organizing Ideas
Students organize ideas and sequence story events when they read, write, view, or listen to stories read aloud. Students organize ideas for writing using clusters and demonstrate comprehension after reading or viewing using other graphic organizers. Students organize ideas differently depending on whether they are exploring stories, informational books, or poetry.

4. Figuring out Unknown Words
Students figure out unknown words as they read, listen, and view. Depending on the particular situation, students choose whether to use word attack skills, context clues, or skip over a word. Writers use "sound it out" and "think it out" strategies to spell unfamiliar words.

5. Visualizing
Students draw pictures in their minds of what they are listening to, reading, or writing. Often film versions of stories are disappointing because they don't match students' visualizations.

6. Making Connections
Students relate what they are listening, reading, or viewing to their own lives and to books they have read. Similarly, students make connections between their writing or oral presentations and books they have read and experiences they have had.

7. Applying Fix-up Strategies
When students are listening, speaking, reading, writing, viewing, or visually representing and something doesn't make sense, they apply fix-up strategies. They may assume that things will make sense soon and continue with the activity, or they may ask a question, go back, or skip ahead when reading or viewing, or speak with a classmate.

8. Revising Meaning
Students continuously revise meaning as they proceed with a language arts activity. When reading, for example, students reread for more information or because something doesn't make sense, they study the illustrations, or they get ideas from classmates during discussions. Writers meet in writing groups to get feedback on their rough drafts in order to revise their writing and make it stronger. Students also get feedback when they create visual representations.

9. Monitoring
Students ask themselves questions to monitor their understanding as they participate in language arts activities. They monitor their comprehension as they read, view, and listen. They recognize when comprehension breaks down and use other strategies to regain comprehension. When they give oral presentations or participate in discussions, students monitor what they are saying and the reactions of classmates.

10. Playing with Language
Students notice figurative and novel uses of language as they listen, read, and view. When they give oral presentations and write, students incorporate interesting language in their presentations and compositions.

11. Generalizing
When students read, view, and listen, they note ideas and put them together to draw conclusions. Generalizing is important because big ideas are easier to remember than lots of details. Writers often state their big ideas at the beginning of a paragraph and then support them with facts. They want their readers to be able to make generalizations. When students give oral presentations and create visual representations, they emphasize generalizations, too.

12. Evaluating
Students make judgments about, reflect on, and value the language arts activities in which they participate. They also think about themselves as language users and reflect on what they do as listeners, speakers, readers, and writers.

These strategies are applied in all six language arts. Consider revising meaning, for example. Probably its best-known application is in writing. Students revise meaning as they add, substitute, delete, and move information in their drafts. Revising meaning in visual or multimedia representations works the same way. But students also revise meaning as they listen to a speaker, view a video, or read a book. They revise their understanding as they continue listening, viewing, or reading and get more information. And students revise meaning while they are talking, on the basis of feedback from the audience.

Skills, in contrast, are information-processing techniques that students use automatically and unconsciously as they construct meaning. Many skills focus at the word level, but some require students to attend to larger chunks of text. For example, readers use skills such as decoding unfamiliar words, noting details, and sequencing events; writers employ skills such as forming contractions, using punctuation marks, and capitalizing people's names. Skills and strategies are not the same thing, since strategies are problem-solving tactics selected deliberately to achieve particular goals (Paris, Wasik, & Turner, 1991). At the heart of accomplished reading is a balance of both—automatic application and use of reading skills with intentional, effortful employment of reading strategies—accompanied by the ability to shift seamlessly between the two when the situation calls for it (Afflerbach, Pearson, & Paris, 2008). The important difference between skills and strategies is how and when they are used.

During the elementary and middle-school grades, students learn to use and refine five types of skills. While many of the skills are oriented to reading and writing, some are used for listening, speaking, viewing, and visually representing. The five types of skills are

1. *Meaning-making skills.* These include summarizing, separating facts and opinions, comparing and contrasting, and recognizing literary genres and structures. Students use these skills as they create meaning using all six language arts.

2. *Decoding and spelling skills.* These include sounding out words, noticing word families, using root words and affixes to decode and spell words, and using abbreviations. Students use these skills as they decode words when reading and as they spell words when writing.

3. *Study skills.* These include skimming and scanning, taking notes, making clusters, and previewing a book before reading. Students use study skills during across-the-curriculum theme study units, while reading informational texts, and while collecting information to use in composing reports.

4. *Language skills.* These include identifying and inferring meanings of words, noticing idioms and other examples of figurative language, dividing words into syllables, and choosing synonyms. Students are continuously interacting with language as they use the language arts, and they use these skills to analyze words when they are listening and reading, and to choose more precise language when they are speaking and writing.

5. *Reference skills.* These include alphabetizing a list of words, using a dictionary or thesaurus, reading and making graphic organizers, and identifying relevant information on the Internet. Elementary and middle-school students learn to use reference skills in order to read a variety of texts efficiently, including locating specific information in printed and digital resources.

Examples of each of the five types of skills are presented in Figure 2-2. Students use these skills for various language arts activities. For example, students use some of the skills when giving an oral report and others when making a digital book trailer

FIGURE 2-2 LANGUAGE ARTS SKILLS

Meaning-Making Skills

Sequence
Summarize
Categorize
Classify
Identify the author's purpose
Separate facts and opinions
Note details
Draw conclusions
Identify cause and effect
Compare and contrast
Determine problem and solution
Use context clues
Notice organizational patterns of poetry, plays, business
    and friendly letters, stories, essays, and reports
Recognize literary genres (traditional stories, fantasies,
    speculative fiction, realistic fiction, historical fiction,
    biography, autobiography, and poetry)
Identify mood
Recognize persuasion and propaganda

Decoding and Spelling Skills

Sound out words using knowledge of phonics
Notice word families
Look for picture cues
Ask a classmate or the teacher
Consult a dictionary or glossary
Apply spelling rules
Write plurals
Use root words and affixes
Use structural clues
Capitalize proper nouns and adjectives
Use abbreviations

Study Skills

Adjust rate of reading
Skim
Scan
Preview
Follow directions
Make outlines and clusters
Take notes
Paraphrase

Language Skills

Choose among multiple meanings of words
Notice compound words
Use contractions
Divide words into syllables
Use possessives
Notice figurative language
Use similes and metaphors
Notice idioms and slang
Use comparatives and superlatives
Choose synonyms
Recognize antonyms
Differentiate among homonyms
Appreciate rhyme, imagery, and other poetic devices
Use punctuation marks (period, question mark, exclamation
    mark, quotation marks, comma, colon, semicolon,
    and hyphen)
Use simple, compound, and complex sentences
Use declarative, interrogative, exclamatory, and imperative
    sentences
Combine sentences
Recognize parts of sentences
Avoid sentence fragments
Recognize parts of speech (nouns, pronouns, verbs, adjectives,
    adverbs, conjunctions, prepositions, and interjections)

Reference Skills

Sort in alphabetical order
Use a glossary or dictionary
Locate etymologies in the dictionary
Use the pronunciation guide in the dictionary
Locate synonyms in a thesaurus
Locate information in print and digital texts
Compare information from more than one source
Use a table of contents
Use an index
Read and make graphs, tables, and diagrams
Read and make timelines
Read newspapers, magazines, and e-zines
Use conventional bibliographic and
    other reference forms
Use digital resource
    catalogues

for a book they have read or comparing several versions of a folktale. It is unlikely that students use every skill listed in Figure 2-2 for any particular language arts activity, but capable students are familiar with most of these skills and can use them automatically whenever they are needed.

Teachers might wonder when they should teach the skills listed in Figure 2-2. Provincial education departments and school districts often prepare curriculum guides that list the skills to be taught at each grade level, and skills are usually listed on scope-and-sequence charts that accompany commercially published language arts series and programs. These resources provide guidelines, but teachers decide which skills to teach based on their students' instructional needs and the activities in which their students are involved.

Teachers use both direct and indirect instruction to provide information that students need to have about skills and strategies. Both skill and strategy instruction are presented in context so that students see a reason to learn them and are able to apply what they learn in meaningful ways.

When teachers model how to do something, scaffold a student's use of a strategy or skill, or respond to a student's question, they are using indirect instruction. In contrast, direct instruction is planned. Teachers often teach minilessons in which they explicitly explain a particular skill or strategy, model its use, and provide examples and opportunities for practice. Then students apply what they have learned using meaningful, functional, and genuine activities.

A Teaching Strategy

Learning theories can be applied in designing a strategy or lesson format to be used in teaching strategies, skills, concepts, procedures, and other types of information. Piaget's concepts of assimilation and accommodation are important because they describe how children learn concepts and add information to their cognitive structures. Similarly, Vygotsky's concept of the zone of proximal development is useful because it explains that teachers can support students and assist them in learning things that they cannot learn by themselves. The six-step teaching strategy in the Step by Step box establishes a sequence of instruction that can be adapted for teaching almost any language arts procedure, concept, strategy, or skill.

Students do not, of course, learn in such neat little steps. Rather, learning is a process of ebb and flow in which the assimilating and accommodating processes move back and forth as the student grasps pieces of information. Students may grasp a new concept in any of the steps of the teaching strategy; some students may not learn it at all. Teachers will plan additional lessons for the students who need more time to learn. Whether or not students learn depends on the closeness of the fit between their schemata and the information being presented. Information that does not in some way relate to an existing schema is almost impossible to learn. Information must be moderately novel to fit students' existing cognitive structures.

Not all lessons lend themselves readily to this six-step sequence of instruction; for certain concepts, one or more of the steps may not be appropriate, and some adjustments may be necessary.

Two applications to illustrate how the teaching strategy can be used are presented in Figure 2-3. The first is a lesson on *fables*—brief stories that teach a lesson. Some of the best-known fables were compiled by Aesop, a Greek slave who lived in the sixth century BCE, but many other civilizations have contributed fables as well. A number of fables have been retold for children, and children's authors such as Arnold Lobel (1980) have written their own books of fables. The goal of this lesson is for students to examine the genre of fables and learn the characteristics of a fable. This lesson might be taught as part of a resource-based unit on fables in which students read and respond to fables and then tell and write some of their own. The lesson is organized around the six steps of the teaching strategy we have presented. For the sake of brevity, other activities that would be part of this two-week unit for a grade 4 class are not included in this plan.

The second application presented in Figure 2-3 focuses on rhyming words. This lesson might be taught after students read Dr. Seuss's *The Cat in the Hat* (1957). The goal of this lesson is for students to create words that rhyme with *cat*, including *bat*, *fat*, *hat*, *mat*, *pat*, *rat*, and *sat*. Other -*at* words requiring consonant digraphs and blends include *flat*, *chat*, *splat*, and *that*. This plan is also organized around the six steps of the teaching strategy. This lesson is a part of a two-week author study on Dr. Seuss, planned for a grade 1 class.

FIGURE 2-3 USING THE TEACHING STRATEGY

Step	Fables Lesson	Rhyming Words Lesson
Initiating	The teacher rereads "The Hare and the Tortoise" and "The Lion and the Mouse" from Hague's *Aesop's Fables* (1985) and explains that these short stories that teach a moral are called *fables*.	The teacher sets out a large hat and passes out a variety of small objects, including a bat puppet, a block, a toy cat, a placemat, a fork, a plastic rat, and a toy horse. Students place the objects with rhyming names in the hat. The teacher explains that rhyming words sound the same at the end: *cat, hat, mat, bat,* and *rat*.
Structuring	Students and the teacher develop a chart listing the characteristics of fables. The list may include these characteristics: • Fables are short. • The characters are usually animals. • The setting is usually rural and not important to the story. • Fables involve only one event. • The moral is usually stated at the end of the story.	The teacher distributes word cards with these *-at* words written on them: *bat, cat, fat, hat, mat, pat, rat, sat, flat, chat, that,* and *splat*. Students read the words and place them in the hat. They also suggest any other *-at* words they can think of, and the teacher writes these words on word cards.
Conceptualizing	The teacher then reads one or two other fables, and the students check that their lists of the characteristics of fables are complete.	The teacher passes out white eraseboards, and students write *-at* family words as the teacher holds up objects from the hat and reads words on the word cards. Students can invent other *-at* words, such as *dat* and *zat*.
Summarizing	The teacher asks students to make a chart in their language arts notebooks explaining what a fable is. Students share their explanations and compare them to the list of characteristics.	Students brainstorm a list of words that rhyme with *hat* and write them on a chart. Students take turns circling the *-at* pattern at the end of each word.
Generalizing	Students read other fables, such as Lobel's *Fables* (1980) or Mollel's *Rhinos for Lunch and Elephants for Supper! A Maasai Tale* (1991). It is important to include some fables that state the moral implicitly rather than explicitly. Students explain why these stories are or are not fables. The teacher also points out that these fables were created—not retold—by Arnold Lobel and Tololwa Mollel.	Students create a rhyming *-at* book. They draw pictures of four rhyming words and write the words beside each picture. After students compile their books, they share them with classmates.
Applying	Students apply what they have learned when they write their own fables. Students may explicitly state the moral at the end of the story or imply it in the story.	Students apply what they have learned about rhyming words with other rhyming patterns. The teacher sets out a pan, a hen, a toy car, and a nail, and students match rhyming objects with these objects: pan: can, man, fan, tan crayon hen: pen, ten, men car: chocolate bar, jar, star nail: mail, pail, sail (on a boat), snail.

Language-Rich Classrooms

Elementary classrooms should be authentic language environments that encourage students to listen, speak, read, write, view, and visually represent; that is, they should be language-rich. The physical arrangement and materials provided in the classroom play an important role in setting the stage for language arts instruction (Morrow, 1996).

In the past, prescribed readers, or **basal reading programs**, were the primary instructional material, and students sat in desks arranged in rows facing the teacher. Now a wide variety of instructional resources are available; often students' desks are arranged in small groups; classroom libraries include comfortable seating and are well stocked with a variety of high-quality trade books; and classrooms are made visually stimulating with teacher- and student-made displays.

Multimedia technology is also changing the face of both language arts instruction and the language arts classroom. Computers and other multimedia devices such as digital cameras, scanners, and projection equipment are commonplace in Canadian classrooms. And if not consistently available in the classroom, such equipment is available in the school. Further, almost all schools and classrooms are linked to the Internet. How does, and how should, technology influence instruction in a language-rich classroom?

These are frequently observed components of a language-rich classroom:

- desks arranged in groups to facilitate cooperative learning
- classroom libraries stocked with a variety of reading materials
- messages posted about the current day
- displays of student work and projects
- displayed signs, labels for items, and quotations
- directions posted for activities or use of equipment
- abundant supply of materials for recording language, both in print and digitally
- spaces designated for reading and writing activities

See Chapter 9 , "Viewing and Visually Representing," pages 334–353 for further discussion of the role and influence of media and technology in teaching the language arts.

STEP BY STEP

Sequence of Instruction for Lessons

1 Initiating   The teacher introduces the strategy, skill, concept, or procedure. The initiating step includes questions, statements, examples, and activities for stimulating interest in the lesson and engaging students' participation.

2 Structuring   The teacher presents information and relates it to what students already know so that students can begin to overcome the cognitive conflict they experienced in the first step. To overcome cognitive conflict, students begin to enlarge or restructure an existing schema to fit the information, or they begin to develop a new schema to organize the information.

3 Conceptualizing   Students experiment with and analyze the information presented in the second step in order to make connections to related information. This step furthers the process of accommodation begun earlier. When the accommodation process is completed, the existing schemata have been enlarged or a new schema has been developed that fits the new information.

4 Summarizing   The teacher and students review the major points of the lesson. The information and examples presented in the structuring step and the relationships established during the conceptualizing step are organized and summarized. This step allows students to make any necessary adjustments in the schema and in the new interrelationships established within their cognitive structures. For students who have not understood the information being presented, summarizing presents another opportunity to accommodate the information.

5 Generalizing   The teacher presents new examples or variations of the information introduced in the first step. This step is a check on students' understanding, and students demonstrate their understanding by generalizing from the first example to this new example.

6 Applying   Students incorporate the information in an activity that allows them to demonstrate their knowledge by using the concept in a novel or unique way.

- reference resources for group and individual use
- multimedia equipment and software for listening, recording, viewing, and reading
- world-related print (e.g., photographs, maps, and calendars)
- reading and writing materials in young children's dramatic play centres

Figure 2-4 elaborates on these components of a language-rich classroom.

FIGURE 2-4 CHARACTERISTICS OF A LANGUAGE-RICH CLASSROOM

1. Classroom Organization
- Desks are arranged in groups.
- The arrangement facilitates group interaction.
- The arrangement facilitates the teacher working with whole class, small groups, and individuals.

2. Classroom Library Centre
- There are at least four times as many books as there are students in the classroom.
- Stories, informational books, and poetry are included.
- Multicultural books and other reading materials are included.
- Information about authors and illustrators is displayed.
- Some of the books were written by students.
- Books related to resource-based units and theme study units are highlighted.
- Students monitor the centre.

3. Message Centre
- Schedules and announcements about the current day are posted.
- Some of the announcements are student-initiated.
- Students are encouraged to write notes to classmates.
- Messages concerning school, community, and world events of interest are posted.

4. Display of Student Work and Projects
- All students have work displayed in the classroom.
- Student work reflects a variety of curricular areas.
- Students' projects and other student-made displays are exhibited in the classroom.
- There is an area where students can display their own work.
- Other student work is stored in portfolios or in digital files accessible to students and the teacher.

5. Author's Chair
- One chair in the classroom has been designated as the author's chair for students to use when sharing their writing.
- The author's chair is labelled and considered a special place of honour.

6. Signs, Labels, and Quotations
- Equipment and other classroom items are labelled.
- Words, phrases, and sentences are posted in the classroom.
- Some signs, labels, and quotations are written by students.
- Displays of words, phrases, and quotations are relevant to units of study and change frequently.

7. Routines and Directions
- Routines are established and followed so students know what to expect and learning time is maximized.
- Directions are provided in the classroom so that students can work independently.
- Some of the directions are written and posted by students.

8. Materials for Writing
- Pencils, pens, paper, journals, books, computers, and other materials are available for recording language.
- Materials are clearly organized and students shown how to care for them.
- Students have easy access to these materials and monitor their use.

(continued)

FIGURE 2-4 CHARACTERISTICS OF A LANGUAGE-RICH CLASSROOM (*continued*)

9. Places for Reading and Writing
- There are special places in the classroom for reading and writing activities.
- These areas are quiet and separated from other areas.
- These areas are welcoming and kept in order.

10. Reference Materials
- Word walls list important words related to study units.
- Lists, clusters, pictures, charts, books, models, and other reference materials are available for content-area study.
- Artifacts and other items related to study units are labelled and displayed.
- Students use these materials as they work on projects related to study units.

11. Multimedia Technology
- A viewing and listening centre with computers or iPods and headphones for students to experience stories, poems, and other literature read by expert readers.
- Computers and iPads for student writing, illustration, and presentations.
- Multimedia resources related to theme studies and resource-based units.
- Camcorder, digital camera, and projection facilities for student use.

12. Dramatic Play Centre
- A puppet stage is set up in the classroom.
- Art materials are available for making puppets and other props.
- An area in the classroom is accessible for presenting plays and telling stories.
- Props are available in the classroom.
- Centres include reading, writing, and drawing materials.

The Physical Arrangement

Any classroom can be configured to include many language-rich characteristics. You can group desks or tables to encourage students to talk, share, and work cooperatively. Designate areas for reading and writing; ideally, these will include accessible computers, a classroom library, a listening and viewing station, areas for materials related to content-area topics that facilitate inquiry-based learning, and a dramatic play centre for young children. Some variations obviously occur across grade levels. For example, older students need more space for independent research than do younger ones. The diagram in Figure 2-5 suggests ways to make the layout for a grade 3 classroom more language-rich.

Canadian elementary schools extensively use a **centres** approach to instruction in kindergarten and grade 1 and even into the higher grade levels. Many classrooms, however, are physically arranged to facilitate ready access to materials and promote a language-rich environment by encouraging and supporting small group interaction among students (again, see Figure 2-5).

Typically, classrooms include three centres or designated areas: a library centre to support reading, a listening centre to make recorded stories and information available, and a writing centre to support writing and publishing. In addition to the specific centres, most classrooms have computers available to facilitate the students' learning across the curriculum. Having ready access to technology and the Internet makes a significant contribution to creating a language-rich classroom.

In addition to generally creating language-rich classrooms, teachers also set up centres that are directly related to a resource-based unit, theme unit, or particular skills. Students work at these centres independently or in small groups to develop skills and explore unit-related literacy concepts. These centres are available for short periods of

FIGURE 2-5 DIAGRAM OF A LANGUAGE-RICH CLASSROOM

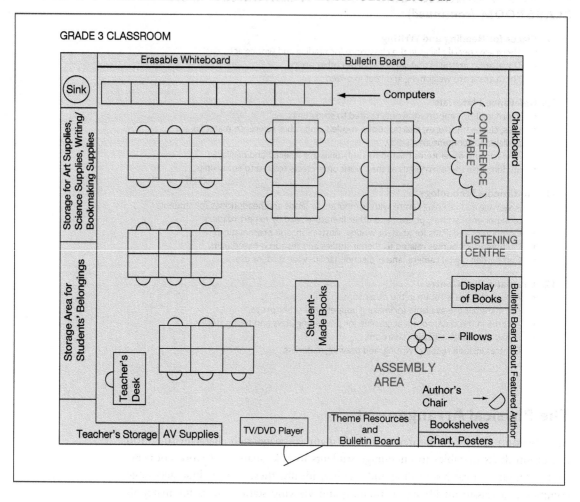

time and often employ baskets or folders that keep the materials organized and easily accessible. Activities are self-directed and can be completed with little teacher involvement, freeing the teacher to work with students on other tasks. Typical activities in these centres for primary-grade students who are just beginning to read include sorting sets of small pictures according to beginning sounds, using pictures or puppets to retell stories, using magnetic letters to spell words from class word lists, playing simple card games that require reading or writing, or completing predetermined web-based activities such as those that involve letter identification. In classrooms where students are capable of more reading and writing, activities might include collaboratively writing a story or a poem, playing computer games that offer practice in using writing conventions, and completing word puzzles. Other centres might encourage exploratory activities such as reading brochures or magazines to learn more about a unit theme, or reinforcement activities focused on spelling or vocabulary building.

Language Arts Programs

Teachers are not on their own when it comes to preparing their language arts programs. Many publishers of both print and non-print resources offer packaged programs of resources for teachers and students. Typically, a program includes a teacher's resource book and student reading materials, together with supplementary materials such as student activity books, resources concerning assessment, and other instructional supports such as DVDs. Historically, prepared programs were referred to as *basal reading programs*. Basal reading programs, however, were more limited than current programs. Most basal programs included a teacher's guide, one reader in which the selections were often written to a formula and were tightly controlled in regard to the level of difficulty, and a student workbook. Informed by research, basal reading programs have evolved to be comprehensive programs that offer teachers a wide base of support to help them meet the expectations of provincial curricula. One significant characteristic is the inclusion of Canadian literature, either as selections within an anthology or as individual texts. Recently published programs offer a wide variety of resources and encourage blending print and non-print resources to support a balanced approach to instruction for teaching all of the six language arts.

Teachers should not assume that packaged programs are equivalent to the total language arts program. Student teachers and beginning teachers, however, may rely heavily on these programs when they start teaching. Published programs approved for Canadian schools have much credibility and can form a solid foundation for language arts instruction. Teachers choose how to use the materials in a program and do not necessarily use all materials. Teachers must be sure that their programs include extensive reading (time and variety of literature) and extensive writing opportunities. Published programs sometimes fall short in these areas.

Children's Literature

Literature is the imaginative shaping of life and thought into the forms and structures of language (Kiefer, 2009). **Children's literature** is literature that appropriately reflects the emotions and experiences of children today. These books are a category of **trade books**, a publishing term used to designate the literature written for a general audience, including children and young adults. Children's literature as a body of work has enjoyed tremendous growth over the past thirty years, to the point where today there are thousands of children's books in print and available to teachers and students. In many Canadian schools, children's and young adult literature is the primary resource for teaching the language arts. Hence, all teachers need to be familiar with the formats and genres of literature, the general characteristics of each, as well to know the value of teaching with literature.

The values of teaching with children's literature are many, including providing delight and enjoyment to children. Children's literature also connects children with storytelling and with narrative ways of thinking. We perceive the world in narrative form (Bruner, 1986; Langer, 1995). Much of our experience is formed by stories, and we tell stories in order to understand our experiences and those of others.

Literature develops the imagination, allowing us to see both ourselves and others in new and different ways. This engagement of the imagination through stories is particularly important in the lives of children, as it nurtures and supports their cognitive development at crucial stages. This engagement of the imagination allows children to vicariously experience the world beyond their own. Children's literature allows us to move through time and space in the reading of a story. We can relive history and we can dream about the future.

Literature allows us to gain insight into human behaviour. It is concerned with feelings, with the quality of life. A story may present us with experiences similar to ones we have experienced, allowing us to see and feel how another person has dealt with a problem we may have encountered. Are we as courageous or as tenacious as the characters we are reading about in the story? What do we learn about ourselves in sharing the experiences of others? Through the reading of stories, we come to understand and appreciate the universality of human experience. Literature asks the big questions about the meaning of life and our relationships with nature and other people.

In terms of the educational development of children, literature plays an important role in oral language development. Children who are exposed to a wealth of literature in the home—who are read to from the beginning stages of life—enjoy significant advantages in later literacy development. This influence of books on children's language and literacy development continues once they begin school. Reading aloud to children throughout their school years and allowing them to have and be with real books also contributes to their growth. It is through exposure to the wealth of children's literature in its various genres that children develop a sense of book language and structure, concepts about print, and their fluency and understanding as readers.

There is also a strong connection between reading and writing. Teachers know that good writers are often avid readers and that good readers are often the best writers. Reading literature presents our students with models of exemplary writing. Part of our responsibility as language arts teachers is to provide students with a range of high-quality children's literature, heard or read, so that exemplary literature will become a resource for writing development and growth.

Formats and Genres of Children's Literature

Children's books are categorized according to their different formats and genres. The aspects of format that makes a children's book unique may include the size, shape, type of binding, arrangement of illustrations, endpapers, cover, typography, and spacing. For example, Ed Young's *Mouse Match* (1997), a retelling of the Chinese Mouse Bride story, is formatted as an accordion book, with the story and illustrations on one side of the page and the story in Chinese script on the other side. The story may be read page by page or stretched out as a many-folded single accordion page. The story may also be shared in Chinese or in translation and compared to the English telling. Children are fascinated with the format of the book and often want to create accordion books for their own writing once they experience this unique format for presenting a story.

Steve Jenkins's Actual Size books have another special format that intrigues young readers. In *Actual Size* (2004) and *Prehistoric Actual Size* (2005), fold-out pages and large illustrations show readers the size of animals and parts of animals as they exist or are understood to have existed prehistorically. Young's and Jenkins's book formats are but two examples of a wide variety of book formats designed to invite and intrigue children as they explore the world of children's books.

Children can also experience *toy books*—books written with some special device for involving the reader (Giorgis & Glazer, 2012). This may include textures for children to feel, smells for them to identify, or pop-up sections to illustrate various shapes or forms. Whether it is *Spot's Playtime Pop-up* (Hill, 2007) or *Cookie Count* (Sabuda, 1997), in which plate after plate of cookies twist and turn into a gingerbread house, children are fascinated with the intricacies and surprises of toy books.

Often a child's first encounter with books is with a board book or picture book. Board books are usually printed on heavy cardboard and are often laminated. They are designed for babies and toddlers who are just learning to handle books. The thickness of the pages makes them easier to turn and less likely to tear. Board books come in a variety of types and sizes, and include such titles as *My Very First Book of Animal Sounds* (Carle, 2007), Sandra Boynton's *Pajama Time* (2000), and *How Do Dinosaurs Learn Their Colors?* (Yolen, 2006).

PICTURE BOOKS

Picture books are those books in which the illustrations and text combine to form meaning. Some authorities consider picture books to be a format, while others consider them a separate genre. Regardless of the category, the distinguishing characteristic of a picture book is that the illustrations are crucial to the meaning of the story. In the longtime favourite *Rosie's Walk* (P. Hutchins, 1968), the minimal text of twenty-five words describing Rosie the hen going for a walk around the barnyard carries only a small part of the meaning of the story. The illustrations are integral to the true meaning of Rosie's walk and the dangers she faces from the fox along the way.

Many picture books are appropriate for young children, but others are written with middle-grade students in mind. Fairytales, myths, and legends have been retold beautifully as picture books, and new versions of these traditional tales have also been created. Examples include three Cinderella tales, *The Tender Tale of Cinderella Penguin* (Perlman, 1993), *The Gift of the Crocodile: A Cinderella Story* (Sierra, 2000), and *Cendrillon: A Caribbean Cinderella* (San Souci, 1998); *The Three Little Javelinas* (Lowell, 1992), which is a Southwestern adaptation of "The Three Little Pigs"; *The True Story of the 3 Little Pigs!* (Scieszka, 1989), the hilarious wolf's version of the story; and *The Girl Who Spun Gold* (V. Hamilton, 2000), a West Indian version of Rumpelstiltskin.

Picture books may have few or no words to complement the illustrations. Wordless picture books are a wonderful way to help develop language and thinking skills in young children. They allow children to explore various experiences without the required language skills of reading text. They also help children develop their narrative skills of identifying sequence, cause and effect, and main ideas and making judgments. Children view the illustrations and supply their own stories from their personal experiences to complete the illustrations. Wordless picture books are also particularly useful when working with children who are learning English as an added language. Books such as *The Snowman* (Briggs, 1980) and *Tabby: A Story in Pictures* (Aliki, 1995) are popular with primary-grade students. Other books, such as *Anno's Britain* (Anno, 1982) and *The Story of a Castle* (J. S. Goodall, 1986), appeal to middle- and upper-grade students because they connect to social studies and science themes. Wordless picture books can range from simple books like *Zoe's Snowy Day* (Reid, 1991a) to more advanced books for older readers, such as *Tuesday* (Wiesner, 1991), in which frogs rise from lily pads, float through the air, and explore nearby houses while their inhabitants sleep.

A *concept book* is a specialized type of picture book in which a single concept is developed with many examples. Concept books are often intended for children under the age of five, focusing on colours, shapes, numbers and counting, and the alphabet (Kiefer, 2009), but concept books can also appeal to older readers. Alphabet books like *Eh? to Zed: A Canadian ABeCedarium* (Major, 2000), in which each letter presents something considered to be uniquely Canadian, or *Animalia* (Base, 1988), in which every illustration on the page begins with that letter of the alphabet, are examples of those that appeal to older students.

Another variety of picture books is *pattern* or **predictable books**. These books are helpful to children at emergent literacy levels. Children are able to quickly learn the pattern in the text and then read the rest of the book. A favourite pattern book, illustrated by Eric Carle, is *Brown Bear, Brown Bear, What Do You See?* (Martin, 1983), in which the question is asked of a series of animals, each a different colour, on one page of the book and answered on the following page. Children enjoy reading the question each time and the predictable responses.

CHAPTER BOOKS

Children move from picture books to **chapter books** as they progress in their literacy development. Chapter books, as the name implies, are books divided into chapters and written in a variety of genres, including:

- traditional literature
- modern fantasy
- poetry
- contemporary realistic fiction
- historical fiction
- nonfiction
- biography

One of our responsibilities as language arts teachers is to ensure that a variety of genres and a range of authors and illustrators are part of our programs as we explore children's literature with our students. Contemporary realistic fiction is probably the most widely read of the genres, although the other genres will be part of a well-rounded exposure to children's literature.

Most chapter books are written for middle- and upper-grade students, but easy-to-read books are also available for those young readers who are gaining independence and who want to read "grown-up" chapter books. Many are written in series, giving children an opportunity to follow the characters while reading short, simple chapter books. Betty Bireny's books about Humphrey the gerbil, beginning with *The World According to Humphrey* (2005), are one example of such a series.

A wide variety of chapter books is available for middle-grade students. Some middle-grade readers choose to read all that a writer, such as Canadian author Deborah Ellis, has to offer. Other students choose to read by genre, such as mysteries, adventure stories, or biographies. Still others choose to read the classics and long-popular titles such as *The Giver* (Lowry, 1993).

Selecting exemplary literature for classroom libraries, and chapter books in particular, can seem like an onerous task, especially for beginning teachers. One way teachers go about making their selections is to choose award winners. For example, the **Newbery Medal** is awarded annually to distinguished American prose, and the Canadian Children's Book Centre in Toronto (www.bookcentre.ca) produces a newsletter that reviews new Canadian literature and manages several awards to honour Canadian literature for children and young adults.

Graphic novels are currently very popular with middle-grade and older students. Today, these books have entered the mainstream of publishing and are aimed at both younger and older audiences (Tunnel, Jacobs, Young, & Bryan, 2012). The Owly series by Andy Runton and Bone series by Jeff Smith are popular among young readers, while titles such as *City of Light, City of Dark* by Avi (2004) and many other paperback graphic novels hold much appeal to middle-school readers, some of whom especially appreciate the comic-like format and different reading demands.

INFORMATIONAL BOOKS

Informational books provide information on a wide variety of topics, including those related to social studies, science, math, art, and music. In informational books, illustrations (often photographs and diagrams) are used to support and extend the text. Informational books usually include a table of contents, a glossary, and an index. Some are written in a story format, such as *The Magic School Bus Inside a Hurricane* (Cole, 1995), *Secrets of the Mummies: Uncovering the Bodies of Ancient Egyptians* (Tanaka, 1999), and *The Buried City of Pompeii* (Tanaka, 2000). Others are written in a more traditional informational style. Some informational books are written for young students, with brief, easy-to-read text presented on each page along with photographs or illustrations. In *Owls* (Mason, 2004), for example, types of owls, their habitats, and how they grow and learn are clearly described and illustrated with colour photographs on every page. Many informational books, such as *Who Eats What? Food Chains and Food Webs* (Lauber, 1995), are published in picture-book format.

Another type of informational book presents language arts concepts, including opposites, homonyms, and parts of speech. One example is Ruth Heller's *Up, Up and Away: A Book about Adverbs* (1998). Many others are listed in Figure 8-6 on page 306. Alphabet books are informational books, too. Although many alphabet books are designed for very young children, others are appropriate for elementary students. An example with appeal to both young and older students is *T Is for Teachers* (Layne & Layne, 2005), and others are listed in Figure 3-8 on page 91.

Biographies are another type of informational book. Most biographies are chapter books, such as *The Man Who Created Narnia: The Story of C. S. Lewis* (M. Coren, 1994), but several authors have written shorter biographies that resemble picture books. Perhaps the best-known biographer for younger children is David Adler, who has written *A Picture Book of Helen Keller* (1990) and other biographies of important historical figures. A few autobiographies have also been written for children, such as *Born Naked* (1995), the story of Farley Mowat's childhood years in Ontario and Saskatchewan, and *The Beet Fields: Memories of a Sixteenth Summer* (2000), the story of Gary Paulsen's life.

POETRY BOOKS

There are many delightful poetry books written especially for children. Some are collections of poems on a single topic written by one poet, such as *There's a Mouse in My House* (Fitch, 1997b) and *Joyful Noise: Poems for Two Voices* (Fleischman, 1988), which is about insects. Other collections of poetry include *Til All the Stars Have Fallen: Canadian Poems for Children* (Booth, 1989), *The New Wind Has Wings: Poems from Canada* (Downie & Robertson, 1987), and *Nothing Beats a Pizza* (Lesynski, 2001). An excellent anthology (a collection of poems written by different poets on a variety of topics) is *The Oxford Book of Children's Poems* (M. Harrison & Stuart-Clark, 2007). Single poems and collections of poems are also published as picture books. Robert Service's *The Cremation of Sam McGee* (1986) is both a 1907 poem and a picture book with Canadian artist Ted Harrison's brilliant paintings on each page. The works of many poets, including Canadian Dennis Lee and the well-known Shel Silverstein, frequently become students' favourites when read to them by their teachers.

All genres of fiction, informational books, and poetry books can be used in teaching the language arts or any content area. By using all types, students learn more about a topic than they could if they read only stories or only informational books or poetry books. Trade books are not sequenced and prepackaged as textbooks are, so teachers must make choices and design activities to accompany the books. The Internet makes a wide variety of supportive resources available to teachers as they plan engaging and challenging encounters with literature for their students. Many websites, such as www.readwritethink.org, offer exemplary lesson plans created by experienced teachers.

Culturally Diverse Literature

Choosing resources is one of the most important components of planning language arts instruction. Teachers must choose a wide variety of print and non-print resources, including fine-quality literature as described above. According to Canadian researchers Joyce Bainbridge and Sylvia Pantaleo (1999), **multicultural literature** "depicts and explores the lives of individuals belonging to a wide range of groups" (p. 110). Culturally diverse literature is a vehicle for fostering cultural awareness and appreciation. It affirms the cultural identity of students of diverse backgrounds and develops all students' understanding of and appreciation for other cultures. Well-written multicultural children's books serve to help students see people living in far-flung parts of the globe or even in their own city as equal and valuable citizens (Tunnell et al., 2012). Students explore and expand their cultural values and beliefs as they read culturally diverse literature (Rasinski & Padak, 1990). They vicariously experience other cultures, and these experiences influence the way they interact with people in our multicultural society (Bainbridge & Pantaleo, 1999).

Culturally Conscious Literature

Educators recommend selecting culturally diverse literature that is also culturally conscious (Sims, 1992)—that is to say, literature that accurately reflects a group's culture, language, history, and values without perpetuating stereotypes. Such literature often deals with issues of prejudice, discrimination, and human dignity. These books should be rich in cultural details, with authentic dialogue, and should present cultural issues in enough depth that readers can think and talk about them. Inclusion of cultural group members should be purposeful. They should be distinct individuals whose lives are rooted in the culture, never simply added to fill a quota.

Culturally diverse literature may be chosen from the previously mentioned genres of children's literature. The different genres will offer a unique perspective on the lives and contributions of each cultural group. Multicultural literature is suggested in the following areas:

1. *Folktales and other traditional stories.* Traditional stories—including folktales, legends, and myths—are a part of every culture, and a wide variety of these stories are available for children. Cinderella stories, for example, come from many different cultures and include *Mufaro's Beautiful Daughters: An African Tale* (Steptoe, 1987); *Yeh-Shen: A Cinderella Story from China* (Louie, 1982); and *Bound* (Napoli, 2004), also from China; *The Egyptian Cinderella* (Climo, 1989); *The Rough Face Girl* (F. Martin, 1992), an Algonquian version; and *The Gift of the Crocodile: A Cinderella Story* (Sierra, 2000). Trickster tales, too, are told in many cultures. *Wisahkechk Flies to the Moon* (Ahenakew, 1999), written in English and Cree, is an example.

2. *Historical fiction.* **Historical fiction**, among other things, can describe the immigration of different cultural groups to North America and the stories of young people in other places and other times. In *Nykola and Granny* (1989), Constance Horne tells the story of a young boy's emigration from the Ukraine to Western Canada at the turn of the century. Similarly, *Silver Threads* (1996), by Marsha Forchuk Skrypuch, also tells of people fleeing the Ukraine and their experiences as new Canadians at the beginning of the World War I. Skrypuch's *Nobody's Child* (2003) tells of orphans' attempts to survive the 1915-1923 Armenian massacres. Deborah Ellis, too, tells an orphan's story in her tale from Afghanistan, *Parvana's Journey* (2002). Kit Pearson, another Canadian author, writes compassionately of young girls leaving their Winnipeg home in 1932 to join their grandmother on a west-coast island in *The Whole Truth* (2011) and *And Nothing but the Truth* (2012).

3. *Contemporary realistic fiction.* **Contemporary realistic fiction** focuses on the experiences of culturally diverse people, including in Canada. *Mina's Spring of Colors* (Gilmore, 2000) describes Mina's difficulties dealing with her recently arrived grandfather's South Asian traditions as perceived by her Canadian classmates. Thomas King's *Medicine River* (1997) and Jan Bourdeau Waboose's *SkySisters* (2000) help young readers to understand the First Nations experience in Canadian society.

4. *Biographies.* These books detail the contributions of people from various cultural groups. Some biographies, such as *James McKay: A Métis Builder of Canada* (Grant, 1995), detail the lives of historical figures; others, such as *Terry Fox: His Story* (Scrivener, 2000), highlight contemporary persons.

5. *Poetry.* A few collections of poems, songs, and chants written by people of various cultural groups are available for children. Some examples are *If You Could Wear My Sneakers* (Fitch, 1997a), *Canadian Poems for Canadian Kids* (J. Hamilton, 2005), *Off to the Sweet Shores of Africa and Other Drum Rhymes* (Unobagha, 2000), and *The Trees Stand Shining: Poetry of the North American Indians* (Jones, 1993).

6. *Informational books.* Other books provide information about various cultures, including information about holidays and rituals, language, cooking, and the arts, as well as information about the country in which the culture originated. *The French* (Horton, 2000), from the We Came to North America series is a good example of such books. *Japan: The People* (2001), from the Lands, Peoples, and Culture series created by Bobbie Kalman, is another example.

Howard Grey/Photodisc/Getty Images

Students read from a variety of informational texts to prepare an oral presentation.

Culturally diverse literature must meet the criteria for good literature as well as for cultural consciousness. That is, books should depict culturally diverse groups in active, rather than passive, roles. One example is *Daniel's Story* (Matas, 1993), which depicts the terrible realities of the discrimination against Jewish people during the World War II. The story is beautifully written, and the details are historically and culturally accurate.

Until recently, most books about First Nations, Métis, and Inuit peoples and other cultural groups have been written by authors who, because of their own ethnicity, represent an "outside" viewpoint. An inside perspective is more likely to give an authentic view of what members of the cultural group believe to be true about themselves, while an outside perspective describes how others see that group's beliefs and behaviours. The difference in perspective means that there is a difference in what the authors say and how they say it, as well as a difference in their purpose for writing (Reimer, 1992). Some authors, however, do successfully write about another culture. Byrd Baylor and Paul Goble are notable examples. They have a sensitivity learned through research about and participation in different cultural groups. Today, more people within each cultural group are writing about their own cultures and are providing more authentic "inside" viewpoints in culturally diverse literature. Christy Jordan-Fenton and Margaret Pokiak-Fenton's *Fatty Legs* (2010) and *A Stranger at Home* (2011), about Margaret's residential school experience, are examples of culturally authentic writing.

There are many reasons to use culturally diverse literature in elementary and middle-school classrooms, whether students represent diverse cultures or not. First, students enjoy reading these stories, informational books, and poems; through reading, they learn more about what it means to be human, and they discover that people of all cultural groups are real people with similar emotions, needs, and dreams. Bainbridge and Pantaleo (1999) indicate that through multicultural literature, students become aware of stereotyping and learn to recognize the contributions various cultural groups make to Canadian society.

Second, students learn about the wealth of diversity through culturally diverse books, and they develop sensitivity to and appreciation for people of other cultural groups (Walker-Dalhouse, 1992). Culturally diverse literature also challenges racial and ethnic stereotypes by providing an inside view of a culture.

Third, students broaden their knowledge of geography and learn different views of history through culturally diverse literature. They read about the countries that minority groups left when they immigrated to Canada, and they gain perspectives about historical events. For example, Joy Kogawa tells of her experiences of relocation and internment in the moving story of *Obasan* (1982). Through reading and responding to culturally diverse books, students challenge traditional assumptions about the history of Canada and gain a more balanced view of historical events and the contributions of people from various cultural groups. They learn that traditional historical accounts have emphasized the contributions of European immigrants, particularly those made by men.

Fourth, culturally diverse literature raises issues of social injustice—prejudice, racism, discrimination, segregation, colonization, anti-Semitism, and genocide.

Using culturally diverse literature has additional benefits for students from various cultural and ethnic backgrounds. When students read books about their own cultural group, they develop pride in their cultural heritage and learn that their culture has made important contributions to Canada and to the rest of the world (Harris, 1992a, 1992b). In addition, students often become more interested in reading because they identify with the characters and events.

Many authors, especially Michael Arvaarluk Kusugak, C. J. Taylor, Leo Yerxa, Thomas King, Tomson Highway, David Bouchard, and Paul Goble, have written sensitively about cultural topics. Some books are retellings of traditional folktales, myths, and legends, such as *The Legend of the Indian Paintbrush* (dePaola, 1988) and *Iktomi and the Boulder* (Goble, 1988). Kusugak's book co-written with Robert Munsch, *A Promise Is a Promise* (1988), is a traditional Inuit legend passed down to him by his grandmother. Tomson Highway's two children's books, *Dragonfly Kites* (2002) and *Caribou Song* (2001), in particular, present beautifully written stories from Canada's North. "The beauty of Canada's north, the extraordinary beauty of the culture of the north, the beauty of language," Highway says, "is an integral part of Canadian culture" (2003). *Dragonfly Kites* is a superbly written story about Joe and Cody, two young Cree brothers living in northern Manitoba, who create stories and games from objects found around them in nature. *Caribou Song* tells the story of two Cree children who follow the caribou by dogsled with their family. A list of literature that features First Nations, Métis, and Inuit (FNMI) culture is presented in Figure 2-6.

FIGURE 2-6 LITERATURE FEATURING FIRST NATIONS, MÉTIS, AND INUIT CULTURE

Ancona, G. (1993). *Powwow*. Orlando, FL: Harcourt Brace. (M–U)

Archibald, J., Friesen, V., & Smith, J. (1993). *Courageous Spirits: Aboriginal Heroes of Our Children*. Penticton, BC: Theytus Books. (M–U) 🍁

Ballantyne, A. (1991). *Wisakyjak and the New World*. Waterloo, ON: Penumbra Press. (P) 🍁

Bouchard, D. (1990). *The Elders Are Watching*. Tofino, BC: Eagle Dancer Enterprises. (M–U) 🍁

Brooks, M. (1997). *The Bone Dance*. Toronto: Groundwood. (U) 🍁

Cameron, A. (1991). *Raven and Snipe*. Madeira Park, BC: Harbour Publishing. (P–M) 🍁

Cardinal, P. (1997). *The Cree People*. Edmonton: Duval House. (M–U) 🍁

Clark, J. (1995). *The Dream Carvers*. Toronto: Viking. (M–U) 🍁

George, J. C. (1972). *Julie of the Wolves*. New York: Harper & Row. (U) (Inuit)

George, J. C. (1997). *Arctic Son*. New York: Hyperion. (U)

Grant, A. (1995). *James McKay: A Métis Builder of Canada*. Winnipeg: Pemmican. (U) 🍁

Highway, T. (2001). *Caribou Song*. Toronto: HarperCollins. (M–U) 🍁

Highway, T. (2002). *Dragonfly Kites*. Toronto: HarperCollins. (P–M) 🍁

Ipellie, A., & MacDonald, D. (2007). *The Inuit Thought of It: Amazing Arctic Innovations*. Toronto: Annick Press. (M–U) 🍁

Jordan-Fenton, C., & Pokiak-Fenton, M. (2010). *Fatty Legs*. Toronto: Annick Press. (M–U) 🍁

Jordan-Fenton, C., & Pokiak-Fenton, M. (2011). *A Stranger at Home*. Toronto: Annick Press. (M–U) 🍁

Jordan-Fenton, C., & Pokiak-Fenton, M. (2013). *When I Was Eight*. Toronto: Annick Press. (P) 🍁

Kalman, B. (1994). *Settler Sayings*. Niagara-on-the-Lake, ON: Crabtree. (M) 🍁

King, T. (1998). *Coyote Sings to the Moon*. Toronto: Groundwood. (M–U) 🍁

Kusugak, M. (1990). *Baseball Bats for Christmas*. Toronto: Annick Press. (P) 🍁

Luenn, N. (1990). *Nessa's Fish*. New York: Atheneum. (P–M) (Inuit)

Martin, J. B. (2001). *The Lamp, The Ice, and the Boat Called Fish*. Boston: Houghton Mifflin. (M–U) (Inuit)

McLellan, J. (1991). *Nanabosho, Soaring Eagle and the Great Sturgeon*. Winnipeg: Pemmican Publications. (P–M) 🍁

McLellan, J. (1993). *Nanabosho Dances*. Winnipeg: Pemmican Publications. (P) 🍁

Munsch, R., & Kusugak, M. (1988). *A Promise Is a Promise*. Toronto: Annick Press. (P) 🍁

O'Dell, S., & Hall, E. (1992). *Thunder Rolling in the Mountains*. Boston: Houghton Mifflin. (U)

Paulsen, G. (1988). *Dogsong*. New York: Bradbury Press. (U)

Plain, F. (1994). *Grandfather Drum*. Winnipeg: Pemmican Publications. (P) 🍁

Richards, D. (1993). *Soldier Boys*. Saskatoon: Thistledown Press. (M–U) 🍁

Schwartz, V. F. (2003). *Initiation*. Toronto: Fitzhenry & Whiteside. (U) 🍁

Seattle, C. (1991). *Brother Eagle, Sister Sky*. New York: Dial. (P–M–U)

Taylor, C. J. (1994). *Bones in the Basket*. Montreal: Tundra Books. (M–U) 🍁

Taylor, C. J. (2004). *Peace Walker: The Legend of Hiawatha and Tekanawita*. Toronto: Tundra Books. (M–U) 🍁

Taylor, H. (1997). *When Bear Stole the Chinook: A Siksika Tale*. New York: Farrar Straus and Giroux. (P–M)

Walters, E. (1998). *The War of the Eagles*. Victoria, BC: Orca. (U) 🍁

Whetung, J. (1996). *The Vision Seeker*. Don Mills, ON: Stoddart Publishing. (M–U) 🍁

P = primary grades (K-2); M = middle grades (3-5); U = upper grades (6-8).

The themes in these books include passing traditions and stories to the next generation, mistreatment and injustice suffered at the hands of Europeans and European Canadians, and a reverence for living things and the Earth. Including FNMI literature in their classrooms is one way teachers show respect for Aboriginal peoples' culture, beliefs, spirituality, and traditions.

LITERATURE FEATURING DIVERSE CULTURAL GROUPS (TRANSCULTURAL LITERATURE)

In addition to Native peoples, there are other underrepresented cultural groups in Canada, including Jewish, Chinese, Japanese, and African Canadians. The book *Struggle and Hope: The Story of Chinese Canadians* (Yee, 1996b) explores events and experiences from Chinese Canadian history. Being the majority culture, Canadians descended from European heritage are sometimes ignored in discussions of cultural groups, but to ignore them denies the distinct cultures of many Canadians (Yokota, 1993)

Within the European-descended Canadian umbrella category are a variety of groups, including German, Italian, Swedish, and Russian peoples. Patricia Polacco's *Thunder Cake* (1990), the story of a Russian grandmother who calms her granddaughter's fear of thunderstorms by making a "thunder cake," is a popular book. Maggi's retelling of a Venezuelan indigenous legend in *The Great Canoe: A Karina Legend* (Maggi & Calderón, 2001) is an important addition to multicultural literature. Figure 2-7 presents a list of books featuring diverse cultural groups.

Engaging and Respecting All Students

By including culturally diverse literature in their classrooms, teachers show respect for all students and acknowledge the diverse cultures, beliefs, languages, and traditions they represent. Many teachers strive to make it possible for all students to identify with or find themselves in the classroom literature. We encourage teachers to include culturally diverse literature in their resource-based units, theme study units, and inquiry-based units to raise students' appreciation for cultural differences and the richness those differences bring to learning communities.

FIGURE 2-7 LITERATURE FEATURING DIVERSE CULTURAL GROUPS

Boraks-Nemetz, L. (1994). *The Old Brown Suitcase*. Brentwood Bay, BC: Ben-Simon. (U) (Polish)

Brosgol, V. (2011). *Anya's Ghost*. New York: First Second. (U) (Russian)

Bunting, E. (2006). *One Green Apple*. New York: Clarion Books. (M) (Muslim)

Czernecki, S., & Rhodes, T. (1994). *The Hummingbirds' Gift*. Winnipeg: Hyperion. (M–U) (Mexican) ✣

Gilman, P. (1992). *Something from Nothing*. Toronto: North Winds Press. (P) (Jewish) ✣

Hearn, E., & Milne, M. (Eds.) 2007. *Our New Home: Immigrant Children Speak*. Toronto: Second Story Press. (M–U) ✣

Kernaghan, E. (1995). *Dance of the Snow Dragon*. Saskatoon: Thistledown Press. (U) (Tibetan) ✣

Khan, R. (1999). *Dahling, If You Luv Me, Would You Please, Please Smile*. Toronto: Stoddart Kids. (U) ✣

Marineau, M. (1995). *Road to Chlifa*. Red Deer, AB: Red Deer College Press. (U) (Lebanese) ✣

Mollel, T. (1990). *The Orphan Boy*. Toronto: Oxford University Press. (P–M) (African) ✣

Mollel, T. (1992). *A Promise to the Sun*. Toronto: Little, Brown & Company. (P) (African) ✣

Oberman, S. (1994). *The Always Prayer Shawl*. Honesdale, PA: Boyd Mills Press. (M) (Jewish)

Walsh, A. (1994). *Shabash!* Victoria, BC: Beach Holme Publishers. (P) (Sikh) ✣

Yee, P. (2006). *What Happened This Summer*. Vancouver: Tradewind Books. (U) (Chinese) ✣

Yee, P. (2009). *Shu-Li and Diego*. Vancouver: Tradewind Books. (P) (Chinese) ✣

Young, B. (2012). *Charlie: A Home Child's Life in Canada*. Vancouver: Ronsdale Press. (M–U) (British) ✣

P = primary grades (K-2); M = middle grades (3-5); U = upper grades (6-8).

Balanced Instructional Frameworks

Many instructional programs in Canadian schools focus on a balanced approach to literacy. These programs recognize that all areas of the language arts need systematic attention with continuity from grade to grade (Brailsford & Coles, 2004). Listening, speaking, reading, writing, viewing, and visually representing are developed in ways that enhance appropriate skill development. Balanced approaches often include shared reading of common texts, class lessons on key reading-comprehension strategies, guided reading and literature circles, reading aloud, and independent reading. Phonics and other word-recognition skills are developed in conjunction with daily writing and the reading of quality literature. The skills and strategies for reading information are developed in appropriate content areas and children learn a variety of ways to respond to text, including writing and visually representing their experiences. All aspects of the language arts are developed in a balanced and integrated way.

Three frameworks for organizing balanced language arts instruction are resource-based units, theme study units, and inquiry-based units. All three approaches embody the characteristics of learning described in Chapter 1, "Learning and the Language Arts," and provide opportunities for students to be involved in meaningful, functional, and genuine activities. Giving students opportunities to participate in all three types of units during each school year is strongly recommended; that is, both teacher-led and student-selected instructional programs provide valuable language-learning opportunities, and neither type of program alone provides all the opportunities that students need.

Resource-Based Units

In **resource-based units**, instruction and learning are organized around a featured selection or several related books or other print or non-print media texts, such as newspapers or videos. Students read, view, or listen to the featured selection using a five-step reading process in which they prepare, read (or listen or view), respond, explore, and extend their study of the text. Because students are working together in groups or as a class, they share their interpretations of the text and become a community of language learners. One popular example of resource-based units is *literature circles*. There are four components of resource-based units:

1. *Reading, listening, viewing texts.* Students read, listen to, or view texts together as a class, in small groups, or independently. In many instances, the teacher guides the listening, viewing, or reading by helping students set purposes for their activity and by offering a schedule or other form of guidance to pace the reading, listening, or viewing.

2. *Responding.* Students respond to the selection to record their initial impressions of it and to develop their comprehension. Typically, students write in response logs, blogs, or wikis and participate in discussions called **grand conversations**.

3. *Teaching minilessons.* Teachers teach **minilessons** on language arts procedures, concepts, strategies, and skills, and connect the lesson to books students are reading or compositions they are writing (Atwell, 1998). Minilessons may also pertain to other types of texts, such as digital texts, whether DVDs or on the Internet. While minilessons are best known in relation to reading and writing,

they may relate to any of the six language arts. They are brief, explicit, teacher-directed lessons usually lasting not more than ten minutes. Some topics may require several minilessons taught over several succeeding days. The six steps in teaching a minilesson are as follows:

a. Introduce the language arts procedure, concept, strategy, or skill.

b. Share examples of the topic or technique using familiar texts or students' writing (presented without identification of particular students).

c. Provide information about the topic and make connections to reading or to children's writing.

d. Have students make notes about the topic, or share with them a classroom poster to remind them about the concept or strategy.

e. Have students practise the procedure, concept, strategy, or skill being taught.

f. Ask students to reflect or speculate on how they can use this information in their reading and writing.

The purpose of minilessons is to highlight the topic or strategy and teach it in the context of authentic literacy activities, not to isolate it or provide drill and practice. Worksheets are rarely used in minilessons; instead, students apply the lesson to their own language arts activities. Minilessons can be conducted with the whole class, with small groups of students who have indicated that they need to learn more about a particular topic, or with individual students. Teachers can also plan minilessons on a regular basis to introduce or review topics.

4. *Creating projects.* Students create projects to extend their engagement with and understanding of the selection (literature, film, etc.). Projects may involve any of the language arts, and often include the use of one or more forms of media to communicate the meaning they have created from the selection. For example, after reading *Dear George Clooney, Please Marry My Mom* (Nielsen, 2010), students in grade 7 worked together to create a movie trailer to tell the story. After hearing Julia Donaldson's *Monkey Puzzle* (2000), grade 1 students chose to dramatize the little monkey's conversations with his rainforest friend, Butterfly.

Theme Study Units

Theme study units are a type of interdisciplinary unit that integrates language arts with one or more of social studies, science, math, and other curricular areas (Altwerger & Flores, 1994; Wiggins & McTighe, 2006). In primary grades, they often extend across most or all of the school day. Students are sometimes involved in planning the direction for the theme, especially in upper grades. Topics for theme study units should be broad and encompass many possible directions for exploration. Example topics include people who make a difference, our green earth, humour in our lives and literature, how natural disasters affect our earth, and civilizations that came before us.

Theme studies become broader and more in-depth as students become familiar with this approach to learning. A theme study at this sophisticated level defines what is to be the centre of attention in the classroom, incorporates many traditional subject areas within it, and develops over a long period of time. It involves thorough study of a topic or theme. The topic or theme must be of interest to the students and wide-ranging enough that it can be subdivided into subtopics, each of which sustains student interest.

Students use all of the language arts as they explore, experiment, synthesize, question, and extend learning during theme study units. They also use language arts to demonstrate their new learning at the end of the theme. Four types of language arts activities are usually included in theme study units:

1. **Reading books and other print and non-print texts.** Students read a range of material, including stories and informational text. Many teachers choose theme-related text sets as core materials for a theme study unit.

2. **Writing.** Various types of writing are done according to the theme. For example, an environmental theme might include making conservation posters, writing informative pamphlets, or writing letters to local media outlets.

3. **Oral language activities.** Oral language activities are focused on one or more aspects of the theme. These include interviewing, listening to guest speakers, debating issues, or dramatizing theme-related literature or events.

4. **Creative projects.** Students engage in creative projects using all six language arts to deepen their understanding of the theme, to extend their learning, and to demonstrate their new knowledge. Theme-related projects often involve working in more than one area of the curriculum. Many projects involve use of technology to enhance and share learning. For example, an environmental theme might include creation of a webpage to show what the students' community does to reduce waste.

Inquiry-Based Units

In **inquiry-based units**, students and teachers learn together. Both grapple with issues out of genuine interest and curiosity. Teachers who facilitate inquiry-based learning believe that shared inquiry is inherently motivating, and they provide time and resources for students to pursue learning individually, in small groups, or as a class. The Internet is a primary source of information for students engaged in inquiry-based learning.

Topics for inquiry-based language arts units develop from students' interests but often grow from shared experiences with literature or non-print media texts. As partners in inquiry, teachers and students share the control and responsibility for learning. Students take active roles in planning and implementing classroom experiences.

Inquiry-based units follow a recursive cycle of activities, including:

1. **Identifying inquiry focus.** Teachers read aloud to students; students read widely and browse informational texts, including websites; teachers and students engage in dialogue, do quickwrites, and ask questions to identify the focus.

2. **Exploring multiple data sources.** Resources for inquiry units must be abundant and diverse. Students need access to fiction and nonfiction, knowledgeable human resources, related Internet sites, and other non-print sources to increase their knowledge, skills, and understanding of the focus.

3. **Sharing what is learned.** All of the language arts can be used to share learning. Students can use writing, drama, music, art, oral presentations, and multimedia to represent their learning.

4. **Reflecting and planning.** Inquiry is a never-ending process. Students need time to reflect on new learning, make connections to what is already known, and begin planning further inquiry.

Readers and Writers Workshops

Readers and writers workshops are ways of structuring classroom reading and writing that facilitate both student-centred and teacher-directed learning. Initially made popular by the research and writings of Nancie Atwell, the term *workshop* now has many interpretations. Donalyn Miller's books, *The Book Whisperer* (2010) and

FIGURE 2-8 COMPONENTS OF READERS AND WRITERS WORKSHOPS

	Time	Purpose	Typical Activities
Teacher Sharing	5 minutes	• Shows teacher as reader and writer, member of learning community	• Sharing of personal writing • Sharing of literature reading for pleasure • Sharing of news article related to classroom reading (e.g., film review or obituary of a writer)
Minilesson	10–15 minutes	• Instruction relates to specific concept or skill or workshop procedure	• Teacher-directed lesson on specific skill using literature as example of a writing technique • Teacher modelling of particular reading skill • Teacher and student demonstration of procedure, such as responding to peer writing
Status-of-Class	2–5 minutes	• Teacher determines intended activities for each student and identifies need for teacher assistance	• Students tell teacher what they will be doing (e.g. will be peer editing draft or will be reading chapter 2 of novel)
Reading/Writing/ Responding	30–45 minutes	• Time for uninterrupted reading and/or writing • Time for organized response to literature or student writing	• Reading of selected literature independently or in groups • Conversations about literature • Sustained writing • Conferencing with teacher about literature read or about writing
Student Sharing	10–20 minutes	• Sharing of reading to invite conversation • Sharing of student writing to attain peer feedback • Sharing of writing for celebration of accomplishments	• Students reading from "author's chair" • Students giving book talks • Students reading each other's writings from classroom library

Reading in the Wild (2013) provide helpful advice to teachers using a workshop approach to reading instruction. The components outlined in Figure 2-8 are the mainstay of workshops as an approach to instruction. Workshops can be implemented within all three of the instructional frameworks presented in this chapter.

READERS WORKSHOP

In a **readers workshop**, students read self-selected books independently or in small groups and respond to books by writing in reading logs or reader notebooks and, if a small group of students is reading the same book, by discussing the book (Atwell, 1998; Calkins, 2010; Miller, 2013). Through readers workshops, students become more fluent readers and deepen their appreciation of books and reading. They develop lifelong reading habits, are introduced to different genres, and choose favourite authors. Most important, students come to think of themselves as readers (Daniels, 1994). The primary components of readers workshop are the following:

1. ***Reading and responding.*** Students spend 30 to 45 minutes independently reading books and other reading materials. They also keep reading logs or notebooks to write responses to their reading and participate in conferences with the teacher or in small discussion groups to extend their understanding of books read. They may engage in other interpretive responses designed to extend their understanding.

Responses might include dramatic interpretations or visual images such as posters, collages, or sketches.

2. ***Sharing.*** For the last 10 to 20 minutes of the readers workshop, the class gathers together to share books and response projects.

3. ***Minilessons.*** The teacher spends approximately 10 to 15 minutes teaching lessons on readers workshop procedures, literary concepts, or reading strategies and skills.

WRITERS WORKSHOP

The **writers workshop** is a way of implementing the writing process (Atwell, 1998; Calkins, 2010; D. H. Graves, 1983). Students usually write on topics they choose themselves or those related to their language arts unit, and they assume ownership of their learning. The goal is for the classroom to become a community of writers in which students come to see themselves as writers. They develop and apply writing skills and strategies and, perhaps most important, they see firsthand the power of writing to entertain, inform, and persuade.

In a writers workshop classroom, students have writing folders, either paper or digital, in which they keep all of their writing. They also keep idea files or notebooks in which they jot down images, impressions, dialogue, and experiences that they can build on for writing projects (Calkins, 2010).

The physical arrangement of the classroom for a writers workshop varies with the availability of resources, especially facilities for writing using computers or other technological devices. Usually a workshop arrangement includes space for students to write individually or in small groups, a space for students to conference with the teacher, a place for reference aids such as dictionaries or thesauruses, and facilities for publishing and displaying writing. The classroom atmosphere is one of support and encouragement for students to share quietly with each other, solving problems within their writing, and making suggestions when writers need assistance.

Writers workshop is a 60- to 90-minute period scheduled each day. During this time the teacher and the students are involved in three primary activities:

For more information on the writing process, see Chapter 5, "The Reading and Writing Processes," pages 160–176.

1. ***Writing.*** Students spend 30 to 45 minutes working independently on writing projects. They move through all stages of the writing process—prewriting, drafting, revising, editing, and publishing—at their own pace. When students reach the publishing stage, they often compile their final copies to make books, but sometimes they attach their writing to artwork, make posters, post their writing on the class website, or perform scripts as skits or readers theatre.

2. ***Sharing.*** The class gathers together for 10 to 20 minutes to share their writing, sometimes to seek help with drafts and often to share new publications and make related announcements of forthcoming publications. In primary classrooms, if an author's chair is available, each student sits in the special chair to read his or her composition. After the reading, classmates offer compliments, ask questions, and make suggestions. When incomplete works are shared, the emphasis is on problem solving and encouragement. When completed works are shared, the focus is on celebrating, not on revising the composition to make it better.

3. ***Minilessons.*** During a 10- to 15-minute period, teachers provide brief lessons on writing workshop procedures, literary concepts, and writing skills and strategies. They often talk about authors of children's trade books and the writing strategies and skills they use.

For more information on readers and writers workshops, see Chapter 11, "Putting It All Together," pages 389–400.

Sometimes teachers add a fourth component to writers workshops, in which they read literature aloud to share examples of good writing with students. Often, teachers choose to read literature that provides a model for the kind of writing that their students are doing. Sometimes teachers choose to read examples from literature as part of a minilesson. For example, recently one of our former student teachers read from Jon Scieszka's *The True Story of the 3 Little Pigs!* (1989) to illustrate point of view. Hearing the wolf's declaration that he would tell readers the way things "really" happened made very clear to her grade 6 students that writers make choices regarding perspective. Sharing literature in this way is referred to as using *mentor texts* as examples. Using mentor texts helps students to feel part of the community of successful writers. Teachers often connect readers workshop with writers workshop and, as a consequence, they engage their students in extended literate activities involving all six language arts.

The Teacher's Role

As may be gleaned from the preceding descriptions of classrooms and instruction, the teacher's role in a language arts classroom is complex and multidimensional. No longer are teachers simply providers of knowledge. Instead, teachers understand that children's literacy develops most effectively through purposeful and meaningful social contexts. These teachers create a classroom environment and a community of learners in which all learners have opportunities to be successful. Teachers plan the language arts curriculum to meet the needs of their increasingly diverse classes of students. Their goal is to help students develop communicative competence and to excite students about literacy. They are instructors, coaches, facilitators, and managers. Figure 2-9 presents a list of some of the roles teachers assume.

ESTABLISHING A COMMUNITY OF LEARNERS

Teachers begin the process of establishing a community of learners when they make deliberate decisions about the kind of classroom culture they want to create (Sumara & Walker, 1991). School is "real" life for students, and they learn best when they see a purpose for learning to read and write. The social contexts that teachers create are key. Teachers must make conscientious decisions about their roles and the kind of language arts instruction they want in their classrooms.

Teachers are more successful when they take the first two weeks of the school year to establish the classroom environment (Sumara & Walker, 1991). Teachers can't assume that students will be familiar with the procedures and routines used in language arts, or that students will instinctively be cooperative, responsible, and respectful of classmates. During this time, teachers explain classroom routines, such as how to access supplies and put them away and how to work with classmates in a cooperative group, and they set the expectation that students will adhere to the routines. They demonstrate literacy procedures, such as how to provide feedback in a writing group and how to participate in a grand conversation or discussion about a book. Also, teachers model ways of interacting with students, responding to literature, respecting opinions, using technology to enhance communication, and working collaboratively.

Teachers are classroom managers or administrators. They explain clearly to students what is expected of them and what is valued in the classroom. Teachers model classroom rules themselves as they interact with students. Teachers manage the process of socialization at the beginning of the school year in planned and deliberate ways to foster success of the language arts program.

FIGURE 2-9 ROLES TEACHERS ASSUME

Role	Description
Organizer	• Creates a language-rich environment • Plans the language arts program • Sets time schedules • Develops resource-based units and theme study units • Schedules readers and writers workshops • Uses the language arts as tools for learning across the curriculum
Facilitator	• Develops a community of learners • Stimulates students' interest in language and literacy • Allows students to choose books to read and topics for projects • Provides opportunities for students to use language for meaningful, functional, and genuine activities • Invites parents to become involved in classroom activities
Participant	• Reads and writes with students • Learns along with students • Asks questions and seeks answers to questions
Instructor	• Provides information about books, authors, and illustrators • Explains language arts procedures • Teaches minilessons on concepts, skills, and strategies • Provides background knowledge before reading, writing, and viewing • Groups students flexibly for instruction
Model	• Demonstrates procedures, skills, and strategies • Reads aloud to students every day
Manager	• Sets expectations and responsibilities • Tracks students' progress during resource-based units • Monitors students' work during readers and writers workshop • Keeps records • Arranges the classroom to facilitate learning • Provides technology hardware and software to support language arts activities
Diagnostician	• Conferences with students • Observes students participating in language arts activities • Assesses students' strengths and weaknesses • Plans instruction based on students' needs
Evaluator	• Assesses students' progress in the language arts • Helps students self-assess their learning • Assigns grades • Examines the effectiveness of the language arts program
Coordinator	• Works with librarians, aides, and parent volunteers • Works with other teachers on grade-level projects, pen pal programs, and cross-age reading programs
Communicator	• Expects students to do their best • Encourages students to become lifelong readers • Communicates the language arts program to parents and administrators • Shares language arts goals and activities with parents and the community • Encourages parents to support the language arts program

Throughout the year, teachers continue to reinforce classroom routines and teach additional literacy procedures, as students are involved in new types of activities; that is, the foundation is laid during the first weeks, but the classroom community evolves during the school year.

When teachers develop a predictable classroom environment with familiar routines and procedures, students feel comfortable, safe, and more willing to take risks and to experiment. It is especially important that all students, regardless of background, previous experiences, cultural and belief differences, and language and linguistic capabilities, feel secure and able to engage in risk-taking, because risk-taking is critical to learning.

WHAT ABOUT TEACHING?

We could say that everything a teacher does, by one definition or another, is teaching. However, at this time we want to look at two contrasting kinds of teaching that are significant within the role of language arts teaching. One kind is called **direct instruction** (Carnine, Silbert, Kame'enui, & Tarver, 2004). In this kind of teaching, teachers provide systematic, planned lessons in which they explicitly present information, provide an opportunity for supervised practice, and then have students apply what they have learned through authentic reading and writing activities. Direct teaching emphasizes use of small groups, face-to-face, and explicit instruction. Teachers often use direct instruction during minilessons in which they teach students about reading and writing procedures, skills, and strategies. Direct instruction has been associated with skill-and-drill activities, but it doesn't have to be. This kind of teaching is necessary to provide information and opportunities for students to apply what they are learning with guidance from the teacher. Examples of direct-instruction lessons include:

- presenting a biographical sketch of poet Dennis Lee during a unit featuring the author and his humorous verse
- highlighting important vocabulary when introducing informational text
- teaching a word-processing lesson on inserting bubble speech when creating cartoons
- demonstrating how to proofread a piece of writing to identify spelling, punctuation, and capitalization errors

The second kind of teaching is **indirect instruction** (Borich, 2010). Indirect instruction involves students in observing, investigating, drawing inferences from data, or forming hypotheses. It takes advantage of students' interest and curiosity and is well suited to concept learning, inquiry learning, and problem-centred learning. In indirect instruction, the role of the teacher shifts from director to facilitator, supporter, and resource person. Teachers use indirect instruction for brief, on-the-spot lessons as they respond to students' questions or when students demonstrate the need to know something. Indirect lessons take place during whole-class activities, during conferences with students, and while working with small groups. Teachers also use indirect instruction as they model reading when reading aloud to the class and as they model writing when writing collaboratively with students. Other examples include:

- demonstrating how to use an index when a student says he or she can't find a particular topic when reading an informational text
- showing the effects of changes in background colour using paint software when students express concern about the impact of the poster they are creating
- explaining why some alphabet books such as *M Is for Maple* (Ulmer, 2007) include both large poetic text and smaller factual informational text
- talking with students about the intertextual connections they are making when reading about Parvana's challenges (Ellis, 2002c) and those of Libertad and Julio (Fullerton, 2008)

Sometimes teachers ask how they should balance the two types of teaching. It is important to remember that most of the instructional time should be devoted to real reading and writing and teacher-led instruction offered as needed to meet students' needs.

Differentiating to Meet the Needs of Every Student

In Canadian schools, it is usual that policies regarding special-needs students call for integration and inclusion; that is, most classes include students of diverse learning abilities and styles. Teachers are expected to meet all students' instructional needs. To do this, teachers must provide flexibly structured programs that can be differentiated as needed to ensure that all students enjoy success. It is particularly important that the language-learning needs of special-needs students be met in classrooms because language development is a significant factor in learning in all curricular areas.

It is our position in this text that students with special learning needs benefit from the same language arts content and teaching strategies that are generally recommended for elementary classrooms but that adaptations are needed to maximize each student's learning. The most common adaptations of instruction involve choosing resources and technology that are appropriate to the student, changing the nature of teacher—student interaction to offer the assistance needed for success, and altering assignments so that successful completion is possible. For example, teachers must choose reading materials suited to the students' reading level, must offer individualized instruction when needed, and must tailor expectations in regard to such things as the length of written assignments and the time available for assignment completion. While it is beyond the scope of this text to provide extensive description, what follows is an overview of the needs of some special-needs students together with suggestions for adapting language arts instruction.

STUDENTS WITH SPECIFIC LEARNING DISABILITIES

Many children who experience significant learning problems have specific learning disabilities. Although there is no universally agreed-upon definition of *learning disability*, educators in Canada generally conceptualize a learning disability as any one of a mixed group of long-lasting disorders that may be the result of a central nervous system dysfunction. These disorders may be evidenced by difficulties in one or more processes such as attention, concentration, perception, memory, reasoning, organization, planning, and problem solving (Andrews & Lupart, 1993). Children with specific learning disabilities are of average or above-average intelligence and can be very able learners when adequate instruction is provided.

In language arts classrooms, specific learning disabilities are evidenced by such behaviours as students' difficulties in learning word-recognition skills such as phonics, difficulties in spelling, underdeveloped vocabulary, poor comprehension skills (such as sequencing material read or heard), and poor organization skills in written work. Further, specific learning disabilities may negatively affect students' self-esteem and consequently their social interactions, especially with peers.

Instruction for students with specific learning disabilities must be clearly structured, and the structure made apparent to the students. Such students do well when routines are followed and when guidelines for tasks are presented sequentially both in writing as well as orally. These students benefit from modifications to length and time of writing and independent reading assignments, and from extensive use of technology to support their learning. Peer and cross-age tutoring also provide advantages, especially as opportunities for reinforcement of concept learning.

STUDENTS WITH DELAYED COGNITIVE SKILLS

Currently, it is widely recognized that children who are considered to have delayed cognitive skills meet three criteria: sub-average intellectual functioning, deficits in adaptive behaviour, and delays observed between conception and eighteen years of age (Andrews & Lupart, 1993). Delays and limitations are exhibited in such areas as communication, self-care, social skills, functional academics, and gross and fine motor development. Although these children may be included in many Canadian classrooms for at least part of each school day, students with delayed cognitive skills need individualized instruction to ensure continuous conceptual and skill development. Most often, their instruction is planned by a team of teachers and is based on an *individual education plan* (IEP). In general, the focus of instruction should be on helping students develop the functional skills considered essential to living independently. In the language arts classroom, the focus is on communication (oral, written, and visual) and enjoyment of literature.

STUDENTS WITH BEHAVIOUR DISORDERS

Students whose behaviour interferes with learning are characterized as having behaviour disorders. They often exhibit inappropriate behaviour and feelings under normal circumstances; they may be either aggressive and disruptive or anxious and withdrawn. These students have difficulty in developing satisfactory relationships with classmates and the teacher. Often, they are unhappy or depressed, and they may develop physical symptoms or fears associated with personal or school problems. Although any student can exhibit one of these behaviours for a brief period, students with behaviour disorders exhibit more than one of these behaviours to a marked degree and consistently over time.

Students with behaviour disorders need a structured and positive classroom environment in order to be successful. For that reason, it is important that all teachers who work with such a student collaborate with parents and teachers with expertise in this area to set behavioural expectations and consequences. In the language arts classroom, open-ended activities such as literature circle discussions may require explicit rule-setting and careful teacher coaching. Similarly, it may be necessary to set time limits for writing, monitor computer use closely, and keep periods of independent reading relatively short.

STUDENTS WITH LANGUAGE DISORDERS

Students who have grown up in an English-speaking community but who have severe difficulty understanding or expressing language are classified as having a language disorder. Often these children talk very little, speak in childlike phrases, and lack the language to understand basic concepts. Such limited ability to communicate has a negative impact on learning as well as on social interaction with classmates and the teacher. Students may require extensive language therapy and specialized programming. It is important to note that students who speak their first language fluently and are learning English as an added language do not have a language disorder.

STUDENTS WITH ATTENTION DEFICIT/HYPERACTIVITY DISORDER

Students with attention deficit/hyperactivity disorder (AD/HD) have great difficulty attending to tasks and activities. While there is much discussion about definition, it is widely accepted that there are at least two variants of attention deficit/hyperactivity disorder—with and without hyperactivity. All students with AD/HD display distractibility, inattention, and mood fluctuations. Their inattention is not wilful, as is sometimes mistakenly thought. In addition to these behaviours, some students are also highly impulsive and physically active. These students are diagnosed as having the hyperactivity variant. Some students are helped by stimulant drugs, but medication must be accompanied by well-structured instruction and efforts to help the students learn to focus on tasks at hand. While success is important for all students, it is crucial that students with AD/HD be successful in the classroom and that teachers structure their environment to minimize their distractibility (Weaver, 1994). In the language arts classroom, it is frequently necessary to modify programs in ways such as arranging for a distraction-free area for writing, shortening independent reading expectations, and encouraging oral contributions rather than written.

STUDENTS WHO ARE LEARNING ENGLISH AS AN ADDED LANGUAGE

Many children in Canadian classrooms come from linguistic backgrounds beyond the official languages of English and French. Many of these children are fluent in one or more languages when they come to school, where they are immersed in English. For children learning English as an added language (English language learners, or ELL), language arts as a curricular subject is especially challenging, and instructional provisions must be made for them. Students learn an additional language in much the way they learned to speak their first language. It is now widely recognized that effective ELL classroom instruction includes sharing the students' first language and culture with classmates. Teachers must include culturally relevant literature in the selections available in their classrooms. Such literature facilitates the sharing of culture that is beneficial to language learning among ELL students.

In Canada, particular consideration must be given to students for whom English is a second dialect (ESD), such as Aboriginal students who have grown up in a mixed linguistic setting, speaking English and an Aboriginal language. The risk is that when languages become confused with one another during development, children may not achieve fluency in either. There is a growing consensus among educators in Canada and elsewhere that a secure grasp of one language provides the optimal basis for all subsequent cognitive development (Piper, 1993).

STUDENTS WHO ARE GIFTED

Gifted students are academically advanced, but giftedness comprises more than a high IQ score. Gifted students are curious, have unusually good memories, express themselves well, enjoy working independently, have a well-developed sense of humour, and are often perfectionists. However, some gifted students are underachievers who do not work up to their potential because of a lack of motivation, peer pressure, or fear of success. Gifted students require special adaptations to meet their needs. Typical adaptations for gifted students include allowance for student choice and design of assignments, often involving independent research and experimentation, increased level of complexity of resource materials including ready access to the Internet, wide selection of literature (fiction and nonfiction) for independent reading, involvement in cross-age study groups, and flexibility in grading criteria.

The information in this text capitalizes on the natural ways children learn, and it can be used effectively with almost all learners, given some adaptations. Special educators continue to point out that there is no one way to teach students with special needs that is different from how other students are taught. Moreover, educators recommend an integrated approach as especially valuable for learning-disabled and remedial learners (Dudley-Marling & Paugh, 2009) and for students learning English as an added language (Xu, 2010).

Review

This chapter focused on how teachers teach the language arts and the resources recommended for teaching the language arts. Establishing a paradigm for language arts instruction and creating a language-rich classroom are important prerequisites. Teachers plan language arts instruction using three instructional approaches: resource-based units, theme study units, and inquiry-based units. Many teachers implement readers and writers workshops as a way of organizing instruction within these units.

The following key concepts are presented in this chapter:

1. Students need opportunities to participate in authentic language arts activities that are meaningful, functional, and genuine.
2. Teachers create a community of learners in their classrooms.
3. Students learn and use language arts strategies and skills.
4. A teaching strategy should include initiating, structuring, conceptualizing, summarizing, generalizing, and applying components.
5. Teachers use all genres and types of children's literature in paper and electronic forms—picture books, chapter books, graphic novels, informational books, and poetry books—related to instructional units.
6. Culturally diverse literature helps students understand the viewpoints of ethnically diverse groups and encourages greater appreciation of other cultures. Its use contributes to creating a sense of belonging among students.
7. Resource-based units include four components: reading, listening, or viewing texts; minilessons; responding; and creative projects.
8. Theme study units are interdisciplinary and integrate language arts with one or more of social studies, science, math, and other curricular areas. They range from simpler theme units at the primary levels to more in-depth study of a topic or theme over a long period of time.
9. Inquiry-based units are based on students' genuine curiosity and include using multiple resources and all of the language arts to discover answers to their questions.
10. Readers and writers workshop components are: reading and responding or writing, sharing, and minilessons.
11. Teachers play many roles during language arts instruction, including organizer, facilitator, participant, instructor, model, manager, diagnostician, evaluator, coordinator, and communicator.
12. Students with special learning needs benefit to greater and lesser extents from the same language arts program as other students, but some adaptations are always necessary.

Theory to Practice

1. Visit an elementary classroom and note which characteristics of a language-rich classroom it exemplifies. What might be changed in the classroom to incorporate other characteristics?

2. Form a literature-sharing club with your peers. For each meeting of the club, choose as your focus one of the following categories of children's literature that were discussed in this chapter: picture books, concept books, chapter books, graphic novels, informational books, and poetry books. Hold lively book talks, and take turns presenting to one another examples of Canadian and award-winning non-Canadian selections.

3. Read a collection of culturally diverse books and create an annotated reading list in which you note connections that could be made between the book and areas of grade-appropriate curriculum. Share one or more books from your collection with age-appropriate students. Include the students' responses in your annotation.

4. Reflect on the advantages and disadvantages of each of the three ways to organize for language arts instruction—resource-based units, theme study units, and inquiry-based units—and think how each type of unit might fit into a year-long program plan for a grade level of your choice.

Chapter 3: Reading and Writing Connections

Procedure

To teach writing is also to teach reading. When I teach children to write, they also learn skills necessary for both efficient writing and reading.

Perhaps the most important thing I do during the day is writing the "daily message" on the chalkboard. Usually we decide together what sentences we want to write, for children are more attentive when they have a say in the content and when they write about things that interest them. Sometimes we compose a poem, write a thank-you letter, or write about a book I've read to them. As I write the words of our chosen sentences on the board, I encourage my students to spell along with me and to answer my questions aloud. Not all are ready to respond orally, but everyone listens and watches. As the younger students gain experience, I'll be hearing their voices too. As we work through our sentences, I explain how our language works: rules of phonics, punctuation, rhyming words, irregular spellings, formation of the letters, and the like. I even throw in the word derivation when I think they'll find it interesting. (Remember the French word *beau*? Here it is in *beautiful*!)

> "It is a challenge to plan activities for students who are at many levels of development, activities that will help each child achieve success and grow in skills and self-confidence. Group writing followed by individual practice, writing conferences, and sharing with classmates meets this challenge."
>
> Linda Pierce Picciotto

Students learn different things from this collaborative writing, depending upon their readiness. Jamie is learning the names of the letters and to be aware of spaces between words. Some of the things I talk about have no meaning for him at this point, but he won't be required to do too difficult a worksheet afterward, and hearing about compound words and apostrophes may make them less mysterious later on. Nicky is learning the concept of root words, how to form contractions, spell irregular words, add suffixes to words, and compose interesting and varied sentences.

When we're finished, we read our message as a group. Some days we do a little editing so they can learn that skill and become aware of more descriptive language.

After the group writing process, students have the chance to practise their writing on special "writing workshop" paper. While drawing their pictures, they think about what sentences to print below. If they have trouble coming up with ideas, I ask them to tell me about their drawing. It's easy to develop sentences with this information. I encourage them to start with something other than "This is . . ." to make their message more interesting. I do not help them with the writing process, for I want them to think carefully about the words, to say them quietly, to listen to the sounds and "feel the letters in their mouths." In the beginning, some only do "pretend writing," or draw strings of letters that have no relationship to sounds. With experience and maturity, they begin to include correct or "good guess" consonants and vowels, start separating words, use more interesting words, write using lowercase letters, and write longer and more complex sentences. Each child works at the level appropriate to his or her own developmental level.

Assessment

When students complete their work, we have a short conference. They read the sentences to me, and we talk a bit about the content. Then I write the sentence in Standard English on the facing page while the students look on and listen as I talk about their use of correct or good guess letters and punctuation. I ask them what additional letters they can hear in certain words I pronounce carefully for them. I always make some positive remarks about their writing progress, and I suggest—or ask them to suggest—things to remember the next time they write. Some students need a little encouragement to write more or with more care.

It is easy to see where each child is in his or her writing development when I conference with each one after a writers workshop. By working with individuals, I can help them with exactly the skills they need and make mental notes about certain concepts to emphasize during group writing time.

Often students share their writing with a partner, a group, or the entire class. I make sure they are supportive of one another when they make their observations. I teach them that different children develop skills at varying rates and in many ways. All students encourage each other without insults or comparisons. We celebrate our differences and our progress!

Reflection

It is a challenge to plan activities for students who are at many levels of development, activities that will help each child achieve success and grow in skills and self-confidence. Group writing followed by individual practice, writing conferences, and sharing with classmates meets this challenge. It provides the teacher with a wealth of information about the needs of his or her students. In addition, most students enjoy the writers workshop and come to be able to talk about their own growth, and to articulate what they need to focus on to continue their progress, a skill that will help them throughout their years in school and beyond.

Books published by Linda Pierce Picciotto: *Evaluation: A Team Effort* (Toronto: Scholastic Canada, Ltd., 1992); *Learning Together: A Whole Year in a Primary Classroom* (Toronto: Scholastic Canada, Ltd., 1993); *Student-Led Parent Conferences* (New York: Scholastic Inc., 1996); *Managing an Integrated Language Arts Classroom (Grades K-3)* (Toronto: Scholastic Canada, Ltd., 1999); and *Scientist of the Day: A Classroom or Home Science Program for Students Ages 6-12* (Toronto: Scholastic Canada Ltd., 2010).

From the classroom of Linda Pierce Picciotto, Primary Teacher
Formerly of South Park School Victoria, British Columbia

CHAPTER 3

Emergent Literacy

LEARNING OUTCOMES

After reading this chapter, you should be able to

1. Describe several ways teachers and other caregivers can foster young children's literacy development

2. Describe key characteristics of young children's development as readers

3. Describe key characteristics of young children's development as writers

4. Compare and contrast read-aloud and shared reading as two ways teachers read with children

5. Describe the core components of the Language Experience Approach

6. Explain guided reading as an instructional strategy

7. Describe the reading and writing resource materials needed in primary-grade classrooms

Marcel Mooij/Fotolia

In a combination grade 2/3 classroom, school-based family literacy activities invite parents to collaborate in learning with their children. The portfolio was developed and maintained in school. During their portfolio conference, parent and child review work in progress, discuss completed assignments, and talk about successes and future learning goals. Portfolios also give parents access to materials that allow them to share in their child's development and performance.

The process of becoming literate begins well before the elementary grades and continues into adulthood and throughout life. In years past, researchers and many educators held the belief that children came to kindergarten to be "readied" for reading and writing instruction, which would formally begin in grade 1. The implication was that there was a particular point in children's development when it was time to begin teaching them to read and write, a concept known as **reading readiness**. The past four decades of research, including very careful observations of what children do and can do when offered stimulation and resources, have discredited this view. Children themselves have demonstrated that they can recognize signs and other environmental print, retell stories, scribble letters, find needed keys on a keyboard, click on designated icons, invent print-like writing, and listen closely to stories read aloud to them. Some children even teach themselves to read.

This perspective on how children become literate is known as **emergent literacy**. New Zealand educator the late Marie Clay is credited with coining the term. Now, researchers look at literacy learning from the child's point of view. The age range has been extended to include children as young as twelve to fourteen months of age, who listen to stories being read aloud; notice labels, icons, and signs in their environment; experiment with a variety of writing tools, such as pencils, crayons, and markers: and playfully engage with digital text on screens. The concept of literacy has been broadened to include the cultural and social aspects of language learning, and children's experiences with and understanding of written language—both reading and writing—are included as part of emergent literacy.

Many researchers (Dickinson & Neuman, 2006; Kendrick, 2003; Morrow, 2015; Teale & Sulzby, 1989) who address children's literacy development point out that:

- Children begin to learn to read and write very early in life.
- Young children learn the functions of literacy through participating in real-life activities and through observing others as they engage in reading and writing activities.
- Young children construct their understanding of reading and writing through active involvement with literacy materials.
- Young children's literacy development and practices reflect the social contexts and communities in which they live.

Fostering Young Children's Interest in Literacy

Most children are introduced to written language before they come to school. Parents, caregivers, and others provide opportunities for them to begin to explore printed language, both text and visual images. They read to young children, and the children observe adults reading. Children learn to read signs and other environmental print in their community. They experiment with writing, both physically with pencils or other markers and digitally on various devices. They also observe adults writing and sometimes write collaboratively with adults. When young children come to kindergarten, their knowledge about written language expands quickly as they participate in meaningful, functional, and genuine experiences with reading and writing. Their literacy development is responsive to the experiences their teachers provide as they share their love for reading and writing.

Children also grow in their ability to reflect on language. The ability to talk about concepts of language is called **metalinguistics** (M. Chapman, 2002). Children's ability to think metalinguistically is developed by their experiences with reading and writing (Smith & Read, 2005; Templeton & Spivey, 1980).

Written Language Concepts

Through experiences in their homes and communities, young children learn that print carries meaning and that reading and writing are used for a variety of purposes. As noted above, they may read signs and menus, write and receive cards, send text and email messages, play simple board and computer games involving print, and read and listen to stories for enjoyment. While reading and writing are part of daily life for most children, families and other community members use written language for different purposes in different communities (Heath, 1983b; Sample Gosse & Phillips, 2007). It is important to realize that children come to kindergarten having had a wide range of literacy experiences. McKeough and her collaborators (2008) consider the special case of Aboriginal children in Canada. They point out the prominent place of oral narrative in the children's experiences and show us how storytelling creates a meaningful frame of reference for experiencing the relationship between written language and the world in which the children live.

The differences in perceptions and uses are important determinants of early childhood curriculum. Teachers and schools must be ready to teach children with different experiences. They must respect, appreciate, and work with what the children know, and be prepared to offer complex and sophisticated literate practices through which all children can achieve things in their immediate and future worlds (Comber, 1999).

Teachers demonstrate the purposes of written language and provide opportunities for students to experiment with reading and writing in many ways other than explicit teaching. Some of those ways include:

- posting signs and labels in the classroom
- including literacy materials in dramatic play centres
- writing notes to students in the class
- reading calendars and daily weather charts
- reading and writing stories, poems, and informational texts
- posting charts to describe class routines, rules, and class helpers
- drawing and writing in journals
- making reading and writing games available on digital devices
- writing morning messages on charts and electronic whiteboards
- recording questions and information on charts
- creating class websites with print, visual, and auditory information
- writing blogs, notes, newsletters, and email messages to parents

CONCEPT OF A WORD

Children's understanding of the concept of a "word" is an important part of becoming literate. Young children have only vague notions of language terms, such as *word*, *letter*, *sound*, and *sentence*, which teachers use in talking about reading and writing (Invernizzi, 2003). Preschoolers equate words with the objects they represent. As they are introduced to reading and writing experiences, children begin to differentiate between objects and words, and finally come to appreciate that words have meanings of their own.

Researchers have investigated children's developmental understanding of a word as a unit of language and their becoming word conscious. Being word conscious refers to being aware and interested in words and their meanings (Anderson & Nagy, 1992; Graves & Watts-Taffe, 2002). It is possible to identify four stages of word consciousness. At the first level, young children do not differentiate between things and the words that name them. At the next level, children describe words as labels for things. They consider words that stand for objects as words, but they do not classify articles and prepositions as words because they cannot be represented by objects. At the third level, children understand that words carry meaning and that stories are built from words. At the fourth level, fluent readers and writers describe words as autonomous elements having meanings of their own with definite semantic and syntactic relationships. Also, at this level children understand that words can be spoken, listened to, read, and written.

ENVIRONMENTAL PRINT

Many young children begin reading by recognizing environmental print such as logos on fast-food restaurants, signs in supermarkets, and commonly used household items within familiar contexts (Harste, Woodward, & Burke, 1984b). They recognize the golden arches of McDonald's and say "McDonald's," but when they are shown the word *McDonald's* written on a sheet of paper without the familiar sign and restaurant setting, they cannot read the word. Researchers have found that young emergent readers depend on context to read familiar words and memorized texts (Sulzby, 1985). Slowly, children link form and meaning as they learn concepts about written language through reading and writing experiences.

When children begin writing, they use scribbles or single letters to represent complex ideas. As they learn about letter names and phoneme–grapheme correspondences, they use one, two, or three letters to stand for a word. At first, they may run their writing together, but they slowly learn to segment words and leave spaces between words. They sometimes add dots or lines as markers before learning conventional text organization. Through experience and with some adult guidance and modelling, they learn about and begin to use writing conventions such as capital letters and other punctuation marks. As children discover that writing helps them understand and communicate with others, their interest in writing increases. They best learn the joy and power of writing when it is integrated in various themes and activities for a variety of purposes (Bowman, Donovan, & Burns, 2000).

DRAMATIC PLAY CENTRES

Young children learn about the functions of reading and writing as they use written language in their play. As they construct block buildings, children write signs and tape them on the buildings and as they play teacher, they read stories aloud to friends who are pretending to be students or to doll and stuffed-animal "students." Housekeeping **centres** are probably the most common play centres in early childhood classrooms, but these centres can be easily transformed to coordinate with units and themes, becoming a grocery store, restaurant, or a medical centre by changing the props. Materials for reading and writing can be included in each of these play centres. When young children plan and communicate through writing during play, they develop both literacy and cognitive skills (Bodrova & Leong, 2001; Burns, Griffin, & Snow, 1999). Ideas for three dramatic play centres and related props are offered in Figure 3-1. Each centre includes authentic literacy materials.

Children use props in dramatic play centres to pretend play.

FIGURE 3-1 THREE DRAMATIC PLAY CENTRES

Restaurant Centre
- Tablecloth
- Dishes
- Glasses
- Silverware
- Napkins
- Menus
- Tray
- Order pad and pencil
- Apron/vest for waitstaff
- Hat and apron for chef
- Placemats with activities for children

Medical Centre
- Appointment book/computer
- White shirt/jacket
- Medical bag
- Telephone
- Stethoscope
- Thermometer
- Bandages
- Prescription pad
- Folders (for patient records)
- Empty prescription bottles and labels
- Children's magazines

Grocery Store Centre
- Grocery cart
- Food packages
- Plastic fruit and artificial foods
- Price stickers
- Cash register (play)
- Money (play)
- Credit and debit cards (play)
- Grocery bags
- Marking pen and pencils
- Cents-off coupons
- Advertisements
- Shopping lists

Alphabet Concepts

Young children need a variety of experiences and several types of information to establish a firm foundation for their literacy development. Knowledge of the alphabet is certainly one type of information they need. (Snow, Burns, & Griffin, 1998). To have full knowledge of a letter, children must know its four components. The four are letter-shape knowledge or letter recognition, letter-name knowledge, letter-sound knowledge, and letter-writing ability (Bradley & Jones, 2007; Mason, 1984). Most children come to school with at least partial alphabet knowledge, and teachers help them add to their knowledge through many play activities such as letter recognition and matching games as well as more explicit instruction in which they learn to recognize and use the letters for reading and writing.

THE ALPHABETIC PRINCIPLE

The one-to-one correspondence between the phonemes (or sounds) and graphemes (or letters), such that each letter consistently represents one sound, is known as the **alphabetic principle**. In phonetic languages, there is a one-to-one correspondence; however, English is not a purely phonetic language. The 26 letters represent approximately 44 phonemes, and three letters—*c*, *q*, and *x*—are superfluous because they do not represent unique phonemes. The letter *c*, for example, can represent either /k/ as in *cat* or /s/ as in *city*, and it can be joined with *h* for the digraph /ch/. To further complicate matters, there are more than 500 spellings to represent the forty-four phonemes. Consonants are more consistent and predictable than vowels: long *e*, for instance, is spelled more than ten different ways in common words!

Researchers estimate that words are spelled phonetically approximately half the time (Hanna, Hanna, Hodges, & Rudorf, 1966). The nonphonetic spellings of many words reflect morphological information. The word *sign*, for example, is a shortened form of *signature*. Spelling the word phonetically (e.g., *sine*) might seem simpler, but the **phonetic spelling** lacks semantic information.

LETTER NAMES

The most basic information that children learn about the alphabet is to identify the letters by name and form the letters in handwriting. They notice letters in environmental print, and they often learn to sing the ABC song. By the time children enter kindergarten, they usually recognize some, if not all, letters, especially those in their own names and in common words in their homes and communities. Many children can write the familiar letters and some can locate particular letters on a keyboard or computer screen when playing games.

Young children associate letters with meaningful contexts—names, signs, T-shirts, and cereal boxes. Children don't learn alphabet letter names in any particular order or by isolating letters from meaningful written language; instead, as McGee and Richgels (2012) conclude, learning letters of the alphabet requires many experiences with meaningful written language. It is crucial that explicit instruction to teach children to identify and print the letters of the alphabet be embedded in meaningful and authentic reading and writing experiences. Routines for teaching the alphabet are described in Figure 3-2.

PHONEMIC AWARENESS

Phonological awareness is an umbrella term used to refer to conscious awareness of the constituent sounds within words. Sounds are categorized by size largest to smallest: syllables, onsets and rimes, and phonemes. Considerable evidence affirms a strong relationship between phonological processing skills and the acquisition of reading and spelling in alphabetic languages (Ehri et al., 2001). **Phonemic awareness**, the basic understanding that speech is composed of a series of individual sounds, is the most difficult aspect of phonological awareness for children to learn. It is typically attained after children develop an awareness of rhyming words, syllables, and onset-rime units (Gonzalez & Gonzalez, 1993) and it provides the foundation for phonics (Cameron, 1998; Yopp, 1992). When children can choose a duck as the animal that begins with /d/ from a collection of toy animals, identify *duck* and *luck* as two rhyming words in a song, or blend the sounds /d/, /u/, and /k/ to pronounce *duck*, they are phonemically aware. The emphasis in these and other activities that illustrate phonemic awareness is on the sounds of spoken words, not reading letters or pronouncing letter names. Developing phonemic awareness enables children to use sound–symbol correspondences to read and spell words. Phonemic awareness is not sounding out words for reading, nor is it using spelling patterns to write words; rather, it is the ability to manipulate sounds within words orally.

Understanding that words are composed of smaller sound units—phonemes—is a significant achievement for young children. Phonemes carry no meaning, and children think of words according to their meanings, not their linguistic characteristics (Griffith & Olson, 1992). When children think about ducks, they think of animals covered with feathers that swim in ponds and make noises we describe as "quacks." They don't think of *duck* as a word with three phonemes or four graphemes, as a word beginning with /d/ and rhyming with *luck*. Phonemic awareness requires that children treat speech as an object and that they shift attention away from the meaning of words to the linguistic features of speech. This focus on phonemes is even more complicated because phonemes are not discrete units in speech. Often they are blended or slurred together in speech. Think about the blended initial sound in *tree* and the ending sound in *eating*.

FIGURE 3-2 ROUTINES TO TEACH THE ABCs

Environmental Print
Teachers collect food labels, pictures of familiar signs, and other examples of environmental print for children to use in identifying letters. Children sort labels and other materials to find examples of a letter being studied.

Alphabet Books
Teachers read aloud alphabet books to build vocabulary and teach the names of words that represent each letter. Then children reread the books and consult them to think of words when making books about a letter.

Magnetic Letters
Children pick all examples of one letter from a collection of magnetic letters or match upper- and lowercase letterforms. They also arrange the letters in alphabetical order and use the letters to spell their names and other familiar words.

Letter Stamps
Students use letter stamps and ink pads to stamp letters on paper or in booklets. They also paint letters using letter-shaped sponges and make modeling clay cookies using letter-shaped cookie cutters.

Key Words
Teachers use alphabet charts with a picture of a familiar object for each letter. It's crucial that children be familiar with the objects or they won't remember the key words. Teachers recite the alphabet with children, pointing to each letter and saying, "a—apple, B—bear, C—cat," and so on.

Letter Sorts
Teachers collect plastic containers or small boxes, one for each letter. They write upper- and lowercase letters on the outside of the containers and place several familiar objects or pictures of objects representing the letter in each one. Teachers use these containers to introduce the letters, and children use them at a centre for sorting and matching activities.

Letter Frames
Teachers make circle-shaped letter frames from tagboard, collect large plastic bracelets, or shape pipe cleaners or Wikki-Stix (pipe cleaners covered in wax) into circles for students to use to highlight particular letters on charts or in big books.

Letter Books and Posters
Children make letter books with pictures of objects beginning with a particular letter on each page. They add letter stamps, stickers, or pictures cut from magazines. For posters, the teacher draws a large letterform on a chart and children add pictures, stickers, and letter stamps.

Whiteboards
Children practice writing upper- and lowercase forms of letters and familiar words on whiteboards and digital whiteboards. Where software is available, writing may begin with tracing dotted forms of the letters before writing each one independently.

Handheld Digital Devices
Children practice letter recognition, matching letters and sounds, and tracing letters while playing games on handheld digital devices.

For most children, phonological awareness develops through their literacy experiences at home and in their early childhood classrooms as they sing songs, play with words, interact with word walls, chant rhymes, and listen to parents and teachers read wordplay books to them (Ehri & Roberts, 2006; Griffith & Olson, 1992). For some children, learning to differentiate sounds within words, especially on the phoneme level, is confusing. They benefit from explicit instruction to help them understand that their speech is composed of sounds (Ball & Blachman, 1991; P. McCarthy, 2008; Snow, Griffin, & Tabors, 2002).

Yopp (1995) recommends that teachers read aloud books with wordplay and encourage students to talk about the books' language. Teachers ask questions and make comments such as "Did you notice how _____ and _____ rhyme?" and "This book is fun because of all the words begin with the /m/ sound." Once students are very familiar with the book, they can create new verses or make other variations. Books such as *Mabel Murple* (Fitch, 1995b) and *It's Raining Pigs and Noodles* (Prelutsky, 2000) stimulate children to experiment with sounds, create nonsense words, and become enthusiastic about reading. When teachers read books with alliterative or assonant patterns, such as *Zigzag: Zoems for Zindergartens* (Lesynski, 2004), children attend to the smaller units of language.

The goal of phonemic awareness activities is to break down and manipulate spoken words. Students who have developed phonemic awareness can manipulate spoken language in these five ways:

- match words by sounds
- isolate a sound in a word
- blend individual sounds to form a word
- substitute sounds in a word
- segment a word into its constituent sounds (Yopp, 1992; Yopp & Yopp, 2000)

Teachers teach minilessons focusing on each of these tasks. These lessons and learning activities should be playful and game-like, emphasizing the oral manipulation of sounds within words. Five types of phonemic awareness activities are described in Figure 3-3. These basic activities can be adapted to make connections with theme study units or other topics of study within the curriculum.

FIGURE 3-3 ACTIVITIES TO DEVELOP CHILDREN'S PHONEMIC AWARENESS

1. **Sound matching.** Children choose words beginning with a particular sound. For matching games, teachers present a collection of familiar objects or toys or pictures of familiar objects and ask children to identify objects that begin with the same sound. Children can also identify rhyming words as part of sound-matching activities. They name a word that rhymes with a given word and identify rhyming words from familiar songs and stories.

2. **Sound isolation.** Children are given a word and are asked to identify the sounds at the beginning, middle, or end of the word or from a collection of objects or group of words, children choose the one that doesn't begin with the given sound. Yopp and Yopp (2009) show how creating variations to sing familiar tunes offers opportunity for such sound manipulation. One example using the tune of "Old MacDonald Had a Farm" goes like this:

   Old MacDonald had a farm,
   Me mi me mi mo! (p.12)
   Teachers and children can change the words to focus on medial and final sounds.

3. **Sound blending.** Children blend sounds in order to combine them to form a word. Teachers can play the "What am I thinking of?" guessing game with children. For example, the teacher says, "It lives in a pond," and then articulates each sound, "/d/ /u/ /k/." The children blend the sounds together and use the semantic and phonological information to guess the word *duck*. Children can take turns giving cues and segmenting to challenge their peers.

4. **Sound addition or substitution.** Children play with words and create nonsense words as they add or substitute sounds in words in songs they sing or in books that are read aloud to them. Teachers read wordplay books such as Pat Hutchins's *Don't Forget the Bacon!* (1976), in which a boy leaves for the store with a mental list of four items to buy. As he walks, he repeats his list, substituting words each time. "A cake for tea" changes to "a cape for me" and then to "a rake for leaves." Bernard Most's *Cock-a-Doodle-Moo* (1996) is another book that stimulates wordplay and laughter as children imitate and suggest other substitutions.

5. **Segmentation.** Segmentation requires children to slowly pronounce or stretch out words, identifying and isolating all the sounds in a spoken word. Stretching words is often closely associated with use of sound or **Elkonin boxes** (McCarthy, 2008) as shown in Figure 3-4. The use of sound boxes to teach segmentation comes from the work of the Russian psychologist D. B. Elkonin. Sound boxes can be drawn and easily manipulated on interactive whiteboards. Winsor and Pearson (1992) suggest a dramatic game in which children help animals to cross the ugly troll's bridge by paying a magic coin for each phoneme in the animals' names. Using toy animals of two, three, and four phonemes, children dramatize paying the troll while orally segmenting the words. The child who assists the dog says "d/o/g" and pays three magic coins.

FIGURE 3-4 USING ELKONIN BOXES FOR SEGMENTATION ACTIVITIES

1. The teacher shows students an object or the picture of an object, such as a cat, a bed, a game, a bee, a cup, or a duck.

2. The teacher prepares a diagram with a series of boxes, corresponding to the number of sounds heard in the name of the object. For example, the teacher draws three boxes side by side to represent the three sounds heard in the word duck. The teacher can draw the boxes on the whiteboard or on small cards for each student to use. The teacher also prepares markers to place on the boxes. If using a magnetic whiteboard, magnetic button markers can be used. If using boxes on a card, any small disks can be used.

3. The teacher and students say the word slowly and move markers onto the boxes as each sound is pronounced.

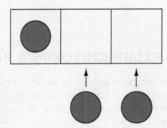

4. Elkonin boxes can also be used when spelling words. The teacher draws a series of boxes corresponding to the number of sounds heard in the word, and then the students and teacher pronounce the word, pointing to each box or sliding markers into each box. Then the students write the letters representing each sound or spelling pattern in the boxes. The teacher emphasizes the representation of sounds and notes that some sounds are represented by more than one letter.

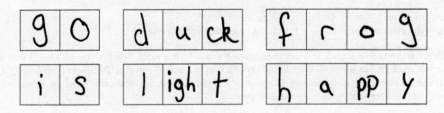

The relationship among oral language, phonemic awareness, learning to read, and later reading achievement is extremely important. Some educators have argued that a child must develop phonemic awareness before learning to read; yet there is strong evidence that phonemic awareness develops as a consequence of learning to read and write (M. Chapman, 2002). Researchers have concluded that at least some level of phonemic awareness is a prerequisite for learning to read (Tunmer & Nesdale, 1985) and that refinement is a consequence of learning to read (Perfetti, Beck, Bell, & Hughes, 1987; K. Stanovich, 1980). As they become phonemically aware, children recognize that speech can be segmented into smaller units, and they use this knowledge to learn the sound–symbol correspondences and spelling patterns they need for reading and writing. Moreover, research evidence suggests that lack of this knowledge is associated with reading difficulties and reading failure (Busink, 1997; Pressley & Allington, 2015).

PHONICS

Phonics is the set of relationships between phonology (the sounds in speech) and orthography (the spelling patterns of written language). Sounds are spelled in different ways for many reasons. One reason is that the sounds, especially vowels, vary according to their location in a word (e.g., *go, got*). Adjacent letters often influence how letters are pronounced (e.g., *bed, bead*), as do vowel markers such as the final *e* (e.g., *bit, bite*) (Shefelbine, 1995).

Phonics is sometimes viewed as a controversial topic. Noted scholar Ken Goodman called it "the most widely misunderstood aspect" of reading instruction (1993, p. 1). Reading is a complex process, and the phonological system works in conjunction with the semantic, syntactic, and pragmatic systems—not in isolation. Therefore, it is essential for students to know phonics (sound–symbol relationships), but that is not all they need to know. It is now widely accepted that phonics should be taught explicitly within a balanced approach that integrates specific instruction in reading skills and strategies with meaningful reading and writing of connected text. Further, phonics instruction should focus on the most useful information for identifying words and be systematic, intensive, and completed by grade 3.

Teachers teach sound–symbol correspondences, how to blend sounds to decode words, how to segment sounds to spell, and the most useful phonics generalizations or "rules." Phonics concepts build on phonemic awareness. The four most important concepts that primary-grade students learn are consonants, vowels, onsets and rimes, and phonic generalizations.

1. ***Consonants.*** Letters are classified as either consonants or vowels. The consonants are *b, c, d, f, g, h, j, k, l, m, n, p, q, r, s, t, v, w, x, y,* and *z.* Most consonants represent a single sound consistently, but there are some exceptions. For example, *c* does not represent a sound of its own. When it is followed by *a, o,* or *u,* it is pronounced /k/ (e.g., *castle, coffee*) and when it is followed by *e, i,* or *y,* it is pronounced /s/ (e.g., *cell, city*). G represents two sounds, as the word *garage* illustrates. It is usually pronounced /g/ (e.g., *glass, go*), but when *g* is followed by *e* or *i,* it is pronounced /j/, as in *giant*. *X* is also pronounced differently according to its location in a word. When *x* is at the beginning of a word, it is often pronounced /z/, as in *xylophone,* but sometimes the letter name is used, as in *X-ray.* At the end of a word, *x* is pronounced /ks/, as in *box*.

   The letters *w* and *y* are particularly interesting. At the beginning of a word or a syllable they are consonants (e.g., *wind, yard*), but when they are in the middle or at the end, they are vowels (e.g., *saw, flown, day, by*).

   Two kinds of combination consonants are blends and digraphs. ***Consonant blends*** are two or three consonants that appear next to each other in words, and their individual sounds are blended together, such as *grass, belt,* and *spring.* ***Consonant digraphs*** are letter combinations that represent single sounds. The four most common are *ch, sh, th,* and *wh.* Another consonant digraph is *ph,* as in *graph* and *photo.*

2. ***Vowels.*** The remaining five letters—*a, e, i, o,* and *u*—are vowels, and *w* and *y* are vowels when used in the middle and at the end of syllables and words. Vowels represent several sounds. Short-vowel sounds are /a/ as in *cat,* /e/ as in *bed,* /i/ as in *win,*

/o/ as in *hot*, and /u/ as in *cup*. Long-vowel sounds are the same as the letter names, and they are illustrated in the words *make*, *feet*, *bike*, *coal*, and *mule*. Long vowels are usually spelled with two vowels, except when *y* is used at the end of a word.

When *y* is a vowel at the end of a word, it is pronounced as long *e* or long *i*, depending on the length of the word. In one-syllable words such as *by* and *try*, the *y* is pronounced as long *i*, but in longer words such as *baby* and *happy*, the *y* is pronounced as long *e*.

When the letter *r* follows one or more vowels in a word, it influences the pronunciation of the vowel sound, as in *car*, *air*, *are*, *ear*, *bear*, *first*, *for*, *more*, *murder*, and *pure*, and these are referred to as *r-controlled vowels*. There are additional vowel combinations representing other sounds. These vowel combinations often represent more than one sound and are used in only a few words:

> *au* as in *laugh* and *caught*
> *aw* as in *saw*
> *ew* as in *sew* and *few*
> *oi* as in *oil*
> *oo* as in *cook* and *moon*
> *ou* as in *about* and *through*
> *ow* as in *now*
> *oy* as in *toy*

Vowel sounds are more complicated than consonant sounds. For children to learn them, teachers must provide explicit instruction and multiple reading and writing experiences.

3. **Onsets and rimes.** One-syllable words and syllables in longer words can be divided into two parts: the onset and the rime. The *onset* is the consonant sound that precedes the vowel, and the *rime* is the vowel and any consonant sounds that follow it. For example, in *show*, *sh* is the onset and *ow* is the rime, and in *ball*, *b* is the onset and *all* is the rime. For *at* and *up*, there is no onset—the entire word is the rime. Research has shown that children make more errors decoding and spelling final consonants than initial consonants and that they make more errors on vowels than on consonants (Treiman, 1985). These problem areas correspond to rimes, and educators now speculate that onsets and rimes could provide the key to unlocking phonemic awareness. This is partly because both the sound and spelling of rimes tend to be fairly predictable (Snow, Burns, & Griffin, 1998).

Children can focus their attention on a rime (sometimes referred to as a *word family*), such as *ay*, and create rhyming words, including *bay*, *day*, *lay*, *may*, *ray*, *say*, and *way*. These words can be read and spelled by analogy because the vowel sounds are consistent in rimes. Thirty-seven rimes can be used to produce nearly 500 words. They can be used in games and other word-work activities to help children master reading and writing them. These rimes and some common words using them are presented in the first Teacher's Notebook.

4. **Phonics generalizations.** Because English does not have a one-to-one correspondence between sounds and letters, both linguists and educators have tried to create rules, or generalizations, to clarify English spelling patterns. One such rule is that *q* is followed by *u* and pronounced /kw/. Only a few phonics generalizations have a high degree of utility for readers. Eight high-utility generalizations are listed in the second Teacher's Notebook. Even though these rules are fairly reliable, very few approach 100 percent utility. It is important, therefore, for teachers to teach children to be flexible when applying the rules, reminding them of the need to always check for contextual meaning when decoding.

Students acquire some phonics knowledge as a natural part of reading and writing activities, but teachers teach about phonics directly in the primary grades. Effective

Thirty-Seven Rimes and Some Common Words Using Them

-ack	black, pack, quack, stack	-ide	bride, hide, ride, side
-ail	mail, nail, sail, tail	-ight	bright, fight, light, might
-ain	brain, chain, plain, rain	-ill	fill, hill, kill, will
-ake	cake, shake, take, wake	-in	chin, grin, pin, win
-ale	male, sale, tale, whale	-ine	fine, line, mine, nine
-ame	came, flame, game, name	-ing	king, sing, thing, wing
-an	can, man, pan, than	-ink	pink, sink, think, wink
-ank	bank, drank, sank, thank	-ip	drip, hip, lip, ship
-ap	cap, clap, map, slap	-ir	fir, sir, stir
-ash	cash, dash, flash, trash	-ock	block, clock, knock, sock
-at	bat, cat, rat, that	-oke	choke, joke, poke, woke
-ate	gate, hate, late, plate	-op	chop, drop, hop, shop
-aw	claw, draw, jaw, saw	-or	for, or
-ay	day, play, say, way	-ore	chore, more, shore, store
-eat	beat, heat, meat, wheat	-uck	duck, luck, suck, truck
-ell	bell, sell, shell, well	-ug	bug, drug, hug, rug
-est	best, chest, nest, west	-ump	bump, dump, hump, lump
-ice	ice, mice, nice, rice	-unk	bunk, dunk, junk, sunk
-ick	brick, pick, sick, thick		

phonics instruction is systematic and explicit. In addition to direct instruction, teachers often explain phonics concepts as they engage children in authentic literacy activities using children's names, titles of books, and environmental print in the classroom. Teachers answer students' questions about words, and they model the use of phonics knowledge to decode and spell words as they engage in classroom routines such as reading big books together and writing class news in morning messages. Phonics instruction, explicit or implicit, is always linked to meaningful reading and writing. Without those links, children see little reason to learn phonics (Cunningham, 2012).

Young Children Become Readers

Learning to read is a process that happens over time, beginning in infancy as children acquire language. Children move through identifiable stages as they learn. In some research, the stages have been labelled *emergent reading*, *beginning reading*, and *fluent reading* (Juel, 1991). In emergent reading, children gain an understanding of the communicative purpose of print. They notice environmental print, dictate stories for the teacher to record, and reread predictable books after they have memorized the pattern. From this foundation, children move into the beginning reading stage where they learn phoneme–grapheme correspondences and begin to decode word

The Most Useful Phonics Generalizations

Pattern	Description	Examples	
1. Two sounds of c	The letter c can be pronounced as /k/ or /s/. When c is followed by a, o, or u, it is pronounced /k/—the hard c sound. When c is followed by e, i, or y, it is pronounced /s/—the soft c sound.	cat cough	cent city
2. Two sounds of g	The sound associated with the letter g depends on the letter following it. When g is followed by a, o, or u, it is pronounced as /g/—the hard g sound. When g is followed by e, i, or y, it is usually /j/—the soft g sound. Exceptions include get and give.	gate go guess	gentle giant gym
3. CVC pattern	When a one-syllable word has only one vowel and the vowel comes between two consonants, it is usually short. One exception is told.	bat cup land	
4. Final e or CVCe pattern	When there are two vowels in a one-syllable word and one of them is an e at the end of the word, the first vowel is long and the final e is silent. Two exceptions are have and love.	home safe cute	
5. CV pattern	When a vowel follows a consonant in a one-syllable word, the vowel is long. Exceptions include the, to, be and do.	go	
6. R-controlled vowels	Vowels that are followed by the letter r are overpowered and are neither short nor long. One exception is fire.	car for birthday	
7. -igh	When gh follows i, the i is long and the gh is silent. One exception is neighbour.	high night	
8. Kn- and wr-	In words beginning with kn- and wr-, the first letter is not pronounced.	knee Write	

Source: Adapted from Clymer, T. (1996). The utility of phonic generalizations in the primary grades. The Reading Teacher, 50, 182–187.
© Gail E. Tompkins

In the fluent reading stage, children have learned how to read, recognize most words automatically, and decode unfamiliar words quickly. They are fluent readers who are able to concentrate their cognitive energy on comprehension and meaning-making.

Primary-grade teachers organize language arts instruction in ways that address the children's developmental needs and take into account the wide variations in experiences they bring to their learning. Typically, instructional programming includes multiple components that change in response to children's progress in acquiring the foundational skills they need to become successful readers and writers. Among the instructional components are read-alouds, shared reading and guided reading. Resource-based units are one way teachers organize multi-faceted instruction. Language experience approach is another way teachers organize instruction for readers.

Children also need opportunities to read some books themselves—independently. Children often begin by reading books with predictable refrains and repetition and then move on to easy-to-read books to practise decoding and to develop fluency. Through a multifaceted language arts program of literature, reading and writing experiences, and explicit instruction in phonics, skills, and strategies, young children develop into fluent readers and writers.

Children learn, too, from their technology-based activities, such as video games, interactive websites, children's television, and digitized toys. Involving young children in digital technology clearly affects their academic success (Wohlwend, 2010). In addition to advanced literacy knowledge, they develop fine motor skills needed for keyboarding, problem-solving necessary for navigating search engines, concentration needed to understand complex concepts, and other abilities. Experiences with digital technology inside and outside classrooms contribute to literacy development.

Teachers plan and teach resource-based units using high-quality books of children's literature. Within the unit of study, instruction and learning activities engage children in using the six language arts as described in Chapter 2. Teachers differentiate activities to make them developmentally appropriate. These include hands-on activities with letters and words, time for children to listen while being read to, time for children to read independently, time for children to read to each other, and mini-lessons on phonics and other specific reading strategies. Sometimes, resource-based units also focus children's attention on a particular theme presented within the literature. Figure 3-5 presents an outline for a resource-based unit focused on Laura Numeroff's books, beginning with *If You Give a Mouse a Cookie* (1985).

Read-Aloud

Reading aloud to children can be a powerful teaching strategy. Teachers read aloud to children in the primary grades for a variety of reasons. Among the reasons are entertainment, sharing of high quality literature beyond the reading level of children, and sharing informational text to support learning across the curriculum. More specifically, teachers sometimes read-aloud to teach specific comprehension strategies, familiarize students with literary genres or language structures, introduce unfamiliar vocabulary and concepts, and provide a model of fluent, expressive reading. Read-aloud is one way for children to experience high quality texts before they are able to read them on their own. For many children, listening while being read to is one of their favourite activities of the school day.

The most powerful read-alouds are interactive. As teachers read to children, they call upon them to make predictions, answer questions, infer ideas from text information, and engage in discussion following the reading. Through interactive read-alouds, teachers can model and encourage the strategies that good readers use (Hilden & Jones, 2013). The steps in interactive read-aloud are explained in the Step by Step box.

Shared Reading

In shared reading, teachers read a book aloud as children follow along in individual books, follow the book as it is projected on an electronic whiteboard, or look at an enlarged version of a picture book, called a **big book**. Teachers use this approach as a first step toward children reading the books independently (Holdaway, 1979). Teachers use the big book to read *with* children rather than *to* children (Bainbridge & Malicky, 2004; Morrow, 2015). Through shared reading, whether in printed or digital text, teachers demonstrate how print works, provide opportunities for students to use the prediction strategy, and increase children's confidence in their ability to read. In many classrooms, the big books are accompanied by a set of small copies of the book for individual reading. After reading the big book with the teacher, often more than once, children read the small copies independently. The steps in shared reading are explained in the Step by Step box on page 85.

FIGURE 3-5 OUTLINE FOR A RESOURCE-BASED UNIT ON LAURA NUMEROFF'S BOOKS.

1. **Preparing**
   - The teacher collects and displays books by Laura Numeroff, including *If You Give a Mousea Cookie* (Numeroff, 1985), *If You Give a Pig a Pancake* (Numeroff, 1998), *If You Give a Moose a Muffin* (Numeroff, 1991), *If You Take a Mouse to the Movies* (Numeroff, 2000), *If You Take a Mouse to School* (Numeroff, 2002), *If You Give a Pig a Party* (Numeroff, 2005), and *If You Give a Dog a Donut* (2011).
   - The teacher brings in several types of cookies for children to sample. Students talk about their favourite cookies, and they create a graph and chart of their favourite cookies.
   - The teacher introduces *If You Give a Mouse a Cookie* as the first of Numeroff's books the class will be reading together. The teacher includes information about the author and tells the children they will be reading several stories written by her.
   - The teacher shares a book box of objects mentioned in the story (cookie, glass of milk, straw, napkin, mirror, scissors, broom, etc.), and children talk about how some of the items might be used in the story.
   - Students and the teacher begin making a word wall with the words cookie and mouse.

2. **Reading**
   - The teacher reads the big book of *If You Give a Mouse a Cookie* using shared reading.
   - The teacher rereads the book, and students join in reading repeated words and phrases.

3. **Responding**
   - The students and teacher participate in a grand conversation about the book.
   - Students dramatize the story using objects in the book box.
   - Students draw pictures in reading logs and add words (using invented spelling) to record their reactions to the book.

4. **Exploring**
   - Students and teacher add interesting and important words to the word wall.
   - Students buddy-read small-size versions of the book with partners and reread the book independently.
   - On successive days, the teacher teaches minilessons on
     - o the /k/ sound using cookie to illustrate two ways it is written
     - o the author, Laura Numeroff
     - o irregular plurals (e.g., *mouse–mice, child–children, moose–moose*).
   - The teacher explains the concept of a circle story, and students sequence picture cards of the events in the stories to make a circle diagram. Some children attempt circle story writing in the writing centre.
   - The teacher sets up centres for students to sort objects related to the phonics lessons, paint pictures of the story characters, to listen to recordings of books by Numeroff.
   - As the unit proceeds and additional books are read, the teacher adapts the responding and exploring activities and minilessons to coordinate with the stories.

5. **Extending**
   - Students write their own stories of adventures of the story characters.
   - Students create projects, including book bags of objects related to the stories.
   - Students share their writing and other projects from the author's chair.

STEP BY STEP

Interactive Read-Aloud

1 **Choose a book.**   Teachers choose both narrative and informational texts depending upon their purpose for reading aloud. Picture books and illustrated informational texts lend themselves to successful reading experiences because they offer both print and visual information. Longer books can be read in two sessions.

2 **Introduce the book.**   Teachers introduce the book by reading the title, exploring the cover illustrations if any, and drawing attention to the name of the author and illustrator. Teachers also provide any background knowledge needed to understand the book. Next, they ask the children to make predictions about the book's content and explain why they are making each prediction.

3 **Read the book with pauses.**   The teacher reads in a fluent, expressive manner until a point is reached when pausing is beneficial for children's listening experience. Pauses are made to closely view illustrations (if present), to clarify, follow through on a prediction or ask for further predictions, and for children to make connections to their lives and other texts. Depending upon purpose, teachers may also stop to point out a particular word or phrase, to draw attention to the author's craft, or simply to seek children's responses. Pauses are intended to heighten children's engagement. Teachers consciously judge when to pause.

4 **Respond to the book.**   Children respond to texts read to them in a number of ways. Teachers encourage responses to broaden and deepen the meaning children make of the story, poem, or other text. Teachers ask questions to prompt critical and creative thinking and invite children's comments, opinions, and general discussion. Other responses to help develop meaning include drawing, painting, drama, various forms of writing such as journal entries, and multimedia projects using text, visuals, and sound.

Shared reading and interactive read-aloud have much in common. The distinction we make is that in read-aloud the teacher reads *to* the children, pausing to share illustrations and other interactions, but the children are not in position to closely follow the text. In shared reading, the teacher reads initially, but the children can see and are expected to follow the text (individual copies, a big book, or on screen) and join in the reading. Not only do procedures vary in respect to following text, but distinctions can be made in respect to primary purposes and types of text chosen. For example, read-aloud is most often the strategy chosen for extending children's experience with literature beyond their reading level whereas shared reading is preferred for specific strategy instruction.

PREDICTABLE BOOKS

The stories and other books used for both shared and guided reading with young children often have repeated words and sentences, rhyme, or other patterns. Books that use these patterns, known as **predictable books**, make a valuable tool for emergent readers because the repetition enables children to predict the next sentence or episode in the story (Heald-Taylor, 1987; Tompkins & Webeler, 1983). Four characteristics of predictable books are

1. *Repetition.* In some books, phrases and sentences are repeated over and over. Examples include *Brown Bear, Brown Bear, What Do You See?* (B. Martin, 1990).

Sometimes each episode or section of the text ends with the same words or a refrain; other times, the same statement or question is repeated.

2. **Cumulative sequence.** In some books, phrases or sentences are repeated and expanded in each episode. In *The Gingerbread Boy* (Galdone, 1975), for example, the Gingerbread Boy repeats and expands his boast as he meets each character. Other examples include *We're Going on a Picnic* (P. Hutchins, 2002) and *Bear Snores On* (K. Wilson, 2002).

3. **Rhyme and rhythm.** Rhyme and rhythm are important devices in some books. Sentences have a strong beat, and rhyme is used at the end of each line or in another poetic scheme. Some books have an internal rhyme within lines. Books in this category include *Chicka Chicka Boom Boom* (Martin & Archambault, 1989) and *A Frog in the Bog* (K. Wilson, 2003). Please see below.

4. **Sequential patterns.** Some books use a familiar sequence—such as months of the year, days of the week, numbers 1 to 10, or letters of the alphabet—to structure the text. For example, *The Very Hungry Caterpillar* (Carle, 1969) combines number and day-of-the-week sequences as the caterpillar eats through an amazing array of foods. Laura Numeroff's *If You Give a Pig a Party* (2005) is another example.

> A list of predictable books illustrating each of these patterns is presented in Figure 3-6.

FIGURE 3-6 BOOKS WITH PREDICTABLE PATTERNS

Repetitive Sentences

Bennett, J. (2000). *Jason Mason Middleton-Tap*. Vancouver: Raincoast. 🍁

Carle, E. (1990). *The Very Quiet Cricket*. New York: Philomel.

Carle, E. (1995). *The Very Lonely Firefly*. New York: Philomel.

Guarino, D. (1989). *Is Your Mama a Llama?* New York: Scholastic.

Hutchins, P. (1986). *The Doorbell Rang*. New York: Morrow.

Kovalski, M. (1987). *The Wheels on the Bus*. Boston: Little, Brown.

Martin, B., Jr. (1983). *Brown Bear, Brown Bear, What Do You See?* New York: Holt, Rinehart & Winston.

Martin, B., Jr. (1992). *Polar Bear, Polar Bear, What Do You Hear?* New York: Holt, Rinehart & Winston.

Stinson, K. (1984). *Red Is Best*. Toronto: Annick Press. 🍁

Tankard, J. (2007). *Grumpy Bird*. Toronto: Scholastic Canada. 🍁

Viorst, J. (1972). *Alexander and the Terrible, Horrible, No Good, Very Bad Day*. New York: Atheneum.

Williams, S. (1989). *I Went Walking*. San Diego: Harcourt Brace Jovanovich.

Repetitive Sentences in a Cumulative Sequence

Beck, A. (2002). *Elliot Gets Stuck*. Toronto: Kids Can Press. 🍁

Brett, J. (1989). *The Mitten*. New York: Putnam.

Galdone, P. (1975). *The Gingerbread Boy*. New York: Seabury.

Kalan, R. (1995). *Jump, Frog, Jump!* New York: Greenwillow.

Karas, G. (1994). *I Know an Old Lady*. New York: Scholastic.

Litzinger, R. (1993). *The Old Woman and Her Pig*. New York: Harcourt Brace Jovanovich.

West, C. (1996). *"I Don't Care!" Said the Bear*. Cambridge, MA: Candlewick.

Rhyme and Rhythm

dePaola, T. (1985). *Hey Diddle Diddle and Other Mother Goose Rhymes*. New York: Putnam.

Fernandes, E. (2002). *Busy Little Mouse*. Toronto: Kids Can Press. 🍁

Fitch, S. (1992). *There Were Monkeys in My Kitchen*. Toronto: Doubleday Canada. 🍁

Gilman, P. (1994). *Jillian Jiggs to the Rescue*. Richmond Hill, ON: Scholastic Canada. 🍁

Lee, D. (2001). *The Cat and the Wizard*. Toronto: Key Porter Books. 🍁

Martin, B., & Archambault, J. (2000). *Chicka Chicka Boom Boom*. New York: Aladdin Books.

Seuss, Dr. (1963). *Hop on Pop*. New York: Random House.

Numeroff, L. (2011). *If You Give a Dog a Donut*. New York: Collins.

Wilson, K. (2003). *A Frog in the Bog*. New York: Simon & Schuster.

Sequential Patterns

Carle, E. (1969). *The Very Hungry Caterpillar*. Cleveland: Collins-World.

Galdone, P. (1986). *Over in the Meadow*. New York: Simon & Schuster.

Godfrey, M. (1992). *Is It OK If This Monster Stays for Lunch?* Toronto: Oxford University Press. 🍁

Kingsley, C. (2001). *Ten Little Puppies*. Toronto: Fitzhenry & Whiteside. 🍁

Numeroff, L. J. (1985). *If You Give a Mouse a Cookie*. New York: HarperCollins.

Numeroff, L. J. (1991). *If You Give a Moose a Muffin*. New York: HarperCollins.

Numeroff, L.J. (2000). *If You Give a Pig a Pancake*. New York: HarperCollins

Numeroff, L. J. (2005). *If You Give a Pig a Party*. New York: HarperCollins.

Shared Reading

1 **Introduce the book.**   The teacher introduces the book by activating children's prior knowledge about the topic or by presenting new information on a topic related to the book, and then by showing the cover of the book and reading the title and author. Then children make predictions about the book. The purpose of these introductory activities is to involve children in the reading activity and to build their anticipation. The book is displayed on an easel in clear view for all.

2 **Read the book.**   The teacher reads the book aloud while children follow the text. The teacher models fluent reading and uses a dramatic style to keep the children's attention. The teacher points to the text and encourages children to chime in on (read chorally) words they can predict and for phrases, sentences, and refrains that are repeated. Periodically, the teacher stops to ask the children to make predictions about the story or to redirect their attention to the text.

3 **Children respond to the book.**   Children respond to the book by drawing and writing in reading logs and by sharing their responses in a grand conversation. While drawing and writing, they may use the book to learn more about written language.

4 **Reread the book.**   Children and the teacher read the book again together in a group. Children reread the book independently or with partners, taking turns using the big book or reading from small copies. Children need to read the book several times in order to become comfortable with the text.

5 **Teach minilessons.**   The teacher uses the book as the basis for minilessons to explore letters, words, and sentences in the text. Minilessons may also focus on rhyme, word-identification strategies, and reading procedures, concepts, strategies, and skills.

6 **Create projects.**   Children extend their understanding of the book through other reading and talking activities and through drama, writing, and multimedia projects.

BIG BOOKS

Teachers use enlarged picture books called *big books* in shared reading, most commonly with primary-grade students. In this approach, developed in New Zealand, teachers use a big book placed on an easel or chart stand where all children can see it; the teacher reads the big book with small groups of children or with the whole class (Holdaway, 1979). When reading big books, teachers follow the shared reading procedures described in the Step by Step: Shared Reading box.

Many picture books are available in big book editions. Some popular ones include *Red Is Best* (Stinson, 1982), *Follow the Polar Bears* (Black, 2001), and *Alphabet Rescue,* 2006). In addition to stories, many informational books associated with particular curriculum topics in science and social studies are available. Shared reading of texts such as *It's about Me, It's about You* (Bryan and Bryan, 2005) facilitates integrated learning of the language arts across curriculum. Some big books are published with accompanying oral readings of the texts along with interactive response activities. Children listen and respond individually and in small groups during

Bob Ebbesen/Alamy Stock Photo

This teacher shares a big book with her students.

literacy-centre time. Another option many teachers choose is to read collaboratively (following the steps for shared reading) from stories and other texts available on the Internet and projected on classroom digital whiteboards.

Teachers and children also make big books together. Publishing software and other production facilities available in many schools make it possible to create personalized, informative, and theme-related big books. One popular authoring activity is creating class "All about Us" big books to which children contribute pages on which they draw large self-portraits and write about their favourite activities. Other types of big books authored and illustrated by teachers and children include collections of favourite poems, retellings of stories, personalized versions of familiar stories, and informative accounts of their learning about specific topics. Writing these books digitally makes it possible to reproduce them in small versions suitable for children to share with their families.

Guided Reading

Guided reading, sometimes referred to as *levelled reading*, involves teachers working with small groups of readers (usually four to six) of similar strengths and instructional needs. They read texts determined to be at the children's instructional level—texts the children can read successfully with some support. Typically, teacher and children each have a copy of the text. The teacher introduces the text and guides the children in a preview or walk-through of the text to note particular vocabulary and language structures, introduce unfamiliar concepts, ask for predictions, and set a purpose for reading. That is, the teacher scaffolds the children's reading before directing them to reread independently. Teachers often embed applicable explicit strategy instruction in the walk-through of the text. During the independent reading, the teacher assists individual readers as needed. After reading, teachers review and reinforce students' strategy use and engage students in discussion that prompts higher-level thinking. Advocated by researchers (Fountas & Pinnell, 1996, 2001), guided reading is widely implemented in primary-grade Canadian classrooms to help students develop and use the strategies needed to be independent readers; it enables them to read progressively more complex texts at increasing levels of difficulty. The steps in guided reading lessons are shown in the Step by Step box.

While it is generally accepted that a guided reading instructional model benefits all students, Avalos, Plasencia, Chavez, and Rascon (2007) have shown that a modified model is especially beneficial to **English language learners (ELLs)**. Their modifications include increasing the time teachers and students interact; adding a shared reading of the guided-reading text, including detailed vocabulary instruction; and paying close attention to language structures and cultural relevance. These modifications offer ELLs opportunities to acquire aspects of language that **native speakers** typically acquire implicitly. Through modified guided reading, teachers can help ELLs achieve the goal of guided reading—to read progressively more challenging texts independently and successfully.

Guided Reading

1 Choose a book. Teachers choose a book that students in a small group can read with 90 to 94 percent accuracy and collect copies of the book for each student in the group.

2 Introduce the book. Teachers show the cover, read the title and author's name, and activate students' background knowledge on a related topic. They use key vocabulary words as they talk about the book but don't always directly teach them. Students also "picture walk" through the book, examining the illustrations.

3 Read the book. Teachers have students read the book independently and ask individual students to take turns reading aloud. They help individual students decode unfamiliar words, deal with unfamiliar sentence structures, and comprehend ideas whenever assistance is needed.

4 Respond to the book. Students talk about the book and relate it to others they've read, as in a grand conversation.

5 Teach concepts. Teachers teach a comprehension strategy or a phonics skill, review vocabulary words, or examine an element of story structure.

6 Do independent reading. Teachers have students reread the book several more times to develop fluency. They often place the book in students' book baskets so students can reread it independently.

LANGUAGE EXPERIENCE APPROACH

The language experience approach (LEA) has long and deep roots as a way of approaching literacy instruction for young children; it first gained popularity in the 1960s (Ashton-Warner, 1965; Stauffer, 1970) when fine-quality children's literature and other resources were not as abundant as they are now in most Canadian classrooms. LEA is based on children's own language and experiences, hence its capacity for differentiation and response to children's interests and instructional needs.

In this approach, stories are usually composed as a group. Children dictate sentences about their experiences to their teacher, who records their language by writing on a large chart or digital whiteboard. The text they develop becomes their reading material. Because the content is familiar, and because the text is their language, children can usually read the chart stories easily. Collaboratively composing, dictating, and then rereading demonstrate to the children the connections between reading and writing. The basic steps in LEA are described in the accompanying Step by Step box.

Teachers and children engage in many variations of the basic steps. One variation is having the children participate in the writing, referred to as *interactive writing*. When children participate or "share the pen" (McCarrier, Pinnell, & Fountas, 2000) by writing some of the letters and words in the chart story, it shows them that writing does not need to be perfect and demonstrates that their contributions to the chart writing are valued. Interactive writing can be used for many types of writing projects in many areas of the curriculum. Examples include morning messages, lists, clusters and other diagrams, collaborative books, classroom newspapers, stories, science experiment reports, and poems. In many Canadian classrooms, the two

Language Experience Approach (LEA)

1 **Provide an experience.**   A meaningful experience is identified to serve as the stimulus or prompt for the writing. For group writing, it can be an experience shared in school, a book read aloud, a field trip, or some other experience—such as having a pet or playing in the snow—familiar to most children. For individual writing, the stimulus can be any experience that is important for the particular child.

2 **Talk about the experience.**   The children and teacher discuss the experience prior to writing. The purpose of the talk is to generate thoughts and words and to review the experience so that the children's written text will be interesting and complete. The teacher often begins with an open-ended question, such as "What do you want to say about _____ ?" As children talk about their experiences, they clarify and organize ideas, use more specific vocabulary, and extend their understanding.

3 **Record the children's expression of ideas.**   Traditionally, the children dictate and the teacher writes what they say. Texts for individual children are written on sheets of writing paper or in small booklets. Group texts are written on chart paper. Where facilities are available, dictations may be composed on an interactive whiteboard or written on a computer keyboard and projected for all to see. The teacher's writing is a model for the students, showing letter forms and correct spelling and punctuation. When writing, teachers preserve the children's language as much as possible. It can be a great temptation to change the children's language, but editing should be kept to a minimum so that children do not get the impression that their language is inferior or inadequate.

For individual texts, the teacher continues to take the child's dictation and writes until the child finishes or hesitates. If the child hesitates, the teacher rereads what has been written and encourages the child to continue. For group texts, the teacher leads children to collaboratively formulate sentences to include their ideas and to take turns dictating sentences. As the teachers take dictation and write, they encourage talk about the words, the spelling patterns, and the punctuation being used. The children can also be engaged in orally spelling and writing individual words. Children can also be invited to contribute to the composition by writing some letters, words, and sentences with careful teacher guidance. Discussion and participation in the writing helps children become observant of the writer's craft and the features of written language.

After writing each sentence, the teacher leads children in choral reading of the sentence. As the chart story progresses, the teacher engages children in choral rereading of all that has been written so far.

4 **Read the text.**   After the text has been written, the teacher leads the children in choral reading of the whole text, reading with the children to encourage fluent reading. This reading reminds children of the content of the text and demonstrates how to read it aloud with appropriate intonation. After reading group texts together, individual children can take turns rereading. Group texts can also be printed and copied to give each child a copy to read independently.

strategies of LEA and interactive writing are combined and, depending on the technology available, the texts written are published in a variety of ways.

Inviting Others to Support Children's Literacy Development

Children benefit from repeated opportunities to listen to stories and to read and reread simple texts. Two ways teachers facilitate these opportunities are cross-age reading buddies and travelling bags of books.

Upper-grade students can be paired with primary-grade children to become reading buddies. Older students read books aloud to younger children, and they also read with the children. The effectiveness of cross-age tutoring is supported by research, and teachers report that students' reading fluency increases and their attitudes toward school and learning become more positive (Caserta-Henry, 1996).

Teachers arranging a buddy reading program decide when the students will get together, how long each session will last, and what the reading schedule will be. Primary-grade teachers explain the program to their students and talk about activities the buddies will be doing together. Upper-grade teachers teach a series of minilessons about how to work with young children, read aloud and encourage children to make predictions, select books to appeal to younger children, and help them respond to books. Older students choose books to read aloud and practise reading them until they can read the books fluently. When primary students begin reading, they too, may read to their buddies. Pending reading abilities, it may be appropriate for reading buddies to choose easy-to-read stories, novels, or informational texts such as those listed in Figure 3-7.

FIGURE 3-7 EASY-TO-READ BOOKS

Stories

Abramson, B. (2006). *Off We Go!* Toronto: Tundra Books. 🍁

Bellingham, B. (2005). *Lilly's Special Gift*. Halifax, NS: Formac. 🍁

Bradford, K. (2005). *Ghost Wolf*. Victoria, BC: Orca Book. 🍁

Chataway, C. (2002). *The Perfect Pet*. Toronto: Kids Can Press. 🍁

Edwards, F. (1997). *Downtown Lost and Found*. Toronto: Firefly Books. 🍁

Gay, M.-L. (2002). *Stella, Fairy of the Forest*. Vancouver: Groundwood Books/Douglas & McIntyre. 🍁

Helmer, M. (2002). *Three Barnyard Tales: The Little Red Hen; the Ugly Duckling; Chicken Little (Once-Upon-a-Time series)*. Toronto: Kids Can Press. 🍁

Higgs, S. (2006). *Best Friends, No Matter What*. Toronto: Scholastic Canada. 🍁

Hood, S. (2005). *Pup and Hound in Trouble*. Toronto: Kids Can Press. 🍁

Hughes, S. (2003). *Bobcat Rescue*. Toronto: Scholastic Canada. (And others in Wild Paw series.) 🍁

Lewison, W. C. (1992). *"Buzz," Said the Bee*. New York: Scholastic

Northey, L. (2002). *I'm a Hop Hop Hoppity Frog*. Don Mills, ON: Stoddart Kids. 🍁

Parish, P. (1963). *Amelia Bedelia*. New York: Harper & Row. (And other books in the series.)

Scrimger, R. (2002). *Princess Bun Bun*. Toronto: Tundra Books. 🍁

Easy Novel Series

Bates, C. (2001). *Shooting Star*. (Sports Stories series). Halifax, NS: James Lorimer & Co. 🍁

Hughes, M. (2001). *Jan's Awesome Party*. (First Novels series). Halifax, NS: Formac Publishing. 🍁

Hutchins, H. (2012). *Think Again, Robyn* (First Novels series). Halifax, NS: Formac Publishing. 🍁

Kerrin, J. (2009). *Martin Bridge Onwards and Upwards*. Toronto: Kids Can. (And others in Martin Bridge series.) 🍁

Langlois, A. (2011). *Mia, Matt and the Lazy Gator* (First Novels series). Halifax, NS: Formac Publishing. 🍁

Little, J. (2001). *Orphan at My Door: The Home Child Diary of Victoria Cape*. (Dear Canada series). Toronto: Scholastic Canada. 🍁

Park, B. (2003). *Junie B., First Grader: Toothless Wonder*. New York: Random House Children's Books.

Staunton, T. (2012). *Morgan Gets Cracking* (First Novels series). Halifax, NS: Formac Publishing. 🍁

Poetry

Heidbreder, R. (2006). *Drumheller Dance*. Toronto: Kids Can Press. 🍁

Heidbreder, R. (2012). *Noisy Poems for a Busy Day*. Toronto: Kids Can Press. 🍁

Lesynski, L. (2004). *Zigzag: Zoems for Zindergarten*. Toronto: Annick Press. 🍁

Lesynski, L. (2007). *Shoe Shakes*. Toronto: Annick Press. 🍁

Yolen, J. (2000). *Color Me a Rhyme: Nature Poems for Young People*. Honesdale, PA: Boyds Mills Press.

Social Studies

Bourgeois, P. (2005a). *Canadian Fire Fighters*. Toronto: Kids Can Press. (And others in the series.) 🍁

Bourgeois, P. (2005b). *Canadian Garbage Collectors*. Toronto: Kids Can Press. 🍁

Bourgeois, P. (2005c). *Canadian Police Officers*. Toronto: Kids Can Press. 🍁

Bourgeois, P. (2005d). *Canadian Postal Workers*. Toronto: Kids Can Press. 🍁

Drake, J., & Love, A. (2009). *Kids Book of the Far North*. Toronto: Kids Can Press. (And other books in the Kids of series.) 🍁

Highway, T. (2003). *Fox on the Ice* (Songs of the North Wind series). Toronto: HarperCollins Canada. 🍁

Rondina, C. (2012). *Lighting Our World*. Toronto: Kids Can Press. 🍁

Weir, R., & Routhier, A. (2003). *O Canada: Our National Anthem*. Toronto: North Winds Press. 🍁

FIGURE 3-7 **EASY-TO-READ BOOKS (continued)**

Science

Bourgeois, P. (2007). *The Jumbo Book of Space*. Toronto: Kids Can Press. 🍁

Berkowitz, J. (2009). *Out of This World*. Toronto: Kids Can Press. 🍁

Bourgeois, P. (2008). *The Dirt on Dirt*. Toronto: Kids Can Press. 🍁

Coren, S. (2006). *Why Do Dogs Have Wet Noses?* Toronto: Kids Can Press. 🍁

Faulkner, M. (2004). *A Day at the Sugar Bush: Making Maple Syrup*. Toronto: Scholastic Canada. 🍁

Hodge, D. (2008). *Who Lives Here? Wetlands*. Toronto: Kids Can Press. (And others in the Who Lives Here series.) 🍁

Mason, A. (2005). *Move It! Motion, Forces, and You*. Toronto: Kids Can Press. 🍁

Mason, A. (2006). *Change It! Solids, Liquids, Gases, and You*. Toronto: Kids Can Press. 🍁

Serafini, F. (2008). *Looking Closely Inside the Garden* (Looking Closely series). Toronto Kids Can Press. 🍁

Swanson, D. (2001). *Burp! The Most Interesting Book You'll Ever Read about Eating*. Toronto: Kids CanPress. 🍁

Wilson, B. (2005). *Izzie: Book Two: Trongate Fury* (Our Canadian Girl series). Toronto: Penguin Books. 🍁

There are significant social benefits to cross-age tutoring programs. Children get acquainted with other children they might otherwise not meet and learn to work with older or younger children. As they talk about books, they share personal experiences and interpretations. They also talk about reading strategies, how to choose books, and their favourite authors or illustration styles. Sometimes reading buddies write notes or email messages back and forth, or the two classrooms share holiday or other celebrations, and these activities strengthen the social connections between the children.

TRAVELLING BAGS OF BOOKS

For more information on LIFT, see Chapter 4 Literacy in Action.

A second way to encourage more one-on-one reading is to involve families in literacy activities through travelling bags of books. Some teachers with whom we work refer to their home literacy support as LIFT (Literacy Is a Family Thing). They create thematically organized bags of books and activities for their students to take home and enjoy with their families. Children keep the bags at home for a few days before returning them for others to borrow. Most bags contain three books, including both narrative and informational texts. Bags also include suggestions for family literary activities and the materials needed for each. The activities included in some travelling thematic bags include references to websites that offer background information about the theme and additional activities related to the books. Parents and children share their responses to the literature and activities with one another and with the teachers by writing in a journal kept in the bag. Examples of text sets for travelling bags of books are listed in Figure 3-8.

Teachers introduce programs like LIFT at a special meeting at which they explain the purpose of the travelling bags of books and how to use the books and materials with the children. It is important that families understand that their children are not expected to read all of the books independently, nor are they expected to complete all of the suggested activities. Teachers also show sample journal entries to encourage parents to share their families' responses by writing in the response journal kept in each bag.

Introduction meetings provide opportunities for teachers to help families and caregivers understand their role in helping children grow into literacy. To be successful in the 21st century, children must become proficient in both traditional (print) and digital literacies (McKenna, Conradi, Young, & Yang, 2013). Teachers explain that programs such as LIFT offer a way for families to help children develop positive associations with reading and writing.

FIGURE 3-8 TEXT SETS FOR TRAVELLING BAGS OF BOOKS

Books by Paulette Bourgeois
Bourgeois, P. (2000). *Franklin Helps Out*. Toronto: Kids Can Press.
Bourgeois, P. (2001). *Franklin Says I Love You*. Toronto: Kids Can Press.
Bourgeois, P. (2002). *Franklin Plays Hockey*. Toronto: Kids Can Press.
Bourgeois, P. (2004). *Franklin Forgives*. Toronto: Kids Can Press.
Bourgeois, P. (2005). *Franklin Celebrates*. Toronto: Kids Can Press.
Bourgeois, P. (2012). *Franklin's Partner*. Toronto: Kids Can Press.

Books about Frogs and Toads
Azore, B. (2007). *Wanda and the Frogs*. Toronto: Tundra Books.
Carney, E. (2009). *Frog!* New York: National Geographic Society.
Donaldson, C. (2006). *Canada's Wetland Animals*. Toronto: Scholastic Canada.
Lobel, A. (1970). *Frog and Toad Are Friends*. New York: Harper & Row.
McLeod, H. (2011). *Kiss Me!* Markham, ON: Fitzhenry & Whiteside.
Pallotta, J. (1990). *The Frog Alphabet Book: And Other Awesome Amphibians*. Watertown, MA: Charlesbridge.

Books about Mice
Asch, F. (2007). *Mrs. Marlowe's Mice*. Toronto: Kids Can Press.
Fagan, C. (2007). *Ten Old Men and a Mouse*. Toronto: Tundra Books.
Fitch, S. (1997). *There's a Mouse in My House*. Toronto: Doubleday Canada.
Hood, S. (2012). *The Tooth Mouse*. Toronto: Kids Can Press.
Steer, D. (2005). *Thank You, Little Mouse*. Toronto: Scholastic Canada.
Lionni, L. (1969). *Alexander and the Wind-up Mouse*. New York: Pantheon.

Books about the Alphabet
Fauchon, J. (2005). *The Métis Alphabet Book*. Saskatoon: The Gabriel Dumont Institute.
Jocelyn, M. (2005). *ABC x 3*. Toronto: Tundra Books.
Lohnes, M. (2007). *F Is for Fiddlehead: A New Brunswick Alphabet*. Chelsea, MI: Sleeping Bear Press.
Major, K. (2000). *Eh? To Zed: A Canadian AbeCedarium*. Red Deer, AB: Red Deer Press.
Moak, A. (2002). *A Big City ABC*. Toronto: TundraBooks.
Ruurs, M. (2001). *A Pacific Alphabet*. Vancouver: Whitecap Books.
Ulmer, M. (2001). *M Is for Maple: A Canadian Alphabet*. Chelsea, MI: Sleeping Bear Press.

Books about Trees
Bralier, T. (2009). *Tess's Tree*. Toronto: HarperCollins Canada.
Eger, D. (2006). *Who's in Maxine's Tree?* Victoria, BC: Orca Book Publishers.
Hickman, P. (1996). *The Kids Canadian Tree Book*. Toronto: Kids Can Press.
McCormick, R. (2002). *Plants and Art Activities*. St. Catharines, ON: Crabtree Publishing.
Silsbe, B. (2001). *A Tree Is Just a Tree?* Vancouver: Raincoast.
Weale, D. (2004). *Three Tall Trees*. Charlottetown, PEI: Acorn Press.

Books about Goldilocks and the Three Bears
Ahlberg, A. (2000). *The Bravest Ever Bear*. Cambridge, MA: Candlewick.
Barnes, L. (1995). *Goldilocks and the Three Bears*. Toronto: Somerville House.
Buehner, C., & Buehner, M. (2007). *Goldilocks and the Three Bears*. New York: Dial.
Campbell, E. (2003). *Goldilocks Returns*. New York: Simon & Schuster.
Smith, S. (2004). *Goldilocks and the Three Martians*. New York: Dutton.
Tolhurst, M. (1990). *Somebody and the Three Blairs*. New York: Orchard Books.
Yolen, J. (1995). *The Three Bears Rhyme Book*. New York: Harcourt.

Book about Families
Downey, R. (2001). *Love Is a Family*. New York: HarperCollins.
Friedrich, M. (2004). *You're Not My Real Mother*. New York: Little Brown.
Horrocks, A. (2010). *Silas's Seven Grandparents*. Victoria, BC: ORCA.
Munsch, R. (2003). *Lighthouse: A Story of Remembrance*. Toronto: Scholastic Canada.
Ohi, R. (2007). *A Trip with Grandma*. Toronto: Annick Press.
Richardson, B. (2007). *The Aunts Come Marching*. Vancouver: Raincoast Books.
Smith, L. (2011). *Grandpa Green*. New York: Roaring Brook Press.
Stinson, K. (2007). *Mom and Dad Don't Live Together Anymore*. Toronto: Annick Press.
Zweilbel, A. (2005). *Our Tree Named Steve*. New York: G. P. Putnam's Sons.

Books about Schools
Chambers, C. (2007). *School Days Around the World*. London: DK Publishing.
Fine, E. H., & Josephson, J. P. (2007). *Armando and the Blue Tarp School*. New York: Lee & Low Books.
Hughes, S. (2011). *Off to Class: Incredible and Unusual Schools Around the World*. Toronto: Owlkids.
Rumford, J. (2010). *Rain School*. Boston: HMH Books for Young Readers.
Ruurs. M. (2009). *My School in the Rainforest: How children attend school around the world*. New York: M. Boyd's Mills Press.
Smith, P., & Shalev, Z. (2007). *A School Like Mine: A Unique Celebration of Schools Around the World*. London: DK Publishing.

Books about FNMI
Ballantyne, E. (2001). *The Aboriginal Alphabet for Children*. Winnipeg, MB: Pemmican Publications.
Lindstrom, C. (2013). *Girls Dance, Boys Fiddle*. Winnipeg, MB: Pemmican.
Kalman, B. (1997). *Celebrating the Pow-wow*. New York: Crabtree Publishing.
McLeod, E. (2002). *Lessons from Mother Earth*. Toronto: Groundwood.
Smith. C. (2000). *Jingle Dancer*. New York: Morrow Junior Books.
Spalding, A. (2006). *Secret of the Dance*. Victoria, BC: ORCA.

In planning for family literacy activities, teachers are aware of the increasing diversity among families in Canadian schools. They are aware that there are wide variations in families' capacities to support young readers and writers, especially to support them in their language of classroom instruction. Schools, therefore, often work collaboratively with community agencies to support families in linguistically and culturally appropriate ways such as multigenerational programs in which children and adult family members read together. Other programs that support **family literacy programs** focus on providing instruction for adults so that they, in turn, are able to read to children. At their core, school-based family literacy programs are parent–teacher partnerships that require open, dependable, and non-intrusive communication directed toward bridging the literacy traditions and practices that are integral to family and classroom life (Paratore, 2006).

Young Children Become Writers

Many young children become writers before entering kindergarten; others are introduced to writing during their first year of school (Bright, 2002). Young children's writing development follows a pattern of stages similar to their reading development: emergent writing, beginning writing, then fluent writing. In the initial, emergent writing stage, children make scribbles to represent writing. At first, the scribbles may appear randomly on a page, but with experience children line up the letters or scribbles from left to right and from top to bottom. Children also begin to "read," or tell what their writing says. The next stage is beginning writing, and it marks children's growing awareness of the alphabetic principle. Children use invented spelling to represent words, and as they learn more about phoneme–grapheme correspondences, their writing approximates conventional spelling. The third stage is fluent writing, in which children use conventional spelling and other conventions of written language, including capital letters and punctuation marks.

EMERGENT WRITING

Emergent writing takes many different forms. It can be scribbles or a collection of random marks on paper. Sometimes children imitate adults' cursive writing as they scribble. Children can string together letters that have no phoneme–grapheme correspondences, or they can use one or two letters to represent entire words. Children who have more experience with written language can invent spellings that represent more sound features of words, and they can apply spelling rules. Figure 3-9 presents examples of writing development. The first example shows scribble writing (not letters yet), the second shows strings of letters to represent words, and the third shows labeling. The fourth example shows the child spelling phonetically and applying a few spelling rules, while the last example shows the child has control over some standard spellings and uses punctuation to mark spaces between words.

Children in kindergarten learn about the alphabetic principle as they collect classmates' autographs at the writing centre.

FIGURE 3-9 **EMERGENT WRITING**

Scribble Writing

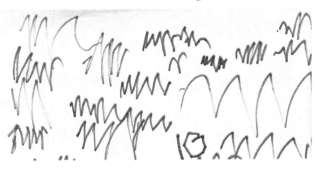

Letter Strings Without Spacing

Labeling

Used with permission from Erin Bright and Kerry Snatic.

FIGURE 3-9 EMERGENT WRITING (continued)

More Sophisticated Invented Spelling With Spacing

To'The tooth fary

I lased anuther tooth.
Will you plesu still give me
sum momey.

Invented/Conventional Spelling with Application of Rules

one day, Stevie and
Sophie were walking in
the Park, They got stolen
by a gobbler.

Used with permission from Erin Bright and Kerry Snatic.

Young children's writing grows out of talking and drawing. As they begin to write, their writing is literally their talk written down, and children can usually express in writing the ideas they talk about. Emergent writing is important to young children's development as writers because it gives them the opportunity to experiment with written language, especially to invent spellings that reflect their knowledge of written language. The spellings they use give teachers a window onto their writing development and suggest the instruction they need to advance toward fluent writing. Understanding and acceptance of emergent writing by adults helps them to encourage children to experiment when they draw and write. Children who are willing to experiment and take risks in their writing move smoothly through the developmental stages.

When children begin writing, teachers accept their writing as it is written and focus on the message. As children gain experience with writing, teachers encourage them to read their work to themselves and to "fix" one or two errors. Revising becomes more formal as children learn about audience and start to want to add more or make other changes to their writing to make it appeal to their classmates. Gradually teachers lead them to experience the writing process as it is described in Chapter 5 concerning experienced writers.

For more information on the five stages of the writing process, see Chapter 5, "The Reading and Writing Processes," pages 160–171.

WRITING CENTRES

Writing centres can be set up in kindergarten and primary classrooms so that children have a special place to write. When classroom space does not permit room for children to write at the centre, the centre may serve as simply a place to keep writing tools and resources handy. The centre may include any combination of a table, chairs with a box of supplies (such as pencils, crayons, a date stamp, and different kinds of paper), and a bank of computers or tablets. The alphabet, printed in upper- and lowercase letters, should be available for children to refer to as they write. This is an important aid for young writers if the keyboards they use show only uppercase letters. In addition, there should be a place for children to file their writing papers as well as routines for saving digital texts. Teachers, assistants, or parent volunteers should be available to encourage and assist children at the centre. They can observe children as they invent spellings and can provide information about letters, words, and sentences as needed.

SHARING WRITING

Researchers have identified many benefits of encouraging and facilitating children sharing their writing. Benefits include creating authentic purposes for writing (McCarrier, Pinnell, & Fountas, 2000), a platform for thinking and learning (Hurst, Scales, Frecks, & Lewis, 2011), and the opportunity to build confidence in reading, writing, and speaking abilities (McCallister, 2008). Sharing has also been found to help children develop a sense of community among their peers.

In primary-grade classrooms, teachers often designate a special chair for sharing writing, The "author's chair" (D. H. Graves & Hansen, 1983) is where children sit to share their writing with the class. One child sits in the author's chair and a group of children sit in front of the author. The author reads the piece of writing aloud and shows the accompanying illustrations. Then children in the audience who want to make a comment raise their hands, and the author chooses several children to ask questions, give compliments, and make comments. Then the author chooses another child to share and takes a seat in the audience. Taking the author's chair and responding to other's writing adds to children's growing awareness of themselves as writers.

Hall (2014) reminds teachers that although there are many benefits to young children sharing their writing, some may be reluctant to read and speak from the authors' chair as described above. There are many reasons why children may be reluctant to occupy the author's chair. Some may be shy to speak to a large group, some may feel their writing is too personal to share, and others, especially English language learners, may lack confidence in their oral communication abilities. Strategies to support those who are reticent include:

- provide children plenty of time to select their piece of writing and prepare to share
- allow children to "pass" sometimes during sharing time
- offer to share children's work anonymously
- allow children to record their work digitally to share
- arrange for different types of audiences such as a small group of friends
- encourage children who have writing skills in another language to share in their primary language

Assessment of Writing

Assessment of young children's writing should take place frequently throughout the school year. By assessing frequently, teachers can monitor progress and plan appropriate instruction. Teachers use observation notes, checklists, and sample pieces of writing to assess young writers' increasing competencies. Checklists help organize assessment of children's emergent and beginning writing. Items such as the following help track children's development as writers:

- Can write own name
- Uses drawing for writing
- Uses scribbles with no letter forms
- Uses random letters
- Uses invented spelling
- Uses a combination of invented and conventional spelling
- Makes message clear
- Stories include beginning, middle, and ending
- Writes for a variety of purposes

To further guide assessment, many teachers choose to maintain a portfolio of samples of children's writing. The collected samples provide evidence of writing development over time and across writing contexts and purposes. Portfolios can be a source of pride for young writers and can be used during parent-teacher interviews to explain achievement.

Review

Emergent literacy is the accepted perspective on how children learn to read and write (Hayden & Kendrick, 2002). Young children learn concepts about written language as they observe teachers' and others' demonstrations and as they experiment with reading and writing. Teachers offer instruction through multiple strategies and approaches. Children gradually become fluent writers; they progress from using graphic symbols (drawing) to represent their thoughts to writing using knowledge of phoneme–grapheme correspondences and other conventions of printed language.

The following key concepts are presented in this chapter:

1. Emergent literacy refers to the concept that young children move into reading and writing through experiences with written language (print and digital).
2. Oral language is the foundation upon which reading and writing develop.
3. Phonological awareness is an essential aspect of oral language development
4. As children learn about words, they move from recognizing environmental print and icons to reading contextualized words in books and on screens.
5. Children use phonics as well as information from the other three language systems (semantic, syntactic, and pragmatic) as they learn to read.
6. Both reading and writing development have three stages: emergent, beginning, and fluent.

7. Three ways teachers read books with young children are read-aloud, shared, and guided reading.

8. In resource-based units, teachers engage children in using the six language arts.

9. The language experience approach employs children's own language to offer meaningful reading and writing experiences.

10. Children use emergent writing, including invented spelling, to experiment with written language concepts before becoming fluent writers.

11. Young children begin writing using an abbreviated form of the writing process.

12. Young children learn about audience as they share their writing from the author's chair.

Theory to Practice

1. Observe how children in a kindergarten or grade 1 classroom are learning concepts about written language. Examine reading materials available in the classroom, including predictable books, big books, picture books, and online digital stories. Also observe opportunities for writing, such as in dramatic play and digital writing activities.

2. Establish and monitor a buddy-reading program between a group of primary-grade readers and upper-grade readers.

3. Collect books and other materials for two travelling bags of books and share them with a small group of grade 1 and 2 students and their families.

4. Compose a language experience story about an event or favourite story with a group of young children and produce it as a book or digital story for their classroom library.

5. Observe a classroom teacher engage children in a guided reading lesson. Take note of how the teacher introduces the book and relevant vocabulary, teaches strategies, and has the children read the text.

Literacy in Action

Chapter 4: Literacy Is a Family Thing

Procedure

As a primary-grade teacher, I have experimented with several ways to motivate children to read for pleasure and to enjoy reading outside their classrooms. Giving extrinsic rewards in the form of stickers and treats has been somewhat effective, but it also sends a message that reading is something you do to earn points or prizes. Literacy Is a Family Thing (LIFT) sends a different message. It says that reading is a pleasurable activity that you anticipate and do with people you love. Since developing LIFT with my own class a number of years ago, I have introduced the program to my colleagues from kindergarten to grade 3. Many of them have now established similar family literacy programs as part of their language arts curriculum.

LIFT is based on sharing book bags, and is similar to other "backpack" programs that support reading and writing by providing families with books and materials. I put together fifteen colourful book bags that the children take home on alternating weeks. Each book bag is centred on a theme and contains a novel, a picture book, and an informational book. A few book bags include theme-related videos. Each bag also contains a letter to adult family members giving suggestions for response activities and materials needed for the suggested activities. Most response activities are designed to require family members' interaction, and include such things as retelling stories using puppets or felt-board characters; following a recipe; doing simple crafts; and writing stories, postcards, or letters.

> "The LIFT program has generated genuine enthusiasm for reading and writing at school and at home. I feel strongly that this is a way to lead children to develop a lasting love of reading."
>
> Samantha Wishewan

The children take the book bags home on Thursday afternoons and bring them back to school the following Thursday morning. When book bags come back to school, the children are always anxious to tell their classmates and me about their reading and to show us the activities they did with their families. They proudly share their stories, crafts, and artwork. I display their products in the classroom as a way of celebrating their family activities. Early Thursday afternoons, I check that all of the books are in place and restock each bag.

Assessment

LIFT is a source of much pleasure and satisfaction for all participants. The parents of my children report that not only my students, but also other children in their family look forward to the bags. A recent survey indicates that the time families spend in literary activities has increased since the implementation of LIFT. In describing LIFT to classroom visitors, the children claim, "I like reading with my family. My mom really likes the pig books," and "I don't like it when it is not my week to have a bag."

Adaptation

The success of the LIFT program has been contagious. Another teacher started along with me, but now several more are interested. Some changes are needed to expand to other grade levels. For example, grade 1 book bags need to include both easy readers and picture books to be read to children, whereas upper–grade-level bags might focus on novels and such response activities as visiting particular Internet sites.

Reflection

The LIFT program has generated genuine enthusiasm for reading and writing at school and at home. For children, receiving a book bag is like opening a present and finding surprises. I feel strongly that this is a way to lead children to develop a lasting love of reading. I can't imagine teaching without LIFT.

Guidelines for LIFT Book Bags

1. When a new book bag arrives in your home, check to see that it contains the materials listed on the contents card. If something is missing, please notify your child's teacher.

2. Encourage family members to handle books, materials, and bags with care. Care is essential if the book bags are to be a lasting addition to our program.

3. Talk about the books before, during, and after reading with your children. Introduce the books to your children, or let the children introduce them to you by examining the covers, talking about the titles, and making predictions about the contents.

4. Encourage your children to ask questions about the books and ask questions of your children, especially questions with more than one possible response and that require children to think about and reflect upon what is being read.

5. Share the reading with your children. Some books require that you or an older child read to your children; others can be read by grade 3 students. When possible, take turns reading among several family members.

6. Read the books more than once if your child asks to repeat the reading. Each time the book is read, there are new things to notice or talk about.

7. Keep a playful tone to all of your activities. The book bags are intended to support you and your family in having literary fun together. Enjoy!

From the classroom of Samantha Wishewan
Pine Street School
Sherwood Park, Alberta

CHAPTER 4

Listening and Speaking in the Classroom

LEARNING OUTCOMES

After reading this chapter, you should be able to

1. Describe the listening process

2. Compare ways that students listen aesthetically and efferently

3. Explain why speaking is important in the learning process

4. Explain how students learn to have authentic conversations in the classroom

5. Identify the types of aesthetic talk activities that are helpful to elementary students

6. Identify the types of efferent talk activities that are helpful to elementary students

7. Explain how listening and speaking can be taught as part of language arts units

123RF

Students listen as their teacher shows and explains lines of latitude and longitude on a globe to find locations of interest.

Students use oral language to explore ideas and communicate with others. Listening and speaking (talking) are the basic communication tools in most human lives. In school, students learn to use their listening and speaking skills to clarify and understand the ideas, thoughts, and perceptions of others and themselves, and to integrate the two to make sense of their world. Teachers who provide time for and instruction in listening and speaking find that their students learn to engage in meaningful talk and responsive listening. The terms *speaking* and *talking* are often used interchangeably to describe aspects of oral language. In this chapter, *speaking* is used to denote formal aspects of oral language and *talking* is used to denote informal aspects.

Listening in the Classroom

Listening is something most people take for granted. It is the first language mode that children acquire, and it is the basis for the other language arts. When children are read to, they begin to see the connection between what they hear and what they see on the printed page. The processes of reading and listening, and the strategies and skills used during reading and listening are similar in many ways.

The Listening Process

Listening is a complex, multistep process "by which spoken language is converted to meaning in the mind" (Lundsteen, 1979, p. 1). As this description suggests, listening is more than just hearing, even though children and adults often use the terms *hearing* and *listening* synonymously. Rather, hearing is an integral component, but only one component, of the listening process. The crucial part is thinking, or converting to meaning what one has heard.

Purposes for Listening

In and beyond classrooms, people have many purposes for listening. Pending their reasons for listening, they engage in different types of listening. Wolvin and Coakley (1996) delineate four types of listening:

- discriminative listening
- aesthetic listening
- efferent listening
- critical listening

We have applied Louise Rosenblatt's (1985b, 1991) terms **aesthetic reading**, meaning "reading for pleasure," and **efferent reading**, meaning "reading to carry away information," for the listening categories. These terms can be applied because reading and listening are similar language modes, except that one is written and the other is oral.

DISCRIMINATIVE LISTENING

People use discriminative listening to distinguish sounds and to develop a sensitivity to nonverbal communication. Teaching discriminative listening involves one sort of activity in the primary grades and a different activity for older students. Having kindergartners listen to recorded animal sounds and common household or outdoor noises is one discriminative listening activity. Most children are able to discriminate among sounds by the time they reach age five or six. Primary-grade students also use discriminative listening as they develop **phonemic awareness**, the ability to blend and segment the sounds in spoken words. Older students use discriminative listening to sound out spellings of words and divide words into syllables.

Students at all levels also learn to "listen" to the nonverbal messages that people communicate. Young children quickly recognize the unspoken message when a parent's expression changes from a smile to a frown or when a teacher expresses puzzlement. Older students learn the meanings of more sophisticated forms of body language, such as folding your arms over your chest, and the ways that teachers emphasize that something is important, such as speaking more loudly, or repeating what was said.

For more information on phonemic awareness, see Chapter 3, "Emergent Literacy," pages 73–77.

When teachers read aloud books such as Anne Villeneuve's *Loula is Leaving for Africa* (2013)) and JonArno Lawson's *Old MacDonald Had Her Farm* (2012) (a song-style read that encourages children to use the twisted refrain: "A-E-I-O-U and at times Y"), they provide opportunities for young children to develop their discriminative listening abilities. Middle- and upper-grade students develop more sophisticated knowledge about language when they read such books as *When I Get Older: The Story Behind "Wavin' Flag"* (K'naan and Guy, 2012) and *The Night the Stars Flew* (Bogart, 2001).

AESTHETIC LISTENING

People listen aesthetically when they listen for enjoyment. Teachers encourage children's aesthetic listening by reading aloud and teaching students how to visualize characters and episodes and notice figurative language. Canadian author and illustrator, Barbara Reid's *Picture a Tree* (2012) and Kit Pearson's *And Nothing But the Truth* (2012) offer strong verbal images for teacher and students to talk about. Pearson writes of young Polly and her classmates meeting Emily Carr for the first time, "Miss Carr's round face was sunburned. Tufts of white hair poked from the wide black bank around her forehead. Her eyes were direct and bright as she examined them" (pp. 168–169). Viewing video or multimedia versions of stories and listening to classmates converse or talk about literature they have read or had read to them are other examples of aesthetic listening. Ensure that multimedia versions of stories are thoughtful reproductions, as these can sometimes oversimplify a story and its illustrations.

As students listen to the teacher read aloud well-crafted stories and poems such as *Heartbeat* (Creech, 2005), *My Life with the Salmon* (Jacobson, 2011), *Wonder* (Palacio, 2012), and *Welcome to the Green House* (Yolen, 1993), they engage with the text and step into the secondary world it creates. In *Heartbeat*, they feel the friendship between Annie and Max, who is sometimes inexplicably moody. In *My Life with the Salmon*, they experience Diane "Honey" Jacobson's action-filled adventure to save the salmon and her personal journey to find meaning and a sense of place in life. In *Wonder*, they are inspired and impacted by Auggie's experiences being different from those around him. And in *Welcome to the Green House*, a book-length poem about the rainforest, they recognize the ecological treasures of the rainforest and appreciate the contribution of rhythmic language to meaning.

EFFERENT LISTENING

People listen efferently to understand a message. This is the type of listening required in many classroom instructional activities. Students determine the speaker's purpose, identify the main ideas, and then organize the information they are listening to in order to remember it. Elementary students usually receive little instruction in efferent listening; rather, teachers assume that students simply know how to listen. Note-taking and web creation/mapping are two efferent listening strategies taught in the elementary grades.

Students often use efferent listening as they listen to teachers read aloud informational books or view videos and multimedia versions of books. As they listen to the teacher read from *Take Action! A Guide to Active Citizenship* (Kielburger & Kielburger, 2002), they learn tips, strategies, and examples to become more socially aware and involved. While listening to *Where Does a Tiger-Heron Spend the Night?*

(M. Carney, 2002), they find out about a wider range of birds than we see in our backyards. Even though these books are informational books, students don't necessarily listen to them only efferently. Louise Rosenblatt (1991) explains that aesthetic and efferent approaches to reading represent two ends of a continuum and that students rarely use one type of reading exclusively. The same is true of listening.

CRITICAL LISTENING

People listen critically to evaluate a message. Critical listening is an extension of efferent listening and is needed to question all messages, whether encountered in the media, in books, or on the Internet. Students listen to understand a message, but they also filter the message to detect propaganda devices, persuasive language, and emotional appeals. Critical listening is used when people listen to debates, commercials, political speeches, and other arguments.

The most important strategy for critical listening is evaluating, because students need to judge the message. As they listen, students consider these "Big Six" questions from Dominic Ali and Michael Cho's book *Media Madness: An Insider's Guide to Media* (2005):

For more information on critical viewing and listening, see Chapter 9, "Viewing and Visually Representing," pages 341–345.

- Who created this message and why are they sending it?
- Who is the target audience and how is the message tailored to them?
- How does this message get your attention?
- What values and lifestyles are shown?
- How might other people read this message differently?
- What's missing from this message that might be important to know? (p. 5)

Students rarely use these types of listening in isolation. As students listen to stories such as *Brothers at War* (Cummer, 2013), set in the years leading up to the War of 1812, or *Amelia and Me* (Stemp, 2013), which takes readers to Newfoundland in 1931, they often use several types of listening simultaneously. They step back into history and imagine they are Jake Gibson, a member of a Loyalist family, or 12-year-old Ginny, who dreams of becoming a pilot like Amelia Earhart, and feel what the characters feel as they listen aesthetically. Students use efferent listening as they think about geographic locations, historical events, historical figures, and other information that authors have carefully researched and included in the story. They use discriminative listening as they notice rhyme, alliteration, and other types of wordplay. Critical listening plays a role, too, as students consider the author's viewpoint, assess emotional appeals, and think about the theme. The four types of listening are reviewed in Figure 4-1.

Teaching Listening Strategies

Activities involving listening go on in every classroom. Students listen to the teacher give directions and instruction, to recorded stories at listening centres, to classmates during discussions, and to someone reading stories and poetry aloud. However, although these activities provide opportunities for students to practise listening strategies and skills they already possess, they do not teach students how to become more effective listeners.

Donohue (2007) provides a framework for teaching *guided listening*. Students are introduced to a variety of teaching strategies for both aesthetic and efferent listening, which can then be applied to reading. These strategies include making inferences

FIGURE 4-1 OVERVIEW OF THE FOUR TYPES OF LISTENING

Type	Characteristics	Example
Discriminative	Distinguish among sounds	Participate in phonemic awareness activities Notice rhyming words in poems and songs Recognize alliteration and onomatopoeia Experiment with tongue twisters Listen to stories and poems read aloud View digital versions of stories
Aesthetic	Listen for pleasure or enjoyment	Listen to stories at a listening centre Watch students perform a play or readers theatre reading Participate in grand conversations
Efferent	Listen to understand a message	Listen to informational books read aloud or at a listening centre Listen to oral reports View informational videos Listen to book talks Participate in writers groups Listen during minilessons Listen to students share projects
Critical	Evaluate messages	Listen to debates and political speeches View commercials and other advertisements Evaluate themes and arguments in books read aloud

and predictions, determining important ideas, making connections, visualizing, asking questions, and synthesizing. The procedure for teaching the strategies for guided listening is as follows:

1. The teacher shares the *purpose* for listening and introduces the strategy.
2. The teacher provides a graphic organizer such as a Venn diagram or a web for students to use to organize and record ideas while listening.
3. The teacher models the strategy. She pauses while reading and records different ideas, depending on the purpose for listening. She asks students to do the same.
4. The teacher asks the students to share their recorded ideas with peers.
5. The teacher reviews the strategy one more time.
6. The teacher asks the students to practise the strategy independently.
7. The teacher assesses the students' learning by looking at their graphic organizers and talking to them about their listening.

This student listens aesthetically to a favourite story.

Imgorthand/E+/Getty Images

Aesthetic Listening

Louise Rosenblatt (1978, 1983, 1991) coined the term *aesthetic reading* to describe one stance readers take. During aesthetic reading, the focus is on the readers' experience during reading and the connections they make to their own lives, the world around them, and other literature. The term *aesthetic listening* can be used to describe the type of listening children and adults do as they listen to storytellers tell stories, poets recite poems, actors perform plays, and singers sing songs.

Strategies for Aesthetic Listening

Three of the most important aesthetic listening strategies are predicting, visualizing, and connecting, all of which contribute to comprehension.

1. **Predicting.** As students listen to a story read aloud, they are predicting or making guesses about what will happen next. They revise their predictions as they continue listening to the story. When teachers read aloud, they help students develop the predicting strategy by asking them what they think will happen in the story before reading and stopping several times while reading to have students predict again.

2. **Visualizing.** Students create an image or picture in their minds while listening to a story that has strong visual images, details, or descriptive words. Students practise this strategy by closing their eyes and trying to draw mental pictures while they listen to a story, and then reproducing these pictures on paper after reading.

3. **Making connections.** Students make personal connections between the story they are listening to and experiences in their own lives. Students might share these connections in reading log entries and in **grand conversations**. They also make connections between the story they are listening to and other ones they have listened to or read themselves. Students make connections between the story they are listening to and another story with the same theme, or a character or episode in this story and a character or episode in another story. Teachers help students use this strategy by asking them to talk about any connections they are making as the story is discussed or by having them make entries in their reading logs. These literary connections are known as *intertextuality*.

Students also use these strategies as they listen aesthetically to poems or informational books read aloud. They create mental images and make connections among what they are listening to, other literature they know, and their own lives. As they think about the powerful figurative language of poems, they consider the impact that alliteration and metaphors have on listeners. When listening to informational books such as Shelley Tanaka's *Climate Change* (2012), students think about how the author's use of factual information, charts, maps, a glossary, and an index help them to create mental images.

Since reading and listening involve many of the same strategies, teachers can teach strategies through listening and then have students use the strategies during reading. As they read aloud, teachers model how to use these strategies, and after listening, students can reflect on how they used the strategies. It is easier for students to focus on strategy use during listening than during reading because students don't have to decode written words when listening.

For more information on intertextuality, see Chapter 6, "Reading and Writing Narrative Text," pages 211, 212.

For more information on the elements of story structure, see Chapter 6, "Reading and Writing Narrative Text," pages 198–205.

Reading Aloud to Students

Sharing stories, poems, and informational books orally with students is a wonderful way to develop an appreciation of literature, model fluent reading, encourage interest in reading, and create a community of learners in the classroom. Sharing literature with students also creates an excellent opportunity to teach listening skills. Strategies such as setting a purpose for listening, asking students to make predictions, and discussing the outcome of their predictions after reading help students develop active listening skills. Reading stories to children is an important component in most kindergarten and first-grade classrooms. Unfortunately, teachers often think they need to read to children only until they learn to read for themselves; however, reading aloud and sharing the excitement of books, language, and reading should remain an important part of the classroom learning at all grade levels. Good literature often provides rich vocabulary and access to ideas and places not ordinarily experienced by readers. David Bouchard and Shelley

Willier's *Drum Calls Softly* (2008) is a wonderful example of a book that shares new language and images with its readers that can be shared with all ages of learners.

Reading aloud is an important instructional activity with these benefits:

- It stimulates children's interest in books and in reading.
- It broadens children's reading interests and developing their taste for high-quality literature.
- It introduces children to the sounds of written language and expands their vocabulary and sentence patterns.
- It shares with children books that are "too good to miss."
- It allows children to listen to books that would be too difficult for them to read on their own or books that are "hard to get into."
- It expands children's background of experiences.
- It introduces children to concepts about written language, different genres of literature, poetry, and elements of story structure.
- It provides a pleasurable, shared experience.
- It models to children that adults read and enjoy reading, to increase the likelihood that children will become lifelong readers.

Guidelines for choosing literature to read aloud are simple: choose books that you like and think will appeal to your students. Trelease (1995) suggests four additional criteria for good read-aloud books: they should be fast-paced to hook children's interest as quickly as possible, contain well-developed characters, include easy-to-read dialogue, and keep long descriptive passages to a minimum. There are a number of annotated guidebooks, journals, and online journals and websites that are useful to teachers to guide their selection of books for reading aloud and independent reading. Figure 4–2 lists some of these resources. Information prepared and published by the Canadian Children's Book Centre is also helpful.

FIGURE 4-2 GUIDES FOR CHOOSING LITERATURE TO READ ALOUD TO STUDENTS

Books

Baker, D. and Setterington, K. (2004). *A Guide to Canadian Children's Books*. Toronto: McClelland & Stewart. ◆

Bishop, R. S. (Ed.). (1994). *Kaleidoscope: A Multicultural Booklist for Grades K–8*. Urbana, IL: National Council of Teachers of English.

Devers, W., & Cipielewski, J. (1993). *Every Teacher's Thematic Booklist*. Toronto: Scholastic. ◆

Edwards, G. and Saltman, J. (2010). *Picturing Canada: A History of Canadian Children's Illustrated Books and Publishing*. Toronto: University of Toronto Press. ◆

Gertridge, A. (2002). *Meet Canadian Authors and Illustrators*. Richmond Hill, ON: Scholastic. ◆

Jobe, R., & Dayton-Sakari, M. (1999). *Reluctant Readers: Connecting Students and Books for Successful Reading Experiences*. Markham, ON: Pembroke. ◆

Jones, R., and Stott, J. (2000). *Canadian Children's Books: A Critical Guide to Authors and Illustrators*. Don Mills, ON: Oxford University Press.

McTeague, F. (1992). *Shared Reading in the Middle and High School Years*. Markham, ON: Pembroke. ◆

Trelease, J. (2013). *The New Read-Aloud Handbook* (7th ed.). New York: Penguin.

Journals and Newsletters

CBC Features. The Children's Book Council, 67 Irving Place, New York, NY 10003.

Children's Book News. Canadian Children's Book Centre, Suite 217, 40 Orchard View Blvd., Toronto, ON M4R 1B9. ◆

The Horn Book. Park Square Building, 31 St. James Avenue, Boston, MA 02116.

Language Arts. National Council of Teachers of English, 1111 Kenyon Road, Urbana, IL 61801.

The New Advocate. Christopher-Gordon Publishers, P.O. Box 809, Needham Heights, MA 02194.

The Reading Teacher. International Reading Association, P.O. Box 8139, Newark, DE 19711.

Online Journals

Books in Canada: The Canadian Review of Books. ◆
http://www.booksincanada.com/

Jeunesse: Young People, Texts, Cultures. ◆
www.jeunessejournal.ca

The Looking Glass: New Perspectives on Children's Literature.
www.the-looking-glass.net

Children's Literature – Electronic Journal and Book Reviews. ◆
www.ucalgary.ca/~dkbrown/journals.html

Quill & Quire.
http://www.quillandquire.com

Books that have received awards or other acclaim from teachers, librarians, and children make good choices. Two of the most prestigious awards are the **Caldecott Medal** and the **Newbery Medal**. Other awards include the Canadian Library Association's (CLA) Book of the Year for Children and Young Adult Canadian Book Award, and the Children's Literature Roundtables of Canada Information Book Award. Several other regional awards are given to celebrate diversity and excellence in Canadian writing for children and young adults. Lists of outstanding books are published annually to publicize the choices of children, young adults, teachers, and librarians. *Our Choice*, an annual review, is published by the Canadian Children's Book Centre and is posted on the centre's website. Three lists—"Children's Choices," "Young Adults' Choices," and "Teachers' Choices"—are published by the International Literacy Association in *The Reading Teacher*.

Teachers in many primary-grade classrooms read one story aloud daily as part of language arts instruction, and later during the day they read informational books aloud as part of social studies or science lessons. Poems, too, are read aloud in connection with content-area themes. It is not unusual for primary-grade students to listen to their teacher read aloud three or more stories and other books during the school day. Students in middle and upper grades should also listen to chapter books, picture books, and poems read aloud as part of language arts units, along with reading and listening to informational books, magazines, and newspaper articles in content-area lessons.

One-School, One-Book is a program designed to have a school community share one book both in school and at home using a read-aloud approach. A copy of the book is provided to every family in the school. Students, together with their teachers and families, share the book and engage in activities that support and enrich the reading experience. Students develop their listening skills, build vocabulary, and feel positive about books and reading.

Students—especially kindergartners and primary-grade students—often beg to have a familiar book reread. Although it is important to share a wide variety of books with children, children benefit in specific ways from repeated readings. Through repetition, students gain control over the parts of a story and are better able to synthesize those parts into a whole, gaining greater understanding.

Teaching Aesthetic Listening

Students must listen aesthetically in many situations both in and out of the classroom to learn simply to enjoy stories and new information. Teachers can help students become effective listeners by making them aware of what they are doing when they are listening. Teachers can speak with students about listening behaviours. They can ask such questions as "What do you think about when a friend tells you about his birthday present?" and "How do you let your friend know that you are interested in what he is saying?" Listening is a social skill as well as a learning skill.

Teachers also teach aesthetic listening when they read aloud a variety of children's literature to students. Before and during reading aloud, **minilessons** help students develop and use aesthetic listening strategies.

STEPS IN READING ALOUD TO STUDENTS

Sometimes teachers simply pick up a book and start reading aloud to students, but for the most meaningful experience, teachers use the five-stage reading process described in this chapter, even though one or more stages might be abbreviated. It is important that teachers help students activate their background knowledge before reading and provide opportunities for students to respond to the book after reading. The steps in reading aloud are presented in the Step by Step box that follows.

MINILESSONS ON AESTHETIC LISTENING

Teachers also teach minilessons to introduce, practise, and review procedures, concepts, and skills related to aesthetic listening. A list of topics for minilessons on aesthetic listening and the other types of listening is presented below. The steps in teaching a minilesson on aesthetic listening strategies are presented in the Step by Step box that follows.

STEP BY STEP

Reading Aloud

1 Prepare to share the story. The teacher activates background knowledge or provides necessary concepts or experiences so that students can understand the story. The teacher may also set the purpose for listening.

2 Read aloud to students. The teacher reads the story aloud to students or shows a digital version of the story. One procedure teachers can use to read the story aloud is the **Directed Listening–Thinking Approach (DLTA)**, in which the teacher asks students to make predictions about the story and then listen to confirm or reject their predictions. DLTA is described in Figure 4–3.

3 Capture an initial response. Immediately after reading, students reflect on the story (or a chapter of a longer book) by talking about the story or writing in a **reading log**. In these initial responses, students focus on voicing their personal feelings, making connections to their own lives, articulating questions and confusions, and identifying favourite characters, events, and quotations. Students need an opportunity to talk about a story after reading. They may talk about it with a partner, in small groups, or with the entire class. The focus is on sharing thoughts while reading the story, not answering the teacher's questions about the story.

Students also capture initial responses to a story by writing entries in a reading log. Primary-grade students keep a reading log by writing the title and author of the story and drawing a picture related to the story. They can also add a few words or a sentence. Figure 4–4 on page 110 presents three entries from a grade 3 student's reading log written during an author study on Eve Bunting. Very young children compose and dictate log entries indirectly or collaboratively. Older students sometimes write an entry after each chapter. After drawing and writing, students often share their reading logs with classmates, and this sharing provides another opportunity for classmates to listen aesthetically.

4 Explore the story. Students explore the text by examining the vocabulary, collecting notable language samples, learning about story structure and authors, and participating in other word-study activities. The teacher also teaches minilessons related to aesthetic listening. This stage is often abbreviated when teachers are reading aloud stories for enjoyment, as they often do after lunch or at the end of the day. Even so, the teacher often needs to clarify difficult words, discuss the structure of the story, or share information about the author or topics related to the book.

5 Extend the response. Students expand their responses through reading, writing, speaking, drama, research, and other projects. Students choose projects they are interested in pursuing to extend their enjoyment and interpretation of a book. These projects include making puppets to use to retell a favourite story, writing letters to authors, creating a mobile for a favourite story, doing a short presentation as a book character, and reading other books by the same author or on a similar theme, to name only a few possibilities.

FIGURE 4-3 THE DIRECTED LISTENING–THINKING APPROACH

The Directed Listening–Thinking Approach (DLTA) is based on the Directed Reading–Thinking Activity, a procedure developed by Russell Stauffer (1975). In DLTA the teacher reads the story or other piece of literature aloud to students, who are actively listening by making predictions and listening to confirm their predictions. After reading, students discuss their predictions and give reasons to support them. The three steps are:

1. Prepare to Read
Teachers provide necessary information related to the story or the author, thereby stimulating students' interest in the story. Teachers might discuss the topic or theme, show pictures, or share objects related to the story to draw on prior knowledge or to create new experiences. For example, teachers might talk about students' knowledge of animal habitats before reading Carl Hiaasen's adventure story, *Hoot* (2004). Then the teacher shows students the cover of the book and reads the title and asks them to make a prediction about the story using questions like these:

- What do you think a story with a title like this might be about?
- What do you think might happen in this story?
- Does this picture give you any ideas about what might happen in this story?

If necessary, the teacher reads the first paragraph or two to provide more information for students to use in making their predictions. After a brief discussion in which all students commit themselves to one or another of the alternatives presented, the teacher asks these questions:

- Which of these ideas do you think would be the likely one?
- Why do you think that idea is a good one?

2. Read Aloud to Students
After students set their purposes for listening, the teacher reads part of the story aloud and then asks students to confirm or reject their predictions by answering questions such as the following:

- What do you think now?
- What do you think will happen next?
- What would happen if . . . ?

The teacher continues reading the story aloud, stopping at several key points to repeat this step.

3. Reflect on Students' Predictions
Students talk about the story, expressing their feelings and making connections to their own lives and experiences with literature. Then students reflect on the predictions they made as they listened to the story being read aloud, and they provide reasons to support their predictions. Teachers ask these questions to help students think about their predictions:

- What predictions did you make?
- What in the story made you think of that prediction?
- What in the story supports that idea?

DLTA is useful only when students are reading or listening to an unfamilar story so that the prediction actively involves them in the story. This strategy can be used both when students are listening to the teacher read literature aloud and when they are doing the reading themselves.

Assessing Students' Aesthetic Listening

Students need to learn how to listen aesthetically so that they can engage more fully with the experience of literature. Teachers assess whether students are listening aesthetically in several ways. They can listen to the comments students make during grand conversations and read entries in students' reading logs to see if they are:

For a list of extending projects, see Chapter 5, "The Reading and Writing Processes," pages 154–156.

- making predictions
- visualizing
- connecting to personal experience and to literature

- revising meaning
- playing with language from the story
- applying knowledge of story structure

Teachers can also convert the list of aesthetic listening procedures, concepts, and strategies and skills presented in the list of minilessons into a checklist and keep track of each topic as it is introduced, practised, and reviewed.

FIGURE 4-4   THREE ENTRIES FROM A GRADE 3 STUDENT'S READING LOG

Fly A way Home by Eve Bunting

This book was so sad I stareted crying. Its sad to be homeless but Andrew has a lot of hope and hes going to get out just like the bird. Hes going to get a home again. I think everone shold have a home to live in.

A Day's Work by Eve Bunting

I liked this book alot. Francesco said his Abuelo was a fine gardner but he didn't know what to do. But they got to keep the jobs because they were honest. Weeds and flowers can look the same if your not a gardner.

The Man Who Could Call Down Owls by Eve Bunting

This was a scary story. The man who could call down owls was a good person who loved the owls and cared for them. Then, an evil man killed him and took his beautiful coat so he could call down the owls. I am glad the owls weren't fooled by him. The little boy was given the power to call the owls instead.

STEP BY STEP

A Minilesson on Aesthetic Listening

❶ Introduce the strategy.   The teacher explains the listening strategy, the way it is used, and the types of listening activities for which it is most effective. The teacher develops a chart with the students to list the characteristics or steps of the strategy. For example, after introducing visualizing, the teacher can list the following steps in creating a mind picture on a chart:

- Close your eyes.
- Draw a picture or make a movie of a scene or character in your mind.
- Listen for details and add them to your picture or movie.
- Add colours to your mind picture or movie.

2 Demonstrate the strategy.   The teacher demonstrates the strategy while reading a story aloud or as students listen to a recording of a story. The teacher stops the presentation periodically to talk about what she is doing or how she is using the strategy. After completing the activity, the teacher discusses the use of the strategy with students. For example, the teacher might demonstrate how to create mind pictures of the characters and story events while reading aloud the first four or five chapters of Pamela Porter's *The Crazy Man* (2005).

3 Practise the strategy.   The teacher provides students with opportunities to practise the strategy as she reads aloud several other stories. The teacher stops reading periodically to ask students to describe how they are using the strategy to listen aesthetically. For example, the teacher might provide opportunities for students to practise creating mind pictures as they continue listening to *The Crazy Man.*

4 Review the strategy.   After using an aesthetic listening strategy, the teacher asks a student to summarize the strategy and explain how he or she used it. Students can also write about how they used what they have learned, or they can draw pictures. For example, after listening to the first few chapters of *The Crazy Man* read aloud, one grade five student explained his visualization strategy:

"I made a picture in my mind of Emaline's farm. She lives there with her mom and dad and her dog Prince. I can tell she is pretty sad that her dad left them. I can see the tractor where the accident happened that used to be the Dad's and I had a picture in my mind of prince running too close to the tractor. I see the fields that need to be seeded so Emmy and her mom can survive. It made me feel sad for Emaline."

5 Apply the strategy.   After students develop a repertoire of the aesthetic listening strategies, they practise the strategies as they listen to stories and other types of literature read aloud.

MINILESSONS

Listening

	Procedures	Concepts	Strategies and Skills
Aesthetic Listening	Listen to a story read aloud Respond to classmates' comments Listen to a poem read aloud Write a response in a reading log Choose favourite quotations from a story Work on projects	Difference between aesthetic and efferent listening Concept of story	Predict Confirm Visualize Connect to personal experiences Connect to other stories Notice the power and beauty of language Apply knowledge of text structure
Efferent Listening	Take notes Do note-taking/note-making Use graphic organizers	The listening process Organizational patterns of informational texts	Categorize ideas Generalize Monitor Ask questions of the speaker
Critical Listening	Write advertisements Make storyboards Film commercials Proofread Make hardcover books Write "About the Author" pages	Three types of persuasion Propaganda Persuasion compared to propaganda Deceptive language Propaganda devices	Ask self questions Note cue words Get clues from the speaker Evaluate the message Determine the speaker's purpose Recognize appeals Recognize deceptive language Identify propaganda devices

Efferent Listening

Efferent listening is listening to understand a message. The term *efferent*, first applied to language arts by Louise Rosenblatt (2005), means "to carry away." It is the most common type of listening students do in school. Students use efferent listening to identify and remember important pieces of information.

Whether students comprehend and remember the message is determined by many factors. Some of these factors occur before listening, others during and after. First, students need a background of knowledge about the content they are listening to. They must be able to relate what they are about to hear to what they already know. Speakers can help provide some of these links. Second, as they listen, students use a strategy to help them remember. They organize and "chunk" the information they receive, and may want to take notes or create a map to help them remember. Then, after listening, students should somehow apply what they have heard so that there is a reason to remember the information.

Strategies for Efferent Listening

Students use a variety of strategies as they listen efferently; some of the strategies are the same as for reading and writing, and others are unique to efferent listening. The purpose of each strategy is to help students organize and remember the information they are listening to. Elementary students use five strategies for efferent listening:

1. *Organizing ideas.* Informational presentations are usually organized in special ways called **expository text** *structures*. The five most common patterns are description, sequence, comparison, cause and effect, and problem and solution. Students learn to recognize these patterns and use them to understand and remember a speaker's message more easily. Speakers often use certain words to signal the organizational structures they are following. Signal words include *first, second, third, next, in contrast,* and *in summary*. Students learn to attend to these signals to identify the organizational pattern the speaker is using.

   Students often use graphic organizers to visualize the organization of the informational presentations (Yopp & Yopp, 2006). When students listen to a presentation comparing amphibians and reptiles, for example, they make T-charts or Venn diagrams to organize the information. Students can draw a two-column T-chart, labelling one column "Amphibians" and the other "Reptiles." Then students write notes in the columns while they listen to the presentation or immediately after listening. A grade 6 class T-chart comparing amphibians and reptiles is shown in Figure 4-5.

   When students are listening to a presentation or hearing an informational book being read that contains information on more than two or three categories, they can make a cluster diagram, write each category on a ray, and then add descriptive information. For example, when students are listening to a presentation on simple machines, they can make a cluster with five rays, one for each type of simple machine. Then students add words and drawings to take notes about each type of simple machine. A grade 5 student's cluster diagram is shown in Figure 4-6.

2. *Summarizing.* Speakers present several main ideas and many details during oral presentations, and students need to learn to generalize or focus on the main ideas.

FIGURE 4-5 A GRADE 6 T-CHART COMPARING AMPHIBIANS AND REPTILES

Amphibians	Reptiles
metamorphosis	only one form
skin is moist	dry skin
smooth or worry skin	lay eggs on land
gills then lungs	just lungs
only males have voices	only gecko has a voice

Otherwise, they try to remember everything and quickly feel overwhelmed. Once students can identify the main ideas, they can then chunk the details to the main idea.

When teachers introduce the summarizing strategy, they ask students to listen for two or three main ideas. They write these ideas on the chalkboard and draw boxes around them. Then, as they give an oral presentation, teachers ask students to raise their hands when they hear the first main idea stated. Students raise their hands when they hear the second main idea, and again for the third main idea. Once students gain practice in detecting already-stated main ideas, teachers give a very brief presentation with one main idea and ask students to identify it. Once students can identify the main idea, teachers give longer oral presentations and ask students to identify two or three main ideas. A grade 5 teacher might make these points when giving an oral presentation on simple machines:

1. There are five kinds of simple machines.
2. Simple machines are combined in specialized machines.
3. Machines make work easier.
4. Almost everything we do involves machines.

FIGURE 4-6 A GRADE 5 STUDENT'S CLUSTER DIAGRAM ON SIMPLE MACHINES

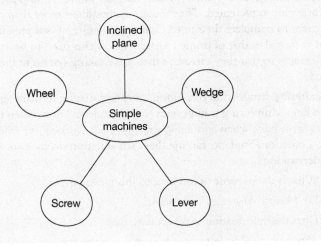

Once students can identify the main ideas during an oral presentation, they can chunk details to the main ideas. This hierarchical organization is the most economical way to remember information, and students need to understand that they can remember more information when they use the summarizing strategy.

3. **Note-taking.** Students are more active listeners when they take notes to help them remember the big ideas while they listen to an oral presentation. Students' interest in note-taking begins with the realization that they cannot store unlimited amounts of information in their minds; they need some kind of external storage system. Many listening strategies require listeners to make written notes about what they are hearing. Note-taking is often thought of as a listing or an outline, but notes can also be written in clusters and other diagrams and may be done by hand or electronically.

    Teachers introduce note-taking by taking notes with the class on the whiteboard, typing or writing them. During an oral presentation, the teacher stops periodically, asks students to identify what important information was presented, and lists their responses on the whiteboard. Teachers often begin by writing notes in a list format, but notes can also be written in outline or cluster formats. Similarly, the teacher can use keywords, phrases, or sentences in recording notes. After an introduction to various note-taking strategies, students develop personal note-taking systems in which they write notes in their own words and use a consistent format.

For other examples of double-entry journals written in two columns, see Chapter 6, "Reading and Writing Narrative Text," pages 222, 223.

    Upper-grade students might try a special kind of note-taking in which they divide their papers into two columns, labelling the left column "Take Notes" and the right column "Make Notes." They take notes in the left column, but, more importantly, they think about the notes, make connections, and personalize the notes in the right column. Students can use this strategy when listening to oral presentations as well as when reading a content-area textbook or an informational book.

    The information students should include in the notes they take depends on their purpose for listening. Teachers set a clear purpose, and during the oral presentation, they stop periodically and ask students to identify the idea being presented and its relationship to other ideas that have been presented. Some listening tasks require noting main ideas or details; others require noting sequence, cause and effect, or comparisons.

    Students can also take notes from informational books and from reference materials; however, taking notes from a speaker is a more complex task. When they are taking notes from a speaker, students cannot control the speed at which information is presented. They usually cannot listen more than once to a speaker in order to complete their notes, and the structure of oral presentations is often not as formal as that of printed materials. Students need to become aware of these differences so that they can adapt their note-taking system to the presentation mode.

4. **Monitoring.** Students need to monitor their listening to make sure they are understanding. Monitoring is important so that students know when they are not listening successfully, when a listening strategy is not working, or when they need to ask a question. Students can use these self-questions to monitor their understanding:

    - What is the purpose of listening to this message?
    - Do I know what _____ means?
    - Does this information make sense to me?

    Students need to learn how to manage comprehension problems during listening rather than becoming confused and frustrated. When readers don't understand something, they often turn back a page or two and reread, but listeners can't turn back unless they are listening to an audio recording, video, or multimedia presentation.

5. ***Getting clues from the speaker.*** Speakers use both visual and verbal cues to convey their messages and direct their listeners' attention. Visual cues include gesturing, writing or underlining important information on the chalkboard, and changing facial expressions. Verbal cues include pausing, raising or lowering the voice, slowing down speech to stress key points, and repeating important information. Surprisingly, many students are not aware of these attention-directing behaviours, so teachers must point them out. Once students are aware of these cues, they can use them to increase their understanding of a message.

For more information on expository text structures, see Chapter 7, "Reading and Writing Expository Text," pages 254–257.

Teaching Efferent Listening

Learning to listen efferently helps students efficiently remember information and better understand the message they are listening to. Teachers need to explain the differences between aesthetic and efferent listening and teach students to use efferent listening strategies. Teachers also need to teach minilessons related to efferent listening.

MINILESSONS ON EFFERENT LISTENING

Teachers teach minilessons to introduce, practise, and review procedures, concepts, and strategies and skills related to efferent listening. The list of topics for minilessons presented on page 111 includes topics related to efferent listening. The teaching strategy discussed in the previous section on aesthetic listening can be used to teach minilessons on efferent listening.

Students need to learn to select appropriate strategies for specific listening purposes. The choice depends on both the listener's and the speaker's purpose. Teachers can suggest which strategy to use before students begin to listen and then help them monitor the use of the strategy during and after listening. Students can generate a list of questions to help guide their selection of strategies and monitor their effectiveness. Asking themselves questions like these before listening will help them select a strategy *before* listening:

To review the steps in teaching a minilesson on aesthetic listening, see "Step by Step: A Minilesson on Aesthetic Listening" in this chapter on page 110, 111.

- What is the speaker's purpose?
- What is my purpose for listening?
- What am I going to do with what I listen to?
- Will I need to take notes?
- Which strategies could I use?
- Which strategy will I select?

    These are possible questions to use *during* listening:
- Is my strategy still working?
- Am I organizing the information effectively?
- Is the speaker giving me cues about the organization of the message?
- Is the speaker giving me nonverbal cues, such as gestures and facial expressions?
- Is the speaker's voice giving me other cues?

    These questions are appropriate *after* listening:
- Do I have questions for the speaker?

- Is any part of the message unclear?
- Are my notes complete?
- Did I make a good choice of strategies? Why or why not?

PRESENTING INFORMATION SO IT IS UNDERSTOOD

Just as students need to use efferent listening to remember the important information that teachers present, teachers need to present information in ways that facilitate learning. The way teachers present information often determines whether students understand the presentation. Too much information overwhelms students and too little may contribute to loss of interest. Using visual representation when presenting information orally can be very helpful to learners who do not remember information that is communicated only through oral language. The steps in presenting information are described in the Step by Step box that follows.

As part of a unit on meteorology, for example, a grade 6 teacher might share a variety of Internet resources related to information about weather. First, the teacher builds background knowledge by asking students to examine images and photographs from websites and identify the type of weather depicted. The teacher uses vocabulary such as *hurricane, typhoon, lightening, wind, hail,* and *flooding.* Then the teacher explains that she will speak about four types of weather: hurricanes, tornadoes, thunderstorms, and typhoons. Students divide a sheet of paper into four sections to take notes as each weather type is discussed.

The teacher gives the first part of the presentation, speaking briefly about the different types of weather in found in various geographical areas of Canada. She

STEP BY STEP

Presenting Information

1 **Build students' background knowledge.**   Before beginning the presentation, the teacher makes sure that students have the necessary background knowledge; then, when the teacher presents the new information, she links it to students' background knowledge. The teacher explains the purposes of the listening activity and reviews one or more strategies students can use to facilitate their understanding. The teacher may also draw a graphic organizer on the whiteboard or give students copies of one to use in taking notes. Examples of graphic organizers include T-charts, Venn diagrams, cluster maps, and timelines.

2 **Present the information.**   While students listen, the teacher can draw a graphic organizer on the whiteboard and add keywords to help students organize the information being presented. This information can also be the basis for the notes students take either as they are listening or immediately after they have listened. The teacher can also pass out sheets with skeleton notes that students complete while they are listening or after they have listened. The teacher uses both visual and verbal cues—writing notes on the whiteboard, using coloured markers, repeating key concepts, raising the voice to highlight conclusions—to direct students' attention to the important information being presented. As the teacher draws the presentation to a close, she summarizes the important points or draws conclusions.

3 **Provide application opportunities.**   After students listen to the presentation, the teacher provides opportunities to apply the new information in a meaningful way.

writes keywords on the whiteboard as she describes the characteristics of different types of weather. She stops for students to take notes using the keywords she has written. She also asks students to monitor their listening, think about what she has said, and ask themselves if they have understood. The teacher repeats this process as she speaks briefly about each topic.

After this presentation, students review their notes with a classmate and add any important information they have not included. Later, during the unit, students will divide into small groups to teach their classmates about other weather types using the same procedure.

Assessing Students' Efferent Listening

Teachers often use formative and summative tests to measure students' efferent listening. For example, if teachers have provided information about planets, they can ask which is nearest to Earth. From students' responses, they can check the students' understanding of the information and infer whether students listened. Teachers should also assess students' listening habits and strategies. Specifically, they should check how well students understand efferent listening procedures, strategies, and skills and how they apply them in listening activities. Asking students to reflect on and talk about the strategies they use and what they do before, during, and after listening provides insights into children's thinking in a way that objective tests cannot.

Differentiating to Meet the Needs of Every Student

Because listening is the language mode used most often, it is especially important that all students be effective listeners. To become effective listeners, students need to

DIFFERENTIATING

Listening Instruction to Meet the Needs of Every Student

1. Identify a Purpose for Listening

Whenever students listen to a lesson or an oral presentation, they need to have a specific purpose for listening and to know what they will be expected to do after listening.

2. Use the Directed Listening–Thinking Approach

The Directed Listening–Thinking Approach is a good way to introduce the aesthetic listening strategies. Many teachers use DLTA when they read aloud to involve their students actively in listening.

3. Teach Students to Use Graphic Organizers and Take Notes

Many students have difficulty identifying the key concepts in order to take useful notes. Teachers demonstrate note-taking by writing notes on chart paper or the whiteboard as they

present lessons and give oral presentations, and afterward they talk about why some points were more important than others.

4. Teach Students to Monitor Their Listening

Often students don't realize that listeners are actively involved in the listening process. It is important for students to learn to monitor themselves as they listen and to ask themselves if they understand what they are listening to and whether or not the listening strategies they are using are working.

5. Make the Listening Process Visible

Listening is an invisible process, but students can make it more visible by speaking, drawing, mapping and writing about what they do when they listen. Teachers encourage students to think about how they vary the way they listen for different purposes and to think about the strategies they use.

learn how to vary the way they listen for different purposes and how to use the listening strategies presented in this chapter. The following Differentiating box presents a list of ways to adapt listening instruction to meet the needs of all students.

Speaking in the Classroom

Students get together in small groups to respond to literature they're reading, talk about each other's writing, organize information they are learning, and work on projects. Of the nearly 3000 languages spoken today, only a fraction of them—fewer than 200—have developed written forms. A recent snapshot of Canadian populations indicates that in the metropolitan area of Vancouver alone, students for whom English is a second language represent close to half of the elementary and secondary population.

When they come to school, most children are fluent oral language users. They have had four or five years of extensive practice talking and listening. Because students have acquired basic oral language competencies, teachers often assume that they don't need to emphasize talk in the elementary school curriculum. However, students learn and refine their strategies for talking with classmates. They learn how to begin conversations, take turns, keep the conversation moving forward, support comments, respond to questions that classmates ask, deal with conflicts, and bring the conversation to a close. Heath (1983a) concluded that children's talk is an essential part of language arts and is necessary for academic success in all content areas. Research now suggests that talk is a necessary ingredient for learning. Teachers must make an extra effort to provide opportunities for socialization and talk.

Talking in Small Groups

Brief, informal conversations are common occurrences in the social environment of school. Students converse with classmates as they work on a mural, as they sort books in the class library centre, and after they listen to a story at the listening centre. Students use talk for different purposes. They try to control the behaviour of classmates, maintain social relationships, convey information, and share personal experiences and opinions. Teachers use conversations with students for socialization. Conversations with students are essential to creating a climate of trust in the classroom. Ketch (2005) indicates, "[conversation] helps to build empathy, understanding, respect for different opinions, and ownership of the learning process" (p. 8).

Other conversations serve instructional purposes. Students meet in small groups to react to literature they have read, respond to each other's writing, work on projects, and explore concepts in resource-based units and theme study units. Students use talk for both aesthetic and efferent purposes, and the most important feature of small-group conversations is that they promote thinking. As students work in groups, they become engaged in the learning process and feel ownership of the knowledge they produce.

Researchers have found that students' learning is enhanced when they relate what they are learning to their own experiences—especially when they do so in their own words Pressley (1992) reported that students' learning was promoted when they had opportunities to elaborate on ideas through talk.

Students use talk to work out problems, accomplish a goal, or generate an interpretation or new knowledge in small-group conversations. These conversations can be used at all grade levels. For example, children in kindergarten might work together

For a list of extending projects, see Chapter 5, "The Reading and Writing Processes," pages 154–156.

FIGURE 4-7 CHARACTERISTICS OF SMALL-GROUP CONVERSATIONS

1. Each group has three to six members. These groups may be permanent, or they may be established for specific activities. It is important that the group be cohesive and courteous to and supportive of each other. Students in established groups often choose names for their groups.

2. The purpose of the small-group conversation or work session is to develop interpretations and create knowledge.

3. Students' talk is meaningful, functional, and genuine. They use talk to solve problems and discover answers to authentic questions—questions that require interpretation and critical thinking.

4. The teacher clearly defines the goal of the group work and outlines the activities to be completed. Activities should require cooperation and collaboration and could not be done as effectively through independent work.

5. Group members have assigned jobs. Sometimes students keep the same jobs over a period of time, and at other times specific jobs are identified for a particular purpose.

6. Students use strategies to begin the conversation, keep it moving forward and ontask, and end it.

7. Students feel ownership of and responsibility for the activities they are involved in and the projects they create.

Source: Adapted from Cintorino (1993); Nystrand, Gamoran, and Heck (1993); Shafer (1993) . © Gail E. Tompkins

in a small group to experiment with objects and sort them according to whether or not they float. Middle-school students might work in a small group to plan a dramatization of a story they have read. Cross-age conversations allow students of different ages talk together when they meet as book buddies. Characteristics of small-group conversations are listed in Figure 4-7.

Teachers play an important role in planning activities for small-group conversations. The activities and projects should be interesting to students, and teachers should ask authentic questions—questions without obvious answers—that require students to interpret or think critically. As students work in small groups, teachers assist and make suggestions, but they do not impose their ideas on students. Teachers are confident of students' ability to create knowledge, respect their ideas, and take their comments and questions seriously.

Guidelines for Talking in the Classroom

Students learn and refine their strategies and skills for socializing and conversing with classmates as they participate in small-group conversations. And, they learn how powerful talk is in making meaning and creating knowledge.

BEGINNING THE CONVERSATION

To begin the conversation, students gather in groups at tables or a meeting place in the classroom, bringing with them any necessary materials. One student in the group begins the conversation with a question or comment; classmates then take turns making comments and asking questions and support the other group members as they elaborate on and expand their comments. The tone is exploratory, and throughout the conversation, the group is progressing toward a common goal: deepening students' understanding of a book they've read, responding to a question the teacher has posed, or creating a project. From time to time, the conversation slows down and there may be a few minutes of silence. Then a group member makes a comment that sends the conversation in a new direction.

KEEPING THE CONVERSATION GOING

Students support one another in groups, and two of the most important ways they do this are by calling each other by name. They also cultivate a climate of trust in the group by expressing agreement, sharing feelings, voicing approval, and referring to comments that group members made earlier. Conflict is inevitable, but students need to learn how to deal with it so that it does not get out of control. They learn to accept that there will be differing viewpoints and to make compromises. Cintorino (1993) reported that her grade 8 students used humour to defuse disagreements in small-group conversations.

ENDING THE CONVERSATION

At the end of a conversation, students reach consensus, conclude that they have explored all dimensions of a question, or completed a project. Sometimes students have a product from the conversation—a brainstormed list, collection of notes, or project. Group members may be responsible for collecting and storing materials or for reporting on the group's work.

Teachers play an important role in making conversations successful, beginning with creating a community of learners in the classroom so that students understand that they're responsible group members. Teachers create a climate of trust by demonstrating to students that they trust them and their ability to learn. Similarly, students learn to socialize with classmates and to respect one another as they work together.

Types of Conversations

Students participate in many types of small-group conversations, and they use talk for both aesthetic and efferent purposes. Here are ten examples of conversation-based activities:

- Analyze propaganda on websites, in commercials, and in advertisements.
- Compare characters in book and multimedia versions of a story.
- Brainstorm questions for an interview.
- Design a blog, mural, or bulletin-board display.
- Assess the effectiveness of a cross-age reading-buddy program.
- Share writing in writers groups and get feedback from classmates about how to revise rough drafts.
- Write a script for a puppet show, design puppets, and plan for the puppet-show performance.
- Discuss reactions and develop comprehension as students read a chapter book.
- Make a cluster diagram or other graphic organizer about information presented in a video.
- Plan a storytelling project.

These sample activities create opportunities to talk with classmates and to listen, argue, and agree. They are authentic and integrate talking with listening, reading, writing, viewing, and visually representing. Students do not hunt for correct answers; they talk to develop interpretations and create knowledge.

Students participate in a grand conversation about The Giver *(Lowry, 1993).*

Teaching Students to Talk in Small Groups

For primary- and middle-school students, reading Diane Stanley's picture book *The Conversation Club* (1990) is a good way to introduce the climate of trust and to explain the roles of speakers and listeners during conversations.

Sorenson (1993) begins the school year by telling her grade 8 students that they will participate in a different type of discussion in her classroom. She hangs a sign in the classroom that says "Teach Each Other," and tells them that it is a quote from one of her students about why this different kind of discussion works. Ferris (2014) shows that students learn that what they say is as important as what the teacher says and that through conversations, students teach each other.

The teacher models working in small groups and discusses how students can begin conversations, sustain them, and bring them to a close. Together the teacher and students summarize what they have learned and develop guidelines for small-group conversations. The teacher observes students as they work in small groups and teaches minilessons on needed procedures, concepts, and strategies and skills.

MINILESSONS ON SPEAKING

Even though most children come to school speaking fluently, they need to learn new ways to use talk. Small-group conversations provide one of these new ways. Students know how to talk, but they may not know how to work in small groups, tell stories, participate in debates, and use talk in other ways. Teachers need to explain and demonstrate various types of talk and teach minilessons on procedures, concepts, and strategies and skills for different types of talk. A list of minilesson topics on talk is presented on page 123. Teachers use the procedure developed in Chapter 1, "Learning and the Language Arts," for these minilessons so that students are introduced to the topic and opportunities to use talk in meaningful ways.

Differentiating to Meet the Needs of Every Student

Talk is a useful learning tool, and it is important that activities be adapted so that every student can speak effectively to learn and get along with others. Small-group conversations and the other talk activities can be adapted in many ways to meet students' needs. Perhaps the most basic way to meet the needs of students who are uncomfortable speaking in a large group, who are hesitant to speak because they are **English language learners**, or who have other language disabilities is to have them work in a small, comfortable group and to keep the language use informal. It is much easier to work in a small group to accomplish a project than to give an oral report in front of the class or participate in a debate.

Farrell (2006) suggests the following classroom activities that appear beneficial to ELL students: story reading, question-and-answer periods, role-playing, detective games with words and sentences, the use of visual aids, making predictions, referring to personal experiences, and drawing on background knowledge as it relates to a particular topic. The authors suggest that, in addition to using these effective teaching practices, it is the teacher's orientation to language that enhances or inhibits an ELL student's language development. Teachers who view a child's first language as a resource see multilingualism as beneficial and enriching to that child and to other children in the classroom. These and other ways to adapt talk activities to meet the needs of every student are presented in the Differentiating box on page 124.

Assessing Students' Talking Abilities

It is important to assess talk, and all of the types of talk discussed in this chapter can be assessed. In small-group conversations, teachers can simply note whether or not students are contributing members of their groups, or they can observe students' behaviour and assess how students contribute to their groups. Teachers can "listen in" on students' conversations to learn about their language competencies and their abilities to work in small groups. Teachers of primary-grade students might assess whether students:

- contribute to the conversation
- share ideas and feelings
- are courteous
- listen carefully to classmates' comments
- call group members by name
- pay attention to classmates when talking to them

Middle- and upper-level students learn more sophisticated procedures, strategies, and skills, and in addition to the six behaviours listed above, teachers of older students might assess whether students:

- volunteer to begin the conversation
- perform their assigned jobs in the group
- extend and expand classmates' comments
- ask questions and seek clarifications
- invite other group members to contribute
- stay on task
- take turns
- deal with conflict within the group

- help to end the conversation
- assume a leadership role in the group

Teachers can create a self-assessment checklist so that students can assess their own contributions to small-group conversations. It is important that students know what is expected of them during conversations and that they reflect on their behaviour and contributions.

Aesthetic Talking

Aesthetic talking, like aesthetic listening, deals with having experiences with literature and creating interpretations. Students use aesthetic talking in discussing literature; telling stories; and participating in interviews, debates, oral reports, and show and tell.

For more information on the teaching strategy on which these minilessons are based, see Chapter 2, "Teaching the Language Arts," pages 37–41.

Conversations about Literature

Students talk about literature they are reading in order to clarify understanding and develop their interpretations of a story. In these conversations, often called **grand conversations** or *literature circles*, students voice their opinions and support their

MINILESSONS

Talking

	Procedures	Concepts	Strategies and Skills
Conversations	Begin a conversation Take turns Expand or extend a classmate's comment Sustain a conversation Deal with conflicts End a conversation	Share published writing Small-group conversations Climate of trust Roles of speakers and listeners	Share ideas and feelings Refer to previous comments Call group members by name Look at classmates Ask questions Extend and expand classmates' comments
Aesthetic talk	Participate in literature conversations Choose a story to tell Prepare and tell a story Make props Select a script for readers theatre	Storytelling Readers theatre Parts of a script	Seek clarification Include the beginning, middle, and end Incorporate interesting or repeated phrases Use dialogue Use props Use facial expressions or gestures
Efferent talk	Participate in theme study unit conversations Do a show-and-tell presentation Prepare and present an oral report Do a book talk and/or a book review Conduct an interview Participate in a debate	Theme study unit conversations Facts and opinions Guidelines for speakers and listeners Persuasion	Present information Vary points of view Support opinions Ask clarifying questions Choose a topic Gather information Organize information Use visuals Rehearse Speak loudly Use note cards Look at the audience

views with examples from the literature. Through these conversations, students take responsibility for learning. They talk about what puzzles them, what they find interesting, their personal connections to the story, and the connections between this story and others they have read. Students also encourage their classmates to contribute to the discussion. Teachers often sit in on conversations about literature as a participant, not as a judge; the talk is primarily among the students. Ketch (2005) points out that it is important for the classroom to be a place where students feel comfortable enough to think out loud.

Literature circles can be held with the whole class or in small groups. Young children usually meet together as a class, while older students often talk in small groups. When students meet together as a class, there is a shared feeling of community, and the teacher can be a part of the group. Both younger and older students meet in small groups when they are reading different books and when they want more opportunities to talk. When the entire class meets together, students have few opportunities to talk, but in small groups they have many more opportunities to share their interpretations.

STEPS IN LITERATURE CIRCLES

Literature circles often have two parts. The first part is open-ended: students talk about their reactions to the book, and the direction of the conversation is determined by students' comments; teachers share their responses, ask questions, and provide information. In the second part the teacher focuses students' attention on one or two aspects of the book not talked about in the first part of the conversation. The steps in literature circles are presented in the next Step by Step box.

DIFFERENTIATING

Talk Activities to Meet the Needs of Every Student

1. Include All Students in Conversations

Conversations have social as well as instructional purposes. As students learn ways to talk with classmates—how to ask questions, share information, and keep the conversation moving—they build a sense of community and a climate of trust.

2. Use Small Groups

Some students may feel more comfortable working with a partner or in small groups of classmates they know well or in the same cultural group. These students might be more successful in small-group conversations, or they might be more articulate in giving book talks to a small group than to the whole class.

3. Give Group Presentations

Instead of preparing oral presentations individually, students can work in pairs or small groups to interview, tell stories, and give oral reports and book talks. When students work with a partner or in a small group, they share the responsibility and the

talking. Students also learn important socialization skills and develop friendships. In addition, students can present to other small groups rather than to the entire class.

4. Use Manipulatives and Visuals

Many students find it easier to talk in front of a group when they are talking about an object they are holding. Young children bring photographs and objects for show-and-tell, and students can make charts, posters, projection slides, or technological displays to support or enhance oral reports. Older students feel more comfortable speaking in front of others if they have an opportunity to write down their thoughts and ideas first.

5. Encourage Students to Relate Personal Experiences

Students are encouraged to share their own personal experiences as these relate to a text being read or written. This strategy provides students with concrete ideas to use when making sense of a story.

Literature Circles

1 Meet in groups. Students meet together as a class or in small groups to talk about a book or a section of a book. When students meet together as a class, they sit in a circle in order to see each other; when they meet in a small group, they sit close together so that they can talk without disturbing their classmates.

2 Share responses. Students share their reactions to the book. To begin the conversation, a student or the teacher asks, "Who would like to begin? What did you think of the story? Who would like to share a reaction?" Students comment on the events in the story, the literary elements, characters they have encountered, or the author's language, and they might make connections to their own lives and to other literature they have read. Each student participates and may build on classmates' comments and ask for clarifications. In order that everyone may participate, teachers often ask students to make no more than three comments until everyone has spoken at least once. Students may refer to the book or read a short piece to make a point, but there is no round-robin reading. Usually students don't raise their hands and are not called on by the teacher or a group leader. Instead, students take turns and speak when no else is speaking, much like adults do when they talk with friends. Pauses and brief silences may occur, and when students indicate they have run out of things to say, the discussion may end or continue onto the next part.

3 Ask questions. The teacher asks open-ended questions to focus students' attention on one or two aspects of the book that have been missed. Four possible directions are:

- Focus on illustrations. After reading the graphic novel *Stone* (7 Generations, vol. 1; Robertson, 2010), the teacher might ask, "What did you think of the illustrations in *Stone*? How did the illustrations show mood during the book? Why do you think the illustrator, Scott Henderson, did that?"
- Focus on authors. During a resource-based unit on J. K. Rowling, the teacher might say, "This is the sixth book we've read in the Harry Potter series by J. K. Rowling. What is so special about her books? Why do we like her books so much? Is there something they all share?"
- Focus on comparison. The teacher asks students to make a comparison: "How did this book compare with _____ ? Did you like the book or the film version better? Why? Which of Kit Pearson's characters is your favourite?"
- Focus on literary elements, stylistic devices, and/or genres. After reading *Odd and the Frost Giants* (Gaiman, 2009), the teacher might ask, "Is the story a myth? Which characters from Norse mythology do you recognize? How is the story enhanced by the illustrations? What was the theme of the book?

4 Provide assistance. If students require assistance, the teacher assists them one on one with word identification and supports their efforts to comprehend the selection, trying not to interrupt students while they are reading.

5 Retell the story. In small groups, students can learn and practise storytelling skills by retelling the story, or parts of it, to interested classmates or even to younger students. Students love to retell the events of Phoebe Gilman's *Something from Nothing* (1992). They especially enjoy retelling the picture story of the mice who live beneath the floorboards in this exceptional picture book.

After the literature–circle conversation, students often write (or draw) in their reading–response journals, or write again if they wrote before the literature circle. Then they continue reading the book. Participating in literature circles and writing entries in reading journals help students think about and respond to what they have read.

The most useful questions about literature cannot be answered with *yes* or *no*, and require students to give personal opinions. After reading *The Case of the Missing Deed* (Schwartz, 2011), a group of grade 4 students wrote their own questions, and spent the first few minutes considering them and deciding which ones to use. Their questions included the following:

- Why do you think Grandpa hid the deed to the property on Otter Island before he passed away?
- How do you think the cousins will be able to help Grandma remember where the deed is?
- What does the Tantalus Mining Company want to do with the property?
- Which of the five cousins is most like me?
- What is your favourite clue that Grandpa left for the cousins to help them find the deed?

BENEFITS OF LITERATURE CIRCLES

Through talk, students extend their individual interpretations of their reading and create a better understanding of it. Students talk about their understanding of the story and can change their opinions after listening to classmates' alternative views. They share personal stories related to their reading in poignant ways that trigger other students to identify with them. Students also gain insights about how authors use the elements of story structure to develop their message.

When students talk in-depth about literature, their writing shows the same level of interpretation (Sorenson, 1993). Students are more successful in literature circles if they have written in journals first, and are more successful in writing journal entries if they have participated in literature circles first.

Efferent Talking

Students use efferent talk to inform and persuade. They use efferent talk in conversations during theme study units and four other types of efferent talk: show and tell, oral reports, interviews, and debates. These activities are more formal, and students prepare and rehearse their talks before giving them in front of an audience.

Talking during Theme Study Units

Talking is an important part of theme study units. Students talk about concepts they are learning and about issues such as homelessness, immigration, nuclear energy, and human rights. These conversations can take place in small groups or as a class. In contrast to literature circles, in which students use primarily aesthetic talk to create and deepen their interpretations, students primarily use efferent talk to create knowledge and understand relationships among concepts. Students gather information to then talk about through: giving or listening to oral presentations; reading informational books and newspapers; researching related websites; and watching television news reports, videos, and films. As they talk—offering information, considering other points of view, searching for additional information to support opinions, and listening to alternative viewpoints—students learn social skills as well as information they want to learn about.

QUESTIONING STRATEGIES

Teachers often use questions to initiate talk during theme study units, and the questions teachers ask go beyond knowledge-level thinking (i.e., those with single correct answers) to authentic questions in which students analyze and synthesize information and make connections to their own lives. Here are some examples for a theme study unit on ancient Egypt:

- To introduce a theme study unit on ancient Egypt, teachers ask if students have seen photos or images of the pyramids. After viewing a short video about the pyramids with students, teachers ask what students already know about these ancient structures.

- After making a list of what the students know about pyramids, such as how they were built and what they were used for, teachers ask students to create their own cardboard pyramid structures using four triangles.

- After sharing a map of Upper and Lower Egypt, teachers ask students to find the locations of the pyramids along the Nile River.

- Together as a class, students brainstorm a list of the reasons that the pyramids had been built along the Nile River and the importance of the Nile floods to Egypt and its people. Then students work in small groups to research the five most important reasons for the pyramids to be built along the Nile River.

  Wilen (1986) offers these suggestions:

- Ask carefully planned questions to organize and direct the lesson.

- Ask clearly phrased questions rather than vaguely worded or multiple questions.

- Sequence questions to move from factual-level to higher-level questions, which require critical thinking.

- Ask questions to follow up on students' responses.

Students need sufficient time to think about questions and plan their responses. Sometimes the most effective way to do this is to have students talk about the question in small groups and then report back to the class. It is important to encourage wide participation and interaction among students and to draw in students who do not volunteer contributions. Seating students in a circle or a horseshoe formation is one technique, and having students work in small groups is another. Other ways to promote student involvement are to have class members create questions, lead the conversation, and follow up on ideas developed during the conversation. The emphasis in these conversations is on creating knowledge and making connections with information students are learning. Students also use persuasive language as they try to convince classmates of the importance of the points they make and the issues they discuss.

K-W-L CHARTS

K-W-L charts are a good way to help students take an active role in talking about what they are learning in theme study units. The letters K, W, and L stand for "What We *K*now," "What We *W*ant to Learn," and "What We *L*earned." Students include two types of information in the Learned column: both "what we learned" and "what we still need to learn." We prefer a variation of the traditional chart, proposed by Sippola (1995), that adds an S column, for "What We Still Want to Know," as shown in Figure 4-8. Teachers use these charts at the beginning of theme study units to help students think and ask questions about what they will study during the theme.

To begin, the teacher asks students to brainstorm what they know about a topic. The teacher records the information in the "K" column—"What We Know"—on a

FIGURE 4-8 A MIDDLE-GRADE STUDENT'S K-W-L-S CHART ON SPIDERS

class chart, as shown in the Teacher's Notebook. As students suggest information and as questions arise, the teacher adds questions in the "W" column—"What We Want to Learn." Students also suggest questions they would like to explore during the theme study unit. Brainstorming information in the "K" column helps students activate prior knowledge, and developing questions in the "W" column provides students with specific purposes for learning.

Next, students look for ways to categorize the information they brainstormed, and use the categories to organize information they are reading or learning from a video presentation. For example, grade 2 students making a K-W-L chart on penguins might identify these categories: what they look like, where they live, how they move, and what their families are like. Older students might use categories such as appearance, habitat, diet, and enemies.

After categorizing, students participate in activities related to the theme study unit, looking for new information and for answers to questions in the "W" column. Later, students reflect on what they have learned and complete the "L" column—"What We Learned." The questions that remain after completing the "L" column can be recorded in the "S" column. Answers can then be sought through research by the whole class, small groups, or individuals, as a way of extending or completing the theme study unit. The K-W-L-S chart helps prepare students to learn, helps them organize their learning, clarifies their misconceptions, and helps them appreciate their learning.

Teachers can make class K-W-L-S charts on chart paper or a bulletin board. Class charts are best for primary-grade students or for older students who have not made K-W-L-S charts before. Older students can also work in small groups to make charts on chart paper, or they can make individual K-W-L-S charts. Students make individual K-W-L-S charts by folding a sheet of paper in half vertically. Then students cut four flaps and label them *K*, *W*, *L*, and *S* as shown in the top drawing in Figure 4-8. Students flip up the flaps to write on the chart as shown in Figure 4-8's lower picture.

For a list of extending projects, see Chapter 5, "The Reading and Writing Processes," pages 154, 155.

FIGURE 4-9 A GRADE 2 CLASS LIST OF RESPONSIBILITIES OF SPEAKERS AND LISTENERS

Our Rules for Show and Tell

What a Speaker Does

Brings something interesting to talk about.

Brings each thing only one time.

Thinks of three things to say about it.

Speaks loudly so everyone can hear.

Passes what he or she brought around so everyone can see it.

What Listeners Do

Show interest.

Pay attention.

Listen.

Ask a question.

Say something nice.

Sharing Time

Daily sharing time, sometimes referred to as "show-and-tell," is a familiar ritual in many kindergarten and primary-grade classrooms. Children bring favourite objects to school and talk about them. Sharing time is a nice bridge between home and school, and a good introduction to speaking in front of a group.

GUIDELINES FOR SPEAKERS AND LISTENERS

If sharing time becomes repetitive, children can lose interest, so teachers must play an active role. Teachers can discuss the roles and responsibilities of both speakers and listeners. A grade 2 class developed the list of responsibilities for speakers and listeners shown in Figure 4-9. This list, with minor variations, has been used with students in upper grades as well.

Some children need prompting even if they have been advised to plan in advance to say two or three things about the object they have brought to school. It is tempting for teachers to speed things up by asking questions and, without realizing it, to answer their own questions, especially for a very quiet child. Sharing time could go like this:

Teacher:	Jerry, what did you bring today?
Justin:	(Holds up a stuffed bear.)
Teacher:	Is that a teddy bear?
Justin:	Yeah.
Teacher:	Is it new?
Justin:	(Nods head yes.)
Teacher:	Can you tell us about your bear?
Justin:	(Silence.)
Teacher:	Jerry, why don't you walk around and show your bear to everyone?

Justin needed prompting, but the teacher in this example dominated the conversation and Justin said only one word—"Yeah." Two strategies may help. First, talk with children like Justin and help them plan something to say. Second, invite listeners to ask the speakers questions using the "5 Ws plus one" questions (*who, what, where, when, why,* and *how*).

A "K-W-L-S" Chart

K What We Know	W What We Want to Learn	L What We Learned	S What We Still Want to Know

Categories of information we expect to use

A.

B.

C.

D.

Source: Adapted from http://www.readwritethink.org/files/resources/printouts/kwls-chart.pdf

Classmates are the audience for sharing activities, but often teachers become the focus. To avoid this, teachers join the audience rather than direct the activity. They also limit their comments and allow the student who is sharing to assume responsibility for the activity and the discussion that follows. Students can ask three or four classmates for comments and then choose which student will share next. It is difficult for teachers to share control of their classrooms, but young students are capable of handling the activity themselves.

ASSESSING SHARING TIME

Students can discuss the effectiveness of their sharing time using the guidelines in Figure 4-9. These guidelines can be converted into a checklist that both speakers and listeners can complete for each presentation. Through the checklists and discussion, students learn to share with confidence when speaking in front of a group.

Sharing time can evolve into an informal type of oral report for middle-grade students. When this method is used effectively, older students gain valuable practice talking in an informal and non-threatening situation. For example, to begin a sharing activity, students can talk about a collection of hockey cards, a program from an Ice Capades show, a recently found snakeskin, or snapshots of a vacation at Banff National Park. Sharing time can lead to informal dramatics and to reading and writing activities. One student may act out routines recalled from the Ice Capades show;

another student may point out the location of Banff National Park on a map or check a website for more information about the park. A third student may write about a prized collection of hockey cards. Experience plus oral rehearsal helps students gear up for other language activities.

Oral Reports

Learning how to prepare and present an oral report is an important efferent talk activity for middle- and upper-grade students. But students are often assigned an oral report without any guidance about how to prepare and give one. Too many students simply copy the report verbatim from a book or website and then read it aloud. The result is that students learn to fear

Students present oral reports to share what they learn during theme study units.

speaking in front of a group rather than build confidence in their oral language abilities. Even young children can be encouraged to read and write informational reports. Read (2005) documents a study of twenty-four grade 1 and 2 students in a multi-age classroom. The students show they are interested in the content of the report, the form and organization of the report, and finally in rereading and reflecting on how the work was done.

We will focus on the steps in teaching students how to prepare and present two types of oral reports. The first type is reports of information—these include reports on social studies or science topics such as the Laurentian Shield, the solar system, or rainforests. The second type comprises book talks, reviews of television shows and films, and even video games. Oral reports have genuine language functions—to inform or to persuade—and are often done as projects during theme study units.

REPORTS OF INFORMATION

Students prepare and give reports of information about topics they are studying in social studies and science. Giving a report orally helps students learn about specific content areas as well as develop their speaking abilities. Students need more than just an assignment to prepare a report for presentation on a particular date; they need to learn how to prepare and present research reports. The four steps in preparing reports, as explained in the next Step by Step box, are choosing a topic, gathering and organizing information, creating visuals, and giving the presentation.

Before the presentations begin, teachers teach minilessons on the characteristics of successful presentations. For example, speakers should talk loudly enough for all to hear, look at the audience, keep to the key points, refer to note cards for important facts, and use the visuals they have prepared.

Students are usually the audience for the oral reports, and members of the audience have responsibilities. They should be attentive, listen to the speaker, ask questions, and applaud the speaker's work. Sometimes students give presentations to the whole class, but it is possible to divide the class into groups so that students can present reports in each group simultaneously.

Preparing and Presenting Reports of Information

1 **Choose a topic.** The class begins with each student or pair of students choosing a topic for a report. For example, if a grade 2 class is studying the human body, each student or pair might select a different part of the body for a report. When students can choose their own topics to research and present, they are more likely to be engaged in the process. After students have chosen a topic, they need to inventory, or think over, what they know about the topic and decide what they need to learn about it. They can learn to focus on the key points for their reports in several ways. One strategy is to create a cluster diagram with the topic written and circled in the centre of a piece of paper; the key points are drawn out from the topic like rays from the sun. Then students write the details on rays drawn from each main idea.

Another strategy is a data chart, in which the teacher provides a chart listing three or more key points to guide students as they gather information for their reports. Figure 4–10 shows a cluster diagram and a data chart for a report on the human body. A third strategy is brainstorming ideas for possible key points by asking questions about the topic prefaced with the "5 W's plus one" question words. The number and complexity of the key points depend on the students' ages or levels of experience.

2 **Gather and organize information.** Students gather information using a variety of reference materials, including, but not limited to, informational books, websites, magazines, podcasts, newspapers, encyclopedias, almanacs, and atlases. In addition to print sources, students can view films and videos, visit websites, or interview people in the community who have special expertise on the topic. In the beginning, students read information that they find interesting. They can tell a peer about what they read as a way to paraphrase the resource and put the knowledge into their own words. From there, they make notes or use point form to record the information.

The preliminary organization—deciding on the key points—completed in the first step gives direction for gathering the information. Now students review the information they have gathered and decide how best to present it so that the report will be both interesting and well organized. Students can transfer the "notes" they want to use for their reports from the cluster diagram or data chart onto note cards. Only keywords—not sentences or paragraphs—should be written on the cards. This helps guard against copying down information verbatim from research sources.

3 **Create visuals.** Students may develop visuals such as charts, diagrams, maps, photos, pictures, models, and timelines. For example, the grade 2 students who gave reports on parts of the body made drawings and clay models of the parts and used a large skeleton hanging in the classroom to show the location of the organ in the body. Visuals provide further information for the speaker to draw upon and add an element of interest for the listeners.

4 **Give the presentation.** The final step is to rehearse and then give the presentation. Students can rehearse several times by reviewing key points and reading over their note cards. They should not, however, read the report directly from the note cards. Students might want to choose a particularly interesting fact to begin the presentation. The teacher can record the presentation so that the presenter can assess his or her own performance at a later time. It is not necessary for students to present in front of the entire class but rather they may present to a small group of their peers as they develop their skills and confidence.

BOOK TALKS AND OTHER REVIEWS

Students give oral reports to review books they have read or television shows and films they have viewed. These book talks and reviews are one type of project students create in resource-based units, readers workshops, and theme study units. The

FIGURE 4-10 A CLUSTER DIAGRAM AND A DATA CHART FOR A REPORT ON THE HUMAN BODY

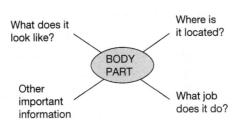

HUMAN BODY REPORT DATA CHART				
Source of information	What does it look like?	Where is it located?	What job does it do?	Other important information

steps in preparing and presenting book talks and other reviews are similar to those for reports of information, as shown in the below Step by Step box.

ASSESSING STUDENTS' ORAL REPORTS

Teachers can assess students' oral reports according to the steps students move through in developing their reports as well as the presentations of their reports in front of the class. Students can also assess their own presentations, considering each of the four

STEP BY STEP

Preparing and Presenting Book Talks and Other Reviews

1 Gather information. Students select information for the report, including a brief summary of the selection and bibliographic information; comparisons to other selections (e.g., with similar themes, written by the same author, starring the same actor); strengths and weaknesses; and opinions and conclusions. They also choose a brief excerpt from the book to read or an excerpt from a video to show.

2 Organize information. Students record and organize the information on a cluster diagram and then copy keywords onto note cards.

3 Create visuals. Students locate or create props to show during the review. Students may show the book in a book talk or show a book trailer or a poster for the film, or they may collect a box or bag of objects related to the book or film to show during the presentation.

4 Give the presentation. Students briefly rehearse the review, and then they give the presentation, referring to the note cards but not reading them, and sharing the props.

steps involved in developing the oral report. These points might be used in developing an assessment checklist:

- Did you choose a narrow topic?
- Did you collect and organize information in a cluster diagram or a data chart?
- Did you prepare a chart or other visual(s) to use in the presentation?
- Did you rehearse the presentation?

  Students can reflect on the presentation and respond to questions such as:
- Did you present the report as you planned?
- Did you speak loudly enough to be heard?
- Did you look at the audience?
- Did you use your visual(s)?
- Did you make your key points?
- How did the audience respond to your presentation?
- What are you most pleased with about your presentation?
- What will you change or do differently when you give another report?

Students should also be asked to comment on what they learned through the process of researching, writing, and presenting the report.

Interviews

Almost all children see interviews on television programs and websites and can be taught the interviewing techniques reporters use. Interviewing is an exciting language arts activity that helps students refine questioning skills and use oral and written language for authentic purposes.

Interviewing is an important language tool that can be integrated effectively in resource-based and theme study units. As part of a theme study unit on school, for example, a grade 1 class invited the local high school principal to visit their class to be interviewed. The principal, who is blind, brought his guide dog with him. The children asked him questions about how visually impaired people manage everyday tasks, as well as how he performed his job as a principal. They also asked questions about his guide dog. After the interview, students drew pictures and wrote summaries of the interview.

During a resource-based unit on the Second World War, grade 5 students can read Joy Kogawa's *Naomi's Tree* (2008) and Kathy Kacer's *The Diary of Laura's Twin* (2008) and interview grandparents and great-grandparents about their memories of the Second World War. After reading excerpts from Deborah Ellis' *Looks Like Daylight: Voices of Indigenous Kids* (2013), a book based on interviews with 45 young people between the ages of nine to 18, students can interview a grandparent or elder to understand the context of their lives in history. After interviewing, students can share the answers with the class. Then students can be encouraged to write reports of their interviews, either in first person or in third person. In small groups, students learn to brainstorm questions before the interviews, and meet again in small gatherings to revise and edit their compositions. Through Ellis' writing and their own interviews, students will be introduced to a wide range of stories and experiences both different from and similar to their own.

One way to introduce interviewing is to watch interviews conducted on television or YouTube and discuss what the purpose of the interview is, what a reporter does before and after an interview, and what types of questions are asked. Interviewers use a variety of questions, some to elicit facts, others to probe for feelings and opinions, but all questions are open-ended. Rarely do interviewers ask questions that require only a yes or no answer.

STEPS IN CONDUCTING INTERVIEWS

There are three steps in the interview process: planning the interview, conducting the interview, and sharing the results, as shown in the below Step by Step box.

ASSESSING STUDENTS' INTERVIEWS

Teachers assess students' interviews by checking that they followed the three steps of the interview process and by examining the quality of their final products. Similarly, students can assess their own use of the interview process and their reports, much like they assess other types of efferent talk projects. One way is through writing reflective journal entries.

Debates

Debates are useful when the whole class is excited about an issue in the news or in a book they are reading together as a class and most or all of the students have taken supporting or opposing positions. As they participate in debates, students learn to use language to persuade their classmates and to articulate their viewpoints. Two types of debates are impromptu debates and formal debates.

IMPROMPTU DEBATES

The class decides on an issue, clarifies it, and identifies positions that support or oppose the issue. Then students who wish to speak in favour of the issue move to the

STEP BY STEP

Conducting Interviews

1 **Plan the interview.**   In the planning step, students arrange for the interview and brainstorm questions to ask the person being interviewed. From this list, students choose which questions they will ask, making sure to avoid questions that require only yes or no answers. Students often write the questions on note cards. Then they sequence the cards in a reasonable order.

2 **Conduct the interview.**   The second step is conducting the actual interview. Students greet the interviewee and conduct the interview by asking questions they have prepared in advance. They take notes or record the answers. They ask follow-up questions about points that are not clear, and if the answer to one question elicits an impromptu, unscripted query, students ask it anyway. Students are polite and respectful of the answers and opinions of the interviewee. Before finishing, students thank the person for participating in the interview.

3 **Share the results.**   Students share the results of the interview by presenting an oral report, writing a report or newspaper article, creating a multimedia presentation, or making a poster.

side of the room designated for supporters, and students who wish to speak against the issue move to the other side. Class members who have not formulated a position sit in the middle.

A lectern is set up in front of the classroom, and the teacher initiates the debate by asking a student from the supporting side to state the position on the issue. After this opening statement, the opposing side counters with a statement. Students take turns going to the lectern and speaking in support of or in opposition to the issue. Students who wish to participate go to the side of the room for the position they support and wait in line for their opportunity to speak. After hearing arguments, students may change their minds and move to the opposite side of the room; if they are no longer certain what side they are on, they take a seat in the middle.

Students who have just made a statement may be asked a question before a student for the other side makes a return statement.

FORMAL DEBATES

A more formal type of debate is appropriate for students in the upper-elementary and middle-school grades. Debates take the form of arguments between opposing sides of a proposition. A proposition is a subject that can be discussed from opposing points of view, such as the following:

> Resolved, that students should have a role in setting standards of behaviour in classes and in disciplining those students who disrupt classes.

After the proposition has been determined, teams of three or four students are designated to support the proposition (the affirmative team) or oppose it (the negative team).

FIGURE 4-11 DEBATE-SCORING RUBRIC

DEBATE RUBRIC

Resolved: There should be more sports for students at Lakeview Middle School.

Rating Code: 1–5;
5 = highest,
1 = lowest

	Appearance	Delivery	Factual information	Keeping to the point	Persuasiveness	Teamwork	Participation in rebuttal	Total
Pro								
Kristen Auch	____	____	____	____	____	____	____	____
James Wilson	____	____	____	____	____	____	____	____
Jeremy Fox	____	____	____	____	____	____	____	____
							Total	____
Con								
Rene LeBlanc	____	____	____	____	____	____	____	____
Whitney Lawson	____	____	____	____	____	____	____	____
Kim Lee	____	____	____	____	____	____	____	____
							Total	____

Depending on the number of members on each team, the debate proceeds in this order:

1. The first student from the affirmative team makes a statement.
2. The first student from the negative team makes a statement.
3. The second student from the affirmative team makes a statement.
4. The second student from the negative team makes a statement.
5. The third student from the affirmative team makes a rebuttal statement.
6. The third student from the negative team makes a rebuttal statement.
7. The fourth student from the affirmative team makes a rebuttal statement.
8. The fourth student from the negative team makes a rebuttal statement.

Sometimes three or four statements are made by each team before beginning to make rebuttal statements rather than just two for each team (steps 1 to 4). Normally there are as many rebuttal statements as there are statements about the position, but teachers may vary the procedure to fit the class and their purposes.

Students can also choose judges to determine the winning team and decide the criteria for judging. They brainstorm questions that form the basis for their criteria and then develop a rubric. The rubric used in one grade 6 class is shown in Figure 4-11. Questions similar to the following might initiate the brainstorming sessions:

- Did the speakers communicate their ideas to the listeners?
- Was a mastery of information evident in the presentations and rebuttals?
- Was the team courteous?
- Did the team work cooperatively?
- Did the second speaker on each team pick up and extend the statement of the first team member?

Review

Listening is the most basic and most used of the language modes. Despite its importance, listening instruction has been neglected in elementary classrooms. Students vary the way they listen for different purposes, and they use different procedures, strategies, and skills for each type of listening. In addition, teachers sustain talk in the elementary classroom because speaking has definite benefits for elementary students. Too often teachers assume that students already know how to speak effectively, so they concentrate on reading and writing. The four types of talk activities—conversations, aesthetic talk, efferent talk, and dramatic activities—are important for developing children's talk, and they also complement students' written language development.

The following key concepts are presented in this chapter:

1. Listening is the neglected language art because it is rarely taught; instead, teachers merely provide practice activities.
2. Students need to learn to use listening strategies to enhance their listening abilities.
3. There are four types of listening: discriminative, aesthetic, efferent, and critical.
4. Students listen aesthetically as teachers read stories aloud and while viewing puppet shows, plays, and digital versions of stories.

5. The Directed Listening–Thinking Approach (DLTA) is one way to actively involve students in aesthetic listening.

6. Students use efferent listening to remember information.

7. Students talk in informal conversations as part of resource-based units and theme study units.

8. Students participate in many types of small-group conversations, and they use talk for both aesthetic and efferent purposes.

9. In literature circles, students use aesthetic talk to respond to a book and develop interpretations.

10. In storytelling and readers theatre activities, students use aesthetic talk to present stories.

11. During sharing time and in oral reports, interviews, and debates, students use efferent talk to inform and persuade listeners.

Theory to Practice

1. Visit a classroom and observe how the purpose for listening is taught or practised. Consider how practice activities might be changed into instructional activities.

2. Interview primary-, middle-, and upper-grade students about strategies they use while listening. Ask questions such as these:

   • What is listening?

   • Why do people listen? Why else?

   • What do you do to help you remember what you are listening to?

   • Do you always listen in the same way, or do you listen differently to stories read aloud and to information your teacher is telling you?

   • How do you know what is important when you are listening?

   • What is the hardest thing about listening?

   • Are you a good listener? Why? Why not?

   • Compare students' responses across grade levels. Are older students more aware of the listening process than younger students are? Can older students identify a greater variety of listening strategies than younger students can?

3. Plan and teach a minilesson on one of the aesthetic listening strategies and on one of the efferent listening strategies discussed in this chapter. Reflect on the lessons and on the differences between aesthetic and efferent listening.

4. Teach students how to participate in literature circles or grand conversations. Then, as you read a chapter book or a collection of picture books with a group of students, have the students participate in a series of literature conversations. Observe students as they talk about the book, and notice how they interact with their classmates as well as how they develop their interpretations.

5. Plan and conduct a debate with a group of upper-grade students. Help them choose a topic from current events, school and community issues, or a theme study unit.

6. In a small group, share several photos of yourself growing up. Notice how the photos serve as a catalyst for you to talk about yourself as you share stories and anecdotes.

7. Have upper-elementary or middle-school students create a list of interesting questions to use to interview a variety of individuals in the school such as the librarian, a parent, the school custodian, the school secretary, a classroom aide, or an administrator. Share the interviews with the class.

Literacy in Action

Chapter 5: Non-Fiction Writing in Grade Three

Procedure

At the end of the school year, one of my favourite writing projects to do with my grade 3 students is to integrate our unit on animal life cycles from our science curriculum, with an expository writing project that gives students the chance to demonstrate the fabulous writing skills that they have been working on all year. For this project, I begin by having students choose an animal that they would like to learn more about. Students have lots of choice and flexibility in this project and as a result they get very excited about researching an animal of their choice. To help students focus on their research, I provide them with a graphic organizer. This graphic organizer helps students keep track of the information they find about their chosen animal. Since students are doing most of their research online, I make sure that students use safe search engines designed for kids when they are completing their research. Students typically need a few computer periods to complete their research and they enjoy finding facts about their chosen animal, looking at pictures of their animal, and watching videos about topics like how their animal survives in its natural habitat.

Once students have gathered facts about their chosen animal, the students and I work together to create an outline of what kind of information should go into each paragraph. In this piece of expository writing we decided to focus on why their chosen animal would make a good pet. The first paragraph was an introduction to the topic; the second paragraph was how they would have to take care of their animal if it was a pet; the third paragraph was a description of why their animal would be a good pet, etc. Once we worked together to create an outline of the paragraphs, students got to work on their rough copies, using the information they had researched about their animal and organizing it into the paragraphs. Finally, I helped students to edit their rough copies and helped them check for mistakes like spelling errors and missing punctuation, before they went on to complete a good copy of their work.

Assessment

To assess students' writing, I focus on the areas of content/organization, sentence structure, vocabulary, and grammar/spelling. I assess students in these key areas across many different types of writing, such as narrative writing, autobiographical writing, etc. To assess content and organization, I am looking at the amount of information the students have included in their work and if they are able to organize their ideas into the paragraphs that we have outlined. To assess sentence structure, I am looking at the quality of the sentences students have used, if their sentences make sense, and if they have used a variety of sentence starters. To assess vocabulary, I am looking at the types of words that students have used in their writing, and am hoping to see lots of descriptive words. Finally, to assess grammar and spelling, I am looking for capital letters and punctuation that is used accurately, and words that are spelled correctly.

Adaptation

This project can easily be modified to give students more or less support, based on their individual writing needs. Students who struggle more with writing can be given a reduced expectation for the amount of information they need to research about their animal or they can receive more support with their writing once they are working on their rough copy or the final copy of their work. Students who need to be challenged will be able to spend time finding a greater number of in-depth facts about their animal, and will be able to produce longer, more detailed pieces of work.

Reflection

I believe it is important to expose students to a variety of different types of text and writing. By integrating our science curriculum and a writing project, students are able to both deepen their knowledge about what we are learning about in science, including learning more about an animal, its lifecycle, habitat, and adaptations, as well as become really engaged in the writing process. It is always amazing for me to watch these grade 3 students become so excited about the whole writing process, from the research to the finished copy!

From the classroom of Lisa Jensen, Grade 3 Teacher
General Stewart Elementary School
Lethbridge, Alberta

The Reading and Writing Processes

Monkey Business Images/Shutterstock

LEARNING OUTCOMES

After reading this chapter, you should be able to

1. Describe five stages of the instructional reading process
2. Describe the stages in the writing process
3. Explain how reading and writing are alike
4. Explain how teachers' knowledge of reading and writing processes affects their teaching of language arts
5. Describe how teachers assess students' learning in the language arts

As part of their pre-service course work in English language arts instruction, student teachers learn about the reading and writing processes by researching children's literature and sharing texts with their students in practicum. After reading, student teachers maintain a blog of the books they have researched, providing a resource for them to use while teaching.

Reading and writing are viewed as processes in which readers and writers create meaning. Readers create meaning, through negotiation with the texts they are reading, and, similarly, writers create meaning through negotiation with the texts they are writing. It is quite common for two people to read the same text and come away with different interpretations and for two writers to write different accounts of the same event. Meaning does not exist within the text that a reader is reading or in the words of the composition that a writer is writing; instead, meaning is created through the transaction between readers and what they are reading or between writers and what they are writing.

The **reading process** involves a series of stages during which readers construct interpretations—known as *comprehension*—as they read and then respond to the text they have read. Provincial curriculum documents address the stages readers go through to read with understanding. Teachers provide instruction to assist students in moving through the stages when reading text. Text comprises all reading materials—paper and electronic—including stories, maps, websites, newspapers, blogs, graphs, cereal boxes, textbooks, and so on.

The **writing process** is a similar recursive process involving a variety of activities as students gather and organize their ideas, draft their compositions, revise and edit the drafts, and, finally, publish their writings.

Assessment is also a component of reading and writing programs. By *assessment*, we specify the ongoing collection of information about students' learning as they read, write, and use all of the language arts to construct meaning and communicate effectively. Teachers use formative assessment information to guide their instruction to help them meet students' needs. This information should be authentic and reflect how children learn. Teachers and students collaborate to document students' learning and to collect artifacts in portfolios. The assessment information contributes to summative evaluation and the assigning of grades. Assigning grades is a fact of life in most classrooms, and teachers must use innovative ways to determine grades and involve students in assessing their own learning.

The Reading Process

Reading is a process in which readers negotiate meaning in order to comprehend or to create an interpretation. During reading, the meaning does not go simply from the page to the reader. Instead, reading involves a complex negotiation between the text and the reader and is shaped by many factors: the reader's knowledge about the topic; the reader's purpose for reading; the language community the reader belongs to, and how closely that language matches the language used in the text; the reader's culturally based expectations about reading; and the reader's expectations about reading based on his or her previous experiences.

Aesthetic and Efferent Reading

Readers read for different purposes, and the way they approach the reading process varies according to their purpose. Often they read for enjoyment, but at other times they read to carry away information. When reading for enjoyment or to be entertained, readers are performing **aesthetic reading**. They concentrate on the thoughts, images, feelings, and associations evoked during reading. Readers also respond to these thoughts, images, feelings, and associations. For example, as children read Cybele Young's story *A Few Blocks* (2011a), they may relate the events in the book to a time when they did not want to go to school; as they read Kathy Stinson's *Highway of Heroes* (2010), they may respond to colour photos and powerful quotations in a nonfiction section of the text; or as they read *Nowhere Else on Earth: Standing Tall for the Great Bear Rainforest* by Caitlyn Vernon (2011), they may focus on the First Nations people who live there and the scientists and conservationists who have joined together to protect this region.

When reading to carry away information, readers are performing **efferent reading**. They concentrate on the public, common referents of the words and symbols in the text. For example, as children read Roberta Bondar's *Touching the Earth*

(1994), with its breathtaking photographs of Earth taken by satellites, their focus is on the information in the text and illustrations, not on the experience of reading.

Almost every reading experience calls for a balance between aesthetic and efferent reading (Langer, 1995; Rosenblatt, 1978; 1991). Readers do not simply read stories and poems aesthetically and informational books efferently. As they progress through a text, readers move back and forth between the aesthetic and efferent stances.

For purposes of instruction, teachers help students to engage in both aesthetic and efferent reading by guiding them through five stages of the reading process: prereading, reading, responding, exploring, and extending. The key features of each stage are presented in the Teacher's Notebook on page 145.

To compare aesthetic and efferent reading with similar stances for listening, see Chapter 4, "Listening and Speaking in the Classroom," pages 104–117.

Stage 1: Prereading

Reading begins before students open a book. The first stage is prereading. Students undertake the following activities in the preparing stage:

- choosing books
- activating background knowledge
- setting purposes
- planning for reading

CHOOSING BOOKS

Readers often begin the reading process by choosing the book they will read. Choosing an appropriate book is not easy. First of all, students need to know about themselves as readers: What types of books do they like? Who are their favourite authors? As they become readers, students learn the answers to these questions. They can also point to books they have read and can tell about them and explain why they enjoyed reading them.

Students need to learn to choose books they can read. Ohlhausen and Jepsen (1992) developed a method called the Goldilocks Strategy for choosing books. These teachers developed three categories of books—"Too Easy," "Too Hard," and "Just Right"—using the Three Bears folktale as their model. The books in the Too Easy category were ones students had read before or could read fluently. Too Hard books were unfamiliar and confusing, and books in the Just Right category were interesting and had just a few unfamiliar words. The books in each category vary according to the students' reading levels. This strategy was developed with a grade 2 class, but the categorization scheme can work at any grade level. Figure 5-1 presents a chart on choosing books using the Goldilocks Strategy with a grade 3 class.

Sometimes teachers choose books for students, but it is important that readers have many opportunities to select the books they are interested in reading. Miller (2014) writes, "Our students must build confidence and competence in choosing their own books to read" (p. 47) in order to foster engagement in and motivation for reading.

ACTIVATING BACKGROUND KNOWLEDGE

Readers activate their background knowledge, or schemata, about the book (or other selection) before beginning to read. The topic of the book, the title, the author(s), the genre, the cover illustration, a comment someone makes about the book, or something

FIGURE 5-1 **A GRADE 3 CHART APPLYING THE GOLDILOCKS STRATEGY**

How to Choose the Best Books for YOU

"Too Easy" Books

1. The book is short.
2. The print is big.
3. You have read the book before.
4. You know all the words in the book.
5. The book has a lot of pictures.
6. You are an expert on this topic

"Just Right" Books

1. The book looks interesting.
2. You can decode most of the words in the book.
3. Mrs. Donnelly has read this book aloud to you.
4. You have read other books by this author.
5. There's someone to give you help if you need it.
6. You know something about this topic.

"Too Hard" Books

1. The book is long.
2. The print is small.
3. There aren't many pictures in the book.
4. There are a lot of words that you can't decode.
5. There's no one to help you read this book.
6. You don't know much about this topic

else may trigger this activation. When students are reading independently—during readers workshop, for example—they choose the books they will read and activate their background knowledge themselves. For example, readers who love sports often choose to read sports books, such as *Breakaway* (Kew, 2011) and *Hockey Girl* (Hyde, 2012).

At other times, such as during resource-based units, teachers teach minilessons to help students activate and build their background knowledge. They share information on a topic related to the book or introduce a book box with a collection of objects related to the book. Or they show a video or film, tell about the author, read the first paragraph aloud, or ask students to make a prediction about the book. For instance, before reading the fourth book in the Submarine Outlaw series by Philip Roy, *Ghost of the Pacific* (2011), teachers talk about submarines, the Pacific Ocean, and environmentalism; before reading Barbara Reid's *Picture a Tree* (2011), teachers help young students use their imagination. The colourful Plasticine art lets children see the tree as a pirate ship, a bear cave, a clubhouse, and anything else they can think of.

Key Features of the Stages of Reading

Stage 1: Prereading
- Choose a book.
- Activate prior knowledge.
- Connect to prior personal and literary experiences.
- Connect to theme study units or special interests.
- Set purposes for reading.
- Make predictions.
- Preview the text.
- Consult the index to locate information.

Stage 2: Reading
- Make predictions.
- Apply skills and strategies.
- Read independently, with a buddy using shared reading, or through guided reading, or listen to the text read aloud.
- Read the illustrations, charts, and diagrams.
- Read the entire text from beginning to end.
- Read one or more sections of the text to learn specific information.
- Take notes.

Stage 3: Responding
- Write in a reading log or blog.
- Participate in a grand conversation.

Stage 4: Exploring
- Reread and think more deeply about the text.
- Make connections with personal experiences.
- Make connections with other literary experiences.
- Examine the author's craft.
- Identify memorable quotes.
- Learn new vocabulary words.
- Participate in minilessons.

Stage 5: Extending
- Construct projects (develop multimedia projects using video, music, and PowerPoint™).
- Use information in theme study units.
- Connect with related content through websites, videos, images, and other texts.

When students are preparing to read a book on an unfamiliar topic, they need to build background knowledge. By being introduced to key vocabulary, students are more likely to be successful when they read. For example, teachers show a video on beavers before reading *The Busy Beaver* (Oldland, 2011); or before reading *That Fatal Night: The Titanic Diary of Dorothy Wilton* (S. Ellis, 2011), from the Dear Canada series, they talk about the trauma experienced by the survivors of the sinking of the *Titanic*.

Another part of activating knowledge before reading is to make connections with personal experiences and with literary experiences. The more connections students make between the book they are about to read and personal experiences, the better. Students who have observed a hermit crab at the seashore, for instance, will be better prepared to read *A House for Hermit Crab* (Carle, 1987) than students who have never seen one. Similarly, students who are familiar with other books by Eric Carle and know about his fabulous collage illustrations will be better prepared for *A House for Hermit Crab* than those who have not experienced Carle's work.

SETTING PURPOSES

The two overarching purposes for reading are pleasure and information. When students read for pleasure or enjoyment, they read aesthetically, to be carried into the world of the text; when they read to locate and remember information or for directions about how to do something, they read efferently. Often readers use elements of both purposes as they read, but usually one purpose is more primary to the reading experience than the other. For example, when students pick up *The Sweetest Fig* (1993) or *Just a Dream* (2011), two Chris Van Allsburg picture book fantasies, their primary purpose is enjoyment. They want to experience the story, but at the same time, they search for the white dog—a trademark that Van Allsburg includes in all of his books—and compare these books with other Van Allsburg titles that they have read. As students search for the white dog or make comparisons, they add efferent purposes to their primarily aesthetic reading experience.

Readers are more successful when they have a single purpose for reading the entire selection. Purpose-setting is usually directed by the teacher during resource-based units, but in **readers workshop** students set their own purposes because everyone is reading different self-selected books. For teacher-directed purpose-setting, teachers explain how students are expected to read and what they will do after reading. Students should always have a purpose for reading, whether they are reading aesthetically or efferently.

PLANNING FOR READING

Students often preview the reading selection as they prepare to read. They look through the selection and check its length, the reading difficulty of the selection, and the illustrations/images in order to judge the general suitability of the selection for them as readers. Previewing serves an important function as students connect with their background knowledge, identify their purpose for reading, and take their first look at the selection.

Teachers set the guidelines for the reading experience. They explain how the book will be read—independently, in small groups, or as a class—and set the schedule for reading. Setting the schedule is especially important when students are reading a chapter book. Often teachers and students work together to create a two- or three-week schedule for reading and responding and then write the schedule on a calendar to which students can refer.

When students are preparing to read informational books, they preview the selection, noting section headings, illustrations, diagrams, and other charts. Sometimes they examine the table of contents to see how the text is organized, or consult the index to locate specific information. They may also notice unfamiliar vocabulary and other words they can check in the glossary, ask a classmate or the teacher about, or look up in a dictionary. Teachers also use the **SQ4R study strategy** (in which students survey, question, read, recite, review, and reflect to remember information), anticipation guides, and other teaching strategies as they work with informational books and content-area textbooks.

Stage 2: Reading

In the second stage, students read the book or other selection. They use their knowledge of word identification, sight words, reading strategies and skills, and vocabulary while they read. Fluent readers are better able to understand what they are reading because they identify most words automatically and use decoding skills when necessary. They also apply their knowledge of the structure of text as they create meaning. They continue reading as long as what they are reading fits the meaning they are constructing. When something doesn't make sense, fluent readers slow down, back up, and reread until they are making meaning again. Applying strategies to reinstate meaning is sometimes referred to as using "fix-up" strategies.

Students may read the entire selection or specific sections. When students are reading aesthetically, they usually read the entire selection, but when they are reading efferently, they may be searching for specific information and read only until they locate that information. It is unrealistic to assume that students will always read entire selections or finish reading every book they begin, even when reading for aesthetic purposes.

Outside of school, readers usually read silently and independently. Sometimes, however, people listen as someone else reads. Young children often sit in a parent's lap and look at the illustrations as the parent reads a picture book aloud. Adults read and listen in group settings such as church services and listen to stories read aloud on podcasts and audiobooks. In the classroom, teachers and students use five types of reading:

- shared reading
- guided reading
- independent reading
- buddy reading
- reading aloud to students

SHARED READING

Students follow along as the teacher reads the selection aloud. Kindergarten teachers and other primary-grade teachers often use **big books**—enlarged versions of the selection—for shared reading (Sampson, Rasinski, & Sampson, 2003). Students sit so that they can see the book, and they either listen to the teacher read aloud or join in and read along. The teacher or a student points to each line of text as it is read to draw students' attention to the words; to show the direction of print on a page; and to highlight important concepts about letters, words, and sentences.

For more information on big books, see Chapter 3, "Emergent Literacy," pages 85, 86.

Teachers also use shared reading when students have individual copies of the reading selection. Students follow along in their copies as the teacher or another fluent reader reads aloud. This "first" reading is preparation for students so that they become familiar enough with the storyline and the vocabulary that they can read the selection independently later.

For more information on using shared reading with young children, see Chapter 3, "Emergent Literacy," page 81.

When students are reading chapter books, shared reading is used as the main reading approach if some students can't read the selection independently. The teacher

For more information on choral reading, see Chapter 6, "Reading and Writing Narrative Text," pages 230–234.

and other fluent readers take turns reading aloud as students follow along in their copies of the selection. To ensure that all the students are following along in their copies of the book, teachers sometimes ask all students or a group of students to read aloud very softly as they read aloud. Sometimes teachers read the first chapter or two of a chapter book together as a class using shared reading, and then students use other types of reading as they read the rest of the book. Only students for whom the book is too difficult continue to use shared reading and read along with the teacher.

There are several variations of shared reading (Slaughter, 1993). One is *choral reading*, when students divide into groups to read poems aloud. Another is **readers theatre**, in which students read play scripts aloud. A third type of shared reading is the **listening centre**, where students can listen to a book read aloud as they follow along in the book. Listening centres are a good way to provide models of fluent reading and additional reading practice to help students become fluent readers.

GUIDED READING

This type of reading is teacher-directed and usually done in small groups with students who read at the same level or use similar reading skills and strategies (Clay, 2001; Fountas & Pinnell, 1996). Teachers often group and regroup students for guided reading so that the book the teacher selects is appropriate for all students in a group using books written at students' **instructional reading levels**—that is, slightly beyond their ability to read the text independently or at their level of proximal development.

Guided reading, as described by Fountas and Pinnell (1996) and outlined here, is a popular practice with beginning readers in Canadian classrooms. Establishing a guided reading program is one way to help meet the varied needs of all students. Although guided reading can take different forms, most involve working with small groups of students at similar levels of development, using texts that are carefully matched to their needs, providing instructional support to build reading strategies and increase independence (Rog, 2003). As the following Step by Step box shows, there are six steps in guided reading, according to Fountas and Pinnell (1996).

A modified form of guided reading is often used when teachers read with students during resource-based and theme study units. When teachers read a featured selection with students, they have opportunities to demonstrate reading strategies, clarify misconceptions as students construct meaning, point out key vocabulary words, and take advantage of many teachable moments. When the reading takes place in a small-group arrangement and each student has a copy of the text, teachers have the opportunity to observe individual students as they read, to monitor their comprehension, and to informally assess their reading progress.

INDEPENDENT READING

Independent reading is an important part of language arts instruction because it is the most authentic type of reading. This is the type of reading that most people do, and this is the way students develop a love of reading and come to think of themselves as readers.

Student comparing digital and print texts.

When students read independently, they read silently by themselves and at their own pace. In order for students to read independently, the selections must be at their reading level or very familiar to them. For beginning readers, independent reading often follows the teacher's reading of the book one or more times during shared reading experiences. It is essential for students to have access to many texts with which they can be successful. Access to books has been repeatedly shown to encourage more frequent reading (Morrow, 2003).

BUDDY READING

In buddy reading, students read or reread a selection with another student. Sometimes students read with buddies because it is an enjoyable social activity, and sometimes they read together to help each other. Often students can read selections together that neither one could read individually. By working together, they are often able to figure out unfamiliar words and talk out comprehension problems.

Teachers sometimes choose to pair older and younger students for buddy reading. For example, upper elementary and middle-school students can be reading buddies with kindergarten and grade 1 students. Both buddies benefit. Older students develop their oral reading skills and serve as tutors to give their younger buddies reading practice.

As teachers introduce buddy reading, they show students how to read with buddies and how to support each other as they read. Unless the teacher has explained and

STEP BY STEP

Guided Reading

1 **Choose a book.**   The teacher chooses a book or other selection for the group to read based on knowledge of students' reading levels and ability to use reading skills and strategies.

2 **Introduce the selection.**   The teacher briefly introduces the selection by activating background knowledge, introducing characters, and setting a purpose for reading. The teacher may also ask students to make predictions about what they think will happen in the selection.

3 **Observe students as they read.**   Students read silently and the teacher observes them as they read. The teacher notices the reading skills and strategies that students exhibit as they read and makes anecdotal notes about these observations. The teacher also notes any words students ask for help with or any questions that students ask.

4 **Provide assistance.**   If students require assistance, the teacher assists them one on one with word identification and supports their efforts to comprehend the selection, trying not to interrupt students while they are reading.

5 **Talk about the selection.**   The teacher encourages students to briefly share their responses to the book. Students talk about the selection, ask questions to clarify misconceptions, and relate the reading to their own lives.

6 **Teach minilessons.**   The teacher introduces, practises, or reviews one or two skills or strategies after reading. The teacher may select topics for minilessons in advance or respond to students' observed needs. In these lessons, the teacher asks students to return to the text to practise word-identification or comprehension skills or strategies. The teacher also has students focus their attention on elements of story structure and the language patterns used in the selection.

Source: Adapted from Fountas, I. C., & Pinnell, G. S. (1996). Guided Reading: Good First Teaching for All Children. Portsmouth, NH: Heinemann. © Gail E. Tompkins

modelled the approach and taught students how to work collaboratively, buddy reading often deteriorates into the better reader reading aloud to the other student, and that is not the intention of this type of reading. Students need to take turns reading aloud to each other or to read in unison. They often stop and help each other identify an unfamiliar word or take a minute or two at the end of each page to talk about what they have read. Buddy reading is a valuable way of providing the practice that beginning readers need to become fluent readers, and it is also an effective way to work with students who have special learning needs and those who are learning English.

READING ALOUD TO STUDENTS

At every grade level, teachers read aloud to students for a variety of purposes each day. Sometimes teachers read aloud featured selections that are appropriate for students' interest level but too difficult for students to read by themselves. Teachers also read aloud featured selections during thematic and resource-based units if they have only one copy of the book or other source available. Sometimes it is also appropriate to read the featured selection aloud before distributing copies of the selection for students to read with buddies or independently. When they read aloud, teachers model fluent and expressive reading and show what good readers do and how good readers use reading strategies such as prediction and other comprehension strategies.

During **readers workshop**, teachers also read aloud stories and other books to introduce students to literature they might not choose to read on their own. The reading-aloud component of a readers workshop provides students with a shared social experience and an opportunity to talk about literature and reading. In addition, teachers also read aloud books related to science, social studies, and other across-the-curriculum themes.

Reading aloud to students is not the same as *round-robin reading*, in which students take turns reading paragraphs aloud as the rest of the class listens. Round-robin reading has been used for reading chapter books aloud, but it is more commonly used for reading chapters in content-area textbooks, even though there are more effective ways both to teach content-area information and to read textbooks.

Round-robin reading is no longer recommended for several reasons. First, if students are going to read aloud, they should read fluently. When less capable readers read, their reading is often difficult to listen to and embarrassing to them personally. Less capable readers need reading practice, but performing in front of the entire class is not the most productive way for them to practise. They can read with buddies and in small groups during guided reading. Second, if the selection is appropriate for students to read aloud, they should be reading independently, not hindered in their reading by the differences in reading rate that naturally occur in group reading. During round-robin reading, students often follow along only just before it is their turn to read. Third, round-robin reading is often tedious and boring, and students lose interest in reading.

The advantages and drawbacks of each type of reading are outlined in Figure 5-2.

Stage 3: Responding

During the third stage, readers respond to their reading and continue to negotiate meaning in order to deepen their comprehension. Two ways that students make tentative and exploratory comments immediately after reading are as follows:

- writing in reading-response logs
- participating in grand conversations

FIGURE 5-2 ADVANTAGES AND DRAWBACKS OF THE FIVE TYPES OF READING

Type	Advantages	Drawbacks
Shared Reading Teacher reads aloud while students follow along using individual copies of book, a class chart, or a big book.	• Students access books they could not read themselves • Teacher models fluent reading • Opportunities given to model reading strategies • Students practise fluent reading • It develops a community of readers	• Multiple copies, a class chart, or a big book needed • Text may not be appropriate for all students • Students may not be interested in the text
Guided Reading Teachers support students as they read texts at their reading levels. Students are grouped homogeneously.	• Teacher provides direction and scaffolding • Opportunities given to practice reading strategies and skills • Students read silently • Students practise the prediction cycle	• Multiple copies of text needed • Teacher controls the reading experience • Some students may not be interested in the text
Independent Reading Students read a text independently and often choose the text themselves.	• Students develop responsibility and ownership • Texts are self-selected • Experience is more authentic	• Students may need assistance to read the text • Teacher has little involvement and control
Buddy Reading Two students read or reread a text together.	• Collaboration takes place between students • Students assist each other • It is used to reread familiar texts • It develops reading fluency • Students talk and share interpretations	• Teacher has limited involvement • Teacher has less control
Reading Aloud to Students Teacher or other fluent reader reads aloud to students.	• Students access books they could not read themselves • Teacher models fluent reading • Opportunities given to model reading strategies • It develops a community of readers • It is used when only one copy of text is available	• No opportunity given for students themselves to read • Text may not be appropriate for all students • Students may not be interested in the text • It does not require students to take turns reading

WRITING IN READING LOGS

Students write and draw thoughts and feelings about what they have read in **reader-response** journals. Rosenblatt (2005) explains that as students write about what they have read, they unravel their thinking and, at the same time, elaborate on and clarify their responses. When students read informational books, they sometimes write in **reading logs** just as they do after reading stories and poems, but at other times they make notes of important information or draw charts and diagrams to use in theme study units.

Students sometimes make reading logs by stapling together several sheets of paper at the beginning of a unit. They decorate the covers in keeping with the topic of the unit, write entries related to their reading, and make notes related to what they are learning in minilessons. They also create blogs to express themselves as well as practise computer, keyboarding, spelling, and grammatical skills.

Students usually choose their own topics for reading journal entries, but at other times teachers offer a list of prompts from which students choose. Students are never expected to respond to all prompts. Many teachers display a list of prompts in the classroom or give the list to students to place in their language arts notebooks. Possible prompts include the following:

I really don't understand …

I like/dislike (character) because …

This book reminds me of …

(Character) reminds me of myself because …

I think (character) is feeling …

I wonder why …

(Event) makes me think about the time I …

If I were (character), I'd …

I noticed that (the author) is …

I predict that …

These prompts are open-ended and allow students to make connections with their own lives, the world, and other literature.

At other times, teachers ask a specific question to direct students' attention to some aspect of a book. For example, as upper-grade students are reading Pamela Porter's *The Crazy Man*, winner of the 2005 **Governor General's Literary Award** for children's literature, teachers might ask questions like these:

Why did Emaline's father react the way he did after the accident?

Would you have Angus as a friend?

How does Angus feel when someone tries to send him away?

What do you think happened to Emaline's father?

These questions, like the prompts listed above, are open-ended and ask for students' interpretations.

Teachers monitor students' entries, often reading and responding to those entries. Because these logs are learning tools, teachers rarely correct students' spelling. They focus their responses on the students' ideas. At the end of the unit, teachers review students' work and often grade the logs based on whether students completed all the entries and on the quality of the ideas in their entries.

PARTICIPATING IN GRAND CONVERSATIONS

Students also talk about the text in discussions called **grand conversations** or *literature circles* (Daniels, 1994; Booth & Schwartz, 2004). R. Peterson and M. Eeds (1990) explain that in this type of discussion, students share their personal responses and tell what they liked about the selection. After sharing personal reactions, they shift the focus to "puzzle over what the author has written and … share what it is they find revealed" (p. 61). Often students make connections between the selection and their own lives or other literature they have read. If they are reading a chapter book, they also make predictions about what will happen in the next chapter.

Stories with dramatic plots or ones that present a problem students can understand, such as *Shin-chi's Canoe* (N. Campbell, 2008), *One on One* (Aker, 2005), and *Dear George Clooney: Please Marry My Mom* (Nielsen, 2010), focus the conversation on the book as experience. Multilayered stories or books in which main characters deal with dilemmas, such as *One Thing That's True* (Foggo, 1997), *Before We Go* (Bright, 2012), and *The Hunger Games* (Collins, 2008), focus the conversation on the message. Books with distinctive structures or language features, such as *Uumajut, Volume Two: Learn More about Arctic Wildlife!* (Awa, Akeeagok, Ziegler, & McDonald, 2011), *Wolves* (Gravett, 2006b), and *Being with Henry* (M. Brooks, 1999), focus the conversation on the object.

Teachers often participate in grand conversations, but they act as interested participants, not leaders. The discussion is primarily among students; teachers ask open-ended questions regarding things they are genuinely interested in learning more about and share information in response to questions students ask. Open-ended questions teachers might ask during grand conversations include the following:

Which character is most like you?

What would you have done if …?

What did that make you think of?

Grand conversations can be held with the whole class or in small groups. Young children usually meet together as a class, while older students often prefer to talk with classmates in small groups. When students meet together as a class, there is a shared feeling of community and the teacher can be part of the group. When students meet in small groups, students have more opportunities to participate in the discussion and share their responses, but fewer viewpoints are expressed in each group and teachers must move around, spending only a few minutes with each group. Some teachers compromise and have students begin their discussions in small groups and then come together as a class and have each group share what their group discussed.

For more information on grand conversations, see Chapter 4, "Listening and Speaking in the Classroom," pages 123–126.

Stage 4: Exploring

During this stage, students go back into the text to explore it more analytically. They participate in some of these activities:

- rereading the text
- examining the author's craft
- focusing on new vocabulary words
- participating in minilessons

REREADING THE TEXT

Through repeated readings, students reread the text and think again about what they have read. Each time they reread, students benefit in specific ways (Yaden, 1988). They enrich their comprehension and make further connections between the text and their own lives or between the text and other literature they have read. Students often reread a text several times. If the teacher used shared reading to read the text with students in the reading stage, students might reread it with a buddy once or twice, read it with their parents, and, after these experiences, read it independently.

EXAMINING THE AUTHOR'S CRAFT

Teachers plan exploring activities to focus students' attention on the structure of the text and the literary language that authors use. Students notice opposites in the story, use **storyboards** to sequence the events in the story, and make **story maps** to visually represent the plot, characters, and other story elements (Bromley, 1996). Older students also examine closely the writing devices used by authors and explore their use in their own writing. They can use technology to do these same activities and create PowerPoint™ or other multimedia presentations. Another way students learn about the structure of stories is by writing books based on the text they have read. Students write sequels, telling what happened to the characters after the story ends. Some stories, such as *Rex Zero and the End of the World* (Wynne-Jones, 2007), *Walk Two Moons* (Creech, 1995), and *Jumanji* (Van Allsburg, 1981), end in a way that seem to invite students to create a sequel. Students also write innovations, or new versions, for the selection by following the sentence pattern. First graders often write innovations for Bill Martin, Jr.'s *Brown Bear, Brown Bear, What Do You See?* (1983) and for *Pussycat, Pussycat, Where Have You Been?* (Bar-el, 2011), and older students write innovations for *The Important Book* (Wise Brown, 1949).

Teachers share information about the author of the featured selection and introduce other books by that author. Sometimes teachers have students compare several books written by a particular author. They use technological resources found on the Internet and in databases to find information about authors and their books.

When students read **picture books**, they also learn about illustration and the illustrator's craft. Students can learn about the media and techniques the artist used and experiment with the media themselves. They can examine the illustrations to find out about the illustrator's stylistic choices and think more deeply about how illustrations affect interpretation of the text.

FOCUSING ON NEW VOCABULARY WORDS

Teachers and students add "important" words to **word walls** after reading and post these word walls in the classroom. Students refer to the word walls when they write, using these words for a variety of activities during the exploring stage. Researchers emphasize the importance of immersing students in words, teaching strategies for learning words, and personalizing word learning (Blachowicz & Fisher, 2006). Students make word **clusters** and posters to highlight particular words. They also make word chains, sort words, create a semantic feature analysis to analyze related words, and play word games.

Teachers choose words from word walls to use in minilessons, too. Words are used to teach phonics skills, such as beginning sounds, rhyming words, vowel patterns, *r*-controlled vowels, and syllabication (Bear, Invernizzi, Templeton, & Johnston, 2008). Other concepts, such as root words and affixes, compound words, and metaphors, can also be taught using examples from word walls. Teachers often teach a minilesson on a particular concept, such as the *-ly* suffix, because five or six words representing the concept are listed on the word wall.

For more information on word walls and vocabulary instruction, see Chapter 8, "Words, Their Meanings, and the Tools to Use Them: Grammar, Spelling, Handwriting, and Word Processing," pages 294–301.

PARTICIPATING IN MINILESSONS

Teachers present minilessons on reading concepts, procedures, strategies, and skills during the exploring stage. A list of topics for minilessons on the reading process is presented on page 159. In a reading minilesson, teachers introduce the topic and make connections between the lesson topic and reading of the featured selection. In this way, students are better able to connect the information teachers are presenting with their own reading process. Students need to learn about the process approach to reading and about ways to develop interpretations.

Stage 5: Extending

During the extending stage, readers move beyond comprehension to broaden and deepen their interpretations, reflect on their understanding, and value the reading experience. Students build on their initial understanding and responses through engaging in exploring activities and extending projects related to their reading. These activities and projects can involve reading, writing, speaking and drama, viewing, visually representing, or research, and are often interactive with other readers. They may take many forms, including murals, readers theatre scripts, oral presentations, and written/digital texts, as well as reading other books by the same author. A list of extending projects is presented in Figure 5-3. The wide variety of project options offers students choices and takes into account that students have preferred

FIGURE 5-3 EXTENDING PROJECTS

Writing Projects

Note that many of these writing projects are completed using various forms of technology to enhance both the process and the products.

1. Write a review of a favourite book for a class review file.
2. Write a postcard or letter about a book to a classmate, friend, or pen pal.
3. Dictate or write another episode or sequel for a book.
4. Create a newspaper with news stories and advertisements based on characters and episodes from a book.
5. Make a five-senses cluster about the book.
6. Write and mail a letter to a favourite author (or participate in a class collaboration letter).
7. Write a simulated letter from one book character to another.
8. Copy five "quotable quotes" from a book and list them on a poster.
9. Make a scrapbook about the book. Label all items in the scrapbook and write a short description of the most interesting ones.
10. Write a poem related to the book. Some types of poems to choose from are acrostics, concrete poems, colour poems, "I wish" or "I am" poems, haiku, or found poems.
11. Write a lifeline related to the book, the era, the character, or the author.
12. Write a business letter to a company or organization requesting information on a topic related to the book.
13. Keep a simulated journal from the perspective of one character from the book.
14. Write a dictionary defining specialized vocabulary in a book.
15. Write the story from another point of view (e.g., write the story of the Little Red Hen from the perspective of the lazy characters).
16. Make a class collaboration book. Each child dictates or writes one page.
17. Write a letter to a famous person from a character in a book.
18. Create an alphabet book on a topic related to the book.
19. Make a cube with information about the book or a related topic.

Reading Projects

20. Read another book by the same author.
21. Read another book by the same illustrator.
22. Read another book on the same theme.
23. Read another book in the same genre.
24. Read another book about the same character.
25. Read and compare two versions of the same story.
26. Read a biography about the author or illustrator of the book.

Speaking and Drama Projects

27. Record a book or an excerpt from it to place in the listening centre.
28. Read aloud a poem that complements the book to the class. Place a copy of the poem in the book.
29. Give a readers theatre presentation of a book.
30. Create a song about a book or choose a tune for a poem and sing the song for the class.
31. Write a script and present a play about a book.
32. Make puppets and use them in retelling a book.
33. Dress as a character from the book and answer questions from classmates about the character.
34. Write and present a rap about the book.
35. Record on video a commercial for a book.

Research Projects

36. Interview someone in the community who is knowledgeable about a topic related to the book.
37. Research the author or illustrator of the book and compile information in a chart or summary. Post the chart or summary in the library centre.
38. Research a topic related to the book. Present the information in an oral or written report.
39. Research the setting or context of the book and share findings with other readers.
40. Conduct a poll among readers of a book (or readers of several sources concerning the same topic). Record and share poll results.

ways of learning and showing knowledge. Usually students choose which projects they will do rather than work as a class on the same project. Sometimes, however, the class decides to work together on a project.

Teaching the Reading Process

Everyone—parents, teachers, researchers—has an opinion about what's important in reading instruction. Most, however, agree that there are four important components in developing capable readers. These are:

For more information on creating a community of learners and arranging the classroom, see Chapter 2, "Teaching the Language Arts," pages 32–64.

- word identification
- vocabulary
- comprehension
- fluency

WORD IDENTIFICATION

Proficient readers have a large bank of works that they recognize automatically because they can't stop and analyze each word as they read. Students learn to read phonetically regular words, such as *baking* and *first*, and high-frequency words, such as *there* and *said*. In addition, they learn to figure out, using phonic analysis, unfamiliar words such as *election* and *jungle*. Through reading instruction and reading practice, students' ability to identify words continues to grow.

VOCABULARY

Strong vocabulary knowledge is essential because it is easier to figure out words that you have heard before and to comprehend what you are reading when you are already familiar with some words related to the topic. Reading is the most effective way that students expand their vocabularies. Proficient readers do more reading than less proficient students, so they learn more words.

COMPREHENSION

Comprehension is a complex process that involves both the reader and text factors (Sweet & Snow, 2003). Proficient readers are strategic. They use predicting, visualizing, connecting, questioning, summarizing, and other strategies to think about and understand what they are reading. Teaching comprehension involves introducing strategies through minilessons, demonstrating how good readers use them, and involving students in guided practice of those strategies (Oczkus, 2009).

FLUENCY

The components of fluency are reading speed, accuracy, and prosody (Rasinski, 2004). During the primary grades, the focus is on word identification, and students learn to identify hundreds of words, but by grade 4, the focus changes to comprehension, and speed begins to be important because it's hard for students to remember what they're reading when they read slowly. Prosody, the ability to read with appropriate phrasing and intonation, is important because when readers read expressively, the text is easier to understand.

Teachers apply the five-stage reading process and teach word identification, vocabulary, comprehension, and fluency in the reading lessons they teach, whether they organize instruction into resource-based units, theme study units, inquiry units, or readers workshops. Teachers bring students together as a community of learners and teach them the procedures for various language arts activities. Each unit requires that teachers carefully structure activities, provide appropriate books and other materials, and create time and space for students to work.

IN RESOURCE-BASED UNITS

In resource-based units, students might read a single book, such as *Becoming Holmes: The Boy Sherlock Holmes, His Final Case* (Peacock, 2012) or *The Nose from Jupiter* (Scrimger, 1998), and as they read they will move through the five stages of the reading process. Or they might read a collection of books on the same theme (e.g., adventure stories), in the same genre (e.g., folktales), or by the same author (e.g., books by Carol Matas). When students read several books together, they move back and forth among the second, third, and fourth stages as they read, respond to, and explore each book before moving on to the extending stage.

Figure 5-4 shows one way to organize a resource-based unit on *Bunnicula: A Rabbit-Tale of Mystery* (D. Howe & Howe, 1979). In this unit, grade 5 students work

FIGURE 5-4 A PLAN FOR TEACHING A RESOURCE-BASED UNIT ON BUNNICULA: A RABBIT-TALE OF MYSTERY (D. HOWE & HOWE, 1979)

Stage 1: Preparing
The teacher shares a book box of objects related to the book with students. Objects include a stuffed rabbit dressed in a vampire costume, plastic vegetables that have been painted white and marked with two small pinpricks, and a children's version of the Dracula story. The teacher shares the objects, and students make predictions about the book.

Stage 2: Reading
The teacher uses the shared reading approach to read the chapter book. Each student has a copy of the book and follows along as the teacher reads the book aloud. One or two chapters are read aloud each day.

Stage 3: Responding
After reading a chapter or two, students write responses in reading logs and share these logs with classmates. Students also participate in grand conversations and make connections between the story and their own lives and other experiences with literature.

Stage 4: Exploring
Students write interesting and important words from the book on a word wall (chart paper hanging on the wall) and use the words in a variety of vocabulary activities, including word sorts. The teacher shares information about the authors, Deborah and James Howe, and a text set of other books by James Howe. The teacher teaches several minilessons on characterization and the meaning-making strategy of identifying with a character. The teacher asks students to choose the character they identify with the most (Harold the dog, Chester the cat, or Bunnicula the rabbit) and explain why they chose that character. Students make an open-mind portrait of one character. Other minilessons include portmanteau words (e.g., *bunny*+ *Dracula* = *Bunnicula*) and homonyms.

Stage 5: Extending (through Fine Arts and Technology)
Each student chooses a project from a list of choices posted in the classroom. A number of students choose to read one of the sequels and other stories about Bunnicula: *Howliday Inn* (1982), *The Celery Stalks at Midnight* (1983), *Nighty-Nightmare* (1987), *Scared Silly* (1989), *The Fright before Christmas* (1989), *Hot Fudge* (1990), *and Return to Howliday Inn* (1992). Other students choose these projects:

- Write and/or email a letter to authors Deborah and James Howe.
- Perform a play about an episode of the book.
- Make a book box and place five items related to the book with explanations in the box.
- Write a sequel to the book.
- Make a tabletop display of the Monroes' house.
- Research Dracula and vampires.

through all five stages of the reading process. The teacher uses a book box with a stuffed rabbit dressed like a vampire, plastic vegetables that have been painted white, and a children's version of the Dracula story. Students use shared reading to read the chapter book; then they respond to their reading and participate in exploration activities. The teacher presents minilessons on homophones (e.g., *steak, stake*) and portmanteau words (*bunny + dracula = Bunnicula; smoke + fog = smog*), and shares information about the authors, Deborah and James Howe. Students also construct projects and engage in dramatizations to extend their study of the book.

IN THEME STUDY AND INQUIRY-BASED UNITS

Teachers coordinate the books and other materials students are reading with what they are studying during theme study units. Theme study units usually include study across curriculum subject areas. For example, during a theme study unit on insects in a grade 2 classroom, students might read *Insect Homes* (Kalman & Crossingham, 2006) at the beginning of the theme. Students move through all five stages of the reading process. First they read the easy-to-read informational book using shared reading; then they read it a second time with reading buddies; and then they read it a third time independently. During the grand conversation held after they read the book the first time, students brainstorm a list of reasons why it's a good thing there are insects. Later they can write their own books about insects. Teachers can also use this book to teach minilessons about the differences between stories and informational books. *Insect Homes* is an excellent example of an informational book because the illustrations are photos, and a glossary and index are included.

Later in the theme study unit the teacher might pair two books about bugs for the students to read: *The Delicious Bug* (Perlman, 2009), a story about two chameleons hunting for lunch who latch on to the same bug, and *Bugs up Close* (Swanson, 2007), an informational book that students or the teacher can read, with colourful photos, a glossary, and an index. If the teacher has enough copies of each book for half the class, the students divide into two groups. One group reads one book and the other group reads the other book; then the two groups trade books. As the students read these two books, the teacher has many opportunities to continue comparing stories and informational books. After reading, students might talk about which book they liked better, and they work on projects to extend their understanding of bugs and other insects.

IN READERS WORKSHOP

Students also work through the stages of reading during readers workshop. In readers workshop, students focus on the prereading, reading, and responding stages of the reading process, but the remaining stages are also involved. Students choose books (often using the Goldilocks Strategy), activate background knowledge, set purposes, and make plans as they begin to read (stage 1). Next, they read the book independently (stage 2). After reading, they may write in reading logs and talk about the books they are reading in conferences with the teacher (stage 3). Sometimes students read three or four books and then choose one book for a project (stage 5). Students also talk about the books they read and show their completed projects to classmates

The Reading and Writing Processes

	Procedures	Concepts	Strategies and Skills
The Reading Process	Choose books to read	Aesthetic reading	Decode words
	Use the Goldilocks Strategy	Efferent reading	Predict
	Listen to books read aloud	Interpretation	Confirm
	Do shared reading		Visualize
	Do buddy reading		Retell
	Do independent reading		Connect to literature
	Respond in reading logs		Connect to life
	Participate in grand conversations		Empathize
	Reread a book		Identify with characters
	Create projects		Monitor
	Participate in readers workshop		
The Writing Process	Choose a topic	Functions of writing	Gather ideas
	Cluster	Writing forms	Organize ideas
	Quickwrite	Audience	Draft
	Participate in writing groups	Focus on content	Revise
	Proofread	Focus on mechanics	Edit
	Make hardcover books	Proofreaders' marks	Identify and correct spelling errors
	Write About the Author pages	Publish writing	Use capital letters correctly
	Share published writing		Use punctuation marks correctly
			Value the composition

during sharing time (stages 3 and 5). In readers workshop, teachers also teach mini-lessons, and during these lessons students learn reading concepts, procedures, strategies, and skills (stage 4). Children's future success depends on reading and so it is essential that teachers create reading communities as supportive spaces for their students.

Differentiating to Meet the Needs of Every Student

Reading instructional activities are flexible and can be adapted to help every student, whether talented or developing, become a more successful reader. For students with limited experiences or for those who are learning English as a second or third language, more time should be spent in the prereading stage. During reading, teachers often read books aloud or use shared reading when working with students who are not yet fluent readers. Many easy-to-read stories and informational books that are well written and enticing to students are currently available, so it is possible to have several books at different reading levels on almost any topic. During the responding stage, students can draw or dramatize rather than write their responses in reading journals, and grand conversations take on an even greater importance for students who need to clarify misconceptions about their reading. Students can reread the text with a buddy or listen to the audiobook version during the exploring stage. The fifth stage is important for all students, and many students who find reading difficult are very successful in creating art projects and dramatic productions. Suggestions for adapting reading instruction to meet the needs of every student are presented in the accompanying Differentiating box.

The Reading Process to Meet the Needs of Every Student

Stage 1: Prereading
- Spend more time activating and constructing background knowledge.
- Use concrete experiences, multimedia presentations, and photos.
- Introduce important vocabulary related to the topic but not limited to the vocabulary in the text. Use independent reading and research skills to develop background knowledge. Share background knowledge with other readers.

Stage 2: Reading
- Read books aloud.
- Use shared reading or buddy reading.
- Listen to a recorded version of the book.
- Break the reading time into smaller chunks.
- Provide easier-to-read or more challenging alternative texts.

Stage 3: Responding
- Have students draw or dramatize responses instead of writing in reading journals.

- Take time in grand conversations to clarify misconceptions. Engage students in critical thinking followed by oral or written presentations.

Stage 4: Exploring
- Role-play important events in the book.
- Reread the text with a buddy.
- Teach minilessons to individual students and small groups of students.
- Engage students in comparisons of texts and views of authors.

Stage 5: Extending
- Encourage students to create art projects.
- Encourage students to produce dramatic productions.
- Set out clear expectations for the projects students develop.
- Encourage students to pursue projects that they are interested in and that challenge them.

The Writing Process

The focus in the writing process is on what students think and do as they write. The five stages are prewriting, drafting, revising, editing, and publishing, and the key features of each stage are shown in the following Teacher's Notebook. The labelling and numbering of the stages does not mean, however, that the writing process is a linear series of neatly packaged categories. Research has shown that the process involves recurring cycles, and labelling is only an aid to identifying and discussing writing activities. In the classroom, the stages merge and recur as students write.

Stage 1: Prewriting

Prewriting is the getting-ready-to-write stage. Writers begin the writing process before they have completely thought out their topic. They begin by talking, reading, or writing to discover what they know and decide what direction they want to take. Calkins (1994) believes that a significant amount of writing time should be spent in prewriting. Students undertake the following activities in the prewriting stage:

- choosing a topic
- considering purpose, audience, and form
- generating and organizing ideas for writing

CHOOSING A TOPIC

Students often choose their own topics so that they write about things they are interested in and knowledgeable about. Helping students find their own topics is

Key Features of the Writing Process

Stage 1: Prewriting
- Students write on topics based on their own experiences.
- Students engage in rehearsal activities before writing.
- Students identify the audience and the purpose of the writing activity.
- Students gather and organize information.

Stage 2: Drafting
- Students write a rough draft.
- Students emphasize content rather than mechanics.

Stage 3: Revising
- Students reread their own writing.
- Students share their writing in writers groups.
- Students participate constructively in discussions about classmates' writing.
- Students make changes in their compositions to reflect the reactions and comments of both teacher and classmates.
- Students make substantive rather than only minor changes.

Stage 4: Editing
- Students proofread their own compositions.
- Students help proofread classmates' compositions.
- Students increasingly identify and correct their own mechanical errors.
- Students meet with the teacher for a final editing.

Stage 5: Publishing
- Students publish their writing in an appropriate form.
- Students share their finished writing with an appropriate audience.

the first step in assisting them in becoming responsible for their own writing. Teachers can help them brainstorm a list of three, four, or five topics and then to identify the one topic they are most interested in and know the most about. Students who feel they cannot generate any writing topics are often surprised that they have so many options. At other times, teachers do provide topics for writing and general guidelines. Sometimes they may specify the writing form and at other times they may establish the function, but students should choose their own specific content.

CONSIDERING PURPOSE

As students prepare to write, they need to think about their purpose for writing. Are they writing to entertain? To inform? To persuade? Understanding the purpose of a piece of writing is important because it influences other decisions students make about audience and form. When students have no purpose in mind other than to complete the assignment, their writing is often lacklustre—without a strong voice or a controlling idea.

CONSIDERING AUDIENCE

Students' writing is influenced by their sense of audience. They may write primarily for themselves—to express and clarify their ideas and feelings—or they may write for others. Possible audiences include classmates, younger children, parents, foster grandparents, children's authors, and pen pals. Other audiences are more distant and less well known. For example, students write blogs to post on the Internet, submit stories and poetry to online publications, and compose emails to send to authors and illustrators they like.

CONSIDERING FORM

One of the most important considerations is the form the writing will take. It could be a story, letter, email, poem, or journal entry. There is an almost endless variety of forms that children's writing may take. A list of these forms is presented in the accompanying Teacher's Notebook. Students need to experiment with a wide variety of writing forms and explore the potential of these functions and formats. Because children are clarifying the distinctions between various writing forms during the elementary grades, it is important that teachers use the correct terminology and not label all children's writing "stories."

GENERATING AND ORGANIZING IDEAS FOR WRITING

Students engage in activities to gather and organize ideas for writing. D. H. Graves (1994) calls what writers do to prepare for writing "rehearsal" activities. When students read books, take field trips, view videos, and dramatize events, they are participating in rehearsal activities and building background knowledge. Young children use drawing and talking to gather ideas for writing and older students often make diagrams or webs to organize their ideas as they prepare for writing. Students also use quickwriting to brainstorm ideas. Through this informal writing activity, they gather ideas they will be able to use as they draft their writing.

Stage 2: Drafting

Students get their ideas down on paper or on the screen during the drafting stage. Because writers do not begin writing with their compositions already composed in their minds, students begin with tentative ideas developed through prewriting activities. The drafting stage is the time to pour out ideas, with little concern about spelling, punctuation, and other mechanical aspects of writing.

When students write their drafts, they may write on only one side of the page and on every other line to leave space for revisions. When writing on notepaper, they may use arrows to move sections of text, cross-outs to delete sections, and scissors and tape to cut apart and rearrange text. They learn to revise and cut and paste using the computer.

Teachers teach students to label their drafts by writing the date and "Draft #1" in ink at the top of the paper, by stamping them with a DRAFT stamp, or by including "draft" in their electronic file name. This label indicates to the writer, other students, and parents that the composition is a draft in which the emphasis is on content, not mechanics. It also explains why the teacher has not graded the paper or marked mechanical errors.

TEACHER'S NOTEBOOK

Writing Forms

"about the author" pages
acrostics
advertisements
"all about ..." books
alphabet books
announcements
anthologies
apologies
applications
autobiographies
awards
bibliographies
biographies
blogs
book jackets
books
brochures
captions
cartoons
catalogues
certificates
character sketches
charts
cinquain poems
clusters
comics
comparisons
complaints
computer programs
concrete poems
crossword puzzles
cubes
definitions
descriptions
diagrams
dialogue journals
dialogues

diamante poems
dictionaries
digital stories
directions
double-entry journals
editorials
emails
essays
evaluations
explanations
fables
fairytales
folktales
formula poems
found poems
greeting cards
haiku poems
hink-pinks
"I am" poems
instructions
interviews
invitations
jokes
lab reports
learning logs
letters
life lines
limericks
lists
lyrics
maps
menus
mysteries
myths
newspapers
notes
obituaries

oral histories
personal narratives
postcards
posters
puzzles
questionnaires
questions
quickwrites
reading logs
recipes
reflections
reports
reviews
riddles
schedules
scripts
sentences
signs
simulated journals
stories
storyboards
study guides
tall tales
telegrams
telephone directories
texts
thank-you notes
thumbnail sketches
timelines
tongue twisters
tweets
valentines
word-finds
wordless picture books
word posters
word walls

During drafting, students may need to modify their earlier decisions about purpose, audience, and, especially, the form their writing will take. For example, a composition that began as a story may be transformed into a report, a letter, or a poem if the new format allows the student to communicate more effectively. The process of modifying earlier decisions continues into the revising stage.

As students write drafts, it is important not to emphasize correct spelling and format. In fact, pointing out mechanical errors during the drafting stage sends students a message that mechanical correctness is more important than content. Later, during editing, students can clean up mechanical errors and put their composition into a neat, final form.

Stage 3: Revising

During the revising stage, writers clarify and refine ideas in their compositions. Students often break the writing process cycle as soon as they complete a draft, believing that once they have jotted down their ideas, the writing task is complete. Proficient writers, however, know that they must turn to others for reactions and revise on the basis of these comments. Revision is not just polishing; it is meeting the needs of readers by adding, substituting, deleting, and rearranging material. The word *revising* means "seeing again," and in this stage writers see their compositions again with the help of their classmates and teacher. Students participate in the following activities in the revising stage:

- rereading the draft
- sharing the draft in writers groups
- revising on the basis of feedback
- conferencing with the teacher

REREADING THE DRAFT

After finishing the first draft, writers need to distance themselves from the draft for a day or two, and then reread it from a fresh perspective, as a reader might. As they reread, students make changes—adding, substituting, deleting, and moving—and place question marks by sections that need work. It is these trouble spots that students ask for help with in their writers groups.

SHARING THE DRAFT IN WRITERS GROUPS

Students meet in writers groups to share their compositions with classmates. Because writing must meet the needs of readers, feedback is crucial. The Step by Step feature describes the procedure for organizing revising groups in the classroom.

Writers groups can form spontaneously when several students have completed drafts and are ready to share their compositions, or they can be formal groupings with identified leaders. In some classrooms, writers groups form when four or five students finish writing their drafts. Students gather around a conference table or in a corner of the classroom and work as authors, sometimes without the teacher. They take turns reading their drafts aloud, and classmates in the group listen and respond, offering compliments and suggestions for revision. Regardless of how the groups are formed, students need instruction, demonstrations, reminders, and time to learn to conference well and to support each other as writers (Atwell, 1998).

In other classrooms the writers group membership is established, usually by the teacher, and maintained for a period of time. Students get together when all students in a group have completed rough drafts and are ready to share their writing. Sometimes the teacher participates in these groups, providing feedback along with the students. At other times, the writers groups can function independently. Four or five students are assigned to each group, and a list of groups and their members is posted in the classroom. The leader changes intermittently to give all group members the opportunity to be leader.

In writers groups, students share their writing through the activities listed in the following Step by Step box.

STEP BY STEP

Writers Groups

1 The writer reads.   Students take turns reading their compositions aloud to the group. All the students listen politely, thinking about compliments and suggestions they will make after the writer finishes reading. Only the writer looks at the composition, because when classmates and teacher look at it, they quickly notice and comment on mechanical errors, even though the emphasis during revising is on content. Listening to the composition read aloud keeps the focus on content.

2 Listeners offer compliments.   Next, writers group members say what they liked about the writing. These positive comments should be specific, focusing on strengths, rather than the often-heard "I liked it" or "It was good." Even though these are positive comments, they do not provide effective feedback. When teachers introduce revision, they should model appropriate responses because students may not know how to offer specific and meaningful comments. The teacher and students can brainstorm a list of appropriate comments and post it in the classroom for students to refer to. Comments may focus on organization, leads, word choice, voice, sequence, dialogue, theme, and so on. Possible comments are

> I like the part where …
> I'd like to know more about …
> I like the way you described …
> Your writing made me feel …
> I like the order you used in your writing because …

3 The writer asks questions.   After a round of positive comments, writers ask for assistance with trouble spots they identified earlier when rereading their writing, or they may ask questions that reflect more general concerns about how well they are communicating. Admitting that they need help from their classmates is a major step in students learning to revise. Possible questions to classmates are

> What do you want to know more about?
> Is there a part that I should throw away?
> What details can I add?
> What do you think the best part of my writing is?
> Are there some words I need to change?

4 **Listeners offer suggestions.** Members of the writers group ask questions about things that were unclear to them, and they make suggestions about how to revise the composition. Almost any writer resists constructive criticism, and it is especially difficult for elementary students to appreciate suggestions. It is important to teach students what kinds of comments and suggestions are acceptable so that they will word what they say in helpful rather than hurtful ways. Possible comments and suggestions that students can offer are

> I got confused in the part about …
> Do you need a closing?
> Could you add more about …?
> I wonder if your paragraphs are in the right order because …
> Could you combine some sentences?

5 **The process is repeated.** The first four steps are repeated for each student's composition. This is the appropriate time for the teacher to provide input as well. The teacher should react to the piece of writing as any other listener would—not error-hunting with red pen in hand. In fact, most teachers prefer to listen to students read their compositions aloud, since teachers may become frustrated by having to contend with the numerous misspelled words and nearly illegible handwriting common in handwritten and unedited drafts.

6 **Writers plan for revision.** At the end of the writers group session, all students make a commitment to revise their writing based on the comments and suggestions of the group members. The final decisions on what to revise always rest with the writers themselves, but with the understanding that their rough drafts are not perfect comes the realization that some revision will be necessary. When students verbalize their planned revisions, they are more likely to complete the revision stage. Some students also make notes for themselves about their revision plans. After the group disbands, students make the revisions.

MAKING REVISIONS

Students make four types of changes: additions, substitutions, deletions, and moves. As they revise, students might add words, substitute sentences, delete paragraphs, and move phrases. Students often use a blue or red pen to cross out, draw arrows, and write in the space left between the double-spaced lines of their rough drafts so that revisions will show clearly. When using a computer for writing, students can print a copy of their rough drafts before making revisions. That way, teachers can examine the types of revisions students make by examining their revised rough drafts and by having students use Track Changes on the computer. Revisions are another gauge of students' growth as writers.

CONFERENCING WITH THE TEACHER

Conferences play an important role in all aspects of literacy learning (Calkins, Hartman, & White, 2005). In writing conferences, the focus is on the student as writer. The particular piece of writing being addressed is the vehicle for coaching the writer. The teacher's role during conferences is to help students make choices and define directions for revision. Barry Lane (2008) offers these suggestions for talking with students about their papers:

- Have students come to a conference prepared to begin talking about their concerns. Students should talk first in a conference.
- Ask questions rather than give answers. Ask students what is working well for them, what problems they are having, and what questions they have.

- React to students' writing as a reader, not as a teacher. Offer compliments first; give suggestions later.
- Keep the conference short and recognize that not all problem areas or concerns can be discussed.
- Limit the number of revision suggestions and make all suggestions specific.
- Have students meet in writers groups before they conference with the teacher. Then students can share the feedback they received from classmates.
- To conclude the conference, ask students to identify the revisions they plan to make.
- Take notes during conferences and summarize students' revision plans. These notes are a record of the conference, and the revision plans can be used in formatively assessing students' revisions.

It is time consuming to meet with every student, but many teachers believe it to be worthwhile. In five-minute conferences, teachers listen to students talk about their writing processes, guide students as they make revision plans, and offer feedback during the writing process when it is most usable.

Stage 4: Editing

Editing is the process of putting the piece of writing into its final form. Until this stage, the focus has been primarily on the content of students' writing. Once the focus changes to mechanics, students polish their writing by correcting misspellings and other mechanical errors. Writers who write for readers understand that if their compositions are not readable, they have written in vain because their ideas will never be read.

Mechanics are the commonly accepted conventions of written Standard English. They include capitalization, punctuation, spelling, sentence structure, usage, and formatting considerations specific to poems, scripts, letters, and other writing forms. The use of these commonly accepted conventions is a courtesy to those who will read the composition.

Mechanical skills are best taught during the editing stage, not through workbook exercises. When editing a composition that will be shared with a genuine audience, students are more interested in using mechanical skills correctly so that they can communicate effectively. In a study of two grade 3 classes, Calkins (1980) found that the students in the class who learned punctuation marks as a part of editing could define or explain more marks than the students in the other class who were taught punctuation skills in a traditional manner, with instruction and practice exercises on each punctuation mark. In other words, the results of this research, as well as other studies (D. H. Graves, 1994; Routman, 1996; Weaver, 1996), suggest that students learn mechanical skills better as part of the writing process than through practice exercises.

Students move through three activities in the editing stage:
- getting distance from the writing
- proofreading to locate errors
- correcting errors

GETTING DISTANCE FROM THE WRITING

Students are more efficient editors if they set the composition aside for a few days before beginning to edit. After working so closely with a piece of writing during drafting and revising, they are too familiar with it to be able to locate many mechanical errors. With the distance gained by waiting a few days, children are better able to approach editing with a fresh perspective and gather the enthusiasm necessary to finish the writing process by making the paper optimally readable.

PROOFREADING TO LOCATE ERRORS

Students proofread their compositions to locate and mark possible errors. Proofreading is a unique type of reading in which students read slowly, word by word, hunting for errors rather than reading quickly for meaning. Concentrating on mechanics is difficult because our natural inclination is to read for meaning. Even experienced proofreaders often find themselves reading for meaning and thus overlooking errors that do not inhibit meaning. It is important, therefore, to take time to explain proofreading and demonstrate how it differs from regular reading.

To demonstrate proofreading, a teacher projects a piece of student writing onto an interactive whiteboard. The teacher reads it several times, each time hunting for a particular type of error. During each reading, the teacher reads the writing slowly, softly pronouncing each word and pointing to focus attention on it. The teacher marks possible errors as they are located.

Errors are marked or corrected with special proofreaders' marks. Students enjoy using these marks, the same ones that adult authors and editors use. Proofreaders' marks that elementary students can learn to use in editing their writing are presented in Figure 5-5. Editing checklists help students focus on particular types of errors. Teachers can develop checklists with two to six items appropriate for the grade level. A grade 1 checklist, for example, might include only two items—perhaps one about

FIGURE 5-5 PROOFREADERS' MARKS

Delete	ℒ	There were cots to sleep on and food to eat on at the shelter.
Insert	∧	Mrs. Kim's cat is the colour of carrots.
Indent paragraph	⌐|	⌐|Riots are bad. People can get hurt and buildings can get burned down but good things can happen too. People can learn to be friends.
Capitalize	=	Daniel and his mom didn't like mrs. Kim or her cat.
Change to lowercase	/	People were Rioting because they were angry.
Add period	⊙	I think Daniel's mom and Mrs. Kim will become friends⊙
Add comma	⋀	People hurt other people, they steal things, and they burn down buildings in a riot.
Add apostrophe	∨	Daniel's cat was named Jasmine.

FIGURE 5-6 A GRADE 3 EDITING CHECKLIST

Editing Checklist

Author Editor

1. I have circled the words that might be misspelled.

2. I have checked that all sentences begin with capital letters.

3. I have checked that all sentences end with punctuation marks.

4. I have checked that all proper nouns begin with a capital letter.

Signatures:

Author:_____   Editor:_____

capital letters at the beginning of sentences and a second about periods at the end of sentences. In contrast, a middle-grade checklist might include items such as using commas in a series, indenting paragraphs, capitalizing proper nouns, and spelling homonyms correctly. Teachers can revise the checklist during the school year to focus attention on skills that have recently been taught.

A sample grade 3 editing checklist is presented in Figure 5-6. First, students proofread their own compositions, searching for errors in each category on the checklist; after proofreading, they check off each item. Then, after completing the checklist, students sign their names and trade checklists and compositions with a classmate. Now they become editors and complete each other's checklist. Having both author and editor sign the checklist helps them to take the activity seriously.

An example of an editing checklist for grade 6 writers is presented in Figure 5-7.

CORRECTING ERRORS

After students proofread their compositions and locate the errors, they correct the errors individually or with an editor's assistance. Some errors are easy to correct, some require use of a dictionary, and others involve instruction from the teacher. It is unrealistic to expect students to locate and correct every mechanical error in their compositions.

When mechanical correctness is crucial, students can meet with the teacher for a final editing conference. Teachers proofread the composition with the student, and they identify and make the remaining corrections together or the teacher makes check marks in the margin to note errors for the student to correct independently. Error correction is an important step in the writing process, one that is significantly simplified by word processing.

FIGURE 5-7 A GRADE 6 EDITING CHECKLIST

Title:

Date Began: Date Finished:

Editor: Peer Editor:

- Have you reread your writing carefully, noting the places where it seems particularly strong and clear?
- Have you reread it carefully, trying to imagine places where readers might be confused?
- Have you underlined words that look as if they may not be spelled correctly and tried to get some help on those words?
- Have you reread your piece aloud, paying attention to the punctuation?
- Have you tried to cut your piece, taking out the extra words that don't add much?
- Have you tried adding to your piece or changing your writing where there is confusion?
- What new risks have you taken with the conventions of written language?
- What questions do you have? What are the issues around which you want help?

—

Source: Adapted from Calkins, L. M. (1994). The Art of Teaching Writing (2nd ed.). Portsmouth, NH: Heinemann. © Gail E. Tompkins

Stage 5: Publishing

In this stage, students bring their compositions to life by publishing them or sharing them orally with an appropriate audience. When they share their writing with real audiences of classmates, other students, parents, and the community, students come to think of themselves as authors. Students undertake activities such as the following in the publishing stage:

- making final copies of their writing
- sharing writing orally and electronically

MAKING FINAL COPIES

One of the most popular ways for children to publish their writing is by making books (King & Stovall, 1992). Simple booklets can be made by folding a sheet of paper into quarters, like a greeting card. Students write the title on the front and use the three remaining sides for their compositions. They can also construct booklets by stapling sheets of writing paper together and adding construction-paper covers. Sheets of wallpaper cut from old sample books also make sturdy covers. These stapled booklets can be cut into various shapes, too. Students can also produce digital manuscripts using computer software that allows integration of text and illustrations. Students can make more sophisticated books by covering cardboard covers with contact paper, wallpaper samples, or cloth. Pages are sewn or stapled together, and the first and last pages (endpapers) are glued to the cardboard covers to hold the book together.

SHARING WRITING

Students read their writing to classmates or share it with larger audiences through hardcover books placed in the class or school library; plays performed for classmates; or letters sent to authors, businesses, and other correspondents. The Internet offers unlimited opportunities for students to publish their writing online, share it with a global audience, and receive authentic feedback from readers (McNabb, 2006). Other ways students might share writing are as follows:

- Read it aloud in class and to other classes.
- Submit it to writing contests.
- Display it as a mobile.
- Contribute it to a class anthology.
- Contribute it to the local newspaper or literary magazine.
- Make a shape book.
- Make an audio recording.
- Read it at a school assembly.
- Share it on a class blog.
- Share it with parents, siblings, or grandparents.
- Produce a video of it.
- Display poetry on a "poet-tree."
- Send it to an e-pal.
- Make a hardbound book.
- Produce it as a roller movie.
- Display it on a bulletin board.
- Make a big book.
- Design a poster about it.
- Share it as a puppet show.
- Create a PowerPoint presentation of it.
- Publish it on the Internet.

Through this sharing, students communicate with genuine audiences who respond to their writing in meaningful ways.

Teaching the Writing Process

Learning to use the writing process is more important than any particular writing project students might be involved in because the writing process is a tool. Students need many opportunities to learn to use the writing process. Teachers model the writing process by writing class collaborations, and they teach minilessons on the writing process that look at the procedures, concepts, strategies, and skills writers use.

WRITING CLASS COLLABORATIONS

One way to introduce the writing process is to write a collaborative or group composition. The teacher models the writing process and provides an opportunity for students to practise the process approach to writing in a supportive environment. As students and the teacher write a composition together, they move through the five stages of the writing process just as writers do when they work independently. With young students, the whole composition may be written collaboratively, whereas with older students, the teacher may choose to write a particular part of the composition or writing project.

The teacher begins by introducing the idea of writing a group composition and by reviewing the project. Students dictate a rough draft, which the teacher records on the chalkboard, on chart paper, or on the computer. The teacher notes any

For more information on writing a class collaborative story, see Literacy in Action in this chapter, "Non-fiction Writing in Grade 3", on pages 139, 140.

misunderstandings students have about the writing assignment or process, and, when necessary, reviews concepts and offers suggestions. Then the teacher and students read the composition and identify ways to revise it. Some parts of the composition will need reworking, and other parts may be deleted or moved. More specific words will be substituted for less specific ones, and redundant words and sentences will be deleted. Students may also want to add new parts to the composition. After making the necessary content changes, students proofread the composition, checking for mechanical errors, paragraph breaks, and sentences to combine. Then the teacher or a student copies the completed composition on to chart paper, a sheet of notebook paper, or the computer. Copies can be made and given to each student.

MINILESSONS ON THE WRITING PROCESS

For more information on minilessons, see Chapter 2, "Teaching the Language Arts," page 57.

Teachers use minilessons to show students how to move through the five stages of the writing process, how to gather and organize ideas for writing, how to participate in writers groups, how to proofread, and how to share their writing. Teachers teach these procedures, concepts, and strategies and skills during minilessons.

Minilessons can be taught as part of class collaborations, during resource-based units and theme study units, and in writers workshop. A list of topics for minilessons on the writing process is presented on page 159. Many teachers use the editing stage as a time to informally assess students' spelling, capitalization, punctuation, and other mechanical skills and to give minilessons on a skill that a student or several students are having trouble with. The teacher notes which students are having difficulty with a particular skill—paragraphing, capitalizing proper nouns, or using the apostrophe in possessives, for example—and conducts an impromptu minilesson using the students' writing as the basis of the lesson. In this brief, five-minute lesson, the teacher reviews the particular skill, and students practise it as they correct their own writing and help to correct their classmates' writing. This procedure individualizes instruction and teaches the skill when learning it matters and is relevant to students.

Applying the stages of the writing process occurs in the various instructional frameworks adopted by teachers.

IN RESOURCE-BASED UNITS

Students use the writing process as they create projects during the extending stage of the reading process. Sometimes the class works together to write a class collaboration; sometimes students work in small groups on the same writing project; and at other times students work on a variety of writing projects. Here are three examples:

- After reading Karma Wilson's bear story *Bear Feels Scared* (2011), a class of grade 1 students worked together to write a retelling of the story, which they published as a big book.
- During an author unit on Kit Pearson, grade 5 students each chose to illustrate a scene from *The Whole Truth* (2011) and wrote a description or story about it.
- As part of a unit on point of view, grade 7 students each rewrote familiar folktales from the viewpoint of one character after reading *The True Story of the 3 Little Pigs!* (Scieszka, 1989), which is told from the wolf's viewpoint.

In each of these projects, students used the writing process and moved through all five stages as they prewrote, drafted, revised, edited, and published their compositions.

Teachers often plan writing projects in connection with theme study units. Frequently, the projects involve writing forms and information from more than one area of the curriculum. For example, a theme study unit concerning protecting the environment might include persuasive writing when students write letters of protest to government officials. A unit concerning historical figures might involve biographical writing. In these cases, teachers review the writing forms required in minilessons and draw upon information learned in other subject areas.

Sometimes all students in the classroom work together on a single project, such as making an alphabet book about the ocean as part of a theme on the environment, or writing a collection of animal poems to display with the animal sculptures they made in art. At other times, however, students choose projects and work independently. For example, during a theme study unit on First Nations, Métis, and Inuit culture and language, students might choose one of the following projects:

- Write about place names in Canada based on Aboriginal words.
- Write a pourquoi (why) folktale.
- Make a map of the historical Aboriginal areas in Canada.
- Create a storyboard for an Aboriginal hero.
- Make a timeline of an Aboriginal author's life (e.g., David Bouchard, Michael Kusugak).

For each of these projects, students use the writing process to develop their compositions. They meet in writers groups to share their drafts and revise their compositions using feedback from peers and their teacher. They also edit their compositions to correct as many mechanical errors as possible. Then they make final copies of their compositions and share them with classmates or other audiences.

IN INQUIRY-BASED UNITS

Students use the writing process in inquiry-based units in the same way they do in resource-based and theme study units. They select topics, gather information, compose drafts, revise, edit, and publish. Students often choose topics in which they have particular interest. Teachers make it possible for students to pursue interests by designing writing projects that are flexible and open-ended yet linked to whole class studies.

In a grade 7 class, students became interested in genealogy after one student reported that his family was able to trace its roots to early settlers in Nova Scotia. Several students in the class read Sheree Fitch's *The Gravesavers* (2005) and were intrigued by twelve-year-old Minn's fight to save the eroding maritime graves of shipwrecked victims who had hoped to be settlers. The teacher asked the students to create a piece of writing that demonstrated their ability to combine fact and fiction. As writers of historical fiction they were to demonstrate knowledge of family and social history. Students wrote letters, diary entries, newspaper articles, ballads, and short stories using the writing process.

ABOUT WRITERS WORKSHOP AND WRITING PROCESS

Sometimes the terms *writers workshop* and *writing process* are confused or mistakenly used interchangeably. We use **writers workshop** to refer to a way of organizing writing instruction that facilitates the writing process. The **writing process** refers to the stages through which writers move a composition from idea generation to publication. It would be convenient if the writing process were equated with an instructional framework that included prewriting on Monday, drafting on Tuesday, revising on Wednesday, editing on Thursday, and publishing on Friday, but it does not. Writers move back and forth through the stages as they develop, refine, and polish their compositions, and they participate in some activities, such as revising, throughout the writing process (Flower & Hayes, 1994). The process for a particular piece often ends during a special time set aside for students to share their published writing projects with an interested audience. Sharing is a social experience, and when students share their writing with real audiences, they feel the satisfaction of a job well done.

The Author's Craft

Spandel (2005, 2008) and her colleagues identified the six traits of effective writing: ideas, organization, voice, word choice, sentence fluency, and conventions. Teachers help students understand what the traits are and how these can be used to improve their writing.

Trait 1: Ideas. Ideas are the "heart of the message" (Culham, 2003, p. 11). When ideas are well developed, the writing is clear and focused. The ideas encompass what the writer has to say and create images in readers' minds. As students examine this trait, they develop the ability to

- choose original and interesting ideas
- narrow and focus ideas
- choose detail to develop an idea
- use the senses to add imagery

Trait 2: Organization. Organization is the internal structure of a piece of writing and shows how information is put together in an order that makes sense to the reader. The logical pattern of the ideas varies according to form; stories, for example, are organized differently than nonfiction or poetry. As students learn about organization, they develop the ability to

- use structural patterns in their writing
- use devices to capture the reader's attention
- use transition words to link ideas together
- write satisfying endings

Trait 3: Voice. Voice is the writer's style; it's what breathes life into the writing. The writer's voice can be humorous or compelling, reflective or persuasive. What matters most is that the author connects with readers. Student develop their voices when they

- retell familiar stories from the viewpoints of different characters
- assume a persona and write from that person's viewpoint
- avoid repetition and vague wording

Trait 4: Word Choice. Carefully chosen words clarify meaning and create mood. It's important for writers to choose words that fit both their purpose and the audience to whom their writing is directed. Students increase their word knowledge through readers workshops and lots of reading. As students experiment with word choice, they

- use precise nouns, vivid verbs, and colourful modifiers
- consult a thesaurus to consider options

Jim Craigmyle/Corbis

This student shares her writing with the teacher and her classmates.

- avoid repeating words and phrases
- use wordplay

Trait 5: Sentence Fluency. Effective sentences vary in structure and length, and students are now encouraged to include some sentence fragments to add rhythm and energy to their writing (Culham, 2003). Teachers teach students about sentence structure so they learn to

- vary sentence structure and length
- include some sentence fragments
- begin sentences in different ways
- combine or expand sentences

Trait 6: Conventions. Writers check that they have used Standard English mechanics—spelling, punctuation, capitalization, and grammar—in order to meet the reader's expectations. They check that their writing uses paragraphing as a way to enhance organization. They also create a visual design for their work and arrange the text to enhance readability. Students learn to

- proofread to identify mechanical errors
- use a dictionary and word wall to correct spelling errors
- check paragraphing
- add design/visual elements

Linking the Six Traits to the Writing Process

The writing process is a series of stages that students use as they draft and refine their writing, but it doesn't specify how to make writing better. That's where the six traits come in: Students apply what they've learned about the traits to improve the quality of their writing, particularly during the revising and editing stages. As students reread their drafts, they can check that their writing exemplifies the writing traits. Teachers also develop rubrics that focus on one or more traits that students can use to self-assess their writing.

The following Teacher's Notebook summarizes the six traits of effective writing and how they connect to the writing process and instructional activity.

For more information on how to adapt the writing process for young children, see Chapter 3, "Emergent Literacy," pages 92–95.

Differentiating to Meet the Needs of Every Student

Teachers differentiate the activities involved in each stage of the writing process to make writing a successful experience for all students. Teachers often shorten the writing process to three stages—prewriting, drafting, and publishing—for young children, for English language learners, and for students with few successful writing experiences. Then, as students become more fluent writers and develop audience awareness, teachers add the revising and editing stages. Teachers also pair students with special needs with older students who act as scribes, recording the story as their partners tell it. When working with talented student writers, teachers extend the scope of writing projects and encourage elaboration at all stages of the process.

Teachers can develop checklists with activities for each stage of the writing process listed so that students with short attention spans or students who have trouble completing an assignment can stay on task. Other suggestions for adapting each stage are listed in the following Differentiating box.

Linking the Six Traits of Effective Writing to the Writing Process and Instructional Activities

Traits	Writing Process	Instructional Activities
Trait 1: Ideas	Prewriting	• Brainstorm, word web, or draw • Create a memory box • Discuss special places and people
Trait 2: Organization	Prewriting/Drafting/Revising	• Practise story leads • Make beginning, middle, and end charts • Discuss transitions
Trait 3: Voice	Drafting/Revising	• Use authors as models • Write from various characters' points of view
Trait 4: Word Choice	Drafting/Revising	• Focus on verbs and "juicy" words • Paint a picture with words • Use word play
Trait 5: Sentence Fluency	Drafting/Revising	• Create super sentences from simple unadorned sentences • Practise writing shorter and longer sentences
Trait 6: Conventions	Editing/Publishing	• Work in pairs to check spelling, punctuation, and grammar • Provide checklists • Add design elements

DIFFERENTIATING

The Writing Process to Meet the Needs of Every Student

Stage 1: Prewriting
- Use drawing as a rehearsal activity.
- Have students "talk out" their compositions before beginning to write.
- Draw a cluster with students, using the ideas and words they suggest.
- Make available multiple sources of topical information.

Stage 2: Drafting
- Have students dictate their drafts.
- Guide students to write on every other line to allow space for revision.
- Reassure students that spelling and other mechanical skills are not important in this stage.
- Have older students act as "scribes" for younger children.
- Have students draft using a computer if handwriting/printing is too difficult.
- Encourage students to explore more than one form of writing to carry their message.

Stage 3: Revising
- Participate in writers groups with older, more capable students.

- Focus on compliments rather than on suggestions for revisions when students begin writers groups.
- Expect students to make only one or two revisions at first.
- Expect talented writers to be astutely aware of audience.

Stage 4: Editing
- Teach students how to proofread.
- Have students mark possible errors; then correct errors with them.
- Have students identify and correct errors on the first page of their compositions; then correct remaining errors for students when edited copy is required.
- Encourage self- and peer-editing among talented writers.

Stage 5: Publishing
- Use a computer for final copies.
- Input the final copy for students.
- Provide opportunities for students to share their writing with a trusted group of classmates.
- Do not correct any remaining errors on the final copy.
- Ensure a wide audience for talented writers' products.

Connections between the Reading and Writing Processes

Reading and writing are both meaning-making processes, and readers and writers are involved in many similar activities. It is important that teachers plan literacy activities so that students can connect reading and writing.

Comparing the Two Processes

The reading and writing processes have comparable activities at each stage. In both reading and writing the goal is to construct meaning, and, as shown in Figure 5-8, reading and writing activities at each stage are similar. For example, notice the

FIGURE 5-8 A COMPARISON OF THE READING AND WRITING PROCESSES

	What Readers Do	What Writers Do
Stage 1	*Preparing*	*Prewriting*
	Readers use knowledge about	Writers use knowledge about
	• the topic	• the topic
	• reading	• writing
	• literature	• literature
	• language systems	• language systems
	Readers' expectations are cued by	Writers' expectations are cued by
	• previous reading/writing experiences	• previous reading/writing experiences
	• format of the text	• format of the text
	• purpose for reading	• purpose for writing
	• audience for reading	• audience for writing
	Readers make predictions.	Writers gather and organize ideas.
Stage 2	*Reading*	*Drafting*
	Readers	Writers
	• use word-identification strategies	• use transcription strategies
	• use meaning-making strategies	• use meaning-making strategies
	• monitor reading	• monitor writing
	• create meaning	• create meaning
Stage 3	*Responding*	*Revising*
	Readers	Writers
	• respond to the text	• respond to the text
	• interpret meaning	• interpret meaning
	• clarify misunderstandings	• clarify misunderstandings
	• expand ideas	• expand ideas
Stage 4	*Exploring*	*Editing*
	Readers	Writers
	• examine the impact of words and literary language	• identify and correct mechanical errors
	• explore structural elements	• review paragraph and sentence structure
	• compare the text to others	
Stage 5	*Extending*	*Publishing*
	Readers	Writers
	• go beyond the text to extend their inter-pretations	• produce the finished copy of their compositions
	• share projects with classmates	• share their compositions with genuine
	• reflect on the reading process	audiences
	• make connections to life and literature	• reflect on the writing process
	• value the piece of literature	• value the composition
	• feel success	• feel success
	• want to read again	• want to write again

Source: Adapted from Butler, A., & Turbill, J. (1984). *Towards a Reading-writing Classroom.* Portsmouth, NH: Heinemann. © Gail E. Tompkins

similarities between the activities listed for responding and revising—the third stage in reading and writing, respectively.

Reading and writing are multidimensional and involve concurrent, complex transactions between writers, between writers as readers, between readers, and between readers as writers. Writers participate in several types of reading activities. They read other authors' works to obtain ideas and to learn about the structure of stories, but they also read and reread their own work in order to problem solve, discover, monitor, and clarify. That is, readers are involved in many of the same activities that writers use—generating ideas, organizing, monitoring, problem solving, and revising. F. Smith (1982) believes that reading influences writing skills because readers unconsciously "read like writers":

> To read like a writer we engage with the author in what the author is writing. We can anticipate what the author will say, so that the author is in effect writing on our behalf, not showing how something is done but doing it with us.... . Bit by bit, one thing at a time, but enormous numbers of things over the passage of time, the learner learns through reading like a writer to write like a writer. (pp. 563–564)

Also, both reading and writing are recursive, cycling back through various parts of the process; and, just as writers compose text, readers compose their meaning.

Classroom Connections

Teachers can help students appreciate the similarities between reading and writing in many ways:

1. Help writers assume alternative points of view as potential readers.
2. Help readers consider the writer's purpose and viewpoint.
3. Point out that reading is much like composing, so that students will view reading as a process, much like the writing process.
4. Talk with students about the similarities between the reading and writing processes.
5. Talk with students about similarities and linkages between reading and writing strategies.

For more information on reading and writing strategies, see Chapter 2, "Teaching the Language Arts," pages 55–58.

Other Considerations in Teaching Reading and Writing Processes

A BALANCED APPROACH

It is important to consider and maintain balance when teaching students to read and write. In a balanced language arts program, teachers devote attention to each component in accordance with its importance to literacy development and students' needs. Our responsibility as teachers is to discern the level and intensity of instruction required for individuals or small groups and then to modify our instruction accordingly. Likewise, students learn at different rates. In a balanced language arts program, the teacher makes adjustments for these and other variables.

Balanced instruction guides a teacher's instructional decision making. Teachers wishing to achieve the highest rate of reading and writing success for their students will continuously seek balance in the following areas:

- teacher-directed explicit instruction and learner-centred discovery learning
- sequenced, prescribed instruction and curriculum based on learner needs
- isolated skill emphasis with meaning-emphasis methods

- unplanned and planned instruction
- student- and teacher-selected materials
- integration of the processes of all the language arts within the context (Blair-Larsen & Williams, 1999)

GENDER DIFFERENCES IN READING AND WRITING

As early as kindergarten and grade 1, the differences in the reading and writing preferences of girls and boys are evident. In writing, stereotypical gender roles and relationships are reflected in the characters, plots, and styles of children's stories (S. Peterson, 2001). In reading, research also shows that some boys resist aesthetic reading of fictional texts and have difficulty expressing their feelings in peer groups about what they have read. It is important to consider gender differences when teaching reading and writing to children and young adults (Cole, 1997).

The following examples illustrate these differences. In their writing, grade 1 girls tend to choose domesticated animals (e.g., cats, horses), while boys choose animals that are dangerous and wild (cougars, monsters). Grade 2 girls choose primary territory as the focus of their writing (home, school, parents, friends), while boys choose secondary territory (professions) or extended territory (wars, space) as the focus of their writing (Newkirk, 2000).

Boys read far less than girls at all age levels. By adolescence, 85 percent of girls read for pleasure compared with only 65 percent of boys (Moffitt & Wartella, 1992). And the choices of what they read differ significantly. Girls are interested in stories that emphasize personal feelings and relationships, and boys prefer scary stories, sports books, adventure stories, comics, and magazines. By adolescence, boys will have spent countless hours reading guides for video games.

Teachers who are sensitive to these needs use strategies that encourage boys in reading and writing what is of interest to them (Young & Brozo, 2001). Reading aloud to boys from texts that reflect their interests will help them continue to develop as competent readers. As well, by introducing texts that reflect the choices and preferences of both genders, teachers help broaden boys' and girls' interests and their appreciation for each other.

A balanced approach to gender issues in reading and writing focuses on what is of interest to students, with activities that students find personally meaningful (Au, 1997). The idea that children learn to read by reading and to write by writing remains true. However, we need to accommodate gender differences by expanding our notions of what is of interest to boys and girls and by valuing those differences as boys and girls grow and develop into mature readers and writers.

Assessing Students' Reading and Writing

Assessing students' learning in the language arts is a complex task. Although it may seem fairly easy to develop and administer a criterion-referenced test, tests measure language skills rather than students' ability to use language in authentic ways. Nor do tests measure listening, speaking, viewing, and representing very well. A test on punctuation marks, for example, does not indicate students' ability to use punctuation marks correctly in their own writing. Instead, such a test typically evaluates students' ability to add punctuation marks to a set of sentences created by someone else, or to proofread and spot punctuation errors in someone else's writing.

Classroom assessment should be authentic, that is, students should be evaluated on how well they can use the six language arts in meaningful activities and projects. Students, too, participate in reflecting on, and self-assessing their learning. Authentic assessment has five purposes:

1. to document progress in students' language and literacy development
2. to identify students' strengths and needs in order to plan for instruction
3. to document students' language arts activities and projects
4. to determine grades
5. to help teachers learn more about how students become strategic readers and writers

Although it seems that increasing attention is given to high-stakes, standardized assessment and test results, authentic assessment is the key to effective instruction. Through authentic assessment, teachers learn about their students, about themselves as teachers, and about the impact of the instructional program. Similarly, when students reflect on their learning and use self-assessment, they learn about themselves as learners and also about their learning. The Teacher's Notebook "Guidelines for Authentic Assessment" describes how teachers use authentic assessment tools in their classrooms.

Monitoring Students' Progress

Teachers monitor students' progress as they are involved in language arts and across-the-curriculum activities during resource-based units, theme study units, and inquiry-based units. Six ways to monitor students' progress are classroom observations, anecdotal notes, conferences, checklists, miscue analyses, and running records. In addition to these informal and teacher-designed classroom assessments, provincial departments of education administer standardized assessments. Teachers and students also engage in portfolio development to monitor progress over time. To determine students' progress and especially to identify reading difficulties that impede progress, teachers conduct miscue analysis as they complete informal reading inventories.

Teachers monitor students' progress through conferences during writers workshops.

Guidelines for Authentic Assessment

1. Choose Appropriate Assessment Tools
Teachers identify their purpose for assessment and choose an appropriate assessment tool. To judge students' spelling development, for example, teachers examine students' spelling in stories they write and their use of proofreading, as well as their performance on spelling tests.

2. Use a Variety of Assessment Tools
Teachers regularly use a variety of authentic assessment tools that reflect current theories about how children learn, including anecdotal notes and reading logs. Using a variety of tools increases the likelihood of identifying growth and instructional needs.

3. Integrate Instruction and Assessment
Teachers use the results of assessment to inform their teaching. They observe and conference with students as they teach and supervise students during language arts activities. When teachers observe that students do not understand, they need to try other instructional procedures.

4. Keep a Positive Focus
Teachers focus on what students can do, not what they can't do. They should focus on how to facilitate students' continuous development as readers, writers, and users of language.

5. Consider Both Processes and Products
Teachers examine both the language processes students use and the products they create. Teachers notice the strategies students use for language activities as well as assess the quality of students' visual representations, oral reading, compositions, and other products.

6. Consider Multiple Contexts
Teachers assess students' language arts development in a variety of contexts, including specific language arts activities and across-the-curriculum learning activities. Multiple contexts are important because students often demonstrate different competencies from one context to another.

7. Focus on Individual Students
In addition to whole-class assessments, teachers make time to observe, conference, and do other assessment procedures, such as running records with individual students to develop a clear understanding of a student's development.

8. Teach Students to Self-Assess Their Learning
Self-assessment is an integral part of assessment. Students need to learn to judiciously reflect on their progress and to recognize their strengths and areas that need further development.

CLASSROOM OBSERVATIONS

Language arts teachers engage in "kid watching," as they informally watch students participating in language arts activities (Owocki & Goodman, 2002). To be an effective kid watcher, teachers must understand how children develop language and the role of errors in language learning. Teachers engage in kid watching spontaneously when they interact with children and are attentive to their behaviour and comments. Other observation times should be planned when the teacher focuses on particular students and makes anecdotal notes about the students' involvement in literacy events and other language arts activities. The focus is on what students do as they use oral and written language, and the effects on the students' language use of any intervention offered by the teacher.

ANECDOTAL NOTES

Teachers write brief notes as they observe students, and the most useful notes describe specific events, report rather than evaluate, and relate the events to other information about the students (Rhodes & Nathenson-Mejia, 1992). Teachers make notes about students' performance in listening, speaking, reading, writing, viewing, and visually representing activities; the questions students ask; and the strategies and skills they use fluently or indicate confusion about. These records document students' growth and pinpoint problem areas for future minilessons and conferences. A year-long collection of anecdotal notes provides a comprehensive picture of a student's learning in the language arts. An excerpt from a grade 5 teacher's anecdotal notes about one student's progress during a unit on Canada in the early 1900s is shown in Figure 5-9.

Several organizational schemes for anecdotal notes are possible, and teachers choose the format that is most comfortable for them. Some teachers make a card file with dividers for each child and write anecdotes on note cards. They jot notes on these small cards or even carry around a set of cards in a pocket. Other teachers divide a spiral-bound notebook into sections for each child and write anecdotes in the notebook, which they keep on their desk. Some teachers write anecdotes on sheets of paper and clip the sheets into students' assessment folders or file them in loose-leaf binders organized with a section for each student. Still others make notes on a tablet and maintain computer files that allow for easy access and additions.

CONFERENCES

Teachers meet with students to monitor their progress in language arts activities as well as to set goals and help students solve problems. Seven types of conferences are

FIGURE 5-9 ANECDOTAL NOTES ABOUT ONE STUDENT'S LEARNING DURING A THEME STUDY UNIT ON CANADA IN THE EARLY 1900s

Notes about Matthew

March 5	Matthew selected Prime Minister William Lyon Mackenzie King as historical figure for Canada in the early 1900s.
March 11	Matthew fascinated with information he has found about M. K. Brought several sources from home. Is completing M. K.'s lifeline with many details.
March 18	Simulated journal. Four entries in four days! Interesting how he picked up language style of the period in his journal. Volunteers to share daily. I think he enjoys the oral sharing more than the writing.
March 25	Nine simulated journal entries, all illustrated. High level of enthusiasm.
March 29	Conferenced about cluster for M. K. biography. Well-developed with five rays, many details. Matthew will work on "contributions" ray. He recognized it as the least-developed one.
April 2	Three chapters of biography drafted. Talked about "working titles" for chapters and choosing more interesting titles after writing that reflects the content of the chapters.
April 7	Drafting conference. Matthew has completed all five chapters. He and Dustin are competitive, both writing on M. K. They are reading each other's chapters and checking the accuracy of information.
April 12	Writers group. Chapters longer and more complete since drafting conference. Compared with autobiography project, writing is more sophisticated. Longer, too. Reading is influencing writing style—e.g.,"I have a great future." He is still somewhat defensive about accepting suggestions except from me. He will make 3 revisions—agreed in writers group.
April 15	Revisions: (1) eliminated "he" (substitute), (2) re-sequenced Chapter 3 (move), and (3) added sentences in Chapter 5 (add).
April 19	Proofread with Dustin. Working hard.
April 23	Editing conference—no major problems. Discussed use of commas within sentences, capitalizing proper nouns. Matthew and Dustin more task-oriented on this project; I see more motivation and commitment.
April 29	Final copy of biography completed and shared with class.

described in the accompanying Teacher's Notebook. The type of conference selected by the teacher is dependent upon the purpose for conferring with the student. Some conferences are brief and impromptu, held at students' desks as the teacher moves around the classroom, whereas at other times the conferences are planned and students meet with the teacher at a designated conference table.

The teacher's role is to be listener and guide. Teachers can learn a great deal about students and their learning if they listen as students talk about their reading, writing, or other activities (Miller, 2014).

When students explain a problem they are having, the teacher is often able to decide on a way to work through it. Teachers balance the amount of their talk with the student's talk during the conference, and, at the end, reflect on what the student has taught them, what responsibilities the student can take on, and whether the student understands what to do next.

CHECKLISTS

Teachers use checklists as they observe students; they track students' progress during instructional units by documenting use of language arts skills, strategies, procedures, and concepts. For example, when students participate in writing conferences in which they read their compositions to small groups of classmates and ask for suggestions for improving their writing, teachers can note whether students participate fully in the group, share their writing with classmates, gracefully accept suggestions about improving their writing, and make substantive changes in their writing based on some of their classmates' suggestions. Students, too, can use checklists to monitor

TEACHER'S NOTEBOOK

Seven Types of Conferences

1. On-the-Spot Conferences
Teachers visit briefly with students to monitor some aspect of the students' work or to check on progress. These conferences are brief; the teacher may spend less than a minute with each student.

2. Prereading or Prewriting Conferences
The teacher and student make plans for reading or writing at the conference. At a prereading conference, they may talk about information related to the book, difficult concepts or vocabulary related to the reading, or the reading log the student will keep. At a prewriting conference, they may discuss possible writing topics or how to narrow a broad topic.

3. Revising Conferences
A small group of students and the teacher meet to provide writers with specific suggestions for revising their compositions. These conferences offer student writers an audience to provide feedback on how well they have communicated.

4. Book Discussion Conferences
Students and the teacher meet to discuss the book they have read. They may share reading log entries, discuss plot or characters,

compare the story with others they have read, or make plans to extend their reading.

5. Editing Conferences
The teacher reviews students' proofread compositions and helps them correct spelling, punctuation, capitalization, and other mechanical errors.

6. Minilesson Conferences
The teacher meets with students to explain a procedure, strategy, or skill (e.g., writing a table of contents, using the visualization strategy when reading, or capitalizing proper nouns).

7. Assessment Conferences
The teacher meets with students after they have completed an assignment or project to talk about their growth as readers or writers. Students reflect on their competencies and set goals.

their performance and progress. Experienced teachers recommend that students participate in constructing checklists so that they understand what is expected of them.

Middle-grade students might complete the sample checklist in Figure 5-10 to monitor their work during readers and writers workshops. Notice that students are directed to write a letter to the teacher on the back of the sheet, reflecting on their work.

MISCUE ANALYSES

Teachers often need to assess students' reading in a focused way to help determine instructional needs, particularly when students are struggling to read fluently and with understanding. One way that teachers can do such assessment is through *miscue analysis*. Miscue analysis involves working individually with one student at a time. The term **miscue**, coined by Goodman (1969), occurs when what the reader says does not match the printed text.

Miscue analysis can help teachers identify what strategies the reader is using and point to the areas where instruction is needed. Miscue analysis can also help teachers determine whether a reader is attending to letters and sounds, to meaning, or to both. In addition, it can point out when the reader is making substitutions, mispronunciations, and omissions. Miscue analysis helps teachers answer two questions: Is the reader attending to print at the word or within-word level? Is the reader attending to meaning?

Miscue analysis involves teacher preparation, student oral reading, and teacher recording and analysis of reading errors. To prepare, the teacher needs to select one or more short passages to be read by the student. Two copies of the text are needed, one from which the student reads and one on which the teacher writes. Choosing the level of text can be challenging, but a rule of thumb is to choose a text with which the teacher anticipates the student will have some success.

FIGURE 5-10 ASSESSMENT CHECKLIST

Readers–Writers Workshop Activity Sheet

Name_____		Week_____	
Read independently	M T W Th F	Made a cluster	M T W Th F
Wrote in a reading log	M T W Th F	Wrote a rough draft	M T W Th F
Listened to the teacher read a loud	M T W Th F	Went to a writing group	M T W Th F
Read with a classmate	M T W Th F	Made revisions	M T W Th F
Read at the listening centre	M T W Th F	Proofread my own writing	M T W Th F
Had a reading conference	M T W Th F	Had a writing conference	M T W Th F
Shared a book with classmates	M T W Th F	Shared my writing with classmates	M T W Th F
Other		Other	
Interesting words read this week		Spelling words needed this week	
Titles of books read		Titles of writings	

Write a letter on the back, thinking about the week and your reading and writing.

The teacher asks the student to read aloud. While the student reads, the teacher records the student's reading errors on the second copy of the text. The teacher uses a system of symbols, as shown in Figure 5-11, that facilitate quick recording. Some teachers record the oral reading so that it can be reviewed.

Following the reading, the teacher reviews the reading errors, observing the types of errors made and looking for patterns in those errors. By observing reading errors, the teacher can hypothesize which cues from the text the student uses and what instruction is needed to improve the student's reading. Figure 5-11 shows miscue analysis of Christopher's reading and the teacher's interpretation.

FIGURE 5-11 MISCUE ANALYSIS: CHRISTOPHER'S READING AND THE TEACHER'S INTERPRETATION

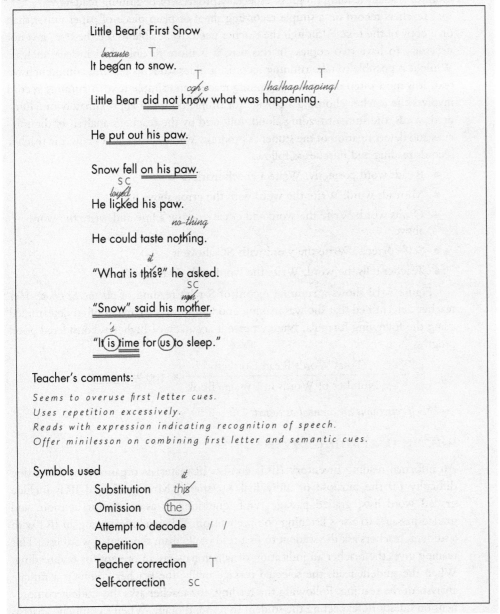

Miscue analysis is a component of two other forms of assessment that are popular in Canadian schools: running records and informal reading inventories (IRIs). Each has unique characteristics, but both are forms of individual assessment. Many schools choose to adopt a system such as the Fountas & Pinnell (2008) Benchmark Assessment System, which provides measurement tools and texts for every grade level to assist teachers with their assessment procedures.

RUNNING RECORDS

A running record (Clay, 1985) is similar to miscue analysis in that it is a way to record what students do while reading a text aloud. Teachers record the reading to see the strengths and weaknesses in the use of cues and strategies. The primary purpose is to determine whether a text is easy, appropriate, or difficult for a student. Teachers use running records to aid them in choosing appropriate materials for students and to monitor student reading progress, especially progress of beginning readers.

Teachers record on a simple recording sheet or plain piece of paper rather than on a copy of the text. Although the teacher needs to be able to see the text, it is not necessary to have two copies. In this way, it is more flexible than miscue analysis. While it is possible to take running records of older students reading comprehensive text, it is most often used with beginning readers and simple text. A running record involves the teacher choosing a passage (or simple book) of approximately one hundred words, the student reading aloud, followed by the teacher's analysis of the miscues and determination of the student's progress. While the student reads, the teacher records reading and miscues as follows:

- Reads word correctly: Write a check mark (✓).
- Misreads word: Write the word with the error above it.
- Omits word: Write the word and circle or draw a line and write the word above.
- Self-corrects: Write the word with *SC* above it.
- Teacher tells the word: Write the word with *T* above it.

Figure 5-12 shows a running record of Sarah's reading of *At the Seashore*. Her teacher determined that she was making good progress. Progress is often determined using the following formula. Ninety percent accuracy or higher is considered good progress.

$$\frac{\text{Total Words Read Correctly*}}{\text{Number of Words in Passage/Book}} \times 100 = \underline{\hspace{2em}}\%$$

Self-corrections are counted as correct.

INFORMAL READING INVENTORIES

An informal reading inventory (IRI) consists of materials organized by increasing difficulty for the purpose of individual assessment. Most published IRIs include graded word lists, graded passages with questions to assess comprehension, and graded passages to assess listening comprehension. When administering an IRI with a student, teachers ask the student to first read orally from the graded word lists. This reading gives the teacher an indication of which passages to present for oral reading. When the student reads the selected passage orally, the teacher conducts a miscue analysis of the reading. Following the reading, the teacher asks the student comprehension questions, expecting the student to respond orally. When the miscue analysis

FIGURE 5-12 RUNNING RECORD: SARAH'S READING OF AT THE SEASHORE

Text: At the Seashore.

I can build a sandcastle.

The castle is white and pink.

I can dig a clam.

The clam is small and round.

I can see the waves.

I cannot catch the waves.

Student: At the Seashore.

I can make a sandcastle.

The castle is white and pink.

I can big a car.

The car is small, is small, and red.

I can see the waves.

I can catch the waves.

Running Record:

✓	✓	✓			
✓	✓	make build	✓	✓	
✓	✓	✓	✓	✓	✓
✓	✓	dig big	✓	car clam	
✓	car clam	R	R		red round
		✓	✓	✓	
✓	✓	✓	✓	✓	✓
✓	can cannot	✓	✓	✓	

Teacher's Analysis:

Attends to meaning and seems to use picture cues. Tends to focus only on first letter cues.

$$\frac{29\ Correct}{35\ Words} \times 100 = 85\%\ Needs\ more\ practice\ at\ this\ level.$$

is complete, the teacher reviews the information to determine the cues the student is using or not using and what instruction is needed. If listening comprehension is included in the analysis, the teacher reads passages to the student and follows the reading with oral questioning.

Despite controversy regarding best practices in reading assessment, IRIs remain popular because they provide information needed for teachers to plan instruction. When administered in their complete form, they give teachers a clear indication of the levels of text with which students will be frustrated, will be able to read with assistance, and those they can read independently. Many published IRIs are available, but teachers can also create their own using classroom reading materials. One criticism often raised is that using published IRIs means asking students to read inauthentic texts—that is, to read the texts prepared especially for testing, as opposed to literature texts in regular use in classrooms. To overcome this potential weakness, yet maintain the strength of IRIs as diagnostic tools, some teachers with whom we work include reading of both test materials and literature selections when they assess their students.

Implementing Portfolios in the Classroom

Portfolios are systematic and meaningful collections of artifacts documenting students' language arts learning and development over a period of time (De Fina, 1992; D. H. Graves & Sunstein, 1992; Porter & Cleland, 1995). Students' work samples provide "windows" on the strategies that students employ as language users—listeners, speakers, readers, writers, viewers, and visual representers.

There are many reasons why portfolio assessment complements language arts instruction. The most important one is that students become involved in the assessment of their work and are reflective about the quality of their reading, writing, and other language use. Other benefits include the following:

- Students feel ownership of their work.
- Students accept responsibility for their work.
- Students set goals and are motivated to work toward accomplishing them.
- Students reflect on their accomplishments.
- Students make connections between learning and assessing.
- Students' self-esteem is enhanced.
- Students recognize the connection between process and product.

In addition, portfolios eliminate the need to grade all student work. Portfolios are useful in student and parent conferences and complement the information provided in report cards.

COLLECTING WORK IN PORTFOLIOS

Portfolios can hold hard copies or electronic copies of students' work and may be folders, large envelopes, binders, or boxes. Teachers often have students label and decorate large folders and then store them in plastic crates or large cardboard boxes. One teacher with whom we work uses presentation binders for portfolios in her classroom. At the beginning of the school year, she takes and prints digital photographs of each child for the portfolio cover. Students date and label items as they place them in their portfolios, and they attach notes to the items to explain the context of the activity and why they selected that particular item for inclusion in the portfolio. Students' portfolios should be stored in the classroom in a place readily accessible to students. Students review their portfolios periodically and add new pieces to them.

Students usually choose the items to place in their portfolios, within the guidelines provided by their teacher. However, teachers may require that particular items be included. In addition to the writing and art samples, students also record electronically audio and video samples of oral language and drama to accompany the work in their portfolios. Large-size art and writing projects can be photographed, and the photographs placed in the portfolio or online. Figure 5-13 lists examples of what might be placed in a portfolio.

Not all work that is placed in a student's portfolio needs to be graded in the same manner that tests are graded. It may be appropriate on some occasions to simply indicate that a piece is "complete" or "satisfactory." Teachers should encourage

FIGURE 5-13 EXAMPLES OF PORTFOLIO ARTIFACTS

Listening
- picture or other interpretation of music
- notes of information presented orally
- pictures showing audience for peer report
- drawings or log entries to represent recorded stories listened to
- pictures showing listening at listening station

Speaking
- puppet show (on video)
- oral reports (on audiotape or video)
- cue cards and audiotape of speech or debate

Reading
- reading logs
- oral reading (recordings of oral reading)
- readers theatre (recording of readers theatre performance)

Writing
- journal entries
- letters
- poems
- reports
- stories

Viewing
- Venn diagrams comparing stories and film versions
- clusters or semantic maps of information, or story of video
- pictures to interpret video watched
- notes comparing paintings viewed

Visually Representing
- multimedia reports on disc
- Venn diagrams of information read
- timelines or life lines
- drawings to communicate information
- illustrations to interpret stories

All items should be accompanied by a brief explanation of what the artifact represents for student learning and the date it was placed in the portfolio.

inclusion of pieces that show process and improvement as well as finished products and "best work."

Finally, the most significant aspect of this kind of assessment is that portfolios involve reflection. Through reflection, students become aware of their strengths as readers, writers, and language users. They use their work samples to identify the language arts skills, strategies, procedures, and concepts they already know, and the ones they need to focus on. (Students include written reflections in their portfolios.) That is, they become metacognitively aware: they understand not only what they know, but also how they learn and what they need to learn.

Assigning Grades

Assigning grades is one of the most difficult responsibilities placed on teachers. The authentic assessment procedures described in this chapter are meaningful and encourage students because they document how students are using the language arts in authentic ways. Reviewing and translating this documentation into grades is the difficult part. Checklists and rubrics are useful tools that teachers use to assign grades.

Students can keep track of assignments by using checklists. Teachers create assignment checklists as they plan a unit, giving students a copy of the checklist at the beginning of the unit to keep in their unit folder. Then, as they complete the assignments, students check them off, sometimes adding notes of their reflections about their learning while doing the assignment. Checklists help both students and teachers make periodic checks of student progress toward completion of unit activities and assignments.

A checklist for a grade 2 theme study unit on hermit crabs is presented in Figure 5-14. Eight assignments included on the checklist include both science and language arts activities. Students put a check in the boxes in the "Student's Check" column when they complete each assignment, and the teacher adds the grade in the right-hand column. Some assignments will be graded as simply "completed" and

FIGURE 5-14 TWO ASSIGNMENT CHECKLISTS

Checklist for Theme Study Unit on Hermit Crabs

Name _____   Begin _____

                                         End _____

	Student's Check	Teacher's Check
1. Keep an observation log on the hermit crab on your table for 10 days.	☐	____
2. Make a chart of a hermit crab and label the parts.	☐	____
3. Make a map of the hermit crab's habitat.	☐	____
4. Read three books about hermit crabs and do quickwrites about them.	☐	____
_____ Hermit Crabs		
_____ A House for Hermit Crab		
_____ Is This a House for Hermit Crab?		
5. Do two science experiments and write lab reports.	☐	____
_____ Wet–Dry Experiment		
_____ Light–Dark Experiment		
6. Write about hermit crabs. Do one:	☐	____
_____ All about Hermit Crabs book		
_____ A poem about hermit crabs		
_____ A story about hermit crabs		
7. Do a project about hermit crabs. Share it.	☐	____
8. Keep everything neatly in your hermit crab folder.	☐	____

Number the Stars Grading Sheet

Name _____   Date _____

_____1. Read *Number the Stars*.	(25)	____
_____2. Write 5 entries in a reading log or simulated journal.	(25)	____
_____3. Talk about your reading in five grand conversations.	(10)	____
_____4. Make a Venn diagram to compare characters. Summarize what you learned from the diagram in an essay.	(5)	____
_____5. Make a cluster about one word on the word wall.	(10)	____
_____6. Make a square with a favourite quote for the story quilt.	(25)	____
_____7. Do a response project.	(100)	____
Total		

others will be graded for quality. When teachers grade for quality, they explain the criteria to students and provide them with a written description of the criteria such as in the rubrics discussed below. The second checklist in Figure 5-14 is for a grade 5 resource-based unit on *Number the Stars* (Lowry, 1989) and could easily be adapted for any novel study. The point value for each activity is listed in parentheses. Students write check marks on the lines on the left side of the grading sheet, and the teacher marks the numerical grades on the right side.

The checklists in Figure 5-14 refer only to completion of projects and assignments.

RUBRICS

Teachers and students develop **rubrics**, or scoring guides, to assess students' growth as writers (Skillings & Ferrell, 2000). Rubrics make the analysis of writing simpler and the assessment process more reliable and consistent. Rubrics may have three, four, five, or six levels, with descriptors related to ideas, organization, language, and mechanics at each level. Some rubrics are general and appropriate for almost any writing project, while others are designed for a specific writing assignment. Figure 5-15

FIGURE 5-15 TWO RUBRICS FOR WRITING ASSESSMENT

Middle-Grade Writing Rubric

5. Exceptional Achievement
- Creative and original
- Clear organization
- Precise word choice and figurative language
- Sophisticated sentences
- Essentially free of mechanical errors

4. Excellent Achievement
- Some creativity, but more predictable than an exceptional paper
- Definite organization
- Good word choice but not figurative language
- Varied sentences
- Only a few mechanical errors

3. Adequate Achievement
- Predictable paper
- Some organization
- Adequate word choice
- Little variety of sentences and some run-on sentences
- Some mechanical errors

2. Limited Achievement
- Brief and superficial
- Lacks organization
- Imprecise language
- Incomplete and run-on sentences
- Many mechanical errors

1. Minimal Achievement
- No ideas communicated
- No organization
- Inadequate word choice
- Sentence fragments
- Overwhelming mechanical errors

(continued)

FIGURE 5-15 **TWO RUBRICS (CONTINUED)**

Rubric for Assessing Reports on Ancient Egypt

4. Excellent Report
_____Three or more chapters with titles
_____Main idea clearly developed in each chapter
_____Three or more illustrations
_____Effective use of Egypt-related words in text and illustrations
_____Very interesting to read
_____Very few mechanical errors
_____Table of content

3. Good Report
_____Three chapters with titles
_____Main idea somewhat developed in each chapter
_____Three illustrations
_____Some Egypt-related words used
_____Interesting to read
_____A few mechanical errors
_____Table of content

2. Average Report
_____Three chapters
_____Main idea identified in each chapter
_____One or two illustrations
_____A few Egypt-related words used
_____Some mechanical errors
_____Sort of interesting to read
_____Table of content

1. Poor Report
_____One or two chapters
_____Information in each chapter rambles
_____No illustrations
_____Very few Egypt-related words used
_____Many mechanical errors
_____Hard to read and understand
_____No table of content

presents two rubrics. One is a general five-level writing rubric for middle-grade students, and the other is a four-level rubric for assessing grade 6 students' reports on ancient Egypt. In contrast to the general rubric, the report rubric includes specific components that students were to include in their reports. Many websites offer helpful assistance with creating rubrics tailored to your goals and projects. One such website, which classroom teachers we know find easy to use, is http://teach-nology. com/web_tools/rubrics.

Teachers and students can assess writing with rubrics. They read the composition and highlight words or check statements in the rubric that best describe the composition. It is important to note that rarely are all the highlighted words or checked statements at the same level. Examine the highlighted words or checked statements to determine the score and which level best represents the quality of the composition.

To assess students' learning fairly and systematically, teachers should use at least three assessment approaches. Approaching evaluation from three viewpoints is called _triangulation_. Triangulation of assessment data fosters accurate and reliable evaluation.

Using a variety of techniques enables students to show their strengths and increases the likelihood of the evaluation accurately representing the students' learning, performance, and skills.

Large-Scale Formal Assessment

Although it is beyond the scope of this text to describe large-scale formal assessment and **standardized achievement tests** or to discuss the topic of setting standards, we would be remiss not to note that most provinces and territories engage in annual assessment of student achievement in the language arts, in particular, reading and writing. Students are required to read narrative and informational text and to respond in both structured and creative ways. They also compose more than one form of writing, showing both their process and their written products.

The goal of provincial testing is to provide a means of assessing student performance against a standard and to improve student learning. For example, in Alberta, reading and writing are formally assessed in grades 6 and 9, while in Newfoundland and Labrador, reading and language skills are assessed in grades 4, 7, 10, and 12. Although policies and practices regarding use and distribution of assessment results vary from province to province, they are generally studied carefully by schools and school jurisdictions to plan their programs. Results are usually shared with parents on the basis of overall grade achievement—not on a per-pupil basis. Standardized tests assess cumulative growth and achievement, not just learning in the grade assessed. It is important, therefore, for teachers of all grades to be guided by their students' results, not just those of the students that write the standardized tests.

Review

Reading and writing are similar processes of constructing meaning. Teachers organize reading and writing instruction using the five stages of the reading and writing processes. Students learn to use the reading and writing processes through resource-based, thematic, and inquiry-based units as well as through readers and writers workshops. Assessment is an integral part of instruction, and should be authentic.

Note: In addition to the overview of authentic assessment presented in this chapter, assessment considerations specific to the content will also be presented in the remaining chapters of the text.

The following key concepts are presented in this chapter:

1. The five stages of reading are: preparing, reading, responding, exploring, and extending.
2. Students use aesthetic reading when they read for enjoyment and efferent reading when they read for information.
3. Students use the Goldilocks Strategy or a modified version of it to choose books at their reading level.
4. Five ways to read a selection are: shared reading, guided reading, independent reading, buddy reading, and reading aloud.
5. The five stages of the writing process are: prewriting, drafting, revising, editing, and publishing.

6. Purpose, form, and audience are three considerations that influence students' compositions.

7. Teachers present minilessons on procedures, concepts, skills, and strategies in the reading and writing processes.

8. There are gender differences in reading and writing that influence effective learning and teaching.

9. The goal of both reading and writing is to construct meaning, and both processes have comparable activities at each stage.

10. Teachers use authentic assessment procedures, including classroom observations, anecdotal notes, conferences, checklists, portfolios, and rubrics.

11. Teachers assess individual students' use of reading cues and strategies by conducting miscue analysis.

12. Running records and informal reading inventories (IRIs) include miscue analysis procedures.

Theory to Practice

1. Observe students using the reading and writing processes in an elementary or middle-school classroom. In what types of preparing, reading, responding, exploring, and extending activities are they involved?

2. Observe students using the writing process. What minilessons would be beneficial to them?

3. Plan a resource-based unit or theme study unit and include a variety of activities on the reading and writing processes.

4. Sit in on a writers group in which students share their writing and ask peers for feedback in revising their compositions. Make a list of the students' questions and comments. What conclusions can you draw about their interactions with each other?

5. Reflect on your own reading and writing processes. Are you conscious of moving through the stages when you are engaged in reading and writing? What strategies do you use at each stage? How do you vary your reading when you read aesthetically and efferently?

6. Observe students writing on a computer. How do they engage in the writing process as they work?

7. Interview an elementary teacher and ask about the kinds of assessment he or she uses.

8. Through your provincial department of education website, research the practices related to standardized testing of the language arts.

Literacy in Action

Chapter 6: Short Story Writing

Procedure

To hook my grade 7 students into short story writing, I begin with a quickwriting activity called "The Neverending Story," in which students are given the beginning of the first line of a story, copy it in their journals, and complete the rest of the sentence on their own. Then they pass their journals to the next person, who reads what has been written and adds another sentence to the story. Students continue to pass journals, read what has been written and add another line until I indicate to end the story. Journals are returned to their owners; students get a chance to read how the story they started developed, and then they share it with the class.

I base my short story writing unit around the picture book *The Mysteries of Harris Burdick* (1996) by Chris Van Allsburg and show animations of the illustrations on YouTube. Students then choose an illustration to base their short story on, keeping in mind that they must use the illustration as a major setting as well as incorporate the caption underneath the illustration into their story.

Having students talk before writing is always important, and so I use the strategy of inner/outer circle, in which students share their chosen illustration and talk about what could be happening in the picture. Then, as part of their brainstorming process, they complete a plot diagram, which they hand in to me for teacher feedback.

> "I want my students to understand that their writing and ideas can evolve through the writing process and to feel empowered as writers to make decisions based on feedback."
>
> Grace Chan

Throughout the week, I have minilessons on the use of literacy devices, which students are required to incorporate in their stories as they write their first drafts. I always emphasize that the first draft is their opportunity to get their ideas down and to try and make sense of how they want their story to develop. It is not the time to worry about the technical aspects of writing. It is at this stage that I run peer-feedback conferences where students receive a peer's story to read and give feedback on ideas and plot development. Students get time to read the feedback and ask questions of their feedback provider. With peer feedback, students are ready to write their second draft, they need to focus not only on revising content but also on the technical aspects of writing (e.g., spelling and grammar) as they prepare for publishing.

Feedback is an important part of the writing process: student writers have the opportunity to see how effectively they have communicated their thoughts and ideas to their readers. This is why, after students have completed a second draft, they have another opportunity to receive peer feedback. They can also request feedback from the teacher. When students receive feedback on their second draft, they then edit their writing for publishing.

Assessment

During the first week of the unit, I develop the success criteria with the class and we establish the categories for the rubric that will be used to mark their final piece. I divide the class into groups and assign them a criterion to develop the descriptors for the four levels. We build the rubric using the descriptors created by the small groups. To address metacognition, students complete a reflection that tells me a strength of their writing piece, an area for improvement, and an area they feel they have grown in. I make anecdotal notes on students' ability to revise and edit using the feedback they received.

Adaptation

Often, English language learner (ELL) students write a shorter story that follows a simple story structure. They can also write using their first language. Some students need support with providing feedback and making revisions. Peer feedback can be done in pairs, and stories can be strategically assigned to feedback providers. Computer programs that read text back to students can help writers with their revisions.

Reflection

Clearly, the stages of the writing process take time and not all writing assignments will go through the process as described. I want my students to understand that their writing and ideas can evolve through the writing process and to feel empowered as writers to make decisions based on feedback. I often emphasize that they can disagree with their feedback providers but that they must keep in mind that the feedback allows them to gauge how well they have communicated their ideas to their readers. It is rewarding when students begin to ask for peer feedback in other writing tasks because they are engaging in the writing process without teacher direction.

From the classroom of Grace Chan, Intermediate Teacher
Kennedy Public School
Toronto, Ontario

Reading and Writing Narrative Text

Students are given many opportunities throughout the day to read and share self-selected texts.

Pressmaster/Shutterstock

Stories and poetry give meaning to the human experience, and are a powerful way of knowing and learning. Preschool children who listen to family members tell and read stories aloud develop a concept about stories by the time they come to school. Students' knowledge about stories is refined as they learn about plot, character, and other elements of story structure. They also learn to write their own stories through responding to others' stories and to events. Developing students' concept of story is crucial because it plays an important role in learning to comprehend and compose stories.

Concept of Story

Children's concept of story begins in the preschool years. Children as young as two years old have a rudimentary sense of story (Applebee, 1978), and older children seem to be instinctively aware of how stories develop. Children acquire this concept of story gradually, by listening to stories, reading stories, and telling and writing stories. The stories children tell and write become increasingly complex, the plot structures more tightly organized, the characters more fully developed.

Students' concept of story plays an important role in interpreting stories they read, and is just as important in writing. As they explore and respond to stories, students learn about elements of story structure and genre.

Elements of Story Structure

Stories have unique structural elements that distinguish them from other forms of literature, elements that include plot, characters, and setting. Authors manipulate the elements to make their stories complex and interesting. We will focus on five elements of story structure—plot, characters, setting, point of view, and theme—and illustrate each element using familiar and award-winning books.

PLOT

The sequence of events involving characters in conflict situations is the *plot*. It is based on the goals of one or more characters and the processes they go through to attain these goals (Lukens, 2006). The main characters want to achieve a goal, and other characters are introduced to oppose or assist them. The story events are put in motion by characters as they attempt to overcome conflict, solve their problems, and reach their goals. The most basic aspect of plot is the division of the story into three parts: *beginning*, *middle*, and *end*. Older students might substitute the terms *introduction*, *development* or *complication*, and *resolution*.

Conflict—the tension or opposition between forces in the plot—motivates readers to continue reading. Conflict usually occurs

- between a character and nature
- between a character and society
- between characters
- within a character (Lukens, 2006)

Conflict between a character and nature occurs in stories in which severe weather or natural disasters play an important role. In *Keeley and the Mountain* (Ellis, 2006b), small-town life in Frank, Alberta, is relatively uneventful until a rockslide buries much of the mining town. The main character, Keeley, must overcome challenges presented by nature in her plight to locate her father. Nature presents intense challenges in stories set in isolated geographic locations, such as *Peak* (R. Smith, 2008), in which the main character, Peak Marcello, travels to an Everest base camp in Tibet prepared to help his father run his adventure/expedition company. In some stories, a character's activities and beliefs differ from those of other members of the society, and the differences cause conflict.

Conflict between characters is common in children's literature. In *Keeper* (Appelt, 2010), ten-year old Keeper decides to search for her missing mother in the rough waters of the Gulf of Mexico during a rare blue moon. Conflict within a character occurs in stories such as *Me and the Blondes* (Toten, 2006) and *Princess Mia* (Cabot, 2009).

In *Me and the Blondes*, Sophie is determined to fit in at her new school but encounters multiple challenges as she devises a plan for making friends. *Princess Mia*, the ninth and penultimate instalment of the Princess Diaries series, features several character conflicts: Mia has broken up with Michael; her best friend, Lily, isn't speaking to her; Mia's parents are so worried about her emotional state that they are making her see a therapist; and Mia seems to have uncovered a secret that could alter Genovia's destiny.

Figure 6-1 lists stories representing the four types of conflict.

Plot is developed through conflict introduced in the beginning of a story, expanded in the middle, and resolved at the end. Plot development involves four components:

1. **A problem.** A problem that introduces conflict is presented at the beginning of a story.

2. **Roadblocks.** In the middle of the story, characters face roadblocks in attempting to solve the problem.

3. **The high point.** The high point in the action occurs when the problem is about to be solved. This high point separates the middle and end of the story.

4. **The solution.** The problem is solved and roadblocks are overcome at the end of the story.

CHARACTERS

Characters are often the most important element of story structure because many stories are centred on a character or group of characters. In *Anne of Green Gables* (Montgomery, 1908/1999), for example, the story focuses on Anne's struggles to

FIGURE 6-1 STORIES THAT ILLUSTRATE THE FOUR TYPES OF CONFLICT

Conflict between a Character and Nature
Bunting, E. (1991). *Fly Away Home*. New York: Clarion. (P–M)
Korman, G. (2001). *Island, Book 1: Shipwreck*. New York: Scholastic. (M–U)
Loyie, L. (2005). *As Long as the River Flows*. Toronto: HarperCollins. 🍁
MacLachlan, P. (1994). *Skylark*. New York: HarperCollins. (M)
Paulsen, G. (1996). *Brian's Winter*. New York: Dell. (M–U)
Poulsen, D. (1996). *Billy and the Bearman*. Toronto: Napoleon Publishing. (M–U) 🍁
Steward, S. (2003). *Raven Quest*. Toronto: Scholastic. (M–U) 🍁
Tullson, D. (2005). *Red Sea*. Victoria, BC: Orca Books. (U) 🍁

Conflict between a Character and Society
Brandis, M. (1985/2003). *The Quarter-Pie Window*. Toronto: Tundra Books. (U) 🍁
Ellis, D. (2002). *A Company of Fools*. Markham, ON: Fitzhenry & Whiteside. (M–U) 🍁
Langston, L. (2003). *Lesia's Dream*. Toronto: HarperTrophy. (M–U) 🍁
Polacco, P. (1994). *Pink and Say*. New York: Philomel. (M–U)
Taylor, C. (1994). *Summer of the Mad Monk*. Vancouver: Greystone Books. (M–U) 🍁
Uchida, Y. (1993). *The Bracelet*. New York: Philomel. (P–M)
Volponi, P. (2009). *Response*. Toronto: Viking. (U) 🍁
Walters, E. (2006). *Stuffed*. Victoria, BC: Orca Books. (M) 🍁

Conflict between Characters
Citra, B. (1999). *Ellie's New Home*. Victoria, BC: Orca Books. (M) 🍁

Ghent, N. (2003). *No Small Thing*. Toronto: HarperCollins. (M) 🍁
Higgs, S. (2006). *Best Friends, No Matter What*. Toronto: Scholastic. (P) 🍁
Lawrence, I. (2006). *Gemini Summer*. New York: Yearling. (M–U)
Naylor, P. R. (1991). *Shiloh*. New York: Atheneum. (M–U)
Paterson, K. (1994). *Flip-flop Girl*. New York: Lodestar. (U)
Rathmann, P. (1995). *Officer Buckle and Gloria*. New York: Putnam. (P)
Wynne-Jones, T. (1995). *The Maestro*. Toronto: Groundwood Books. (M–U) 🍁
Zelinsky, P. O. (1986). *Rumpelstiltskin*. New York: Dutton. (P–M)

Conflict within a Character
Cumyn, A. (2002). *The Secret Life of Owen Skye*. Toronto: Groundwood Books. (M–U) 🍁
Henkes, K. (1991). *Chrysanthemum*. New York: Greenwillow. (P)
Hudson, J. (1984). *Sweetgrass*. Edmonton: Tree Frog Press. (U) 🍁
Matas, C. (1995). *The Primrose Path*. Winnipeg: Blizzard Publishing. (U) 🍁
Nicholson, S. (2005). *Against the Boards*. Toronto: James Lorimer. (M–U) 🍁
Resau, L. (2007). *Red Glass*. New York: Delacourte Press. (M)
Skrypuch, M. (2001). *Hope's War*. Toronto: Boardwalk Books. (U) 🍁
Trottier, M. (2006). *Three Songs for Courage*. Toronto: Tundra Books. (U) 🍁

P = primary grades (K–2); M = middle grades (3–5); U = upper grades (6–8).

FIGURE 6-2 STORIES WITH FULLY DEVELOPED MAIN CHARACTERS

Character	Story
Lee	Bell, W. (2006). *The Blue Helmet*. Toronto: Doubleday. (U) 🍁
Jolene	Beveridge, C. (2003). *Shadows of Disaster*. Vancouver: Ronsdale Press. (M–U) 🍁
Franklin	Bourgeois, P. (2003). *Franklin's Reading Club*. Toronto: Kids Can Press. (P) 🍁
Mary Ann Alice	Doyle, B. (2001). *Mary Ann Alice*. Vancouver: Douglas & McIntyre. (M–U) 🍁
Ellen	Givner, J. (2004). *Ellen Fremedon*. Toronto: Groundwood Books. (M–U) 🍁
Chrysanthemum	Henkes, K. (1991). *Chrysanthemum*. New York: Greenwillow. (P)
Travis	Huser, G. (2003). *Stitches*. Toronto: Groundwood Books (M) 🍁
Logan	Langston, L. (2006). *Exit Point*. Victoria, BC: Orca Books. (U) 🍁
Blake	McNaughton, L. (2006). *The Raintree Rebellion*. Toronto: HarperTrophy. (U) 🍁
Marty	Paulsen, G. (1999). *Brian's Return*. New York: Delacourte Press.
Harry	Rowling, J. K. (2007). *Harry Potter and the Deathly Hallows*. London: Bloomsbury. (M–U)
Matthew	Slade, A. (2001). *Dust*. Toronto: HarperCollins. (U) 🍁
Miriam	Skrypuch, M. (2003). *Nobody's Child*. Toronto: Dundurn Press (M–U) 🍁
Stargirl	Spinelli, J. (2000). *Stargirl*. New York: Knopf. (U)
Casey	Thayer, E. L. (2006). *Casey at the Bat*. Toronto: Kids Can Press. (M) 🍁
Winston	Walters, E. (2003). *Run*. Toronto: Viking. (M) 🍁

P = primary grades (K–2); M = middle grades (3–5); U = upper grades (6–8).

settle into her new life in Avonlea, her antics with Diana, the trials she presents to Marilla, and ultimately, her devotion to both Matthew and Marilla.

Usually, one or two well-rounded characters and several supporting characters are involved in a story. Fully developed main characters have many traits, both good and bad. By understanding or inferring a character's traits, we get to know that figure well, and the character seems to come alive. Figure 6-2 presents a list of stories with fully developed main characters.

Anne is the main character in *Anne of Green Gables*, and readers get to know her as a real person. She is a bright young girl with a vivid imagination and a tremendous desire to live a life filled with adventure and excitement. Her day-to-day existence in the village of Avonlea pales in comparison to the magical poetic land of her imagination. L. M. Montgomery takes readers into Anne's world through monologues in which the young woman transforms the natural surroundings of the Cuthbert place into inviting places of some mystique. Through dialogue and reports of Anne's antics at home and at school, readers come to know her quick wit, mischievous scheming, and quick temper. Readers come to know the supporting characters through their contrasts to Anne.

Characters are developed in four ways—via appearance, action, dialogue, and monologue. Readers notice these four types of information as they read in order to understand the characters.

Authors generally provide some physical description of the characters—their facial features, body shapes, habits of dress, mannerisms, and gestures. Early in *Anne of Green Gables*, much emphasis is placed on Anne's appearance, especially her long braids of flaming red hair and her forlorn, worried expression as she waits at the train station's platform to be collected to go to her new home.

What a character does is often the best way to know about that character. Readers are endeared to Anne through her actions. As she ventures to the ice cream social, dyes her hair, studies diligently, and cracks her slate over Gilbert's head when he calls her "Carrots," readers come to know her vivaciousness.

Dialogue is the third way character is developed. What characters say is important, but so is the manner in which they speak. A character might speak less formally with friends than with respected elders or characters in positions of authority. The geographic location of the story, the historical period, and the characters' socio-economic status also determine how characters speak. Anne's incessant talking frequently provides readers with a social commentary on life in Avonlea, including a glimpse of current fashion when Anne describes her Christmas gift:

> I'd rather feast my eyes on that dress. I'm so glad that puffed sleeves are still fashionable. It did seem to me that I'd never get over it if they went out before I had a dress with them. I'd never have felt quite satisfied, you see. (p. 214)

Authors provide insight into characters by revealing their thoughts, or inner dialogue. Anne does not need an audience to share her thoughts. With no apparent listeners, she chatters on in metaphoric **discourse** about such things as how she is invigorated by the arrival of mornings, her pleasure in knowing that there is a lively brook at Green Gables, and how utterly humiliated she feels having been reprimanded at school.

Students can draw *open-mind portraits* to examine characters and reflect on story events from the character's viewpoint. These portraits have two parts: the face of the character is on one page, and the mind of the character is on the second page. The two pages are stapled together, with the "mind" page under the "face" page. A grade 7 student's open-mind portrait of Anne is shown in Figure 6-3. The student divided Anne's thinking into two groups: Anne's likes and dislikes. In each picture she has shown some of the things and people that Anne repeatedly tells the reader she likes and dislikes.

SETTING

In some stories, the settings are merely backdrops. Many folktales, for example, simply use the convention "Once upon a time ..." to set the stage. In other stories, the setting is elaborate and integral (Lukens, 2006).

Location is an important dimension in many stories. For example, life in Afghanistan under Taliban control in the Breadwinner trilogy, including the fourth book, *My Name Is Parvana* (2012), is integral to the stories' effectiveness. The settings are artfully described and add something unique to the story. Other stories take place in predictable settings that do not contribute to the story's effectiveness.

The time period is an important element in stories set in the past or future. If *The Quarter-Pie Window* (Brandis, 1985/2003) and *Archipelago* (Ward, 2008) were set in different eras, for example, they would lose much of their impact. For instance, in

FIGURE 6-3 AN OPEN-MIND PORTRAIT OF ANNE IN ANNE OF GREEN GABLES

Used with permission from Jane Sanden.

Achipelago, setting the plot 14 000 years ago, accomplished through excellent descriptions of the land, what animals existed, and even what it smelled like long ago, makes the plot much more plausible. In stories that take place in the future, such as *Divergent* (Roth, 2011), things are possible that are not possible today. Figure 6-4 presents a list of stories with integral settings.

The fourth dimension, time, includes both time of day and the passage of time. Most stories ignore time of day, except for scary stories that take place after dark.

FIGURE 6-4 STORIES WITH INTEGRAL SETTINGS

Brandis, M. (1985/2003). *The Quarter-Pie Window*. Toronto: Tundra Books. (P–M) 🍁

Carter, A. L. (2002). *Under a Prairie Sky*. Victoria, BC: Orca Books. (M) 🍁

Chan, G. (2004). *An Ocean Apart*. Toronto: Scholastic. (M–U) 🍁

Ellis, D. (2002). *Parvana's Journey*. Toronto: Groundwood Books. (M–U) 🍁

Godkin, C. (2002). *When the Giant Stirred: Legend of a Volcanic Island*. Toronto: Fitzhenry & Whiteside. (P–M) 🍁

Greenwood, B. (2001). *Gold Rush Fever: A Story of Klondike, 1898*. Toronto: Kids Can Press. (M–U) 🍁

Gutirrez, E. (2005). *Picturescape*. Toronto: Simply Read Books. (P–M–U) 🍁

Lebox, A. (2002). *Salmon Creek*. Toronto: Groundwood Books. (P–M) 🍁

Prince, B. (2004). *I Came as a Stranger: The Underground Railroad*. Toronto: Tundra Books. (U) 🍁

Reid, B. (2003). *Subway Mouse*. Toronto: Scholastic. (P–M) 🍁

Scrimger, R. (2002). *Noses Are Red*. Toronto: Tundra Books. (M–U) 🍁

Skreslet, L., & MacLeod, E. (2001). *To the Top of Everest*. Toronto: Kids Can Press. (M) 🍁

Spring, D. (2005). *The Righteous Smuggler*. Toronto: Second Story Press. (M–U) 🍁

Stenhouse, T. (2001). *Across the Steel River*. Toronto: Kids Can Press. (M–U) 🍁

Taylor, C. (2002). *Buffalo Hunt*. Toronto: Penguin Books. (M) 🍁

P = primary grades (K–2); M = middle grades (3–5); U = upper grades (6–8).

In stories such as *The Graveyard Book* by Neil Gaiman (2008), a story about a boy's adventures and dangerous encounters while growing up in a graveyard, time is important because night makes things scarier.

Many short stories span a brief period of time. In *Jumanji* (Van Allsburg, 1981), Peter and Judy's bizarre adventure, during which their house is overtaken by exotic jungle creatures, lasts only the several hours their parents are at the opera. Other stories, such as *Charlotte's Web* (White, 1952/1980) and *The Graveyard Book* (Gaiman, 2008), span a long enough period for the main character to grow to maturity.

Students can draw maps to show the setting of a story. These maps may show the path a character travelled or the passage of time.

POINT OF VIEW

Stories are written from a particular viewpoint, and this focus determines to a great extent readers' understanding of the characters and the events of the story. The four points of view are first-person viewpoint, omniscient viewpoint, limited omniscient viewpoint, and objective viewpoint (Lukens, 2006). Figure 6-5 presents a list of stories written from each viewpoint.

The first-person viewpoint tells a story through the eyes of one character using the first-person pronoun "I." The reader experiences the story as the protagonist/

FIGURE 6-5 STORIES THAT ILLUSTRATE THE FOUR POINTS OF VIEW

First-Person Viewpoint

Bagdasarian, A. (2000). *Forgotten Fire*. New York: Dorling Kindersley. (M–U) 🍁

Brouwer, S. (2007). *Titan Clash*. Victoria, BC: Orca Books. (M–U) 🍁

MacLachlan, P. (1985). *Sarah, Plain and Tall*. New York: Harper & Row. (M)

Naylor, P. R. (1991). *Shiloh*. New York: Atheneum. (M–U)

Tanaka. S. (2006). *Wings*. New York: Purple Bear Books. (M–U)

Omniscient Viewpoint

Andrews, J. (1996). *Keri*. Toronto: Groundwood Books. (U) 🍁

Badami, R. A. (2000). *The Hero's Walk*. Toronto: Vintage. (M–U). 🍁

Bishop, M. H. (2005). *Tunnels of Tyranny*. Regina, SK: Coteau Books. (M–U) 🍁

Mott, A. S. (2005). Reality Television. In *Haunting Fireside Stories: Ghostly Tales of the Paranormal*. Edmonton, AB: Ghost House Books. (U) 🍁

Ward, D. (2008). *Archipelago*. Red Deer, AB: Red Deer Press. (M–U) 🍁

Limited Omniscient Viewpoint

Baxter, J. R. (2007). *The Way Lies North*. Vancouver, BC: Ronsdale Press. (M–U) 🍁

Harlow, J. H. (2004). *Thunder from the Sea*. New York: McElderry Books. (M)

Stratton, A. (2008). *Leslie's Journal*. Toronto: Annick Press. (U) 🍁

Taylor, C. (2005). *Angelique, Book Two: The Long Way Home*. Toronto: Penguin. (M–U) 🍁

Wallace, I. (2000). *Duncan's Way*. Toronto: Douglas & McIntyre. (M) 🍁

Objective Viewpoint

Got, Y. (2001). *Sam's Little Sister*. San Francisco, CA: Chronicle. (P)

Kurtz, J. (2004). *Goldilocks and the Three Bears*. New York: Hyperion. (P)

Lunn, J., & Gál, L. (1979). *The Twelve Dancing Princesses*. Toronto: Methuen. (P–M) 🍁

Mollel, T. (1990). *The Orphan Boy*. Toronto: Oxford University Press. 🍁

Willems, M. (2005). *Leonardo the Terrible Monster*. New York: Hyperion. (P)

Multiple and Alternating Viewpoints

Appelt, K. (2008). *The Underneath*. New York: Atheneum (M)

Hegerat, B. J. (2006). *Running toward Home*. Edmonton, AB: NeWest Press. (U) 🍁

Knox, E. (2007). *Dreamquake*. (Dreamhunter Duet, Book Two). Toronto: Viking. (M) 🍁

McFarlane, L. (2005). *Hockey Stories*. Toronto: Key Porter Books. (M–U) 🍁

McNicoll, S. (2006). *Beauty Returns*. Markham, ON: Fitzhenry & Whiteside. (U) 🍁

P = primary grades (K–2); M = middle grades (3–5); U = upper grades (6–8).

narrator tells it. For example, in *The Great Unexpected* (Creech, 2012), Naomi tells about living in the small town of Blackbird Tree with her best friend Lizzie, and meeting a mysterious new boy named Finn, and in *Angelique, Book Two: The Long Way Home* (C. Taylor, 2005), ten-year-old Angelique and her Métis family are hunting buffalo across the prairies when horse thieves raid their camp. Angelique, along with her brother, Joseph, and friend François, is determined to bring their beloved horses home. Many children's books are written from the first-person viewpoint. One limitation is that the narrator must remain an eyewitness in all scenes of the story.

In the omniscient viewpoint, the author is godlike, seeing and knowing all about the characters in the story. Using the third-person viewpoint, the author tells readers about the thought processes of each character without worrying how the information is obtained. Most stories told from the omniscient viewpoint are chapter books. Examples of chapter books written from the omniscient viewpoint are *Saving Armpit* (Hyde, 2011) and *Coram Boy* (Gavin, 2000).

The limited omniscient viewpoint is used to reveal the thoughts of one character. The story is told in the third person, and the author concentrates on the thoughts, feelings, and significant past experiences of the main character or another important character. Many picture book and chapter book stories are told from this viewpoint. Lois Lowry uses the limited omniscient viewpoint in *The Giver* (1993), concentrating on the main character, Jonas, using his thoughts to explain Jonas's "perfect" community to readers. Later, Jonas's thoughts reveal his growing dissatisfaction with the community and his decision to escape to Elsewhere with the baby Gabriel.

In the objective viewpoint, readers are eyewitnesses to the story and are confined to the immediate scene. They learn only what is visible and audible, without knowing what any character thinks. Many folktales, such as *Cinderella* (Galdone, 1978) and *The Little Red Hen* (Zemach, 1983), are told from the objective viewpoint. Other picture book stories, such as *Duck in the Truck* (Alborough, 2005) and *The Orphan Boy* (Mollel, 1990), are told from this eyewitness viewpoint. The focus is on recounting events, not on developing the personalities of the characters.

Younger children can experiment with point of view to understand how the author's viewpoint affects a story. One way to demonstrate point of view is to contrast *The Three Little Pigs* (Galdone, 1970), the traditional version of the story told from an objective viewpoint, with *The True Story of the 3 Little Pigs!* (Scieszka, 1989), a self-serving narrative told by Mr. A. Wolf from a first-person viewpoint. In this unusual and satirical retelling, the wolf tries to explain away his bad image.

Another way to demonstrate the impact of different viewpoints is for students to retell or rewrite a familiar story, such as *Little Red Riding Hood* (Hyman, 1983), from specific points of view—through the eyes of Little Red Riding Hood; her sick, old grandmother; the hungry wolf; or the hunter. Compare this version with *Little Red Riding Hood: A Newfangled Prairie Tale* (Ernst, 2005), in which Grandma is far from frightened and the wolf is reformed. To help them appreciate how these changes affect a story, take a story such *as Oink?* (Palatini, 2006) and ask the students to imagine things from other perspectives. How do the pigs feel? How do the chickens feel? The duck? The rabbit? As students shift to other points of view, they must decide how to tell the story from different viewpoints.

A few stories are written from multiple viewpoints. In flip picture books, one version of the story begins at the front of the book, and another begins at the back of the book. In Rowland's *Little Red Riding Hood/The Wolf's Tale* (1991), the traditional version begins on one side of the book, the wolf's version on the other. In some chapter books, such as *The Underneath* (Appelt, 2008), alternating chapters are written from different characters' perspectives—in this case, from the point of view of a calico cat and a hound named Ranger.

Asking students questions about point of view helps them to develop critical literacy skills. For instance, in Anthony Browne's *Voices in the Park* (2000), young children quickly recognize that the way a story is told may leave out important information that changes its meaning. Other stories written from multiple or alternating viewpoints are listed in Figure 6-5.

THEME

The underlying meaning of a story, the theme, embodies general truths about human nature (Lehr, 1991). It usually deals with the characters' emotions and values. Explicit themes are stated openly and clearly in the story. Lukens (2006) uses *Charlotte's Web* to point out how one theme of friendship—the giving of oneself for a friend—is expressed as an explicit theme:

> Charlotte has encouraged, protected, and mothered Wilbur, bargained and sacrificed for him, and Wilbur, the grateful receiver, realizes that "friendship is one of the most satisfying things in the world." And Charlotte says later, "by helping you perhaps I was trying to lift up my life a little. Anyone's life can stand a little of that." Because these quoted sentences are exact statements from the text they are called explicit themes. (p. 94)

Implicit themes are implied rather than explicitly stated, emerging through the thoughts, speech, and actions of the characters as they seek to resolve their conflicts. Lukens also uses *Charlotte's Web* to illustrate implicit themes:

> Charlotte's selflessness—working late at night to finish a new word, expending her last energies for her friend—is evidence that friendship is giving oneself. Wilbur's protection of Charlotte's egg sac, his sacrifice of first turn at the slops, and his devotion to Charlotte's babies—giving without any need to stay even or to pay back—leads us to another theme: true friendship is naturally reciprocal. As the two become fond of each other, still another theme emerges: one's best friend can do no wrong. In fact, a best friend is sensational! Both Charlotte and Wilbur believe in these ideas; their experiences verify them. (p. 95)

Sketch-to-stretch activities are used to help students better understand the plot, characters, theme, or other elements of a story. Many teachers use sketch-to-stretch activities as responses to texts they read to students, asking the students to sketch as they listen. When the reading is finished, students explain their drawings to one or more peers. Through drawing and explaining, the students can transform or extend meanings, discover new insights, clarify misunderstandings, or construct new meanings about the text. Students may also include short sentences or captions as part of their drawings. In sketch-to-stretch, the emphasis is on representing the students' ideas and feelings, not on artistic technique. Sketch-to-stretch can also be used across curricula to respond to nonfiction information texts. The steps in sketch-to-stretch are presented in the accompanying Step by Step box.

Sketch-to-Stretch

1 Read and respond orally to a story. Students read a story or several chapters of a longer book and respond to the story in a **grand conversation** about literature or in reading logs.

2 Talk about the themes in the story and ways to symbolize meanings. The teacher reminds students that there are many ways to represent the meaning of an experience, and that students can use lines, colours, shapes, symbols, and words to visually represent what a story means to them. Students and the teacher talk about possible meanings and ways they might visually represent these meanings.

3 Students draw sketches. Students work in small groups to draw sketches that reflect what the story means to them. The teacher emphasizes that students should focus on the meaning of the story, not their favourite episode, and that there is no single correct interpretation of the story.

4 Students share their sketches with classmates. Students meet in small groups to share their sketches and talk about the symbols they used. The teacher encourages classmates to study each student's sketch and tell what they think the student is trying to convey.

5 Some students share with the class. Each group chooses one sketch from their group to share with the class.

6 Revise sketches and make final copies. Some students will want to revise and add to their sketches based on feedback and ideas they received from classmates. Also, students may make final copies if the sketches are being included in larger projects concerning the book.

Teaching Students about Stories

Teachers help students expand their concepts of story through **minilessons** that focus on particular story elements. Minilessons are usually taught during the exploring stage of the reading process, after students have had an opportunity to read and respond to a story and share their reactions.

MINILESSONS ON STORIES

Teachers adapt the teaching strategy set out in Chapter 1 to teach minilessons on the elements of story structure and other procedures, concepts, and strategies and skills related to stories. The steps in teaching a minilesson on stories are presented in the following Step by Step box.

A list of topics for minilessons about stories is presented on page 209. These topics include procedures, concepts, and strategies and skills for reading and writing stories.

Differentiating to Meet the Needs of Every Student

Teachers find ways to involve all students in successful reading and writing experiences with stories. A list of suggestions for differentiating the information presented in this chapter to meet the needs of every student is presented on page 210. These suggestions emphasize the importance of allowing students to respond to stories before exploring them, and of finding ways to support students as they read and write.

A Minilesson on Stories

1 Introduce the element. The teacher introduces the element of story structure using a chart or the smart board to define and list the characteristics of the element. Figure 6-6 shows examples of charts that can be developed for some story elements. Next, students think about stories they have read recently that exemplify the element, and talk about how these stories were organized.

2 Analyze the element in stories. Students read or listen to one or more excerpts from stories that illustrate the element. Students analyze how the author used the element in the story and tie their analyses to the information about the element presented in the first step. Students can write the information from the chart in their reading logs.

3 Explore example stories. Students participate in exploring activities to investigate how authors use the element in particular stories. Activities include the following:

- Retell a story with emphasis on an identified element.
- Dramatize a part of a story to focus on a particular element.
- Create a visual storyboard to illustrate one or more elements.
- Draw and label clusters or other diagrams to visually represent one or more elements within the story structure.

As students participate in these activities, the teacher draws their attention to the particular element being studied.

4 Review the element. The teacher reviews the information about the element, using the charts introduced in the first step. Students explain the element in their own words, using one story they have read as an example.

FIGURE 6-6 CHARTS FOR THE ELEMENTS OF STORY STRUCTURE

Chart 1	Chart 2	Chart 3
Stories	**Beginnings of Stories**	**Middles of Stories**
Stories have three parts: 1. A beginning. 2. A middle. 3. An end.	Writers put these things in the beginning of a story: 1. The characters are introduced. 2. The setting is described. 3. A problem is established. 4. Readers get interested in the story.	Writers put these things in the middle of a story: 1. The problem gets worse. 2. Roadblocks thwart the main character. 3. More information is provided about the characters. 4. The middle is the longest part. 5. Readers become engaged with the story and empathize with the characters.

(continued)

FIGURE 6-6 CHARTS FOR THE ELEMENTS OF STORY STRUCTURE (continued)

Chart 4

Ends of Stories

Writers put these things in the end of a story:

1. The problem is resolved.
2. The loose ends are tied up.
3. Readers feel a release of emotions that were built up in the middle.

Chart 5

Conflict

Conflict is the problem that characters face in the story. There are four kinds of conflict:

1. Conflict between a character and nature.
2. Conflict between a character and society.
3. Conflict between characters.
4. Conflict within a character.

Chart 6

Plot

Plot is the sequence of events in a story. It has four parts:

1. A Problem: The problem introduces conflict at the beginning of the story.
2. Roadblocks: Characters face roadblocks as they try to solve the problem in the middle of the story.
3. The High Point: The high point in the action occurs when the problem is about to be solved. It separates the middle and the end.
4. The Solution: The problem is solved and the roadblocks are overcome at the end of the story.

Chart 7

Setting

The setting is where and when the story takes place.

1. Location: Stories can take place anywhere.
2. Weather: Stories take place in different kinds of weather.
3. Time of Day: Stories take place during the day or at night.
4. Time Period: Stories take place in the past, at the current time, or in the future.

Chart 8

Characters

Writers develop characters in four ways:

1. Appearance: How characters look.
2. Action: What characters do.
3. Dialogue: What characters say.
4. Monologue: What characters think.

Chart 9

Theme

Theme is the underlying meaning of a story.

1. Explicit Themes: The meaning is stated clearly in the story.
2. Implicit Themes: The meaning is suggested by the characters, action, and monologue.

Chart 10

Point of View

Writers tell the story according to one of four viewpoints:

1. First-Person Viewpoint: The writer tells the story through the eyes of one character using "I."
2. Omniscient Viewpoint: The writer sees all and knows all about each character.
3. Limited Omniscient Viewpoint: The writer focuses on one character and tells that character's thoughts and feelings.
4. Objective Viewpoint: The writer focuses on the events of the story without telling what the characters are thinking and feeling.

MINILESSONS

Reading and Writing Stories

Procedures	Concepts	Strategies and Skills
Make a beginning–middle–end cluster diagram	Concept of story	Predict and confirm
Make a setting map	Beginning–middle–end	Monitor understanding
Make a plot profile	Plot	Visualize
Make an open-mind portrait	Characters	Identify with characters
Create a sketch-to-stretch drawing	Setting	Empathize with characters
Create storyboards	Theme	Write dialogue for characters
Make comparison charts	Point of view	Summarize
Plan an innovation on a text	Genre	Retell the story
Plan a story sequel	Mentor text	Connect to one's own life
Assume roles to foster discussion of a text	Writers voice	Compare to previously read
Prepare to give peer feedback	Authors' choices	literature
Read expressively	Types of illustrations	Note uses of literary devices
	Illustrators' choices	Question the author
	Sequels	Elaborate on the plot
	Aesthetic reading	Evaluate the story
	Efferent reading	

Assessing Students' Concept of Story

Teachers assess students' concept of story in many ways. They observe students as they read and respond to stories. They can make anecdotal notes about whether or not students are sensitive to story elements as they talk during grand conversations. Students talk about the character who is most like them, or compare two stories. Teachers note whether students use terminology related to story elements. Do they talk about conflict, or the way a story ends? If they are talking about point of view, do they use that term? Teachers also ask questions about story elements during grand conversations and note students' responses. Students' **reading logs** also provide evidence of the same sorts of comments and reactions.

Students demonstrate their understanding of story elements by making cluster diagrams, charts, and other diagrams. These activities are a natural outgrowth of students' responses to a story, not the reason students read stories (Oczkus, 2009). Teachers document students' understanding of story elements by examining stories they write to see how they apply their knowledge.

Reading Stories

Students read stories, and their concept of story informs and supports their reading. They read popular and award-winning stories together during resource-based units, stories they choose themselves in readers workshop, and other stories as part of **theme study units**. Students use the reading process to read, respond to, explore, and extend their reading. Reading stories with students is more than simply a pleasurable way to spend an hour; it is how classroom communities are created and can be accomplished by linking reading with school-wide events such as "one school, one book" initiatives or a community astronomy night (Johnson, Rezak, Hodges, Lawrence, Tippins, &

Reading and Writing Stories to Meet the Needs of Every Student

1. Read Aloud to Students

Teachers make accessible stories that students cannot read independently by reading aloud to students or by having them read to by older students or classroom volunteers. Engagement in active listening can be fostered by clarifying unfamiliar vocabulary and by having students make predictions as the reading proceeds. When students listen together in a class or small group, they develop strong bonds as readers, providing support for less able readers.

2. Make Stories Available for Independent Listening

Stories and other written materials can be made available in digital format to students for listening. Make the text available so listeners can read along as they listen.

3. Encourage Students to Choose a Variety of Stories to Read Independently

Teachers regularly schedule time for sustained reading. Classroom libraries are well stocked with a variety of books (and ebooks) at various reading levels. Teachers introduce books and entice readers to read a wide range of literature through book talks and by having digital stories available.

4. Dramatize or Digitalize Stories

Drama and digital storytelling are effective techniques students can use to understand stories they are reading and to create stories they will write. When students are reading a complex story, they can role-play important scenes and use multimedia to record these in order to better understand the characters and events.

5. Write Retellings or Fanfiction

Students write retellings of favourite stories or retell the story from a particular character's viewpoint. Writing retellings of favourite stories provides the support that some writers need to write successfully. Retellings can involve writing new settings, new endings, changes to characters, and changes of perspective. Fanfiction allows students to use characters and situations from their favourite writers to develop their own storyline preferences. This writing can be securely posted online to share with others.

6. Work in Collaborative Readers and Writers Groups

Students work together in pairs or in small groups to support each other as they read and write. Sharing responses to reading prompts comprehension and having an audience gives purpose to writing.

Bongkotphet, 2008). Reading, writing, and talking about stories are natural extensions of the relationships that students have built together.

Another way to share stories is through digital storytelling. Digital storytelling encourages children of all ages to use multimedia to share, record, and value stories from their own lives. Brenneman Eno (2004) suggests that when young children use digital storytelling, their imaginative play is validated and they are empowered to share their stories.

Strategies for Reading

Students use a number of strategies to respond to and comprehend stories. Our role as teachers is to teach students to use specific strategies to enhance their understanding and enjoyment. Lori Oczkus, in *Interactive Think-Aloud Lessons: 25 Surefire Ways to Engage Students and Improve Comprehension* (2009), offers a creative and fun approach to teaching comprehension strategies using props, gestures, and mentor texts. Students might use the following strategies to comprehend stories:

- *Visualizing.* Students create images or pictures of the story in their minds.
- *Predicting.* Students anticipate or make predictions about what will happen in the story. Students consider the impact of what they have read on what they are reading.

- **Engaging.** Students become so involved they feel transported through time and space into the story.
- **Empathizing.** Students respond with their feelings as they read.
- **Identifying.** Students make connections between a character and themselves.
- **Elaborating.** Students make inferences and add information to what they read.
- **Noticing opposites.** Students note tensions or contrasts in the story.
- **Monitoring.** Students make sure that what they are reading makes sense to them.
- **Connecting to life.** Students make connections between events, characters, and other aspects of the story with their own lives.
- **Connecting to literature.** Students make connections between the story they are reading and other stories they have read.
- **Evaluating.** Students make judgments about why they liked a story or whether it was worth reading.
- **Analyzing.** Students analyze the author's use of the elements of story structure. (Duke, 2005; Duke & Pearson, 2002; Lipson, 2007).

With practice and guidance, students learn to use these strategies as they read and participate in response activities.

Comprehension develops gradually. As students pick up a book or e-book by a favourite author or look at the cover of a book, they call to mind past experiences and make predictions. Comprehension continues to develop as students read, respond to, and explore the story, and it deepens as they discuss the story and write responses in reading logs. Students move beyond the actual text as they work on projects and extend their comprehension further.

Teachers encourage reading and comprehension by sharing stories, teaching mini-lessons, planning responses, and exploring activities. Guidelines for enhancing comprehension in the classroom are presented in the accompanying Teacher's Notebook.

INTERTEXTUALITY

As students comprehend and create interpretations, they make connections to books read previously. These connections are called **intertextuality** (Hartman, 1995). Students use intertextuality as they respond to books by recognizing similarities between characters, plots, and themes, and incorporate ideas and structures from the stories they have read into the stories they are writing. Intertextuality has five characteristics (Cairney, 1990, 1992):

1. **Individuality and uniqueness.** Students' literary experiences and the connections they make among them are different.
2. **Dependence on literary experiences.** Intertextuality is dependent on the types of books students have read, their purpose for and interest in reading, and the literary communities to which they belong.
3. **Metacognitive awareness.** Most students are aware of intertextuality and consciously make connections among texts.
4. **Links to concept of story.** Students' connections among stories are linked to their knowledge about literature.
5. **Reading–writing connections.** Students make connections between stories they read and stories they write.

The sum of students' experiences with literature—including the stories parents have read and told to young children, the books and audiobooks students have read or listened to, the film or YouTube versions they have viewed, their concepts of story and knowledge about authors and illustrators, and the texts students have written—constitutes their intertextual histories (Cairney, 1992). One way in which teachers encourage students to make intertextual links is by grouping literature into text sets: collections of three or more books that are related in some way. Possible text sets include:

- stories written by the same author
- stories featuring the same character
- stories illustrating the same theme
- different versions of a folktale
- stories in the same genre
- stories and other books related to a theme study unit

As students read and discuss these books, they make connections and share these connections, allowing classmates to gain insights about literature and build on classmates' ideas. Teachers prompt students and ask them to describe commonalities among the books. Students make charts and other diagrams to compare authors, characters, and other aspects of stories. Teachers provide other texts for students to examine as well, such as films, YouTube videos, fanfiction and author blogs to help students make sense of the many kinds of print they encounter in their daily lives.

Teaching Stories

Teachers plan resource-based units featuring award-winning books for children and adolescents to read and respond to stories. Some resource-based units feature a single book, others a text set of books. Students may focus on the story or they might learn about a particular genre, or category, of literature by reading stories illustrating the genre. They might also be involved in an author study where they read and respond to stories written by a particular author. Activities to explore stories are presented in the accompanying Teachers' Notebook.

For more information on readers workshops, see Chapter 5, "The Reading and Writing Processes," pages 146, 150, 158, 159

Readers workshop is another way of organizing instruction that provides time for students to engage in independent or shared reading and to respond through conversation and writing, and for teachers to offer instruction. In a typical setting, students choose what they read from literature introduced by their teachers or recommended by their classmates. Readers workshop simulates reading outside of school.

Students often read stories as part of theme study units or inquiry-based units. Stories are useful because they give life to information and make it more memorable than many informational texts. For example, **historical fiction** helps children experience the past, bringing them to fuller understanding of human problems and human relationships, and to see that times change but human needs remain relatively unchanged (Kiefer & Tyson, 2010). Many stories have been written to describe life on the prairies and to show how living on the dusty, wind-swept open plains is distinctive from living elsewhere. Here is a sampling:

- Poetic description of prairie life—*If You're Not from the Prairie . . .* (Bouchard, 1995).
- Ruination of fertile soil—*Grandpa's Alkali* (Bannatayne-Cugnet, 1993).
- Travel across the prairies—*Dandelions* (Bunting, 1995).
- Family life on the prairies—*The Dust Bowl* (Booth & Reczuch, 1996).
- Immigrating to live on the prairies—*Josepha: A Prairie Boy's Story* (McGugan, 2003).
- Unusual weather for a prairie Christmas—*Chinook Christmas* (Wiebe, 1992).

Activities to Explore and Comprehend Stories

Storyboards

Students create visual depictions of story events or **storyboards.** They identify important events in sequence, then draw or choose digital visuals to illustrate the events. They can also add brief statements to more fully tell the story. Students can also work together to create storyboards for a chapter book. After reading the book, each student chooses a chapter, rereads it, creates a representative visual, and writes a summary of it. The pictures are then sequenced and displayed in order.

Story Boxes

Students and the teacher collect items related to a story and place them in a box. The box cover is decorated with the title and author, pictures of scenes from the story, pictures of the characters, and memorable quotes. Making the box is a good way to focus students' attention on what is important about the story, and students can examine the items in a box prepared by students in a previous class as they talk about the story and what it means to them.

Create Word and Quotation Walls

To focus on the author's craft and language use, students identify unfamiliar or particularly descriptive words along with memorable quotations to create a word wall. Students write words, phrases, and quotations in a variety of fonts and then display them on a bulletin board for easy reference as they engage in their own writing. Alternatively, students can create word displays using available software and then explain their word choices to a peer.

Open-Mind Portraits

In order to probe a character, students draw portraits of the character and cut around the face so that the head flips up. Next they back the page with another sheet of paper. Then they write words and draw pictures in the "open mind" behind the face that reflect the character's thoughts. When completed, students discuss their portraits with peers.

Setting Maps

Students draw setting maps to illustrate a character's journey in a story. Other types of maps are beginning–middle–end cluster diagrams, Venn diagrams to compare characters (see www.readwritethink.org/files/resources/interactives/venn_diagrams), and plot profiles. Using available art materials and software, students can elaborate on their maps, incorporating techniques learned in art and other lessons.

Sketch-to-Stretch

Students make sketch-to-stretch drawings to represent the theme of a story. These drawings are not illustrations of particular events in the story; they symbolize the story's message. After making their sketches, students share them with classmates and talk about the symbols and messages they have included in the drawings.

Internet Research

Students explore websites linked to the story they are reading. They share information they discover about the author, the content of the story, versions of the storyline, and other background knowledge. Teachers can design an online research tool to guide students to specific sites and to organize the information they find there. For example, see www.davidbouchard.com, for a biography, books, and links related to Canadian author David Bouchard.

- Sale of a family farm—*The Auction* (J. Andrews, 1990).
- Family history—*Potato: A Tale from the Great Depression* (Lied, 2002).
- Summer work and play—*Harris and Me* (Paulsen, 1993).
- Prairie nature and activities in winter—*A Prairie Boy's Winter* (Kurelek, 1973).
- Drought on the prairies—*Out of the Dust* (Hesse, 2001).

Assessing Students' Understanding of Stories

Students' interpretations are unique and personal. Having students answer comprehension questions or fill in the blanks on worksheets is not an effective assessment technique. Teachers can better assess students' interpretation in these ways (Cairney, 1990):

- Listen to students as they talk about stories during grand conversations and other literature discussions.
- Read students' entries in reading logs.

- Ask about and note students' use of reading strategies.
- Observe students' participation in exploring activities.
- Examine the projects that students do.

Teachers also ask students to reflect on their interpretations during reading conferences or in reading log entries.

Teachers expect students to go beyond literal recall to critique the stories through making connections and comparisons among texts, identifying personal meanings of text, and recognizing story structure and the writing techniques used.

Writing Stories

As students read and talk about literature, they learn how writers craft stories. Writers draw from stories they have read as they create their own stories, intertwining several story ideas and adapting story elements to meet their own needs. Cairney (1990) found that students do think about stories they have read as they write, and Blackburn (1985) describes a cycle of intertextuality: students read and talk about books, weave bits of stories they have read into stories they write, and share their compositions, and bits of these compositions make their way into classmates' compositions. Students make intertextual links in different ways, such as

- using specific story ideas without copying the plot
- copying the plot from a story but adding new events, characters, and settings
- using a specific genre they have studied for a story
- using a character borrowed from a story read previously
- writing a retelling of the story
- incorporating content from an informational book into a story
- combining several stories into a new story

The first two strategies were the ones most commonly used in Cairney's study of grade 6 students (Cairney, 1990). Interestingly, the penultimate strategy was used only by less capable readers, and the last only by more capable readers.

Students incorporate what they have learned about stories when they write stories, and use the writing process to draft and refine their work. They write stories as part of resource-based units, during theme study units, and in **writers workshop**. Stories are probably the most complex writing form that elementary students use. It is difficult to craft well-formed stories incorporating plot, character development, and other elements of story structure.

Writing Retellings

Students often write retellings of stories they have read and enjoyed. As they retell a story, they internalize the structure of the story and play with the language the author used.

Students work together as a group to write or dictate the retelling, or they divide the story into sections or chapters and each student or pair of students writes a small part. Then the parts are compiled. A grade 1 class worked together to dictate their retelling of *Where the Wild Things Are* (Sendak, 1963), which was published as a big book:

Page 1:   Max got in trouble. He scared his dog and got sent to bed.

Page 2:   This room turned into a jungle. It grew and grew.

Page 3:   A boat came for Max. It was his private boat.

Page 4:	He sailed to where the wild things lived.
Page 5:	They made him king of all the wild things.
Page 6:	The wild things had a wild rumpus. They danced and hung on trees.
Page 7:	Max sent them to bed without any supper.
Page 8:	Then Max wanted to come back home. He waved goodbye and sailed home on his boat.
Page 9:	And his dinner was waiting for him. It was still hot from the microwave.

As the grade 1 students dictated the retelling, their teacher typed it and projected it onto the interactive whiteboard. Then they read over the story several times, making revisions. Next, the students divided the text into sections, recopied the text onto each page for the big book, drew pictures, and added a cover and title page. Students also wrote their own books, including the major points at the beginning, middle, and end of the story.

Sometimes students change the point of view in their retellings. A grade 4 student wrote this retelling of "Goldilocks and the Three Bears" from Baby Bear's perspective:

One day mom got me up. I had to take a bath. I hate to take baths, but I had to. While I was taking my bath, Mom was making breakfast. When I got out of the tub breakfast was ready. But Dad got mad because his breakfast porridge was too hot to eat. So Mom said, "Let's go for a walk and let it cool." I thought, "Oh boy, we get to go for a walk!" My porridge was just right, but I could eat it later.

When we got back our front door was open. Dad thought it was an animal so he started to growl. I hate it when Dad growls. It really scares me. Anyway, there was no animal anywhere so I rushed to the table. Everybody was sitting down to eat. I said, "Someone ate my porridge." Then Dad noticed someone had tasted his porridge. He got really mad.

Then I went into the living room because I did not want to get yelled at. I noticed my rocking chair was broken. I told Dad and he got even madder.

Then I went into my bedroom. I said, "Someone has been sleeping in my bed and she's still in it." So this little girl with long blond hair raises up and starts to scream. Dad plugged his ears. She jumped up like she was scared of us and ran out of the house. We never saw that little girl again.

Retelling of stories gives teachers the opportunity to explore or develop and review different story elements with students. Using different perspectives helps students think critically about the texts they read and write even at very early ages.

INNOVATIONS

Many stories have a repetitive pattern or refrain, and students can use this structure to write their own stories. As part of a resource-based unit on mice, a grade 1 class read *If You Give a Mouse a Cookie* (Numeroff, 1985) and talked about the circle structure of the story. The story begins with giving a mouse a cookie and ends with the mouse getting a second cookie. Grade 1 students wrote stories about what they would do if they were given a cookie. A student named Michelle drew the circle

Types of Journals

Personal Journals

Students write about events in their own lives and other topics of special interest in personal journals. These journals are the most private type. The teacher responds as an interested reader, often asking questions and offering comments about his or her own life.

Dialogue Journals

Dialogue journals are similar to personal journals except that they are written to be shared with the teacher or a classmate. The person who receives the journal reads the entry and responds to it. These journals are like a written conversation.

Reading Response Journals

Students respond to stories, poems, and informational books they are reading in reading logs. They write and draw entries after reading, record key vocabulary words, make charts and other diagrams, and write memorable quotes.

Double-Entry Journals

Students divide each page of their journals into two columns and write different types of information in each column. Sometimes they write quotes from a story in one column and add reactions to the quotes in the other, or write predictions in one column and what actually happened in the story in the other.

Learning Logs

Students write in learning logs as part of theme study and inquiry-based units. Their log writing helps them to make sense of and retain information they have gathered. They write quickwrites, draw diagrams, take notes, and write vocabulary words they will use throughout the theme study. Students also write learning logs during subject-based lessons especially social studies, science, and math lessons.

Simulated Journals

Students assume the role of a book character or a historical personality and write journal entries from that person's viewpoint. Students include details from the story or historical period in their entries.

Students use journals for a variety of purposes, just as adults do. Types of journals are described in the Teacher's Notebook on page 218. In each type of journal, the focus is on the writer, and the writing is often done for a specific purpose. Students' writing in these types of journals is spontaneous and loosely organized and it often contains mechanical errors because students are focusing on thinking, not on spelling, capitalization, and punctuation. Some of the purposes for journal writing are to:

- record experiences
- stimulate interest in a topic
- explore thinking
- personalize learning
- develop interpretations
- wonder, predict, and hypothesize
- engage the imagination
- ask questions
- activate prior knowledge
- assume the role of another person
- share experiences with trusted readers

Personal Journals

Personal journals are usually the first type of journal writing that young children do. Kindergarteners begin writing in journals early in the school year, and their writing becomes more conventional as they learn about written language, letters of the

FIGURE 6-8 GRADE 4 AND 5 STUDENTS' LIST OF POSSIBLE JOURNAL-WRITING TOPICS

Things to Write about in Personal Journals

my favourite place in town	if I had three wishes
things that make me happy or sad	TV shows I watch
music I like	my favourite holiday
an imaginary planet	if I were stranded on an island
cars I'd like to drive	what I want to be when I grow up
magazines I like to read	how to be a superhero
dreams I have	my mom/my dad
places I've been	my friends
favourite movies	if I were an animal or something else
if I were a movie/rock star	books I've read
poems	favourite things to do
pets	my hobbies
football or other sports	if I were a skydiver
the prime minister	if I had a lot of money
jokes I like to tell	dolls
things that happen in my school	if I were rich
current events	favourite colours
things I do on weekends	questions answered with "never"

or

ANYTHING else I want to write about

alphabet, and phonics. It is normal for students to misspell a few words in their entries; when students write in personal journals, the emphasis is on what they say, not how correctly they write.

It is often helpful to develop a list of possible journal-writing topics on a chart in the classroom or on sheets of paper for students to clip inside their journal notebooks. For personal journals, they choose their own topics. Although they can write about almost anything, some students will complain that they don't know what to write about, so a list of topics gives them ideas. Figure 6-8 shows a list of possible journal-writing topics developed by a class of grade 4 and 5 students. Students can add topics to their lists throughout the year, which may include more than a hundred topics by the end of the school year. Referring students to the list or asking them to brainstorm a list of topics alone or with others encourages them to become more independent writers and discourages them from relying too heavily on teachers for writing topics.

Classroom Blogs

Teachers set up classroom *weblogs*, or *blogs*, to develop students' understanding of online communication and to allow them to safely engage in writing for their classmates. In addition, blogs are an online instructional tool in which students may respond to books they are reading, publish their writing, and work with classmates on projects.

Teachers use blogs in a variety of ways to support their instructional programs. They ensure that the applications are relevant to language arts instruction and theme study units; students respond to books and texts they are reading in resource-based units, publish their writing during writers workshop, and create online learning logs during **inquiry-based units**.

Teachers are responsible for teaching students to conduct themselves safely and responsibly online, and for monitoring that they practise good digital citizenship. They are also responsible for addressing privacy, inappropriate comments, cyberbullying, and safety while considering grade-level-appropriate lessons.

When students share personal information with teachers through their journals or blogs, sometimes teachers learn details about students' problems and family life that the children do not know how to deal with. Entries about child abuse, suicide, or drug use may be the child's way of asking for help. Although teachers are not counsellors, they do have a legal obligation to protect their students and report possible problems to appropriate school personnel. Occasionally, a student invents a personal problem in a journal entry as an attention-getting tactic; however, asking the student about the entry or having a school counsellor do so will help to ensure that the student's safety is fully considered.

Dialogue Journals

Students use dialogue journals to have a written conversation with the teacher or with a classmate. These journals are interactive and conversational in tone. Most important, dialogue journals are an authentic writing activity and provide the opportunity for real communication between students or between a student and the teacher. They can be done on paper or online. Students write informally about something of interest, a concern, a book they are reading, or what they are learning in a theme study unit.

Teachers' responses do not need to be lengthy; a sentence or two is often enough. Even so, it is time-consuming to respond to twenty-five, thirty, or more journal entries every day. As an alternative, many teachers read and respond to students' journal entries on a rotating basis. They might respond to one group of students one week and another group the next week.

In this grade 5 student's dialogue journal, Daniel shares the events and problems in his life with his teacher, and she responds sympathetically. Daniel writes:

> Over spring break I went down to my grandma's house and played basketball in their backyard and while we were there we went to see some of my uncles who are all Aboriginal. Out of my whole family down there they are all Aboriginal except Grandpa Russell.

And Daniel's teacher responds:

> What a fun spring break! That is so interesting to have Aboriginal peoples in your family. I think I might have some Aboriginal ancestors too. Do you still plan to go to Vancouver Island for the summer?

The next day Daniel writes:

> My family and I plan to go to Vancouver Island in June and I imagine we will stay there for quite a while. I think the funnest part will probably be swimming or camping or something like that. When we get there my mom says we will probably stay in a nice motel.

Daniel's teacher responds:

> That really sounds like a fun vacation. I think swimming is the most fun, too. Who will go with you?

This journal is not a series of teacher questions and student answers. Instead, the student and teacher are having a **dialogue**, or conversation, and the interchange is built on mutual trust and respect.

Additional to informing instructional decisions, using dialogue journals allows teachers the opportunity to get to know their students (Hanrahan, 1999). As the journal excerpts between Daniel and his teacher demonstrate, strong relationships with students may develop through writing back and forth.

Dialogue journals are especially effective in promoting the writing development of children who are **English language learners**. Researchers have found that these students are more successful writers when they choose their own topics for writing and when their teachers contribute to the dialogue with requests for a reply, statements, and other comments (Parsons, 2001). Not surprisingly, researchers found that students wrote more when teachers requested a reply than when teachers made comments that did not require a response. Also, when a student was particularly interested in a topic, it was less important what the teacher did, and when the teacher and the student were both interested in a topic, the topic seemed to take over as they shared and built on each other's writing.

This approach is especially effective in readers workshop classrooms when students are reading different books. Students are often paired and write back and forth with their reading buddies. This activity provides the socialization that independent reading does not. Depending on whether students are reading relatively short picture books or longer chapter books, they can write dialogue journal entries every other day or once a week, and then classmates write back.

Grade 4 students wrote these entries to classmates and their teacher about informational books they were reading during readers workshop:

Dear Adam,

I'm reading the coolest book. It's about snakes and it's called <u>A Snake's Body</u> [Cole, 1981]. Look at the pictures on pages 34, 35, 36, 37, 38, 39, 40, 41, and 42 to see how a python strangles and eats a chick. It's awesome.

Your Friend, Todd

Dear Mrs. Parker,

I just finished reading <u>Totally Human: Why We Look and Act the Way We Do</u> [Nicolson, 2011]. I think you would like it, too, because it's about the things people do. It has lots of facts and tells why we laugh and even why we eat junk food. The book takes a long time to read because it has lots of cartoons and extra things to read and look at. I'd say it was one of the best books I've ever read. I think everyone in our class should read it. What do you think?

Love, Ali

Trevor,

The book I'm reading is <u>Hold the OXO! A Teenage Soldier Writes Home</u> [Brooker, 2011]. It's about a boy who volunteered to go to war as a soldier and he was only 17 years old. There's letters written by the boy named Tim and photos, too. Have you ever heard of it?

From your friend, David

Before the students began writing dialogue journal entries, the teacher taught a minilesson about how to format their entries, about how to capitalize and underline book titles, and about the importance of asking questions in their entries so that respondents could answer them in their replies. In their entries, most students incorporated what they had learned in the minilesson.

Reading Response Journals

Students write in **reading response journals** about the stories and other books they are reading or listening to the teacher read aloud during resource-based units and readers workshop. Students relate their reading to their own lives or to other literature they have read. Students may also list interesting or unfamiliar words, jot down memorable quotes, and take notes about characters, plot, or other story elements; but the primary purpose of these journals is for students to think about the book, connect literature to their lives, and develop their own interpretations. Journals like these go by a variety of names. They are sometimes called *reading journals* or *literature logs* (Cooper & Kiger, 2006); but no matter what they are called, their purpose remains the same.

Grade 7 students' reading journal entries about *The Graveyard Book* (Gaiman, 2008) are shown in Figure 6-9. In these entries, students react to the book, make predictions, deepen their understanding of the story, ask questions, assume the role of the main character, and value the story.

When students begin writing entries in reading logs, their first entries are often retellings and plot summaries, but as students gain experience reading and responding to literature, their entries become more interpretive and personal. Teachers model writing "I wonder" reactions, share student entries that are interpretive, and respond to students' entries by asking questions (Collins, Dickson, Simmons, & Kameenui, 2006).

Double-Entry Journals

For double-entry journals, students divide each entry into two parts (Barone, 1990; Berthoff, 1981). They divide their journal pages into two columns; in the left column, they write quotes from the story or other book they are reading, and in the right column, they relate each quote to their own lives and to literature they have read.

FIGURE 6-9 ENTRIES FROM GRADE 7 STUDENTS' READING RESPONSE JOURNALS ABOUT *THE GRAVEYARD BOOK*

I think the book *The Graveyard Book* is very scary because when you start reading you know something bad has happened to a family. I think it would be terrible to lose your family like that and wonder what to do.

I think I would like to be friends with Bod. I was angry that Scarlett didn't like him at the end because he seems like a perfect friend. I would also like to live in the graveyard like Bod because I liked the way the ghosts became his family.

I am wondering how the Owenses are going to look after Bod.

I love how all the ghosts come together to help Bod, especially when they name him. "Bod" short for Nobody.

I felt sad when Bod couldn't go to school anymore. He had to stay unnoticed and invisible to fit in, even when he is special enough that he should be noticed.

Well, I am pretty sure that Mr. Frost is the one who killed Bod's family but I hope not because he's going to find a way to get to Bod.

The ending was very sad. I know Bod had to leave the graveyard behind, but it is still sad to think of him in the world somewhere on his own. I guess that means that it's very happy at the same time, but I think those are the worst endings when they are happy and sad and you don't know which way to feel.

FIGURE 6-10 EXCERPTS FROM A GRADE 5 STUDENT'S DOUBLE-ENTRY JOURNAL ABOUT *THE LION, THE WITCH AND THE WARDROBE*

In the Text	My Response
Chapter 1	
Lucy felt a little frightened, but she felt very inquisitive and excited as well.	I felt like this when I came to my new school. I was scared because I didn't know anyone. I was excited, too, because it was a big school and had lots of art up on the walls.
Chapter 3	
"A jolly good hoax, Lu," he said as he came out again; "you have really taken us in. I must admit. We half-believe you."	This reminds me when it was April Fool's Day and my mom told me there was no school. I was so happy and then she said, "April Fools." And I had to get dressed and make my lunch and still go to school. Lucy isn't joking though.
Chapter 14	
Forward they went again and one of the girls walked on each side of the Lion. But how slowly he walked! And his great, royal head drooped so that his nose nearly touched the grass. Presently he stumbled and gave a low moan.	I am so sad for Aslan right now. He is going up the hill to the Stone Table and I know it is not going to be good. This reminds me when we had to take my dog to the Vet when he was sick and I didn't want to let go of him.

Through this type of journal, students become more engaged in what they are reading, note sentences that have personal connections, and become more sensitive to the author's language.

Students in a grade 5 class kept a double-entry journal as they read C. S. Lewis's classic *The Lion, the Witch and the Wardrobe* (1950/2005). After they read each chapter, they reviewed it and selected one, two, or three brief quotations. They wrote these excerpts in the left column of their journals, and they wrote reactions beside each quotation in the right column. Excerpts from a grade 5 student's journal are presented in Figure 6-10. This student's responses indicate that she is engaged in the story and is connecting it to her own life as well as to another story she has read.

Double-entry journals can be used in several other ways. Instead of recording quotations from the book, students can write "Reading Notes" in the left column and then add "Reactions" in the right column. In the left column students write about the events they read about in the chapter. Then, in the right column, they make personal connections to the events.

As an alternative, students can use the heading "Reading Notes" for one column and "Discussion Notes" for the second column. Students write reading notes as they read or immediately after reading. Later, after discussing the story or chapter of a longer book, students add discussion notes. As with other types of double-entry journals, it is in the second column that students make more interpretive comments.

Younger students can use the double-entry format for a prediction journal (Macon et al., 1991). They label the left column "Predictions" and the right column "What Happened." In the left column they write or draw a picture of what they predict will happen in the story or chapter before reading it. Then, after reading, they draw or write what actually happened in the right column.

Simulated Journals

Some children's books, such as *Light at the Edge of the World* (Davis, 2001), *The Time Traveler's Journal* (Masessa, 2007), and *Dear Mrs. LaRue* (Teague, 2002), are written as journals, and the authors assume the role of a character and write from the character's point of view. We call these books *simulated journals*. They are rich with details and feature examples of both words and phrasing of the period. At the end of the book, authors often include information about how they researched the period and explanations about the liberties they took with the character, setting, or events that are recorded.

Students, too, write simulated journals. They can assume the role of another person and write from that person's viewpoint. For example, they can assume the role of a historical figure when they read biographies or as part of social studies theme study units (Tompkins, 1995). As they read stories, students can assume the role of a character in the story. In this way, students gain insight into other people's lives and into historical events.

Students use simulated journals in two ways: as a tool for learning or as a project. When students use simulated journals as a tool for learning, they write the entries as they are reading a book in order to get to know the character better or during the theme study unit as they are learning about the historical period. In these entries, students are exploring concepts and making connections between what they are learning and what they already know. These journal entries are less polished than when students write a simulated journal as a project. Students might choose to write a simulated journal as a culminating project for a resource-based unit or a theme study unit. As a project, students plan out their journals carefully, choose important dates, and use the writing process to draft, revise, edit, and publish their journals.

One variation of simulated journals is simulated letters (Roop, 1995). Students assume the role of a book character or historical figure, as they do for simulated journals, but students write a letter—not a journal entry—to another character in the book or to another historical figure. Students can exchange letters with classmates or the teacher and write replies.

Exploring Poetry—Playing with Words

Poetry "brings sound and sense together in words and lines," according to Donald Graves (1992, p. 3), "ordering them on the page in such a way that both the writer and reader get a different view of life." Children are natural poets, and poetry surrounds them as they chant jump-rope rhymes on the playground, clap out the rhythm of favourite poems, and dance in response to songs. Gill (2007) believes that poetry is something people do and that teachers can design lessons to help children understand and appreciate it.

Songs for young children and English language learners like "Row, Row, Row Your Boat," "Twinkle, Twinkle, Little Star," and others are particularly good to introduce poetry in a fun and easy way. Older students enjoy looking at favourite song lyrics and raps like "Anybody Listening" by Classified and "New Divide" by the group Linkin Park. Teachers share examples of poetic devices and writing techniques used in songwriting.

Georgia Heard calls language "the poet's paint" (1989, p. 65). As students experiment with words, they learn to create images, play with words, and evoke feelings.

FIGURE 6-11 WORDPLAY BOOKS FOR ELEMENTARY STUDENTS

Booth, D. (1993). *Doctor Knickerbocker*. Toronto: Kids Can Press. (P–M)

Fitch, S. (1994). *I Am Small*. Toronto: Doubleday. (P–M)

Fitch, S. (1999). *If I Were the Moon*. Toronto: Doubleday. (P)

Hutchins, P. (1976). *Don't Forget the Bacon*. London: Bodley Head. (P–M)

Lee, D. (1974). *Alligator Pie*. Toronto: Macmillan. (P–M)

Lee, D. (2000). *Bubblegum Delicious: Poems*. Toronto: Key Porter Books. (M–U)

Lesynski, L. (1999). *Dirty Dog Boogie*. Toronto: Annick Press. (M)

Lewis, J. P. (1996). *Riddle-icious*. New York: Knopf. (M)

Most, B. (2001). *Cock-a-doodle moo!* Orlando, FL: Harcourt Brace. (P)

New, W. (1998). *Vanilla Gorilla: Poems*. Vancouver: Ronsdale Press. (P–M)

O'Connor, J. (2005). *Fancy Nancy*. New York: Harper Collins. (P)

Parish, P. (2012). *Amelia Bedelia 50th Anniversary Library*. New York: Greenwillow Books. (P–M)

Silverstein, S. (2005). *Runny Babbit: A Billy Book*. New York: Program and Genres. (P–M)

Soule, J. (1964). *Never Tease a Weasel*. New York: Dragonfly Books. (P)

Terban, M. (1992). *Funny You Should Ask: How to Make Up Jokes and Riddles with Wordplay*. New York: Clarion. (M–U)

Van Allsburg, C. (1987). *The Z Was Zapped*. Boston: Houghton Mifflin. (M)

P = primary grades (K–2); M = middle grades (3–5); U = upper grades (6–8).

They laugh with language, experiment with rhyme, and invent new words. These activities provide students with a rich background of experiences for reading and writing poetry, and they gain confidence in choosing the "right" word to express an idea, emphasizing the sounds of words, and expressing familiar ideas with fresh comparisons. Figure 6-11 lists wordplay books that elementary students enjoy.

DIFFERENTIATING

Journal Writing to Meet the Needs of Every Student

1. **Draw Journal Entries**

   Students can draw their thoughts and ideas in journal entries instead of writing them, or they can draw pictures before writing. What is important is that students explore their thoughts and feelings or record important information they are learning.

2. **Talk before Writing**

   Students can talk about topics to generate and narrow ideas before beginning to write. As they talk, students find the words and sentences to express their ideas, and they use these words and expand on them as they write.

3. **Dictate Entries**

   Teachers or cross-age tutors can take students' dictation and write the entries for students. Then students reread their dictation with the teacher's or cross-age tutor's assistance. They can also pick key words and phrases from the dictated text and use the words to label drawings.

4. **Share in Small Groups**

   Sharing is an important part of writing, but some students may not feel comfortable sharing with the whole class. These students may prefer sharing their journal entries with a partner or in small groups, which are less threatening than large groups.

5. **Focus on Ideas**

   Students focus on ideas, not mechanical correctness, as they write journal entries because they use journal writing to develop writing fluency and explore the ideas they are learning. Similarly, when teachers assess students' entries, they should consider whether or not students have developed their ideas and not correct their mechanical errors.

6. **Use Flow Writing**

   Children listen to a story, such as Kobi Yamada's (2014) *What Do You Do With An Idea?* (1985) or David Smith's *If: A Mind-Bending New Way of Looking at Big Ideas and Numbers . . .* (2014), and then write for 10 minutes using a prompt from the story such as "My idea is. . ." or "If there were a million . . . ."

Chanting

Twinkle, twinkle little star,

How I wonder what you are,

Up above the world so high,

Like a diamond in the sky.

Twinkle, twinkle, little star,

How I wonder what you are.

Children need to hear the rhythms and patterns of English over and over, until the regular syntactic patterns are as familiar to them as their everyday language. Poetry is an excellent way to allow children that repeated practice, especially if it begins with music and chanting. Children love to chant the poems in Dennis Lee's "Alligator Pie" (1974) because the rhythm of the language evokes a response that is compelling to them. In addition, poetry has been used successfully in the classroom to help build students' confidence and improve their reading skills and attitudes (Wilfong, 2008).

In a grade 2 class, children begin each morning with songs such as Sharon, Lois, and Bram's "The Smile on the Crocodile," which combines music with actions, or "Good Day, Good Day to You," which includes clapping rhythms with the words and music. These activities introduce children to a variety of language patterns and give them the practice they need while engaging in an enjoyable activity. They learn patterns and rhythms with words that are essential for their future development as readers and writers.

From songs, children can proceed to chanting favourite poems for their own enjoyment, moving eventually to chanting with expression that reflects a public performance standard. Children need to chant frequently and repetitively.

Experimenting with Rhyme

Because of their experience with Dr. Seuss, Shel Silverstein, and Robert Munsch stories; with finger plays, and with and nursery rhymes; kindergartners and primary-grade students enjoy creating rhymes naturally. But when rhyme is equated with poetry, it can get in the way of wordplay and vivid images. The following three-line poem shows a grade 5 student's effective use of rhyme:

Thoughts After a 40-Mile Bike Ride

My feet

And seat

Are beat.

A small group of grade 1 students wrote their own version of *Oh, A-Hunting We Will Go* (Langstaff, 1974):

Oh, a-hunting we will go,

a-hunting we will go.

We'll catch a little bear

and curl his hair,

and never let him go.

Oh, a-hunting we will go,

a-hunting we will go.

We'll catch a little mole

and put him in a hole,

and never let him go.

Oh, a-hunting we will go,

a-hunting we will go.

We'll catch a little bug

and give him a big hug

and never let him go.

Oh, a-hunting we will go,

a-hunting we will go.

We'll catch a little bunny

and fill her full of honey,

and never let her go.

Oh, we'll put them in a ring

and listen to them sing

and then we'll let them go.

The grade 1 students wrote this collaboration with the teacher taking dictation. After the rough draft was written, students reread it, checking the rhymes and changing a word here or there. Then each student chose one stanza to copy and illustrate. The pages were collected and compiled to make a book. Students shared the book with their classmates, with each student reading his or her "own" page.

Other Poetic Devices

Poets choose words carefully. They craft powerful images when they use unexpected comparisons, repeat sounds within a line or stanza, imitate sounds, and repeat words and phrases. These techniques are called *poetic devices*. Students learn to appreciate the poet's ability to manipulate devices in poems and to apply the devices in their own writing (Cullinan, Scala, & Schroder, 1995). The terminology is also helpful in response groups when students talk about poems, and in writers groups.

COMPARISON

One way to describe something is to compare it to something else. Students can compare images, feelings, and actions to other things using two types of comparison—similes and metaphors. A *simile* is an explicit comparison of one thing to another—that one thing is like something else. In contrast, a *metaphor* is used in poetry and other writing to compare two *unlike* things. Differentiating between the two terms is less important than using comparisons to make writing more vivid. For example, children can compare anger to a thunderstorm. Using a simile, they might say, "Anger is like a thunderstorm, screaming with thunder-feelings and lightning-words." Or, as a metaphor, they might say, "Anger is a volcano, erupting with poisonous words and hot-lava actions." Songs like Simon and Garfunkel's "I Am a Rock," provide examples of metaphor in music lyrics.

ALLITERATION

Alliteration is the repetition of the initial consonant sound in consecutive words or in words in close proximity. Alliteration makes poetry fun, and children enjoy reading and reciting lines from *Lickety-Split* (Heidbreder, 2007) and *The Z Was Zapped* (Van Allsburg, 1987). After reading one of these books, children can create their own versions.

ONOMATOPOEIA

Onomatopoeia is a device in which poets use "sound words" to make their writing more sensory and vivid. These words (e.g., *crash, slurp, varoom, me-e-e-ow*) sound like their meanings. Students can compile a list of sound words to refer to when they write their own poems.

Spier has written the long-time popular book of sound words, *Gobble Growl Grunt* (1971), about animal sounds, and Munsch has written *We Share Everything* (2000) using words like BLUMPH, GAWCK, and AAAAAAHHHHHH! Students can use these books to select sound words for their writing. Comic strips are another good source of sound words.

In *Wishes, Lies, and Dreams* (1980), Koch recommends having children write noise poems that include a noise or sound word in each line. These first poems often sound contrived (e.g., "A dog barks bow-wow"), but the experience helps children learn to use onomatopoeia, as this poem dictated by a kindergartner illustrates:

Elephant Noses

Elephant noses

Elephant noses

Elephants have big noses

Big noses

Big noses

Elephants have big noses

through which they drink

SCHLURRP

REPETITION

Repetition is another device used to structure writing as well as to add interest. Edgar Allan Poe's use of the word *nevermore* in "The Raven" (Poe, 2009) is one example, as is the gingerbread boy's boastful refrain in "The Gingerbread Boy" (Galdone, 1975).

Reading Poetry

Poems for children assume many different forms. One type of poetry is rhymed verse, such as Robert Louis Stevenson's "Where Go the Boats?" (in Stevenson, 1985), Ernest Thayer's "Casey at the Bat" (1888/2006), and John Ciardi's "Mummy Slept Late and Daddy Fixed Breakfast" (1992). **Narrative** poems tell a story; examples are Clement Moore's "The Night before Christmas" (1823/1995), Robert

Browning's "The Pied Piper of Hamelin" (1842/1993) Robert W. Service's "The Cremation of Sam McGee" (1907/1986), and Sheree Fitch's "There's a Mouse in My House" (1987b). A Japanese form, haiku, is a three-line poem that contains seventeen syllables. Because of its brevity, it has been considered an appropriate form of poetry for children. Free verse has lines that don't rhyme, and rhythm is less important than in other types of poetry. Images take on greater importance in free-form verse. Langston Hughes's "Subway Rush Hour" and William Carlos Williams's "This Is Just to Say" are two examples. Other forms of poetry include limericks, a short, five-line rhymed verse form popularized by Edward Lear (1995b), and concrete poems, which are arranged on the page to create a picture or an image.

Poetry books published for children include picture book versions of single poems such as Alfred Noyes's *The Highwayman*, freshly illustrated by Murray Kimber (2005); specialized collections of poems written by a single poet or related to a single theme, such as dinosaurs or Halloween; and comprehensive anthologies featuring 50 to 500 or more poems arranged by category. A list of poetry books written for children is presented in Figure 6-12.

Some poetry written for adults can be used effectively with elementary students, especially at upper-grade levels. Poems written for adults use more sophisticated language and imagery and provide children with an early introduction to poems and poets they will study later. For example, upper-grade students enjoy Shakespeare's "The Witches' Song" from *Macbeth* and Robert W. Service's "The Shooting of Dan McGrew." Many poems that appeal to both children and adults have been published in colourfully illustrated picturebook formats. The illustrations add to their appropriateness for use with elementary students. *Canadian Railroad Trilogy* by Gordon Lightfoot (2010) is an example.

CHILDREN'S FAVOURITE POEMS

Children have definite preferences about poems, just as adults do. Kutiper and Wilson (1993) found that the humorous poetry of Shel Silverstein and Jack Prelutsky was the most popular with students. The three most widely circulated books in school libraries were *The New Kid on the Block* (Prelutsky, 1984), *Where the Sidewalk Ends* (Silverstein, 1974), and *A Light in the Attic* (Silverstein, 1981). Both Silverstein

FIGURE 6-12 POETRY BOOKS WRITTEN FOR CHILDREN

Booth, D. (Ed.). (1989). *Til All the Stars Have Fallen: Canadian Poems for Children.* Toronto: Kids Can Press. (P–M–U) 🍁

Booth, D. (Ed.). (1990). *Voices on the Wind: Poems for All Seasons.* Toronto: Kids Can Press. (P–M–U) 🍁

Brand, D. (2006). *Earth Magic.* Toronto: Kids Can Press. (M) 🍁

Brenner, B. (2000). *The Earth Is Painted Green: A Garden of Poems about Our Planet.* Toronto: Scholastic. (M) 🍁

Cohen, L. (1995). *Dance Me to the End of Love.* New York: Welcome Enterprises. (U) 🍁

Harrison, T. (2002). *O Canada.* Toronto: Kids Can Press. (P–M–U) 🍁

Hopkins, L. B. (2011). *I Am the Book.* New York: Holiday House. (P)

Lesynski, L. (2007). *Shoe Shakes.* Toronto: Annick Press. (P) 🍁

Salas, L. (2011). *BookSpeak! Poems about Books.* New York: Clarion Books. (M)

Service, R. (1907/1986). *The Cremation of Sam McGee.* Illus. T. Harrison. Toronto: Kids Can Press. (M–U) 🍁

Service, R. (1907/1988). *The Shooting of Dan McGrew.* Illus. T. Harrison. Toronto: Kids Can Press. (U) 🍁

Shapiro, S., & Shapiro, S. (2011). *Better Together.* Toronto: Annick Press. (P) 🍁

P = primary grades (K–2); M = middle grades (3–5); U = upper grades (6–8).

Students share their favourite poems from anthologies of poetry.

and Prelutsky use rhyme and rhythm effectively in their poems and write humorous narrative poems about familiar, everyday occurrences.

POETS WHO WRITE FOR CHILDREN

Many poets write for children today, among them Arnold Adoff, Byrd Baylor, David Booth, David Day, Sheree Fitch, Paul Fleischman, Lee Bennett Hopkins, Lilian Moore, and Jack Prelutsky. Children are interested in learning about favourite poets, and Loris Lesynski's *"I Did It Because . . .": How a Poem Happens* (2006) offers tips for writing poems for children. When children view poets and other writers as real people, people whom they can relate to and who enjoy the same things they do, they begin to see themselves as poets—a necessary criterion for successful writing. Information about poets is available in *Speaking of Poets: Interviews with Poets Who Write for Children and Young Adults* (Copeland, 1993), *Speaking of Poets 2: More Interviews with Poets Who Write for Children and Young Adults* (Copeland & Copeland, 1994), and *A Jar of Tiny Stars: Poems by NCTE Award-Winning Poets* (Cullinan, 1996).

Teaching Students to Read Poems

The focus in reading poems with students is on enjoyment. Students should have many opportunities to read and listen to poems read aloud, and should learn a variety of approaches for sharing poetry. Teachers should share poems they especially like with students. Students are not expected to analyze them; instead, they read poems they enjoy and share their favourite ones with classmates. Students use the reading process as they read and respond to poems, and they often read poems during readers workshop and in connection with resource-based and theme study units. Guidelines for reading poems with children are presented in the accompanying Teacher's Notebook.

Guidelines for Reading Poems with Children

1. Read Aloud
Children and teachers read poetry aloud, not silently. Both teachers and children need to rehearse before reading to an audience. Rehearsing enables then to read fluently and with expression. Even if students are reading independently, they should speak each word, albeit softly or in an undertone.

2. Read with Expression
The teacher teaches students how to read a poem with expression, how to emphasize the rhythm and feel of the words, and where to pause.

3. Sing Poems to Familiar Tunes
Children sing poems to familiar tunes such as those of "Twinkle, Twinkle Little Star" or "I've Been Working on the Railroad." Children experiment to find a tune that fits the line structure of the poem and then sing the poem to the tune.

4. Listen to Digital Recordings
Digital recordings of poets and other professional readers provide students with examples of exemplary reading. Listening independently and in groups gives students the opportunity to experience the sounds of poetic language.

5. Include Poetry Books in the Classroom
A collection of poetry books should be included in the classroom library for children to read during readers workshop and other independent reading times.

6. Avoid Requiring Memorization
Children should not be assigned to memorize a particular poem; rather, children who are interested in learning a favourite poem should be encouraged to do so and share it with class members.

7. Avoid Analysis
Children do not analyze the meaning of a poem or its rhyme scheme; instead, they talk about poems they like and why they like them. They can be encouraged to talk about aspects of a poem such as choice of vocabulary, form, use of metaphor, and others when expressing their preferences.

8. Teach Units on a Poet
The teacher teaches author units to focus on a poet, such as Robert Service, Jack Prelutsky, Sheree Fitch, Dennis Lee, Gary Soto, or Loris Lesynski.

IN READERS WORKSHOP

Students sometimes choose collections of poetry to read during readers workshop, or teachers can plan a special poetry workshop. Poetry workshop can have the same components as regular readers workshop, or it can integrate both readers and writers workshops (Tompkins & McGee, 1993).

During a poetry workshop, the reading time is often divided into two parts. During the first part, students spend time browsing in collections of poetry in traditional texts and online and selecting poems they want to share with classmates. During the second part of reading time, students read poems aloud to partners or small groups of classmates. Students need to have the opportunity to read poems aloud. They also write responses to poems in reading logs and do projects to extend their poetry experience. Projects can include using multimedia to create poetry presentations with images, music, and computer-generated animation.

IN RESOURCE-BASED UNITS

Teachers share poems with students in conjunction with stories and other books they read aloud. For example, they might read Langston Hughes's poem "Dreams" (Prelutsky, 1983) together with *Number the Stars* (Lowry, 1989), or read Lee Bennett Hopkins's "Night Bear" (1984) before or after reading *Bear Snores On* (K. Wilson, 2002). Sometimes, teachers read a poem as a preparing activity; other times, as an exploring activity. Students may also locate a poem related to a story or other book and share it with the class as a project during the extending stage.

Poetry can be read and written as part of all units, but sometimes teachers choose to teach an entire unit on poetry. During the unit, students read and respond to a collection of poems. In this unit, poetry is at the centre. Teachers choose some poems that all students will read and respond to; students select others.

Teachers read many poems to students, and students read other poems themselves. One way for students to read poems is choral reading, in which students take turns reading a poem together. Students need multiple copies of the poem for choral reading, or the poem must be displayed on a chart or smart board so that everyone can read it. Four possible approaches to reading poems (Stewig, 1981) are as follows:

1. *Echo reading.* The leader reads each line, and the group repeats it.
2. *Leader and chorus reading.* The leader reads the main part of the poem, and the group reads the refrain or chorus in unison.
3. *Small-group reading.* The class divides into two or more groups, and each group reads one part of the poem.
4. *Cumulative reading.* One student or one group reads the first line or stanza, and another student or group joins in as each line or stanza is read so that a cumulative effect is created. Music and other multimedia can be used to accompany these readings.

Choral reading makes students active participants in the poetry experience, and helps them learn to appreciate its sounds, feelings, and magic. Two books of award-winning authors written specifically for choral reading are *Big Talk: Poems for Four Voices* (Fleischman, 2008) and *Til All the Stars Have Fallen: Poems for Children* (Booth, 1989). Many other poems can be used for choral reading; try, for example, Shel Silverstein's "Boa Constrictor," Karla Kuskin's "Full of the Moon," Laura E. Richards's "Eletelephony," and Sheree Fitch's "Sleeping Dragons All Around."

Students respond to the poem they have read or listened to. Sometimes students talk informally about the poem, sharing connections to their own lives or expressing whether they liked it. For instance, they may say they liked the humour, the rhyme, or the visualizations they create in response to the poem. They might write responses in reading logs or quickwrites. Or students may explore the poem, choose favourite lines, or illustrate it. A list of ways students respond to poems is presented in the accompanying Teacher's Notebook.

One way students explore familiar poems is to sequence the lines of the poem. Teachers copy the lines of the poem on sentence strips (long strips of chart paper), and students sequence the lines in a pocket chart or using the smartboard. Teachers can enlarge the text of the poem and then cut the lines apart. Students arrange the lines in order on a tray and read the familiar poem. As students sequence the poem, they practise reading and check their understanding. For a more challenging activity, teachers can cut apart the words on each line so that students "build" the poem word by word. Through these sequencing activities, students have opportunities to practise word-identification skills and experiment with the syntactic structure of poems.

Students often create projects, using drama, art, music, and multimedia activities to extend their interpretations. For example, students can role-play Kuskin's "I Woke Up This Morning" or construct monster puppets for the Lurpp creature in Prelutsky's "The Lurpp Is on the Loose."

Students may compile digital versions of narrative poems. Using available software, they create illustrations and voice recordings, then combine the two to present their versions of favourite or newly discovered poems.

Some students enjoy compiling anthologies of their favourite poems. They collect favourite poems to keep, and either staple their collections together to make books or maintain them in a file on the computer. In *Pass the Poetry, Please!* (1987), poet and anthologist Lee Bennett Hopkins suggests setting up a tree branch or an artificial Christmas tree in the classroom as a "poetree" on which students can hang copies of their favourite poems.

TEACHER'S NOTEBOOK

Ways to Respond to a Poem

1. Students rehearse and read the poem aloud to classmates.

2. Students perform the poem using puppets or dramatization as a recording is played aloud.

3. Students write a reading journal entry, discussing what the poem brings to mind or why they like it.

4. Students arrange the poem for choral reading, using multimedia to present images and music, and with classmates present it to the class.

5. Students identify a favourite line in a poem and explain why they like it, either by talking to a classmate or in a reading journal entry.

6. Students work collaboratively to make a picture book with lines or a stanza of the poem written on each page and illustrated.

7. Students read other poems written by the same author.

8. Students investigate the poet and, perhaps, write an email to the poet.

9. Students make a cluster diagram on a topic related to the poem.

10. Students write a poem on the same topic or follow the format of the poem they have read.

11. Students make a paper or digital poster to illustrate the poem and attach a copy of the poem to it.

12. Students add the poem to an electronic file of favourite poems to be shared during a poetry café.

FIGURE 6-13 POETRY BOOKS FOR THEME STUDY AND RESOURCE-BASED UNITS

Theme	Poetry Books
Being Healthy	Gabbitas, C., & Barritt, L. (Eds.) (2015). *Poems and Pictures Children's Poems-Exercise and Healthy Food: An Invitation that Captured the Primary School Nation: Volume 3.* Selby, UK: Poems and Pictures Ltd. Kennedy, C. (2013). *Poems to Learn By Heart.* New York: Hyperion Books. Prelutsky, J. (2007). *Good Sports: Rhymes about Running, Jumping, Throwing, and More.* New York: Knopf. Singer, M. (2012). *A Stick is an Excellent Thing: Poems Celebrating Outdoor Play.* New York: Clarion.
Caring for the Environment	Alderson, S. (2007). *The Eco-Diary of Kiran Singer.* Vancouver, BC: Tradewind Books. 🍁 Brand, D. (2006). *Earth Magic: Poems.* Toronto: KCP Poetry. 🍁 Levy, C. (2002). *Splash. Poems of Our Watery World.* London, UK: Orchard. Singer, M. (2002). *Footprints on the Roof: Poems about the Earth.* New York: Knopf. Woods, F. (Ed.). (2007). *The Green Book of Poetry: An Anthology of Children's Poetry About the Environment.* Oswestry, UK: Scemes Limited. Yerxa, L. (1993). *Last Leaf, First Snowflake to Fall.* Toronto: Douglas & McIntyre. 🍁
Poet Sheree Fitch and Her Verse	Fitch, S. (1992). *There Were Monkeys in My Kitchen.* Toronto: Doubleday. 🍁 Fitch, S. (1995). *Mabel Murple.* Toronto: Doubleday. 🍁 Fitch, S. (1997). *There's a Mouse in My House.* Toronto: Doubleday. 🍁 Fitch, S. (2005). *If I Had a Million Onions.* Vancouver, BC: Tradewind Books. 🍁 Fitch, S. (2013). *Night Sky Wheel Ride.* Vancouver, BC: Tradewind Books. 🍁 Fitch, S. (2014). *Singily Skipping Along.* Halifax, NS: Nimbus. 🍁

P = primary grades (K–2); M = middle grades (3–5); U = upper grades (6–8).

IN THEME STUDY UNITS

Teachers often share poems in connection with theme study units. They select poems individually or in groups from themed collections such as *Good Sports* (Prelutsky, 2007) during a theme study unit on athletics. We recommend that text sets of books and other resources for theme study units always include poetry books or copies of poems written on charts. A list of poetry collections that can be coordinated with theme study units and holiday celebrations is presented in Figure 6-13. Including poems in theme study units is important for two reasons. It helps students appreciate poetry as a meaningful genre and poetry gives students a different perspective on social studies and science concepts.

Both teachers and students can share poems during theme study units. Teachers read poems aloud to students or put copies of a poem on the interactive whiteboard for students to read. Students can add these poems to their learning logs or poetry collections. Teachers can display poems related to a theme on a bulletin board. Students can select poems to share as projects, or write a favourite poem related to a theme.

Assessing Students' Experiences with Poems

Teachers assess students' experiences with poetry by observing as they read poems, by keeping anecdotal notes of students as they read and respond to poems, and by reading students' reading logs and monitoring their projects. Teachers conference with students and ask them about favourite poems and poets to assess their interest in poetry. They notice students' attention to the ways poets use wordplay and poetic devices. Students can also write reflections about their learning and work habits during the poetry activities, providing valuable metacognitive information.

During poetry units, teachers prepare assessment checklists and keep track of students' reading and response activities. For example, grade 4 students might be assessed on these activities:

- Read twenty poems.
- Keep a list of the twenty poems read.
- Write in a reading log about five favourite poems.
- Participate in choral reading activities.
- Participate in minilessons about choral reading techniques, rhyme, and word pictures.
- Make a page for a class book on a favourite poem.
- Do a project about a poem including a digital recording of reading the poem.

It is difficult to grade students on reading poetry, but students can earn points for these activities, and the points can be added together for a grade.

Writing Poetry

Students write funny verses, vivid word picture, powerful comparisons, and expression of deep sentiment. To encourage successful poetry writing, poetic formulas can serve as scaffolds so students focus on ideas rather than form and mechanics.

An excellent place to begin is with children's literature that evokes patterned responses. For example, after reading Cynthia Rylant's *All I See* (1988), children can then write their own responses using the stem "All I see is _____." Another favourite book is Barbara Reid's *The Party* (1997). Grade 2 students listened to the story, talked about different times in their lives when their families had parties or other special gatherings, and then wrote using the sentence frame "I remember …"

Five types of poetic forms are formula poems, free-form poems, syllable- and word-count poems, rhymed verse poems, and model poems.

Formula Poems

Poetic formulas may seem like recipes to be followed rigidly, but that is not how they are intended; rather they provide a scaffold, organization, or skeleton for students' writing. These formulas call for students to begin every line the same way or to insert a particular kind of word in every line. The formulas use repetition, a stylistic device that is more effective for young poets than rhyme. Some forms may seem more like sentences than poems, but the dividing line between poetry and prose is a blurry one, and these poetry experiences help children move toward poetic expression.

"I WISH …" POEMS

Children begin each line of their poems with the words "I wish" and complete the line with a wish (Koch, 1980).

COLOUR POEMS

Students begin each line with a colour. They can repeat the same colour in each line or choose a different colour (Koch, 1980).

Writing colour poems can be coordinated with teaching young children to read and write colour words. Instead of having students in kindergarten and grade 1 read worksheets and colour pictures in the designated colours, students can create colour poems in booklets. They write and illustrate one line of the poem on each page.

FIVE-SENSES POEMS

Students write about a topic using each of the five senses. Sense poems are usually five lines long, with one line for each sense, as this poem written by a student in grade 6 demonstrates:

> **Being Heartbroken**
>
> Sounds like thunder and lightning
>
> Looks like a carrot going through a blender
>
> Tastes like sour milk
>
> Feels like a splinter in your finger
>
> Smells like a dead fish
>
> It must be horrible!

It is helpful to have students develop a five-senses cluster diagram and collect ideas for each sense. Students select from the cluster the strongest or most vivid idea for each sense.

"IF I WERE ..." POEMS

Children write about how they would feel and what they would do if they were something else—a tyrannosaurus rex, a hamburger, or sunshine ((Koch, 1980). They begin each poem with "If I were" and tell what it would be like to be that thing.

DEFINITION POEMS

In definition poems, students describe what something is or what something or someone means to them. To begin, the teacher or students identify a topic to fill in the blank, such as anger, a friend, liberty, or fear; then students start each line with "... is" and describe or define that thing. A group of grade 2 students wrote the following poem as a part of their weather unit:

> **Thunder Is ...**
>
> Thunder is someone bowling.
>
> Thunder is a hot cloud bumping against a cold cloud.
>
> Thunder is someone playing basketball.
>
> Thunder is dynamite blasting.
>
> Thunder is a brontosaurus sneezing.
>
> Thunder is people moving their furniture.
>
> Thunder is a giant laughing.

Thunder is elephants playing.

Thunder is an army tank.

Thunder is Bugs Bunny chewing his carrots.

Students often write powerful poems using this formula once they move beyond the cute "Happiness is …" and "Love is …" patterns.

ACROSTIC POEMS

Students write acrostic poems by choosing a keyword and writing it vertically on a sheet of paper. Then they create lines of poetry, each beginning with a letter of the word. Students can use their names during a unit on autobiography or names of characters during a resource-based unit. For example, after reading *Officer Buckle and Gloria* (Rathmann, 1995), grade 1 students wrote this acrostic using the dog's name, Gloria, for the keyword.

Gloria

Loves to do tricks.

Officer Buckle tells safety

Rules at schools.

I wish I had

A dog like Gloria.

Students also write acrostics using keywords from social studies and science theme study and inquiry-based units. A grade 6 student wrote,

Every

Golden treasure lies still

Young in beauty and

Precious in value beneath the earth

The Egyptians adorned themselves in never-ending splendour.

Free-Form Poems

In free-form poems, children choose words to describe something, express a thought, or tell a story, without concern for rhyme or other arrangements. The number of words per line and the use of punctuation vary. In the following poem, a grade 8 student uses only fifteen well-chosen words:

Loneliness

A lifetime

Of broken dreams

And promises

Lost love

Hurt

My heart

Cries

In silence

Students can use several methods for writing free-form poems. They can select words and phrases from brainstormed lists and cluster diagrams, or they can write a paragraph and then "unwrite" it by deleting unnecessary words. They arrange the remaining words to look like a poem.

CONCRETE POEMS

Students create concrete poems through art and the careful arrangement of words on a page. Words, phrases, and sentences can be written in the shape of an object, or word pictures can be inserted within poems written left to right and top to bottom. The website Wordle (www. wordle.net) can be used when writing concrete poems on the computer; it generates a "word cloud" from the text provided by the students. Students can experiment with different fonts, layouts, and colour schemes, which can then be printed out or saved to the Wordle Gallery. In "Ants," the words *ants*, *cake*, and *frosting* create the image of a familiar picnic scene, and in "Cemetery," repetition and form create a reflection of peace. Three books of concrete poems are *Splish Splash: Poems* (Graham, 1994), *Blue Lipstick: Concrete Poems* (Grandits, 2007), and *A Poke in the I* (Janeczko, 2001).

Students are proud to share their own poems with the teacher and other students.

FOUND POEMS

Students create poems by culling words from other sources, such as stories, songs, and newspaper articles. A grade 3 class created a lengthy found poem, with a section for each chapter, as they read *Sarah, Plain and Tall* (MacLachlan, 1985). This section is from Chapter 3, "The Arrival":

> Papa drove off,
>
> New wife,
>
> New mother.
>
> Maybe? Maybe?
>
> Rocking on the porch,
>
> Rolling the blue marble,
>
> Back and forth,
>
> Back and forth.
>
> Caleb saw it too,
>
> Not smiling.
>
> We do not have the sea here.
>
> Perfect? Perfect?

Syllable- and Word-Count Poems

Haiku and other syllable- and word-count poems provide a structure that helps students succeed in writing; however, the need to adhere to these poems' formulas may restrict freedom of expression. The exact syllable counts force students to search for just the right words and provide an opportunity for students to use thesauruses and dictionaries.

HAIKU

Haiku (high-KOO) is a Japanese poetic form consisting of 17 syllables arranged in three lines of five, seven, and fivesyllables. Haiku poems present a single, clear image. A grade 4 student wrote this haiku poem:

> Spider web shining
> Tangled on the grass with dew
> Waiting quietly.

Books of haiku to share with students include *Haiku—One Breath Poetry* (Wakan, 1993), *Black Swan/White Crow* (J. P. Lewis, 1995), *Spring: A Haiku Story* (Shannon, 1996), *Shadow Play: Night Haiku* (Harter, 1994), *The Sound of Water* (Hamill, 1995), *The Essential Haiku: Versions of Basho, Buson, & Issa* (Hass, 1995), and *The Classic Tradition of Haiku: An Anthology* (Bowers, 1996). The photographs and artwork in these books may give students ideas for illustrating their haiku poems.

TANKA

Tanka (TANK-ah) is a Japanese verse form containing thirty-onesyllables arranged in five lines, 5-7-5-7-7. A grade 8 student wrote this tanka poem:

> The summer dancers
> Dancing in the midnight sky,
> Waltzing and dreaming
> Stars glistening in the night sky.
> Wish upon a shooting star.

CINQUAIN

A cinquain (SIN-cane) is a five-line poem containing twenty-two syllables in a 2-4-6-8-2 syllable pattern. Students ask themselves what their subject looks like, smells like, sounds like, and tastes like, and record their ideas using a five-senses cluster as follows:

Line 1:_A one-word subject with two syllables

Line 2:_Four syllables describing the subject

Line 3:_Six syllables showing action

Line 4:_Eight syllables expressing a feeling or an observation about the subject

Line 5:_Two syllables describing or renaming the subject

Here is a cinquain poem written by an upper-grade student:

> Wrestling
> skinny, fat
> coaching, arguing, pinning
> trying hard to win
> tournament

Some lines in this poem are short a syllable or two. The student bent some of the guidelines to create a powerful image of wrestling; however, the message of the poem is more important than adhering to the formula.

DIAMANTE

Tiedt (1970) invented the diamante (dee-ah-MAHN-tay), a seven-line contrast poem written in the shape of a diamond. This poetic form helps students apply their knowledge of opposites and parts of speech. The formula is as follows:

Line 1:_One noun as the subject

Line 2:_Two adjectives describing the subject

Line 3:_Three participles (ending in -*ing*) telling about the subject

Line 4:_Four nouns (the first two related to the subject and the second two related to the opposite)

Line 5:_Three participles telling about the opposite

Line 6:_Two adjectives describing the opposite

Line 7:_One noun that is the opposite of the subject

A grade 3 class wrote this diamante poem:

Baby

wrinkled tiny

crying wetting sleeping

rattles diapers money house

caring working loving

smart helpful

Adult

Notice that the students created a contrast between *baby*, the subject in the first line, and *adult*, the opposite in the last line. This contrast gives students the opportunity to play with words and apply their understanding of opposites. The third word in the fourth line, *money*, begins the transition from *baby* to its opposite, *adult*.

Rhymed Verse Forms

Rhymed verse forms such as limericks can be used effectively with middle- and upper-grade students. It is important that teachers try to prevent the forms and rhyme schemes from restricting students' creative and imaginative expression.

LIMERICKS

The limerick is a form of light verse that uses both rhyme and rhythm. The poem consists of five lines; the first, second, and fifth lines rhyme, while the third and fourth lines rhyme with each other and are shorter than the other three. The rhyme scheme is a-a-b-b-a, and a limerick is arranged this way:

Line	Rhyme
1 _____	a
2 _____	a
3 _____	b
4 _____	b
5 _____	a

The last line often contains a funny or surprise ending, as in this limerick written by a grade 8 student:

> There once was a frog named Pete
>
> Who did nothing but sit and eat.
>
> He examined each fly
>
> With so careful an eye
>
> And then said, "You're dead meat."

Writing limericks can be a challenging assignment for many upper-grade students, but middle-grade students can also be successful with this poetic form, especially if there is a class collaboration.

Limericks were first popularized over a century ago by Edward Lear (1812–1888). Poet X. J. Kennedy (Kennedy & Kennedy, 1982) described limericks as the most popular type of poem in the English language today. Teachers can introduce students to limericks by reading aloud some of Lear's verses so that students appreciate the rhythm of the verse. Two collections of limericks are *Daffy-Down-Dillies: Silly Limericks* by Edward Lear (1995a) and *Lots of Limericks* (Livingston, 1991). John Ciardi has written *The Hopeful Trout and Other Limericks* (1992) for grades 3 to 6, and Arnold Lobel has also written a book of unique pig limericks, *The Book of Pigericks* (1983). After reading Lobel's pigericks, students will want to write "birdericks" or "fishericks."

Teaching Students to Write Poems

As they write poems, students use what they have learned about poetry through reading poems and the information presented in minilessons on the poetic forms.

Teachers often simply explain several poetic forms and then allow students to choose a form and write a poem. This approach ignores the teaching component; it's back to the "assign and do" syndrome. Instead, students need to experiment with each poetic form. After these preliminary experiences, they can apply what they have learned and write poems that adhere to any of the forms they have learned during writers workshop or as part of resource-based units, theme study units, and inquiry-based units. Class collaborations are crucial because they are a practice run for children who are not sure what to do. The five minutes it takes to write a class collaboration poem can be the difference between success and failure for would-be poets.

Teachers teach many other poetry minilessons on wordplay, arranging lines of poetry for the greatest impact, punctuating poems, and how to read poems, for example. A list of topics for minilessons related to reading and writing poetry is presented on page 242.

The accompanying Teacher's Notebook summarizes some guidelines for teaching children to write poetry.

IN WRITERS WORKSHOP

After students learn about various poetic forms, they often choose to write poems during writers workshop. They write poems about favourite topics or to express their feelings. They also experiment with forms introduced during recent minilessons. Students who especially like to write poems can publish collections of their poems during writers workshop and share them with their classmates. This sharing often stimulates other students to write poetry.

Reading and Writing Poetry

	Procedures	Concepts	Strategies and Skills
Wordplay	Craft riddles Create word pictures Invent words Craft tongue twisters	Word picture Metaphors Similes Alliteration Onomatopoeia Repetition Rhyme	Rhyme Compare Use alliteration Use onomatopoeia Use repetition
Reading Poetry	Read a poem interpretively Do choral reading Share poems in pairs Visualize while reading Use simple gestures	Rhymed verse Narrative poems Free verse Concrete poems Information about poets	Vary tempo Emphasize rhythm Vary pitch Stress juncture Interpret poets' message
Writing Poetry	Write formula poems: • "I wish ..." poems • colour poems • five-senses poems • "If I were ..." poems • contrast poems • definition poems • preposition poems Craft found poems Write free-form poems Design concrete poems Write haiku poems Write cinquain poems Write diamante poems Write limericks Write model poems	Poetic forms Alignment of form, content, and purpose	Use poetic forms Create sensory images Paint word pictures Unwrite Use model poems Write rhymes Punctuate poems Capitalize poems Arrange poems on the page

For more information on readers and writers workshops, see Chapter 2, "Teaching the Language Arts," pages 55–58, and Chapter 11, "Putting It All Together," pages 389–400.

Teachers also plan poetry workshops that incorporate components of both readers and writers workshops. Students read and respond to poems during the readers workshop component, and then they write poems during the writers workshop component. One possible schedule for a poetry workshop is as follows:

10 minutes	The teacher leads a whole-class meeting to; • Give a book talk on a new poetry book • Talk about a poet • Read several favourite poems using choral reading • Talk about a "difficult" or "confusing" poem
20 minutes	Students read poems independently.
10 minutes	Students share poems with classmates.
10 minutes	The teacher teaches a poetry minilesson.
25 minutes	Students write poems using the writing process.
10 minutes	Students share poems they have written.

Guidelines for Writing Poems

1. Explain the Concept of Poetry
The teacher explains what poetry is and what makes a good poem. Too often students assume that all poems must rhyme, are written on topics such as love and flowers, must be punctuated in a particular way, or have other restrictions.

2. Include Poetry Books in the Classroom
Poetry books are set out in a special section of the classroom library. Students learn about poetry through reading, and some poems can serve as models for the poems students write.

3. Teach Formulas
Students learn five to ten formulas to use when they write poems so that they have a range of formulas from which to choose. At the same time, it is important that students know that they can break the formulas in order to express themselves more effectively.

4. Teach Minilessons on Poetic Devices
The teacher presents minilessons on comparison, alliteration, onomatopoeia, and repetition; and encourages students to use poetic devices other than rhyme.

5. Encourage Wordplay
The teacher encourages students to play with words, invent new words, and create word pictures as they write poems.

6. Write Poetry
Students write poetry as part of resource-based units, thematic units, and inquiry-based units. Students can write found poems using excerpts from books, write poems about characters in stories, and write poems about topics related to themes. They use multimedia to create demonstrations and performances that can be shared with others.

7. Create a Class Anthology
The teacher and students create a class anthology of students' poems and duplicate copies of the anthology for each student.

IN RESOURCE-BASED UNITS

Students often write poems as part of resource-based units. They write poems together as a class during the exploring stage, or individually or in small groups as projects during the extending stage. Sometimes poetry writing activities are planned, and at other times they happen spontaneously. To explore the language of a book, students might write found poetry using a paragraph from a favourite book. Or students might write acrostic poems about a book title or a character's name. This acrostic poem about *Jumanji* (Van Allsburg, 1981) was written by a grade 4 student:

> **J**ungle adventure game and
> f**U**n for a while.
> **M**onkeys ransacking kitchens
> **A**nd boa constrictors slithering past.
> **N**o way out until the game is done—
> **J**ust reach the city of Jumanji,
> **I** don't want to play!

Students also write poems as projects during theme study units. A small group of grade 3 students composed the following found poem after reading *Sarah Morton's Day: A Day in the Life of a Pilgrim Girl* (Waters, 1989):

This Is My Day

Good day.

I must get up and be about my chores.

The fire is mine to tend.

I lay the table.

I muck the garden.

I pound the spices.

I draw vinegar to polish the brass.

I practise my lessons.

I feed the fire again.

I milk the goats.

I eat dinner.

I say the verses I am learning.

My father is pleased with my learning.

I fetch the water for tomorrow.

I bid my parents good night.

I say my prayers.

Fare thee well.

God be with thee.

To compose the found poem, the students collected their favourite words and sentences from the book and organized them sequentially to describe the pilgrim girl's day.

Differentiating to Meet the Needs of Every Student

Poetry should be an important part of reading and writing, and teachers must find ways to involve all students in poetry activities. Poetry written for children is available today that will evoke strong feelings and powerful images in students. Writing poetry is a valuable way for students to play with language and express themselves. As teachers plan poetry workshops and connect reading and writing poetry activities to resource-based and theme study units, they must find ways to adapt the activities to meet the needs of every student. Some suggestions are offered here. A list of additional poetry resources can be found in Figure 6-14.

Assessing Poems That Students Write

As teachers read, respond to, and assess the poems that students write, they need to recognize the nuggets of promise in the poems and support and build on them. Hughes (2007) recommends that teachers focus on the passion and wonder in students' writing and on students' ability to make the common seem uncommon. Teachers can also notice the specific details, strong images, wordplay, comparisons, onomatopoeia, alliteration, and repetitions of words and lines that students incorporate in their poems.

FIGURE 6-14 WRITING POETRY RESOURCES

Fitch, S. (2000). *Writing Maniac: How I Grew Up to be a Writer and You Can Too.* Markham, ON: Pembrooke Publishers. 🍁

Fletcher, R. (2002). *Poetry Matters: Writing a Poem from the Inside Out.* New York: Harper Collins.

Fletcher, R. (2005). *A Writing Kind of Day: Poems for Young Poets.* Honesdale, PA: Wordsong.

Lesynski, L. (2006). *"I Did It Because . . .": How a Poem Happens.* Toronto: Annick Press. (M) 🍁

Prelutsky, J. (2008). *Pizza, Pigs, and Poetry: How to Write a Poem.* New York: Greenwillow Books.

Prelutsky, J. (2009). *Read a Rhyme, Write a Rhyme.* New York: Dragonfly Books.

The poetic formulas discussed in this chapter provide options for students as they experiment with ways to express their thoughts. Although children experiment with a variety of forms during the elementary grades, it is not necessary to test their knowledge of particular forms. Knowing that haiku is a Japanese poetic form composed of seventeen syllables arranged in three lines will not make a child a poet. Descriptions of the forms should instead be posted in the classroom or added to language arts notebooks for students to refer to as they write.

Assessing the quality of students' poems is especially difficult, because poems are creative combinations of wordplay, poetic forms, and poetic devices. Instead of trying to give a grade for quality, teachers can assess students on other criteria:

- Has the student experimented with the poetic form presented in a minilesson?
- Has the student used the process approach in writing, revising, and editing the poem?
- Has the student used wordplay or another poetic device in the poem?

Teachers also ask students to assess their own progress in writing poetry. Students choose their best efforts and poems that show promise. They can explain which writing strategies they used in particular poems and which poetic forms they used.

Students keep copies of their poems in their writing folders or poetry booklets so that they can review and assess their own work. They may also place copies of some poems in their language arts portfolios. If a grade for quality is absolutely necessary, students should choose several of the poems in their writing folders for the teacher to evaluate.

Review

During the elementary and middle-school grades, students learn about five elements of story structure: plot, characters, setting, point of view, and theme. Students apply this knowledge as they listen to stories teachers read to them and as they read independently. They also use their knowledge of the elements as they write stories. Students develop interpretations as they read and respond to stories. Students read and write stories as part of resource-based units, readers workshop, and theme study units. They use the writing process and their knowledge of new literacies to write and share retellings of familiar stories, new versions of stories, sequels, and original stories. They also use journal writing and blogging to share events in their lives and record what they are learning both in language arts units and during lessons across the curriculum.

Poetry is also an important part of the language arts curriculum. Students participate in wordplay activities and read and write poetry as part of resource-based units, readers and writers workshops, and theme study units. Experiences with poetry give students a variety of perspectives on language and other subject matter.

The following key concepts are presented in this chapter:

1. Students acquire a concept of story by listening to, reading, and writing stories and by learning about the elements of story structure.

2. Stories have unique structural elements that distinguish them from other forms of writing: plot, characters, setting, point of view, and theme.

3. Students use the following strategies to respond to stories: visualizing, predicting, engaging, empathizing, identifying, elaborating, noticing opposites, monitoring, and connecting to personal experiences.

4. Storyboards, story boxes, open-mind portraits, setting maps, sketch-to-stretch, and multi-media productions are six ways to explore stories.

5. Students use intertextuality as they incorporate ideas from the stories they have heard and read into the stories they write.

6. Students write in many different kinds of journals: personal journals, dialogue journals, reading response logs, double-entry journals, learning logs, simulated journals, and blogs.

7. Dialogue journals are especially useful for students learning English as a second language.

8. Reading response journals, double-entry journals, simulated journals and blogs are often used during resource-based units.

9. The focus in journal writing is on developing writing fluency and using writing as a tool for learning.

10. Wordplay activities with riddles, comparisons, rhyme, and other poetic devices provide the background of experiences students need for reading and writing poetry.

11. The focus in teaching students to read and respond to poems is enjoyment.

12. Students can write poems successfully using a variety of poetic formulas such as beginning each line with particular words or counting syllables.

13. Because rhyme is a sticking point for many students, they should be encouraged to experiment with other poetic devices in their writing.

14. Multimedia, songs, and publishing websites support students' efforts to read and write poetry.

Theory to Practice

1. Compile a list of books to use in teaching about story elements at the grade level you teach or plan to teach. Write a brief summary of each book, commenting specifically on the element of story structure or genre that the book exemplifies.

2. Interview several students about their concept of story and what they think about as they read and write stories. Ask questions such as these:

   - Tell me about a story you have read that is really a good one.

   - What things do authors include in stories to make them good?

   - Tell me about some of the stories you have written.

3. Plan a resource-based unit on a picture book or a chapter book. Include reading and writing poetry in your plans.

4. Collect samples of children's stories and examine them to see how students use the elements of story structure in their writing.

5. Using dialogue journals and/or blogs, write back and forth with three students in your classroom who are having difficulty. Continue for several weeks. What changes do you see in students' entries and your own over the period?

6. Teach a small group of students to write several types of poems, and have students share their poems by posting them to a secure class website or compiling their poems in a class anthology added to the class library.

Literacy in Action

Chapter 7: Changing Information into Knowledge

Procedure

In a five-week unit called Exploring Ancient Egypt, my goal was to motivate students to research areas of ancient Egypt that interested them and to give them the skills to sift through masses of resources and synthesize information into a concise, useable, and memorable project. It was all about changing information into knowledge. What fun we had! We chose ancient Egypt because all of the students were very interested in that topic. The grade 7 social studies curriculum included culture, and because the ancient Egyptian culture was so different from our Canadian one, it made for great comparisons when I later taught the regular social studies topic.

> "This unit was so much fun to teach because... I was able to choose skills from both the language arts and social studies curricula to integrate into the learning."
>
> Dawn King-Hunter

We started out by taking a 17 × 11 piece of paper and folding it in half three times. This gave us a tracking sheet with eight equal squares on each side. As a class, we brainstormed topics that people wanted to explore. Students wrote a topic at the top of each square, coming up with many different ones, including ancient Egyptian food, religion, clothing, farming, lifestyles, language, writing, pharaohs, the Nile, holidays, festivals, art, class system, housing, architecture, transportation, education, mummification, and burial ceremonies. One of the squares was entitled "Bibliography," and students recorded each informational resource they used.

As a facilitator, I then tried to inundate them with all sorts of different information material. We examined library books, flipped through *National Geographic* magazines, and surfed the Internet. On day 1, I read information from a few different books and as a class we practised how to pinpoint the main idea and copy a point-form phrase on our tracking sheet. I modelled this on the board. Day 2 gave the students an opportunity to share the materials we had in the classroom and take more notes. Students were allowed to work with a partner reading the information, but both students needed to record important points. On day three, we accessed a class set of laptop computers and students used a variety of search engines to find more information. Throughout our research, students recorded information in point

form in the appropriate square on their own tracking sheets. We continued researching this way for about a week. At one point, we invited one of our ESL students to
teach us basic Egyptian Arabic.

From the beginning of the unit, all students were extremely interested in the
mummification process, so we researched how this was done and everyone participated in a hands-on chicken mummification experience. After completing a mummification game on the Internet at http://www.bbc.co.uk/history/interactive/
games/mummy_maker/index_embed.shtml, students divided into groups and each
group was given a chicken to mummify. After five weeks of processing the chickens,
each group wrapped the mummy in gauze bandages and adorned the bodies with
precious gems. By this time, each mummy had been named (for instance, King
Cluck, Princess Cluckopatra) and students had turned a shoebox into a beautifully
designed sarcophagus. We had a classroom burial ceremony and the mummies were
placed in the G. S. Lakie School resident tomb (the classroom back closet).

Assessment

Students were required to create a project to present the information they gleaned
during the unit to the rest of the class. Each specific project was left open-ended so
students could choose a project and method of presentation that appealed to their
strongest intelligence. For example, a student with a strong visual intelligence chose
to present information in poster format and another built an intricate 3-D model of
the pyramids. Three students worked together on a video "mockumentary" showing
a new discovery of an ancient tomb. One student with a strong proficiency in writing composed a fictional story of a slave girl's life of catering to a famous pharaoh.
The entire unit was based on a pass/fail grade, so if students participated in the
research and had a final project, they passed.

Reflection

This unit was so much fun to teach because, first of all, the students were really interested in ancient Egypt. Second, it was a topic that lent itself well to the integration
of many different subjects. I was able to choose skills from both the language arts and
social studies curricula to integrate into the learning. As a group, we learned together,
and I adjusted my lessons according to the information we were unearthing on a
daily basis. The tracking sheet is an extremely useful tool because it teaches students
to organize research material all in one place. Insisting that students write the main
idea in point form rather than copying reams of sentences directly from the resources
also teaches them how to make the knowledge their own, without plagiarizing.
Finally, the real learning comes through having participated in individual research,
creating a final project, and then observing and experiencing everyone else's
presentation.

From the classroom of Dawn King-Hunter
G. S. Lakie Middle School
Lethbridge, Alberta

Reading and Writing Expository Text

LEARNING OUTCOMES

After reading this chapter, you should be able to

1. Describe the types and features of informational text

2. Explain how informational text differs from stories

3. Describe the five most common expository text structures

4. Explain how teachers can teach students to read and learn from expository text

5. Explain how teachers facilitate students' writing of various types of informational prose, including reports and letters

Tyler Olson/Shutterstock

Students enjoy learning from both visuals and printed text when reading informational books.

Stories and informational books are different genres, although they overlap. In this chapter, we will focus primarily on reading and writing informational texts. To read and write informational text effectively, students need to develop knowledge of how texts are structured and develop strategies that help them identify and remember the information authors present. Similarly, to write informational text, students imitate the structures they have read and learn to present their information in ways that engage their readers.

Janet Lunn, co-author of *The Story of Canada* (Lunn & Moore, 1992), the first illustrated history of Canada for young people, talks about how children become engaged in reading informational books. She suggests that adults and children together share this type of literature. Lunn says, "I can't see too many kids sitting down and reading it from beginning to end, but they will dip into it, and read this and that story" (Reed, 1992, p. 295). In addition, she notes the important role that illustrations play in an informational book, indicating that these "in large part are responsible for the book's appeal" (p. 295).

As students read informational books and listen to them read aloud, they learn about the world around them and many other things as well. They learn how to vary their reading depending on their purpose. Sometimes they read informational books from beginning to end like stories, or they may use the index to locate a specific topic and then read just that section. They learn how to use an index and a table of contents, and how to read charts, graphs, maps, and diagrams. On the Internet, they also notice the different ways **expository texts** are organized and how writers develop interrelationships among the pieces of information being presented. In Chapter 1, we discussed that students require new skills and strategies, called *new literacies*, to identify information, critically evaluate that information, and communicate effectively on the Internet (Leu, Kinzer, Coiro, & Cammack, 2004).

Reading informational text from the Internet requires some of the same skills as reading linear print text, but it also requires other skills. Reading from the Internet has been described as 3-D (D. Fisher, Lapp, & Wood, 2011). That is, like reading print, readers read from left to right and from top to bottom, but they also have the option of leaving the original text to go to other screens—the third dimension. Clicking on related links may take the reader deeper into the web, but it takes away from simply progressing through a text. The reader is essentially in control: he or she decides what to read next—whether to merely skim or to read the entire text, when, and in which direction to move. Being in control means that readers must be prepared to make decisions that help them achieve their purposes for reading. The strategies teachers teach must prepare students to read both print and three-dimensional informational text.

Students also write informational books about concepts and information they are learning during theme study units and in lessons in other areas of the curriculum. The informational trade books they read serve as models, or *mentor texts*, for their writing. Similarly, the informational websites they have consulted serve as examples for the multimedia presentations and websites they create. Students organize the information that they present using the same types of patterns or structures used in informational sources from which they gather information. As discussed in Chapter 9, "Viewing and Visually Representing," they learn to visually represent information in the ways they experience them in these sources.

Not all texts are simply expository or **narrative**. Some are both. Chapman and Sopko (2003) refer to the books in which information and story overlap as *combined texts*. Combined texts, also referred to as *narrative nonfiction* or *creative nonfiction*, such as *The Magic School Bus inside a Hurricane* (Cole, 1995) and *Mimi's Village and How Basic Health Care Transformed It* (Milway, 2012), use a story-like format, but the emphasis is on providing information (E. B. Freeman & Person, 1992).

Types of Informational Books

A new wave of engaging and artistic informational books is now available, and these books show increased respect for children's interest in learning about the world in which they live. Peter Roop (1992) explains that for years informational books were the "ugly duckling" of children's literature, but now they have grown into a beautiful swan. Each year, outstanding Canadian nonfiction for young people is recognized through the awarding of the *Norma Fleck Award for Canadian Children's Non-Fiction*. Winners and finalists are listed on Canadian Children's Book Centre's website, www.bookcentre.ca.

The best informational books exemplify four qualities:

Accuracy. The information is factual, objective, and current, avoiding stereotypes and anthropomorphism—that is, attributing human characteristics to animals and inanimate objects. The text distinguishes between fact and opinion. The author's qualifications are emphasized through evidence of research, information about how the author studied the topic, and suggestions for further reading and related websites.

Organization. Ideas are developed logically using sequence, cause and effect, or another expository pattern, and the author's purpose is clear. Reader-friendly nonfiction features, including table of contents, diagrams, and margin notes, make the information more accessible.

Design. The design is appealing, and illustrations complement the text, making the book more engaging. Margin notes, headings, feature boxes, and other reader-friendly nonfiction features make the book easier to comprehend.

Style. The style reveals the author's curiosity and enthusiasm for the topic. The tone suits the topic, and the text is written at appropriate interest and reading levels for the intended audience.

The same four characteristics are true of informational texts presented in other contexts, such as in magazines like *Canadian Geographic Kids*, *OWL*, and *Chickadee*, and on the Internet.

A wide variety of informational books is available today. Topics include the biological sciences, the physical sciences, the social sciences, the arts, and biographies. *Media Madness: An Insider's Guide to Media* (Ali & Cho, 2005) is a fine informational book about media literacy that urges young readers to critically evaluate messages on television; in music, magazines, comic books, newspapers, and video games; and on the Internet. Another book—*Chew on This: Everything You Don't Want to Know about Fast Food* (Schlosser & Wilson, 2006)—documents the far-reaching negative effects of the fast-food industry. Books like *Move!* (Jenkins & Page, 2006) show how a variety of animals move, with bright colourful illustrations and simple yet engaging text.

Other books present historical and geographic concepts. The "Our Canadian Girl" and "I Am Canada" series help readers experience facets of Canadian history through the eyes of early inhabitants and historical figures. The books contain fact, fiction, and some illustrations. Another fine book, *Amelia Earhart: The Legend of the Lost Aviator* (Tanaka, 2008) presents Earhart's many accomplishments in a flowing narrative accompanied by photographs and colourful illustrations. These books are exciting to read, and they provide an engaging and enriching reading experience for elementary students.

Life stories, both biography and autobiography, are another type of informational book. Life stories being written today are more realistic than in the past, and they present well-known personalities, warts and all. Linda Granfield's portrait of John McCrae in *In Flanders Fields: The Story of the Poem by John McCrae* (1995) is among the best known. *John Lennon: All I Want Is the Truth* (Partridge, 2005) is an award-winning biography of Lennon's life and death. Lian Goodall's book *Photographing Greatness: The Story of Karsh* (2007) is another amazing story, about the life of a successful Canadian photographer. Two other publications, *Capturing Joy: The Story of Maud Lewis* (Bogart, 2002) and *Breaking Free: The Story of William Kurelek* (Ebbit-Cutler, 2002), make a significant contribution to information available to young readers regarding Canadian art and artists. Authors often include notes in the back of books to explain how the details were researched and to provide additional information.

Although few autobiographies are available to elementary students today, more are being published each year. Autobiographies by authors, such as Jean Little's *Little by Little* (1987), and by talented performers, such as Olympia Dowd, who wrote *A Young Dancer's Apprenticeship: On Tour with the Moscow City Ballet* (2002), provide insight into courage, perseverance, and talent, and are popular with students. These examples show how other subject areas such as science and social studies can be enhanced through books and reading.

In addition to these main types of informational books, there are other, more specialized, types. Four types that elementary students read are

1. ***Alphabet and counting books.*** While many alphabet and counting books with pictures of familiar objects are designed for young children, others provide a wealth of information on various topics. In *Eh? to Zed: A Canadian ABCedarium,* Kevin Major (2000) focuses on uniquely Canadian objects and artifacts to produce his alphabet book; in *A Northern Alphabet* (1982), Ted Harrison uses many elements from the Cree culture to inform his work; Denise Fleming uses handmade paper artwork to create an alphabet book highlighting construction activities in *Alphabet under Construction* (2002); and in *Loonies and Toonies: A Canadian Number Book* (2006), Mike Ulmer uses poetry and prose to explain many numerical facts of Canadian history. In some of these books, new terms are introduced and illustrated, and in others, new terms are explained in a sentence or a paragraph.

2. ***Books that present information through a song or poem.*** In these powerful books, songs and poems are illustrated with a word, line, or stanza on each page. Together, the text and illustrations provide information. Young readers and listeners are invited to learn about math in nature in Lizann Flatt's poetic series, including *Counting on Fall* (2012) and *Sorting through Spring* (2013). In *Mummer's Song* (1990), Bud Davidge's song—well known in Newfoundland and Labrador—is accompanied by Ian Wallace's captivating pictures of that province's mummering tradition; old-fashioned dress-ups and Christmas traditions are described and celebrated through pictures and song. Joyce Sidman's poetry and Beckie Prange's illustrations combine to describe the life of ponds through melodic verse and woodcut art in *Song of the Water Boatman and Other Pond Poems* (2005). *Ann and Seamus* (2003), the story of an Irish shipwreck off the coast of Newfoundland and Labrador, is told by award-winning author Kevin Major and exquisitely illustrated by East Coast artist David Blackwood.

3. ***Books that present information within a story.*** Authors are devising innovative strategies for combining information with a story in combined texts. Michele Martin Bossley's *The Perfect Gymnast* (1996) provides detailed and powerful information about gymnastics, bulimia, and interpersonal relationships. In *Selina and the Bear Paw Quilt* (1995), Barbara Smucker documents a Mennonite family's move to Upper Canada to avoid the U.S. Civil War, and *Arizona Charlie and the Klondike Kid* (2003), by Julie Lawson, is set during the Yukon Gold Rush era. These books present factual material through interesting and thought-provoking stories. Flashback is another useful technique for presenting information. In *Just Like New* (Reczuch & Manson, 1995), flashback is used to contrast Canada with war-torn England in the 1940s. Karen Reczuch cleverly uses black-and-white and colour illustrations to contrast the settings in these two countries.

Some combination informational/story books are imaginative fantasies. The Magic School Bus series, written by Joanna Cole and illustrated by Bruce Degen, is perhaps the best known. In *The Magic School Bus inside a Hurricane* (1995), for example, Ms. Frizzle and her class study weather up close as their bus survives both a hurricane and a tornado on its way to a weather station. Charts and reports with factual information and suggestions for projects are presented throughout the book.

Other authors use the story format to tell about experiences in their own lives or their families' lives. *Ryan and Jimmy and the Well in Africa That Brought Them Together* (Shoveller, 2006) tells the story of six-year-old Ryan Hreljac's wish to build a well to supply villagers in Agweo, Uganda, with safe, clean water. Told by his great-uncle, the story explains how Ryan's will and determination led to a cherished friendship between Ryan, his family, and Akana Jimmy. The blending of factual information with story events makes *Ryan and Jimmy* more than a story of friendship—it gives young readers a true account of one family's success in being caring global citizens. Still other authors use combined texts to write autobiographically. For example, Jacqueline Briggs Martin (1998) tells the life story of Wilson Bentley in narrative while also detailing the development of specialized photography technique through marginal notes in *Snowflake Bentley*, a Caldecott Medal winner.

4. ***Journals and letters.*** Journals and letters are types of informational books, and these artifacts provide a glimpse into historical periods and the lives of historical personalities. One all-encompassing example is the previously mentioned *The Story of Canada* (Lunn & Moore, 1992). This encyclopedic volume follows the buffalo hunt, tells the story of the Klondike Gold Rush, and features information about the lives of such notable Canadians as Terry Fox and Roberta Bondar. The book is well researched and contains paintings, historical photographs, maps, and posters, making it visually appealing to children and adults alike.

Some journals and collections of letters are authentic accounts, but others are fictionalized. Shelley Tanaka's *I Was There: On Board the* Titanic (1996) is an award-winning informational book that focuses on the lives of two young men who actually survived the sinking of the *Titanic*. The author weaves together memories and factual information to produce an outstanding account of the voyage and its tragic demise. From *Zlata's Diary: A Child's Life in Wartime Sarajevo* (Filopovic, 2006), a true account and bestseller, readers learn of a young girl's hardships as war engulfs Sarajevo. Even the fictionalized accounts can be used in conjunction with informational books, but teachers and students should be aware of the differences between the two types.

Expository Text Structures

Just as stories are structured using plot, characters, and the other elements of story structure, informational books are organized or patterned in particular ways called *expository text structures*. These structures are commonly found in textbooks, in informational trade books, on the Internet, in magazines, and in newspapers. Five of the most common organizational patterns are description, sequence, comparison, cause and effect, and problem and solution (Allen, 2004; Sejnost & Thiese, 2010). Figure 7–1 describes these patterns and presents sample passages and cue words that signal use of each pattern. In stories, the elements of story structure interact together to create the story framework; however, in informational text, each expository text structure may be used separately.

DESCRIPTION

In this pattern, the author describes a topic by listing characteristics, features, and examples. Phrases such as *for example, characteristics are,* and *consists of* cue this structure. When students delineate any topic, such as volcanoes, wolves, or the Rocky Mountains, they use description.

SEQUENCE

In this pattern, the author lists items or events in numerical or chronological order. Cue words include *first*, *second*, *third*, *next*, *then*, and *finally*. Students use the sequence pattern to write directions for completing a math problem, the stages in an animal's life cycle, or events in a biography.

COMPARISON

In this pattern, the author explains how two or more things are alike and/or different. *Different, in contrast, alike, same as,* and *on the other hand* are cue words and phrases that signal this structure. When students compare and contrast book and video versions of a story, reptiles with amphibians, or life in ancient Greece with life in ancient Egypt, they use this organizational pattern.

CAUSE AND EFFECT

In this pattern, the author describes one or more causes and the resulting effect or effects. *Reasons why, if... then, as a result, therefore,* and *because* are words and phrases that cue this structure. Students use the cause-and-effect structure when they write such explanations as why dinosaurs became extinct or the effects of pollution on the environment.

PROBLEM AND SOLUTION

In this pattern, the author states a problem and offers one or more solutions. A variation is the question-and-answer (or Q&A) format, in which the author poses a question and then answers it. Cue words and phrases include *problem is, dilemma is, puzzle is, solve,* and *question ... answer*. Students use this structure when they write about why money was invented, saving endangered animals, or building dams to stop flooding. They often use the problem–solution pattern in writing advertisements and in other persuasive writing.

These organizational patterns correspond to the traditional organization of main ideas and details within paragraphs. The main idea is embodied in the organizational pattern, and the details are the elaboration; for example, in the sample passage of the comparison pattern in Figure 7-1, the main idea is that the modern Olympic games are very different from the ancient Olympics. The details are the specific comparisons and contrasts.

Graphic organizers can help students organize and visually represent ideas for the five organizational patterns (Neufeld, 2005/2006). Teachers use software such as Inspiration (http://www.inspiration.com), Kidspiration, or free online tools that generate graphic organizers to demonstrate text structure to students. Students might use a **cluster** for description, a Venn diagram or T-chart for comparison, or a series of boxes and arrows for cause and effect (Yopp & Yopp, 2006). Diagrams of a variety of graphic organizers also appear in Figure 7-1.

Even though the expository text structures are used with informational texts, some books that are classified as stories also involve sequence, cause and effect, or one of the other expository text structures. Teachers can point out these structures or use graphic organizers to help students look more closely at the story. The popular *The Very Hungry Caterpillar* (Carle, 1969), for example, involves two sequences. Eric Carle uses sequence to show the development of the caterpillar from egg to

FIGURE 7-1 THE FIVE EXPOSITORY TEXT STRUCTURES

Pattern	Description	Cue Words	Graphic Organizer	Sample Passage
Description	The author describes a topic by listing characteristics, features, and examples.	*for example* *characteristics are* *consists of*		The Olympic symbol consists of five interlocking rings. The rings represent the five continents—Africa, Asia, Europe, North America, and South America—from which athletes compete in the games. The rings are coloured black, blue, green, red, and yellow. At least one of these colours is found in the flag of every country sending athletes to compete in the Olympic games.
Sequence	The author lists items or events in numerical or chronological order.	*first, second, third* *next* *then* *finally*	1. 2. 3. 4. 5.	The Olympic games began as athletic festivals to honour the Greek gods. The most important festival was held in the valley of Olympia to honour Zeus, the king of the gods. It was this festival that became the Olympic games in 776 BC. These games were ended in AD 394 by the Roman Emperor who ruled Greece. No Olympic games were held for more than 1500 years. Then the modern Olympics began in 1896. Almost 300 male athletes competed in the first modern Olympics. In the games held in 1900, female athletes were allowed to compete. The games have continued every four years since 1896 except during World War II, and they will most likely continue for many years to come.
Comparison	The author explains how two or more things are alike and/or how they are different.	*different* *in contrast* *alike* *same as* *on the other hand*		The modern Olympics is very unlike the ancient Olympic games. Individual events are different. While there were no swimming races in the ancient games, for example, there were chariot races. There were no female contestants and all athletes competed in nude. Of course, the ancient and modern Olympics are also alike in many ways. Some events, such as the javelin and discus throws, are the same. Some people say that cheating, professionalism, and nationalism in the modern games are a disgrace to the Olympic tradition. But according to the ancient Greek writers, there were many cases of cheating, nationalism, and professionalism in their Olympics, too.
Cause and Effect	The author lists one or more causes and the resulting effect or effects.	*reasons why* *if ... then* *as a result* *therefore* *because*		There are several reasons why so many people attend the Olympic games or watch them on television. One reason is tradition. The name *Olympics* and the torch and flame remind people of the ancient games. People can escape the ordinariness of daily life by attending or watching the Olympics. They like to identify with someone else's individual sacrifice and accomplishment. National pride is another reason, and an athlete's or a team's hard-earned victory becomes a nation's victory. There are national medal counts and people keep track of how many medals their country's athletes have won.
Problem and Solution	The author states a problem and lists one or more solutions for the problem. A variation of this pattern is the question-and-answer format in which the author poses a question and then answers it.	*problem is* *dilemma is* *puzzle is* *solved* *question ... answer*		One proble with the modern Olympics is that it has become very big and expensive to operate. The city or country that hosts the games often loses a lot of money. A stadium, pools, and playing fields must be built for the athletic events, and housing is needed for the athletes who come from around the world. And all of these facilities are used for only two weeks! In 1984, Los Angeles solved these problems by charging a fee for companies who wanted to be official sponsors of the games. Companies like McDonald's paid a lot of money to be part of the Olympics. Many buildings that were already built in the Los Angeles area were also used. The Coliseum where the 1932 games were held was used again, and many colleges and universities in the area became playing and living sites.

256　CHAPTER 7　READING AND WRITING EXPOSITORY TEXT

butterfly and to list what the caterpillar ate each day of the week. Problem and solution is illustrated in *Missuk's Snow Geese* (Renaud, 2008), a story of a young Inuk girl who unknowingly helps her father find his way home in a winter storm with a trail of snow angels she made in the snow earlier that day.

Much of students' reading of expository text is from the Internet, where text structures differ from the five basic ones previously described. They differ because they contain text features such as hyperlinks, pull-down menus, animated graphics, videos, and other site-specific components. These variations increase the complexity of the text from a structural point of view, but they may make reading easier. When a group of grade 6 students read from their city's newspaper website about the potential impact of climate change on coffee production, they not only learned from the written text, which exemplified cause-and-effect structure, they were also able to expand their research by following embedded hyperlinks to world coffee growers' blogs. Like combination books that include both narrative and expository text, many websites provide readers with more than one text structure.

Teaching Students to Read and Learn from Expository Text

Reading expository text, just like reading narrative text, requires students to monitor their reading to make sure that what they read makes sense. Ruddell (2001) suggests students need to do six things to read and learn from expository text. Figure 7-2 explains those six things.

Students also need to learn about the five expository text structures and how to use them to improve their reading comprehension as well as to organize their writing (Neufeld, 2005/2006; Serafini, 2004). Teachers teach students about expository text structure by presenting **minilessons**. The informational books listed in Figure 7-3 exemplify each of the expository text structures. They can be used as examples when teachers present minilessons. The steps in teaching minilessons on expository text structure are presented in the accompanying Step by Step box.

FIGURE 7-2 WHAT STUDENTS NEED TO DO TO READ AND LEARN FROM EXPOSITORY TEXT

To read and learn from expository text, students need to

1. **Organize information before reading.** Students think about what they know, raise questions, and predict.
2. **Organize information while reading.** Students confirm or adjust predictions, relate new information to that known, and visualize concepts presented.
3. **Organize information after reading.** Students respond to text in an important way (e.g., mapping, writing) and perceive relationships with prior knowledge.
4. **Synthesize and articulate new learning.** Students arrive at new understandings and integrate new information with known, prepare for further learning.
5. **Learn vocabulary that labels important concepts, elements, and relationships.** Students identify new words and concepts and use them in meaningful ways.
6. **Produce or create something new and apply new information.** Students work through new ideas in writing; build or create something new; perform.

Source: Adapted from Ruddell, M. R. (2001). *Teaching content reading and writing* (3rd ed.). New York: John Wiley & Sons. © Gail E. Tompkins

FIGURE 7-3 INFORMATIONAL BOOKS REPRESENTING THE EXPOSITORY TEXT STRUCTURE

Description

Amosky, J. (2002). *All about Frogs*. New York: Scholastic. (P–M)

Dixon, N. (1995). *Kites*. Toronto: Kids Can Press. (P–M) 🍁

Hughes, S. (2011). *Off to Class: Incredible and Unusual Schools Around the World*. Toronto: Owlkids Books. (M–U) 🍁

Jenkins, S. (2005). *Prehistoric Actual Size*. New York: Houghton Mifflin. (P) 🍁

Kaner, E. (1995). *Towers and Tunnels*. Toronto: Kids Can Press. (M–U) 🍁

Scowen, K. (2006). *My Kind of Sad: What It's Like to Be Young and Depressed*. Toronto: Annick Press. (U) 🍁

Stinson, K. (2009). *Love Every Leaf: The Life of Landscape Architect Cornelia Hahn Oberlander*. Toronto: Tundra Books (M–U) 🍁

Swanson, D. (2007). *Bugs up Close*. Toronto: Kids Can Press. (M) 🍁

Szpirglas, J. (2005). *They Did What?! Your Guide to Weird & Wacky Things People Do*. Vancouver: Maple Tree Press. (M–U) 🍁

Tanaka, S. (1996). *I Was There: On Board the Titanic*. Illus. K. Marshall. Toronto: Scholastic Canada. (M–U) 🍁

Sequence

Bateman, R. (2005). *Backyard Birds: An Introduction*. Toronto: Scholastic Canada/Madison Press. (P–M) 🍁

Loxton, D. (2010). *Evolution: How We and All Living Things Came to Be*. Toronto: Kids Can Press. (M–U) 🍁

Reid, B. (1991). *Zoe's Snowy Day*. Toronto: HarperCollins Publishers. (P) 🍁

Reid, B. (1991). *Zoe's Sunny Day*. Toronto: HarperCollins Publishers. (P) 🍁

Reid, B. (1991). *Zoe's Windy Day*. Toronto: HarperCollins Publishers. (P) 🍁

Ritchie, S. (2009). *Follow That Map! A First Book of Mapping Skills*. Toronto: Kids Can Press. (M) 🍁

Steltzer, U. (1995). *Building an Igloo*. New York: Holt. (P–M)

Thornhill, J. (2006). *I Found a Dead Bird: The Kids' Guide to the Cycle of Life & Death*. Toronto: Maple Tree Press. (M) 🍁

Vande Griek, S. (2011). *Loon*. Toronto: Groundwood Books. (P–M) 🍁

Comparison

Barretta, G. (2006). *Now & Ben: The Modern Inventions of Benjamin Franklin*. New York: Holt. (P)

Becker, H. (2012). *AlphaBest*. Toronto: Kids Can Press. (M) 🍁

Chaconas, D. (2006). *Cord & Fuzz: Short and Tall*. New York: Viking. (P)

Lee, D. (2011). *Biomimicry: Inventions Inspired by Nature*. Toronto: Kids Can Press. (M–U) 🍁

Markle, S. (1993). *Outside and Inside Trees*. New York: Bradbury Press. (M)

Singer, M. (1995). *A Wasp Is Not a Bee*. New York: Holt. (P)

Cause and Effect

Acer, D. (2008). *Gotcha! Mystery Hunters: 18 Amazing Ways to Freak Out Your Friends*. Toronto: Kids Can Press. 🍁

Andrews, W. (1995). *Understanding Global Warming*. Toronto: Health Canada Ltd. (M–U) 🍁

Bateman, R. (2010). *Vanishing Habitats*. Toronto: Scholastic Canada. (M–U) 🍁

Cole, J. (2010). *The Magic Schoolbus and the Climate Challenge*. New York: Scholastic. (P–M)

Dixon, N. (1995). *Kites*. Toronto: Kids Can Press. (M) 🍁

Fromer, L., & Gerstein, F. (2012). *My Itchy Body*. Toronto: Tundra Books. (P–M) 🍁

Godkin, C. (2006). *Fire! The Renewal of a Forest*. Markham, ON: Fitzhenry & Whiteside. (M) 🍁

Golick, M. (1995). *Wacky Word Games*. Markham, ON: Pembroke Publishers. (M–U) 🍁

Gryski, C. (1993). *Boondoggle: Making Bracelets with Plastic Lace*. Toronto: Kids Can Press. (M) 🍁

Gryski, C. (1995). *Favourite String Games*. Toronto: Kids Can Press. (M) 🍁

Lauber, P. (1995). *Who Eats What? Food Chains and Food Webs*. New York: HarperCollins. (M)

Milway, K. S. (2008). *One Hen: How One Small Loan Can Make a Big Difference*. Toronto: Kids Can Press. (M–U) 🍁

Souza, D. M. (1994). *Northern Lights*. New York: Scholastic.

Zoehfeld, K. W. (1995). *How Mountains Are Made*. New York: HarperCollins. (M)

Problem and Solution

Arnosky, J. (1995). *I See Animals Hiding*. New York: Scholastic. (P)

Bourgeois, P. (1990). *The Amazing Dirt Book*. Toronto: Kids Can Press. (P) 🍁

Dyer, H. (2010). *Watch This Space: Designing, Defending, and Sharing Public Spaces*. Toronto: Kids Can Press. (M–U) 🍁

Hickman, P. (1985). *Bugwise*. Toronto: Kids Can Press. (P–M) 🍁

Hughes, S. (2010). *Case Closed? Nine Mysteries Unlocked by Modern Science*. Toronto: Kids Can Press. (M–U) 🍁

Savan, B. (1991). *Earthcycles and Ecosystems*. Toronto: Kids Can Press. (M–U) 🍁

Sayre, A. (2010). *Turtle, Turtle, Watch Out!* Watertown, MA: Charlesbridge. (P–M)

Things to Do

Bell-Rehwoldt, S. (2009). *The Kids' Guide to Building Cool Stuff*. Mankato, MN: Capstone Press. (M–U)

Bucholz, D. (2010). *The Unofficial Harry Potter Cookbook*. Avon, MA: Adams Media. (M–U)

Davies, H. (2009). *The Games Book: How to Play the Games of Yesterday*. New York: Scholastic. (M–U)

Kaner, E. (1995). *Towers and Tunnels*. Toronto: Kids Can Press. (M) 🍁

Luxbacher, I. (2003). *The Jumbo Book of Art*. Toronto: Kids Can Press. (P–M) 🍁

Luxbacher, I. (2006). *The Jumbo Book of Outdoor Art*. Toronto: Kids Can Press. (P–M) 🍁

Petronis, P., & Lisle, A. (2010). *Sewing School: Handsewing Projects Children Will Love to Make*. North Adams, MA: Storey Publishing. (M)

Schendlinger, M. (2005). *Prepare to be Amazed: The Geniuses of Modern Magic*. Toronto: Annick Press. (M–U) 🍁

Teaching Minilessons on Expository Text Structure

1 Introduce an organizational pattern. The teacher explains the pattern and when writers use it, noting cue words that signal the pattern. Then the teacher shares an example of the pattern and describes the graphic organizer for that pattern.

2 Analyze examples of the pattern in informational texts similar to those the students will be reading. Figure 7-3 lists books that illustrate each of the five expository text structures. Sometimes the pattern is signaled clearly by means of titles, topic sentences, and cue words, and sometimes it is not. Students learn to identify cue words, and they talk about why writers may or may not explicitly signal the structure. They also diagram the structure using a graphic organizer.

3 Write paragraphs using the pattern. The first writing activity may be a whole-class activity; later, students can write paragraphs in small groups and individually. Students choose a topic, gather information, and organize it using a graphic organizer. Next they write a rough draft of the paragraph, inserting cue words to signal the structure. They revise, edit, and write a final copy of the paragraph. Then they share the paragraphs they have written and explain how and why they have used the particular organizational pattern in their writing.

4 Repeat steps 1 to 3 for each pattern. The teacher and students repeat the first three steps for each of the five expository text structures.

5 Use the patterns appropriately. After students have learned about the five patterns through the above steps, they need to learn to use the structure to guide their comprehension when reading and to choose the most appropriate pattern to communicate effectively in their writing. Students can experiment further with using the various patterns by creating graphic organizers to make notes while they read and by writing paragraphs about one set of information using different organizational patterns. For example, information about early inventions might be written as a description or as problem and solution telling why the invention was needed and how it was developed.

Teachers also teach students specific strategies to help them read expository text comprehensively, a skill especially important to upper-elementary and middle-school students, who are expected to read and study independently with textbooks and other sources of informational text. Three strategies they teach are mapping, SQ4R (survey, question, read, recite, review, reflect), and summarizing. These strategies work well when students apply them to build their understandings of expository texts from content area or subject textbooks, informational trade books, magazines for young readers, or informational websites such as National Geographic for Kids (http://kids.nationalgeographic.com/kids/) or CBC.ca/kids (www.cbc.ca/kids/).

MAPPING

Visual structures are powerful tools for comprehension instruction because they offer concrete, memorable representations of abstract thinking processes (Neufeld, 2005/2006). Visual structures, sometimes referred to as *clusters*, *maps*, or *graphic organizers*, help students organize large amounts of textual information in ways that show relationships and connections among the ideas and concepts contained in the text.

Each expository text structure lends itself to meaningful visual mapping, as shown in Figure 7-1.

Students learn to construct maps through viewing examples, teacher modeling, and experimenting with creating maps. After presenting minilessons focused on learning each text structure, teachers show students how to graphically represent text. As noted earlier, software such as Inspiration can be used to create complex and sophisticated visual representations of information.

Concept maps are one of the most basic visual structures that teachers show students how to construct. They are often used to help students understand concepts and ideas that are foundational to understanding extended selections of expository text or informational books.

SQ4R: SURVEY, QUESTION, READ, RECITE, REVIEW, REFLECT

Traditionally, teachers taught students the **SQ3R study strategy** (Robinson, 1946), perhaps the oldest study strategy ever presented—survey, question, read, recite, and review. Currently, several derivatives of the strategy are popular in elementary and middle-school classrooms. With increasing attention to reflection as a valid form of learning, it is popular to add a fourth *R—reflect—*to the processing of text. We have also explored *represent* as the fourth *R*, but have no experimental data at this point to demonstrate its effect. Slavin (1997) changed the first step from *survey* to *preview* (PQ3R). Regardless of labels, all versions of the strategy engage students in essentially the same systematic and thorough processing of text. Teaching students to use SQ4R, like teaching most strategies, requires time, modeling, and guided practice before students can be expected to use it independently. The SQ4R study strategy consists of the following steps:

1. **Survey.** The reader scans and skims the text, seeking a general overview of content and message; reading headings and subheadings; and noting illustrations, charts, graphs, and other text features.
2. **Question.** The reader poses questions by converting headings and subheadings into questions.
3. **Read.** The reader reads the entire text to answer the questions posed.
4. **Recite.** The reader states answers to the questions either to him- or herself or to a reading partner.
5. **Review.** The reader goes back over what has been learned, reading summaries or other features such as text boxes that recapture highlights, and rereading as necessary.
6. **Reflect.** The reader thinks about the reading, writes journal entries, writes two-column notes of statements and interpretations, or makes notes using passage headings or questions to clarify and aid memory of learning from the text.

Students need step-by-step guidance to learn to effectively apply the strategy to their reading. Teachers provide this instruction through minilessons concerning each step, and then follow the lessons with opportunities for practice. Only after practice can students be expected to use the strategy independently.

Summarizing is perhaps the most important subskill involved in comprehension (Pressley, 2000). It has been shown to improve students' overall comprehension (Duke and Pearson, 2008/2009). Summarizing helps students increase their understanding of text through organizing and restating information to reduce a text to its main points. To become adept at summary writing, student must be able to discern and analyze text structure. Good summarizers are able to distinguish important from less important information and guard against including less important information in their summaries. Good organizers write in their own words but are careful to maintain the author's point of view and to stick closely to the sequence of ideas or events presented in the text being summarized (Vacca, Vacca, & Bogoray, 2005). Teachers teach students how to summarize through minilessons in which they explain the value and purposes of summarizing, then model the procedures. To help elementary and middle-school students summarize effectively, teachers begin with summarizing short passages, such as a paragraph or brief section of text from a website. When students have grasped the essential skills, they can move on to working with longer texts.

When a group of grade 5 students read from Coulter's *Secrets in Stone: All about Maya Hieroglyphs* (2001), they learned a great deal about the writing of the ancient civilization and about how difficult it was for both the Maya and their Aztec neighbours in what is now Mexico to fight against the Spanish. They read details about the differences in the two groups' weapons and discovered that the Spaniards had a secret weapon. After reading, they composed the following summary statements to include in a PowerPoint project, which they shared with their class:

- The Maya and Aztecs fought against the Spaniards.
- The Spaniards had better weapons.
- The Spaniards even had a secret weapon.

The basic steps in summarizing were presented many years ago by Kintsch and van Dijk (1978). In the intervening years, they have been modified only slightly. Students can easily produce a summary if they first analyze the text structure to discern how the ideas are interrelated to convey a message to the reader. This process involves looking at key words, subheadings, and other text features that reveal the structure (Dymock & Nicholson, 2010). To summarize well, students should follow these procedures:

1. **Include no unnecessary detail.** Delete all trivial and repetitious information from the text.

2. **Collapse lists.** Condense examples, details, actions, or traits into broader categories of information. Think of key words or phrases that describe the concept. For example, a list such as *social studies*, *mathematics*, *science*, *music*, and *art* could be referred to as "school subjects."

3. **Use topic sentences.** Include explicit topic sentences contained in the text. When no topic sentences appear in the text, students must create sentences.

4. **Integrate information.** Integrate the ideas identified in the first three procedures into a coherent piece of writing.

5. **Polish the summary.** Revise the draft summary to create an organized, smoothly structured piece of writing. Rethinking while polishing helps students get a firmer grasp on the information in the text.

In addition to these four strategies to support learning from informational text, teachers teach students to ask questions of themselves and each other. They model asking questions to show students how to generate questions that require readers to integrate information and think before, while, and after they read. Questions before reading help readers to set purposes for reading; questions while reading help readers make connections from one part of the text to another and to prior knowledge; questions following reading guide readers to think critically or to evaluate the information read. Using the revised version of Bloom's taxonomy for learning, teaching, and assessing (Anderson & Krathwohl, 2001) as a guide is one way teachers ensure

FIGURE 7-4 ASKING QUESTIONS BASED ON BLOOM'S REVISED TAXONOMY

Asking Questions and Prompting Discussion Based on Bloom's Revised Taxonomy

Creating: What if . . .? Tell me another . . . Does this mean . . .? How else could . . .?

Evaluating: Decide whether . . . Assess . . . Write your opinion (with evidence) of . . .

Analyzing: Why? What is the difference between . . .?

Applying: Show me . . . Could . . .? Imagine if . . .

Understanding: Say more about . . . Summarize . . . What do you predict? Why did . . .?

Remembering: Tell . . . Describe . . . Who? What? When? Where?

Source: Based on Anderson, I. W., & Krathwohl, D. R. (Eds.). (2001). A taxonomy for learning, teaching, and assessing: A revision of Bloom's taxonomy of educational objectives (complete ed.). New York: Longman. © Gail E. Tompkins

that they model a broad range of questions and prompt students to engage in discussion of the texts they have read. Figure 7-4 shows some key words and phrases that teachers use to formulate questions and discussion prompts at each level.

Learning to ask and answer questions at all levels of the taxonomy is beneficial to students. Generating and answering questions helps them develop thorough knowledge of the texts they read, whether informational books, textbooks, or selections on the Internet.

Reading Content-Area Textbooks

Content-area textbooks are often used as the primary print resource in social studies and science. Although the quality of textbooks available for use in Canadian classrooms is generally high, typically they are employed as only one resource. Other resources are needed and used to provide depth and expanded understanding. Students need to read, write, and discuss topics. A variety of excellent nonfiction books are available to support the teaching of curriculum topics. It is most effective to use the reading process and then extend students' learning with projects. Developing **theme study units** or **inquiry-based units** using content-area textbooks together with additional print and multimedia resources is recommended.

Content-area textbooks are often difficult for students to read—more difficult, in fact, than many informational books. One reason textbooks are difficult is that they briefly mention many topics without developing any of them. A second reason is that content-area textbooks, like all expository text, are read differently from stories. Teachers need to show students how to approach content-area textbooks and teach students how to use specific expository text reading strategies and procedures to make comprehension easier. The first Teacher's Notebook presents guidelines for using content-area textbooks and these guidelines can also be applied to reading content-area texts on the Internet.

Teachers can make content-area textbooks more readable and show students ways to remember what they have read. Some activities are used before reading and others after reading. The before-reading activities are used to help students activate prior knowledge, set purposes for reading, or build background knowledge. The after-reading activities help students identify and remember main ideas and details.

Guidelines for Using Content-Area Textbooks

1. Use Comprehension Aids

The teacher teaches students how to use the comprehension aids in content-area textbooks, including chapter overviews; headings that outline the chapter; helpful graphics such as maps, charts, tables, graphs, diagrams, photos, and drawings; technical words defined in the text; end-of-chapter summaries; and review questions.

2. Have Students Revise Section Headings into Questions

The teacher divides the reading of a chapter into sections. Before reading each section, students turn the section heading into a question and read to find the answer to the question. As they read, students take notes about the section and then answer the question they created using the section heading after reading.

3. Teach Expository Text Structures

The teacher teaches students about expository text structures and assists students in identifying the patterns used in the reading assignment, especially cause and effect or problem and solution, before reading.

4. Introduce Vocabulary

The teacher introduces only the key terms as part of an introductory presentation or discussion before students read the textbook assignment. The teacher presents other vocabulary during reading, if needed, and after reading, develops a **word wall** with important words.

5. Focus on Key Concepts

The teacher has students focus on key concepts or the big ideas instead of having students try to remember all the facts or details.

6. Use Content-Area Reading Techniques

The teacher uses content-area reading techniques, such as PReP, SQ4R, exclusion brainstorming, or anticipation guides, to help students identify and remember main ideas and details after reading.

7. Encourage Students to Use Headings

The teacher encourages students to use headings and subheadings to select and organize relevant information. Headings can be used to create a **semantic map**, and students add details as they read.

8. Apply the Listen–Read–Discuss Format

First, the teacher presents the key concepts orally, and then students read and discuss the chapter. Or the teacher has students read the chapter as a review activity rather than as the introductory activity.

Other activities are used when students want to locate specific information. Seven activities to make content-area textbooks more readable are

1. *Previewing.* Teachers introduce the reading assignment by asking students to note main headings in the chapter and then skim or rapidly read the chapter to get a general idea about the topics covered in the reading assignment.

2. *Prereading plan (PReP).* Teachers introduce a key concept discussed in the reading assignment and ask students to brainstorm words and ideas related to the concept before reading. After reading, they ask students to write about the topic to explore it further (Tompkins, 2013).

3. *Anticipation guides.* Teachers present a set of statements on the topic to be read. Students agree or disagree with each statement and then read the assignment to see if they were right (Head & Readence, 1992).

4. *Exclusion brainstorming.* Teachers distribute a list of words, most of which are related to the key concepts to be presented in the reading assignment. Teachers ask students to circle the words that are related to a key concept and then read the assignment to see if they circled the right words (Wormeli, 2001; Tompkins, 2013).

5. *Clusters.* Teachers distribute a cluster, map, or other graphic organizer with main ideas marked. Students complete the graphic organizer by adding details after reading each section.

6. *Note-taking.* Students develop an outline by writing the headers and then take notes after reading each section.

7. *Scanning.* Students reread quickly to locate specific information.

Content-area texts are no longer viewed as the only source for learning, but they continue to be useful tools for learning across the curriculum and are available in most classrooms. In many school jurisdictions, where textbooks are supplied, the expectation is that teachers use the textbooks as one of their resources. That is, they are expected to teach *with* textbooks but also to include other types of reading materials and other types of activities in their instructional programs.

Reading and Writing Digital Text—A Special Form of Expository Text

Students read from many sources, including the Internet. Their reading from the Internet requires that they be able to process text that is not linear. In other words, linear text in books, magazines and newspapers is essentially structured with a definitive beginning and ending with identifiable structure and order of information (see Figure 7-1, p. 256). **Hypertext**, on the other hand, is not linear and not sequential. Hypertext comprises any nonlinear text that provides readers with options to explore links among individual segments of text **Hypermedia**, or multimedia text, is a broader term used to describe hypertext that includes visual and audio components. Readers of hypertext and hypermedia must make decisions regarding the order in which they read and the connections they form among pieces of information presented. As noted earlier, readers take control of text construction. It could be said that they become authors in that they decide which links to follow and thus they shape or create the text that they read.

Imagine two grade 6 students beginning to research the rainforest from a well-constructed website. Together they read the introduction and then must make a choice. They can "click here" to learn about the animals of the rainforest or "click here" to learn more about the overarching canopy and lower structures of trees and plants. They choose to read about the animals and click to take them to that webpage. They are anxious to solve their curiosity concerning the preying nature of the jaguar. Within minutes they are attempting to print the picture of the sleek beast, thinking that it will make an attractive cover for their report.

Scenarios such as this are common. The plethora of information available in highly attractive formats—print and digital on the Internet—can be highly motivational and engaging for students, but can also be confusing and somewhat overwhelming if they are not able to systematically process the text. Teachers need to guide students' reading and help them develop the strategies required to follow a variety of texts. Students use many of the same thinking strategies whether reading print or digital texts (Schmar-Dobler, 2003). Two strategies that are especially important to reading from the Internet are skimming and scanning. The volume and nonlinear organization of Internet text can be overwhelming for students without skills to identify pertinent text. Students must also learn to navigate Internet text to make efficient use of its features.

Teachers help students purposefully read from the Internet by designing WebQuests. A WebQuest is a web-based instructional technique that integrates research with embedded links and current online resources. Simply, "the Quest has a purpose, a problem that puts reading and study in an entirely new light" (Spires & Estes, 2002, p. 118). Students follow an inquiry process with supports that allow them to work collaboratively to understand material and create something for others to respond to.

Given the great diversity of written material available, reading comprehension is by nature so sophisticated that no single teaching strategy is sufficient for all readers with all texts in all learning situations The teaching strategies previously described in this chapter and elsewhere in this text are applicable not only to traditional print but also to hypertext and hypermedia. However, teaching students how to read hypertext and hypermedia requires that the nature of electronic text be considered. Karchmer (2001) points out four characteristics of electronic text:

1. **It is interactive and malleable.** Reading material on the computer can be manipulated and modified through such things as adding pronunciations, graphing, and video.

2. **It seamlessly incorporates audiovisual features.** Graphics are integral within an electronic environment, whereas they are considered supplementary in traditional printed text.

3. **It makes it possible to access multiple related resources.** Through electronic links, authors can make relevant supplementary information easily available to readers.

4. **It is not linear.** Readers have a more active role in the navigation of electronic text than in traditional text.

In addition, it is important to help students understand that electronic texts need to be read critically (Coiro, 2003). Don Tapscott says, "Never before has it been more necessary that children learn to read, write and think critically. It's not just point and click. It's point, read, think, click" (1998, p. 63).

Two strategies we have seen students use effectively when reading from the Internet to complete research projects are graphic organizers and study guides. Graphic organizers may follow the expository text structures shown in Figure 7-1 (p. 256) or may take the form of data charts, as illustrated in Figure 7-5. Data charts help students organize information from various sections of one website or from multiple sources.

Study guides are a way for teachers to guide students through the reading of a particular text—traditional print or electronic. They help students identify important

FIGURE 7-5 DATA CHART ON CANADIAN WILDFLOWERS

Name	Appearance	Size	Where It Grows	Flower Family
Buttercup	• Five yellow waxy petals • Long thin green stems	30–40 cm tall	Fields and roadside ditches	Buttercup
Dog-toothed Violet (or Glacier Lily)	• Yellow flowers on green stems • Each flower has six petals and six stamens • Two long green leaves	15–30 cm tall	Alpine meadows	Lily
Mountain spirea	• Dense, flat-topped deep pink flower clusters • Leaves are oval; stems are light brown	50–90 cm tall	Wet meadows and boggy ground	Rose
Indian Paintbrush	• Narrow, tubular flowers with many little petals like a brush—pink, red, orange; rarely yellow or white	10–60 cm tall	Well-drained areas and rocky slopes	Figwort

FIGURE 7-6 A STUDY GUIDE FOR A READING FROM THE INTERNET

Structure of the Government of Canada
http://Canada.gc.ca

Purpose for Reading
The purpose for your reading is to learn about the Government of Canada and its structure. Also, read any aspect of the site you think appropriate to answer the challenge questions. By answering them, you will learn about other important and interesting facts related to the Government of Canada.

Go to **http://Canada.gc.ca**
Click on English Click on About Government
Click on Canada's System of Government
Click on Governors General Since Confederation

1. During what year was the first Governor General appointed?
2. What was his name?
3. Describe an interesting fact about the Right Honourable Jeanne Mathilde Sauvé.

Go back to the first page. (Use the Back button to go back one page.)

www.Canada.ca/home.html
Click on Canada's system of government
Click on About Canada, then Canadian History
Click on Canadian Prime Ministers

1. Who was the first Prime Minister?
2. When was he appointed?
3. Describe one interesting fact about the second prime minister.

Go back to the main page. (Use the Back button to go back.)
Click on About Government
Click on Provincial and Territorial Governments

1. Find your province or territory.
2. Draw and colour its flag.
3. Locate and name the capital city of your province or territory.

Fill in the chart:

Flag	Name the capital city

Challenge Questions
1. If our class went to Rideau Hall, whose home would we be visiting?
2. What would we see in the home?

information (key concepts and supporting details) and focus on the content that the teacher considers essential to their learning and meeting curricular objectives. See Figure 7-6 for a sample study guide for a reading from the Internet. The steps in preparing and using study guides are presented in the accompanying Step by Step box.

Students also write hypertext and create multimedia texts. Increasingly, classrooms are equipped to support students' creation of the kinds of texts they experience on the Internet. Teachers facilitate their writing in at least two ways. First, they provide them with models and the opportunity to discover the characteristics of the models through such activities as discussion of the decisions authors make about how to present their texts—print, visual, and audio—singularly or in combination. Second, teachers make time and equipment available during each

Preparing and Using Study Guides

1 **Select the text to be read.** If a text is on the Internet, the teacher bookmarks it for easy access by students.

2 **Identify the purpose or purposes for the reading.** The teacher states, in simple terms, the objectives of the students' reading.

3 **Identify the information most crucial to student understanding.** The teacher points out to students the key concepts about which they will be reading.

4 **Develop questions to guide students through the text.** The teacher identifies the segments of text where students can find answers to the questions. If necessary, the teacher indicates which links to follow. Question format can be extended to include having students make note of particular information. For example, students might be asked to list information or draw and label a diagram to show information read.

5 **Have students complete the study guide as they read.** The teacher provides space in the study guide for students to include questions that arise as they seek answers to the questions provided.

6 **Discuss students' answers in large or small groups.** If disputes over students' interpretation of the text arise, the teacher clarifies the information so that students are left with accurate notes for future reference.

stage of the writing process for students to compose digital and multimedia texts. Students we recently observed were deeply involved in producing an animated, interactive retelling of Clement Moore's *The Night before Christmas*. Their work was complete with their drawings and digital photos to let readers know "to their wondering eyes did appear … a shiny SUV loaded with hockey gear!" The interactive and nonlinear characteristics of hypertext and multimedia texts extend the ways in which meaning can be made and thought represented (Hammerberg, 2001). Whether students are writing independently or collaboratively, they benefit from opportunities to take writing beyond the limitations of traditional print.

Assessing Students' Use of Expository Text Structures

Teachers can assess how students use expository text structures to comprehend as they read and listen to informational books read aloud. Students should learn to recognize the structural patterns and use graphic organizers to classify information, take notes, and generalize main ideas. Teachers can monitor students as they participate in discussions about informational books and review students' learning log entries during theme study units to assess their understanding of key concepts and their use of graphic organizers.

Teachers can also assess how well students organize information when they write paragraphs, reports, and other across-the-curriculum pieces. When students write to present information, they

- choose the most appropriate structure
- develop a graphic organizer before writing
- write a topic sentence that identifies the structure
- use cue words to signal the structure

These four components can be used to develop a checklist or rubric to assess students' use of expository text structures.

Reports

Students in the elementary grades—even in the primary grades—write both class collaborative and individual reports (Flynt & Brozo, 2009). Early successful experiences with informative writing teach students about content-area topics as well as how to collect data from multiple sources and how to prepare and share reports. Not only do primary and elementary students write traditional text-based reports, they also transform their reports into multimedia presentations.

Young Children's Reports

Contrary to the popular assumption that young children's first writing is narrative, educators have found that kindergartners and first graders write many non-narrative compositions in which they provide information about familiar topics, such as "Signs of Fall," or directions for familiar activities, such as "How to Feed Your Pet" (Bright and Smith, 2014). Many of these writings might be termed "All about …" books, in which an entire booklet is written on a single topic. "All about …" books usually include one piece of information and an illustration on each page. A grade 2 student wrote an "All about …" book called *Snowy Thoughts*, shown in Figure 7-7, as part of a theme on the four seasons. Even though the student omitted some capital letters and punctuation marks and used **invented spelling** for a few words in his book, the information can be easily deciphered. Using simple software, teachers can publish children's writing such as this and add the books to the classroom library.

Another way for young children to write informational text is to dictate reports to their teacher, who serves as scribe to record them. Writing informational text in this way is similar to chart story writing discussed in Chapter 3 in the Language Experience Approach (LEA). The dictated reports show the children the structures and conventions of writing informational text. A class of kindergartners compiled this book-length report on police officers when they focused on learning about the people who help in their community:

Page 1:   Police officers help people who are in trouble. They are nice to kids. They are only mean to robbers and bad people. Police officers make people obey the laws. They give tickets to people who drive cars too fast.

Page 2:   Men and women can be police officers. They wear blue uniforms like Officer Jerry's. But sometimes police officers wear regular clothes when they work undercover. They wear badges on their uniforms and on their hats. Officer Jerry's badge number is 3407. Police officers have guns, handcuffs, whistles, sticks, and cell phones. They have to carry all these things.

Page 3:   Police officers drive police cars with flashing lights and loud sirens. Their cars have computers so the officers can connect to other police officers at the police station. Sometimes they ride on police motorcycles or on police horses or in police helicopters or in police boats.

Page 4:   Police officers work at police stations. The jail for the bad people that they catch is right next door. One police officer sits at the computer to talk to the police officers who are driving their cars. The police chief works at the police station, too.

Page 5:   Police officers are your friends. They want to help you so you shouldn't be afraid of them. You can ask them if you need some help.

Page 6:   How We Learned about Police Officers for Our Report 1. We read this book: Bourgeois, Paulette (2004). *Canadian Police Officers.* Illustrated by Kim LaFave. Toronto: Kids Can Press. 2. We interviewed Officer Jerry. 3. We visited the police station.

The teacher read two books aloud to the students, and Officer Jerry visited the classroom and talked to the students about his job. The students also took a field trip to the police station. The teacher took photos of Officer Jerry, his police car, and the police station to illustrate the report. With this background, the students and the teacher together developed a cluster with these five main ideas: what police officers do, what equipment police officers have, how police officers travel, where police officers work, and police officers are your friends. The students added details to the five main ideas until each one developed into one page of the report. The background of experiences and the clustering activity prepared students to compose their report. After students completed the report, added a bibliography called "How We Learned about Police Officers for Our Report," and inserted the photographs, it was ceremoniously presented to the school library to be enjoyed by all students.

Collaborative Reports

A successful report-writing experience for middle- and upper-grade students is a class collaboration research report. Reports can be limited to written text or expanded to include digital forms of recording and sharing. Small groups of students work together to prepare sections of the report, which are then compiled. Students benefit from working as a group to write a report in two ways: first, they learn the steps in writing a research report—with the group as a scaffold or support system—before tackling individual reports; second, working in groups lets them learn from each other while they share the laborious parts of the work.

A quartet of grade 4 students wrote a collaborative report on hermit crabs. The students sat together at one table and watched hermit crabs in a terrarium. They cared for the crustaceans for two weeks, observing them closely. They took digital pictures and made notes of their observations in learning logs. After this period, the students were bursting with questions about the hermit crabs and eager for answers. They wanted to know about the crabs' natural habitat, what the best habitat was for them in the classroom, how they breathed air, why they lived in "borrowed" shells, why one pincer was bigger than the other, and so on. Their teacher provided some answers and directed them to books and websites that would provide additional information. As they collected information, they created a cluster that they taped to the table next to the terrarium. The cluster became inadequate for reporting information, so they decided to share their knowledge by writing a book entitled *The Encyclopedia about Hermit Crabs.* Chapters from their book and the cluster they

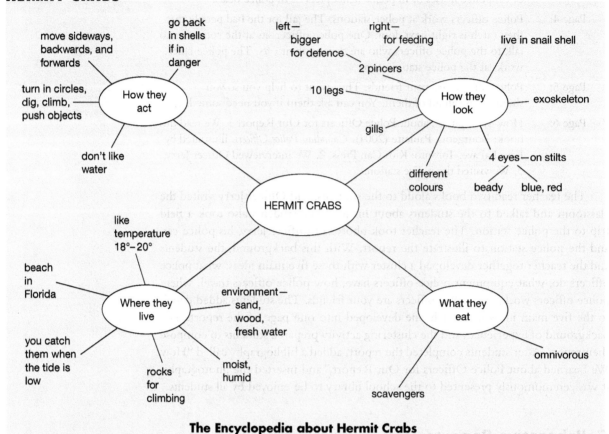

The Encyclopedia about Hermit Crabs

How They Look
Hermit crabs are very much like regular crabs but hermit crabs transfer shells. They have gills. Why? Because they are born in water and when they mature they come to land and kill snails so they can have a shell. They have two beady eyes that look like they are on stilts. Their body is a sight! Their shell looks like a rock. Really it is an exoskeleton which means the skeleton is on the outside. They have two pincers. The left one is bigger so it is used for defence. The right one is for feeding. They also have ten legs.

Where They Live
Hermit crabs live mostly on beaches in Florida where the weather is 18°–32°. They live in fresh water. They like humid weather and places that have sand, wood, and rocks (for climbing on). The best time to catch hermit crabs is at low tide.

What They Eat
Hermit crabs are omnivorous scavengers which means they eat just about anything. They even eat leftovers.

How They Act
Hermit crabs are very unusual. They go back into their shell if they think there is danger. They are funny because they walk sideways, forward, and backward. They can go in circles. They can also get up when they get upside down. And that's how they act.

used in gathering the information appear in Figure 7-7. The students decided to share the work of writing the book, and they chose four main ideas, one for each participant to write: what hermit crabs look like, how they act, where they really live, and what they eat. A different student wrote each section and they then returned to the group to share their respective rough drafts. The students gave each other suggestions and made revisions based on the discussion. Next, they edited their report with the teacher and added an introduction, a conclusion, and a bibliography. Then they chose which pictures they wanted to include and decided where to insert them before printing and binding their informational text. Finally, they read their book to each class in the school before adding it to the school library.

Students can organize reports in a variety of formats—formats they see used in informational books. One possibility is a Q&A format; another possibility is an alphabet book like *Z Is for Zamboni* (Napier, 2007), which explains many of the intricacies of Canada's favourite sport.

Individual Reports

Although there is value in students' working collaboratively, they also benefit from learning independently. Julie Coiro (2003) recommends that students do "authentic" research in which they explore topics that interest them or hunt for answers to questions that puzzle them through web-based inquiry projects. When students become immersed in content-area study, questions arise that they want to explore. Teachers help them discover answers by guiding them through a research process using both web-based and print resources. Once they have learned the answers to their questions, the students are then eager to share their new knowledge. They share through written and multigenre reports.

Teaching Students to Write Reports

Students learn how to write research reports through experience. Whether working collaboratively or independently, they follow the same basic research, writing, and sharing process. The Step by Step box that follows explains seven steps from initial idea to project completion. Teachers make some adjustments in how these basic steps are followed in response to students' need for guidance and the availability of resources, including computer access, but the sequence remains constant. Teachers also present minilessons on procedures, concepts, and strategies related to writing research reports to help students develop effective research skills. Teachers and students sometimes use the K–W–L–S strategy as described in Chapter 8 to guide their inquiries and prepare for report writing. It can be especially helpful to structure collaborative inquiry when a whole class is working together.

Multigenre Projects

Written reports are just one form of reporting student learning from inquiry. Students frequently create multigenre projects to explore a topic from several perspectives and through several genres. "Research comes alive when students explore a range of alternate genres instead of writing the traditional research report" (Grierson, Anson, & Baird, 2002, p. 51). Figure 7-8 lists genres that students use to share knowledge in multigenre projects. Tom Romano (1995) explains, "Each genre offers me ways of seeing and understanding that others do not" (p. 109). Students collect a variety of nonfiction materials, including books, textbooks, Internet articles, charts, diagrams, and photos, and then they study them. Students write several pieces, such as feature articles, letters, journal entries, stories, and poems; collect photos, charts, and other visual representations; and compile them in a book or display them on a poster. For example, for a multigenre project on the planet Mars, fourth graders included these pieces:

FIGURE 7-8 GENRES FOR MULTIGENRE PROJECTS

Artifacts	Students gather or create a collection of objects, photos, postcards, time lines, and other items about a topic.
Biographical sketches	Students write biographical sketches of people related to the topic.
Cartoons	Students draw cartoons or copy published cartoons from a book or Internet site.
Clusters	Students draw clusters or other diagrams to display information concisely.
Cubes	Students examine a topic from six perspectives.
Data charts	Students create data charts to present and compare information.
Essays	Students write essays to describe a topic, examine an issue, or persuade readers to take a course of action.
Feature articles	Students bring a human-interest slant to the news or a nonfiction topic in these creative compositions.
Found poems	Students collect words and phrases from a book or article and arrange them to make poems.
Games	Students create cardboard or digital games and puzzles about a topic for classmates to play.
Letters	Students write simulated letters or make copies of real letters related to the topic.
Life lines	Students draw life lines and mark important dates related to a person's life.
Maps	Students make copies of actual maps or draw maps related to a topic.
Newspaper articles	Students make copies of actual newspaper articles or write simulated articles related to the topic.
Open-mind portraits	Students draw open-mind portraits of people related to the topic.
Photos	Students download photos from public domain sites on the Internet.
Podcasts	Students create podcasts to share information they've learned or stories and poems they've written.
Poems	Students write list poems, poems for two voices, "I am ..." poems, and other types of poems about the topic.
Postcards	Students create picture postcards related to the topic.
PowerPoint presentations	Students prepare a set of pages or slides for a PowerPoint presentation.
Quotes	Students collect quotes about the topic from materials they're reading.
Simulated journals	Students write simulated journal entries from the viewpoint of a person related to the topic.
Slideshows	Students prepare slideshows with photos and other images related to the topic.
Timelines	Students draw timelines to sequence events related to the topic.
Venn diagrams	Students draw Venn diagrams to compare two components of the topic or the topic with something else.
WebQuests	Students create digital inquiry projects called WebQuests.
Websites and wikis	Students display information they've collected about a topic in an online database.
Word clouds	Students create word clouds related to the topic at www.wordle.net.

STEP BY STEP

Writing Research Reports

1 **Identify a topic.** Students choose topics for research reports from a content area, theme study unit, inquiry unit, or other interests. After choosing a general topic, they need to narrow the topic so that it is manageable for independent work, or divide the topic into subtopics for group inquiry.

2 **Design research questions.** Students design research questions by brainstorming a list of questions. They review the list, combine some questions, delete others, and finally arrive at four to six questions worthy of response. When they begin their research, they may add new questions and delete others.

3 **Gather information.** Students use websites and informational texts as their primary resources. They may also interview experts or elders or collect information from other multimedia sources. They record the information collected in a number of ways, including notecards, clusters, and data charts. Upper-grade students may use online note-making tools.

4 **Organize information.** Students must read their collected information critically, planning ways to organize it that will clearly portray responses to their questions. If gaps in information are discovered, further inquiry will be required. Students can follow mentor texts to assist with organization.

5 **Draft the report.** Students write a draft from the information they have gathered. When word processing, students use spell- and grammar-checking devices as they draft. At the same time, they begin to plan any features other than text they will include to display their information. For example, they might plan to include illustrations, diagrams, or charts.

6 **Revise and edit the report.** Students meet in writers' groups to share their drafts and get feedback from their classmates. Using their peers' suggestions, they revise and then use an editing checklist or other checklist supplied by the teacher to proofread their reports, readying them for publication. Upper-grade students include a bibliography and notation of all sources used.

7 **Publish the report.** Students have many options for publishing their research. They may publish simple information text documents or they may create multimedia texts as ways of sharing their learning. Teachers guide students in making choices of the most effective ways of publicizing their information then provide opportunities for students to share with appropriate audiences.

- A feature article about the planet written collaboratively by the class
- A data chart comparing Mars to other planets taken from a nonfiction book
- A photograph located at: www.nationalgeographic.com
- A found poem about Mars with phrases taken from a book students have read
- A simulated journal written from the perspective of an astronaut who is exploring the planet

Through these five pieces, students presented several kinds of information, written from varied viewpoints. The project was much more complete than it would have been with just one genre.

Assessing Students' Reports and Projects

Students need to know the requirements for the research project and how they will be assessed or graded and have input into developing these. Many teachers distribute a checklist of requirements for the project before students begin working so that the students know what is expected of them and can assume responsibility for completing each step of the assignment. The checklist for an individual report might include these observation behaviours and products:

- Choose a narrow topic.
- Identify four or five research questions.
- Use a cluster or other graphic organizer to gather information to answer the questions.
- Use a checklist to critically evaluate the information.
- Write a draft with a section or a chapter to answer each question.
- Write a summary to conclude the report.
- Meet in writers' groups to share your report.
- Make at least three changes in your draft.
- Complete an editing checklist with a partner.
- Add a bibliography to show the resources used, including the Internet.
- Write and format the final copy of the report.
- Publish and share the report with someone.

The checklist can be simpler or more complex depending on a student's age and experiences and the intended learning outcomes of the research. A checklist enables students to monitor their own work and learn that writing is an involved process, not just a final product. It also helps teachers assess students' progress as work on extended projects continues. Teachers use a variety of ways to manage assessment over time. Written reports may be collected in **portfolios**, as described in Chapter 5. Multimedia projects maybe filed electronically for further sharing and assessment. In many Canadian classrooms, teachers choose a combination of ways to collect and assess so that their evaluation is based on a broad representation of student achievement.

Letters

While much communication, both personal and business, is now conducted electronically, elementary and middle-school students benefit from knowing letter conventions and this form of writing appears in most provincial curriculum documents.

Letters are typically classified as friendly or business letters. Formats for friendly and business letters are shown in the second Teacher's Notebook. Teaching students in elementary and middle schools about letter formats is often done in conjunction with teaching word processing and the various features used in the particular programs available to the students. Students need only be taught essential formatting. In particular, they need to learn to distinguish between friendly and business formats, how to write using each conventional arrangements, and that the choice of format depends on the purpose of the letter. Friendly letters might be informal, chatty letters to friends or e-pals or thank-you notes to family or to parent volunteers who have assisted in the classroom. Business format would be used when students write to agencies requesting information or send letters to public officials expressing an opinion about current events or issues of concern to them.

Friendly and business letter formats are accepted writing conventions, and most teachers simply explain the formats to students and prepare a set of charts to illustrate them. Attention to format should not suggest, however, that form is more important than content; rather, it should highlight formatting considerations of letter writing that elementary students are typically unfamiliar with.

Writing Letters

After teachers have introduced the formats for friendly and business letters, students need to apply them in writing to real people for authentic reasons. Writing authentic letters that will reach a real audience is much more valuable than writing practice letters to be graded by the teacher. One way of facilitating authentic letter writing is to make linkages to seeking information from or expressing opinions to appropriate audiences as part of theme studies or inquiry in other curriculum areas. Friendly letter writing can occur through communicating with pen pals traditionally or electronically. Teachers often arrange for their students to exchange letters with students in another class by contacting a teacher in a nearby school or by making connections on the Internet. Another possibility in some areas is for students to communicate with student teachers. The children have the opportunity to be pen pals with university students, and the university students have the opportunity to get to know an elementary student and examine students' writing. Remember that receiving replies to letters, paper or electronic, is the reward for writing!

Figure 7-9 shows a cluster with four rays developed by a grade 3 class for pen pal letters. As a class, the students brainstormed a list of possible topics for their first letters and decided on the four main-idea rays (me and my family, my school, my hobbies, and questions for my pen pal). Then students completed the clusters by adding details to each main idea. After creating their organizational clusters, their teacher guided them through the writing process to help each student compose a letter to be sent.

Teachers use a series of minilessons to teach students how to write letters and to show them how the format and style of letters differs from stories, informational books, and journals. Topics for minilessons include using the letter-writing forms, focusing on your audience, organizing information in the letter, and asking questions. Teachers also teach minilessons on capitalizing proper nouns in titles and names, addressing an envelope, using paragraphs, and being courteous.

LETTERS TO AUTHORS AND ILLUSTRATORS

One special type of letter students write is to favourite authors and illustrators. Students write to share their ideas and feelings about the books they have read. They ask questions about how a particular character was developed or why the illustrator used a certain art medium. Students also describe the books they have written. Students should be encouraged to write genuine letters to share their thoughts and feelings about the author's writing or the illustrator's artwork.

Most authors and illustrators reply to students' letters when possible. However, authors and illustrators receive thousands of letters from children every year. Correspondence, therefore, is usually managed by their publishers or agents. Teachers can check individual authors' websites for details concerning communication from readers. We suggest the following guidelines for students writing to authors and illustrators:

FIGURE 7-9 A GRADE 3 STUDENT'S CLUSTER AND PEN PAL LETTER

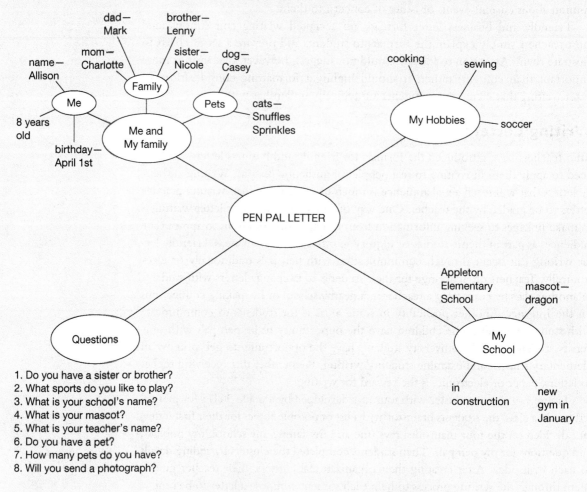

1. Do you have a sister or brother?
2. What sports do you like to play?
3. What is your school's name?
4. What is your mascot?
5. What is your teacher's name?
6. Do you have a pet?
7. How many pets do you have?
8. Will you send a photograph?

December 10

Dear Annie,

I'm your pen pal now. My name is Allison and I'm 8 years old. My birthday is on April 1st.

I go to Appleton Elementary School. Our mascot is a dragon. We are in construction because we're going to have a new gym in January.

My hobbies are soccer, sewing, and cooking. I play soccer, sewing I do in free time, and I cook dinner sometimes.

My pets are two cats and a dog. The dog's name is Casey and he's a boy. He is two years old. The cat is a girl and her name is Snuffles. She is four years old. The kitten is a girl and her name is Sprinkles. She is two months old.

My dad's name is Mark and my mom's name is Charlotte. Her birthday is the day after Mother's Day. My brother's name is Lenny. He is 13 years old. My sister's name is Nicole. She is 3 years old.

I have some questions for you. Do you have a sister or a brother? What sports do you like to play? Mine aren't. What is your school's name? What is your mascot? What is your teacher's name? Do you have a pet? How many pets do you have? Will you send me a photograph of yourself?

Your friend,
Allison

Forms for Friendly and Business Letters

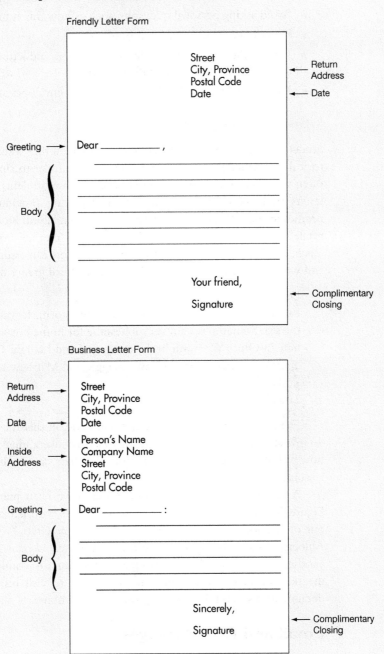

Friendly Letter Form

Street
City, Province
Postal Code
Date

→ Return Address
→ Date

Greeting → Dear _____ ,

Body

Your friend,

Signature

→ Complimentary Closing

Business Letter Form

Return Address →
Street
City, Province
Postal Code

Date →
Date

Inside Address →
Person's Name
Company Name
Street
City, Province
Postal Code

Greeting → Dear _____ :

Body

Sincerely,

Signature

→ Complimentary Closing

- Follow business letter format, with return address, greeting, body, closing, and signature.
- Use the process approach to write, revise, and edit the letter. Be sure to proofread and correct errors before writing or printing the final copy.
- Be polite in the letter; use the words *please* and *thank you*.
- Avoid asking personal questions, such as how much money he or she earns.
- Do not ask for free copies of books.
- Include the return address on both envelope and letter. Use the school address to avoid sharing personal information.
- Follow publishers' guidelines in respect to envelopes and addresses for replies.

SIMULATED LETTERS

Students can also write simulated letters, in which they assume the identity of a historical or literary figure. Simulated letters are similar to simulated journals and are often written as a form of response to the literature students read. Writing simulated letters can be combined with dramatic role-playing, providing students with opportunities to share letters and sometimes read them aloud. Students can write to a fairytale character, or from one book character to another. For example, after reading *Sarah, Plain and Tall* (MacLachlan, 1985), students can assume the persona of Sarah and write a letter to her brother William, as a third grader did in this letter:

> Dear William,
> I'm having fun here. There was a very big storm. It was so big it looked like the sea. Sometimes I am very lonesome for home but sometimes it is very fun here in Ohio. We swam in the cow pond and I taught Caleb how to swim. They were afraid I would leave. Maggie and Matthew brought some chickens.
> Love,
> Sarah

Even though these letters are not authentic, in that they are never mailed, they do give students experience in writing to a particular audience and they show clearly how well students comprehend the story. Teachers can use them to monitor students' learning.

A variety of books that include letters have been published for children (see Figure 7-10 for some). Some of these are stories with letters that children can take out of envelopes and read. *The Jolly Postman, or Other People's Letters* (Ahlberg & Ahlberg, 1986) has been a long-time favourite. *Meerkat Mail* (Gravett, 2006) is another popular storybook example of writing for communication. Sunny, the meerkat, decides to leave the Kalahari Desert to visit his mongoose cousins and documents his travels by sending postcards back home.

Email and Text Messages

Students write email and text messages to correspond with others. Students learn to use informative subject lines, begin with the most important information, and use short sentences and paragraphs. They also learn to avoid using too many capital letters, different fonts, exclamation marks, abbreviations, acronyms, or icons to communicate in a semi-formal email. Students use email and text messages for social purposes, but teachers also use them as a form of writing responses to literary texts. McKeon (2001) studied the email messages an elementary class wrote about the books they were

FIGURE 7-10 BOOKS THAT INCLUDE LETTERS

Books That Include Letters

Ablett, B. (2007). *Dear Polar Bear*. New York: Scholastic. (P)

Ada, A. (1998). *Yours Truly, Goldilocks*. New York: Atheneum. (M)

Ahlberg, J., & Ahlberg, A. (2007). *The Jolly Postman or Other People's Letters* (20th anniversary ed.). Boston: Little, Brown. (P)

Ahlberg, J., & Ahlberg, A. (2012). *The Jolly Christmas Postman*. London: Puffin. (P)

Durant, A. (2007). *Dear Santa Claus*. Somerville, MA: Candlewick Press. (P)

Gravett, E. (2006). *Meerkat Mail*. New York: Simon & Schuster Books for Young Readers. (P)

Hedderwick, M. (2010). *Katie Morag Delivers the Mail*. New York: Red Fox Picture Books. (P–M)

Hesse, K. (1992). *Letters from Rifka*. New York: Holt. (U)

Husband, A. (2009). *Dear Miss*. London, UK: Meadowside Children's Books. (M)

Husband, A. (2012). *Dear Class*. London, UK: Meadowside Children's Books. (M)

James, S. (2002). *Dear Greenpeace*. Somerville, MA: Candlewick Press. (M)

Keats, E. J. (1968). *A Letter to Amy*. New York: Harper Row. (P)

Kitagawa, M. (1986). *This Is My Own: Letter to Wes and Other Writings on Japanese Canadians, 1941–1948*. Vancouver: Talonbooks. (M–U) ✦

Langen, A., & Droop, C. (1994). *Letters from Felix: A Little Rabbit on a World Tour*. New York: Abbeville Press. (M)

Moss, M. (2007). *Amelia Writes Again*. New York: Simon & Schuster Children's Books. (M)

Moss, M. (2011). *Amelia's BFF: Amelia's Notebook*. New York: Simon & Schuster Children's Books. (M)

Neering, R. (1990). *Pioneers* (Canadian Lives series). Markham, ON: Fitzhenry & Whiteside. (M–U) ✦

Orloff, K. (2004). *I Wanna Iguana*. New York: Putnam. (P)

Potter, B. (1995). *Dear Peter Rabbit*. New York: Warne. (P–M)

Teague, M. (2008). *LaRue for Mayor: Letters from the Campaign Trail*. New York: Blue Sky Press. (P–M)

P = primary grades (K–2); M = middle grades (3–5); U = upper grades (6–8)

---

reading and concluded that email is a constructive way to enhance students' learning as well as an effective strategy for teachers to interact with their students. We, too, verified that email message exchanges fostered meaningful discussion about books when our student teachers partnered with students in local schools and shared opinions about the books they were reading. Both elementary and university students engaged in thoughtful exchanges that demonstrated their sustained engagement as readers.

Assessing Students' Letters

Traditionally, students wrote letters and turned them in for the teacher to grade, but they were never mailed. Educators now recognize the importance of authenticity in student writing and the benefit of students having an audience other than the teacher for their writing. One way that teachers can give feedback on letters that are to be sent is by completing checklists concerning the key criteria and letter features. A grade 3 teacher developed the checklist for assessing students' pen pal letters in Figure 7-11; it identifies specific behaviours and measurable products. The completed checklist can be added to the students' writing folders.

Differentiating to Meet the needs of Every Student

Teachers can make adaptations as students read and write informational books so that every student can be successful. A list of recommendations is presented in the Differentiating box below. It is important to teach students about the genre of informational books and the characteristics of expository text from multiple sources and the unique conventions they have to help readers—including diagrams, glossaries, and indexes. Students also need to learn about the five expository text structures because research has shown that less fluent readers are not as conscious of them as better readers are. Informational books are available on a wide variety of topics and at a range of reading levels, so selecting reading materials to meet the needs of every student should not be too difficult.

FIGURE 7-11 A CHECKLIST FOR ASSESSING STUDENTS' PEN PAL LETTERS

Pen Pal letter Checklist

Name _____

	Yes	No
1. Did you complete the cluster?	☐	☐
2. Did you include questions in your letter?	☐	☐
3. Did you put your letter in the friendly letter form?	☐	☐
_____ return address		
_____ greeting		
_____ three or more paragraphs		
_____ closing		
_____ salutation and name		
4. Did you write a rough draft of your letter?	☐	☐
5. Did you revise your letter with suggestions from people in your writers group?	☐	☐
6. Did you proofread your letter and correct as many errors as possible?	☐	☐

DIFFERENTIATING

Reading and Writing Information to Meet the Needs of Every Student

1. Examine Informational Books with Students

Informational books are organized differently than stories, and they often have unique conventions. Teachers can help students examine this genre and compare these books with stories so that they can recognize the differences. Point out to students such features as glossaries, marginal textboxes, and picture captions that are designed to help readers construct meaning.

2. Teach Students How to Read Hypertext

Approach reading from the Internet as a guided reading lesson. Work with a small group of students, preferably each with a computer screen. Begin with a carefully selected website on which text is clearly organized. Set a purpose for reading and then guide readers to locate information to fulfill the purpose. A series of minilessons can highlight hypertext features useful to students as they read. A modified SQ4R strategy can be followed under teacher direction. Another alternative is to pair less capable readers with more able readers to read selections from the Internet.

3. Provide Students with Reading Guides

Written study guides or outlines may be provided to help readers follow a logical path and/or to make clearly organized notes. Guides should follow the organization of the text to be read from books or the Internet. Guide readers in small steps by directing them to read brief sections at a time followed by structured note-making.

4. Provide Frameworks for Student Writing

Less experienced writers can compose reports and projects similar to those of their peers if given a writing framework to follow. For example, when writing an "All about …" book, a framework might be a six-page booklet with a sentence starter on each page to support writing about six aspects of the topic. Writing frameworks for informational reports might resemble extended fill-in-the blanks structure. Students write information they are learning during theme study or inquiry units as well as in social studies and science. Young writers can combine pictures and words to create their reports. As students gain skills, the frameworks can be modified to shift responsibility to the students.

5. Arrange for Students to Write Authentic Letters

Teachers can arrange for students to write friendly and business letters so that students can have the experience of writing to a real audience. Receiving a reply is one of the best ways to stimulate students' interest in writing and to motivate reluctant writers to persevere. To ensure replies and understanding of the developmental nature of inexperienced writers' compositions, teachers can arrange for students to write to older students or to student teachers at a nearby university.

Review

Research suggests that reading and writing information should be as much a part of students' reading and writing as stories. Much of students' reading of informational or expository text is from the Internet, informational magazines, informational trade books, and life stories. Students write informational text when they compose reports, life stories, and letters.

The following key concepts are presented in this chapter:

1. Students read expository texts to learn information (from books, the Internet, newspapers, and magazines), and they write expository text (in reports, informational books, posters, and so on) to share information with others.

2. Informational writing is organized into five expository text structures: description, sequence, comparison, cause and effect, and problem and solution.

3. Students use their knowledge of expository text structures when reading and writing informational texts.

4. Reading and writing digital text requires students to use many of the same strategies as traditional print, but also requires them to make decisions regarding structure and links across text, and to read information critically.

5. Students write both collaborative and individual reports using the stages of the writing process.

6. Students can organize reports in a variety of formats and often extend them to include multimedia such as visuals, sound, or other digital features.

7. The friendly and business letters that students write should be mailed to authentic audiences.

8. Students write simulated letters as a response to the literature they read during theme studies, resource-based units, or in conjunction with social studies or science.

Theory to Practice

1. Follow the guidelines in this chapter to write a class collaborative report with a group of elementary students on a social studies topic, such as Canadian communities, or on a science topic, such as the solar system.

2. Choose a topic related to teaching language arts, such as writing in journals or the uses of drama. Research the topic and create a brief multimedia report to share with colleagues.

3. With students in a local elementary school, write biographies of Canadian heroes, using graphic organizers to collect the information.

4. Help a group of students write friendly letters and email messages to friends in another school.

Literacy in Action

Chapter 8: Integrating Technology into Performance Tasks

Procedure

Integrating technology into instruction "not only increases student learning, understanding, and achievement but also augments motivation to learn and supports the development of critical thinking and problem-solving skills. [Furthermore], it allows teachers to differentiate instruction more efficiently by providing a wider variety of avenues for learning" (Pitler, Hubbell, Kuhn & Malenoski, 2007, p. 3). Given the increased access to technology within my school district in recent years, I was eager to integrate technology into an existing English language arts performance task based on Lois Lowry's novel *The Giver* (1993).

Following the class novel study, in which the implications of conformity and the elimination of personal freedom were explored, students worked collaboratively to design their own utopian community. Three essential questions formed the basis of the exploration and the subsequent creation of the community:

- What makes an ideal society?

- To what extent should a government control individual rights for the benefit of society?

- How can information be delivered effectively using digital media?

Each group received an invitation to attend the École St. Joseph School Utopian Symposium to showcase their community and attract potential members. Students were responsible for developing a slideshow (created in PowerPoint) and an oral presentation.

> "Integral in the performance task as well was the integration of technology.... Technology enhanced the interest, motivation, and effort of the majority of my students."
>
> Janice Beland

Communities were designed using the following guidelines:

- Group members are responsible for one or two of the project roles. Task cards describing role responsibilities were provided for: mayor, educator, employer, builder, health & public safety officer, transportation & technology expert, and entertainment director.

- Each member is individually responsible for his/her role(s); however, the group must approve the ideas.

- The community (and subsequent presentation) must include an education system, a government with laws, an employment system, some type of currency (money), transportation and technology, housing, recreation/entertainment, and health care.

- In addition to researching and creating information based on specific roles, each group must work together to create a community name; flag or logo; and motto or slogan.

- Groups are also encouraged to include any additional aspects of the society that members feel are relevant.

- Equal participation is mandatory: each member of the group must create his/her own slide or slides and must participate in the oral presentation.

Assessment

Students were required to keep a journal recording daily goals and progress reports. Completion of goals and reports increased student accountability. Individuals or groups struggling to meet goals were provided with additional teacher support.

Use of anecdotal notes and checklists helped me to track the progress of individuals and groups. Individual skills were assessed informally throughout the project. Assessment of technology focused on use of graphics, layout and design, and transitions and effects.

Each group assessed their group work skills and their slideshow and oral presentation using the same rubric I used to assess the task. Each student was also individually assessed on his/her slide(s) and oral presentation.

Adaptation

I used only *The Giver*, but other novels could be used to address varying reading levels and interests. Novels such as *City of Ember* (DuPrau, 2003) and *The Hunger Games* (Collins, 2008) present similar community scenarios. They could be used to stimulate discussion about the restriction of personal freedoms and the subsequent consequences.

The performance task could also be completed effectively using alternative presentation applications such as VoiceThread (web-based) or Explain Everything (an iPad app). Each application is able to capture images and audio.

Reflection

Prior to this performance task, students had opportunities to work collaboratively, to familiarize them with the routines of group work. Understanding collaborative group processes contributed to their overall success.

Providing the rubrics to students before beginning the task was also crucial.

Integral too, was the integration of technology. Having utilized the task previously without technology, it was evident during both the process and the presentations that technology enhanced the interest, motivation, and effort of the majority of my students.

From the classroom of Janice Beland, Literacy Coach
École St. Joseph School
Yellowknife Catholic Schools

Words, Their Meanings, and the Tools to Use Them: Grammar, Spelling, Handwriting, and Word Processing

LEARNING OUTCOMES

After you read this chapter you should be able to

1. Identify what teachers teach young students about the meanings of words

2. Explain how teachers focus on words during resource-based units, thematic units, and inquiry-based units

3. Discover selections of children's literature to share with students to explore words and how they work

4. Explain how teachers teach spelling and grammar in the elementary grades

5. Describe handwriting and word-processing minilessons

6. Explain why use of the language tools is best learned through meaningful and functional, language arts activities

Monkey Business Images/Shutterstock

Middle grade students use their digital thesaurus to improve their writing.

Words are the meaning-bearing units of language. Many people estimate there are over a million words in the English language. Although some linguists insist it is impossible to count actual words, during a project looking at words in digitized books, researchers from Harvard University and Google in 2010 estimated a total of 1,022,000 existed words and that the number would grow by several thousand each year. Questions about number are raised because considerations must be made concerning what counts as a word. For example, how many forms of a word should be counted and should archaic words, no longer used, be counted? More easily understood, perhaps, are the number of words in current use and the number native speakers of

English actually use. In talking about how many words there are in English, then, there are three key numbers to remember: more than a million total words, about 170,000 words in current use, and 20,000–30,000 words used by each adult person (English Live, 2014).

To construct meaning, readers and writers need to know many words, how to choose the right words, and how to connect words together in ways that are understood by others; that is, they need to have and use rich vocabularies and know and use Standard English grammar. If they are to communicate with others, they also need to know how to use the tools of language—spelling, handwriting, and word processing. Traditionally, the use of Standard English grammar, conventional spelling, and neat handwriting have been considered the hallmarks of an educated person. Today, people see grammar, spelling, handwriting, and word processing as tools for communicating *through* language—as means to an end, rather than the goal of education. These tools continue to be important parts of language arts instruction. In this chapter, we will first look at some types of words and students' vocabulary development. Then we will discuss the language tools of spelling, grammar, handwriting, and word processing, along with how to teach students to use them.

Words and Their Meanings

Learning about words and how to choose the right one to express the meaning you intend is what vocabulary is all about. Vocabulary is not decoding or word identification; rather, the focus is on meaning. Choosing the best word to express meaning is important to all language users. When we listen and read, we must understand the meaning that someone else intends, and when we speak and write, we must choose exactly the right word so that our audience will understand our message.

Students begin kindergarten with approximately 5000 words in their vocabularies, and their vocabularies grow at a rate of about 3000 words a year (M. Graves, 2006; Nagy & Herman, 1985). Through being read to, reading, and other experiences with language, students not only learn more words, but also their word knowledge becomes more sophisticated. They learn about words and word parts, words that mean the same as and the opposite of other words, words that sound alike, words with multiple meanings, the figurative language of idioms, and how words have been borrowed from languages around the world. They also learn about how words are created and they have fun playing with words (Tompkins, 1994). What follows is a teacher's guide to those aspects of words most often explored in elementary classrooms.

Root Words and Affixes

A *root word* is a **morpheme**, the basic and meaning-bearing part of a word to which affixes are added. Some root words are whole words, and others are parts of words. Many words are developed from a single root word; for example, the Latin word *portare* ("to carry") is the source of at least nine Modern English words: *deport*, *export*, *import*, *port*, *portable*, *porter*, *report*, *support*, and *transportation*. Latin is one source of English root words, and Greek and Old English are two other sources. A list of root words appears in the first Teacher's Notebook. Students can compile lists of words developed from these root words, and they can draw root word **clusters** to illustrate the relationship of the root word to the words developed from it. Figure 8-1 shows a root word cluster for the Greek root *graph*, which means "to write." Recognizing

FIGURE 8-1 A CLUSTER FOR THE ROOT WORD GRAPH

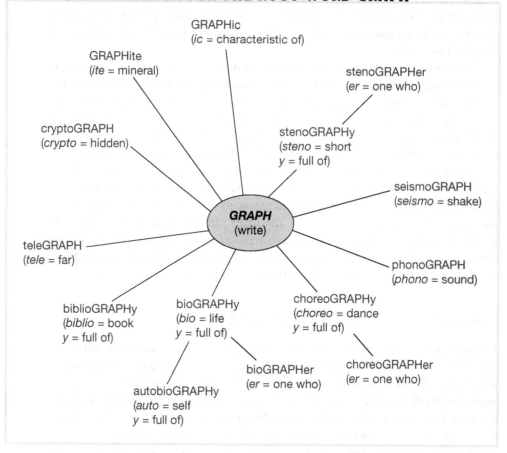

GRAPHic
(*ic* = characteristic of)

GRAPHite
(*ite* = mineral)

stenoGRAPHer
(*er* = one who)

cryptoGRAPH
(*crypto* = hidden)

stenoGRAPHy
(*steno* = short
y = full of)

GRAPH
(write)

seismoGRAPH
(*seismo* = shake)

teleGRAPH
(*tele* = far)

phonoGRAPH
(*phono* = sound)

biblioGRAPHy
(*biblio* = book
y = full of)

bioGRAPHy
(*bio* = life
y = full of)

choreoGRAPHy
(*choreo* = dance
y = full of)

autobioGRAPHy
(*auto* = self
y = full of)

bioGRAPHer
(*er* = one who)

choreoGRAPHer
(*er* = one who)

basic elements from word to word helps students cut down on the amount of memorizing necessary to learn meanings and spellings.

Affixes are morphemes, or meaning units, that are added to words and root words. They influence meaning but are never stand-alone words. Affixes can be prefixes or suffixes. Prefixes are added to the beginning of words, such as *re-* in *reread*, and suffixes are added to the ends of words, such as *-ful* in *hopeful* and *-er* in *player*. Like root words, affixes come from Old English, Latin, and Greek. They often change a word's meaning, such as adding *un-* to *happy* to form *unhappy*. Sometimes they change the part of speech, too. For example, when *-ion* is added to *attract* to form *attraction*, the verb becomes a noun.

When an affix is "peeled off" or removed from a word, the remaining word is usually a real word. For example, when the prefix *pre-* is removed from *preview*, the word *view* can stand alone; and when the suffix *-ful* is removed from *careful*, the word *care* can stand alone. One caution should be pointed out to students. Some words include letter sequences that look like affixes, but because the remaining word cannot stand alone, they are not affixes. For example, the *in-* at the beginning of *include* is not a prefix because *clude* is not a word. Such "phantom" affixes can be confusing to students when they are using the affixes to unlock the meaning of unfamiliar words.

A list of prefixes and suffixes is presented in the second Teacher's Notebook. Those that are most commonly used in English words (White, Sowell, & Yanagihara, 1989) are marked with an asterisk in the Teacher's Notebook.

Synonyms and Antonyms

Synonyms are words that have the same or nearly the same meanings as other words. Synonyms are useful because they provide options, allowing us to express ourselves with more exactness. Students can check a dictionary or thesaurus to locate synonyms for words to assist them to clearly and expressively present their ideas in their writing.

Antonyms are words that express opposite meanings. For example, antonyms for *loud* include *soft, subdued, quiet, silent, inaudible, sedate, sombre,* and *dull.* These words express shades of meaning just as synonyms do, and some opposites are more appropriate for one meaning of *loud* than for another.

Teachers teach students to use dictionaries and thesauri, both hard texts and online editions. Beginning with pictionaries, students can learn to use these resources as soon as they begin to read and write. Examples of reference books teachers find useful in working with young readers and writers are annotated in Figure 8-2.

FIGURE 8-2 REFERENCE BOOKS FOR ELEMENTARY STUDENTS

Dictionaries

Gage Canadian Beginner's Dictionary. (2004). Toronto, ON: Nelson Education Canada. (P) 🍁
- This dictionary is intended for use in schools in kindergarten through grade 3. It contains 550 of the most commonly used words in the English language together with full-colour illustrations.

Collins Gage Canadian Intermediate Dictionary. (2005). Toronto: Nelson Education. (U) 🍁
- Recently revised and updated, it is ideal for grades 6 to 10 and ESL students. It offers definitions, pronunciation, homonyms, usage information, synonyms, etymologies, and example sentences.

Shannon, R. (2004). *Franklin's Picture Dictionary.* Toronto: Kids Can Press. (P) 🍁
- This dictionary contains over 1000 words withfull-colour illustrations from the Franklin series along with simple sentences and language building suggestions for parents and teachers. It is intended for ages 5–8.

Gage Canadian First Book of Words. (2002). Toronto: Nelson Education Canada. (P) 🍁
- This book includes over 550 of the most commonly used words in the English language along with full-colour illustrations.

McIlwain, J. (2003). *Children's Illustrated Dictionary* (Canadian ed): Toronto: Dorling Kindersley. (P) 🍁
- This dictionary has 12,000 word entries written with Canadian spellings accompanied by clear definitions, examples of usage, colour photographs, and illustrations.

Gage Canadian Junior Dictionary. (2005). Toronto: Nelson Thomson Learning Education Canada. (M) 🍁
- This dictionary contains 3000 word entries, many illustrated, along with grammar and usage guides. Canadian entries are highlighted. It is intended for grades 3–6.

My First Canadian Oxford Dictionary. (2009). Don Mills, ON: Oxford University Press Canada. (P) 🍁
- This dictionary is intended for children ages 5 and up. It contains lively, colourful illustrations of over 550 words.

Oxford Canadian Spelling Bee Dictionary. (2008). Toronto: Oxford University Press. (U) 🍁
- Based on the *Canadian Oxford Dictionary* this book provides over 36,000 words difficult to spell and fundamental to competitors. It includes etymologies, pronunciations, primary definitions, and homophones.

Parnwell, E., & Grennan, M. (1996). *The Canadian Oxford Picture Dictionary: Monolingual.* Toronto: Oxford University Press. (P–M) 🍁
- This useful dictionary is designed to be a basic tool to aid acquisition of Canadian English vocabulary. It contains over 2400 words and full-colour illustrations portraying Canadian culture.

Canadian Oxford Dictionary (2nd ed). (2004). Toronto: Oxford University Press. (T) 🍁
- This dictionary presents 300,000 words and senses, including 2200 uniquely Canadian words and Canadian preferred spellings.

Student's Oxford Canadian Dictionary (2nd ed). (2007). Toronto: Oxford University Press. (M–U) 🍁
- This dictionary contains 185 000 words, phrases, and definitions with 2000 uniquely Canadian words and senses. It is suitable for grades 9–12.

Thesauruses

Bollard, J. (2006). *Scholastic Children's Thesaurus.* Richmond Hill, ON: Scholastic. (M–U) 🍁
- This comprehensive thesaurus provides a sample sentence for each synonym listed. It also includes an extensive index.

Collins Gage Canadian Intermediate Thesaurus. (2006). Scarborough, ON: Nelson Canada. (U) 🍁
- Word choices include Canadian vocabulary and slang in Canadian preferred spellings. It is intended for grades 7–12.

Collins Primary Thesaurus. (2004). New York: HarperCollins. (M)
- This clear, user-friendly thesaurus is intended for grades 3–6. It shows words in context.

My First Canadian Oxford Thesaurus. (2003). Don Mills, ON: Oxford University Press Canada. (P–M) 🍁

(continued)

- This thesaurus includes 100 headwords and more than 1000 alternative words, including opposites. It is intended for children 5 years and up.

Oxford Learner's Thesaurus. (2008). London: Oxford University Press. (M–U) (T)
- This pack contains book and CD-ROM with over 15,000 words and expressions from written and spoken English. It illustrates correct uses, especially helpful to English learners.

Roget's Student Thesaurus (Rev. ed). (2001). Toronto: Pearson Scott Foresman. (U) (T)
- Over 4000 synonyms with sample sentences are listed in this thesaurus. The pronunciation guide is listed in the index. It is intended for ages 9–12.

—

P 5 primary grades (K–2); M 5 middle grades (3–5); U 5 upper grades (6–8); T 5 teacher.

TEACHER'S NOTEBOOK

Root Words

ann/enn (year): anniversary, annual, biennial, centennial, perennial

ast (star): aster, asterisk, astrology, astronaut, astronomy

auto (self): autobiography, automatic, automobile

bio (life): autobiography, biodegradable, biography, biology

cent (hundred): cent, centennial, centigrade, centipede, century

circ (around): circle, circular, circus, circumspect

corp (body): corporal, corporation, corps

cycl (wheel): bicycle, cycle, cyclist, cyclone, tricycle

dict (speak): contradict, dictate, dictator, predict, verdict

geo (earth): geography, geology, geometry

gram (letter): diagram, grammar, monogram, telegram

graph (write): biography, graphic, paragraph, phonograph, stenographer

grat (pleasing, thankful): congratulate, grateful, gratitude

jus/jud/jur (law, right): injury, judge, justice

man (hand): manacle, manual, manufacture, manuscript

mand (order): command, demand, mandate, remand

mar (sea): aquamarine, marine, maritime, submarine

meter/metre (measure): barometer, centimetre, diameter, speedometer, thermometer

min (small): miniature, minimize, minor, minute

mort (death): immortal, mortal, mortality, mortician, post-mortem

ped/pod (foot): pedal, pedestrian, podiatry, tripod

phon (sound): earphone, microphone, phonics, phonograph, saxophone, symphony

photo (light): photograph, photographer, photosensitive, photosynthesis

quer/ques/quis (seek): query, question, inquisitive

rupt (break): abrupt, bankrupt, interrupt, rupture

scope (see): horoscope, kaleidoscope, microscope, periscope, telescope

struct (build): construction, indestructible, instruct

tele (far): telecast, telegram, telegraph, telephone, telescope, telethon, television

terr (land): terrace, terrain, terrarium, territory

tract (pull, drag): attraction, subtract, tractor

vict/vinc (conquer): convict, convince, evict, victor, victory

vis (see): television, visa, vision, visual

viv/vit (live): survive, vitamin, vivid

volv (roll): involve, revolutionary, revolver

(continued)

Affixes

Prefixes

a/an- (not): atheist, anaerobic
amphi- (both): amphibian
anti- (against): antiseptic
bi- (two, twice): bifocal, biannual
contra- (against): contradict
de- (away): detract
di- (two): dioxide
***dis-** (not): disapprove
***dis-** (reversal): disinfect
ex- (out): export
hemi- (half): hemisphere
***il-/im-/in-/ir-** (not): illegible, impolite, inexpensive, irrational
***in-** (in, into): indoor
inter- (between): intermission
kilo/milli- (one thousand): kilometre, milligram
micro- (small): microfilm
***mis-** (wrong): mistake
mono- (one): monarch
multi- (many): multimillionaire
omni- (all): omnivorous
***over-** (too much): overflow
poly- (many): polygon
post- (after): postwar
pre-/pro- (before): precede, prologue
quad-/quart- (four): quadruple, quarter
re- (again): repay
***re-/retro-** (back): replace, retroactive
***sub-** (under): submarine
super- (above): supermarket
trans- (across): transport
tri- (three): triangle
***un-** (not): unhappy
***un-** (reversal): untie

Suffixes

-able/-ible (worthy of, can be): lovable, audible
***-al/-ial** (action, process): arrival, denial
-ance/-ence (state or quality): annoyance, absence
-ant (one who): servant
-ard (one who is): coward
-ary/-ory (person, place): secretary, laboratory
-dom (state or quality): freedom
-ed (past tense): played
-ee (one who is): trustee
***-er/-or/-ar** (one who): teacher, actor, liar
-er/-or (action): robber
-ern (direction): northern
-et/-ette (small): booklet, dinette
-ful (full of): hopeful
-hood (state or quality): childhood
-ic (characterized by): angelic
-icle/-cule (small): particle, molecule
-ify (to make): simplify
-ing (participle): eating, building
-ish (like): reddish
-ism (doctrine of): communism
-less (without): hopeless
-ling (young): duckling
-logy (the study of): zoology
***-ly** (in the manner of): slowly
-ment (state or quality): enjoyment
***-ness** (state or quality): kindness
-s/-es (plural): cats, boxes
-ship (state, or art or skill): friendship, seamanship
***-sion/-tion** (state or quality): tension, attraction
-ster (one who): gangster
-ure (state or quality): failure
-ward (direction): homeward
***-y** (full of): sleepy

* = most commonly used affixes

Source: Based on White, T. G., Sowell, J., & Yanagihara, A. (1989). Teaching elementary students to use word-part clues. The Reading Teacher, 42, 302–308. © Gail E. Tompkins

Homonyms

Homonyms, words that have sound and spelling similarities, are divided into three categories: homophones, homographs, and homographic homophones. *Homophones* are words that sound alike but are spelled differently. Most homophones, such as *right* and *write*, developed from entirely different root words, and it is only by accident that they have come to sound alike.

Homographs are words that are spelled the same but pronounced differently. Their meaning is dependent on the pronunciation. Examples of homographs are *bow, close, lead, minute, record, read,* and *wind.*

Homographic homophones are words that are both spelled and pronounced alike, such as *bark, bat, bill, box, fair, fly, hide, jet, mine, pen, ring, row, spell, toast,* and *yard.* Some are related words; others are linguistic accidents.

There are many books of homonyms for children. One is Barretta's *Dear Deer* (2007), in which short news vignettes from the zoo tell of amusing characters, such as the moose who ate eight bowls of mousse. Students enjoy reading these books and making their own word books and illustrative posters.

Multiple Meanings and Ambiguity

Many words have more than one meaning. Such words are referred to as *polysemous* words. The word *bank,* for example, has as many as twelve meanings. Why does this happen? One possibility is word origin, such as when words of similar pronunciation but different meanings were borrowed from different languages. Another possibility is the evolution of meanings as society became more complex and needed finer shades of meaning. Other polysemous words may be linguistic accidents.

Teachers help students become aware of potential ambiguities created by multiple meanings and syntactical structures. Zipke (2008) points out that ambiguity training improves students' reading comprehension. She recommends reading and writing riddles for learning how to manipulate language. Students can also create posters with word clusters to show multiple meanings of words (Bromley, 1996).

Idioms and Metaphors

Many words have both literal and figurative meanings. *Literal* meanings are the explicit, dictionary meanings, and *figurative* meanings are metaphorical or use figures of speech. For example, to describe winter as the coldest season of the year in Canada is literal, but to say that winter has icy breath is figurative. Two types of **figurative language** are idioms and metaphors.

Idioms are groups of words, such as "let the cat out of the bag," that have a special meaning. There are hundreds of idioms in English, and we use them every day to create word pictures that make language more colourful. Some examples are "out in left field," "a skeleton in the closet," and "stick your neck out." Some of these idioms are new, and others are hundreds of years old.

Idioms can be confusing to students because they must be interpreted figuratively rather than literally. They can be particularly troublesome to students learning English as an added language. It is important that children move beyond the literal meanings to learn flexibility in using language. One way teachers help students learn flexibility is to use literature to introduce figurative language. Young students enjoy the clever use of homonyms and idioms made by the author Peggy Parish in her series of books about Amelia Bedelia. The wordplay in *Teach Us, Amelia Bedelia* (Parish, 2004) and others often creates laughter as well as meaningful experience with potentially confusing vocabulary. Older students enjoy sharing books such as *My Teacher Likes to Say* (Brennan-Nelson, 2004) to discover both figurative and literal meanings of idioms and clichés. Other excellent books of idioms are shown in Figure 8-3. A good reference book for teachers is *Canadian Words and Sayings* (Casselman, 2007). This book provides meanings and examples of idioms that are used every day in Canada.

FIGURE 8-3 RIDDLE BOOKS AND BOOKS ABOUT AMBIGUOUS LANGUAGE

Alda, A. (2006). *Did You Say Pears?* Toronto: Tundra Books. 🍁

Cleary, B. (2009). *Skin Like Milk, Hair of Silk: What Are Similes and Metaphors?* Minneapolis, MN: Millbrook Press.

Cleary, B. (2014). *A Bat Cannot Bat, A Stair Cannot Stare.* Minneapolis, MN: Millbrook Press.

Dahl, M. (2001). *The Everything Kids' Joke Book.* Avon, MA: Adams Media.

Helmer, M. (2004). *Funtime Riddles.* Toronto: Kids Can Press. 🍁

Helmer, M. (2004). *Recess Riddles.* Toronto: Kids Can Press. 🍁

Leedy, L. (2003). *There's a Frog in My Throat! 440 Animal Sayings a Little Bird Told Me.* New York: Holiday House.

Leedy, L. (2009). *Crazy Like a Fox: A Simile Story.* New York: Holiday House.

Leedy, L. (2010). *My Teacher Is a Dinosaur and Other Prehistoric Poems, Jokes, and Amazing Facts.* Tarrytown, NY: Marshall Cavendish Children.

Loewen, N. & Wu, D. (2011). *You're Toast and Other Metaphors We Adore.* Mankato, MN: Picture Window Books.

Moses, W. (2008). *Raining Cats and Dogs.* New York: Philomel Books.

Terban, M. (1990). *Punching the Clock: Funny Action Idioms.* New York: Clarion.

Terban, M. (1992). *Funny You Should Ask: How to Make Up Jokes and Riddles with Wordplay.* New York: Clarion.

Terban, M. (1993). *It Figures! Fun Figures of Speech.* New York: Clarion.

O'Connor, E. (2005). *101 Cool Canadian Jokes.* Markham, ON: Scholastic Canada. 🍁

Regan, L. (2015). *Riddles at School.* New York: Windmill Books.

Terban, M. (2007). *In a Pickle and Other Funny Idioms.* New York: Sandpiper.

Thomas, L. (2008). *Ha! Ha! Ha! And Much More: The Ultimate Round-up of Jokes, Riddles, Facts, and Puzzles.* Toronto: Maple Tree Press. 🍁

Waldman, D. (2009). *Clever Rachel.* Victoria, BC: Orca Books. 🍁

Metaphors and similes compare something to something else. A *simile* is a comparison signalled by the use of *like* or *as*. "The crowd was as rowdy as a bunch of marauding monkeys" and "In the moonlight, the dead tree looked like a skeleton" are two examples. In contrast, a *metaphor* compares two things by implying that one *is* something else, without using *like* or *as*. "The two old men were snails crossing the street" is an example.

Differentiating between the terms *simile* and *metaphor* is less important than understanding the meaning of comparisons in books students are reading and having students use comparisons to make their writing more vivid.

Sources of New Words

Knowing the history of English and how words entered the language contributes greatly to understanding the language and its words—their meanings and spelling patterns. When teachers know about the language and its history, they can help students understand some of the complexities of English.

The fact that English is a historic language accounts for word meanings and some spelling inconsistencies. English has a variety of words for a single concept, and the history of English in general, and the etymology of the words in particular, explains apparent duplications. Consider these words related to water: *aquatic, hydrant, aquamarine, waterfall, hydroelectric, watercress, watery, aquarium, waterproof, hydraulic, aqualung,* and *hydrogen,* to name a few. These words have one of three root words that each means "water": *water* is English, of course, while *aqua* is Latin and *hydro* is Greek. The root word that is used depends on the people who created the word, the purpose of the word, and when the word entered English. Helping children understand and appreciate the origins of words is an excellent way to help build meaning vocabulary. In some instances, it also helps them understand the complexities of English orthography.

Dating back to Old English times, the most common way of expanding English is to borrow words from other languages. Perhaps as many as 75 percent of our words have been borrowed from other languages and incorporated into English.

New words continually appear in English. Not all are borrowed. Many are created to describe new phenomena, inventions, and scientific projects. They are created in a variety of ways, including coining, compounding, and clipping.

Creative people have always coined new words. Lewis Carroll, author of *Alice in Wonderland* and *Through the Looking Glass*, is perhaps the best-known inventor of words. He called his inventions *portmanteau words* (borrowing from the British word for a suitcase that opens into two halves) because they blended two words into one. His most famous example, *chortle*, a blend of *snort* and *chuckle*, is from the poem "Jabberwocky." Other examples of blended words include *brunch* (*breakfast + lunch*), *guesstimate* (*guess + estimate*), and *smog* (*smoke + fog*).

In addition to blending, some new words are created through compounding, or combining two existing words to create a new word. *Friendship* and *childhood* are two words the Anglo-Saxons compounded, while recent compoundings include *latchkey kids*, *skateboard*, and *software*. Canadian author Jane Barclay (1998) shows the playfulness of combining words in *How Cold Was It?* when she writes of a "freezing, sneezing, goosebumpy, teeth-chattering, can't-get-out-of-bed, blanket-over-my-head kind of cold."

Clipping, the process of shortening existing words, is another way of creating new words. For example, *bomb* is the shortened form of *bombard*, and *zoo* comes from *zoological park*. Most clipped words are only one syllable and are used in informal conversation.

Two other types of coined words are trademarks and acronyms. An example of a well-known brand name used generically is *Kleenex* (to mean tissue). Acronyms are words formed by combining the initial letters of several words, such as *scuba*, formed by combining the initial letters of "self-contained underwater breathing apparatus." Additional coining of words involves changes in how words are used. For example, the word *Google*, initially the noun that names a popular search engine, is now readily used as a verb to describe seeking information from the Internet.

Authors also create new words in their stories, and students should be alert to the possibility of finding a created word when they read or listen to stories. J. K. Rowling (1997) introduced readers to Harry Potter's associates *Dumbledore* and Lord *Voldemort*, whose wizardry was aided by a *portkey*. Although it is unlikely that your students will create new words that will eventually appear in the dictionary, they do create words to add pizzazz to their speech and their writing, and some invented words become part of the everyday jargon in families and classrooms. For instance, a young wordsmith in kindergarten in rainy Halifax told her teacher that for her birthday she wanted a *rainbrella*.

Teaching Students about Words

Students' vocabularies grow at an astonishing rate—about 3000 words a year, or roughly seven to ten new words every day (Nagy & Herman, 1985). By the time students finish high school, their vocabularies are in excess of 30,000 words. Students learn words in many ways. They learn some through specific instruction, but they also learn through independent reading and writing projects and from their interactions with media, including the Internet. It remains true, however, that encouraging students to read is probably the most important way teachers promote vocabulary growth (Nagy, 1988). Repeated exposure to words is crucial because students need to see and use a new word many times before it becomes a part of their ownership dictionaries—words they understand and use competently.

Learning a word isn't as simple as you might think. It's not that you either know a word or you don't; instead, there's a continuum of word knowledge, moving from never having seen or heard the word to being able to use it effectively in a variety of contexts (Allen, 1999). Beck, McKeown, and Kucan (2002) suggest this continuum of word knowledge that moves from not knowing a word at all to knowing it well:

Level 1: No Knowledge. Students aren't familiar with the word.

Level 2: Incidental Knowledge. Students have seen or heard the word, but they don't know its meaning.

Level 3: Partial Knowledge. Students know one definition for the word or can use it in one context.

Level 4: Full Knowledge. Students have a deep understanding of the word's multiple meanings and are able to use it effectively in multiple contexts.

It takes time for students to move from having little or no knowledge of a word to full knowledge. During a week's study of a word, for example, students may move one or two levels, but it's unlikely that they'll reach the fourth level. In fact, it may take several years of using a word to develop a rich, decontextualized understanding of its meaning and related words. When they reach the full-knowledge level, students develop "ownership" of the word, meaning that they can do these things:

- Pronounce the word correctly.
- Understand the word's multiple meanings.
- Use the word appropriately in sentences.
- Identify related noun, verb, and adjective forms.
- Recognize related words that come from the same root word.
- Name synonyms and antonyms.

With this knowledge, students will be able to understand the word when they're listening and reading and use it to express ideas in talk and writing. Even though students learn hundreds or thousands of words incidentally through reading and content-area study each year, teaching high-utility vocabulary explicitly is an essential part of language arts instruction for all students, even prekindergartners, and especially for struggling students and English learners (M. Graves, 2006). Blachowicz and Fisher (2006) have reviewed the research on effective vocabulary instruction and identified these guidelines for teaching vocabulary:

Word-Rich Environment. Teachers create a word-rich environment in the classroom because when teachers display words, students are more likely to learn them incidentally and through direct instruction.

Independent Word Learners. Teachers prepare students to become independent word learners. When teachers involve students in choosing some of the words they'll study and teach word-learning strategies, such as how to use root words to analyze words and how to use a dictionary, students are more likely to take control of their own learning.

Word-Learning Strategies. Teachers explicitly teach students how to use **context cues**, **morphology**, and other word-learning strategies to figure out the meaning of words, and they also model word-learning strategies when they come across words that students don't know.

Assessment. Teachers assess both the depth and the breadth of students' vocabulary knowledge. When teachers choose assessment techniques based on their instructional goals, they can evaluate both how well students understand the words they've studied and the range of words they learned.

Word Learning

❶ Reread the sentence. Students reread the sentence containing the unfamiliar word.

❷ Use context cues. Students use context cues to figure out the meaning of the word, and if that doesn't work, they continue to the next step.

❸ Analyze word parts. Students use morphological information to examine word parts, looking for familiar root words and affixes to aid in figuring out the meaning. If they're still not successful, they continue to the next step.

❹ Pronounce the word. Students pronounce the word to see if they recognize it when they say it. If they still can't figure it out, they continue to the next step.

❺ Check a dictionary or ask the teacher. Students locate the word in a dictionary or ask the teacher for help.

The goal of vocabulary instruction is to develop students' *word consciousness*, their interest in learning and using words (Graves & Watts-Taffe, 2008). According to Scott and Nagy (2004), word consciousness is "essential for vocabulary growth and comprehending the language of schooling" (p. 201). Students who have word consciousness exemplify these characteristics:

- Students use words skilfully, understanding the nuances of the word meanings.
- Students gain a deep appreciation of words and value them.
- Students are aware of differences between social and academic language.
- Students understand the power of word choice.
- Students are motivated to learn the meaning of unfamiliar words.

Developing students' word consciousness is important because vocabulary knowledge is generative—that is, it enhances their learning of other words. Vocabulary instruction can take many forms in classroom instruction and may be included in many curriculum areas, not just the language arts. Teachers present vocabulary in minilessons and engage students in other word-study activities. The most successful activities are meaningful to students and involve students in manipulating words from books they are reading or words related to themes they are studying. Teachers also need to teach students how to independently figure out the meaning of unfamiliar words (Blachowicz & Lee, 1991). To discover word meaning while they are reading students need to systematically use all information available to them. Following the steps shown in Step by Step helps students become independent in figuring out word meanings.

Stahl and Nagy (2006) explain that effective vocabulary instruction requires repeated encounters with words in which students must exercise creativity and deep processing, and make multiple connections between the word being learned and concepts and experiences already familiar to them. Teachers engage students in many such activities to bolster vocabulary and reading comprehension.

Word Walls

One important way to focus students' attention on words is to create **word walls**, or displays of keywords. As they plan a unit, teachers identify vocabulary essential

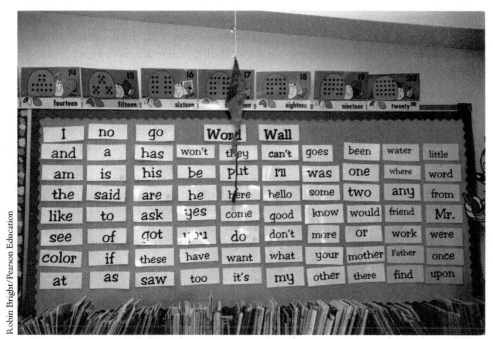

I	no	go	Wor	Wall					
and	a	has	won't	they	can't	goes	been	water	little
am	is	his	be	put	I'll	was	one	where	word
the	said	are	he	here	hello	some	two	any	from
like	to	ask	yes	come	good	know	would	friend	Mr.
see	of	got	you	do	don't	more	or	work	were
color	if	these	have	want	what	your	mother	Father	once
at	as	saw	too	it's	my	other	there	find	upon

Word walls like the one shown here display high-frequency words and other vocabulary in a prominent place in the classroom. Students access the word wall for reading, writing, and word study activities.

Robin Bright/Pearson Education

to understanding the unit concepts. For example, in a science unit concerning food production in plants key terms such as *photosynthesis* might be identified. In introducing classic Canadian literature such as *Anne of Green Gables* (Montgomery, 1908/1999), the word *orphan* would be identified as a keyword. As the unit proceeds, students and the teacher use the word wall to record interesting, confusing, and important words related to the topic and from the books they are reading or from other media texts they are using. Words are added to the word wall as they come up during unit activities. Words remain visible throughout the unit and are available for easy reference as students read, write, and engage in other unit activities.

In many primary classrooms word walls are used for an additional purpose. Teachers display the words the students regularly encounter and those they frequently want to include in their writing. In one grade 1 classroom we visit often, the word wall is divided into two sections. One section lists high-frequency words alphabetically so the young writers can easily locate words such as *here* and *said*. In the other section, words related to current classroom areas of study are posted, often with simple pictures to indicate meanings. Teachers choose from the words listed on the word wall for word-study activities, including spelling of keywords when appropriate.

Word-Study Activities

Word-study activities provide students with opportunities to expand their vocabulary and knowledge of words. Word study occurs in all subject areas when students need to extend their understanding of words and terms. In many language arts classrooms, word study includes spelling instruction and their word-study activities may engage students in using available technology, especially computer software for drawing, writing, and games. Word-study activities that engage students in oral, written, and other uses of the words maximize their learning. Here are eight types of word-study activities:

1. *Word posters.* Students choose a word from the word wall, write it, and illustrate it. They may also add a sentence or two to their poster. Words and pictures may be created by hand or by using word-processing or drawing and paint software. Teachers might also want to choose a "word of the day" from the wordwall and have students work together to illustrate it.

2. *Word clouds.* Students use Wordle (http://www.wordle.net) or similar software to design word clouds with the text they provide. Word clouds are a particular type of word poster. They give greater prominence to more frequently used words. Students can tweak the clouds using a variety of fonts, layouts, and colour schemes. Students make Wordles featuring selected vocabulary, definitions, synonyms, antonyms, and related words.

3. *Word clusters.* Students choose a word to explore and explain, and then write it in the centre of a cluster. They write information about the word and make connections between the word and the literature they are reading or the concepts they are studying. Word clusters can be hand-drawn or created with software. Illustrations of words and meanings are also referred to as *word maps*. They are sometimes created together by students and teachers to expand word knowledge. Figure 8-4 shows three types of word clusters. Grade 1 students made the first cluster after reading Phoebe Gilman's *Something from Nothing* (1992). The second is a cluster made by a group of grade 3 students after reading *A Day at the Sugar Bush* (Faulkner, 2004) and *At Grandpa's Sugar Bush* (Carney, 1997) in preparation for a spring field trip. The third cluster illustrates grade 6 students' clarification of the meaning of *hurricane* before they read *Rain Tonight: A Story of Hurricane Hazel* (Pitt, 2004) as part of their thematic study of natural disasters in Canadian history.

4. *Dramatizing words.* Students choose a word from the word wall and dramatize it using gestures and physical actions to illustrate its meaning. Classmates guess the word and indicate their guesses either verbally or in writing. Writing guesses on individual whiteboards gives practice in spelling.

5. *Word sorts.* Students sort a collection of words taken from the word wall into two or more categories (Bear, Invernizzi, Templeton, & Johnston, 2011). Usually students decide which categories they will use for the sort, but sometimes the teacher chooses. For example, words from a story might be sorted by character, or words from a theme on machines might be sorted according to type of machine. The words can be written on cards, and then students sort a pack of word cards into piles, or students can work together to sort words presented on an interactive whiteboard.

6. *Books about words.* Teachers often include sharing books about words in their unit activities and as the focus of **minilessons**. For example, a minilesson to raise young children's word consciousness might focus on *Fancy Nancy's Favourite Fancy Words: From Accessories to Zany* (O'Connor, 2008), or one addressing collective nouns might include *A Cache of Jewels and Other Collective Nouns* (Heller, 1987). Jesse Sheidlower answers questions about the origin of words and explains strange expressions like "by the skin of one's teeth" in *Jesse's Word of the Day* (1998). Katherine Barber explores various influences on the English language and challenges readers to discover connections among words in *Six Words You Never Knew Had Something to Do with Pigs and Other Fascinating Facts about*

FIGURE 8-4 THREE WORD CLUSTERS

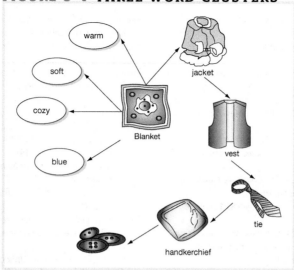

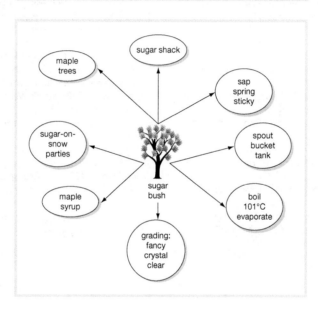

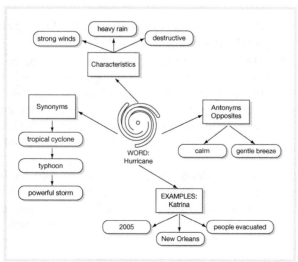

FIGURE 8-5 BOOKS ABOUT WORDS

Banks, K. (2006). *Max's Words*. New York: Farrar, Strauss, Giroux. (P–M)

Bannatyne-Cugnet, J. (1992). *A Prairie Alphabet*. Illus. by Y. Moore. Montreal: Tundra Books. (M) 🍁

Barber, K. (2006). *Six Words You Never Knew Had Something to Do with Pigs and Other Fascinating Facts about the Language from Canada's Word Lady*. Toronto: Oxford University Press. (U) 🍁

Barnette, M. (2003). *Dog Days and Dandelions*. New York: St. Martin's Press. (M–U)

Base, G. (1988). *Animalia*. Toronto: Stoddart. (M) 🍁

Blades, A. (1985). *By the Sea: An Alphabet Book*. Toronto: Kids Can Press. (P) 🍁

Browne, P. (1996). *A Gaggle of Geese: The Collective Names of the Animal Kingdom*. New York: Atheneum. (M)

Casselman, B. (2007). *Canadian Words and Sayings*. Toronto: McArthur & Company. (U) 🍁

Cleary, B. (1999). *A Mink, a Fink, a Skating Rink: What is a Noun?* (and other books in the Words are Categorical series). Minneapolis, MN: Millbrook Press. (P–M)

Dewey, A. (1995). *Naming Colors*. New York: HarperCollins. (M)

Ehlert, L. (1990). *Feathers for Lunch*. Orlando, FL: Harcourt Brace. (P–M)

Escoffer, M. (2014). *Take Away the A*. Brooklyn, NY: Enchanted Lion Books. (P–M)

Feder, J. (1995). *Table, Chair, Bear: A Book in Many Languages*. New York: Ticknor. (P–M)

Fowler, J. (2010). *What's the Point? A Book about Multiple Meaning Words*. Fort Worth, TX: AuthorHouse. (M)

Frasier, D. (2000). *Miss Alaineus. A Vocabulary Disaster*. New York: Harcourt. (M–U)

Garg, A. (2002). *A Word a Day*. London: Wiley. (M–U)

Gibbons, G. (1990). *Weather Words and What They Mean*. New York: Holiday House. (P–M)

Glasser, R. (2006). *Fancy Nancy*. New York: HarperCollins Children's Books. (P).

Graham-Barber, L. (1995). *A Chartreuse Leotard in a Magenta Limousine: And Other Words Named After People and Places*. New York: Hyperion. (M–U)

Heller, R. (1983). *The Reason for a Flower*. New York: Grosset & Dunlap. (And other books in the series by this author.) (M)

Hepworth, C. (1992). *Antics! An Alphabetical Anthology*. New York: Putnam. (M–U)

Hills, T. (2008). *What's Up, Duck? A Book of Opposites*. New York: Schwartz & Wade Books.

Hopkins, L. B. (2004). *Wonderful Words*. New York: Simon & Schuster. (P)

Lobel, A. (1990). *Alison's Zinnia*. New York: Greenwillow. (M)

Moss, L. (1995). *Zin! Zin! Zin! A Violin*. New York: Simon & Schuster. (P–M)

Most, B. (1991). *A Dinosaur Named After Me*. Orlando, FL: Harcourt Brace. (P–M)

Onyefulu, I. (1993). *A Is for Africa*. New York: Cobblehill Books. (M)

Pallotta, J. (1994). *The Desert Alphabet Book*. Watertown, MA: Charlesbridge. (And other alphabet books by the same author.) (M–U)

Palmer, S. (2000). *A Little Alphabet Book*. London: Oxford University Press. (P–M)

Pearson, D. (2005). *Kids Do, Animals Too: A Book of Playground Opposites*. Toronto: Annick Press. (P–M) 🍁

Rand, A. (2006). *Sparkle & Spin: A Book about Words*. San Francisco, CA: Chronicle Books. (P)

Schotter, R. (2006). *The Boy Who Loved Words*. New York: Schwartz & Wade Books. (M–U)

Sheidlower, J. (1998). *Jesse's Word of the Day*. New York: Random House. (M–U)

Terban, M. (1988). *Guppies in Tuxedos: Funny Eponyms*. New York: Clarion. (M–U)

Terban, M. (1989). *Superdupers! Really Funny Real Words*. New York: Clarion. (M–U)

Woop Studios. (2011). *A Zeal of Zebras: An Alphabet of Collective Nouns*. San Francisco: Chronicle Books.

P = primary grades (K–2); M = middle grades (3–5); U = upper grades (6–8); T = teacher.

the Language from Canada's Word Lady (2006). These and other books about words are listed in Figure 8-5.

7. **Word chains.** Students choose a word from the word wall and then identify three or four words to sequence before or after the word to make a chain. For example, the word *tadpole* can be chained this way: *egg, tadpole, frog*; and the word *aggravate* can be chained like this: *irritate, bother, aggravate, annoy*. Students can write or type their chains on a sheet of paper, or write words on cards and place them in order in a pocket chart, or they can make a construction paper chain with the words on each link.

8. **Word puzzles.** Students create crossword puzzles using free software available on the Internet. They choose vocabulary related to a unit of study or literature and compose descriptive clues. Teachers may indicate essential vocabulary from the word wall to be included as core terms along with others of the students' choice. When puzzles are complete, students challenge classmates to solve the puzzles either individually or in relay teams.

Minilessons on Word Meanings

Vocabulary instruction helps students learn the meaning of new words. Researchers identify two major dimensions of vocabulary instruction: learning and remembering words, or *word knowledge*, and learning how to learn words, or strategies for figuring out words (Asselin, 2002). Decades of research about vocabulary development inform teachers about instruction concerning both dimensions. The following six principles are identified as essential (Assselin, 2002; Blachowicz & Fisher, 2000; Rupley, Logan, & Nichols, 1998/1999):

1. Build background experiences, then talk about them and focus on relevant new words.
2. Relate new words to students' background knowledge.
3. Develop relationships between words.
4. Personalize word learning.
5. Immerse students in a word-oriented environment.
6. Build on multiple sources of information to learn words through repeated exposures.

The previously described word-study activities are ways to put these principles into practice. In addition, the minilesson teaching strategy presented in Chapter 1 embodies these guidelines of effective vocabulary instruction. It, too, can be used to teach minilessons on strategies for unlocking word meanings, on specific keywords and groups of related words, or on a lexical concept such as idioms, prefixes, or homonyms.

Students need to know about the English language, words and their meanings, and strategies to figure out the meanings of words independently. Students in the elementary grades learn about multiple meanings as well as about root words and affixes; homonyms, synonyms, and antonyms; and figurative meanings of words, such as idioms. Word study is multidimensional, and teachers provide a variety of activities to meet the needs of every student.

Differentiating to Meet the Needs of Every Student

Because learning about words is an important part of language arts, it is crucial that teachers find ways to help all students use the words they are learning. Having a word wall to accompany every unit is one of the simplest and best ways to focus students' attention on words. Teachers also need to provide a variety of word-study activities to meet the needs of every student. A list of suggestions for adapting vocabulary instruction is presented below. These suggestions focus on using vocabulary in meaningful, functional, and genuine ways.

Assessing Students' Use of Words

Teachers assess students' use of words in a variety of ways. They listen while students participate in discussions, examine students' writing and projects, and ask students to speak or write about the literature and themes and what they have learned. Here are some specific strategies to determine whether students have learned and are applying new words:

- Check reading logs, learning logs, or journals for words related to the unit.
- Use unit-related words in a conference and note the student's response.
- Listen for vocabulary when students give oral reports.

- Note students' use of language tools such as dictionaries and thesauruses.
- Ask students to make a cluster or do a **quickwrite** about some aspect of the unit or about specific words.
- Ask students to brainstorm a list of words and phrases about the unit.
- Check students' reports, biographies, poems, stories, or other writings for unit-related words.
- Ask students to write a letter to you, telling what they have learned in the unit.

Teachers can also give tests on the vocabulary words, but this is probably the least effective approach, because a correct answer on a test does not indicate whether students have ownership of a word or whether they are applying it in meaningful and genuine ways.

Grammar

Children learn the structure of the English language—its grammar—intuitively as they learn to talk; the process is an unconscious one. They have almost completed it by the time they enter kindergarten. The primary purpose of grammar instruction, then, is to make this intuitive knowledge about the English language explicit and to provide labels for words within sentences, parts of sentences, and types of sentences.

Grammar instruction has long been a controversial area of language arts. Some people believe that formal instruction in grammar is unnecessary. Others believe that grammar instruction should be a key component of language arts instruction. They argue that knowing how to use Standard English is essential to success in oral and written communication. In keeping with conventional wisdom, they think knowledge about grammar and usage improves students' oral language and writing. Still others believe that to teach or not to teach grammar is not the question. It is a matter of what to teach and how to teach it (Weaver, McNally, & Moermann, 2001). Research since the beginning of the century has failed to confirm that formal instruction has a positive effect on students' language use. In contrast, much recent research has demonstrated positive effects of teaching grammar in the context of writing (Cramer, 2004; Feng & Powers, 2005; Weaver, 1998).

Before going further, let's clarify the terms *grammar* and *usage*. **Grammar** is the description of the syntax or structure of a language and prescriptions for its use (Weaver, 1996). It involves principles of word and sentence formation. In contrast, *usage* is correctness, or using the appropriate word or phrase in a sentence. It is the socially preferred way of using language within a dialect. Fraser and Hodson explain the distinction between grammar and usage this way: "Grammar is the rationale of a language; usage is its etiquette" (1978, p. 52).

Why Teach Grammar?

Teachers, parents, and the community at large cite many reasons for teaching grammar. Many feel that teaching grammar will help students understand sentence structure and form sentences to express their thoughts. Some teachers explain that they teach grammar to prepare students for the next grade or for instruction in a foreign language. Others pragmatically rationalize grammar instruction because it is a part of some norm-referenced achievement tests.

Despite the controversy about teaching grammar and its value for elementary students, grammar is a part of the language arts curriculum in most provinces and

DIFFERENTIATING

Vocabulary Instruction to Meet the Needs of Every Student

1. Highlight Keywords on Word Walls

Highlight a few keywords pertinent to a unit of study on word walls by writing them with coloured pens. Add pictures to illustrate the words or word translations in students' first languages to benefit students learning English.

2. Use Word Sorts

Provide additional opportunities to categorize words or learn relationships among words. Complete word sorts in pairs to facilitate peer tutoring and discussion of categorization possibilities. Simplify sorts by using a limited number of words.

3. Teach Idioms

Explain that some phrases in English have two meanings. These phrases are called *idioms*. Provide many opportunities for students to hear, learn about, and use idioms through peer dramatizations and shared reading of books. During reading about idioms, allow for discussion and oral wordplay to make them memorable.

4. Teach Multiple Meanings of Words

Provide experience with multiple meanings through solving riddles and other word puzzles, reading books about words, and making posters to illustrate multiple meanings.

5. Introduce New Concepts

When introducing new concepts and vocabulary, provide opportunities for developing meaning and using words in context. Activities might include hands-on experiences, dramatic activities, or viewing and discussing video or pictures. Introduce one concept at a time and allow for guided and independent practice.

6. Read Aloud and Facilitate Silent Reading

Vocabulary is learned through being read to and reading. Establish daily read-aloud time for students to hear literature that may be beyond their independent reading level. Also, provide blocks of time for uninterrupted silent reading. Students who struggle to read independently can listen to interactive DVD recordings.

7. Create Challenges

Challenge students to add to their vocabularies through schemes such as "word of the day" or "expression of the week" in which a student or teacher presents a word, word pair, figure of speech, or idiom and all attempt to use it correctly throughout the day or week. Correct uses can be awarded cumulative points. Other challenges could involve word games such as Scrabble.

---

will undoubtedly remain so for some time. Given this, it is only reasonable that grammar should be taught in the most beneficial manner possible. Researchers suggest that integrating grammar study with reading and writing produces the best results (Noguchi, 1991; Noyce & Christie, 1983; Weaver, 1998). L. M. Calkins has argued for over four decades that "basic skills belong in context" (1980, p. 567). Scholars of writing view grammar as a tool for writers and recommend integrating grammar instruction with the revising and editing stages of the writing process. We concur with this recommendation.

Grammatical Concepts

As we did earlier in this chapter concerning the aspects of words and figurative language most often explored in elementary classrooms, we will now offer a brief teacher's guide to grammar and the teaching of grammar.

The four most common types of information about grammar taught during the elementary grades are parts of speech, parts of sentences, types of sentences, and usage.

PARTS OF SPEECH

Grammarians have sorted English words into eight groups, called *parts of speech*: nouns, pronouns, verbs, adjectives, adverbs, prepositions, conjunctions, and interjections.

Words in each group are used in essentially the same way in all sentences. Nouns and verbs are the basic building blocks of sentences, and pronouns substitute for nouns. Adjectives, adverbs, and prepositions build on and modify the nouns and verbs. Conjunctions connect individual words or groups of words, and interjections express strong emotion or surprise.

PARTS OF SENTENCES

A *sentence* is made up of one or more words to express a complete thought and, to express the thought, must have a subject and a predicate. The *subject* names who or what the sentence is about, and the *predicate* includes the verb and anything that completes or modifies it. In a simple sentence with one subject and one predicate, everything that is not part of the subject is part of the predicate.

TYPES OF SENTENCES

Sentences are classified in two ways. First, they are classified according to structure, or how they are put together. The structure of a sentence may be simple, compound, complex, or compound-complex according to the number and type of clauses. A *clause* consists of a subject and predicate, and there are two types of clauses. If the clause presents a complete thought and can stand alone as a sentence, it is an *independent clause*. If the clause is not a complete thought and cannot stand alone as a sentence, it is a *dependent clause* because it depends on the meaning expressed in the independent clause. A *simple sentence* contains only one independent clause, and a *compound sentence* is made up of two or more independent clauses. A *complex sentence* contains one independent clause and at least one dependent clause. A *compound-complex sentence* contains more than one independent clause and at least one dependent clause.

Second, sentences are classified according to the type of message they contain. Sentences that make statements are *declarative*, those that ask questions are *interrogative*, those that make commands are *imperative*, and those that communicate strong emotion or surprise are *exclamatory*.

USAGE

Usage is the customary or "correct" way in which a language is spoken or written. Using a single negative, not a double negative, in the sentence "I don't have any money" (rather than "I don't have no money") or subjective pronouns, not objective pronouns, for the subject in the sentence "He and I have dirt bikes" (rather than "Him and me have dirt bikes") are examples of **Standard English** usage. Students who speak nonstandard dialects learn Standard English forms as alternatives to the forms they already know. Rather than trying to replace nonstandard forms with standard forms, teachers can explain that Standard English is the language of school and the language expected in most student writing. It is the language used in books, and students can easily locate Standard English examples in books they are reading. Referring to Standard English as "school language" or "book language" helps students understand expectations and to avoid condemnation of nonstandard dialects.

Teaching Grammar in the Elementary Grades

An effective approach to teaching grammar to elementary students is to connect grammar with reading and writing activities and to teach minilessons about the

TEACHER'S NOTEBOOK

Guidelines for Teaching Grammar

1. Teach Minilessons on Grammar and Usage
The teacher teaches minilessons on grammar and usage concepts and has students locate examples of the concepts in books they are reading and pieces they are writing.

2. Share Concept Books
The teacher shares concept books when students are studying parts of speech, and students also create their own concept books.

3. Manipulate Sentences
Students use sentences from books they are reading for grammar activities, such as sentence slotting, sentence expansion, sentence manipulation, and combining sentences.

4. Collect Sentences
Students collect favourite sentences from books they are reading and use the sentences for grammar and usage activities.

5. Use Sentence Frames
Students write innovations, or new versions of books, using sentence frames or patterns in books they have read.

6. Make Grammar Posters
Students can make grammar posters to visually represent parts of speech, sentence types, or usage rules they are learning.

7. Teach Students to Proofread
Students need to learn how to proofread so that they can locate and correct grammar and usage errors in their own writing.

8. Acknowledge Alternatives to Standard English
The teacher explains that Standard English is the language of school and is one way of speaking and writing. It is important that students understand that the purpose of grammar instruction is to expand their repertoire of language options, not to replace their home language.

---

function of words in sentences and ways of arranging words into sentences (Cullinan, Jaggar, & Strickland, 1974; Tompkins & McGee, 1983). Guidelines for teaching grammar are listed in the third Teacher's Notebook.

TEACHING GRAMMAR THROUGH READING

Students learn many things about the structure of the English language through reading. Some learn simply through experience and others need teachers' guidance to learn from the language of the books they are reading. Teachers bring the features of text to students' attention through reading aloud examples or drawing attention through discussion. Students learn more sophisticated language, a more formal register than they speak, and sophisticated ways of phrasing ideas and arranging words into sentences when they read literature. Students reading Lois Burdett's Shakespeare for Kids series, for example, gain experience with language rich in vocabulary and variations of word order. Many opportunities for conversation about grammar and language arise when students read passages of Shakespearean dialogue, such as when Oberon approaches the sleeping Titania in *A Midsummer Night's Dream* (Burdett, 1997):

> What thou see'st when thou dost wake
>
> Do it for thy true-love take;
>
> Be it lynx or cat or bear,
>
> Leopard, or boar with bristled hair,
>
> When thou wak'st, it is thy dear.
>
> Wake when some vile thing is near. (p. 38)

Students often read sentences that are longer than the ones they speak and learn new ways to string words into sentences. In *Chrysanthemum* (Henkes, 1991), the story of a mouse named Chrysanthemum who loves her name until she starts school and is teased by her classmates, the author uses a combination of long and short sentences very effectively: "Chrysanthemum could scarcely believe her ears. She blushed. She beamed. She bloomed" (n.p.).

Students read sentences exemplifying all four sentence message types in many books. One example is Julie Lawson's (1998), *Midnight in the Mountains,* the story of a family's cold and snowy dogsled ride. "It's quiet in the mountains. So quiet, I hear the cold." (n.p.) and "Mom worried about frostbite" (n.p.) are statements, or declarative sentences. "How does frost bite?" and "How cold is the coldest cold?" (n.p.) are questions, or interrogative sentences. The huskies imagined command to the wolves, "Come set us free!" (n.p.), is an imperative sentence. The children's observation of their pet dog, Trouble, "He wants to be a sled dog, too!" (n.p.) is an example of an exclamation, or exclamatory sentence.

Students also read all sentence structure types—simple, compound, complex, and compound-complex sentences. Kevin Henkes includes all of these types of sentences in his wonderful book *Lilly's Purple Plastic Purse* (1996).

Some authors write dialogue and other text in nonstandard English that is appropriate to the characters and setting they are creating. Understanding that authors (and all language users) make choices about Standard and nonstandard English according to the situation in which it is used is important in helping students become aware of Standard English options and to appreciate that "book language" is often a more formal register than general conversation.

One way to help students focus on sentences in the text they read is through sentence collecting (Speaker & Speaker, 1991). Students collect favourite sentences and share them with classmates. They copy their sentences on chart paper or display them digitally. Students and the teacher talk about the merits of each sentence, focus on word choice, and analyze the sentence types. Through this discussion, students gradually learn to comprehend more syntactically complex sentences. These sentences can also be used in the minilessons described later in this section.

TEACHING GRAMMAR THROUGH WRITING

Not only do students notice the way sentences are phrased in the books they read or listen to read aloud, they also imitate the structures in their writing. Kathy Egawa (1990) reports that a grade 1 student used the structure and rhythm of Jane Yolen's *Owl Moon* (1987) in writing a book called *Salamander Sun. Owl Moon* begins this way: "It was late one winter night, long past my bedtime when Pa and I went owling." The child's book, written in invented spelling, begins this way: "It was lat one spring afternoon a long time after lunch when ma tact me sawlumendering" (p. 586). This grade 1 student was not plagiarizing Yolen's book, but adapting and incorporating the structure in his own writing.

Because students' knowledge of grammar and usage is dependent on the language they experience in their homes and neighbourhoods, some primary- and middle-grade students do not recognize instances of nonstandard usage. Using a problem-solving approach during the editing stage can be effective in helping them recognize Standard English structures and usage. During editing, students identify errors and try to make their papers "optimally readable" (F. Smith, 1982). Sometimes, however, they do not recognize errors because what is written "sounds right" to them. For example, grade 5 students who read "The pie was real good" and "The car was going real fast" did not recognize the errors. *Real* sounded better than *really* because it was more familiar. An explanation that adverbs rather than adjectives modify adjectives was not useful either, even though the students were familiar with the parts of speech. Correction of nonstandard English errors can be perceived as a repudiation of the language spoken in homes and must be done with sensitivity. Rather than any suggestion of right and wrong, teachers can explain that written or "book language" requires a somewhat formal language register. The goal in helping students identify instances of dialect and nonstandard English usage is not to imply that the students' language is inferior, but to add Standard English to their language options.

MINILESSONS AND OTHER GRAMMAR LESSONS

Teachers identify topics for grammar minilessons in two ways. The preferred way is to identify concepts by assessing students' writing and noting what types of grammar and usage errors they are making. At other times, teachers choose topics from lists of skills they are expected to teach at their grade level. The topics can be taught to the whole class or to small groups of students, but only to students who don't already know them. Using minilessons is highly recommended because of their immediate connections to reading and writing (Atwell, 1987; Calkins, 1994).

Worksheets are not recommended; instead, excerpts from books students are reading or from students' own writing are used. Teachers introduce a concept and its related terminology, and then they provide examples and opportunities for students to experiment with sentence construction. Several approaches to teaching grammar are presented in the following paragraphs.

1. *Parts of speech.* Students work in small groups to identify words representing one part of speech or all eight parts of speech from books they are reading or from their own writing. Similarly, students can hunt for parts of speech or sentence types in the literature they are reading.

    After collecting words representing parts of speech or sentence types, students can share with the class using word cards or available projection facilities. Students can also create posters, wordles, or books using some of the words they collected.

2. *Grammar concept books.* Students examine concept books that focus on one part of speech or another grammatical concept. For example, students in a grade 8 class divided into small groups to read Ruth Heller's books about parts of speech, including *Up, Up and Away: A Book about Adverbs* (1991), *Behind the Mask: A Book of Prepositions* (1995), and *Mine All Mine: A Book about Pronouns* (1999). After reading one of her books, each group of students made word cards to contribute to a word sort challenge. The cards were collected and each group given a mixed deck to sort according to part of speech. Students who completed the sort first were declared the grammar experts. Books that illustrate grammar concepts are listed in Figure 8-6.

3. *Sentence slotting.* Students experiment with words and phrases to see how they function in sentences by filling in sentences that have slots, or blanks. Sentence slotting teaches students about several grammatical concepts. They can experiment with parts of speech using a sentence like this:

The snake slithered _____ the rock.

> over
>
> around
>
> under
>
> to

Students brainstorm a number of words to fill in the slot, all of which will be prepositions; adjectives, nouns, verbs, and adverbs will not make sense. This activity can be repeated to introduce or review any part of speech.

FIGURE 8-6 **BOOKS THAT ILLUSTRATE GRAMMAR CONCEPTS**

Nouns

Cleary, B. (1999). *A Mink, a Fink, a Skating Rink: What Is a Noun?* Minneapolis, MN: Millbrook Press. (P–M)

Crystal, D. (2001). *Language and the Internet.* Cambridge: Cambridge University Press.

Dahl, M. (2006). *If You Were a Noun.* Minneapolis, MN: Picture Window Books. (P)

Heller, R. (1987). *A Cache of Jewels and Other Collective Nouns.* New York: Grosset & Dunlap. (M–U)

Heller, R. (1990). *Merry-go-round: A Book about Nouns.* New York: Grosset & Dunlap. (M–U)

MacCarthy, P. (1991). *Herds of Words.* New York: Dial. (M)

Pulver, R. (2007). *Nouns and Verbs Have a Field Day.* New York: Holiday House. (M)

Terban, M. (1986). *Your Foot's on My Feet! And Other Tricky Nouns.* New York: Clarion. (M)

Walton, R. (2011). *Herd of Cows, Flock of Sheep: Adventures in Collective Nouns* (Rev. ed.). Layton, UT: Gibbs Smith. (P–M)

Verbs

Cleary, B. (2001). *To Root, to Toot, to Parachute: What Is a Verb?* Minneapolis, MN: Millbrook Press (P–M)

Crystal, D. (2001). *Language and the Internet.* Cambridge: Cambridge University Press.

Dahl, M. (2006). *If You Were a Verb.* Minneapolis, MN: Picture Window Books. (P)

Heller, R. (1988). *Kites Sail High: A Book about Verbs.* New York: Grosset & Dunlap. (M–U)

Parrish, T. (2002). *The Grouchy Grammarian.* London: Wiley. (M)

Rotner, S. (1996). *Action Alphabet.* New York: Atheneum. (P–M)

Schneider, R. M. (1995). *Add It, Dip It, Fix It: A Book of Verbs.* Boston: Houghton Mifflin. (M)

Terban, M. (1984). *I Think I Thought and Other Tricky Verbs.* New York: Clarion. (M)

Adjectives

Boynton, S. (1983). *A Is for Angry: An Animal and Adjective Alphabet.* New York: Workman. (M–U)

Cleary, B. (2001). *Hairy, Scary, Ordinary: What Is an Adjective?* Minneapolis, MN: Millbrook Press. (P–M)

Dahl, M. (2006). *If You Were an Adjective.* Minneapolis, MN: Picture Window Books. (P)

Heller, R. (1989). *Many Luscious Lollipops: A Book about Adjectives.* New York: Grosset & Dunlap. (M–U)

Hubbard, W. (1990). *C Is for Curious: An ABC Book of Feelings.* San Francisco: Chronicle Books. (M)

Adverbs

Cleary, B. (2005). *Dearly, Nearly, Insincerely: What Is an Adverb?* New York: First Avenue Editions. (P–M)

Dahl, M. (2006). *If You Were an Adverb.* Minneapolis, MN: Picture Window Books. (P)

Heller, R. (1991). *Up, Up and Away: A Book about Adverbs.* New York: Grosset & Dunlap. (M–U)

Walton, R. (2011). *Suddenly Alligators: Adventures in Adverbs.* Layton, UT: Gibbs Smith. (P–M)

Prepositions

Ayres, K. (2008). *Up, Down, and Around.* Sommerville, MA: Candlewick. (M)

Berenstain, S. & Berenstain, J. (1968). *Inside, Outside, Upside Down.* New York: Random House. (M)

Cleary, B. (2002). *Under, Over, by the Clover: What Is a Preposition?* Minneapolis, MN: Millbrook Press. (P–M)

Heller, R. (1995). *Behind the Mask: A Book about Prepositions.* New York: Grosset & Dunlap. (M–U)

Hoban, T. (1973). *Over, Under, and Through and Other Spatial Concepts.* New York: Macmillan. (P)

Hoban, T. (1991). *All about Where.* New York: Greenwillow. (P)

Lillie, P. (1993). *Everything Has a Place.* New York: Greenwillow. (P)

Walton, R. (2011). *Around the House the Fox Chased the Mouse: Adventures in Prepositions.* Layton, UT: Gibbs Smith.

Interjections and Conjunctions

Heller, R. (1998). *Fantastic! Wow! and Unreal! A Book about Interjections and Conjunctions.* New York: Puffin Books. (M–U)

Park, L. S. (2005). *Yum! Yuck!: A Fold-out Book of People Sounds.* Watertown, MA: Charlesbridge.

P = primary grades (K–2); M = middle grades (3–5); U = upper grades (6–8).

Sentence slotting also demonstrates to students that parts of speech can substitute for each other. In the following sentence, common and proper nouns as well as pronouns can be used in the slot:

_____ knew more wizardry than anyone else in Hogworts.

> The man
>
> Harry
>
> He
>
> The professor

A similar sentence-slotting example demonstrates how phrases can function as an adverb:

The dog growled _____.

> ferociously
>
> with his teeth bared
>
> daring us to reach for his bone

In this example, the adverb *ferociously* can be used in the slot, as well as prepositional and participial phrases.

Sentences with an adjective slot can be used to demonstrate that phrases function as adjectives. The goal of this activity is to demonstrate the function of words in sentences. Many sentence-slotting activities, such as the last example, also illustrate that sentences become more specific with the addition of a word or phrase. The purpose of these activities is to experiment with language; they should be done with small groups of students or the whole class, not as individual worksheets.

4. **Sentence expansion.** Students expand simple sentences, such as "a frog leaps" or "the car raced," by adding modifiers. The words and phrases with which they expand the sentence can add qualities and attributes, details, and comparisons. Using the "5 *W*s plus one" (*who, what, when, where, why,* and *how*) helps students focus on expanding particular aspects of the sentence; for example:

Sentence	A frog leaps.
Who?	A frog
What kind?	green, speckled
When?	noon
How?	high into the air
Where?	from a half-submerged log and lands in the water with a splash
Why?	to retreat from the hot noon sun
Expanded Sentence	To retreat from the hot noon sun, a green, speckled *frog leaps* high into the air from a half-submerged log and lands in the water with a splash.

Depending on what questions are asked and students' answers, many other expanded sentences are possible from the same basic sentence. Students enjoy working in small groups then comparing their expanded versions with those of other groups. Instead of using the "5 *W*s plus one" questions to expand sentences, teachers can ask older students to supply a specific part of speech or modifier at each step of expansion. Students' expanded sentences may vary greatly. By comparing versions, they come to realize the power of modifiers to transform a sentence.

5. **Sentence manipulation.** Students experiment with or manipulate sentences when they rearrange words and phrases in a sentence, combine several sentences to make a single stronger sentence, or write sentences following a particular sentence pattern. They begin with a sentence and then apply four operations to it: add, delete, substitute, and rearrange. Through these activities, students learn about the structure of sentences and experiment with more sophisticated sentences than they might otherwise write. With the sentence "Children play games," these manipulations are possible:

Add:	Children play computer games at home.
Delete:	Children play.
Substitute:	Adults play games.
	Children like games.
	Children play Nintendo.
Rearrange:	Games are played by children.

Practice with sentence manipulation can be closely linked to revising students' writing. Through sentence manipulation, teachers show students how their writing can be strengthened and enriched. Examples for collaborative manipulation may be taken from the students' writing and become the focus for a minilesson. Without naming the student author, teachers display sentences on a whiteboard or on word cards in a pocket chart and ask students to make suggestions for revisions. Students then discuss the effect of each suggestion on the meaning and impact of the sentence.

6. **Combining sentences.** In sentence combining, students combine and rearrange words in sentences to make the sentences longer and more conceptually dense (Strong, 1996). The goal of sentence combining is for students to experiment with different combinations. Sentences can be joined or embedded in a variety of ways. In the following example, two sentences (S) about *Sylvester and the Magic Pebble* (Steig, 1969) are transformed or combined to create two combined sentences (C1 and C2):

(S)	Sylvester found a red pebble.
(S)	The pebble was magic.
(C1)	Sylvester found a red pebble that was magic.
(C2)	Sylvester found a magic red pebble.

The two combined sentences illustrate embedding the adjective *magic*. The first combined sentence uses a relative clause transformation; the second uses an adjective transformation. Neither combined sentence is right or wrong; rather, they provide two options. Teachers and students can create many other sentences to combine. They can take examples from books they are reading or from their own writing, or they can create the sentences themselves on a variety of topics.

Sentence-combining activities give students opportunities to manipulate sentence structures. Much research points to their value in helping students improve fluency, clarity, and style (Hillocks, 1995); however, they are rather artificial. We caution that they should never be used as substitutes for actual writing. They are most effective when combined with genuine writing assignments.

7. **Sentence frames.** Students in the primary grades often create new books or "innovations" using the structure in repetitive books. Young children write their own versions of *Brown Bear, Brown Bear, What Do You See?* (Martin, 1983) and *The Very Hungry Caterpillar* (Carle, 1969). Teachers often write these collaboratively with groups of children. Similarly, middle-grade students write new verses following the rhyming pattern in Laura Numeroff's *Dogs Don't Wear Sneakers* (1993) and the sequel, *Chimps Don't Wear Glasses* (1995).

A grade 3 class used Numeroff's frame to write verses, and one small group composed this verse, rhyming *TV* and *bumblebee*:

Ducks don't have tea parties,

Lions don't watch TV,

And you won't see a salamander being friends with a bumblebee.

Middle-and upper-grade students can take a favourite sentence and imitate its structure by plugging in new words. Dunning and Stafford (1992) call this procedure "copy changes." For example, grade 8 students chose sentences from *The Giver* (Lowry, 1993) for copy changes. The original sentence was "Dimly, from a nearly forgotten perception as blurred as the substance itself, Jonas recalled what the whiteness was" (p. 175). A student created this sentence using the sentence frame: "Softly, from a corner of the barn as cozy and warm as the kitchen, the baby kitten mewed to its mother."

Differentiating to Meet the Needs of Every Student

The goal of grammar instruction is to increase students' ability to structure and manipulate sentences and to expand their repertoire of sentence patterns. Teaching grammar is a controversial issue, and it is especially so for students whose

Grammar Instruction to Meet the Needs of Every Student

1. **Encourage Reading and Writing of Standard English**

   Provide multiple texts as models of Standard English in the classroom: posters, books, newspapers, magazines, and digital texts. Point out to students how authors use a variety of language structures and help students identify structures that are particularly effective in communicating thoughts and ideas.

2. **Identify Grammar and Usage Concepts to Teach by Examining Students' Writing**

   Analyze students' writing to identify topics for individual, small group, and class grammar minilessons.

3. **Teach Students How to Proofread**

   Provide frequent, short minilessons each focused on only one or two aspects of effective proofreading. Then, provide guided practice on writing samples before leading students to proofread

their own writing. Students may benefit from reading their writing aloud as they edit or working with classmates as editing partners.

4. **Have Students Write Innovations on Texts**

   Present mentor texts as models and encourage students to write innovations, or new versions, of familiar patterned texts. As they use the author's sentence forms to create new versions, students practise using more complex syntactic structures than they might normally use themselves.

5. **Correct Grammatical Errors in Students' Writing, Not in Their Speech**

   Students make grammatical and usage errors both when they speak and when they write. Focus on errors in writing to avoid risk of damaging students' self-confidence as may occur if speech is corrected because speech is so personal.

---

native language is not English or for students who speak a nonstandard form of English. The best way to encourage students' language development and the acquisition of Standard English is to encourage students to talk without fear of embarrassment. Teachers and classmates model Standard English through their talk, and students also learn Standard English syntactic patterns and usage from the books they read and videos they watch. Teachers can address nonstandard English and other grammatical issues found in older students' compositions during the editing stage of the writing process. They can teach minilessons and provide explicit examples.

Students with limited language fluency especially benefit from creating innovations on repetitive books so that they can expand their repertoire of sentence forms and lengthen the sentences they speak and write. Building and manipulating sentences are other useful activities to help these students increase their ability to use a variety of sentence types. A list of recommendations for differentiating grammar instruction to meet the needs of every student is presented in the accompanying Differentiating box.

Assessing Students' Knowledge about Grammar

The best gauge of students' knowledge of grammar is how they arrange words into sentences as part of genuine communication. Teachers can develop checklists of grammar and usage skills to teach at a particular grade level, or they can list errors they observe in students' oral and written communication. When formal knowledge of grammar concepts is deemed important, teachers can ask students to identify and label parts of speech in either written or manipulative activities. For example, students can be asked to highlight all the nouns in a sentence presented on an interactive whiteboard. Following assessment, teachers plan and teach minilessons based on students' needs. They plan and teach minilessons to give young authors the support they need to write accurately and effectively. Records of students' performance as shown in samples of their writing collected over time are the best the best evidence of their knowledge of grammar.

Spelling

Spelling is a tool for writers that allows them to communicate conventionally with readers. As D. H. Graves explains, "Spelling is for writing. Children may achieve high scores on phonic inventories, or weekly spelling tests. But the ultimate test is what the child does under 'game conditions,' within the process of moving toward meaning" (1983, pp. 193–194). Students need to learn to spell words conventionally so that they can communicate effectively through writing. English spelling is complex, and attempts to teach spelling through weekly lists have not been consistently successful. Recent research informs teachers of more effective practices. Ability to use skills such as spelling conventionally is best fostered by teaching the skills in the context of their use (Routman, 1996) and as part of comprehensive word study involving other aspects of knowing a word (Bear et al., 2011). In fact, we recommend that all language tools—grammar, spelling, handwriting, and word processing—be taught as part of integrated reading and writing instruction.

For more information on young children's writing, see Chapter 3, "Emergent Literacy," pages 92–95.

Children's Spelling Development

The **alphabetic principle** suggests a one-to-one correspondence between phonemes and graphemes, but English spelling is phonetic only about half the time.

Elementary students learn to spell the phonetic elements of English as they learn about phoneme–grapheme correspondences, and they continue to refine their spelling knowledge through reading and writing. Children's spelling that reflects their growing awareness of English orthography is known as **invented spelling**. During their development, children move from using scribbles and single letters to represent words through a series of stages until they adopt conventional spellings.

INVENTED SPELLING

As young children begin to write, they create unique spellings, called *invented spellings*, based on their knowledge of English orthography. Other names for invented spelling include *temporary spelling* and *kid spelling*. Charles Read (1975, 1986), one of the first researchers to study preschoolers' efforts to spell words, discovered that they used their knowledge of phonology to invent spellings. These children used letter names to spell words such as U (*you*) and R (*are*), and they used consonant sounds rather consistently: GRL (*girl*), TIGR (*tiger*), and NIT (*night*). These and other observations led Read to identify five stages of invented spelling. The stages are presented with their key characteristics in Figure 8-7.

In summary, Read found that children developed strategies for their spellings based on their knowledge of the **phonological system** and of letter names, their judgments of phonetic similarities and differences, and their ability to abstract phonetic information from letter names. He noted that developing through the stages typically leads children to write using conventional English spelling.

FIGURE 8-7 CHARACTERISTICS OF THE FIVE CONVENTIONAL STAGES OF INVENTED SPELLING

Stage 1: Precommunicative Spelling
Child uses scribbles, letter-like forms, and sometimes numbers to represent a message.
Child shows no understanding of phoneme–grapheme correspondences.

Stage 2: Semiphonetic Spelling
Child shows beginning awareness that letters are used to represent sounds.
Child uses abbreviated one, two, or three-letter spelling to represent a whole word.
Child uses letter-name strategy to spell words.

Stage 3: Phonetic Spelling
Child represents all essential sound features in a word in spelling.
Child develops spellings for long and short vowels and plural and past-tense markers.
Child represents sounds without consistent regard for English conventions.

Stage 4: Transitional Spelling
Child adheres to basic conventions of English orthography, but not all.
Child begins to use morphological and visual information in addition to phonetic information.
Child uses a high percentage of correctly spelled words.

Stage 5: Conventional Spelling
Child knows how to spell a large number of words conventionally.
Child demonstrates growing accuracy in writing affixes, contractions, compound words, homonyms, and in using silent letters.
Child recognizes when a word doesn't "look right" and can consider alternative spellings.

—

Source: Adapted from multiple sources, Gentry, J. R. (1982). Developmental spelling: Assessment. Diagnostique, 8 , 52–61; Gentry, J. R., & Gillet, J. W. (1993). Teaching kids to spell . Portsmouth, NH: Heinemann. © Gail E. Tompkins

Stages of Spelling Development

Based on Read's seminal work, other researchers began to systematically study how children learn to spell. After examining students' spelling errors and determining that their errors reflected their knowledge of English orthography, Bear, Invernizzi, Templeton, and Johnston (2008) identified these five stages of spelling development that students move through as they learn to read and write: emergent spelling, letter name–alphabetic spelling, within-word spelling, syllables and affixes spelling, and derivational relations spelling. The characteristics of each of the stages are summarized in Figure 8-8.

As they continued to study students' spelling development, Bear and his colleagues also noticed three principles of English orthography that students master as they move through the stages of spelling development:

- The alphabetic principle—which explains that letters represent sounds.
- The pattern principle—which explains that letters are combined in predictable ways to spell sounds.
- The meaning principle—which explains that related words have similar spellings even when they're pronounced differently.

Young children focus on the alphabetic principle as they learn to represent sounds with letters. They pronounce words and record letters to represent sounds they hear, spelling *are* as *r* and *bed* as *bad*, for example. Children learn the pattern principle next, as they study **phonics**. They spell consonant and vowel patterns; for example, they learn to spell the /k/ at the end of short-vowel words with *ck* so that they spell *luck* correctly, not as *luk*. They also learn the pattern for adding inflectional suffixes, so that they spell the plural of *baby* as *babies*, not *babys*. The third principle

FIGURE 8-8 THE STAGES OF SPELLING DEVELOPMENT

Stage 1: Emergent Spelling

Children string scribbles, letters, and letter-like forms together, but they don't associate the marks they make with any specific phonemes. This stage is typical of three- to five-year-olds who learn these concepts:

- The difference between drawing and writing
- The direction of writing on a page
- Some letter–sound matches
- The formation of letters

Stage 2: Letter Name-Alphabetic Spelling

Children represent phonemes in words with letters. At first, their spellings are quite abbreviated, but they learn to use consonant blends and digraphs and short-vowel patterns to spell words. Spellers are five- to seven-year-olds who learn these concepts:

- The alphabetic principle
- Short vowel sounds
- Consonant sounds
- Consonant blends and digraphs

Stage 3: Within-Word Spelling

Students learn long-vowel patterns and *r*-controlled vowels, but they may confuse spelling patterns and spell *meet* as METE and reverse the order of letters, such as FORM for *from* and GRIL for *girl*. Spellers are seven- to nine-year-olds who learn these concepts:

- Long-vowel spelling patterns
- Complex consonant patterns
- *r*-controlled vowels
- Diphthongs

Stage 4: Syllables and Affixes Spelling

Students learn to spell multisyllabic words. They also add inflectional endings, use apostrophes in contractions, and differentiate between homophones, such as *your–you're*. Spellers are often nine- to eleven-year-olds who learn these concepts:

- Inflectional endings
- Homophones
- Syllabication
- Possessives

Stage 5: Derivational Relations Spelling

Students explore the relationship between spelling and meaning and learn that words with related meanings are often related in spelling despite sound changes (e.g., *wise–wisdom*). They also learn Latin and Greek root words and derivational affixes (e.g., *amphi-, -tion*). Spellers are eleven- to fourteen-year-olds who learn these concepts:

- Consonant and vowel alternations
- Greek affixes and root words
- Latin affixes and root words
- Etymologies

Source: Based on Bear, D. R., Invernizzi, M., Templeton, S., & Johnston, F. (2008). Words Their Way: Word Study for Phonics, Vocabulary, and Spelling Instruction (4th ed.). Upper Saddle River, NJ: Merrill/Prentice Hall. © Gail E. Tompkins

focuses on meaning; students learn, for example, that the words *oppose* and *opposition* are related in both spelling and meaning. Once students understand the meaning principle, they're less confused by irregular spellings because they don't expect words to be phonetically regular.

EMERGENT SPELLING

Young children, typically ages three to five, string scribbles, letters, and letter-like forms together, but they don't associate the marks with any specific phonemes. Emergent spelling represents a natural, early expression of the alphabet and other concepts about writing. Children write from left to right, right to left, top to bottom, or randomly across the page. Some emergent spellers have a large repertoire of letterforms to use, but others repeat a small number of letters over and over. Children use both upper- and lowercase letters, but they show a distinct preference for uppercase letters. Toward the end of this stage, children begin to discover how spelling works and that letters represent sounds in words.

LETTER NAME–ALPHABETIC SPELLING

Children learn to represent phonemes in words with letters, indicating they have a rudimentary understanding of the alphabetic principle—that a link exists between letters and sounds. Spellings are quite abbreviated and represent only the most prominent features in words. Examples of this stage spelling are DA (*day*), KLZ (*closed*), BAD (*bed*), and CLEN (*clean*). Many children continue to write mainly with capital letters. These spellers use a letter-name strategy: they slowly pronounce words they want to write, listening for familiar letter names and sounds. Spellers at this stage are five- to seven-year-olds.

WITHIN-WORD SPELLING

Children's understanding of the alphabetic principle is further refined in this stage as they learn to spell long-vowel patterns, diphthongs and the less common vowel patterns, and *r*-controlled vowels (Henderson, 1990). Examples of within-word spelling include LIEV (*live*), SOPE (*soap*), HUOSE (*house*), and BERN (*burn*). Children, typically seven- to nine-year-olds, experiment with long-vowel patterns and learn that words such as *come* and *bread* are exceptions. Children often confuse spelling patterns and spell *meet* as METE, and they reverse the order of letters, such as FORM for *from* and GRIL for *girl*. They also learn about complex consonant sounds, including -*tch* (*match*) and -*dge* (*judge*), and about diphthongs (*oi/oy*) and other less common vowel patterns, including *au* (*caught*), *aw* (*saw*), *ou* (*house*), and *ow* (*cow*). Children also compare long and short-vowel combinations (*hop–hope*) as they experiment with vowel patterns.

SYLLABLES AND AFFIXES SPELLING

The focus in this stage is on two-syllable words and the spellings used where syllables join together. Students, generally nine- to eleven-year-olds, apply what they've learned about one-syllable words to longer words, and they learn to break words into syllables. They learn about inflectional endings (-*s*, -*es*, -*ed*, and -*ing*) and rules about consonant doubling, changing the final *y* to *i*, or dropping the final *e* before adding an inflectional suffix. They also learn about compound words, possessives, homophones, and contractions, as well as some of the more common derivational prefixes and suffixes. Examples of syllables and affixes spelling include EAGUL (*eagle*), MONY (*money*), GETING (*getting*), BABYIES (*babies*), THEIR (*there*), CA'NT (*can't*), and BE CAUSE (*because*).

DERIVATIONAL RELATIONS SPELLING

Older students explore the relationship between spelling and meaning during the derivational relations stage, and they learn that words with related meanings are often related in spelling despite changes in vowel and consonant sounds (e.g., *wise–wisdom*, *sign–signal*, *nation–national*). Examples of spelling errors include CRITISIZE (*criticize*), APPEARENCE (*appearance*), and COMMITTE or COMMITEE (*committee*). The focus in this stage is on morphemes, and students learn about Greek and Latin root words and affixes. They also begin to examine etymologies and the role of history in shaping how words are spelled. They learn about eponyms (words from people's names), such as *maverick* and *sandwich*. Some students reach this stage at age eleven or twelve, but others don't attain it until age fourteen or fifteen.

Teachers do many things to scaffold students' learning as they move through the stages of spelling development, and the kind of support they provide depends on students' developmental level. As young children scribble, for example, teachers encourage them to use pencils, not crayons, for writing, to differentiate between drawing and writing. Letter name–alphabetic spellers notice words in their environment, and teachers help children use these familiar words to choose letters to represent the sounds in the words they're writing. As students enter the syllables and affixes stage, teachers teach syllabication rules, and in the derivational relations stage, they teach students about root words and the variety of words created from a single Latin or Greek root word. For example, from the Latin root word *-ann* or *-enn*, meaning "year," students learn these words: *annual*, *centennial*, *biannual*, *millennium*, *anniversary*, *perennial*, and *sesquicentennial*. Figure 8-9 presents suggestions for supporting students' spelling development.

FIGURE 8-9 WAYS TO SUPPORT STUDENTS' SPELLING DEVELOPMENT

Stage 1: Emergent Spelling
- Allow the child to experiment with making and placing marks on the paper.
- Suggest that the child write with a pencil and draw with a crayon.
- Model how adults write.
- Point out the direction of print in books.
- Encourage the child to notice letters in names and environmental print.
- Ask the child to talk about what he or she has written.

Stage 2: Letter Name-Alphabetic Spelling
- Sing the ABC song and name letters of the alphabet with children.
- Show the child how to form letters in names and other common words.
- Demonstrate how to say a word slowly, stretch it out, and isolate beginning, middle, and ending sounds in the word.
- Use Elkonin boxes to segment words into beginning, middle, and ending sounds.
- Post high-frequency words on a word wall.
- Teach lessons on consonants, consonant digraphs, and short vowels.
- Write sentences using interactive writing.

Stage 3: Within-Word Spelling
- Teach lessons on long-vowel spelling rules, vowel digraphs, and *r*-controlled vowels.
- Encourage students to develop visualization skills in order to recognize whether a word "looks" right.
- Teach students to spell irregular, high-frequency words.
- Focus on silent letters in one-syllable words (e.g., *know*, *light*).
- Have students sort words according to spelling patterns.
- Have students make words using magnetic letters and letter cards.
- Introduce proofreading so students can identify and correct misspelled words in compositions.
- Write sentences using interactive writing.

Stage 4: Syllables and Affixes Spelling
- Teach how to divide words into syllables and the rules for adding inflectional endings.
- Teach the schwa sound and spelling patterns (e.g., *handle*).
- Teach homophones, contractions, compound words, and possessives.
- Sort two-syllable words and homophones.
- Have students make words using letter cards.
- Teach proofreading skills, and encourage students to proofread all writings.

Stage 5: Derivational Relations Spelling
- Teach root words and derivational affixes.
- Make clusters with a root word in the centre and related words on rays.
- Teach students to identify words with English, Latin, and Greek spellings.
- Sort words according to roots or language of origin.
- Have students check the etymologies of words in a dictionary.

Teaching Spelling in the Elementary Grades

Spelling instruction is more than learning to spell a given list of words and writing weekly tests. Too often, parents and teachers equate spelling instruction with word lists and spelling tests, but spelling instruction within a word study program includes much more. Most important, it includes teaching students about English orthography; applying phonics concepts and patterns to spelling; and providing students with opportunities to read and write for meaningful, functional, and genuine purposes.

When they design their classroom spelling instruction, teachers consider many factors, especially the spelling development stages of the students. They know students who are not yet at the conventional spelling stage—that is, who do not spell at least 90 percent of words correctly and whose errors are not mostly at the transitional level—do not benefit from formal spelling instruction. Classroom programs, therefore, need to be developmentally appropriate for all students.

COMPONENTS OF THE SPELLING PROGRAM

A comprehensive spelling program has ten components, including reading and writing opportunities and minilessons about English orthography and spelling procedures.

1. *Provide daily writing opportunities.* Providing opportunities for students to write every day is a prerequisite for any spelling program. Spelling is a writer's tool, and it is best learned through the experience of writing. When they write, students use their developing knowledge of sound–symbol correspondences and spelling patterns. Students who write daily and invent spellings for unfamiliar words move naturally toward conventional spelling. Learning to spell is a lot like learning to play the piano. Daily writing opportunities are the practice sessions that lead to achievement.

2. *Provide daily reading opportunities.* Reading plays an enormous role in students' learning to spell. As they read, students store the visual shapes of words. The ability to recall how words look helps students decide when a word they are writing is spelled correctly When students decide that a word doesn't look right, they can rewrite the word several different ways until it does look right, ask the teacher or a classmate who knows the spelling, or check the spelling using spell-checker or by locating the word in a dictionary.

3. *Post words on word walls.* One way to direct students' attention to words in books they are reading is through the use of word walls as described earlier in this chapter. Seeing the words posted on word walls, clusters, and other charts in the classroom and using them in their writing help students to learn to spell the words.

    Researchers have identified the most commonly used words and recommend that elementary students learn to spell these words because of their usefulness. The 100 most frequently used words represent more than 50 percent of all the words children and adults write (Horn, 1926)! The next Teacher's Notebook lists the 100 most frequently used words and suggests ways teachers can teach these words, including creating a wall chart.

4. *Provide opportunities for students to build words.* Students can arrange and rearrange a group of letter cards to build words or create words by manipulating letters on interactive whiteboards. Primary-grade children can be given a limited number of selected letters to simplify their task. They begin by building two-letter words, then progressively longer words. They can work in small groups and record the words they build on a chart, in columns according to the length of the word. Teachers often introduce these activities as a whole-class lesson and then make the letters and word list available for students to use again independently or in small groups.

Teachers can use almost any words for word-building activities, but words related to literature students are reading or topics they are studying work well.

Given the letters *a, e, b, d, t, s,* and *g,* one group of grade 2 students made the following list:

2-Letter Words	3-Letter Words	4-Letter Words
at	bat	date
be	tea	dead
	sea	seat
	ate	babe
	bad	

Students in intermediate grades can increase their knowledge of English orthography and the meanings of affixes and root words by creating new words and their definitions. In one grade 5 classroom, the students called this "Riddlethaurus." The word-building activity requires three packs of word cards, one each of prefixes, root words, and suffixes. Students take one card from each of three piles to form a new word and then they create a definition and sometimes an illustration. One of their favourite inventions is *biphonester*—a person who talks on two telephones at once.

5. ***Teach students to proofread.*** Proofreading is a special kind of reading that students use to locate misspelled words and other mechanical errors in their drafts.

   Proofreading should be introduced in the primary grades. Young children and their teachers proofread class collaborative and dictated stories together, and students can be encouraged to reread their own compositions and make necessary corrections soon after they begin writing. This way, students accept proofreading as a natural part of both spelling and writing.

6. ***Teach students to use a dictionary.*** Students need to learn how to locate the spelling of unknown words in both print and online dictionaries. Developing use of a dictionary has the potential to provide self-teaching opportunities to improve spelling (Beech, 2004). While it is relatively easy to find a "known" word in the dictionary, it is hard to locate an unfamiliar word, and students need to learn what to do when they don't know how to spell a word. One approach is to predict possible spellings based on letter sounds, roots and affixes, then check the most probable spellings in a dictionary. When students use an online dictionary they can use strategies similar to those they use with a conventional dictionary.

7. ***Teach students to use a spell checker.*** When using a word processor to compose, students need to know how to use the spell checker. Most spell checkers offer the writer a variety of choices depending on the type of error made in the original text. Spell checkers frequently fail to produce the intended word as the first option (Montgomery, Karlan, & Coutinho, 2001) and often offer options unrelated in meaning to the intended word. Frequently, options offered include homophones (*to, too, two* and *their, there*). Teachers must teach students how to choose the correct alternative spelling.

   One effective way to teach students how to use the spell checker is by showing examples. Teachers and students look carefully at the options offered on the computer screen and discuss why each one is correct or incorrect. By showing examples of the types of errors students frequently make, teachers lead students to make correct choices. Teachers must also teach students what to do when the intended word does not appear and when the word in text is correct, but not recognized by the spell checker. Spell checkers and grammar checkers help students reduce mechanical errors, especially non-word errors, but do not replace the need to develop spelling strategies. Spell checkers treat the symptom, not the problem; they help correct, not teach spelling.

8. ***Teach spelling options.*** In English there are alternative spellings for many sounds because many words have been borrowed from other languages. There are many more options for vowel sounds than for consonants. Spelling options sometimes vary according to position in the word. For example, *ff* and *gh* are never used to represent /f/ at the beginning of a word.

Teachers can also use a series of minilessons to teach upper-grade students about these options and patterns. During each minilesson, students can focus on one phoneme, such as /f/ or /ar/, and as a class or small group develop a list of the various ways the sound is spelled in English, giving examples of each spelling. In Canadian classrooms, teachers also teach students spelling options related to the national heritage of the orthography. For example, students learn that *cancelled* can be spelled *cancelled* or *canceled* and *honour* as *honour* or *honor*. Generally, the double consonant and *-our* (versus *-or*) patterns are considered Canadian, coming from British heritage, and the single-consonant and *-or* patterns are identified with the United States. With increasing globalization and instantaneous communication systems, however, decreasing attention is paid to such spelling attributes.

9. ***Teach spelling strategies through minilessons.*** Good spellers have a repertoire of spelling strategies (Snowball & Bolton, 1999). Students need to develop strategies in order to spell unfamiliar words (Laminack & Wood, 1996; Wilde, 1993). Through minilessons, teachers teach students strategies such as the following:

- Invent spellings for words based on phonological, semantic, and historical knowledge of words as writing proceeds, then check in a dictionary.
- Visualize words as seen when reading and write best attempt.
- Proofread to locate and correct spelling errors.
- Locate words on word walls and other charts.
- Predict the spelling of a word by generating possible spellings and choosing the best alternative.
- Apply affixes to root words.
- Spell unknown words by analogy to known words.
- Locate the spelling of unfamiliar words in a dictionary or other reliable resource.
- Write a string of letters as a placeholder to stand for an unfamiliar word in a rough draft.
- Ask the teacher or a classmate how to spell a word.
- Use a spell checker effectively.

Instead of giving the traditional "sound it out" advice when students ask how to spell an unfamiliar word, teachers should help them use a strategic approach. We suggest that teachers encourage students to "think it out" and to apply one or more of the above strategies.

10. ***Develop students' spelling conscience.*** The goal of spelling instruction is to help students develop what Hillerich (1977) calls a "spelling conscience"—a positive attitude toward spelling and a concern for using standard spelling. Three dimensions of a spelling conscience are: understanding that standard spelling is a courtesy to readers; developing the ability to proofread to spot and correct misspellings; and appreciating that spell checkers are not infallible.

For more information on proofreading and editing, see Chapter 5, "The Reading and Writing Processes," pages 167–170.

Teachers help students develop a spelling conscience by teaching them to be strategic in their approach to spelling and proofreading and by providing meaningful opportunities to write for genuine audiences.

Many teachers question the use of spelling tests to teach spelling, since research suggests that spelling is best learned through reading and writing (Gentry & Gillet, 1993; Wilde, 1993). In addition, teachers recognize that lists of spelling words in published programs are often unrelated to the words students need at any given time for their writing. We recommend that weekly spelling tests, when they are used, be customized so that students learn to spell the words they need.

In a customized approach to spelling instruction, students and teachers choose the words to be studied. The master list composed by the teacher and students may include words from one or more of the following sources: published spelling programs, topics of study in other areas of curriculum, writing projects specific to language arts, and published lists of frequently misspelled words. In addition to the master list, students can individualize their lists by adding words that they need for their writing projects or that they have misspelled in their writing. In many classrooms, instruction is organized on a weekly basis. Teachers and students compose lists on Monday, study and use the words during the week, and end their study with a test on Friday.

On Monday, the teacher administers a pretest by dictating the master list to the whole class. Students then form pairs and dictate to each other the words they have added to the master list to individualize their lists. Students correct their own pretests and determine the words they must learn throughout the week. One way to organize the lists for the pretest and self-correction is by using test sheets divided into three columns, as shown in Figure 8-10. In the first column, the teacher writes the master list and leaves enough space for students to add their individual words. In the second column, students write the pretest. In the third column, students write any words misspelled on the pretest. The first column is folded under so it is not visible while the pretest is being given. It is then unfolded to guide the students when they are

FIGURE 8-10 TEST SHEET FOR PRETEST OF SPELLING LIST

Master List	Pretest	Correction
volcano	*volcano*	
earthquake	*earthquake*	
lava	*lava*	
spew	*spew*	
ashes	*ashis*	*ashes*
spaghetti	*spaghti*	*spaghetti*
veterinarian	*veternarian*	*veterinarian*

self-correcting their tests. Students circle the part of the word they misspelled before writing the word correctly in the third column. These lists are used for study at school and at home during the week.

Researchers have found that the pretest is a critical component in learning to spell. The pretest eliminates words that students already know how to spell so that they can direct their study toward words that they don't know yet. As long ago as 1957, Ernest Horn recommended that the best way to improve students' spelling is for them to get immediate feedback by correcting their own pretests. His advice is still sound today.

Students spend approximately five to ten minutes studying the words on their study lists each day during the week. Instead of "busy-work" activities, such as using their spelling words in sentences or gluing yarn in the shape of the words, research shows that it is more effective for students to use the following strategy to practise spelling words:

1. Look at the word and say it to yourself.
2. Say each letter in the word to yourself.
3. Close your eyes, visualize the word, and spell it to yourself.
4. Write the word, and check that you spelled it correctly.
5. Write the word again, and check that you spelled it correctly.

This strategy focuses on the whole word rather than breaking it apart into sounds or syllables. It can be adapted for advanced students who are learning multisyllabic words. During a minilesson at the beginning of the school year, teachers explain how to use the strategy, and then post a copy of the strategy in the classroom. In addition to this study strategy, sometimes students trade word lists on Wednesday or Thursday and give each other a practice test.

A final test is administered on Friday. The teacher dictates the master list, and students dictate their individual lists to each other. Any words that students misspell should be included on their lists the following week. Remember, the real test of the students' ability to spell conventionally is in their use of the words in their writing.

Typically, in Canadian classrooms, spelling instruction is embedded in the writing program. Published spelling programs, in which words are grouped by spelling patterns or phonic generalizations, are used as only one teaching and learning resource. Within the writing program, customized lists and specific spelling strategies are only part of more broadly conceived word study. Word study engages students in active exploration of the principles of English orthography. Students compare words, note patterns of consistency, and identify contrasts. The goal is to understand how English words "work." Students do not just learn words; they learn word knowledge that can be applied more generally to their reading and writing (Bear et al., 2011).

Comprehensive instruction offers students multiple opportunities to learn about words, and to apply word knowledge in their writing. Teachers help students use word knowledge and spelling strategies as effective writing tools.

Differentiating to Meet the Needs of Every Student

Spelling and the other language tools can be adapted to meet the needs of all students, and the single most important adaptation teachers can make is to understand the relative importance of language tools in the language arts program. Communicative competence is the goal of language arts instruction, and language tools support communication, but they do not equal it. For spelling instruction, that means encouraging students to use invented spelling so that they can communicate with others

The 100 Most Frequently Used Words

a	did	in	out	time
about	didn't	into	over	to
after	do	is	people	too
all	don't	it	put	two
am	down	just	said	up
an	for	know	saw	us
and	from	like	school	very
are	get	little	see	was
around	got	man	she	we
as	had	me	so	well
at	have	mother	some	went
back	he	my	that	were
be	her	no	the	what
because	him	not	them	when
but	his	now	then	who
by	home	of	there	will
came	house	on	they	with
can	how	one	things	would
could	I	or	think	you
day	if	our	this	your

Ways to Use This List of Words

1. List all or some of these words on bookmarks or tagboard cards that students keep at their desks and refer to when writing. As students learn the words, change the list to include others.
2. Explain to students the importance of knowing how to spell these words: these 100 words are used again and again, and when students know how to spell them, they will be able to spell half of all the words they write.
3. Make a wall chart with these words and have students add other frequently used words during the school year.
4. Use words from this list in minilessons and word sorts to contrast "sight words" with words that can be sounded out.
5. Choose words from this list for spelling words since these words are the most frequently used.
6. These words are also high-frequency reading "sight words." Use this list in activities to develop reading fluency.

before they reach the stage of conventional spelling. Students who are learning English as an added language may take longer to move through the five stages of spelling development, and their invented spelling will reflect their pronunciation of words and use of inflectional endings. Students with special needs may experience pervasive and persistent spelling difficulties and should be taught compensatory strategies, including efficient use of dictionaries and spell checkers. A list of recommendations for differentiating spelling instruction is presented in the accompanying Differentiating box.

Assessing Students' Progress in Spelling

Grades on spelling tests are the traditional measure of progress in spelling, and they provide a convenient way to assess students. For example, Bear and his colleagues (2011) provide tests that help teachers assess students' general level of spelling proficiency and to determine instructional needs. Teachers need to be mindful that assessing student progress by writing word lists, however, is somewhat limited, because the goal of spelling instruction is not simply to spell words correctly on tests but to use the words, spelled conventionally, in writing. It is essential that teachers keep anecdotal information and samples of student's writing to monitor their overall progress in spelling. To determine the carry-over from tests to writing, samples of student writing should be collected periodically. If words that were spelled correctly on tests are not correctly spelled in students' writing, alternative instructional and study strategies should be developed.

Handwriting

Like grammar and spelling, handwriting is a tool for writers. While it is easily argued that extensive attention to handwriting cannot be justified given the prominence of word processing, including voice-activated processing, however, handwriting instruction should not be ignored. Reutzel (2015) makes a compelling argument

DIFFERENTIATING

Spelling Instruction to Meet the Needs of Every Student

1. Read and Write Every Day for Short Periods

Students who are poor spellers need to read and write every day just as those who write easily need to write daily. Poor spellers benefit from frequent, short writing periods.

2. Encourage Invented Spelling

Encourage students to use invented spelling, no matter how old they are, because it allows them to write independently. Their invented spellings provide valuable insights into what students know about English orthography and what kind of instruction they need. Older students can be taught to underline their best guesses as they write, then to use resource tools to edit their work.

3. Teach High-Frequency Words

Help poor spellers to master the spelling of the 100 most frequently used words because of their usefulness. Knowing the 100 most frequently used words allows students to spell correctly approximately half of all words they write.

4. Teach the Think-It-Out Strategy

Teach students how to think out and predict the spelling of unfamiliar words, using multiple strategies. Teach them to apply the same strategies they use to read words: phonics, word structure, and analogies.

5. Teach the Efficient Use of Spell Checkers

Teach students how to employ the spell-checking features of the word-processing programs available in the classroom. Offer short guided practice sessions, each one focused on a particular aspect of using the spell checker effectively.

6. Recognize That Errors Are Part of Learning

Recognize that students and teachers can learn from errors. Errors indicate what students know and what they need to learn. By working together to identify and correct errors on writing projects that will be published students can gain both skill and confidence. Too much emphasis on what students misspell does not help them to spell; it teaches them that they cannot spell.

7. Plan for Success

Modify expectations within weekly class spelling programs by dividing longer lists into several shorter ones. Provide multiple short periods for study of the shorter lists and many opportunities for using the words in written communication.

8. Play Interactive Word Games

Provide practice for poor spellers and challenge for proficient spellers through interactive word games during which they can learn from each other. Games may be on computers or more traditional card games.

9. Challenge Champion Spellers

Following general procedures used in national spelling competitions, friendly competitions can be organized among interested students, especially proficient spellers. Using the *Oxford Canadian Spelling Bee Dictionary* (Barber, 2008) as a resource, student teams can engage in occasional, short, and friendly competitions to incite interest in orthography and etymology.

to include handwriting in language arts instruction stating that when handwritten letter transcription becomes fluent, young students can turn their attention to higher-level cognitive processes that allow them to compose higher quality written texts.

The goal in handwriting instruction is for students to develop skills that enable them to communicate effectively through writing. The two most important criteria in determining quality in handwriting are legibility (the writing can be easily and quickly read) and fluency (the writing can be easily and quickly written). It is imperative to recognize the functional purpose of handwriting and convey to students the importance of developing legible handwriting.

Handwriting Forms

Two forms of handwriting are currently used in most Canadian elementary schools: manuscript, or printing, and cursive, or connected writing. Typically, students in the primary grades learn and use the manuscript form; they switch to cursive handwriting in grade 2 or 3. In the middle and upper grades, students use both handwriting forms.

MANUSCRIPT HANDWRITING

Until the 1920s, students learned only cursive handwriting. Marjorie Wise is credited with introducing the manuscript form for primary-grade students in 1921 (Hildreth, 1960). **Manuscript handwriting** is considered better for young children because the letters require only vertical lines, horizontal lines, and circles, the components of their early drawings. Their drawing practice makes manuscript writing easier when they reach school age (Farris, 1997). In addition, most letter forms in manuscript handwriting are similar to the font in many primary-level books. The similarity is assumed to facilitate young children's introduction to reading and writing.

Students' use of the manuscript form usually diminishes in the middle grades after they have learned cursive handwriting. The need to develop greater writing speed is often given as the reason for the transfer to cursive handwriting, but research does not show that one form is necessarily written more quickly than the other.

CURSIVE HANDWRITING

When most people think of handwriting, **cursive writing**, the connected and slanted form, comes to mind. The letters in cursive handwriting are joined together to form a word with one continuous movement. Children often view cursive handwriting as the "grown-up" type. Primary-grade students often attempt to imitate this form by connecting the manuscript letters in their names and other words before they are taught how to form and join the letters. Awareness of cursive handwriting and interest in imitating it are indicators that students are ready for instruction.

D'NEALIAN HANDWRITING

D'Nealian handwriting is an innovative manuscript and cursive handwriting program developed by Donald Neal Thurber, a teacher in Michigan. The D'Nealian handwriting forms are shown in Appendix B. In the manuscript form, letters are slanted and formed with a continuous stroke; in the cursive form, the letters are simplified, without the flourishes of traditional cursive. Both forms were designed to increase legibility and fluency and to ease the transition from manuscript to cursive handwriting.

The purpose of the D'Nealian program was to mitigate some of the problems associated with the traditional manuscript form (Thurber, 1987). D'Nealian manuscript uses the same basic letter forms that students will need for cursive handwriting, as well as the slant and rhythm required for cursive. Another advantage of the D'Nealian style is that the transition from manuscript to cursive involves adding only connective strokes to most manuscript letters. Only five letters—*f, r, s, v,* and *z*—are shaped differently in the cursive form. Research (Graham, 1992; Kuhl & Dewitz, 1994) considering its ease of learning and use raises some concerns, but is not conclusive. Some Canadian school districts have adopted the use of D'Nealian handwriting across the grades. Teachers report much satisfaction and appreciate the ease of transition from manuscript to cursive letter forms.

Teaching Handwriting in Kindergarten and the Elementary Grades

Children's handwriting grows out of their drawing activities. Teachers must be mindful that young children enter kindergarten with greatly differing backgrounds of drawing and handwriting experience. Handwriting instruction in kindergarten typically is somewhat informal and includes four types of activities: stimulating children's interest in writing, developing their ability to hold writing instruments, refining their fine motor control, and letter formation of both upper- and lowercase letters. A hallmark of kindergarten writing is children learning to write their name using one uppercase letter and the rest in lowercase. Most kindergarten children also learn letter forms for upper- and lowercase letters.

In many Canadian schools, formal handwriting instruction begins in grade 1. Students learn how to form manuscript letters and space between them, and they develop skills related to the six elements of legibility. In the middle grades, after students have learned both manuscript and cursive handwriting, they need to review both forms periodically. By this time, too, they have firmly established handwriting habits, both good and bad. Instruction at the middle- and upper-grade levels focuses on helping students diagnose and correct their handwriting trouble spots so that they can develop a legible and fluent handwriting style. Older students both simplify their letter forms and also add unique flourishes to their handwriting to develop their own "trademark" styles.

Special pencils and other aids are sometimes provided for handwriting instruction for young children. Research indicates that beginner pencils are not better than regular-sized pencils for young children (Graham, 1992). Likewise, there is no clear evidence that specially shaped pencils and small writing aids that slip onto pencils to improve children's grip are effective, but some children appear to be helped, at least temporarily, by them.

Many types of paper, both lined and unlined, are used in elementary classrooms. The few research studies that have examined the value of lined paper in general and paper lined at specific intervals offer conflicting results. One study suggests that younger children's handwriting is more legible when they use unlined paper and that older children's is better when they use lined paper (Lindsay & McLennan, 1983). In practice, we believe it is best to provide students with experiences with a variety of types of paper as best suited to their writing projects.

TRANSITION TO CURSIVE HANDWRITING

Students' introduction to cursive handwriting typically occurs in the second semester of grade 2 or the first semester of grade 3. Teachers and students often attach great importance to the transition from manuscript to cursive. Usually, the basic strokes that make up the letters (e.g., slant stroke, undercurve, downcurve) are taught first. Next, the lowercase letters are taught in isolation, and then the connecting strokes are introduced. It is usual practice to cluster letters of similar shape and to teach them over a short space of time. For example, one cluster includes those with "tails" or strokes that descend below the base line: *f, g, j, p, q, y,* and *z.* Uppercase letters are taught later because they are used far less often and are considered more difficult to form.

The practice of changing to cursive handwriting only a year or two after children learn the manuscript form is sometimes criticized. The argument has been that students need to learn cursive handwriting as early as possible because of their increasing need for handwriting speed. Research several decades ago, however, established that manuscript handwriting can be written as quickly as cursive handwriting (Jackson, 1971). The controversy over the benefits of the two forms of handwriting is tempered by concerns for teaching word processing to facilitate students' writing fluency.

LEFT-HANDED WRITERS

Approximately 10 percent of our population is left-handed. In the past, left-handed writers were thought to have inferior handwriting skills. In fact, research has shown that there is no significant difference in the quality or speed of left- and right-handed students' writing (Groff, 1963). Teachers and parents should support children's natural tendencies, making any accommodation needed.

Teaching handwriting to left-handed students is not simply the reverse of teaching handwriting to right-handed students (Howell, 1978). Left-handed students have unique handwriting needs, and special adaptations of the procedures for teaching right-handed students are necessary. In fact, many of the difficulties that left-handed students face can be made worse by using the procedures designed for right-handed writers (Harrison, 1981). Special adjustments are necessary to allow left-handed students to write legibly, fluently, and with less fatigue.

The basic difference between right- and left-handed writing is physical orientation. Right-handed students pull their arms toward their bodies as they write, whereas left-handed writers push away. As left-handed students write, they move their left hands across what they have just written, often covering it. Many children adopt a "hook" position to avoid covering and smudging what they have written. Because of their different physical orientation, left-handed writers need to make three major types of adjustments:

1. ***Holding pencils.*** Left-handed writers should hold pencils or pens an inch or more farther back from the tip than right-handed writers do. This change helps them see what they have just written and avoid smearing their writing. Left-handed writers need to work to avoid "hooking" their wrists. Have them keep their wrists straight and elbows close to their bodies to avoid the awkward hooked position.

2. ***Tilting paper.*** Left-handed students should tilt their writing papers slightly to the right, in contrast to right-handed students, who tilt their papers to the left. Sometimes it is helpful to place a piece of masking tape on the student's desk to indicate the proper amount of tilt.

3. *Slanting letters.* Whereas right-handed students are encouraged to slant their cursive letters to the right, left-handed writers often write vertically or even slant their letters slightly to the left. Some handwriting programs recommend that left-handed writers slant their cursive letters slightly to the right as right-handed students do, but others advise teachers to permit any slant between vertical and 45 degrees to the left of vertical (Howell, 1978).

PLANNING HANDWRITING INSTRUCTION

Handwriting is best taught in separate periods of direct instruction and teacher-supervised practice. As soon as skills are taught, they should be applied in real-life writing activities.

Handwriting instruction and practice periods should be brief; fifteen-minute periods of instruction several times a week are more effective than a single lengthy period weekly or monthly. Regular short periods of handwriting instruction are necessary when teaching the manuscript form in kindergarten and grade 1 and the cursive form in grades 2 or 3. The minilesson that follows outlines the steps in teaching letter formation. In the middle and upper grades, instruction continues in short, specific lessons, but focuses on particular skills or problem-solving to help students continue to develop writing fluency.

MINILESSONS ON HANDWRITING

The teaching strategy presented in Chapter 2 can be adapted to teach minilessons on handwriting. The strategy is multisensory, with visual, auditory, and kinesthetic components, and is based on research in the field of handwriting (Askov & Greff, 1975; Furner, 1969; Graham, 1992; Hirsch & Niedermeyer, 1973). Research has shown the importance of the teacher's active involvement in handwriting instruction and practice. Observing "moving" models—that is, having students watch the teacher write the handwriting sample—is of far greater value than copying models that have already been written (Wright & Wright, 1980). As in the writing process, the teacher's assistance is far more useful while the students are writing than after they have completed writing. The steps in teaching a minilesson on handwriting are shown in the Step by Step box.

ELEMENTS OF LEGIBILITY

In order for students to develop legible handwriting, they need to know what qualities or elements determine legibility and then analyze their own handwriting according to these elements (Hackney, 1993). The six elements of legible and fluent handwriting are as follows:

1. *Letter formation.* Letters are formed with specific strokes. Letters in manuscript handwriting are composed of vertical, horizontal, and slanted lines plus circles or parts of circles. The letter *b*, for example, is composed of a vertical line and a circle, and *M* is composed of vertical and slanted lines. Cursive letters are composed of slanted lines, loops, and curved lines. The lowercase cursive letters *m* and *n*, for example, are composed of a slant stroke, a loop, and an undercurve stroke. An additional component in cursive handwriting is the connecting stroke used to join letters.

2. *Size and proportion.* During the elementary grades, students' handwriting becomes smaller, and the proportional size of uppercase to lowercase letters increases. Beginning writers' uppercase manuscript letters are twice the size of lowercase letters.

A Minilesson on Handwriting

1 Introduce the Letter   Demonstrate the formation of a single letter or family of letters (e.g., the manuscript circle letters—*O, o, C, c, a, e, Q*) on the whiteboard while explaining how the letter is formed.

2 Explain How to Form the Letter   Have students describe how the letter is formed while you or a student forms the letter on the whiteboard. At first you may need to ask questions to direct students' descriptions. Possible questions include

- How many strokes are used in making the letter?
- Which stroke comes first?
- Where do you begin the stroke?
- In which direction do you go?
- What size will the letter be?
- Where does the stroke stop?
- Which stroke comes next?

Students will quickly learn the appropriate terminology, such as baseline, left-right, slant line, counterclockwise, and so on, to describe how the letters are formed.

3 Review the Steps   Review the formation of the letter or letter family with students while demonstrating how to form the letter on the whiteboard.

4 Have Students Practise Writing the Letter   Have the students print the letter at the whiteboard, in sand, and with a variety of other materials such as clay, shaving cream, finger paint, pudding, and pipe cleaners. As students form the letter, they should softly describe the formation process to themselves.

Have students practise writing the letter on paper with the accompanying verbal descriptions.

Circulate among students providing assistance and encouragement. Demonstrate and describe the correct formation of the letter as the students observe.

5 Provide Authentic Writing Activities   After the students have practised the letter or family of letters, have them apply what they have learned in authentic writing activities. This is the crucial step!

When students first begin cursive handwriting, the proportional size of letters remains 2:1; later, the proportion increases to 3:1 for middle- and upper-grade students.

3. ***Spacing.*** Students should leave adequate space between letters in words and between words in sentences. Spacing between words in manuscript handwriting should equal one lowercase letter *o*, and spacing between sentences should equal two lowercase *o*'s. The most important aspect of spacing within words in cursive handwriting is consistency. To correctly space between words, the writer should make the beginning stroke of the new word directly below the end stroke of the preceding word. Spacing between sentences should equal one uppercase letter *O*, and the indent for a new paragraph should equal two uppercase letter *O*'s.

4. ***Slant.*** Letters should be consistently parallel. Letters in manuscript handwriting are vertical, and in the cursive form letters slant slightly to the right. To ensure the correct slant, right-handed students tilt their papers to the left, and left-handed students tilt their papers to the right.

5. **Alignment.** For proper alignment in both manuscript and cursive handwriting, all letters should be uniform in size and consistently touch the baseline.

6. **Line quality.** Students should write at a consistent speed and hold their writing instruments correctly and in a relaxed manner to make steady, unwavering lines of even thickness.

Correct letter formation and spacing receive the major focus in handwriting instruction during the elementary grades. Although the other four elements usually receive less attention, they, too, are important in developing legible and fluent handwriting.

Differentiating to Meet the Needs of Every Student

The goal of handwriting instruction is for every student to develop legible and fluent handwriting. Students who experience difficulty producing written work that is easily read may require significant intervention. One possibility is that students with severe handwriting problems can be taught to use word-processing programs to produce most of their written work. Consultation with an occupational therapist is often appropriate to determine the best choices for individual children. Instructional decisions regarding students with severe writing difficulties are made to help the students achieve the goals of fluency and legibility, bearing in mind that handwriting and word processing are tools for communication. The Differentiating box presents other recommendations for adapting writing instruction.

Assessing Handwriting

Students and teachers use the six elements of legibility to assess handwriting progress. For primary-grade students letter formation and spacing are most important. Older students can examine a piece of handwriting to assess it in respect to all six elements. A checklist for assessing manuscript handwriting is shown in Figure 8-11. Checklists can also be developed for cursive handwriting. It is important to involve students in developing the checklists so that they appreciate the need to make their handwriting legible and learn to monitor their progress in writing legibly and fluently. When students experience persistent problems, they require remediation.

FIGURE 8-11 A CHECKLIST FOR ASSESSING MANUSCRIPT HANDWRITING

Handwriting Checklist

Name_____

Writing Project_____

Date_____

_____	1.	Did I form my letters correctly?
		Did I start my line letters at the top?
		Did I start my circle letters at 1:00?
		Did I join the round parts of the letters neatly?
		Did I join the slanted strokes in sharp points?
_____	2.	Did my lines touch the midline or top line neatly?
_____	3.	Did I make all my letters sit on the baseline?
_____	4.	Did I make my letters straight up and down?
_____	5.	Did I space evenly between letters?
_____	6.	Did I leave enough space between words?

Word Processing in the Elementary Grades

Word processing is a writing tool for students not unlike handwriting. That is, it enables students to express themselves with fluency and legibility. Students use word processing at all stages of writing: to compose, draft, revise, edit, and publish. Research has shown that students who write using word processing software derive motivation for writing from using the computer and they write more (D'Odorico & Zammuner, 1993). Further, students writing on computers make fewer spelling errors and make more positive changes from first to final drafts (Black, 1989; Lewis, Ashton, Haapa, Kieley, & Fielden, 1999). Increasingly, voice response software programs are becoming available that eliminate the need to write or type. Although software is improving, to date response to children's voices remains somewhat problematic and is not an easy option until children are moving into adolescence (Pollock & Missiuna, 2005).

For young students to use word processing efficiently, they must learn keyboarding. Learning the placement of keys on the computer keyboard is fundamental for writing fluency. The hunt-and-peck technique places students in a similar handicapped position in respect to fluency as when they were first learning to print. Some educators recommend that students begin to acquire keyboarding skills as soon as they begin using computers, but many teachers delay teaching this skill. Curriculum requirements in many provinces support teaching keyboarding in grades 2 and 3. Stoecker (quoted in Langhorne, Dunham, Gross, & Rehmke, 1989) states that a typical unpractised student types at a rate of 6.5 words per minute. With touch-typing instruction for twenty-five half-hour periods, typing speed increased to twenty-eight to thirty words per minute. Students in grade 3 who learned to type an average of twenty-six words per minute were able to record thoughts faster than they could by hand (Hiebert, 1989). More recent research reinforces these earlier findings, reaffirming that keyboarding instruction has positive impact on children's written communication (Christensen, 2004).

DIFFERENTIATING

Writing and Word-Processing Instruction to Meet the Needs of Every Student

1. Accommodate the need for repetition to learn letter forms by making additional time available for practice. Offer multiple materials such as a whiteboard, large sheets of paper, and a variety of writing instruments to entice students to practise. Make models available to reinforce correct forms during practice.

2. Adjust time available to complete written work so students perceive they have time to write legibly or word-process with attention to both writing text and formatting.

3. Modify the quantity of written work. Supplement student writing with dictation to teacher's aides, providing frameworks (fill in the blanks) to compose notes to facilitate focusing on ideas, and, when feasible, integrate use of technology for recording.

4. Provide tutorial assistance in learning to keyboard fluently to help students develop lifelong communication skills. Employ alternative programming if students experience difficulty with the software adopted for the class.

5. Modify writing tools (pens, pencils, crayons, and markers) and materials to meet student needs. For example, left-handed writers may find loose-leaf paper easier to use than spiral-bound notebooks.

6. Seek assistance from an occupational therapist for students with severe difficulties.

Teachers and schools must make a commitment to teach students word processing, including fluent keyboarding. Even very young students can learn keyboarding and the simple processes of add, delete, highlight, and move. Students require explicit keyboarding instruction to develop keyboarding fluency and to unlock the full potential of word processing for their writing (Connelly, Gee, & Walsh, 2007).

Learning to keyboard can be compared with learning to play musical instruments that require brain and fingers to work together. For people who memorize quickly and have good finger dexterity, keyboarding can be easy to learn. Speed can usually be increased through practice (Hallows, 2002). Teachers can use the typing tutorials in software packages or more traditional methods of typing instruction to teach children. The letter combination drills help memorization of key locations. Software programs can be effective and many provide games and activities that are highly appealing to children while they learn and practise the fundamental skills. A review of instructional programs can be found at www.superkids.com/aweb/pages/reviews/typing. It provides teachers with the information they need to choose for their classes and schools. Many teachers ask their assistants or parent volunteers to supervise classroom use of typing programs to ensure students develop effective keyboarding skills and habits.

In all keyboard teaching, teachers need to remember that three factors help students succeed in keyboarding: position (sitting up, hands over home row at natural angle), memorization (key locations on keyboard), and motivation (reasons to write fluently). Although we choose not to recommend particular programs, we prefer those that integrate developing keyboarding fluency with authentic reading and writing. Further, we recommend that teachers devote the necessary instructional time to keyboarding and other fundamental aspects of word processing to facilitate students' writing fluency. Without keyboarding fluency, students' composition skills are hampered. When students have keyboarding fluency, the quality of their writing is superior to handwritten compositions (Connelly et al., 2007). Helping students develop fluent keyboarding as a writing tool is an essential component of writing instruction.

Review

Learning about words is an important part of the language arts. Few words have only one meaning, and students in the elementary grades learn about multiple meanings as well as about root words and affixes; homonyms, synonyms, and antonyms; and figurative meanings of words, such as idioms and metaphors. The best measure of students' learning of words is their ability to use the words in meaningful, functional, and genuine activities. In order to engage in meaningful activities, students must develop their abilities to use the tools of language—grammar, spelling, handwriting, and word processing. During the elementary grades, students learn the fundamental structures of English, such as types of sentences and parts of speech. They learn to spell conventionally and to proofread their writing. They develop legible and fluent handwriting to facilitate communication and also learn fundamentals of word processing, including use of spell checkers.

The following key concepts are presented in this chapter:

1. English is a historic language, and its diverse origins account for word meanings and some spelling inconsistencies.

2. The fact that students' vocabularies grow at a rate of about 3000 words a year suggests that students learn many words incidentally, especially through reading and writing.

3. Students learn about words, parts of speech, and figures of speech through a variety of word-study activities (word walls, word posters, word clusters, word sorts, and word chains).

4. All words are not equally difficult or easy to learn; the degree of difficulty depends on what the student already knows about the word.

5. Students learn to use reference resources, including dictionaries and thesauri in print and digital forms, to support and advance their writing.

6. Grammar is the structure of language, while usage is the socially accepted way of using words in sentences. Study of grammar for elementary students includes learning parts of speech, parts of sentences, types of sentences, and figures of speech.

7. Students move from using scribbles and single letters to represent words through a series of stages that lead to conventional spelling.

8. The five stages of spelling development are described as emergent, letter name–alphabetic, within word, syllables and affixes, and derivational relations. Conventionally the stages were labelled precommunicative, semiphonetic, phonetic, transitional, and conventional.

9. Spelling instruction includes opportunities to read and write as well as explicit minilessons about spelling procedures, concepts, strategies, and skills.

10. The two traditional handwriting forms are manuscript and cursive; manuscript is usually learned first, cursive later. D'Nealian is an alternative form, considered easier than cursive.

11. The primary purpose of handwriting instruction is to help students develop legible and fluent handwriting.

12. The six elements of legible and fluent handwriting are letter formation, size and proportion, spacing, slant, alignment, and line quality.

13. Students should be taught keyboarding to facilitate fluency in writing.

14. Handwriting and word processing are best learned through short, frequent lessons and practice time.

15. Fluent word processing enhances students' writing. Word processing aids students' expression of ideas, spelling, use of Standard English, and production of attractive documents.

Theory to Practice

1. Choose a piece of literature (narrative, poem, or nonfiction) for a particular grade level and identify a list of possible words for the word wall. Which words do you think will be sight words, new words, new concepts, or new meanings for students?

2. Observe in an elementary classroom and note how vocabulary is formally taught and informally learned. Compare those with the information presented in this chapter.

3. Read and analyze a set of stories, reports, or journals written by a class of middle- or upper-grade students. From them, identify five possible grammar and usage topics for minilessons. Choose one of the topics and create a plan for a minilesson to address the writers' instructional needs.

4. Observe how spelling is taught in an elementary classroom. How is the spelling program organized? Which components described in this chapter are used in this classroom?

5. Collect samples of a primary-grade student's writing and analyze the spelling to determine the student's stage of spelling development and instructional needs.

6. Visit a primary grade classroom. Take note of the handwriting charts displayed in the classroom. Compare your handwriting with the models on the charts. Practise forming the manuscript and cursive letters until you can imitate the models. When working in elementary classrooms, be sure to note the handwriting style familiar to the students because several handwriting programs are used in Canadian classrooms.

7. Observe students learning to keyboard and to use word-processing programs, including spell checkers. Note the types of errors they make. How are they helped by the program activities and checkers? What other instruction might they need?

Literacy in Action

Chapter 9: Writing Our Class Story

Procedure

Storytelling is a part of me. It is what I do when I visit friends and when I share about my day, so naturally I use stories as a teaching tool to reach the diverse children in my grade 1 classroom. Like many Canadian teachers, each year I see an increasing number of students in the classroom who are learning English as an additional language (EAL). I realized I needed to meet this new growing population and plan my instruction to affirm students' cultural and life experiences. As a result, I make deliberate planning choices that focus on the lives of the children, beyond their academic needs, to create an environment which is welcoming and inviting to all.

One way I create a positive atmosphere is to engage the children in writing and recording "Our Class Story." This project welcomes the children's backgrounds, experiences, and lives into the classroom as they share their own personal journeys that led them to our grade 1 community. Over many months we work toward the goal of creating a movie and a book that share each student's journey with our class.

To begin the project, I share my own journey with our grade 1 classroom. I bring several photos ranging of myself, from me as a baby, to setting up my first classroom, and my present life as their teacher. As I share each picture, I talk about how it led me to our classroom. Then I invite them to share their stories in many different ways.

We begin by creating "personal museums" out of boxes. Children paint and decorate a box that shares their interests, family, and journey to our room. Students take their boxes home to their families and fill them with the treasures, photos, and written stories of their journeys to bring back to our classroom. Next, we spend time sharing our museums in gallery walks, labelling them, and finally writing about our past experiences. Students also create timelines of important events in their lives, write poetry about what makes them Canadian, and create a quilt that shares their interests and hobbies. When we are well rehearsed and ready to tell our stories, I begin the final project of creating a movie and a book.

To create the book, each child has one page to write a story and one page to choose the layout for the pictures. The movie is created from the photos the students select. I use iMovie because it has a great visual feature that creates animated airplanes flying from different points around the globe to our classroom. Once the photos are loaded in order, the students record their stories to match their pictures and add animated airplanes if they have travelled from another city or country to our classroom. It takes many weeks for students to perfect their stories and prepare to share them with the school community. To celebrate our work, we invite families and the school to attend our movie premiere. I love watching the children's stories play across the screen to show how far we all travelled to become a community of learners.

Assessment

Assessment happens on a daily basis in grade 1. I begin each experience by ensuring that students know their task and the purpose of our work. Our final conversation before we begin is to create a set of criteria to guide our work.

> "Students create timelines of important events in their lives, write poetry about what makes them Canadian, and create a quilt that shares their interests and hobbies."
>
> Katie Devlin

Knowing our task, the intent, and the criteria help students focus on the important skills I am highlighting. As an example, when we began sharing our personal museums, the grade 1 students knew that their job was to share at least three things with their "guest." The criteria for sharing was to use a voice that their "guest" could hear, to share three objects, and to tell at least one thing about each object.

Spending time talking to students and recording my observations enables me to see when the students are ready to move on to the next stages of writing about their experiences and how those experiences are woven together to complete the stories of their journeys to our classroom.

Adaptation

I never know the adaptations I need to make until I am working "in the moment" with grade 1 students. The important thing is to remain flexible and to create an experience that scaffolds students' abilities. Every year that I engage students in Our Class Story, I learn a new way to support their learning. Slowing down the writing process, allowing time for students to rehearse their stories, labelling personal museum objects to create a word bank, and providing individualized supports are strategies that have made this project successful.

Reflection

It is a big responsibility for teachers to guide EAL students as they learn a new language, build friendships, embrace a new culture, and ultimately, we hope, find acceptance in their new classroom. This project has helped me accomplish this and more.

The Our Class Story project has welcomed the children's backgrounds, experiences, and lives into the classroom. This, in turn, has supported the goal of meeting the children's educational, emotional, and social needs. Three things I have learned that have helped me understand and support this project are to trust, to be sensitive, and to honour the child. I need to establish a relationship of trust so that I can share my journey alongside the stories of my students. I need to be sensitive to the lives and stories of the students as we share. And by honouring the child, I am able to validate his or her experience, language, and culture in our classroom. Honouring and valuing the experiences of the children I teach sends a strong message: it does not matter what language you speak— you are welcome here, where you are respected and accepted alongside your peers.

From the Classroom of Katie Devlin, Primary Teacher
Harrow School
Winnipeg, Manitoba

Viewing and Visually Representing

LEARNING OUTCOMES

After reading this chapter, you should be able to

1. Define visual and media literacy

2. Describe the viewing and visually representing processes

3. Explain how viewing and visually representing support and enhance listening, speaking, reading, and writing

4. Consider the place of multimedia in students' communication and learning, and the implications it has for planning and teaching language arts units

5. Explain how the concepts of aesthetic, efferent, and critical information processing described in Chapter 4 apply to viewing and representing

6. Describe how viewing and representing are integral to teaching of language arts units

Jules Selmes/Pearson Education

Gallery of children's representations of story characters.

For decades, listening, speaking, reading, and writing were considered the language arts. With the introduction and increased availability of computers and other digital equipment, educators acknowledged the need to recognize viewing as an essential communication art. Hence, *viewing* became the fifth language art. As technological advances made possible the easy production of print and nonprint media, educators recognized the role of representation of knowledge in meaning construction and communication, and visually representing became the sixth language art. Most recently, the more general term, *representing*, is sometimes used to recognize that knowledge is frequently represented in multimedia formats, blending sounds and images to communicate. *Viewing* and *representing* refer to **visual literacy**, a powerful way of learning that supports oral and written language.

This chapter will focus on how teachers teach the two newest language arts—viewing and representing—and how they contribute to students' learning.

Viewing is a way students acquire, appreciate, and critique information, thoughts, ideas, and feelings that are visually conveyed. Students encounter many opportunities to view a variety of formats, including visuals (such as photographs, illustrations, and charts), drama (puppets, tableaux, and skits), and multimedia (television, videos, DVDs, blogs, and websites). Viewing enhances listening when students attend to nonverbal communication or visual elements of presentations.

Visually representing is a way for students to convey information learned, thoughts, and ideas through the creation of visual texts and art forms. Students create meaning through multiple sign systems such as drawings, videos, digital images, animation, drama, sculptures, models, and posters. Often, visual representation projects lead students to deeper understanding of texts they have read or heard. Visually representing also enhances speaking when students support their oral presentations with visuals. Similarly, speaking and using music can enhance visual images.

Viewing and representing broaden the ways in which students can understand and communicate their learning. Traditionally, the emphasis in language arts has been on representing thoughts, ideas, and feelings in written and spoken forms, but currently in Canadian classrooms students also use visual, dramatic, and multimedia formats, both independently and as support for their written and spoken messages.

Technology and access to the Internet have changed what it means for students to be literate and what language arts strategies and skills teachers need to help them develop. Whereas the term **literacy** traditionally refers to the ability to read and write, it is now readily accepted that literacy includes construction of meaning from multiple information sources, not just text. Hence, the concepts of visual literacy and media literacy have evolved to refer to the ability to create, read, evaluate, and respond to visual images.

Visual Literacy

Visual literacy is an area of literacy that deals with what can be seen and how what is seen is interpreted. *Visual literacy* can be defined as the ability to understand communications composed of visual images as well as being able to use visual imagery to communicate with others. In other words, visual literacy is the ability to see, understand, think, create, and communicate graphically. There is a proliferation of images in our students' worlds—in books; on television; in newspapers, magazines, video games, and movies; on billboards, social networking sites, and the web. As students are exposed to more and more information and entertainment through nonprint media, their ability to think critically and visually about the images they see becomes a vital life skill. Teachers must help students develop the skills to read and create visually in thoughtful and critical ways.

Visual literacy is learned, just as reading and writing are learned. Students learn to process visual images efficiently and understand the impact they have on viewers. The visually literate student looks at images carefully and critically to discover the intention of the image creator, just as a skilled reader discovers the intention of the author. Visual literacy allows students to gather information and ideas contained in images, put them in context, and determine their meaning in relation to that context and beyond. Visually literate students can apply their skills to reading a variety of images including (but not limited to) photographs, charts and graphs, drawings, graphics, paintings, films, sculptures, maps, book illustrations, and web pages.

Visual texts make meaning with images or with a combination of images and words. Think of a map, for instance. The words are needed to name the places, while the images are needed to show where those places are and the relationship of one place to another. Some kinds of information are best expressed in words, others in images, while still others are best expressed in a combination of words and images. As students learn to view and represent, they must learn to distinguish types of information and how they are most clearly communicated.

Teachers work with students in many ways to help them see, read, and create visual images. Just as verbally literate students must be able to manipulate the basic components of written language—the letters, words, spelling, grammar, and syntax—visually literate students must be able to recognize the use of and employ the basic visual elements. The way these elements are arranged can make or break a good picture idea. Being familiar with the basic elements of visual communication makes it possible for students to read and use many visual forms and media. Although there is variation among visual artists in regard to which elements are considered basic, we know that knowledge of the elements and how they function helps students understand and compose meaningful visual messages. Figure 9-1 provides a guide to the visual elements and their functions that students use to interpret and construct visual messages.

FIGURE 9-1 ELEMENTS OF VISUAL ART AND CONCEPT DESIGN

Dot is the most basic of visual elements. It is a pointer or a marker of space. A dot standing alone can direct attention to a specific point. A group of dots can suggest motion or direction. Contemporary visual media such as television, video, digital movies, inkjet and laser printouts, and animation are patterns of dots.

Line is a simple, but powerful, visual tool. Line comprises a series of very closely spaced dots that can show motion and direction. Horizontal lines create a sense of equilibrium; diagonal lines create visual stress and imply movement.

Hue refers to colour. All the colours of the rainbow are actually different hues in the visible spectrum of light. Hues are warm (red, orange, and yellow) and cool (blue and closely related colours). Warm hues imply warmth, comfort, and ease, while cool hues imply distance, anxiety, and tension.

Lighting refers to the use of varying levels of light and colour to create mood and feelings or show change in mood or time.

Sound is the presence or absence of music or special sounds to create a mood, convey action, or signal change.

Composition is the arrangement of masses and spaces, including the arrangement of objects, people, and places within a scene or screen.

Shapes may be the outlines of objects or may be the negative shapes (spaces) between objects. Circle and curvy shapes suggest warmth, comfort, and calm. Squares can be read as dull, stable, or lacking imagination. Triangles are interpreted as action, tension, or conflict.

Form is three-dimensional quality, as in height, width, and depth. Dimension is created through use of linear perspective, often enhanced by colour manipulation. Two-dimensional visual objects such as photographs, drawings, and paintings are created such that they imply that three-dimensional, real objects are being seen.

Perspective is the illusion of distance and point of view created by techniques such as size, overlapping, atmosphere, sharpness or blurriness, and angles.

Texture is the feel of an object's surface, both to the touch of fingers and the way the viewer's eyes *feel* a visual image. Visual texture is interpreted through minute variations in dimension. Viewers perceive visual texture because their sense of touch cooperates with their eyes to help them better understand their surroundings.

Source: Adapted from Cornett, C., & Smithrim, K. (2001). The arts as meaning makers: Integrating literature and the arts throughout the curriculum (Canadian ed.). Don Mills, ON: Prentice Hall; Bartel, M. (1999) "Some Ideas About Composition and Design" Retrieved April 2, 2009, from www.goshen.edu/art/ed/Compose.htm. © Gail E. Tompkins

Responses to visual texts are a form of personal expression, just as written responses to literature are unique to the reader. Teachers help students respond to visual texts by creating a climate of trust and respect for the opinions of all students. Having many students share their perspectives enhances all students' understanding and helps students appreciate the importance of nonverbal communication. To make viewing images a meaningful experience, teachers guide students to consider the ways the elements of design are used and the effect the image has upon viewers. Similarly, teachers guide students to create visual messages attending to the same elements. Students can be asked, for example, to apply these principles when they create their own interpretation of a poem or story through a visual art activity such as drawing a picture, making a collage, or creating their own multimedia productions.

Media Literacy

Students are bombarded with visual language—picture books, 3-D animation, commercials, advertisements, billboards, and more. In addition, they use digital tools and multimedia to create images and to communicate. Media literacy is having the knowledge and skills needed to understand, use and evaluate a variety of media forms. In K–8 classrooms, instruction in media literacy includes helping students understand ideas such as their own personal consumption of media, how to distinguish different types of media, and the content of media messages. Students must learn how to think critically and to reflect on the visual images and messages they receive and create. Ultimately, the goal is to help students make ethical decisions about the messages surrounding them.

Across Canada, provincial and territory curricula have developed to address media literacy in English language arts, information and communication technology, and other subject areas. The Western and Northern Canadian Protocol for Collaboration in Education (which includes British Columbia, Alberta, Saskatchewan, Manitoba, Yukon, Nunavut, and Northwest Territories) refers to texts not only in print form, but also in oral and visual forms. Media literacy in these Canadian provinces and territories encompasses the study of the relationship between text and audience, and the analysis of radio, television, film, website content, and the many forms of advertising. Ontario introduced a new language curriculum in 2006 for grades 1 to 8 with a strand entitled "Media Literacy" that mandates the study of media texts, media audiences, and media production. Quebec curriculum offers media-related concepts that help students understand media messages as both viewers and producers of texts. Media literacy is addressed by the Atlantic Provinces Education Foundation, particularly in the English language arts curriculum. Students examine images in music videos, newspapers, and advertising in order to develop critical thinking skills about the world around them. In addition, provincial and territorial education departments strongly advocate for an approach that fully integrates media literacy throughout curricula in elementary and secondary schools. It should be noted that many experts agree that more attention is needed in media instruction throughout the grades (MediaSmarts, 2012).

Given the complex nature of students' digital experiences with a variety of modes of communication, including texting, instant messaging, Facebook, Twitter, Tumblr, and YouTube, it is important for teachers to promote media education. Teachers use teachable moments to help students question media. For instance, when comparing a book and a movie, teachers can ask students to consider the commercial appeal of a movie and how this affects meaning. They can ask students to reflect on their own media devices and consumption, while focusing the discussion on responsible and ethical uses and decision-making strategies. Such questions help students to develop the ability to think critically about messages from these sources.

The Viewing Process

More than a decade ago, Neil Postman (1992) claimed that children needed no instruction to watch television: there are no skills involved, and "that is why there is no such thing as remedial television-watching" (p. 152). While he was correct about there being no remedial television watching, we disagree regarding the skills needed for viewing. Viewing is more than just seeing. Students must be taught *how* to view. They need to learn that visual images, like words, convey ideas, beliefs, and values. Hence the important place of viewing and media literacy across Canadian provincial and territorial language arts curricula, and its close association with curriculum concerning technology.

Viewing, like reading and writing, is an active process of constructing meaning. By attending to and comprehending visual information, students broaden the ways in which they interpret and understand their worlds.

Steps in the Viewing Process

Viewing involves three steps: receiving, attending, and assigning meaning. In the first step, the viewer receives the visual stimuli. In the second step, the viewer attends to the attributes of the stimuli, such as colour and shape. Stimuli are always present in a context, and viewers must be aware of the influence of the context as they develop meaning. Attributes and context contribute to the viewer's interpretation. In the third step, the viewer, like a reader, assigns meaning to a text based on previous experience and prior knowledge. Teachers provide experiences for students to view a variety of materials, both print and nonprint, for a variety of purposes. Students view in different ways for different purposes. Many parallels can be drawn between the viewing process and **efferent listening** and **aesthetic listening**.

Purposes for Viewing

Little teaching and learning in any discipline is bereft of the use of visual images. Visual images enhance students' understanding and motivation for learning. Because visual images are complex and multilayered, they require skill in their interpretation. Students need to learn to analyze visual images and to understand the image creator's technique and intent to be able to respond to them. In language arts units, students view for at least three primary purposes. First, they often view to deepen their understanding of text composed by others. For example, when students examine picture book illustrations, comics, and graphic novels, seeing the illustrator's interpretation of the text deepens their understanding. Second, students also view and consider the effects of visual images to create visual texts that enrich the messages they wish to convey. For example, when they create cover pages for written project reports or design labels for personally created DVDs, they plan ways to catch viewers' attention. Finally, students view print and nonprint media to gain more information or a fuller understanding of topics. For example, they may seek information from picture galleries, virtual pinboards, or animated diagrams on the Internet to be included in their writing projects or their studies in content areas of the curriculum.

Teaching Viewing Strategies

Although students must be taught how to view and teachers must pay specific attention to the viewing process, opportunities for viewing alone are rare. Students are usually involved in viewing and listening simultaneously when they listen to teachers read aloud from picture books and see the illustrations, watch videos, watch television, engage with interactive websites, and attend dramatic productions. A few exceptions for viewing alone would include watching mime, viewing art objects or models, viewing images online, and reading wordless picture books. During these activities, students must rely only on the visual information alone to construct meaning.

Students often view videos, DVDs, or augmented reality versions of **children's literature** as part of language arts units, and it is important that teachers take advantage of the unique capabilities of this technology. Some precautions, however, are necessary to make the most of both the students' reading (or being read to by the teacher) and the viewing of the literature selection. In many classrooms we visit, it is usual for the book to be read first and the video watched when the reading is complete. While this may sometimes be appropriate, we stress that other options should be considered. Teachers decide upon the purpose for viewing and they decide whether students view the video before or after reading or whether the viewing is interspersed with the reading. They also decide how much of the video students watch in the classroom. Purpose and students' needs and interests guide all of these decisions.

English language learners and other students with limited background knowledge often benefit from viewing before reading or listening to a book read aloud, but for other students, watching a video before reading would curtail their interest in reading the book. Showing a short clip of the video or a book trailer to introduce the book, however, can be instructive concerning some aspects such as unfamiliar settings and can heighten student interest in reading. Similarly, showing clips as reading progresses can clarify aspects of plot or character development and can facilitate discussion and deepening of meaning. Showing the complete video upon completion of reading can also deepen meaning and raise many points for discussion. One example of an augmented reality children's book that can be shared both traditionally and digitally is *The Fantastic Flying Books of Mr. Morris Lessmore*, by William Joyce (2012). This book developed in an unusual sequence of film-to-book and includes an app that animates the images for readers. As Golden (2001) reminds us, students tend to be visually oriented and able to see significant aspects of visual media, and many of the skills they use to decode visual images are the same skills they use for written text. Presenting both visual and written text maximizes the possible transfer of decoding and analytical skills.

In language arts units, teachers often ask students to make comparisons between the book and video versions of a story and to choose the one they like better. Interestingly, less capable students who don't visualize the story in their minds often prefer the video version, while more capable readers often prefer the book version because the video doesn't meet their expectations. Students can also examine some of the conventions used in video productions, such as narration, music, and sound effects; the visual representation of characters and the setting; the camera's perspective; and any changes from the book version. Making comparisons between video and writing techniques deepens understanding of both meaning of the story and effect of techniques. General guidelines for using visual media in the classroom are listed in the accompanying Teacher's Notebook.

Guidelines for Using Visual Media in the Classroom

1. Preview
Before showing a video, YouTube clip, or DVD, taking a virtual field trip, or viewing a website or blog, make sure it is suitable for students and contributes significantly to making information available to them. It may be necessary to skip some portions due to excessive length or unsuitable content when showing visual media to students.

2. Plan How to Use
Plan how the media will be used. Plan an introduction, interaction during the viewing, and a follow-up. Plan how it will be shown—all at once or in short segments. Students who have little background knowledge on the topic or students for whom the sentence structure or vocabulary is difficult may benefit from previewing, with or without sound, with guidance from the teacher or teacher assistant before viewing and listening as a class or independently.

3. Set the Purpose and Give Students Viewing Guidelines
Explain the purpose for viewing and explain whether students should use primarily aesthetic, efferent, or critical listening. Indicate to students what will be expected of them during and after viewing. It is important that students are not asked questions after viewing that they have not been prepared for before viewing.

4. Use the Pause Function
Stop the presentation periodically in order for students to make predictions, reflect on their use of a listening strategy, talk about the story or information, or compare the book and digital versions. If students are listening and viewing an informational presentation, they may need to stop periodically to take notes.

5. Re-view
Consider showing the video, YouTube clip, or DVD more than once because re-viewing is as beneficial as rereading. Teachers can show particular segments twice during the initial showing, or teachers can show the video without interruption the first time and then play it a second time.

6. Vary the Procedure Used
Teachers sometimes show the beginning of a story on the video or DVD and then read the entire book aloud. Afterwards, students view the entire video or DVD. Or teachers can alternate reading and viewing sections of text.

7. Consider the Visual and Sound Elements and Effects
Depending upon the content of the video, YouTube clip, or DVD—story or expository information—students can examine the impact of the narration, music, sound effects, lighting, camera angles, and the visual representation of the characters and setting as appropriate.

8. Provide Opportunities for Response
Provide opportunities for students to respond to visual media presentations. Students can respond in many ways, including participating in grand conversations and writing in reading logs or on blogs.

Besides making comparisons of book and digital versions of a story, students can also compare two digital versions or plan and create their own digital version. Many digital storybooks include the same illustrations and printed text, with the added feature of being able to animate the illustrations in some way, often with a click of the mouse. By providing a multisensory reading experience, multimedia versions of storybooks aid comprehension. Further, Pearman (2008) explains that because these types of books decrease or eliminate the need to concentrate on decoding, listening and reading along allow students to focus on the construction of meaning from text. She recommends that multimedia books would be valuable tools for allowing struggling readers to become familiar with texts that are to be read and discussed in the classroom in a whole-group situation.

Viewing strategies can be learned through many activities. Projects that help students learn to comprehend visual information can be closely linked to reading and responding to literature, and to learning across the curriculum. Figure 9-2 lists projects that allow students to learn viewing and visually representing strategies while engaged in meaningful integrated language arts tasks.

FIGURE 9-2 VIEWING AND VISUALLY REPRESENTING PROJECTS

The Viewing Process

Viewing Projects

1. View a video, website, or graphic novel and analyze use of some of the visual elements and their use in portraying meaning.
2. Compare the illustrations in several versions of the same story. Multiple versions of folktales and other traditional stories are available and appropriate for comparison.
3. Analyze the illustrator's craft and medium to discover the questions illustrators must ask and answer as they work.
4. Ask students to choose a piece of art (e.g., painting or sculpture) that relates to a book or other text (e.g., poem) and share their interpretation of the art with the class.
5. View a digital version of a book. Note how the text is made interactive and discuss the effects of the interactive components on meaning construction.
6. View artifacts or pictures related to a book and use them to predict story plot and events. After reading, use the artifacts to retell the story.
7. View the work of one illustrator in several books. Look for commonalities. The websites of many illustrators provide insight into their work.
8. Ask students to solve visual puzzles such as identifying differences between two similar pictures.
9. View a series of Images or illustrations of characters in books or in the media and discuss how the artistic styles of the visuals contribute to character development and overall meaning.
10. View the same picture in black and white and in colour. Discuss differences and effects upon meaning.

Visually Representing Projects

1. Experiment with the illustration techniques (e.g., collage, watercolour, line drawing) used in favourite books. Examine other books illustrated with the same technique.
2. Make a map, diagram, or model using information from a book.
3. Create a collage with digital photographs, print pictures, text, and other objects to represent the theme of a book or mood of a poem.
4. Design a book jacket, laminate it, and place it on the book.
5. Make a diorama or other miniature scene of an episode from a favourite book. Use toys, clay figures, or other objects to represent characters and objects in the story. Include a display sign to describe the scene.
6. Make a set of storyboards with one card (print or nonprint media) for each episode, chapter, or scene of a text. Show the boards in sequence to retell the text.
7. Create a blog about a favourite author.
8. Make a comic strip to illustrate the sequence of events in a book.
9. Prepare bookmarks for a book and distribute them to classmates.
10. Create a media presentation using pictures, video, and sound from the Internet to retell a story.
11. Experiment with colour, font, and other design techniques when publishing students' written work. Note effects on impression, mood, and meaning of the text.
12. Create a Venn diagram, digitally or in print, to compare the book and film versions of a story.
13. Make a series of digital photographs to depict the setting of a novel or short story.
14. Make a character cluster or sociogram showing relationships among characters.
15. Create brochures with text and pictures to summarize information learned from expository text, videos, and websites.
16. Create movies to retell instances in stories or novels read. Movies can be stitched in sequence to retell the story.
17. Create a PowerPoint™ presentation to report information. Include text, digital pictures, and video as appropriate.
18. Create masks or 3-D models (life size or smaller) of characters or significant story objects from clay, Plasticine, papiermache, cardboard, or other collected materials. Use a 3-D printer if technology is available.

Critical Viewing and Listening

Students—even those in the primary grades—need to develop **critical literacy** skills, both viewing and listening, because they are exposed to many types of persuasion and propaganda in books and media. Interpreting and constructing meaning from books and media requires critical thinking, listening, and viewing. As will be pointed out later in this chapter, students must also be able to apply their critical thinking, listening, and viewing skills to their representation activities. Critical thinking, viewing, and listening are not limited to language arts. Social studies and science lessons on topics such as the environment, political candidates, and health and wellness demand that students think critically.

For more information on critical listening, see Chapter 4, "Listening and Speaking in the Classroom," page 103.

Persuasion and Propaganda

Advertisements on television, in magazines, and on the Internet are prominent forms of persuasion and sources of propaganda in students' lives. Because many commercials are directed at children, it is essential that they be able to listen and view critically and learn to judge advertising claims. Teachers often choose to teach critical listening and viewing through projects focused on advertisements. Teachers extend such language arts units to include **persuasive writing** and identification of writers' techniques in printed text.

Advertisers use many devices, gimmicks, and strategies to attract attention and persuade viewers and listeners. There are, however, three basic ways to persuade people. The first is by reason. People seek logical conclusions, whether from facts or from strong possibilities; for example, people can be persuaded to practise more healthful living based on medical research. It is necessary, of course, to distinguish between reasonable arguments and unreasonable appeals. For instance, to suggest that diet pills will bring about extraordinary weight loss is an unreasonable appeal.

The second way to persuade people is by an appeal to character. We can be persuaded by what another person recommends if we trust that person. Trust comes from personal knowledge or the reputation of the person who is trying to persuade. We must always question whether we can believe the persuader.

The third way to persuade people is by appealing to their emotions. Emotional appeals can be as strong as intellectual appeals. We have strong feelings and concern for ourselves, other people, and animals. Fear, a need for peer acceptance, and a desire for freedom of expression are all strong feelings that influence our opinions and beliefs.

Any of these three types of appeals can be used to try to persuade someone. Students need to learn to recognize and appropriately use all three types. To persuade classmates to read a particular book in a book report "commercial," a student might argue that it is short and interesting (reason); or it is the most popular book in grade 5 and everyone else is reading it (character); or it is hilarious and they'll laugh (emotion).

Students need to learn to become critical consumers of media, especially advertisements, and, more specifically, to understand the symbiotic relationship between words and images (Burmark, 2002). Students who know how to critically analyze mass media text also recognize how it manipulates the public (Hobbs & Frost, 2003). Increasingly, children are bombarded with clever advertising on television and the Internet. Integrating the techniques of "adbusting" into our curricula will equip students with the critical awareness they need to be discriminating consumers (Curry-Tash, 1998).

In addition to techniques of persuasion used by advertisers, students also need to learn about propaganda. As previously discussed, advertisers use appeals to reason, character, and emotion to promote products, ideas, and services; however, advertisers may also use propaganda to influence our beliefs and actions. Propaganda suggests something shady or underhanded. Like persuasion, propaganda is designed to influence people's beliefs and actions, but propagandists may distort, conceal, and exaggerate. Two propaganda techniques are *deceptive language* and *propaganda devices*.

People seeking to influence us often use words that evoke a variety of responses. They claim that something is "improved," "more natural," or "50 percent better"—loaded words and phrases that are deceptive because they are suggestive. When a product is advertised as 50 percent better, for example, consumers need to ask, "50 percent better than what?" Advertisements rarely answer that question.

Doublespeak is another type of deceptive language characterized as evasive, euphemistic, confusing, and self-contradictory. It is language that "pretends to communicate but really does not" (Lutz, 1991, p. 17). Lutz (1991) cites a number of kinds

FIGURE 9-3 EXAMPLES OF DECEPTIVE LANGUAGE

Loaded Words	Doublespeak
best buy	bathroom tissue (toilet paper)
carefree	correctional facility (jail, prison)
discount	genuine imitation leather (vinyl)
extra strong	inner city (slum, ghetto)
guaranteed	passed away (died)
improved	personal preservation flotation device (life preserver)
longer lasting	pre-owned or experienced (used)
more natural	sanitation engineer (garbage collector)
ultra	senior citizen (old person)

Source: Based on Lutz, W. (1989). Doublespeak. New York: HarperCollins. © Gail E. Tompkins

of doublespeak, including euphemisms and inflated language. *Euphemisms* are words or phrases that are used to avoid a harsh or distasteful reality (e.g., "passed away"), often out of concern for someone's feelings rather than to deceive. *Inflated language* includes words intended to make the ordinary seem extraordinary. Thus, garbage collectors become "sanitation engineers," and used cars become "pre-owned" vehicles. Examples of deceptive language are listed in Figure 9-3. Students need to learn that people sometimes use words that only pretend to communicate; sometimes they use words to intentionally misrepresent, as when someone advertises a vinyl wallet as "genuine imitation leather" or a ring with a glass stone as a "faux diamond." Students need to be able to interpret deceptive language and to avoid using it themselves.

To sell products, advertisers use propaganda devices such as testimonials, the bandwagon effect, and rewards. Ten propaganda devices that students can learn to identify are listed in Figure 9-4. Students can view and listen to commercials to find examples of each propaganda device and discuss the effect the device has on them. They can also investigate to see how the same devices vary in commercials directed toward different audiences. For example, a snack food commercial with a sticker or toy in the package will appeal to young children while a cellphone advertisement offering a factory rebate will appeal to teenagers and adults. The propaganda device for both ads is the same: a reward! Propaganda devices can be used to sell ideas as well as products. Public service announcements about smoking or wearing seatbelts, as well as political advertisements, endorsements, and speeches, use these devices. Lessons and units that help students think critically about media elements understand aspects of their own consumption of media.

Strategies for Critical Viewing and Listening

Viewing and listening critically means evaluating the message. Students learn to use evaluating strategies to determine and judge the author's message. Teachers guide students to ask questions concerning appeal to their reasoning, character, and emotions to evaluate advertisements. The Center for Media Literacy (www.medialit.org) suggests that viewers and listeners ask the following key questions to deconstruct the message:

- Who created this image?
- What creative techniques are used to attract my attention?

FIGURE 9-4 PROPAGANDA DEVICES

1. Glittering Generality
Generalities such as "motherhood," "healthy lifestyle," and "*All Canadian*" are used to enhance the quality of a product or the character of a political figure. Propagandists select a generality (such as motherhood or healthy lifestyle) so attractive that viewers and listeners do not challenge the real point.

2. Testimonial
To convince people to purchase a product, an advertiser associates it with a popular personality such as an athlete or movie star. Viewers and listeners assume that the person offering the testimonial has the expertise to judge the quality of the product.

3. Transfer
Persuaders try to transfer the prestige, good looks, or ideas of a person or object to another person or object that will then be accepted. A celebrity, for example, is shown using Super Soap, and viewers are to believe that they can have youthful skin if they use this soap. Likewise, politicians appear with famous athletes or entertainers so that the lustre of the stars will rub off on them.

4. Name-Calling
Advertisers try to pin a bad label or negative Image on something they want viewers and listeners to dislike. The purpose is to cause unpleasant associations to rub off on the competition, whether a product, person, political party, or company.

5. Card Stacking in Comparisons
Persuaders choose only items that favour one side of an issue. Unfavourable facts are ignored. Viewers and listeners are led to believe one product or person or political party is better than another on basis of the limited information included.

6. Bandwagon
This technique appeals to people's need to be a part of a group. Advertisers claim that everyone is using this product or is part of this group and you should be, too. Viewers and listeners must ask if this is the case and if so, why.

7. Snob Appeal
Persuaders use snob appeal to attract the attention of people who want to be part of an exclusive group. Advertisements for expensive clothes, cosmetics, and gourmet foods often use this technique. Viewers and listeners must consider whether the product is of high quality or merely has an expensive nametag.

8. Rewards
Advertisers often offer rewards or rebates for buying their products. Viewers and listeners must consider the value of rewards and how they increase the product's cost.

9. Faulty Cause and Effect
Advertisers portray that use of a product or technique results in a positive effect when no real evidence of causality is shown. Viewers and listeners are intended to take the message at face value.

10. Repetition
Advertisers repeat the name or key words or phrases several times to invoke a lasting Image and associate the particular brand name or quality with the product.

Source: Adapted from Devine (1982), pp. 39–40 and ThinkQuest, www.think.com.
© Gail E. Tompkins

- How might different people understand this message differently?
- What values, lifestyles, and points of view are represented in, or omitted from, this message?
- Why is this message sent?

Asking these questions helps students learn to critically view print and nonprint media. In evaluating, students learn to be mindful that messages contain particular

FIGURE 9-5 **BOOKS THAT ENCOURAGE CRITICAL LISTENING**

Bright, A. (2012). *Before We Go*. Markham, ON: Red Deer Press. (U) 🍁
Creech, S. (2000). *The Wanderer*. New York: HarperCollins. (U)
Creech, S. (2001). *Love That Dog*. New York: HarperCollins. (M)
Duchesne, C., & Kunigis, P. (2012). *W Is for Wapiti! An Alphabet Songbook*. Montreal: The Secret Mountain. (P) 🍁
Edwards, W. (2004). *Monkey Business*. Toronto: Kids Can Press. (P–M) 🍁
Lawson, J. (2012). *Down in the Bottom of the Bottom of the Box*. Erin, Ontario: The Porcupine's Quill. (P–M) 🍁
Porter, P. (2005). *The Crazy Man*. Toronto: Groundwood Books. (U) 🍁
Tamberg, U. (2012). *The Darkest Corner of the World*. Toronto: Dancing Cat Books. (U) 🍁
Uluadluak, D. (2013). *Kamik: An Inuit Puppy Story*. Iqaluit, Nunavut: Inhabit Media. (P–M) 🍁
Wynne-Jones, T. (2003). *Ned Mouse Breaks Away*. Toronto: Groundwood Books. (P) 🍁

P = primary grades (K–2); M = middle grades (3–5); U = upper grades (6–8).

points of view about the world, are produced for commercial (and not educational) purposes, and are designed to attract and appeal to certain audiences.

As students listen to books read aloud; hear and view commercials and advertisements; listen to speakers; and view documentaries, videos such as those on YouTube, and other forms of public media, they need to ask themselves questions such as those above in order to critically evaluate the message.

Students use efferent listening strategies while evaluating because critical listening is an extension of efferent listening. They organize ideas, generalize main ideas, and monitor their understanding of a presentation. Figure 9-5 lists books that encourage critical listening. Few messages are presented in one medium; therefore, teachers help students use multiple questions and criteria to become critical viewers and listeners.

This teacher assists her students to ask critical questions about the texts they are reading in class.

wavebreakmedia/Shutterstock

The Visually Representing Process

Visual art has long been associated with literacy, but only recently has visually representing been recognized in curriculum documents as the sixth language art. *Visually representing* (or just *representing*) involves creating, constructing, and communicating meaning through a variety of media and forms, including drawings, sounds, pictures, illustrations, charts, graphs, posters, murals, photographs, dioramas, puppets, mime, sculptures, models, dramas, videos, and digital text with graphics. Visually representing is a way for students to construct both original meaning and their interpretations of text or other nonprint media. It enables students to communicate information and their ideas and understandings through alternative ways, often enhancing what they might communicate through oral or written text alone. Visually representing is not easily separated from the other language arts. Together with one or more other processes, it is a powerful means of communicating and learning. It allows students to both understand and employ the many ways in which images and language can be used to convey ideas, values, and beliefs.

Traditionally, the emphasis in language arts has been on representing thoughts, ideas, and feelings in written or spoken forms. Today, a broader concept of literacy and the availability of communication technology and multimedia have placed more emphasis on expression through multiple forms of communication. Language arts units give students opportunities to use visual, dramatic, and multimedia formats as both support their written and spoken messages and as stand alone forms of communication.

Purposes for Visually Representing

Students in language arts classrooms use a wide variety of representation for many purposes, mostly to help conceptualize and organize ideas, thoughts, or beliefs. They use concept maps, sets of images, sketches, and diagrams to help organize, often before writing. They enhance the meaning they construct of text or other media by constructing models, creating collages, creating illustrations and animations, and producing dramatic presentations. They demonstrate their interpretation of text through drama, visual arts, and multimedia presentations. Teachers encourage students to construct meaning of whole pieces of text, develop their conceptual understandings, and show their interpretation of theme or characters using visual media. Increasingly, students use multiple forms of media such as digital pictures and sound recordings to illustrate their understanding or interpretation of a text and to create their own original texts.

Integrating Representation Strategies

Learning to represent is not limited to language arts lessons. The strategies and techniques involved are often considered a part of art, technology, and drama curricula, but they are integrated into language arts units. During a thematic unit on penguins, a grade 1 class made an information quilt. One quilt square is shown in Figure 9-6. It is an example of children using technology to bring visual images and text together to represent their knowledge. Before making the quilt, the teacher read aloud to the children from several informational books, and they viewed videos of both real and animated penguins. They recorded what they learned on a class chart and referred to the chart as they created their quilt squares.

When teachers teach how to understand and use visual symbols, they involve students in thinking about and expressing what is often beyond their linguistic capabilities. That is, imagery and metaphor are keys to thinking and learning that are used from early childhood—initially unconsciously and later consciously. Students involved in using multiple sign systems declare that having a range of systems available gives them opportunity to think more broadly, to consider other ideas, to connect to memories, and to think through feelings (Short, Kauffman, & Kahn, 2003). Through representation, they often create sophisticated meaning and stretch their understanding past what they might do in writing or oral presentations. Also, for students who are frustrated by print-dominated learning, visuals and 3-D representations can be venues to access content and construct meaning (Wu & Newman, 2008). The representations students create

FIGURE 9-6 **A SQUARE FOR A GRADE 1 INFORMATION QUILT ON PENGUINS**

Penquens like to eat lots of fish.

Gail E. Tompkins

are a way of teachers knowing what students think, understanding their thoughts, and assessing their thinking. In doing so, respect for diversity and creativity are developed.

Teachers do not need to be artists or dramatists to facilitate students' visual representations. Students, too, need only basic skills and materials to create their representations. Ready access to the Internet and design software in most classrooms enhances the options available to students, as do apps for digital devices. After students are taught the essential elements of visual art and design through experience and example, they can apply these elements to create both visual art products and multimedia products. The elements and concepts shown in Figure 9-1 apply to both visual art products (such as watercolour paintings) and multimedia products (such as PowerPoint™ presentations and 3-D websites). Students can learn to critique their own and their classmates' products. Even young children can become aware of the impact on their communication of each of the elements. Individuals, small groups, or whole classes may do visually representing projects. One grade 6 class that read David Skuy's *Undergrounders* (2011) created digital retellings to depict twelve-year-old Jonathon's experience of living on the streets and playing hockey with the regular kids. The class became aware of the passage of time in the plot by describing

Jonathon's problems while trying to survive. Project suggestions in Figure 9-2 describe the kinds of representation students undertake.

Teachers can teach students about visual representation by making connections to the literature they are reading. For example, students in grade 6 in one neighbourhood school experienced the power of visual representation to enhance the meaning of printed text. Through reading and viewing Susan Bosak's *Dream: A Tale of Wonder, Wisdom & Wishes* (2004), they examined creations by fifteen internationally acclaimed artists who each used a different medium to illustrate each of the poems. Picture books provide excellent examples of one or more forms of representation and various art media. Figure 9-7 lists picture books according to medium.

FIGURE 9-7 PICTURE BOOK EXAMPLES OF A VARIETY OF ART MEDIA

Cartoons and Caricature
Clement, G. (2010). *The Great Poochini,* Toronto: Groundwood Books.
Gilmore, D. and Gay, M.-L. (2001). *Yuck, a Love Story.* Markham, ON: Fitzhenry & Whiteside.
Levert, M. (2001). *Island in the Soup,* Toronto: Groundwood Books.

Collage
Carle, E. (1998). *Hello, Red Fox.* New York: Simon & Schuster.
Jocelyn, M. (2000). *Hannah's Collections.* New York: Dutton Children's Books.
Oppenheim, J. (1996). *Have You Seen Bugs?* Richmond Hill, ON: Scholastic Canada.

Crayons and Coloured Pencils
Gregory, N. (1995). *How Smudge Came.* Red Deer, AB: Red Deer College Press.
McFarlane, S., & Lightburn, R. (1993). *Waiting for the Whales* Victoria, BC: Orca Book Publishers.
Zeman, L. (1999). *Sinbad: From the Tales of the Thousand and One Nights.* Montreal: Tundra Books.

Drawing
Greenwood, B. (1999). *Pioneer Thanksgiving.* Toronto: Kids Can Press.
Macaulay, D. (1977). *Castle.* Boston: Houghton Mifflin.
Munsch, R. (1992). *Purple, Green and Yellow.* Toronto: Annick Press.
Winstanley, N. (2011). *Cinnamon Baby.* Toronto: Kids Can Press.

Mixed Media
Goble, P. (2003). *Mystic Horse.* New York: HarperCollins.
Lewis, W. (2003). *In Abby's Hands.* Calgary: Red Deer Press.
Schotter, R. (2006). *The Boy Who Loved Words.* New York: Schwartz & Wade.

Painting
Bouchard, D. (2006). *Nokum Is My Teacher.* Calgary: Red Deer Press.
Harrison, T. (2002). *O Canada.* Toronto: Kids Can Press.
Lee, D. (2011). *Biomimicry: Inventions Inspired by Nature.* Toronto: Kids Can Press.

Pastels (Chalk)
Coerr, E. (1993). *Sadako.* New York: Putnam.
Dewey, A. (1995). *The Sky.* Seattle, WA: Green Tiger Press.

Sisulu, E. (1996). *The Day Gogo* Went to Vote. Boston: Little, Brown.
Van Allsburg, C. (1985). *The Polar Express.* Boston: Houghton Mifflin.

Pen and Pencil/Ink
Meyrick, J. (2007). *Gracie, the Public Gardens Duck.* Halifax: Nimbus.
Sís, P. (1998). *Tibet: Through the Red Box.* New York: Farrar, Straus & Giroux.
Stinson, K. (1982). *Red Is Best.* Toronto: Annick Press.

Photography
Gerszak, R. (2011). *Beyond Bullets: A Photo Journal of Afghanistan.* Toronto: Annick Press.
Hoban, T. (2000). *Cubes, Cones, Cylinders* and Spheres. New York: Greenwillow.
Levine, K. (2002). *Hana's Suitcase.* Toronto: Second Story Press.

Plasticine
Reid, B. (2003). *The Subway Mouse.* Toronto: Scholastic Canada.
Reid, B. (2006). *Fox Walked Alone.* Toronto: Scholastic Canada.
Reid, B. (2011). *Picture a Tree.* Toronto: North Winds Press.

Printmaking
Ballantyne, A. (1991). *Wisakyjak and the New World.* Waterloo, ON: Penumbra Press.
Bouchard, D. (1990). *The Elders Are Watching.* Tofino, BC: Eagle Dancer Enterprises.
Martin, J. B. (1998). *Snowflake Bentley.* Boston: Houghton Mifflin.

Sculpture and Paper Sculpture
Fleming, D. (1994). *Barnyard Banter.* New York: Henry Holt.
Hoyt-Goldsmith, D. (1990). *Totem Pole.* New York: Holiday House.
Ruurs, M. (2007). *In My Backyard.* Toronto: Tundra Books.

Watercolour
Bouchard, D. (1996). *The Dust Bowl.* Toronto: Kids Can Press.
Chase, E. (1996). *Secret Dawn.* Richmond Hill, ON: North Winds Press.
Gay, M. L. (2000). *Stella Queen of the Snow.* Toronto: Douglas & McIntyre.

Teaching Critical Listening, Viewing, and Visually Representing

The steps in teaching students to be critical listeners, viewers, and visual representers are similar to the steps in teaching aesthetic and efferent listening strategies. In the following teaching strategy, students view commercials to examine propaganda devices and persuasive language. Later they can create their own commercials and advertisements using available digital technologies. The steps in a listening, viewing, and visually representing strategy are presented in the following Step by Step box:

USING ADVERTISEMENTS

Students can use the same step-by-step procedures and activities to critique print and nonprint advertisements. Students can collect their favourite advertisements from a variety of sources, including magazines, Internet websites, and product packages. They can also collect advertisements for such activities as attending concerts and adopting lifestyle changes or habits such as being environmentally conscious. They examine advertisements and then decide how the writer is trying to persuade them to purchase the product or make choices. They can identify techniques used such as varying the proportion of text and pictures in the advertisements. Toy advertisements often feature large, colourful pictures; cosmetic advertisements feature large pictures of beautiful women; but advertisements for medicines devote more space to text. Students point out sports stars and entertainment personalities in many advertisements. Even primary-grade students recognize intellectual, character, and emotional appeals in these advertisements.

MINILESSONS ON CRITICAL LISTENING, VIEWING, AND VISUALLY REPRESENTING

Teachers teach minilessons to introduce, practise, and review procedures, concepts, and strategies and skills related to critical listening and viewing. Chapter 4, "Listening and Speaking in the Classroom," presents topics for minilessons on critical listening. These topics can be taught when students are studying advertisements as part of language arts units, social studies, health, or science lessons.

USING PICTURE BOOKS AND GRAPHIC NOVELS TO TEACH CRITICAL VIEWING

In picture books and graphic novels, the message depends upon the pictures as much as or more than the text. The pictures and images must be accurate and synchronized with the text, but they extend the text. When students view picture books, they first see each picture as a whole, and then notice the individual details that make up the whole. When they read graphic novels, they are attracted by the visual images and develop an appreciation for artistic styles. Books that mix both text and graphics are considered a hybrid form. Brian Selznick's *The Invention of Hugo Cabret* (2007) is an example of a book that switches back and forth between text and illustrations. When teachers present these books to children, they provide time and guidance for careful viewing, pointing out the illustrator's use of such

Listening, Viewing, and Visually Representing Strategy

1 Introduce advertisements. The teacher shows the students a collection of advertisements including those familiar to students from print and nonprint media, as well as those from award-winning advertisements. The teacher leads discussion about the purpose of each, and uses these questions to probe students' thinking about persuasion and propaganda:

- What is the purpose of the advertisement?
- Who is the intended audience?
- Does the advertisement appeal to character, reason, or emotion?
- Does the advertisement make sweeping generalizations or unsupported inferences?
- Does the advertisement make use of any propaganda devices?
- Do you accept the message?

2 Explain persuasion and propaganda. The teacher presents the terms *persuasion* and *propaganda*. The teacher introduces the persuasion and propaganda devices and shows the advertisements again to look for examples of each device.

Then the teacher introduces the terms *loaded words* and *doublespeak*, and shows the advertisements a third time to look for examples of deceptive language.

3 Analyze deceptive language. The teacher has students work in small groups to critique an advertisement (print or nonprint) in respect to the types of persuasion, propaganda devices, and deceptive language used. Students might also want to critique the techniques of visual design used or test the claims made in the advertisement.

4 Review concepts. The teacher reviews the concepts about persuasion, propaganda devices, and deceptive language introduced in the first three steps. It may be helpful for students to make charts about these concepts.

5 Provide practice. The teacher presents a new set of advertisements for students to critique. The teacher asks students to identify persuasion, propaganda devices, and deceptive language in them.

6 Have students create advertisements. The teacher has students apply what they have learned about persuasion, propaganda devices, and deceptive language by creating their own products and writing and producing their own advertisements to sell them. Possible products include breakfast cereals, toys, beauty and diet products, and sports equipment. Students might also create homework and pet-sitting services to advertise, or choose community or environmental issues to campaign for or against. As the students present the commercials, classmates act as critical listeners and viewers to detect persuasion, propaganda devices, loaded words, and doublespeak.

techniques as line, colour, space, and shape for particular effects. For example, a teacher might draw attention to how the black and white cartoons in the graphic novel Bone series (beginning with *Out from Boneville*, J. Smith, 1995) was converted into colour, and how colour, shape, and space are used together to represent characters in *Smile* (Telgemeier, 2012). Young children's attention is also drawn to special effects such as how some characters are rendered in grey and blue and others through colour in Dave Whamond's *Oddrey* (2012), and the soft-to-touch feel of Arctic bear in *Snow Bear* (Harper, 2002). Children not only notice the textual features, but also make links to their own experiences, interpret and predict new information, and make affective and evaluative responses. They make meaning from images in texts regardless of whether they can decode the words of the text (Walsh, 2003).

The techniques and materials used in picture book illustrations are often difficult for classroom teachers to determine. Some information can be found in a foreword or afterword, or on the jacket flap, cover, or last page of the book. Teachers also learn about illustrations by consulting the author's and illustrator's websites. Figure 9-8 lists award-winning picture books that teachers use to teach illustration media and critical viewing.

FIGURE 9-8 RECENTLY PUBLISHED AWARD-WINNING PICTURE BOOKS TEACHERS USE TO TEACH ILLUSTRATION MEDIA AND CRITICAL VIEWING

The **Amelia Frances Howard-Gibbon Illustrator's Award** honours excellence in children's illustration in a book published in Canada.

2005	Wallace Edwards. *Monkey Business*. Toronto: Kids Can Press, 2004.
2006	Leslie E. Watts *The Baabaasheep Quartet* Markham, ON: Fitzhenry & Whiteside, 2005.
2007	Melanie Watt. *Scaredy Squirrel*. Toronto: Kids Can Press, 2006.
2008	Melanie Watt. *Chester*. Toronto: Kids Can Press, 2007.
2009	Dušan Petričić. *Mattland* by Hazel Hutchins and Gail Herbert. Toronto: Annick Press, 2008.
2010	Barbara Reid. *Perfect Snow*. Toronto: North Winds Press, 2009.
2011	Marie-Louise Gay. *Roslyn Rutabaga and the Biggest Hole on Earth!* Toronto: Groundwood Books, 2010.
2012	Matthew Forsythe. *My Name Is Elizabeth!* by Annika Dunklee. Toronto: Kids Can Press, 2011.
2013	Soyeon Kim. *You Are Stardust* by Elin Kelsey. Toronto: Owlkids Books, 2012.
2014	Klassen, J. *The Dark* by Lemony Snicket. Toronto: HarperCollins Publishers.
2015	Gay, M. L. *Any Questions?* Toronto: Groundwood Books.

The **Elizabeth Mrazik-Cleaver Canadian Picture Book Award** is presented annually to a Canadian children's book illustrator whose work on a new book is deemed both original and worthy.

2004	Stéphane Poulin. *Un chant de Noël* by Lucie Papineau. Saint-Lambert, QC: Dominique et compagnie, 2004.
2005	Geneviève Côté. *The Lady of Shalott* by Alfred Lord Tennyson. Toronto: KidsCan Press, 2005.
2006	Kady MacDonald Denton. *Snow* by Joan Clark. Toronto: Groundwood Books, 2006.
2007	Stéphane Jorisch. *The Owl and the Pussycat* by Edward Lear. Toronto: Kids Can Press, 2006.
2008	Christine Delezenne. *La Clé* by Angèle Delaunois. Montreal: Éditions de L'Isatis, 2008.
2009	Oleg Lipchencko. *Alice's Adventures in Wonderland* by Lewis Carroll. Toronto: Tundra Books, 2008.
2010	Julie Flett. *Owls See Clearly at Night: A Michif Alphabet*. Vancouver: Simply Read Books, 2010.
2011	Cybèle Young. *A Few Blocks*. Toronto: Groundwood Books, 2011.
2012	Isabelle Arsenault, *Virginia Wolf* by Kyo Maclear. Toronto: Kids Can Press, 2012.
2013	Morstad, J. How To. Vancouver: Simply Read Books.
2014	Tekavec, H. and Pratt, P. *Stop, Thief!* Toronto: Kids Can Press.

For a complete list of each award since its inception, see the Canadian Children's Book Centre website, at www.bookcentre.ca.

Differentiating to Meet the Needs of Every Student

Because students of all ages and all reading abilities are bombarded with visual images, it is especially important that all students be thoughtful and critical viewers. Students need to learn not only the specific critical viewing skills related to persuasion and propaganda, but also the more general skill of varying the way they view images in accordance with the purposes for which they are viewing. To do this, they must learn to recognize the elements that affect their viewing, and the ways those elements affect the meanings they construct from the visual texts. The Differentiating box lists ways to adapt viewing and visually representing instruction to meet the needs of every student.

Assessing Students' Critical Viewing and Visually Representing

Teachers can assess students' knowledge of critical listening, viewing, and visually representing by having them first view and listen to advertisements or other oral and visual presentations, and then note their recognition of techniques used and their effects.

DIFFERENTIATING

Viewing and Visually Representing Instruction to Meet the Needs of Every Student

1. Identify a Purpose for Viewing

When students view images, they need to have a specific purpose for viewing and to know what they will be expected to do after viewing. Ask students to state their purpose and how they will use the information gathered. Because viewing can be a passive activity if not structured, teachers need to help students clarify the reason for viewing and how the information will be used.

2. Provide Frequent Opportunities to View

Learning to view, like learning to read, requires time on task. Provide students with frequent opportunities to view for multiple purposes followed by an opportunity to discuss what was viewed. Teachers can include words that describe visual elements and techniques in the classroom word wall to assist students in using appropriate vocabulary in discussions.

3. Make the Viewing Process Visible

Viewing is an invisible process. Teachers can help students make it visible by asking them to speak and write about what they do when they view. Teachers encourage students to think about how the author of the visual image perceived the information, what techniques the author chose to convey information, and why those techniques were chosen. Helping students talk about websites they are viewing also helps to make the process visible.

4. Explore Many Examples of Visual Images

Teachers guide students to explore and read the many visual images they encounter, including, but not limited to the visual images in their textbooks (graphs, illustrations, charts, and so on), in graphic novels and comics, and in digital texts they read in school, such as websites. Teachers provide practice in interpreting the information and opportunity to share their interpretations.

5. Provide Frequent Opportunities to Represent

Students need many opportunities to communicate their ideas and demonstrate their learning in a variety of forms. They need to explore use of various media and forms to discover the characteristics, purposes, and effects of using each one. For some students, visual communication may be a means of significantly clarifying or enhancing the message they are able to convey.

6. Give Students Guidance and Explicit Instruction

Although much is learned by observing and exploring, students also need explicit instruction in the strategies used for visually representing. Well-paced instruction in specific strategies needed for story mapping, storyboarding, graphing, charting, role-playing, and creating models, pictorial displays, and images helps students develop effective visually representing skills. Similarly, students also need explicit and well-paced instruction to enable them to use technology to visually represent and communicate their thoughts and ideas.

Teachers can also evaluate their students' recognition and use of critical techniques in their own productions of advertisements, images, 3-D displays, or other visual presentations. A third way to assess students' understanding of critical viewing is to have them critique picture book illustrations or the visuals presented in nonprint media such as DVDs. Critical listening and viewing are interrelated in such tasks, and teachers should consider both when assessing students' knowledge and skills. Further, the production of illustrations and images for a variety of purposes and the creation of multimedia presentations requires application of critical analysis and can provide assessment information regarding student learning.

For assessing and evaluating media literacy work, it is important to identify the key concepts of media literacy, such as that media is constructed by others, and then examine the ability of students to identify issues related to this and other concepts. Teachers should consider how students apply what they have learned about media when viewing and creating videos, multimedia presentations, websites, advertisements, and blogs. In assessing and evaluating, not only students' use of media, but their understanding of it is also critical.

Review

Viewing and visually representing are the most recent additions to the language arts and are referred to as visual literacy. A broader concept of literacy and the ready availability of communication technology and multimedia in students' lives have made them essential parts of the curriculum. Media literacy is about teaching students how to understand, use, and evaluate the media—music, comics, television, video games, the Internet, and ads—surrounding them. Through viewing and visually representing activities, students learn to vary the way they view for different purposes, and they learn the various ways authors produce and use visual images to convey information and ideas. In turn, they learn to create their own visual images, to visually represent, using different procedures, strategies, and skills to communicate their knowledge, understandings, and beliefs.

The following key concepts are presented in this chapter:

1. Viewing and visually representing are essential language arts.
2. Visual literacy is the ability to see and understand, and to think, create, and communicate graphically.
3. Students need to learn viewing strategies to make the most of their learning from visual images.
4. Students need to learn to use visually representing strategies to enhance their communication abilities.
5. Media literacy is the ability to critically evaluate media in order to reflect and make ethical decisions in today's world.
6. Critical viewing, like critical listening, involves students in evaluation of messages from others.
7. Picture books, graphic novels, comics, commercials, and advertisements are excellent resources for teaching visual literacy.

8. Students need to learn elements of visual art and design and techniques of propaganda and persuasion to view critically and create meaning through representation.

9. Students need multiple opportunities to visually represent their learning using a variety of strategies because representation enhances learning not only of the language arts, but also other areas of curriculum.

Theory to Practice

1. Visit a classroom and observe how viewing and visually representing are taught and how students use their viewing and representing skills.

2. Interview primary students about how they read picture books. Ask questions such as these:
   - When you read a picture book, do you look at the pictures first?
   - What do you think the illustrator was thinking when he or she created these pictures? (Show the students a particular picture from a familiar book.)
   - Do you use the pictures to help with words you do not recognize?

3. Read a wordless picture book with primary students. Take note of how they read the illustrations to compose a story. What elements of the illustrations do they attend to, in order to help compose their stories?

4. Work with middle- and upper-grade students to create illustrated stories using pictures and symbols available as clipart on the Internet.

5. Work with students to enhance written informational text with visual images. As they work, talk with students about their choices of text forms such as graphs, diagrams, images, and charts, and the effect they have on the message.

6. Study the illustrations of one or more graphic novels. Read the illustrators' websites to gain insights into the techniques used.

7. Experiment with software and apps designed to create visual images to help you depict your understandings of a topic related to learning and teaching the language arts.

8. Work with upper-grade students to create multimedia advertisements for products and services they use. Take note of the decisions they make and skills they use as they incorporate visuals and sounds to deliver their message.

Literacy in Action

Chapter 10: Meaningful Connections between Visual Art and Literature

Procedure

It is my goal as an elementary teacher, and also as an artist, to help students make linkages between literature and visual art. Few of the art lessons I use are my original inventions. I attend workshops; exchange units with other teachers; and scan teacher resource publications, and various websites for relevant, skill-based art ideas; but I strive to create a meaningful context, the right teaching moment, to introduce the art so that other realms of learning can be applied and reinforced while students are engaged in artistic endeavours that exercise distinct domains of thinking and intelligence. One of my favourite lessons integrates curriculum expectations from the language arts, visual art, and social studies. It involves the students in oral reading, art-making, and procedural writing.

> "I find the writing they produce is confident, well organized, and descriptive. It is also a great way for me to learn about the connections they have made, the concepts they have internalized, and their thoughts and opinions about what we are doing."
>
> Heidi Jardine-Stoddart

I plan this lesson for after students have spent time in social studies developing mapping skills and familiarity with distinguishing physical features of the provinces and territories. At this time, in the language arts my students and I are in the midst of a week-long focus on great Canadian picture books. On maps in the classroom, we indicate the home of each author we read. Students are also near the end of a visual art unit on colour

At this point, I introduce the writing of Robert Service and the art of Ted Harrison. I read to the students *The Cremation of Sam McGee* (Service, 1907/1986) and they are captivated by the haunting words and mesmerizing pictures. Toward the end of the poem, some are whispering along with me, "There are strange things done in the midnight sun by the men who moil for gold…." This leads to energetic discussion about the setting (Yukon Territory), plot, main characters, form, and what it was about this book that caught their attention. We then make connections between the work of the author and of the artist. We talk about how they have created a feeling or mood through their choice of vocabulary or colour. We then brainstorm a list of questions we have about this author, and students break into small groups, to research. Shortly we regroup and record the groups' answers and responses on a chart profile of the author. We display our collection of profiles to remind us of all the authors we have read.

The next day, I read *O Canada*, another text illustrated by Ted Harrison (2002). We focus on the illustrations and discuss pertinent vocabulary, such as *landscape*. I guide students to pay particular attention to the artist's unusual colour choices, his application of colour, and how he creates a feeling of space or depth in his artwork.

As one young student later explained at home, "Mom, did you know that trees can be pink and the sky can be green? It all depends on how you look at it and how you feel." Armed with these insights, I have students identify a specific location or region that they want to depict and we set to work on a very prescriptive, step-by-step lesson designed for the successful creation of Ted Harrison–like landscapes. Once students have settled into the absorbing task of filling in the sections, soft classical or new age music facilitates their concentration; an instrumental version of "O Canada" suits perfectly.

Assessment

An important part of my job is to design lessons so that students experience success. This includes identifying the skills and concepts I intend to teach and making them clear to my students right from the start. To more objectively assess their work, whether written or visual, I use a rubric that outlines the skills and concepts that students are expected to demonstrate. Students use the rubric as a checklist to monitor their progress, and I use it to assess their use of the identified skills and concepts.

Another assessment I use is our weekly art journals—a regular part of our classroom routine that enriches my assessment of students' understanding. Art journal writing is a great way for me to learn about the connections students have made, the concepts they have internalized, and their thoughts and opinions about what we are doing.

Adaptation

This lesson can be adapted to other authors/illustrators. Eric Carle's stories are well suited to early primary grades, and his technique of illustrating can be modified to accommodate young students working at painting, cutting, and pasting. I've also introduced the concepts of relief sculpture and texture using Barbara Reid's stories and Plasticine illustrations.

Reflection

Opportunities for integrating curriculum grow increasingly evident as my students and I develop our sense of interconnectedness through such experiences as the one presented here. I find art-related experiences contribute to students' positive outlook, their enthusiasm, and the meaningfulness of their learning.

In this instance, integration resulted in student recollections that intermingle the poetry of Robert Service, the artwork of Ted Harrison, the geography of Canada, and the concept of free expression. I became aware of this several months later when our class was visiting a local art gallery. A young student stood gazing at a painting, "Oh my gosh, Ms Jardine," he whispered, "it's a real Ted Harrison." He then turned and looked at me. "Remember, he's the guy who did the pictures in that book you showed us and we maked pictures like him with all the different colours . . . remember?" he asked. Yes, I remembered, and more importantly, so did he.

From the classroom of Heidi Jardine-Stoddart
Elementary Visual Arts Mentor/Itinerant Teacher
Anglophone School District–South
New Brunswick

The Language Arts and the Fine Arts

Students scan their city's newspaper for stories of musical and dramatic performances.

Nan Austin/Modesto Bee/ZUMA Press Inc/Alamy Stock Photo

LEARNING OUTCOMES

After you read this chapter, you should be able to

1. Relate children's learning of the Language Arts to all of their intelligences

2. Identify some of the important reasons for integrating the fine arts with the language arts

3. Explain how to use children's literature to help children develop their visual artistic abilities

4. Describe strategies that will encourage students to make linkages between literature and music

5. Explain ways to incorporate drama in the day-to-day language arts experiences of the classroom

" In this century, literacy is more than reading and writing—it is a person's ability to thoughtfully identify, gather, analyze and use information so that they can control the decisions they make in their lives" (Hansen, 2003). Teaching the language arts in an integrated way is important in developing children's literacy. Children do not learn language skills in isolation from each other. Although we separate the language arts to speak about them and to discuss the content and structure of each process, it is clear that children learn their language best in an integrated way. Ability as a writer is enhanced by ability as a reader, and proficiency in listening and viewing enhances ability to represent visually. Also, children can expand their capacity to listen as they learn music and to establish a greater understanding of their physical and emotional selves as they learn through drama and dance.

Integrating the Fine Arts

The arts have long been valued for their aesthetic contributions to education, and studies demonstrate their contribution to academic performance (Baker, 2013). Other forms of **integration,** too, enhance a child's literacy development. Gardner's research on intelligence (Blythe & Gardner, 1990) suggests that we don't have one fixed intelligence, but at least seven separate ones (see Figure 10-1). Gardner defines *intelligence* as our capacity to solve problems and create products that would be valued in a cultural setting. Four of the seven intelligences (verbal, visual, musical, and kinesthetic) parallel the fine arts areas of visual art, music, dance, and drama. The other intelligences are also connected to the language arts and the fine arts: logical, interpersonal, and intrapersonal.

Our ability to communicate effectively not only through language but also through visual art, music, dance, and drama is an indicator of our capabilities as effective human beings participating fully in our cultural setting. We want to develop these intelligences in our children primarily through the language arts, teaching them to be effective users of language in all its forms. We also want to enhance their abilities by integrating the skills they have learned in the language arts with the fine arts.

FIGURE 10-1 GARDNER'S SEVEN INTELLIGENCES

Category	Likes, Needs, Is Good At ...
Verbal "Word lovers"	Seeing and hearing words, talking and discussing, telling stories, reading and writing (e.g., poetry, literature), memorizing (e.g., places, names, facts), using or appreciating humour, using word play, doing word puzzles
Visual "Imagers"	Thinking in pictures and seeing spatial relationships, drawing, building, designing and creating, day-dreaming and imagining, looking at pictures, watching movies, reading maps and charts, doing mazes and puzzles
Musical "Music lovers"	Singing, humming and listening to music, playing instruments, responding to music (e.g., likes to tap out rhythms), composing music, picking up sounds, remembering melodies, noticing pitches and rhythms, timbre
Interpersonal "People-people"	Lots of friends, joining groups, talking out or mediating and resolving conflicts, empathetic and understanding, sharing, comparing, relating, cooperating, interviewing others, leadership, and organizing
Intrapersonal "Loners"	Aware of inner self (e.g., feelings, intentions, goals), working alone, having own space and self-pacing, focuses on own feelings and dreams, pursuing own interests and goals, original thinking, self-reflecting
Logical "Reasoners"	Experimenting, asking questions, problem-solving, figuring out how things work, exploring abstract relationships and discovering patterns, categorizing and classifying, reasoning and using logic (inductive and deductive), math, playing logic games
Kinesthetic "Body movers"	Moving and using body to communicate, touching and using nonverbal communication (e.g., hands, face, gestures, hands-on learning), kinesthetic-tactile learning, sports, dancing, drama, and acting

Source: Based on Gardner, H. (1993). *Multiple intelligences: The theory in practice.* New York: HarperCollins.
© Gail E. Tompkins

Reasons for Integrating the Fine Arts with the Language Arts

There are a number of reasons for integrating the fine arts with the language arts:

1. *The fine arts are fundamental components of all cultures and time periods.* Literature and fine arts are a part of our cultural legacy. It is through our stories, music, art, and drama that we define our cultural heritage and allow our students the opportunity to link our culture with other cultures around the world. Our tradition in the language arts of providing students with the opportunity to read stories from different cultural traditions ought to expand to include the music, art, dance, and drama of these other cultures.

2. *The fine arts teach us that what we think or feel cannot be reduced to words.* As important as language is as an expression of who and what we are, it is equally important to remember that our feelings and emotions are often better communicated through the fine arts. We recognize the value of high-quality children's literature in part because of the visual art that the illustrator has created to enhance our experience of the story. It is this combination of story read or heard and story seen that creates the aesthetic experience we call literature.

3. *Students who engage in the fine arts have the opportunity to "be smart in different ways."* We run the risk as language arts teachers of placing too much emphasis on the role of language in learning in the sense that we sometimes ignore the place and value of other expressive arts in the learning of children. It is important that children be given opportunities to experience their own learning in a variety of ways, moving beyond intellectual approaches to more intuitive, reflective, or hands-on approaches. The arts can be a gateway to learning. Integrating arts into literacy teaching benefits students in innumerable ways (Delacruz & An, 2014).

4. *The fine arts develop the brain.* We need to find the balance in our teaching so that those entrusted to our care can develop all of their abilities. It is true that children need to develop their ability to think logically and analytically. They also need to learn to trust gifts from their senses and cultivate their intuitive abilities. It is important that we accommodate all learners in our approach to teaching the language arts. All the initiatives we undertake to integrate the fine arts with the language arts will enhance development of the whole learner.

5. *The fine arts provide avenues of achievement for students who might not be otherwise successful.* Allowing students to demonstrate their abilities in a variety of ways ensures that students will find appropriate and relevant expressions for their abilities and interests. In an integrated language arts unit on memory, for example, students were exposed to Steven Gammel's art through his illustrations of Mem Fox's story *Wilfrid Gordon McDonald Partridge* (1996). They also listened to the music of Shirley Eikhart's her song "Emily Remembers," and explored informational books such as *How Does Your Brain Work* (2003), by Don Curry. Students were given choices in how they responded to the various artifacts. Some responded by visually representing in response to the music (in digital and non-digital forms); others chose to write in response to the stories. Still others gathered facts, wrote reports, and shared information with the class.

6. *The fine arts develop the values of perseverance and hard work.* "The self-discipline required to master an instrument or learn lines from a school play can transfer to academic learning" (Cornett & Smithrim, 2001).

7. *The fine arts are a necessary part of life.* The fine arts help students cultivate their abilities as thinkers and doers. They learn to focus through the fine arts on the broad pictures as well as minute details and learn to see and listen in different ways.

They cultivate an aesthetic sense of the world and can then use that new insight to solve problems in other areas of their lives.

8. ***There is a strong positive relationship between the fine arts and academic success.*** The fine arts are participatory. They engage students physically, emotionally, intellectually, and spiritually. They help children integrate their lives and, as such, offer tremendous potential for enhancing academic achievement.

9. ***The fine arts offer alternative forms of assessment and evaluation.*** Extensive use of **portfolios** as assessment tools in music, art, drama, and writing provides us with examples of effective ways of measuring growth and achievement beyond the traditional tests.

10. ***Canada's National Symposium on Arts Education calls for arts education for all children.*** The symposium's vision is based on the following principles (Cornett & Smithrim, 2001):

   - that participation in the arts is a fundamental right of all citizens
   - that all Canadians should have access to quality arts education through publicly financed education programs
   - that arts education programs should be delivered by teachers who have the capacity to deliver quality programs
   - that communities should promote and support participation in the arts
   - that the arts are vital to life and learning

The Language Arts and Visual Art

"The arts make vivid the fact that neither words in their literal form nor numbers exhaust what we can know. The limits of our language do not define the limits of our cognition" (Eisner, 2002, p. 72). Language carries meaning beyond the literal "facts" of a story and metaphor is more than a literary device. It is a conceptual framework by which we organize our experience. One of our goals as language arts teachers is to teach children to understand and appreciate the metaphors that guide the ways in which they view the world, and one of the important avenues to exploring metaphor in this sense is through art and stories.

A starting point to integrate art and language is through **children's literature**. In children's literature, illustrator and author work together to produce an integrated aesthetic work that children can experience on many levels. The illustrator represents the story in visual form, illuminating and expanding the words to create a work that is visually responsive to the text, thereby enhancing and elaborating its meaning. Illustrators choose the media that best represents and enhances the story. Children can begin exploring their own sense of visual representation through an introduction to the work of illustrators and through exposure to the vast collection of exemplary art in the literature they read and explore.

The books of Toronto artist, writer, and illustrator Barbara Reid are excellent examples of creative artistic ability. Reid's Plasticine artwork has won her many awards and readers around the world. In her book *The Party* (Reid, 1997, 2012), children are invited to explore the many facets of attending a family reunion (see page 362). The story captures all the fun of a family summer picnic—the games, food, family, and friends. The illustrations allow children to explore the story through their other senses, and often children will be seen touching Reid's illustrations, wanting the tactile experience of the Plasticine artwork as they visually explore the story.

FIGURE 10-2 BOOKS TO LINK LITERATURE AND ART

Carle, E. (2011). *The Artist Who Painted a Blue Horse*. New York: Philomel Books. (P)

Daywalt, D. (2013). *The Day the Crayons Quit*. New York: Philomel Books. (P–M)

Daywalt, D. (2015). *The Day the Crayons Came Home*. New York: Philomel Books. (P–M)

Guitierrez, E. (2005). *Picturescape*. Toronto, ON: Simply Read Books. (M–U) ✦

Hooper, M. (2006). *Celebrity Cat: With Paintings from Art Galleries Around the World*. London: Frances Lincoln. (P–M)

Johnson, C. (1955, 2015). *Harold and the Purple Crayon*. New York: Harper Collins. (P)

McDonnell, P. (2006). *Art*. New York: Little Brown. (P)

Novak, B. (2014). *The Book With No Pictures*. New York: Dial Books. (P–M)

Raczka, B. (2006). *Here's Looking at Me: How Artists See Themselves*. Minneapolis, MN: Millbrook Press. (M–U)

Rodriguez, R. (2007). *Through Georgia's Eyes*. New York: Henry Holt. (P–M)

Rosenstock, B. (2014). *The Noisy Paint Box: The Colours and Sounds of Kandinsky's Abstract Art*. New York: Knopf. (P)

Stoll, E. (2000). *Mouse Paint*. New York: Harcourt. (P)

Thomas, P. (2007). *Nature's Paintbox*. Minneapolis, MN: Millbrook Press. (M–U)

Tougas, C. (2008). *Art Supplies*. Victoria, BC: Orca Book Publishers. (M) ✦

Tullet, H. (2014). *Mix it Up*. San Francisco, CA: Chronicle Books. (P)

VandeGriek, S. (2002). *The Art Room*. Toronto, ON: Douglas & McIntyre. (U) ✦

Winter, J. (2013). *Henri's Scissors*. New York: Beach Lane Books. (P)

Cornett and Smithrim (2001) suggest that visual art needs to be experienced as a whole before it is broken down into its component parts, which means that children need to view and make art first, so that a desire to want to know more is developed in them. Through exposure to the literature written and illustrated for them, children learn about visual art elements and design concepts. Specifically, they learn about colour, line, shape, texture, form, pattern, space, contrast, light, composition, perspective, balance, and symmetry. The literature presented in Figure 10-2 provides children with exemplary examples of artists' use of visual art elements and a variety of media.

Having experienced exceptional art in books such as Barbara Reid's books, students want to create art for themselves using various techniques. Giving students opportunities to work with many media to produce illustrations for their own stories helps them develop their artistic sensibilities and their awareness of how ideas and concepts can be visually represented. Regardless of the medium they use, students need to have many opportunities to express themselves in words and pictures. Teachers need to help them see that the goal is not perfect art, but meaning-making. Like the children in Vande Griek and Milelli's *The Art Room* (2002), who learn to express themselves when they paint with Emily Carr, all students need to know that their creative expressions are valued. The website www.thatartistwoman.org contains a variety of creative ideas for teachers and parents that combine visual art with writing.

Students can learn a great deal by viewing the work of accomplished artists. Sharing books such as Elisa Gutiérrez's *Picturescape* (2005), in which the main character goes on a field trip to an art gallery, is one way to introduce them to some of Canada's well-known artists—e.g., Emily Carr, William Kurelek, Tom Thompson, Alex Colville, Christopher Pratt, and David Blackwood. While sharing this wordless picture book and absorbing the illustrations, students can compose their own stories inspired by the art. Examining books illustrated by Bill Slavin, such as the award-winning *Transformed* (2007), shows how cartooning can communicate detailed information in a fun way.

The Profile at the beginning of this chapter provides another example of an activity that combines language and art. Heidi Jardine-Stoddart helps her grade 4 class explore the artwork of Ted Harrison. Children enjoy the illustrations of

"Want to play sharks?" Danny asks.
Yes we do!
"I'll be It. If I catch you,
then you're a shark too!"

The Party: The Party © 1997 by Barbara Reid. Used by permission of Scholastic Canada Ltd

The lawnchairs are lifeboats,
the grass is all water.
Kate leaps to the birdbath —
too late! Danny's got her.
We're all in the game at the party.

The Party: The Party © 1997 by Barbara Reid. Used by permission of Scholastic Canada Ltd

Robert Service's poems "The Cremation of Sam McGee" and "The Shooting of Dan McGrew." Ted Harrison's unique artistic style is one that children enjoy and often wish to emulate. As language arts teachers, we can support and extend our students in their artistic development by encouraging them in the study of Ted Harrison's painting style and in the replication of his style through their own stories and poetry. Students can also explore their visual artistic abilities using digital drawing programs such as Kid Pix or other paint-and-draw software.

Students display their visual artistic talents through illustrating stories or poetry that they read. Writers who use particularly vivid and descriptive language can be the vehicles for this development. Natalie Babbitt's engaging novel *Tuck Everlasting* (1975) is an example of this quality of writing. Eleven-year-old Winnie Foster, one of the central characters in the story, meets a remarkable family, the Tucks, who live forever, frozen in time, sharing a secret that must be kept. Winnie discovers their secret and is taken by Mae Tuck and her two sons, Jesse and Miles, to their small cottage in the woods, where she must be convinced not to reveal to anyone what she knows. Natalie Babbitt's description of the Tucks' house is particularly memorable as this part of the story unfolds.

Winnie had grown up with order. She was used to it. Under the pitiless double assaults of her mother and grandmother, the cottage where she lived was always squeaking clean, mopped and swept and scoured into limp submission. There was no room for carelessness, no putting things off until later. The Foster women had made a fortress out of duty. Within it they were indomitable. And Winnie was in training.

So she was unprepared for the homely little house beside the pond, unprepared for the gentle eddies of dust, the silver cobwebs, the mouse who lived—and welcome to him!—in a table drawer. There were only three rooms. The kitchen came first, with an open cabinet where dishes were stacked in perilous towers without the least regard for their varying dimensions. There was an enormous black stove, and a metal sink, and every surface, every wall, was piled and strewn and hung with everything imaginable, from onions to lanterns to wooden spoons to washtubs. And in a corner stood Tuck's forgotten shotgun.

The parlor came next, where the furniture, loose and sloping with age, was set about helter-skelter. An ancient green-plush sofa lolled alone in the center, like yet another mossy, fallen log, facing a soot-streaked fireplace still deep in last winter's ashes. The table with the drawer that housed the mouse was pushed off, also alone, into a far corner, and three armchairs and an elderly rocker stood about aimlessly, like strangers at a party, ignoring each other (Natalie Babbitt, Tuck Everlasting) (Farrar, Straus and Giroux, 1975).

Much can be done with the language in this description of the Tucks' cottage. Upper–elementary-level students can be asked to choose their favourite phrases or sentences from this passage to help them appreciate the quality of the description, the use of simile and metaphor, the pure richness of the language. Children can be asked to illustrate this section of the story using their visual artistic skills and their choice of media to see how they would capture Babbitt's description.

Meaningful integration of visual art with language arts means more than simply drawing something after reading or listening to a story. Cornett and Smithrim (2001) suggest that integration maintain the integrity of each area being integrated. A critical question when integrating is "What did my students learn about all the areas being integrated?"—in our example, "What did they learn about story, about describing, about metaphor as a tool in writing?" or "What did they learn about drawing, about interpreting?" Cornett and Smithrim tell us that the classroom teacher doesn't necessarily have to know how to draw well to integrate visual art principles and practices, but the teacher needs a basic knowledge and skill level to use language and present examples of possibilities to students. They suggest the following guidelines to help students "do" art successfully:

- Teach how to use a variety of media, tools, and techniques—printing, collage, watercolour, chalk, tempura, original stencilling, mobiles, sculpting, rubbings, papier-mache—and use different surfaces (e.g., fabric, wood).
- Use an *explore–practice–express* lesson sequence. Demonstrate ways to use materials and tools and give time to explore and experiment.
- Limit direction-giving.
- Similar to responding to writing, give more descriptive feedback than praise as students work.
- Create an atmosphere and expectation for appropriate behaviour. Art-making should be a time for focus and concentration. Play music without lyrics, or make a rule about quiet.
- Invite students to write or tell stories about their art or find music that goes with their art.

In addition, many art teachers use new media technologies such as digital art, computer graphics, virtual art, and computer robotics to help students visually represent their ideas in creative ways. Collaboration among art teachers, English language arts teachers, industrial arts teachers, and computer teachers will provide opportunities for students to engage in publishing, digital imaging, web design, and video production in order to meaningfully integrate visual art with language in the future (Delacruz, 2009).

The Language Arts and Music

Many children enter school with some background in music gained through their preschool play and family activities. Because the introduction to music generally occurs in powerful social contexts like singing with family and friends, listening to iPods or the radio while traveling, or experiencing music in church or community, the result for most children is strong ties to styles and genres of music. Children whose parents sing to them and who participate musically through the family via either singing or learning to play a musical instrument are more likely to sing and play music well and have diverse tastes. According to Cornett and Smithrim (2001),

> The elementary and middle school years need to be musically rich. Young children are more open to types of music—from classical to country—and it is what they hear the most that becomes what they like and value. The teaching implication is to take advantage of this openness to musical diversity by providing experiences with an eclectic range of styles, types, periods and cultural music experiences. Such variety sustains interest, engenders a flexibility of attitude, and builds respect for the diverse expressions of people. (p. 300)

As language arts teachers, we have a responsibility to integrate music with the language arts. Music study can help promote literacy skills such as vocabulary, articulation, pronunciation, grammar, fluency, writing, sentence patterns, rhythm, parts of speech, auditory processing, and prosody (Frasher, 2014). Integration of music in the language arts curriculum makes it possible for children to make the connection between their spoken and written language and the language of music. As we explore musical notation and composition, we help children see how a different language, musical expression, can also enhance their understanding of the world around them. Teachers make learning and composing songs as well as listening to curriculum-related music a regular part of the language arts curriculum. Music can be integrated and become integral to children's language learning experiences in many ways. See the Teachers Notebook for ways to integrate music with the language arts.

The following activity is an example of how music and the language arts can be integrated in a classroom. The children in grade 4 listen attentively to Ms. Lacey as she reads them Margot Fonteyn's retelling of *Swan Lake*, illustrated by Trina Schart Hyman (Fonteyn, 1989). Ms. Lacey also shares information about the author, Dame Margot Fonteyn, her illustrious career as a ballerina, and her particular interest in dancing the ballet *Swan Lake*. The children construct a plotline for the story and work in small groups to imagine the scenes for presenting this story as a ballet. What parts of the story would they include? They then listen to Tchaikovsky's musical score for the ballet, discovering the familiar parts of the story as it is told by the music. Students finish by comparing this version of *Swan Lake* with other versions, noting where the differences are in the various stories and speculating about the reasons for those differences. The children then listen to *Tchaikovsky Discovers America* (Classical Kids, 2000), part of the Classical Kids series on CD that combines dramatic stories and classical music to captivate, engage, and entertain them with the life and music of Pyotr Tchaikovsky.

Ways to Integrate Music with the Language Arts

1. Encourage musical responses to literature by including music as one resource in language arts units, especially theme study units, to enhance understanding of the unit concepts.

2. Use music, vocal or instrumental, as a way of introducing a piece of literature. Encourage students to see likenesses in theme.

3. Teach songs from diverse cultures and for holidays (traditional ones and others that are part of themes or units).

4. Share literature and other activities that support awareness of musical elements and concepts to help students use musical intelligence and develop musical vocabulary.

5. Invite guests to play musical instruments, sing, or share about unique aspects of music.

6. Involve students in making and playing instruments as a means of creative expression.

7. In the classroom, play, and make available for individual listening, a variety of types of music to stretch students' sense of the familiar.

8. Explore the music and other sound effects of commercially produced videos, especially digital versions of stories and poems.

9. Listen to music and ask students to represent through new media, drawings, drama, or dance the images it stimulates for them.

10. Explore the rhythm of poetry through musical activities such as drumming.

11. Sing with students to show the value of all voices.

12. Share personal musical tastes and preferences as a way of celebrating diversity.

13. Collaborate with the music specialist to integrate music throughout the curriculum, especially the fine arts.

14. Present songs and rhythmic activities for pure enjoyment.

This same class continues its musical explorations by listening to another of the stories of great composers presented in this series, *Beethoven Lives Upstairs* (Nichol, 1999). Set in the autumn of 1822, in this story Christoph writes letters to his uncle about the strange person who has rented the upstairs part of his house. He begins his first letter, "I hope you will remember me. It is Christoph, your nephew, who writes. As for the reasons, I will not keep you in suspense. I write, Uncle, because something terrible has happened. A madman has moved into our house" (Nichol, 1999). The "madman" in question is the eccentric Ludwig van Beethoven. Through reading the letters and listening to the story and music on the CD, children explore some of the aspects of Beethoven's life and his music. The children finish their exploration by listening to and learning to play "Ode to Joy," one of Beethoven's famous choral pieces, on simple keyboards.

Earlier in this chapter we explained that children's literature is a rich resource for helping students learn about visual representation. So too, literature is a valuable resource for learning the language and concepts of music. Teachers include

FIGURE 10-3 **BOOKS TO LINK LITERATURE AND MUSIC**

Bang-Campbell, M. (2008). *Little Rat Makes Music*. New York: Houghton Mifflin. (P)

Celenza, A. (2006). *Gershwin's Rhapsody in Blue*. Watertown, MA: Charlesbridge. (P–M)

Engle, M. (2015). *Drum Dream Girl: How One Girl's Courage Changed Music*. New York: Houghton Mifflin Harcourt. (P–M)

Garriel, B. (2004). *A Know a Shy Fellow Who Swallowed a Cello*. Honesdale, PA: Boyds Mills. (P–M)

Gerhard, A. (2013). *Listen to the Birds: An Introduction to Classical Music*. Chicago, IL: The Secret Mountain. (U)

Lach, W. (2006). *Can You Hear It?* New York: Harry N. Abrams. (P–M)

Levine, R. (2000). *Story of the Orchestra: Listen While You Learn About the Instruments, the Music, and the Composers Who Wrote the Music*. New York: Black Dog & Leventhal. (M)

Moss, L. (2000). *ZinZinA Violin*. New York: Aladdin Picture Books. (P)

Schulman, J. (2004). *Sergei Prokofiev's Peter and the Wolf: With A Fully Orchestrated and Narrated CD*. New York: Knopf. (P–M)

Shlasko, R. (2011). *Molly and the Sword*. New York: Jane & Street Publishers. (P–M)

Stinson, K. (2013). *The Man with the Violin*. Toronto, ON: Annick Press. (P–M) 🍁

Thien, M. (2001). *The Chinese Violin*. Vancouver, BC: Whitecap Books. (P) 🍁

Yarrow, P., & Lipton, L. (2007). *Puff the Magic Dragon*. New York: Sterling. (P)

books such as those in Figure 10-3 in the class library and use them as resources during resource-based and theme study units to help students link music to the language arts.

The Language Arts and Drama

Drama integrates all of the arts (music, art, dance, and literature), so it has the potential to play a very significant role in language arts development. Drama enhances these other areas of the curriculum. Students can begin to explore characters and their relationships to one another and to areas such as social studies, science, and health. In the language arts and other subjects, creative drama can be used to help students make sense of the world around them.

Drama helps students enhance their oral language skills and bring congruence between word and action. It is a powerful means of self-expression through speaking and listening. Drama develops social skills and assists students in appreciating and understanding group process. Drama is also a form of entertainment by which students find enjoyment in the exploration of their worlds through representation.

Similar to the other arts, successful integration of drama into the language arts curriculum depends on the skill level of the teacher. Language arts teachers need a repertoire of strategies to teach students how to interact with and respond to each other.

There is a difference between putting on rehearsed plays a few times a year and the daily use of drama in the language arts classroom. According to Cornett and Smithrim (2001), drama in this sense "is participant driven and process centred with a teacher or leader guiding children through explorations of personal experiences, social issues or pieces of literature" (p. 213).

Readers Theatre

A place to begin integrating drama in the language arts curriculum is with **readers theatre**, a language arts technique through which any piece of literature or other material is divided into parts that are read orally. This technique enables children of varying levels of ability to participate in a group presentation and to practise and improve reading fluency. The children do not memorize their lines, but do practise them so that the reading is fluent and expressive, making it a worthwhile activity for improving reading, too. The use of voices, restrained gestures, and facial expression project the mood. Action or physical movement is merely suggested.

Children, regardless of their levels of competency, are grouped together and roles are assigned according to the abilities and interests of those participating. There are usually two kinds of speaking parts—narrator(s) and characters. Narrators are assigned the parts in the story that do not belong to characters. Large segments of narration may be divided among several narrators, thus allowing more children to participate in each performance. The narrator links the various segments together, providing what is necessary to the comprehension of the play. There are as many children involved in each presentation of readers theatre as there are characters and narrator roles.

One way to perform readers theatre is to have all the performers, each with a complete script in hand, stand in a row with backs to the audience. Each time a character speaks, she or he turns to face the audience, reads the part, then turns away from the audience until her or his turn comes up again.

Another suggestion for performance is to have the readers stand at strategic points in the classroom in order to focus the audience's attention on each speaker as the play unfolds. Readers theatre presentations may be enhanced by selective and limited use of scenery and costumes, the use of simple masks or makeup rather than full costumes, and the use of very simple props.

The richest source of material for readers theatre is literature from which a story or poem, in whole or in part, can be adapted. Any story with a range of characters and sufficient dialogue is suitable. Often, all that is required is the marking of the various parts in the text so that children see where their various parts are found. Jan Andrews' book *When Apples Grew Noses and White Horses Flew: Tales of Ti-Jean* (2011) presents three stories that introduce French Canadian folktale hero Ti-Jean. The stories are rich sources of material for readers theatre and are enjoyable to perform for both young and older children. Other stories that can easily be adapted for readers theatre include Doreen Cronin's *Click, Clack, Moo* (2000) and *Giggle, Giggle, Quack* (2002). Older students can also perform using their own writing. While adapting their writing, stories, or other types of work does not give children experience with the rich texts of celebrated literature, it does allow them to have valuable integrated language learning experiences.

Readers theatre offers a rich experience in both speaking and listening. The actors practise before any presentation and improve their fluency, accuracy, and phrasing. Readers theatre provides children of all reading abilities the opportunity to participate in a meaningful activity. The focus in readers theatre is primarily on the speaking of the text and not on the performance. Children are given many opportunities to practise their reading and/or speaking voices as a prelude to developing other dramatic skills.

Story Vines

Story vines are visual representations of stories that teachers and children create or retell in order to engage in storytelling. Using braided rope or other materials to create the vine, the storyteller chooses items to hang on the vine to help him or her tell the story. In this way, they share artifacts important to the story and these help the storyteller remember and retell the story (M. Mackay, 2006). The story is told in the teacher's or student's own words, and is not an exact reading of the text.

Story Dramas

A range of drama activities can be used in exploring a story. For instance, one or two drama activities can be used to teach a particular concept in a unit of study. A drama activity can be an isolated exercise that enhances a specific aspect of a lesson or a series of activities around a certain theme in a piece of literature. For example, the teacher might read from the book *The One and Only Ivan* (2012), by Katherine Applegate. The story features the trials and tribulations of a circus-bound silverback gorilla named Ivan. Rather than replicating actual scenes from the book, students are encouraged in their story dramas to continue a storyline by answering the question "What might happen next?" or by changing the plot to show other possible scenarios using similar characters.

Story dramas and other dramatic activities are highly participatory learning activities. They provide students opportunities to not only increase their understanding of literature, but also to develop as responsible, contributing members of a learning community. To monitor their growth, teachers and students themselves can fill out a checklist like the one shown in Figure 10-4 to reflect on their participation

FIGURE 10-4 PARTICIPATION CHECKLIST

Participation Checklist for: Name: _____

5 = Excellent   0 = Poor

Category	Comment	5	4	3	2	1	0
Do I arrive in class mentally and physically prepared to participate fully?							
Am I able to maintain focus in class?							
Do I challenge myself for improvement, take risks to stretch myself?							
Can my work in class be perceived as enthusiastic?							
Do I take responsibility and share my thoughts and ideas with the whole class?							
Am I flexible? Do I adapt to changes and try new things?							
Do I take initiative and offer new directions during group activities?							
Do I recognize myself as just one of the group and not monopolize?							
Do I accept feedback as an invitation to grow?							
Do I offer feedback in a constructive manner?							
Do I respond authentically, thoughtfully, spontaneously to others?							
Do I take the time to really listen and try to understand what others are saying?							
Am I willing to put in that required "extra" that makes a group function effectively?							
Could I be considered a strong team member?							

Tableaux

A *tableau* is a frozen picture or action that focuses the meaning of an event. It is not posed like a family portrait, but is a frozen event in time. One example of using this strategy is first having the students walk around the room and then playing the game Traffic Lights. As they walk about, the teacher calls out one of the colours of the traffic light. *Green* means to continue walking or begin running around the space. *Yellow* means to stop and stand on one leg as still as possible. *Red* means to lie down on the ground. Once students have mastered the movement and stillness activities, other games can be played. For instance, students can be placed in groups of four or five and given five minutes to create a still image of a particular event, such as a birthday party, a concert, or a campfire. When students are familiar with the process, they can then move to presenting tableaux representing instances from the literature they are reading. As each group presents, the rest of the class observes as in an art gallery looking at the sculptures.

Socio-dramatic Play (Role-Play)

Socio-dramatic play uses the natural make-believe or "pretend" activities that we all do. With children, this type of play is often made public and occurs with others. Young children naturally engage in play to make sense of their world and doing so contributes to their intellectual, physical, social, and emotional growth. Opportunities that build on children's natural tendency to want to play include providing a safe environment and the freedom to try out roles and situations. The most important aspect of socio-dramatic play is the focus on process and not product. Teachers can provide opportunities for role-playing, puppetry, and fantasy play by making time and very simple props available.

Improvisational play tends to emerge naturally among children, but dramatic play can be more structured by offering children input into the kind of environment they want to create and structuring it with a particular text. Stories, especially well-known ones like fairytales, can be used to help students use and become excited about the language of texts. Choosing a character to portray will help students show a deeper understanding of the text. Having that character then move into new settings and situations will further develop students' imagination and creativity. When children create their own stories to act out, they develop their language and communication skills.

The Language Arts and Dance

The language arts are the primary vehicle for knowing and expressing ourselves in the world. Using our physical bodies as a form of expression through sport, movement, or dance allows us to engage a creative, non-rational part of our minds in our learning.

Twenty-five second-graders have gathered on the carpet in the reading area. Their teacher begins to share Ellen Stoll Walsh's picture storybook *Hop Jump* (1993) with them, a story about frogs who only know how to hop and jump until Betsy tries leaping, turning, and twisting like the leaves. "It's called dancing," she says. And soon most of the frogs join in. The children are invited to hop and jump like the frogs and then to leap and turn and twist like the leaves. Soon they are all dancing with the frogs in the story.

The children then listen to the story *Rap a Tap Tap: Here's Bojangles—Think of That* (2002) by Leo and Diane Dillon. The story shares the spirit and exuberance of the legendary dancer Bill "Bojangles" Robinson. Written in verse, each page spread ends with "Rap a tap tap—think of that." The children are invited to tap out the rhythm with their hands and feet as the story is read again and again.

Through dance, children have the opportunity to respond to literature in a way that recognizes their internal need to use movement as a means of expression. Dance study and integration include ideas related to dance elements, creation and composition, presentation and performance, dance history, and dance genres and forms. As language arts teachers, we can build a repertoire of information and examples of various dance forms, such as ballet and jazz, and about important dancers and choreographers. Sharing Karen Kain's (2005) book, *The Nutcracker*, is just one example of how teachers can bring famous Canadian dancers and their art to their classroom. Many aspects of dance can be integrated into the language arts curriculum where it is appropriate.

Cornett and Smithrim (2001) suggest starting small and growing from there. Teachers can start with a single lesson using one dance/movement tool to explore how we move, where, when, and to what effect. This might be a lesson connected to a story, a lesson on the shapes we can make with our bodies, or the use of warm-ups to shift the energy in a group. Providing children with carefully structured experiences that honour the medium and help them develop their own skills will allow for continued growth and development.

There is also a wealth of children's literature that lends itself to integrating dance. Figure 10-5 presents titles appropriate for all elementary students. Some focus on movement. For example, in Rosemary Mastnak's *Dancing with Grandma* (2011), Anya and her grandmother dress up and dance around the house and encourage the participation of the cat and the dog. Others present the history of dance and its place in various cultures. For example, *Drumbeat in Our Feet* (Keeler & Julio, 2006) provides an overview of the origins of African dance traditions and *Secret of the Dance* (Spalding, 2006) tells the history of the Aboriginal dance, the Potlatch, and the Canadian law that forbid it. *Jingle Dancer* (Smith, 2000) tells Jenna's story of securing the jingles she needs so her dress will sing to the beat of the pow-wow drums. These stories and others can stimulate many movement explorations during and after reading.

FIGURE 10-5 BOOKS TO LINK LITERATURE AND DANCE

Andrae, G. (1999). *Giraffes Can't Dance*. New York: Orchard Books. (P)

Ehrlich, A. (2009). *The Girl Who Wanted to Dance*. Somerville, MA: Candlewick Press. (M)

George, J. (2011). *Princess of the Midnight Ball*. New York: Bloomsbury. (M–U)

Heidbreder, R. (2004). *Drumheller Dinosaur Dance*. Toronto: Kids Can Press. (P–M) ✻

Janni, R. (2012). *Jammy Dance*. New York: FSG Kids. (P)

Kain, K. (2005). *The Nutcracker*. Toronto: Tundra Books. (P–M) ✻

Keeler, P., & Julio, L. (2006). *Drumbeat in our Feet*. New York: Lee and Low. (M–U)

Mastnak, R. (2011). *Dancing with Grandma*. Richmond, Australia: Hardie Grant Egmont. (P)

Siegel, S. (2006). *To Dance: A Ballerina's Graphic Novel*. New York: Simon and Schuster. (M–U)

Smith, C. (2000). *Jingle Dancer*. New York: Morrow Junior Books. (P–M)

Spalding, A. (2006). *Secret of the Dance*. Victoria, BC: Orca. (P–M) ✻

Willems, M. (2009). *Elephants Cannot Dance*. New York: Hyperion. (P)

Young, A. (2006). *Belinda and the Glass Slipper*. New York: Penguin Young Readers.

Review

Integrating the fine arts with the language arts is important for the well-rounded intellectual, emotional, physical, and spiritual development of children. Many of our cultural traditions are rooted in the fine arts and students need opportunities to explore our cultural heritage through visual art, music, drama, and dance. The fine arts also allow students to be successful in ways that allow them to engage a variety of intelligences. And success in the fine arts enhances overall academic achievement.

The development of children's visual artistic ability invites them to explore meaning at deeper symbolic levels and encourages them to expand their interpretations of text. Reading descriptive passages or stories and then interpreting them visually contributes to the child's writing ability as each learns to represent meaning in this expanded way. So too, integration of music in the language arts curriculum invites expanded and creative interpretation of text.

Drama and dance give students a further opportunity to construct meaning, both individually and in groups using texts and movement. These activities require students to work together and to develop cooperative learning skills.

Theory to Practice

1. Take a new piece of literature that you wish to include in a unit of study and design two drama activities you might use to teach the piece. Make a list of the language arts, drama, and social skills that could be learned from the experience.

2. Assemble a set of children's books that represent a variety of media used for illustrations. Plan a visual art lesson that will allow children to explore one or more of the styles and the media employed by the artists.

3. Invite children to select music to accompany oral renditions of stories or poems they have written. Explore a range of styles of music from modern to baroque.

4. Keep a record of poems, stories, and other literature that can be used to encourage and support drama, visual art, and dance activities in your classroom. Share your record with a colleague to gain further suggestions.

5. Seek out examples of lessons and units of study that employ the arts (visual art, music, and drama) to enrich students' learning in curriculum areas such as social studies and science.

Literacy in Action

Chapter 11: A Literacy Journey Around the Globe

Procedure

When educators and students read together, doors open onto real and imaginary worlds. As Kiefer and Tyson (2010) remind us, "Books can be the avenues to travel the globe as well as the neighbourhood, to find the glorious diversity that exists in human culture as well as the unifying commonalities" (p. 88). Together, our school library assistant, my grade two students, and I took a literary journey around the globe. Through shared reading from the Global Micro-Library, a collection of international picture books held in the local university library, we grew as readers, writers, and global citizens.

Once a week for seven weeks, we read together, each time focusing on one continent. To help us envision the setting, we began by locating the continent on a world map or a globe, and then looked at pictures on a relevant website. To discover facts, our library assistant read aloud from the *Explore the Continent* series. These introductions opened the way to make general observations and to share personal connections with the region. Students, for example, who had been on holiday in Mexico linked their experiences to *Armando and the Blue Tarp School* (Fine & Josephson, 2007).

Prior to beginning our journey, I issued each student a literary passport designed to resemble our Canadian passports, complete with photos. The children wrote their identification information, carefully managing first and last names in the small spaces. The passports have two facing pages for each continent. The students recorded facts on the left and their retelling of story events on the right. Passports became their journey diaries, prompting their writing skill development and their understandings.

When our global journey finished, the students were well aware of the seven continents. In conversation, they frequently referred to the culturally diverse stories, the characters, and sayings we encountered during our shared reading. They eagerly awaited the day they were to take home their passports, anxious to tell their families about their literary adventures.

The books we read are shown below. The teacher's guide accompanying the collection includes many suggestions for further reading. Those suggested titles will enable the children to continue their journey during independent reading time.

Assessment

Assessment took many forms, but the most tangible measures were the students' contributions to discussions and their writing in their passports. After each reading, we talked together about the stories, the characters, and the likenesses and differences the children observed between their lives and those portrayed in the literature. Their

North America
Fine, E. H., & Josephson, J. P. (2007). *Armando and the Blue Tarp School.* New York: Lee & Low Books.

South America
Javaherbin, M. (2014). *Soccer Star.* S.I.: Cambridge, MA: Candlewick Press.

Antarctica
Geraghty, P. (1995). *Solo*. London, UK: Red Fox (Random House).

Europe
King, D. (2014). *I See the Sun in Russia*. Hardwick, MA: Satya House Publications.

Williams, K. L., Mohammed, K., & Chayka, D. (2007). *Four Feet, Two Sandals*. Grand Rapids, MI: Eerdmans Books for Young Readers.

Africa
Walters, E. (2013). *My Name is Blessing*. Toronto, ON: Tundra Books.

Australia
Scillian, D. (2010). *D is For Down Under: An Australian Alphabet*. Ann Arbour, MI: Sleeping Bear Press.

comments and questions showed me their insights and ability to compare the lives of the children they met and their own. Their recollections, expressed in pictures and words, were clear indications of their grasp of both factual information and their story interpretations.

Adaptation

Our global literary journey was a mere beginning. Future journeys could involve wider reading from the collection and other sources. Many titles are suggested in Worlds of Words, available at wowlit.org. Sharing the literature through read-alouds and writing creates opportunities for meeting curricular expectations in many subject areas, especially social studies, art, and drama.

Reflection

My young students will become adults in a global community. Already, they enjoy friendships with classmates who have joined us from other countries. I hope their childhood experiences with international literature will foster their understanding of the world and help them develop a global perspective. Students connected emotionally with characters of different cultures. Their connections stimulated empathetic discussions which in turn, sparked appreciation for their own good fortune. Their comments and questions such as "I want to cry because she lost her family," or "Can he not afford shoes?" showed me they were developing awareness of global issues in impactful, yet age-appropriate ways. Because of the connections they made students linked our curriculum to the stories. Our shared reading enriched student learning and encouraged positive global citizenship. I recommend it to all educators and their students.

From the classroom of Cheryl Miller, Grade 2 teacher
St. Catherine's School,
Picture Butte, Alberta.

CHAPTER 11

Putting It All Together

LEARNING OUTCOMES

After you have read this chapter, you should be able to

1. Explain the identifying characteristics of resourced-based, theme study, and inquiry-based units

2. Explain how teachers develop resource-based, theme study, and inquiry-based units

3. Explain the benefits to students of the readers and writers workshop approach to reading and writing

4. Explain how teachers set up readers and writers workshops

For more information on instructional frameworks, see Chapter 2, "Teaching the Language Arts," pages 53–64.

Teacher and students collaborate on questions to guide an inquiry-based unit.

Teachers often search for the single best way to develop English language arts units and lessons, but there isn't just one way! First and foremost when planning, teachers consider their students, their instructional needs, and how to make the language arts programs meaningful for all students. In most Canadian classrooms, students represent a range of abilities and instructional needs as well as a variety of linguistic and cultural groups. Diversity permeates classrooms. Teachers want to provide rich and rewarding educational opportunities for all students, introduce challenges to very capable students, provide necessary support to those who struggle, and offer engaging and informative instruction to everyone. Further, they endeavour to promote tolerance for and an appreciation of diversity. One way teachers do those things is to provide instruction through a combination of the three types of instructional frameworks—resource-based, theme study, and inquiry-based—over the course of a school year. Readers and writers workshops are often included within the instructional framework.

FIGURE 11-1 TEN EVIDENCE-BASED BEST PRACTICES FOR COMPREHENSIVE LITERACY INSTRUCTION

1. Create a classroom culture that nurtures literacy motivation by integrating choice, collaboration, and relevance into literacy tasks.
2. Provide students with scaffolded instruction in phonemic awareness, phonics, fluency, and vocabulary to support the development of deep comprehension.
3. Provide students with opportunities to engage with texts across a wide range of narrative and informational genres.
4. Provide students with opportunities to engage in close reading for deep comprehension.
5. Provide students with literacy instruction using appropriately leveled texts to support the reading of increasingly complex materials.
6. Teach literacy with and across all content areas for authentic purposes.
7. Balance teacher and student-led discussions.
8. Use formative and summative assessments that reflect the complex and dynamic nature of literacy.
9. Promote literacy independence by providing time for self-selected reading and writing.
10. Integrate technologies that link and expand concepts and modes of communication.

Source: Based on Gambrell, Malloy, Marinak,& Mazzoni, 2015 in Best Practices in Literacy Instruction (5th Ed), New York: The Guilford Press. © Gail E. Tompkins

Most importantly, teachers must choose from thousands of books and other print and nonprint resources, activities, and assignments as they plan. They bear in mind that their programs must engage their students in learning and effectively use both traditional and new literacies. As the decision makers about instruction, teachers depend upon well-grounded and respected research to guide their choices. Figure 11-1 shows ten research-based best practices (Gambrell, Malloy, Marinak, & Mazzoni, 2015) to be included in well-designed language arts programs. Teachers incorporate these practices in resource-based, theme study, and inquiry-based units as well as in language activities across curriculum.

In this text, you've read about each of the six language arts, how they are learned, and many components of language arts instruction. In this chapter, you will see how teachers bring these together to create programs of instruction. You will be introduced to instructional frameworks for **unit** planning and steps to take in planning readers and writers workshops. Teachers planning language arts programs are like jugglers who balance many and different-sized balls with rhythm and agility, keeping all in the air. They give just the right amount of time and attention to each of the components to create programs that entice and meet the needs of all students. Teachers begin with frameworks for an instructional approach and then choose the literature, other print and nonprint resources, activities, and assignments based on their instructional goals and their beliefs about how children learn. Throughout their planning they pay close attention to the expectations and requirements of their provincial curriculum. They may also choose from a variety of commercially produced programs, such as the "6 Traits of Effective Writing Program" (Spandel, 2008) or the "Daily Five" (Boushey & Moser, 2006), to help them construct comprehensive programs of English language arts instruction. It is a complex task and one that benefits from experience.

As teachers gain experience developing units, they often go beyond "What shall I do with this book or this video?" or "What shall I teach in this unit?" to think about how the choices they make shape the literate experiences of their students. Teachers need to remember that to be authentic, the literacy experiences they provide in their classrooms need to resemble those their students have outside their classrooms. Teachers need to think about why students should choose many of the books they read and why skill and strategy instruction should be taught in context. Typically, teachers plan resource-based units, theme study units, or inquiry-based units and use readers and writers workshop to complement these approaches.

Resource-Based Units

Teachers plan resource-based units featuring popular and award-winning literature for children and adolescents. In today's society, students engage effectively in multiliteracies and technologies (Leu, 2000). It is therefore appropriate that resource-based units also include a variety of print and nonprint media and texts, such as magazines, video, and material on the Internet. Some resource-based units feature a single book, either a **picture book** or a **chapter book**, while others feature sets of books for a **genre** unit or an author study unit, and include accompanying Internet resources, such as YouTube videos, blogs, digital stories, and images. A novel study is but one example of a resource-based unit. Figure 11-2 presents a list of recommended **trade books** and authors and illustrators for resource-based units for kindergarten through grade 8.

FIGURE 11-2 RECOMMENDED TRADE BOOKS AND AUTHORS AND ILLUSTRATORS FOR RESOURCE-BASED UNITS

Trade Books	Authors and Illustrators
Primary Grades (K–2)	
Brett, J. (1989). *The Mitten*. New York: Putnam.	Jo Ellen Bogart 🍁
Carle, E. (1969). *The Very Hungry Caterpillar*. Cleveland, OH: World.	Paulette Bourgeois 🍁
	Jan Brett
Gilman, P. (1999). *Jillian Jiggs and the Secret Surprise*. Markham, ON: Scholastic Canada. 🍁	Eric Carle
	Donald Crews
Gregory, N. (2000). *Wild Girl and Gran*. Red Deer, AB: Red Deer Press. 🍁	Lois Ehlert
	Sheree Fitch 🍁
Lawson, J. (1996). *Whatever You Do, Don't Go Near That Canoe*. Richmond Hill, ON: Scholastic Canada. 🍁	Mem Fox
	Marie-Louise Gay 🍁
McLeod, E. (2002). *Lessons from Mother Earth*. Toronto: Groundwood/Douglas & McIntyre. 🍁	Phoebe Gilman 🍁
	Tana Hoban
McLeod, H. (2011). *Kiss Me! (I'm a Prince)*. Markham, ON: Fitzhenry & Whiteside. 🍁	Sharon Jennings 🍁
	Steven Kellogg
Rylant, C. (1985). *The Relatives Came*. New York: Bradbury Press.	Julie Lawson 🍁
	James Marshall
Spires, A. (2011). *Small Saul*. Toronto: Kids Can Press. 🍁	Robert Munsch 🍁
Trottier, M. (2011). *Migrant*. Toronto: Groundwood Books. 🍁	Barbara Reid 🍁
Underwood, D. (2010). *The Quiet Book*. Boston: Houghton Mifflin Books for Children.	Dr. Seuss
	Kathy Stinson 🍁
Vaage, C. (1995). *Bibi and the Bull*. Red Deer, AB: Red Deer College Press. 🍁	Maxine Trottier 🍁
	Melanie Watt 🍁
Young, C. (2011). *Ten Birds*. Toronto: Kids Can Press. 🍁	Werner Zimmerman
Middle Grades (3–5)	
Brewster, H. (2011). *Deadly Voyage: RMS Titanic*. Toronto: Scholastic Canada. 🍁	Byrd Baylor
	Karen Cushman
Coerr, E. (1977). *Sadako and the Thousand Paper Cranes*. New York: Putnam.	Deborah Ellis 🍁
	Jean Fritz
Fagan, C. (2011). *Banjo of Destiny*. Toronto: Groundwood Books. 🍁	Paul Goble

(continued)

Horvath, P. (2002). *Everything on a Waffle*. Toronto: Groundwood Books. 🍁

Hyde, N. (2011). *Saving Armpit*. Markham, ON: Fitzhenry & Whiteside. 🍁

Little, J. (2002). *Birdie, for Now*. Vancouver: Orca Books. 🍁

McTighe, C. (2007). *The Sakura Tree*. Calgary: Red Deer Press. 🍁

Montgomery, L. M. (1908/1999). *Anne of Green Gables*. New York: HarperFestival. 🍁

Naylor, P. R. (1991). *Shiloh*. New York: Macmillan.

Paterson, K. (1977). *Bridge to Terabithia*. New York: Crowell.

Pearson, K. (2003). *The Guests of War Trilogy*. Toronto, ON: Puffin Books. 🍁

Schwartz, E. (2011). *The Case of the Missing Deed*. Toronto: Tundra Books. 🍁

Smith, D. J. (2011). *This Child, Every Child: A Book about the World's Children*. Toronto: Kids Can Press.

Walsh, A. (2001). *Heroes of Isle aux Morts*. Toronto: Tundra Books. 🍁

Walters, E. (1997). *Trapped in Ice*. Toronto, ON: Puffin Books. 🍁

Ye, T. X. (2002). *White Lily*. Toronto: Doubleday Canada. 🍁

Karen Hesse
Natalie Hyde 🍁
Jean Little 🍁
L. M. Montgomery 🍁
Shane Peacock 🍁
Kit Pearson 🍁
Patricia Polacco
Jack Prelutsky
Cynthia Rylant
David Skuy 🍁
David J. Smith 🍁
William Steig
Shelley Tanaka 🍁
Marvin Terban
Chris Van Allsburg
Eric Walters 🍁
Budge Wilson 🍁
Paul Yee 🍁
Jane Yolen

Upper Grades (6–8)

Appelt, K. (2008). *The Underneath*. New York: Antheneum.

Babbitt, N. (1975). *Tuck Everlasting*. New York: Farrar, Straus & Giroux.

Bedard, M. (2001). *Stained Glass*. Toronto: Tundra Books. 🍁

Buffie, M. (1998). *Angels Turn Their Backs*. Toronto: Kids Can Press. 🍁

Friesen, G. (2000). *Men of Stone*. Toronto: Kids Can Press. 🍁

Hiassen, C. (2006). *Hoot*. New York: Yearling.

Greenwood, B. (2007). *Factory Girl*. Toronto: Kids Can Press. 🍁

Johnston, J. (2001). *In Spite of Killer Bees*. Toronto: Tundra Books. 🍁

Jordan-Fenton, C., and Pokiak-Fenton, M. (2011). *A Stranger at Home: A True Story*. Toronto: Annick Press. 🍁

Lowry, L. (1993). *The Giver*. Boston: Houghton Mifflin.

Ostlere, C. (2011). *Karma*. Toronto: Puffin Canada. 🍁

Robertson, D. (2010). *Stone (7 Generations, vol. 1)*. Winnipeg: Highwater Press/Portage & Main Press. 🍁

Skuy, D. (2011). *Undergrounders*. Toronto: Scholastic Canada. 🍁

Slade, A. (2001). *Dust*. New York: HarperCollins. 🍁

Toten, T. (2001). *The Game*. Calgary: Red Deer Press. 🍁

Watts, I. (2000). *Remember Me*. Toronto: Tundra Books. 🍁

Lloyd Alexander
Alison Baird
Sharon Creech
Paula Danziger
Deborah Ellis 🍁
Gayle Friesen 🍁
Rachna Gilmore 🍁
Virginia Hamilton
Anita Horrocks 🍁
Glen Huser 🍁
Gordon Korman 🍁
David Macaulay
Carol Matas 🍁
Walter Dean Myers
Scott O'Dell
Kenneth Oppel 🍁
Katherine Paterson
Gary Paulsen
J. K. Rowling
Jerry Spinelli
Cora Taylor
Yoshiko Uchida
Tim Wynne-Jones 🍁
Laurence Yep
Paul Zindel

During these units, students move through the five stages of reading as they read and respond to texts, learn reading and writing skills and strategies, and engage in language arts activities.

How to Develop a Resource-Based Unit

Teachers develop a resource-based unit through a multistep series of activities. Planning a unit of instruction is a complex process that requires teachers to think about many aspects of facilitating students' learning at the same time. For clarity, we describe the process in sequential steps; in practice, it is often a recursive process in which teachers frequently plan then reconsider how the learning outcomes, the resources, the activities, and the assessment strategies will work together. Teachers often begin with choosing the literature and other resources for the unit. Then they identify the activities and possible goals and outcomes that can be met. Teachers then continue to plan and schedule learning and assessment activities. They plan how they will collect assessment information about students' learning during the unit and how they will evaluate students' learning upon completion of the unit. Whether teachers are using trade books, anthology selections, videos or other digital texts, or sources from the Internet, their planning process involves multiple steps. Canadian teachers also consult the provincial curriculum documents that describe the requirements for the grades and programs they are teaching. Effective teachers do not simply follow directions in commercially published teachers' manuals and planning guides. While they may consult such guides, they build their own programs to design instruction especially for the students whom they teach. While there are many online resources for teachers to examine, it is very important that they make the plans themselves because they are the ones who best know their students, the resources they have available, the time available for the unit, the curriculum outcomes they want students to achieve, and the language arts strategies and activities they want to use.

The length of time involved in teaching a resource-based unit varies widely depending upon grade level and complexity of the resource. Usually resource-based units featuring a picture book are completed in one week, and units featuring a chapter book and other resources are completed in two, three, or four weeks. Genre and author units may last two, three, or four weeks. Only occasionally do teachers continue resource-based units beyond four weeks. Longer units risk losing students' interest in a particular book or, worse yet, their love of literature.

STEP 1: SELECT THE LITERATURE

Teachers select the reading material for the unit. The literature may be a story in a picture book format, a chapter book, a story selected from a reading series anthology, or online. The reading materials should be high-quality literature and should often include culturally diverse selections. Sometimes teachers select several related pieces of literature—books representing the same genre, books written by the same author for an author study, or books illustrated by the same artist for an illustrator study. Teachers collect multiple copies of the book or books for the resource-based unit. In some schools, class sets of selected trade books are available for classroom use. In others, class sets are made available through lending programs across the school district. In still other situations, teachers purchase multiple copies of books through book clubs and gradually develop class sets. When teachers use picture books, they usually use read-aloud strategies so that multiple copies are not required.

Once the book (or books) is selected, teachers collect related resources for the unit. Related resources include the following:

- other versions of the same story
- other books written by the same author or illustrated by the same artist
- books with the same theme or settings
- books in the same genre
- informational books on a related topic

- books trailers and images of book covers
- digital versions of the story for listening or viewing
- webpages about the author or illustrator or author or illustrator websites

Teachers collect one or two copies of ten, twenty, thirty, or more books as resources, which they add to the classroom library during the unit. These resources are placed on a special shelf or in a crate readily available to students. At the beginning of the unit, teachers do a book talk to introduce the resources, and then students look at them and read them during independent reading time.

STEP 2: BEGIN TO DEVELOP A SERIES OF LESSON PLANS OR UNIT PLAN

Teachers read or reread the selected book or books and then think about the focus for the unit. Sometimes teachers focus on an element of story structure, the historical setting, wordplay, the author or genre, a reading comprehension strategy (i.e., predicting, summarizing, questioning), or a concept or topic related to the book, such as weather or life in the desert. At this stage in their planning, teachers often consult the Internet to determine the approach taken by other teachers and to seek resources others have used that might be useful.

After determining the focus, teachers think about which activities they will use at each of the five stages of the reading process. For each stage, teachers ask themselves these questions:

1. *Preparing*
   - What background knowledge do students need before reading?
   - What key concepts and vocabulary should I teach before reading?
   - How will I introduce the story and stimulate students' interest in reading?

2. *Reading*
   - How will students read this story?
   - What reading comprehension strategies and skills will I model or ask students to use?
   - How can I make it challenging for more capable readers, and accessible for less capable readers and students learning English as a second language? At this point, it may be necessary to select different reading material in order to differentiate instruction appropriately for some students.

3. *Responding*
   - Will students write in reading logs or blogs? How often?
   - Will students participate in grand conversations? How often?
   - What scenes from the book will students want or need to dramatize?

4. *Exploring*
   - What words might be added to the word wall?
   - What vocabulary activities might be used?
   - Will students reread the story to increase fluency?
   - What skill and strategy minilessons might be taught?
   - How can I focus students' attention on words and sentences in the book?
   - How will other resources be used?
   - What can I share about the author, illustrator, or genre?

5. *Extending*
   - What projects might students choose to pursue?
   - How will other resources be used?
   - How will students share projects?

Teachers often brainstorm ideas and jot notes on a chart divided into sections for each stage. Then they use the ideas they have brainstormed as they plan the unit. Usually, they do not use all of the brainstormed ideas. Rather, teachers select the most important ones according to their focus, students' needs and interests, and the available time.

STEP 3: IDENTIFY LANGUAGE ARTS STRATEGIES AND SKILLS (CURRICULUM) TO TEACH DURING THE UNIT

For more information on language arts strategies, see Chapter 2, "Teaching the Language Arts," pages 33–35. Also, see the lists of minilesson topics in Chapters 3 to 11.

Teachers decide which strategies and skills to teach using the resources. Their choice is dependent on the students' observed needs, opportunities afforded by the book, and school district and provincial requirements. Sometimes teachers plan **minilessons** to directly teach skills and strategies, and at other times they plan to model how to use the skills and strategies as they read aloud or to ask students to share how they use the skills and strategies during **grand conversations**.

STEP 4: LOCATE MULTIMEDIA MATERIALS AND WEBSITES RELATED TO THE UNIT

Teachers locate multimedia materials to use in the unit. Multimedia materials include film and digital versions of stories to view and compare with the book version; audio versions of stories to use at listening centres; sequential pictures to aid retelling of the story; and author information and interviews on video, in podcasts, or in other digital forms on the Internet. Teachers also plan how they will use available technology for unit activities, especially writing, researching, and visually representing activities. Frequently, preparation includes bookmarking relevant websites for teacher and student use and planning for use of other equipment such as cameras and recorders.

STEP 5: INCORPORATE ACTIVITIES EMPLOYING ALL SIX LANGUAGE ARTS

For more information on the six language arts, see Chapter 1, "Learning and the Language Arts," pages 24–27.

Teachers review the plans they are developing to make sure that students have opportunities to engage in listening, speaking, reading, writing, viewing, and visually representing during the unit. Of course, not all six language arts fit into every unit, but for most units they do.

STEP 6: COORDINATE GROUPING PATTERNS WITH ACTIVITIES

Teachers think about how to incorporate whole-class, small-group, paired, and individual activities into their unit plans. It is important that students have opportunities to read and write independently as well as to work with small groups and to come together as a class. This is important in both elementary and middle-school classrooms. If the piece of literature that students are reading will be read together as a class, then students need opportunities to reread it with a partner or independently, or to read related books independently. These grouping patterns should be alternated during various activities in the unit. Teachers often go back to their planning sheet and highlight activities with coloured markers according to grouping patterns.

STEP 7: CREATE A TIME SCHEDULE

Teachers create a time schedule that allows students sufficient time to move through the five stages of the reading process and to complete the activities planned for the unit. Resource-based reading programs require large blocks of time, often more than an hour each day, in which students read, listen, talk, and write about the literature they are reading.

Teachers complete weekly lesson plans to guide students' use of this block of time. The activities they include in their plans represent each of the five stages of the reading process. The stages are not clearly separated and they overlap, but preparing, reading, responding, exploring, and extending activities are included in the plans.

STEP 8: PLAN FOR THE ASSESSMENT OF THE RESOURCE-BASED UNIT

Teachers collect information about students' processes in language learning as well as the products of their learning. The information they collect helps them design instruction. Students, too, participate in assessment of their own learning by reflecting on their processes and products. To help make assessment a manageable, consistent, and effective process, teachers often begin a unit by distributing unit folders. Students keep all work, **reading logs**, reading materials, and related materials in the folder. Periodically during the unit and again at the end, students turn in their completed folders for teachers to evaluate. Keeping all the materials together makes the unit easier for both students and teachers to manage and provides a picture of progress and achievements.

Teachers also plan specific ways to document students' learning and assign grades. One form of record keeping is an assignment checklist. This sheet is developed with students and distributed at the beginning of the resource-based unit. Students keep track of their work during the unit and sometimes negotiate to change the sheet as the unit evolves. Students keep the lists in unit folders, and they mark off each item as it is completed. At the end of the unit, students turn in their completed assignment checklist and other completed work. An assignment checklist for an upper-grade resource-based unit on the book *Dust* by Arthur Slade (2001), a **fantasy** set in rural Saskatchewan during the Great Depression of the 1930s, is presented in Figure 11-3. While this list does not include every activity students were involved in, it does list the activities and other assignments that the teacher holds students accountable for. Teachers also create and distribute **rubrics** showing the criteria on which assignments will be graded. Rubrics are also kept in the unit folders. For primary grades, the rubrics are simple and include few criteria easily understood by the children. In upper grades, the rubrics are more detailed. Students in upper grades often contribute to compilation of the rubrics. The checklist shown in Figure 11-3 includes a point system as a way of assigning value. Students complete the checklist on the left side of the sheet and add titles of books and other requested information. Teachers award points (up to the number listed in parentheses) on the lines on the right side of the sheet, and total the number of points on the bottom of the page. The points can be correlated with the criteria on the rubric. Then the total score can be translated into a letter grade or other type of grade as required in any particular school system.

Some teachers engage in an informal ninth step. When their unit plans are complete, they carefully rethink what they are expecting of students and how they will assist students in achieving those goals. They try to identify the aspects of the unit

> For more information on assessing students' learning in the language arts, see Chapter 5, "The Reading and Writing Processes," pages 179–193.

Dust

Name _____

Student's Check		Teacher's Check
_____	1. Read Dust.	_____
_____	2. Write at least 10 entries in your reading log. Use a double-entry format with quotes and your connections. (20)	_____
_____	3. Participate in small-group grand conversations.	_____
_____	4. Create a storyboard. Chapter # _____ (10)	_____
_____	5. Make an open-mind portrait of Robert with four mind pages. (10)	_____
_____	6. Write an essay about the theme of the book. (10)	_____
_____	7. Choose and analyze 10 words from the word wall according to prefix, root word, and suffix. (10)	_____
_____	8. Read one book from the text set. Write a brief summary in your reading log and compare what you learned about fantasy with Dust. (10)	_____
	Title _____	
	Author _____	
_____	9. Engage in a grand conversation about the book. (5)	_____
_____	10. Create a project and share it with the class. (25)	_____
	Project _____	
	Date shared _____	
	Total	_____

that are its strengths and those that are sources of possible difficulties. By taking time to identify these features in advance, they are better prepared to make decisions as the unit proceeds and the students engage in the planned activities.

A Primary-Grade Resource-Based Unit on *The Mitten*

Jan Brett's *The Mitten* (1989), a cumulative picture book story about a series of animals who climb into a mitten that a little boy has dropped in the snow on a cold winter day, is the featured selection in resource-based units taught in many primary-grade classrooms. A planning cluster for a resource-based unit on *The Mitten* is shown in Figure 11-4 on page 383. Teachers introduce students to the unit and the author by listening to and watching the video *Jan Brett at Home*, available on her website at www.janbrett.com. They use the big book version of *The Mitten* to introduce Brett's books and to examine her innovative use of borders. Students use the teacher's collection of stuffed animals and puppets representing the animals in the story—a mole, a rabbit, a hedgehog, an owl, a badger, a fox, a bear, and a mouse—as they retell the story. Students read the story several times—in small groups with the teacher, with partners, and independently. The teacher also reads aloud several other versions of the story, including *The Woodcutter's Mitten* (Koopmans, 1990) and *The Mitten* (Tresselt, 1964), and students make a chart to compare the versions. The teacher presents minilessons on phonemic awareness and phonics skills, creates a **word wall**, and involves students in word-study activities. Students participate in sequencing and writing activities, and learn about knitting from a parent volunteer. The teacher also

Word Wall

Nicki	grandmother
Baba	mitten
glove	mole
cozy	tunnelling along
snowshoe rabbit	big kickers
hedgehog	prickles
owl	commotion
swooped down	glinty talons
badger	diggers
fox	trotted
drowsy	muzzle
bear	lumbered by
swelled	stretched
meadow mouse	acorn
wriggled	bear's nose
whiskers	enormous sneeze
yarn	knitted
wool	sheep
Ukraine	borders

Word-Study Activities

- Word posters
- Word sorts
- Individual word cards
- Semantic feature analysis to compare animals

Maps and Globes

- Locate the Ukraine setting for this book on a map or globe.

Phonemic Awareness and Phonics

- Collect rhyming objects and pictures related to the story for students to match (e.g., mitten–kitten, fox–box, bear–hair–pear–chair, mouse–house).
- Have students "stretch" these words from the story: *mole, snow, owl, mouse, cozy, nose.*
- Focus on a consonant sound: /m/ for *mitten,* /y/ for *yarn,* or /n/ for *Nicki.*
- Teach the r-controlled vowel sound using *yarn.*
- Focus on a vowel sound: short *i* for *mitten,* long *o* for *snow.*

Illustration Techniques

- Examine Brett's use of borders in many of her books, and encourage students to create borders in the books they write.
- Also, note the side mitten panels with looking back and looking forward scenes on each page of *The Mitten.*

Compare Versions of the Story

Read these versions and make a chart to compare them with Brett's version:

Koopmans, L. (1990). *The Woodcutter's Mitten.* New York: Crocodile Books.
Tresselt, A. (1964). *The Mitten.* New York: Lothrop, Lee & Shepard.

Big Book

Introduce the story using the big book version of the book (published by Scholastic) and shared reading.

The Mitten

Research

- Research one of the animals— mole, rabbit, hedgehog, owl, badger, fox, bear, mouse— mentioned in the story and create posters or a class book about the animal.
- Research sheep, wool, and yarn using these books:

Fowler, A. (1993). *Woolly Sheep and Hungry Goats.* Chicago: Children's Press.
Mitgutsch, A. (1975). *From Sheep to Scarf.* Minneapolis: Carolrhoda.

Sequencing Activities

- Dramatize the story with puppets or stuffed animals.
- Create a circle diagram of the story. Have students draw pictures of each event and post them in a circle, beginning and ending with the grandmother.

Other Books by Jan Brett

(1985). *Annie and the Wild Animals.* Boston: Houghton Mifflin.
(1991). *Berlioz the Bear.* New York: Putnam.
(1992). *Trouble with Trolls.* New York: Putnam.
(1995). *Armadillo Rodeo.* New York: Putnam.
(2004). *The Umbrella.* New York: G. P. Putnam's Sons.
(2006). *Hedgie Blasts Off.* New York: G. P. Putnam's Sons.
(2008). *Gingerbread Friends.* New York: G. P. Putnam's Sons.
(2009). *Jan Brett's Snow Treasury.* New York: G. P. Putnam's Sons.

Writing Activities

- Write a reading log entry.
- Write a class collaboration retelling of the story.
- Create a found poem using words and phrases from the book.
- Create a story quilt with a mitten design on each square and a sentence about the book.

Extending Activities

- Compare mittens and gloves.
- Have a parent demonstrate how to knit a mitten.
- Learn to draw the animals in the story. See www.janbrett.com

Meet the Author

- Watch video *Jan Brett at home* at www.janbrett.com

sets out other books by Jan Brett and reads some of the books aloud to students. As their extension projects, students divide into small groups to research one of the animals mentioned in the story, then learn to draw the animal following the directions provided on Brett's website. Grade 5 students work with the primary-grade students as they research and draw the animals, then share what they learn on large posters that are displayed on the classroom bulletin board.

A Middle-Grade Resource-Based Unit on Deborah Ellis and Her Books

For more information on resource-based units, see Chapter 5, "The Reading and Writing Processes," pages 157, 158, 172. Also, see Chapter 6, "Reading and Writing Narrative Text," pages 231–234 and 243.

Students begin the unit by reading *The Breadwinner* (D. Ellis, 2000) together as a class. This Rocky Mountain Book Award–winning book tells the story of a young girl named Parvana who lives with her family in one room of a bombed-out apartment in Kabul, Afghanistan. When her father is arrested by the Taliban, things become desperate. Forbidden to earn money as a girl, Parvana must transform herself into a boy and become her family's breadwinner. After students read this book together, they read other books by Deborah Ellis in small groups and independently. Teachers focus on strategies and skills, teaching both by modelling and through planned minilessons. Students keep reading logs in which they write after reading each of the books. They participate in a variety of visually representing activities, including making open-mind portraits of favourite characters, and learn about story structure. Many of Ellis's stories focus on theme, and students have opportunities to think deeply about the meanings of the stories. Students learn about Deborah Ellis and they may choose to write letters to the author as a project. Students create a graph to determine their favourite book written by Deborah Ellis and pursue group and individual projects. A planning cluster for this unit is presented in Figure 11-5 on page 385.

An Upper-Grade Resource-Based Unit on *The Crazy Man*

Upper-grade students spend three or four weeks reading, responding to, exploring, and extending their understanding of Pamela Porter's **Governor General's Literary Award**–winning book *The Crazy Man* (2005). Porter tells the story of twelve-year-old Emaline, who loves her home on the prairie. One day, Emaline tries to stop her dog, Prince, from chasing a hare into the path of the tractor her father is driving. A terrible accident ensues, leaving her with a permanent disability. In his grief and guilt, her father shoots Prince and then leaves Emaline and her mother on their own. The novel focuses on Emaline's physical and emotional healing. She faces her pain and loss with help from a stern teacher the children call the Dragon Lady, a shy classmate, and most of all from a gentle giant named Angus, a patient from the local mental hospital.

Students can read the story together as a class, in small groups with the teacher, or in literature study groups, with buddies, or independently. Students come together to discuss the story in grand conversations and deal with the complex issues presented in the book in both small groups and whole-class discussions. They also write in reading journals or on blogs. Teachers identify skills and strategies to model during reading and to teach in minilessons. Students write important words from the story on the word wall and engage in a variety of word-study activities. Students also

FIGURE 11-5 A PLANNING CLUSTER FOR A MIDDLE-GRADE RESOURCE-BASED UNIT ON DEBORAH ELLIS AND HER BOOKS

Author Study

- Learn about Canadian author Deborah Ellis at the Canadian Children's Book Centre website: **www.bookcentre.ca**

Types of Reading

- Read books together as a class.
- Read books in small literature study groups.
- Read books with a partner.
- Read books individually.
- Listen to books read aloud at the listening centre.

Visually Representing Activities

- Create a graph with photocopies of the book covers of each of Ellis's books at the top of each column. Have students choose their favourite books and colour in a square in that column.
- Make a diorama using a shoebox to create a scene from one of Deborah Ellis's books.
- Have students make open-mind portraits to examine characters from the books they are reading.

Strategies and Skills

- Focus on connecting to personal experiences, generalizing themes, and monitoring own reading strategies.
- Encourage students to use meaning-making skills such as summarizing, inferring, noting details, and predicting.

Talk and Drama

- Have students dress up as one of the characters from a book written by Deborah Ellis and be interviewed by the class.
- Write an "I Am" poem from the viewpoint of one character and read it aloud to the class.
- Have a small group of students dramatize a scene from one of her books and tell why that scene was chosen.

Reading Logs

- Have students keep a double-entry journal by copying one or two quotes from a book and their connections or reactions to the quote.
- Have students write several journal entries as if they were one of the characters in a Deborah Ellis book.
- Students can create a web of the characters encountered in a book, using lines to show how they are related to one another.

Story Structure

- Focus on the theme of the book. Ask students to identify the theme—loyalty, family, survival and friendship—and then have them expand on the concept.
- Ask students to reflect on reasons Deborah Ellis uses a backdrop of Afghanistan for many of her books.

Deborah Ellis and Her Books

Books by Deborah Ellis

(2000). *The Breadwinner*. Toronto: Groundwood Books.
(2002). *Parvana's Journey*. Toronto: Groundwood Books.
(2003). *Mud City*. Toronto: Groundwood Books.
(2004). *The Heaven Shop*. Markham, ON: Fitzhenry & Whiteside.
(2004). *Three Wishes: Palestinian and Israeli Children Speak*. Toronto: Douglas & McIntyre.
(2006). *I Am a Taxi*. Toronto: House of Anansi Press.
(2007). *Bifocal*. Markham, ON: Fitzhenry & Whiteside.
(2007). *Sacred Leaf*. Toronto: House of Anansi Press.
(2011). *No Ordinary Day*. Toronto: Groundwood Books.
(2012). *Kids From Kabul*. Toronto: Groundwood Books.
(2014). *Moon at Nine*. Toronto: Pajama Press.
(2015). *My Name is Parvana*. Toronto: Groundwood Books.

Word Wall

The Breadwinner

Afghanistan	Shalwar kameez
Taliban	nan
marketplace	distinguish
forbade	penmanship
collapsed	disappeared
marvelled	concentration
rocket attack	customers
burqas	vegetable stand
belongings	adjustments
lavatory	Pakistan
handsome	street vendors
surrender	athletics

Projects

- Have students work together as a class to select a social action or community project to participate in, such as helping refugees integrate into their community, after reading *The Breadwinner* by Deborah Ellis.
- Have students design their own individual projects about favourite books.
- Also, find information about this author in the book *Writing Stories, Making Pictures: Biographies of 150 Canadian Children's Authors and Illustrators*, published by the Canadian Children's Book Centre.
- Have students make a poster with information about the author to display in the library centre next to the text set of books.

FIGURE 11-6 A PLANNING CLUSTER FOR AN UPPER-GRADE RESOURCE-BASED UNIT ON *THE CRAZY MAN*

Introducing the Book

- The novel is set in rural Saskatchewan in the 1960s. Introduce the book when studying the Canadian prairies.
- Explore how people respond to loss and what contributes to healing.
- Investigate how our attitudes toward intellectually challenged people have changed since the 1960s.
- *The Crazy Man* is written in the unusual style of free verse. Children might also be interested in Karen Hesse's Out of the Dust (2001), which is also written in free verse.

Story Structure Activities

- Create a set of storyboards, one for each chapter, with a picture representing the chapter and a summarizing paragraph.
- Analyze the theme of the book.
- Create a plot diagram to graph the highs and lows of the book.
- Make an open-mind portrait with several mind pages to track Emaline's emotional responses through the book.

Word Wall

Emaline	Angus
churning	meadowlarks
catty-cornered	seeder
caragana bushes	sprayer
discing	laundromat
pester	clothesline
Tommy Douglas	vow
machinery shed	kneaded
grain elevators	hailstorms
spring wheat	Medicine Hat
crutches	mental patient
rummaged	constabulary

Author Information

Search for information about author Pamela Porter and about *The Crazy Man*. Include information from the Governor General's Literary Awards jury for 2005.

Writing Projects

- Write a sequel to this story using the same style of free verse.
- Write found poems, "I Am" poems, or other poems.
- Write an essay comparing attitudes toward intellectually challenged people in Emaline's time and now.
- Write a response to this quote: "Healing comes about in unexpected ways. "

Reading Log

- Keep a simulated journal written from Emaline's viewpoint after reading each section of the book.
- Write a double-entry journal with quotes from the story in one column and personal connections or predictions in the other column.

The Crazy Man (2005 Governor General's Literary Award)

Word-Study Activities

- Create word clusters.
- Sort a set of words.
- Collect powerful sentences and write them on posters.

Characters With Challenges

Have students read a book about children who are challenged or have disabilities and compare them with Angus in *The Crazy Man*.

Hunt, L. (2015). *Fish in a Tree*. New York: Nancy Paulsen Books.

Martin, A. (2014). *Rain Reign*. New York: Macmillan (Feiwel & Friends).

Niner, H. (2005). *I Can't Stop!: A Story about Tourette Syndrome*. New York: Albert Whitman.

Palacio, R. (2012). *Wonder*. New York: Knopf.

Rose, C. (2012). *May B*. New York: Schwartz & Wade.

Thompson, L. (2015). *Emmanuel's Dream: The True Story of Emmuel Ofosu Yeboah*. New York: Schwartz & Wade.

Strategies and Skills

- Model monitoring and revising strategies. Ask students to reflect on their use of strategies when reading.
- Focus on decoding longer words by' peeling off affixes and breaking words into syllables.

Grand Conversations

Hold grand conversations after reading each section of the book. Begin grand conversations in small groups and then come together for a whole class discussion.

Choral Reading

To celebrate Pamela Porter's writing have students prepare and present choral readings of favourite sections of *The Crazy Man*, or of Sky (2004). They may also want to prepare and read aloud *Yellow Moon, Apple Moon* (2008) as a favourite bedtime storybook.

---

learn about the author and examine the story structure in the book. After reading, they can do a choral reading, investigate how attitudes about disabilities have changed since the 1960s, report on Canadian laws regarding discrimination, and create other projects. Figure 11-6 on page 386 shows a planning cluster for *The Crazy Man*. Only words from the first three chapters are listed in the cluster due to space limitations.

Theme Study Units and Inquiry-Based Units

Theme study units and **inquiry-based units** are interdisciplinary units that integrate reading and writing with social studies, science, math, and other curricular areas. Topics for these extended theme study units are broad and encompass many possible directions for exploration, such as what it means to be Canadian, our changing environment, or people who have changed the lives of others.

Teachers usually involve students in planning the theme study units or inquiry-based units and identifying some of the questions they want to explore and activities that interest them. By being involved, student interest in and commitment to unit activities is heightened. Textbooks might be used as a resource, but only as one of many available resources. Students explore topics that interest them and research answers to questions they have posed and are genuinely interested in answering. Students share their learning during and at the end of the unit and are assessed on what they have learned as well as the processes they used in learning and working together.

For more information on theme study units, see Chapter 5, "The Reading and Writing Processes," pages 158, 173, 182. Also see Chapter 6, "Reading and Writing Narrative Text," pages 234, 244.

How to Develop a Theme Study Unit or an Inquiry-Based Unit

The starting point for many Canadian teachers in planning a theme study or an inquiry-based unit is the required curriculum for their province or program. When selecting topics, teachers consider the language arts requirements together with the requirements in other areas such as science, social studies, and the fine arts. They combine this information with their students' interests and the resources they have or can make available. Theme study and inquiry-based units provide the framework for integrated instruction and learning, but make it possible for students to engage in diverse activities and achieve similar, but not identical outcomes. Teachers usually choose the general topic and then identify three or four key concepts that they want to develop as well two or three core outcomes they want all students to achieve through the unit. Other times, teachers help students ask their own questions to research and study. Teachers choose themes that are broad general concepts and allow for multiple interpretations. Ten important considerations in developing a theme study or inquiry-based unit are as follows:

1. *Collect a set of stories, informational books, and poems.* Teachers collect stories, poems, informational books, magazines, newspaper articles, and reference books related to the theme or topic of study. The resources are placed in the special area for materials related to the theme in the classroom library. Teachers read aloud some books to students, some will be read independently, and others students will read together as shared or **guided reading**. These materials can also be used for minilessons—to teach students, for example, about reading strategies and expository text structures. Other books can be used as models or patterns for writing projects. Teachers also write the poems on charts to share with students or arrange a bulletin board display of the poems.

2. *Set up a listening centre.* Teachers select digital recordings to accompany stories, poems, or informational books. They can also create their own recordings to enhance students' experiences with the literature or so that absent students can catch up on a book being read aloud daily.

3. *Coordinate content-area textbook readings.* Teachers can teach theme study units or inquiry-based units without textbooks; however, when information is available in a

literature series anthology or content-area textbook, it can be used. Upper-grade students, in particular, read and discuss concepts presented in textbooks or use them as a reference for further study.

4. ***Locate multimedia materials, including websites.*** Teachers plan the use of digital texts and other multimedia materials to be used in the theme study unit. In particular, teachers select appropriate websites and make them available through links on a class webpage or by creating bookmarks on classroom computers. Students use these resources to learn background knowledge about the theme, and to explore key concepts. Commercially prepared multimedia materials can be viewed or displayed in the classroom, and students can make others during the theme study unit.

5. ***Identify potential words for the word wall.*** Teachers preview books and other resources and identify potential words for the word wall. This list of potential words is useful in planning vocabulary activities, but teachers do not simply use their word lists for the classroom word wall. Students and the teacher develop the classroom word wall together as they read and discuss the key concepts and other information related to the theme.

6. ***Plan how students will use learning logs or blogs.*** Teachers plan for students to keep learning logs, in which students take notes, write questions, make observations, clarify their thinking, and write reactions to what they are learning during theme study units and inquiry-based units. Students also write **quickwrites** and make **clusters** to explore what they are learning.

7. ***Identify literacy skills and strategies to teach during the theme.*** Teachers plan minilessons to teach literacy skills and strategies based on curriculum requirements. Examples include expository text structures, how to use an index, skimming and scanning, how to write an alphabet book, and interviewing techniques. Minilessons are taught using a whole–part–whole approach so that students can apply what they are learning in reading, writing, and representing activities.

8. ***Plan oral and visually representing activities related to the theme.*** Students use talk and visually representing to learn during the theme study unit or the inquiry-based unit and to demonstrate their learning. Possible talk and visually representing activities are as follows:

   - Give oral, illustrated reports, using PowerPoint or other digital illustrations.
   - Interview someone with special expertise on the theme.
   - Participate in a debate related to the theme.
   - Create charts or diagrams or use a web-based presentation tool (e.g., Prezi) to display information.
   - Role-play a historical event.
   - Assume the role of a historical figure giving a speech.
   - Participate in a readers theatre presentation of a story or poem.
   - Tell or retell a story, biography, or event through a simulated newscast.
   - Use a puppet show or animate Plasticine or clay characters to tell a story, biography, or event.
   - Write and perform a skit or play.

For more information on extending projects, see Chapter 5, "The Reading and Writing Processes," pages 154–159.

9. ***Brainstorm possible projects students may complete to extend their learning.*** Teachers think about possible projects students may choose to develop to extend and personalize their learning during these units. As ideas for projects are composed, teachers develop criteria to assess student learning as represented through the project. This advance planning makes it possible for teachers to collect needed supplies and to have suggestions ready to offer to students who need assistance in choosing

a project. Students work on projects independently or in small groups and then share the projects with the class at the end of the theme. Projects involve one or more of the six language arts. Some project suggestions are as follows:

- Read a biography or informational text related to the unit.
- Create a poster or digital images to illustrate a key concept.
- Write and mail a letter or send an email message to get information related to the theme.
- Write a story related to the theme; for example, write **historical fiction**.
- Perform a readers theatre production, puppet show, or other dramatization.
- Write a poem, song, or rap related to the theme and perform for an audience.
- Write an "All about ..." book or report about one of the key concepts.
- Create and videotape a commercial or advertisement related to the theme.
- Create a multidimensional display about the theme, using objects, text, and other media.
- Create a WebQuest for peers to pursue information related to the theme.
- Create a podcast, taking on the role of expert concerning a particular aspect of the theme.

10. ***Plan for the assessment of students' learning during the unit.*** Teachers consider how they will assess students' learning as they make plans for activities and assignments. In this way, teachers can explain to students how they will be assessed at the beginning of the unit, and check that their assessment will emphasize students' learning of the key concepts and important ideas.

The goal in developing plans for a theme study unit or an inquiry-based unit is to consider a wide variety of resources that integrate listening, speaking, reading, writing, viewing, and visually representing with the content of the theme.

Readers and Writers Workshops

Readers workshops and **writers workshops** may be used in conjunction with a resource-based unit, a theme study unit, or an inquiry-based unit. Readers and writers workshops are a way of organizing instruction and learning. They offer opportunities for students themselves to make decisions about what to read and write and how to monitor their own processes within a predictable framework managed by teachers.

Nancie Atwell (2007) introduced readers workshop as an alternative to traditional reading instruction. In readers workshop, students read books that they choose themselves and respond to books through writing in reading logs and conferencing with teachers and classmates. This approach represents what we believe about how children learn and how literature can be used effectively in the classroom. Atwell developed readers workshop with her middle-school students, but it has been adapted and used successfully at every grade level, from grades 1 through 8. There are several versions of readers workshop, but they usually contain these components: reading, responding, sharing, minilessons, and reading aloud to students.

Writers workshop is similar to readers workshop, except that the focus is on writing. Students write on topics that they choose themselves, and they assume ownership of their writing and learning. At the same time, the teacher's role

FIGURE 11-7 WRITERS WORKSHOP SCHEDULE

	Time	Typical Activities
Teacher Sharing	5–10 minutes	• reading aloud • sharing writing experiences
Minilesson	5–10 minutes	• teacher-directed instruction • focus on workshop procedures or writing technique
Writing	30–45 minutes	• students writing (all stages of writing process) • teacher conferencing with students
Sharing	10–15 minutes	• students sharing writing in process • students sharing published writing • sharing in small groups or whole class

changes from being a provider of knowledge to serving as a facilitator and guide. The classroom becomes a community of writers who write and share their writing. When students choose to share their writing through the Internet, their audience is extended beyond the classroom. There is a spirit of pride and acceptance among the students in knowing that they have communicated with interested audiences.

Writers workshop is a 60- to 90-minute period scheduled each day (a typical writers workshop schedule is shown in Figure 11-7). During this time, students are involved in three primary components: writing, sharing, and minilessons. The writing component involves students in all stages of the writing process, prewriting through publication. The sharing takes place in conferences with the teacher as well as with peers. Minilessons provide teacher-led instruction concerning the craft of writing and the procedures of writers workshop. Sometimes a fourth component, reading aloud to students, is added when reading and writing workshops are combined.

For more information about the writing process, see Chapter 5, "The Reading and Writing Processes," pages 160–176.

Establishing a Workshop Environment

Teachers begin to establish the workshop environment when their students are reading and writing from the first day of the school year by providing students with choices, time to read and write, and opportunities for response. Through their interactions with students, the respect they show to students, and the way they model reading and writing, teachers establish the classroom as a community of learners.

For more information on establishing a community of learners and a language-rich environment, see Chapter 2, "Teaching and the Language Arts," pages 38–43, 58–60.

Teachers develop a schedule for readers and writers workshops with time allocated for each component, or they alternate between the two types of workshops. In their schedules, teachers allot as much time as possible for students to read and write. Part of developing the schedule, is planning for blocks of time when computers are available for writing. Teachers teach the workshop procedures and continue to model the procedures as students become comfortable with the routines. As students share what they are reading and writing at the end of workshop sessions, their enthusiasm grows and the benefits of the workshop approaches are reinforced.

Students keep two folders—one for readers workshop and one for writers workshop. In the readers workshop folder, students keep a list of books they have read, notes from minilessons, reading logs, and other materials. In the writers workshop folder, they keep all drafts and other compositions. They may also keep a list of all compositions, topics for future pieces, and notes from minilessons. Filing procedures differ according to what computer facilities are available, but most schools provide ways for students to electronically file their drafts and published compositions so they can return to their work on repeated occasions. Students also keep language arts notebooks in which they jot down images, impressions, **dialogue**, and experiences that they can build upon for writing projects.

Teachers use a workshop activity chart to monitor students' work on a daily basis. At the beginning of readers workshop, students or the teacher record what book (or chapter) they are reading, or if they are writing in a reading journal, sharing with their reading group, or working on an extended response project. For writers workshop, students identify the writing project they are involved in or at which the stage of the writing process they are. A sample writers workshop chart is shown in Figure 11-8. Teachers can also use the chart to award weekly "effort" grades, to have students indicate their need to conference with the teacher, or to have students announce that they are ready to share the book they have read or publish their writing. Atwell (2007) calls this chart "the state of the class." Teachers can review students' progress and note which students need to meet with the teacher or receive additional attention. When students fill in the chart themselves, they develop responsibility for their actions and a stronger desire to accomplish tasks they set for themselves.

FIGURE 11-8 "STATUS OF THE CLASS" CHART FOR WRITERS WORKSHOP

Writers Workshop Chart

Names	Dates 10/18	10/19	10/20	10/21	10/22	10/25	10/26	10/27
Anthony	4 5	5	5	6	7	8	8	8 9
Brooke	2	2	2 3	2	2	4	5	6
Charles	8 9 1	3 1	1	2	2 3	4	5	6 7
Dina	6	6	6	7 8	8	9 1	1	2 3
Dustin	7 8	8	8	8	8	8	9 1	1
Eddie	2 3	2	2 4	5 6	8	9 1	1 2	2 3
Elizabeth	7	6	7	8	8	8	9	1 2
Elsa	2	3	4 5	5 6	6 7	8	8	9 1

Code:
1 = Prewrite   4 = Writers Group   7 = Conference
2 = Draft   5 = Revise   8 = Make Final Copy
3 = Conference   6 = Edit   9 = Publish

To monitor primary-grade students, teachers often use a pocket chart and have students place a card in their pocket, indicating whether they are reading or responding during readers workshop or at which stage of the writing process they are working during writers workshop.

How to Set Up a Readers Workshop

Teachers move through a series of steps as they set up their schedules to prepare students to work independently, and for them to provide instruction. The steps in setting up a readers workshop are presented in the Step by Step box that follows.

STEP BY STEP

Setting Up a Readers Workshop

1 **Collect texts for readers workshop.** Students read all sorts of books during readers workshop, including e-books and online **hypertexts**. They read stories, informational books, biographies, poetry books, and magazines. Most of their reading materials are selected from the classroom or school library, but students also bring books from home and borrow books from the public library and classmates, depending on the particular way the teacher chooses to implement readers workshop. Over the course of a school year, the teacher and students need to have available literally hundreds of books, including books written at a range of reading levels, in order to have appropriate books for all students. Primary teachers often worry about finding books that their emerging readers can handle independently. Alphabet and number books, pattern and predictable books, and books the teacher has read aloud several times are often the most accessible for kindergartners and grade 1 students. Primary-grade children often read and reread easy-to-read books.

The teacher introduces students—especially reluctant readers—to the books to be read during workshop so that they can more effectively choose books to read independently. The best way to preview books is using a very brief book talk to interest students in the book. In book talks, the teacher tells students a little about the book, shows the cover, and perhaps reads the first paragraph or two. The teacher also gives book talks to introduce new books, and students give book talks as they share books they have read with the class during the sharing part of readers workshop.

2 **Teach students readers workshop procedures.** Students need to learn how to access and choose books, write responses to books they are reading, share books they have finished reading, and conference with the teacher, as well as other procedures related to readers workshop. Workshop procedures will vary according to whether students are reading hard-copy books or electronic texts. Some of these procedures need to be taught before students begin readers workshop, and others can be introduced and reviewed as minilessons during readers workshop.

3 **Identify topics for minilessons.** Minilessons are an important part of readers workshop because the workshop approach is more than reading practice. Instruction is important, and minilessons are the "teaching" step. The teacher presents minilessons on readers workshop procedures and on reading concepts, strategies, and skills. The teacher identifies topics for minilessons based on what students do during readers workshop, the questions students ask, and the skills and strategies that are expected to be introduced, practised, or reviewed at the grade level. The teacher uses examples from books students are reading, and students are often asked to reflect on their own reading processes. These minilessons can be taught to the whole class, small groups, or individual students, depending on which students need the instruction.

4 **Choose books to read aloud to students in conjunction with readers workshop.** The teacher carefully chooses the books when a reading aloud component is included in readers workshop. The teacher may choose books that are more difficult than those that students can read independently, or ones that introduce students to a genre, an author, or a literary element. Sometimes the teacher reads the first book in a series aloud to students and then invites students to continue reading the sequels themselves. Whatever the reason, teachers choose books to read aloud for specific instructional purposes.

For more information on reading aloud to students, see Chapter 4, "Listening and Speaking in the Classroom," pages 105–108.

5 **Design a schedule for readers workshop.** The teacher examines the daily and weekly schedules, considers all of the language arts activities in which students are involved, decides how much time is available for readers workshop, and allocates time to each of the readers workshop components. Some teachers make readers and writers workshops their entire language arts program. Others engage in workshop approach on a regular schedule such as two or three times a week, balancing with more teacher-directed lessons. They begin by reading aloud a book to the class, chapter by chapter, and talking about the book in a grand conversation. During this time, teachers focus on modelling reading strategies and talking about elements of story structure. Minilessons often follow and are related to teacher read-alouds. Next, students read self-selected books independently. The teacher conferences with small groups of students as they read and then presents minilessons as needed. Then students spend fifteen to twenty minutes writing in reading journals about their reading. Often, teachers have students keep double-entry journals in which students record quotations from the story in one column and react to the quotations in the second column. Sharing is held during the last fifteen minutes, sometimes in small groups and sometimes as a whole class. During sharing in small groups, students typically share their responses to the books they are reading. When sharing as a whole class, students do book talks about books they have finished reading or present extended response projects. Although schedules vary to meet the capabilities and needs of students, all schedules provide extended periods of time for uninterrupted reading.

6 **Plan for extended response projects.** The purpose of students engaging in response projects during and after they read is to help them think in critical and creative ways about the meaning or some particular aspect of the book. Students sometimes complete response projects independently and sometimes collaboratively in small groups. Many popular response projects combine forms of visually representing ideas from the book with talking or creating other sound effects that help portray the students' interpretations. Dramatizations, readers theatre, and multimedia projects, such as creating short movies that depict a particular scene or event, are popular responses. Other projects, such as creating informative podcasts about the setting of the book, involve students in research about times and places described by the author. Teachers usually give students choices about which projects they will complete, but may limit the choices to manage the time spent on any one book.

7 **Plan for conferencing and monitoring.** During readers workshop, students are reading and responding independently and the teacher must find ways to monitor students' progress. Many teachers keep individual records of reading achievements. They include what the student reads as well as anecdotal notes from observations and conferences. Teachers create conference schedules and meet with students individually and in small groups on a regular basis, usually once a week, to talk about their reading and their reading skills and strategies. They listen to students read excerpts aloud, and make plans for the next book. Teachers add the notes they make during these conferences to the folders they keep for each student.

Variations of Readers Workshop

In Canadian classrooms, teachers often integrate readers workshop into resource-based units, theme study units, or inquiry-based units. That is, workshop is an organizational approach to instruction and learning. In other instances, readers workshop is more of a stand-alone component of the language arts program. In one adaptation, students choose and read books from a special themed set of resources. Books may focus on a social studies or science theme such as the ocean or ancient Egypt, or the books may be written by one author or represent one genre, such as tall tales or time-warp stories. In adaptations like this, readers workshop complements other language arts and curricular activities.

Other variations are referred to by other names. For example, another variation (discussed in detail at the beginning of this chapter) is *literature circles*, also called *literature study groups* and *book clubs*, in which students read in small groups. Students divide into small groups to read one of five or six related books. For example, grade 3 students might read different versions of a fairytale, such as "The Three Little Pigs," and grade 6 students might read survival stories such as Gary Paulsen's *Hatchet* (1987). A list of text-set suggestions for literature circles is presented in Figure 11-9.

In a literature circle, small groups of students read a book (each with a copy of the same book), participate in one or more grand conversations in which they talk about the book and their reflections, and write in reading journals.

Teachers collect books for literature circles with five, six, or seven related titles and collect a few copies of each book. Then the teacher gives a book talk about each

FIGURE 11-9 TEXT-SET SUGGESTIONS FOR LITERATURE CIRCLES

Primary Grades

Author Study — Barbara Reid Stories
Reid, B. (2015). *Two by Two*. Toronto: Scholastic Canada. 🍁
Reid, B. (2011). *Picture a Tree*. Toronto: North Winds Press. 🍁
Reid, B. (2012). *The Party*. Richmond Hill, ON: North Winds Press. 🍁
Reid, B. (2012). *Zoe's Year*. Toronto: Scholastic Canada. 🍁

Theme Study — Canadians Live in Many Places
Carter, A. L. (2003). *My Home Bay*. Red Deer, AB: Red Deer Press. 🍁
Hartry, N. (1997). *Hold On, McGinty!* Toronto: Doubleday Canada. 🍁
Jardine–Stoddart, H. (2009). *Back to the Beach*. Halifax, NS: Nimbus. 🍁
Kusugak, M. A. (1998). *Arctic Stories*. Willowdale, ON: Annick Press. 🍁
McFarlane, S. (1991). *Waiting for the Whales*. Victoria, BC: Orca Books. 🍁

Middle Grades

Author Study — Carol Matas Stories
Matas, C. (2012). *Behind Enemy Lines: World War II: Sam Frederiksen, Nazi-Occupied Europe, 1944* (I Am Canada series). Toronto: Scholastic Canada. 🍁
Matas, C. (2013). *Pieces of the Past: The Holocaust Diary of Rose Rabinowitz* (Dear Canada series). Toronto: Scholastic Canada. 🍁
Matas, C. (2013). *Greater Than Angels*. Toronto: Scholastic Canada. 🍁
Matas, C. (2013). *In My Enemy's House*. Toronto: Scholastic Canada. 🍁

Theme Study — Folktales are Part of Our History
Arsenault, G. (2002). *Acadian Legends, Folktales, and Songs from Prince Edward Island* (S. Ross, Trans.). Charlottetown, PEI: Acorn Press. 🍁
Barton, B. (2003). *The Bear Says North: Tales from Northern Lands*. Toronto: Groundwood Books. 🍁
Jorisch, S. (2001). *As for the Princess? A Folktale from Quebec*. Toronto: Annick Press. 🍁
Qitsualik-Tinsley, R. and Qitsualik, S. (2014). *Skraelings*. Toronto: Inhabit Media Inc. 🍁
Yee, P. (2003). *Tales from Gold Mountain: Stories of the Chinese in the New World*. Toronto: Groundwood Books. 🍁

Upper Grades

Author Study — Susan Juby
Juby, S. (2006). *Alice, Realist At Last*. Toronto: HarperTrophy. 🍁
Juby, S. (2007). *Another Kind of Cowboy*. New York: HarperCollins. 🍁
Juby, S. (2010). *Getting the Girl*. New York: HarperCollins. 🍁
Juby, S. (2015). *The Truth Commission*. Toronto: Penguin Canada. 🍁

Theme Study — Literature Takes Us Beyond Our Borders 🍁
Bell, W. (1999). *Forbidden City*. Toronto: Doubleday. 🍁
Coates, J. (2010). *A Hare in the Elephant's Trunk*. Markham, ON: Red Deer Press. 🍁
Maes, N. (2011). *Crescent Star*. Toronto: Dundurn Press. 🍁
Ostlere, C. (2011). *Karma*. Toronto: Puffin Canada. 🍁
Ye, T. X., & Bell, W. (2003). *Throwaway Daughter*. Toronto: Doubleday Canada. 🍁

book, to introduce them to the students. One way to do this is to set each book on the chalk tray after the book talks and have students sign their names on the chalkboard above the book they want to read. Or, teachers can set the books on a table and place a sign-up sheet beside each book. Students take time to preview the books, and then select the book they want to read.

The books vary in length and difficulty to accommodate diversity among students, but students are not always placed in groups according to reading level. Students choose the books they want to read, and as they preview the books they consider how good a "fit" the book is and which one they find most interesting. Students can usually manage whatever book they choose because of support and assistance from their group or through determination. Once in a while, teachers counsel students to choose another book or provide an additional copy for reading with a tutor or at home to enable keeping pace with the literature circle group.

When students finish reading the book or the selected chapter, they engage in conversation to broaden and deepen their understanding. Sometimes teachers participate in the conversations and sometimes they don't. When the teachers are participants, they participate as fellow readers who share joys and difficulties, insights and speculations. They also help students develop literary insights by providing information, asking insightful questions, and guiding students to make comments.

Students talk about the characters, the plot, the theme—all the important issues in a story. They also make connections between the story and their own lives and the story and other stories they have read. They also notice literary language and read memorable passages aloud.

As students read and engage in grand conversations, the teacher circulates and meets with each group. During group meetings, the teacher may read along with students, read their reading journal entries, or participate in grand conversations. While the teacher is meeting with one group, the other groups read independently or write in reading journals.

Students in literature circles often make only one journal entry when reading a picture book, but they make entries after reading every chapter or periodically when reading longer books. Sometimes they write their journal entries before discussing their reading and sometimes after. In many classrooms, students write in notebook journals, but in others, students write blogs and carry on their conversations electronically. When they write before, their writing helps them clarify ideas to contribute to the conversation. When they write after, their entries often reflect what was heard in the grand conversation or what they have gleaned from reading the online conversation. Both help readers develop meaning. Writing in reading journals or blogs and talking about the book replace traditional workbook activities.

There are advantages and disadvantages to students participating in online discussions or blogging rather than face-to-face conversations. The two approaches impose different expectations for what happens during literature circles and workshops in classrooms. Some students have reported that they found it easier to stay on topic when writing online than in face-to-face conversations, while some have suggested that reading other group members' responses inspires deeper and more meaningful transactions with the text (Larson, 2008). One of the difficulties teachers encounter, even in classrooms where every student has a laptop computer, is managing students' postings of journal entries on a schedule that enhances their classroom interactions with their literature circle group. Communicating online, however, has the added advantage of widening the circle of those with whom students can discuss their reading and makes it possible to share responses to literature with students in other schools in Canada and worldwide.

For years teachers have devoted ten, twenty, or thirty minutes a day to silent reading in the classroom. Lyman Hunt (1970) called it **uninterrupted sustained silent reading (USSR)**, McCracken and McCracken (1972) called it **sustained silent reading (SSR)**, and teachers have created their own acronyms, such as **DEAR (Drop Everything and Read)** time. Students read self-selected library books during these practice periods. The idea behind these programs is that students need lots of reading practice in addition to reading instruction to become strategic, fluent readers. These programs were initially developed because research showed that students had few opportunities to transfer the skills and strategies they were learning to genuine reading activities and to read for sustained periods in school. In *The Book Whisperer*, Donalyn Miller (2009) explains that achievement in reading is a "by-product" of students' engagement. As they encounter and digest books, their competence in reading grows. Hence, the value of extended time for reading is clear, but it is important to note that these practice programs are not the same as readers workshop, because they lack instructional components.

How to Set Up a Writers Workshop

As teachers set up a writers workshop classroom, they collect writing supplies and informational resources as well as other materials their students will need. These include different kinds of paper: various writing instruments, and references such as dictionaries and thesauri. They also set up access to the word-processing, printing, and publishing facilities available in their school. They may collect bookmaking supplies as well, to make it possible to publish student writing as durable books to be added to the classroom or school library. Teachers also add to the classroom library and encourage students to use it as a resource for information and ideas. Many times students' writing grows out of favourite books they have read.

Teachers think about classroom arrangement. They maximize access to computers to facilitate writing productivity, but ask students to sit at desks or tables arranged in small groups when they write on paper or conference with each other. The teacher circulates around the classroom, conferencing briefly with students, and the classroom atmosphere is conducive to students writing independently, conversing quietly with other writers, moving around the classroom to collect materials, assisting classmates, or sharing ideas as needed in various stages of the writing process. There is a space, usually with a table available, for students to meet together in writing groups or with the teacher for conferences, proofreading, and minilessons.

In addition to collecting supplies and arranging the classroom, teachers need to prepare students for writers workshop and make plans for the instruction. In classrooms where workshop routines are well established and students are familiar with the writing process, students assume much of the responsibility for the smooth running of the workshop. The steps in setting up a writers workshop are presented in the following Step by Step box:

Variations of Writers Workshop

Sometimes teachers set up writers workshop for a limited period of time when their students are working on a project and need lengthy periods of time for writing. For example, as grade 3 students write weather reports after reading *Hurricane*

Setting Up a Writers Workshop

1 **Teach the stages of the writing process.**   Teachers begin writers workshop by teaching or reviewing the five stages of the writing process, setting guidelines for writers workshop, and taking students through one writing activity together. In their discussion of the writing process and guidelines, teachers remind students that not all pieces of writing are taken through all stages, including publication. Students will make many decisions, including those concerning publication as they engage in writing each piece. A set of guidelines for writers workshop that one grade 7 class developed is presented in Figure 11-10.

2 **Teach writers workshop procedures.**   Teachers need to explain how students will meet in groups to revise their writing, how to sign up for turn-taking at computers or a conference with the teacher, how to proofread, how to use the publishing centre, and other procedures used in writers workshop.

3 **Identify topics for minilessons.**   As with readers workshop, teachers teach minilessons during writers workshop. The minilessons are on procedures related to writers workshop and writing concepts, strategies, and skills that students can apply in their own writing. Some topics for minilessons come from teachers' observations of students as they write, questions students ask, and topics identified in grade-level curriculum guides.

   Teachers also share information about authors and how they write during minilessons. In order for students to think of themselves as writers, they need to know what writers do. Each year there are more autobiographies written by authors. Popular Canadian author Sheree Fitch has written *Writing Maniac: How I Grew Up to Be an Author and You Can Too* (2002), telling readers about her growth as a writer and showing students that writing well takes time and experience. Jean Little, author of *From Anna* (1991), has written an autobiography called *Little by Little: A Writer's Education* (1987), in which she reflects on her writing processes and why she writes about contemporary issues. Some of the other books in the "Meet the Author" series are *Firetalking*, by Patricia Polacco (1994), *Hau Kola/Hello Friend*, by Paul Goble (1994), and *Surprising Myself*, by Jean Fritz (1992). Films and videos about authors and illustrators are also available. For example, in the 27-minute video *Eric Carle: Picture Writer* (1993), Eric Carle demonstrates how he uses paint and collage to create the illustrations for his popular picture books.

4 **Design a writers workshop schedule.**   An important instructional decision that teachers make is how to organize their daily schedule and what portion of the language arts block to allocate to readers and writers workshops. In doing this, their priority is to provide students a block of time for uninterrupted writing. During writers workshop students move through the writing process as they write on self-selected or curriculum-related topics for forty-five or fifty minutes. The teacher meets with small groups of students or individual students as they draft, revise, and edit their compositions during this writing time. Teachers use a ten- to fifteen-minute block of time, often prior to writing time, for giving minilessons on writers workshop procedures and writing concepts, strategies, and skills to the whole class. Other minilessons for small groups of students, or individual students are given as needed while other students write. Sharing is usually held during the last fifteen minutes. (See the writers workshop schedule in Figure 11-7 on page 390.)

   Other teachers coordinate writers workshop with resource-based, theme study, and inquiry-based units. For example, they may allocate the last hour of their language arts block for readers or writers workshop, and alternate readers workshop and writers workshop month by month or grading period by grading period. Some teachers allocate time for writers workshop during the last week of a resource-based unit when students are developing a writing project. For example, in the resource-based unit on *The Mitten* discussed earlier, primary-grade students use a writers workshop approach as they research one of the animals mentioned in the story and create posters to share what they learn.

5 **Plan for conferencing.** Teachers conference with students as they write. Many teachers prefer moving around the classroom to meet with students rather than having the students come to a table to meet with the teacher. Too often a line forms as students wait to meet with the teacher, and students lose precious writing time. Some teachers move around the classroom in a regular pattern, meeting with one-fifth of the students each day. In this way they can conference with every student during the week.

Other teachers spend the first fifteen to twenty minutes of writers workshop stopping briefly to check on ten or more students each day. Many use a zigzag pattern to get to all parts of the classroom each day. In primary classrooms, teachers often kneel down beside each student or carry their own stool to each student's desk. During the one- or two-minute conference, teachers ask students what they are writing, listen to students read a paragraph or two, and then ask what they plan to do next. Then these teachers use the remaining time during writers workshop to more formally conference with students who are revising and editing their compositions.

Students often sign up for these conferences. The teachers make comments to find strengths, ask questions, and discover possibilities during these revising conferences. Some teachers like to read the pieces themselves, while others like to listen to students read their papers aloud. As they interact with students, teachers model the kinds of responses that students are learning to give to each other.

As students meet together to share their writing during revising and editing, they continue to develop their sense of community. They share their drafts with classmates in writers groups composed of four or five students. In some classrooms, teachers join in the writers groups whenever they can, but students normally run the groups themselves. They take turns reading their drafts to each other and listen as their classmates offer compliments and suggestions for revision. In contrast, students usually work with one partner to edit their writing, whether on paper or onscreen.

Teacher and student discuss author's craft while having a reading conference.

After proofreading their drafts with a classmate and then meeting with the teacher for a final editing, students make the final copy of their writings. Depending upon the facilities available, students usually want to print their writing on the computer so that their final copies will appear professional, hence the strong recommendation to develop students' fluency in their handwriting and keyboarding skills. Many times students compile their final copies to make books during writers workshop, but sometimes they attach their writing to artwork, make posters, write letters that are mailed, or perform scripts as skits or puppet shows. Not every piece is necessarily published, however. Sometimes students decide not to continue with a piece of writing. They file the piece in their writing folders and start something new.

For more information on handwriting and keyboarding, see Chapter 8, "Words, Their Meanings, and the Tools to Use Them: Grammar, Spelling, Handwriting, and Word Processing," pages 321–329.

6 Plan for assessment of student writing. Teachers' assessment of student writing should focus on both the writing process and the completed product. By collecting information while they are writing, teachers learn about the students' process, the strategies they use, the difficulties they encounter, and can identify the instruction they need. Teachers often use checklists to help them keep track of students' skill development. Others make anecdotal notes each time they conference with a student. They note what things the student does well and where instruction is needed. To assess pieces of writing, teachers often use rubrics that they create themselves or that are commercially available.

7 Include sharing. For the last ten to fifteen minutes of writers workshop, the class gathers together to share their writing, both work in progress and published pieces. Works in progress are often shared when writers seek peer assistance to help them overcome obstacles and move forward. Published pieces are shared to celebrate accomplishments. Younger students often sit in a circle or gather together on a rug for sharing time. If an author's chair is available, each student sits in the special chair to read his or her composition. After reading works in progress, authors ask for and classmates provide suggestions. When published pieces are read, classmates clap and offer compliments. They may also make other comments and suggestions, but the focus is on celebrating completed writing projects, not on revising the composition to make it better. Published pieces are often added to the classroom library, available for reading by classmates.

FIGURE 11-10 A GRADE 7 CLASS'S GUIDELINES FOR WRITERS WORKSHOPS

Ten Writers Workshop Rules

1. Keep everything in your writing folder (paper or digital).
2. Save draft files clearly labeled "draft". Number your drafts.
3. Keep all drafts.
4. Double-space all drafts so you will have space to revise and edit.
5. Show self-edits in blue.
6. Show peer-edits in red.
7. Keep track of all sources used. Record authors, date, title, and publishers.
8. Keep a record of the compositions you write in your writing folder. Include date and title of each one.
9. Support your peers. Give them helpful feedback.
10. Work hard!

For more information on reading and writing poetry, see Chapter 6, "Reading and Writing Narrative Text," pages 228–245.

(Weisner, 1990), or as upper-grade students write simulated journals or reports, they may participate in writers workshop for a week or two. During these project-oriented writers workshops, teachers sometimes teach minilessons on topics related to the assignment, but usually all of the writers workshop time is used for writing and then for sharing when students complete their projects.

Another variation is a combined readers-writers workshop. Teachers sometimes use this format when studying a literary genre. For example, students can read and write biographies, read and write tall tales or *pourquoi* tales, or read and write collections of letters or journals. Poetry, too, is sometimes experienced through combined workshops. After students learn about various poetic forms and read and listen to many examples, they often choose to write poems during writers workshop.

Overall, readers and writers workshops offer teachers and students opportunities to engage in meaningful literacy activities for extended periods of time. Some teachers use readers and writers workshops as organizational frameworks for their entire language arts programs. However, many teachers use workshops to support and enhance their resource-based units, their theme study units, and their inquiry-based units. The teacher, as instructional decision maker, chooses an organizational approach based on knowledge about and experience with students, resources, and curriculum.

Review

Designing language arts instruction that reflects the theory and research about language and how students learn is an important responsibility. Choosing resources and approaches to instruction involves critical decision making. In planning language arts programs, teachers consider students' interests and needs, curriculum requirements, and all language learning activities—those during language arts blocks and those associated with other subject areas such as social studies and science. They also consider the ways students can use technologies as tools for language learning. They plan for broad, rich learning through resource-based, theme study, and inquiry-based units and engage students in authentic, meaningful reading and writing through readers and writers workshops.

The following key concepts are presented in this chapter:

1. Three instructional frameworks are resource-based units, theme study units, and inquiry-based units.

2. Teachers can adapt and combine resource-based units, theme study units, and inquiry-based units to fit the needs of their students and their curriculum.

3. Plans for all units include the core components: focus and desired outcomes, learning activities, lists of resources, and plans for assessment of learning.

4. Students use all six language arts in all three units, often making cross-curriculum linkages with subject areas such as social studies, science, and the fine arts.

5. Teachers should select high-quality print and nonprint resources, including high-quality literature, digital texts and images, and carefully selected websites, for inclusion in all three units. Textbooks may be used as one resource, but they should never be the only resource.

6. Readers and writers workshops are ways of organizing instruction that include reading, writing, minilessons, and sharing.

7. Readers and writers workshops are often used as ways of organizing a large part of a teacher's instruction and may be used in conjunction with resource-based units, theme study units, and inquiry-based units.

8. Teachers organize readers and writers workshops to give students blocks of uninterrupted time for reading and writing, preferably on a daily basis.

9. Teachers plan for assessment of student learning throughout units of instruction and use the information collected to plan future instruction.

Theory to Practice

1. Read a collection of award-winning literature and create an annotated reading list Share one or more books from your collection with age-appropriate students. Include the students' responses in your annotation.

2. Create a planning cluster for a resource-based unit featuring a picture book or a chapter book or a theme study unit concerning a topic of interest. Incorporate activities involving all six language arts. Share your cluster with colleagues.

3. Observe in a classroom using the readers and writers workshop approach. Note how the teacher manages the routine and conferences with students. Write a journal entry or blog to share your observations with others.

4. Compile a text set of ten or more related books, including stories, informational books, and poems. Design an assignment checklist to engage students in reading at least three books from the text set.

5. Plan a minilesson to teach one writing technique to help students improve their writing. Employ at least one example from good quality literature to illustrate the author's use of the technique.

APPENDIX A

Basic Grammar, Punctuation, and Syntax

Subject–Verb Agreement

The **subject** and the **verb** must agree in number: A singular subject needs a singular verb; a plural subject needs a plural verb. The **subject** tells what or whom the sentence is about and the verb describes what the subject does.

X	✓	WHY?
The **list** of names **were circulated** to the staff.	The **list** of names **was circulated** to the staff.	The subject is **list**, not names. **List** is singular. Use the singular verb **was circulated**.
The **software** in the computers **are** the latest program.	The **software** in the computers **is** the latest program.	The subject is **software**, not computers. **Software** is singular. Use the singular verb **is**.
The **leaves** on the maple tree **turns** red in the fall.	The **leaves** on the maple tree **turn** red in the fall.	The subject is **leaves**, not maple tree. **Leaves** is plural. Use the plural verb **turn**.
The **books** on the shelf **is gathering** dust.	The **books** on the shelf **are gathering** dust.	The subject is **books**, not shelf. **Books** is plural. Use the plural verb **are gathering**.
TIP Ignore the words that come between the subject and the verb.		
The finance **committee have approved** a new budget.	The finance **committee has approved** a new budget.	The members of the group are acting as **one unit**, not as individuals. Use the singular verb **has approved**.
After four days of deliberation, the **jury remains** divided.	After four days of deliberation, the **jury remain** divided.	The members of the group are acting as **individuals**, not as one unit. Use the plural verb **remain**.
Everyone in the audience **were moved** by the performance.	**Everyone** in the audience **was moved** by the performance.	Use a singular verb after words such as **any, anybody, anyone, anything, each, every, everybody, everyone, everything, no one, nobody, nothing, somebody, someone, something**.
Only a **few is staying** to the end.	Only a few **are staying** to the end.	Use a plural verb after words such as **all, both, few, many, several, some**.

402

The Apostrophe (')

The apostrophe has two main functions: to show possession and to form contractions. Knowing when to use an apostrophe and whether to put it before or after the letter *s* is a key to avoiding a frequently made mistake in punctuation.

X	✓	WHY?
The tire on **Terrys** bike has a puncture.	The tire on **Terry's** bike has a puncture.	**Terry** is singular. Add the **'s** to show the bike belongs to Terry.
James computer is loaded with state-of-the-art software.	**James's** computer is loaded with state-of-the-art software.	**James** is singular and ends in **s**. Add an **'s** to show possession if the word isn't awkward to pronounce.
Ulysses travels played a significant role in Greek mythology.	**Ulysses'** travels played a significant role in Greek mythology.	**Ulysses** is singular and ends in **'s**. Add only an **'** after the last **s** when the word is awkward to pronounce.
The **ladies** tennis match attracted a sell-out crowd.	The **ladies'** tennis match attracted a sell-out crowd.	**Ladies** is plural and ends in **s**. Add an **'** after the **s** to show possession.
They watched the **mens'** golf tournament on TV.	They watched the **men's** golf tournament on TV.	**Men** is plural and doesn't end in **s**. Add an **'s** to show possession.
Terry and Robin's cars were vandalized.	**Terry's and Robin's** cars were vandalized.	**Terry** and **Robin** are singular and separate: Each person has a car. Add an **'s** after each name to show possession.
Terry's, Lynn's, and Robin's apartment was painted before they moved in. They decided to rent two **video's** for the weekend.	**Terry, Lynn, and Robin's** apartment was painted before they moved in. They decided to rent two **videos** for the weekend.	**Terry, Lynn, and Robin** are one singular unit: They jointly possess the apartment. Add the **'s** after the last person's name to show possession. The **s** in **videos** is used to make a plural and not to show possession. Do not use the **'** to make the word plural.

Commonly Confused Words I

Many words in the English language are frequently confused one for the other. The word pairs below are called *homonyms*—words that sound alike but have different meanings.

WORD	DEFINITION	EXAMPLE
ascent	the act of rising	The balloon's ascent was rapid.
assent	agreement or acceptance	He gave his assent to the proposal.
bloc	a group of people, companies, or countries with a common interest	The members of the political party voted as a bloc. How quickly will the block of ice melt?
block	a solid piece (e.g., wood, ice); to obstruct	Did the felled tree block the road?
canvas	a strong, heavy cloth	Canvas makes a good protective cover.
canvass	to solicit opinions or views	She phoned residents to canvass their views.
check	to verify; to restrain or impede; a bank draft (used in the U.S.)	Check your letter carefully for careless errors. The flood was held in check by sandbags along the shore. The Chicago office awaited the check from its New York affiliate.
cheque	a bank draft (used in Canada, Britain)	She cashed the cheque as soon as it arrived.
coarse	rough or crude	The book contained coarse language.
course	direction or action; part of a meal; a series of lessons	The wind blew the sailboat off course. The five-course gourmet meal was a delight. Which language arts course are you enrolled in?
complement	one of two things that go well together or suit each other	Wine and food should complement each other.
compliment	to congratulate or to praise	Please compliment the chef on a wonderful meal.
dependant	one who relies on the support of another	Are you a dependant of your parents?
dependent	unable to do without	He was dependent on drugs to ease the pain.
flair	an instinct or knack for doing something well	Her flair for photography earned wide recognition.
flare	a bright flame or light	He launched a flare to signal an emergency.
foreword	a preface or introduction in a book	She wrote a foreword to her latest novel.
forward	ahead or to advance	They looked forward to their winter vacation.
forth	to go forward, set out	They put forth some good ideas.
fourth	a number that follows third	It's her fourth attempt to beat the record.
hoard	to amass or collect; to overstock in scarce times	They put aside a hoard of food before winter's onset.
horde	a throng of people or a swarm of insects, animals	A horde of invaders swept across the land.
it's	a contraction of it is	It's all over but the shouting.
its	indicates possession	The dog wagged its tail when it saw me.
lean	not much fat; to rest against something	She always purchased lean meat. Lean the board against the wall.
lien	a legal claim against property	A lien was issued against his car to cover the debt.
lightening	brightening; reducing in weight	The sky was lightening after the storm. Her mailbag began lightening after 15 minutes of deliveries.
lightning	a flash of bright light during a thunderstorm	A flash of lightning illuminated the sky.

Commonly Confused Words 2

Many words in the English language are often confused one for the other. The word pairs below have similarities in spelling or in meaning.

WORD	DEFINITION	EXAMPLE
accept	to receive; to agree to an action	We accept courier parcels at the reception desk. I accept your offer of a free gift.
except	to exclude; not including	She was excepted from the meeting. Everyone went to the movie except me.
affect	to influence; to move or touch, as in feelings	Computers affect the way we work. Her kindness affected him deeply.
effect	a result or outcome	Staff cuts had a deep effect on morale.
aggravate	to worsen something that already exists	You'll aggravate your injury if you exercise.
irritate	to annoy or to vex	You irritate me when you arrive late.
alternate	a substitute way of doing things	We found an alternate solution to the problem.
alternative	two or more options; a matter of choice	We took the alternative route home. I had no alternative but to replace the broken lamp.
among	involves more than two things or two persons	Among all my discs, this one is my favourite.
between	involves only two things or two persons	Between the two, I like this one better.
anyone	any kind of a person	Anyone can go to the dance.
any one	any single person or thing	The ticket was valid for any one of the games.
assure	to express certainty or confidence	Can you assure me that the rain will stop?
ensure	to make sure or to guarantee	Success at work helps to ensure promotion.
balance	difference between a credit and a debt	The balance owing is seven dollars.
remainder	a small amount left over	I'll eat the remainder of the cookies tomorrow.
beside	by the side of	We picnicked beside the lake.
besides	in addition to	Besides you, there will be five of us.
biannual	twice a year	The craft show has become a popular biannual event.
biennial	once every two years	The biennial games are held on even-numbered years.
bring	to come with something or someone	Please bring some snacks for the party.
take	to remove or carry something or someone elsewhere	Please take my coat to the dry cleaners.
can	indicates a physical or mental ability to do something	I can do anything better than you.
may	indicates permission	You may borrow my car for a few hours.
client	uses professional services	The lawyer's office was filled with clients.
customer	uses commercial services	Customers flocked to the clothing sale.
colleague	business associate	I consider my boss a good colleague.
partner	legally constituted member of partnership	She joined the firm as a full partner.
continual	repeated again and again over a period of time	Mowing the lawn is a continual activity.
continuous	no break in the action or the process	The well produced a continuous flow of oil.

Source: Copyright © 1999 from The Write Guide series, The Writing Edge, 35 Merton St. #1607, Toronto, ON, M4S 3G4.

APPENDIX B

Manuscript and Cursive Handwriting Forms

FIGURE B-1 D'NEALIAN MANUSCRIPT AND CURSIVE HANDWRITING FORMS

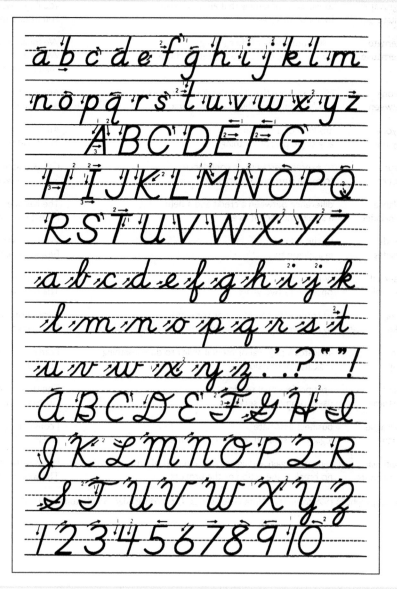

Glossary

Accommodation: one of the two cognitive processes (see also *assimilation*) by which children learn concepts and add information to their cognitive structures (Piaget, 1969). *Accommodation* refers to new information or experience that disrupts the existing schemata by which children understand the world and to how it is acted on, absorbed, or accommodated, and results in a different, more complex capacity to understand.

Aesthetic listening: see *aesthetic reading*.

Aesthetic reading: reading for pleasure, for meaning-making, and for the deep personal engagement that connects the reader's life with the textual experience (Rosenblatt, 1978, 1991). *Aesthetic response* is the involvement of the reader's personal, emotional, often empathetic (rather than cerebral) response to the imaginative and expressive qualities of language. See also *efferent response*.

Alphabetic principle: the one-to-one correspondence between phonemes (or sounds) and graphemes (or letters), so that each letter represents one sound. English is not a purely phonetic language, only approximately half its words being spelled phonetically.

Amelia Frances Howard-Gibbon Illustrator's Award: given since 1971 by the Canadian Library Association, this award honours excellence in children's illustration in a book published in Canada. The award must go to a citizen or resident of Canada.

Assimilation: the cognitive process by which new information in the environment is integrated into existing schemata (Piaget, 1969). Students learn when their existing schemata are enlarged because of assimilated learning. See also *accommodation*.

Basal reading programs: resources for teaching language arts concepts, strategies, and skills. (They are so called because they were originally intended to provide the basis for reading-instruction programs.) They provide information about language arts topics and a sequence of topics, models, examples, and practice activities for each grade level.

Big books: enlarged picture books used in shared reading with emergent (usually primary-grade) readers.

Book of the Year for Children Award: given by the Canadian Library Association to recognize the year's most distinguished children's book by a Canadian citizen.

Caldecott Medal: named for the British illustrator of children's books, Randolph Caldecott (1846–1886), and awarded annually since 1938 to the preceding year's "artist of the most distinguished American picture book for children." The winning book receives the Caldecott Medal, and one or more runners-up are also recognized as "Honor" books.

Chapter books: stories, beginners' novels, and informational books with few, if any, illustrations. They are written in chapter format, mainly for middle-school and upper-elementary readers, as they move from a reliance on illustrations to a focus on text.

Children's literature: literature intended for young people. Children's literature, like all literature, has inherent imaginative and artistic qualities that offer pleasure and understanding.

Literature has the power to evoke strong emotions; to engage the intellect, to express feelings; to share beautiful language; and to allow the vicarious experience of different times, places, and characters. Language used with skill and artistry gives pleasure to readers of all ages, deepens their thinking and feeling, and encourages them to explore the nature of humankind at an appropriate level. The Children's Choice Awards are awarded regionally in Canada (and at the state level in the United States) on the basis of students' votes, and are regarded highly by authors and illustrators. The students' choices are selected from recent titles compiled by teachers and librarians. Awards include Manitoba Young Reader's Choice Award, given by the Manitoba School Library Audio Visual Association for the favourite Canadian book of Manitoba's young readers; the Red Cedar Book Award, given by the Young Readers' Choice Awards Society of BC for British Columbia schoolchildren's favourite fiction and nonfiction books; the Silver Birch Award, given by the Ontario Library Association for the best books chosen by Ontario students in grades 4 to 6; the Red Maple Award, also given by the Ontario Library Association for the best Canadian children's fiction chosen by Ontario students, grades 7, 8, and 9; the Ruth Schwartz Children's Book Award, given by the Ontario Arts Council and Canadian Booksellers Association for the best book selected by Ontario schoolchildren. See also *Amelia Frances Howard-Gibbon Illustrator's Award*, *Book of the Year for Children Award*, *Caldecott Medal*, *Governor General's Literary Awards*, and *Newbery Medal*.

Clusters: a pre-writing strategy by which students gather and organize information and ideas. The topic is written at the centre of a web-like diagram; main ideas supporting the topic are drawn out from the centre like rays, with details added as information is gathered.

Constructivist framework: a learning theory showing how learners participate actively in their own learning. Piaget (1969) views learning as processes of assimilation and accommodation, with learners modifying their cognitive structures as they interact with and adapt to their environment. Because learners construct their own knowledge from personal experience (which arises from particulars of culture, home, and community), the meanings readers construct from the texts they negotiate will be as varied as their background experience.

Contemporary realistic fiction: fiction that offers an imaginative reflection of the concerns and dilemmas of contemporary life. Set in the world as we know it and governed by natural laws as we understand them, contemporary realistic fiction is intended to provide a believable mirror of life. Fictional situations within a child's understanding encourage involvement and empathy, and provide a vision of the human condition. Believable characters who solve real problems suggest models for living in the contemporary world and offer the opportunity for the safe exploration of human relations and varied cultures through the imagination.

Context cues: cues that assist children to construct their understanding of reading material in terms of what makes sense and seems "right." Prior knowledge offers a context for new information, while linguistic cues include syntactic (grammar or word order) and semantic (meaning) aspects of language.

Critical literacy: reading that goes beyond the *what* of written language to the *how, why,* and *so what?* It goes beyond the reader's competency and comprehension to require a capacity for reflective insight, to "read" the symbolism, the relations of power, the cultural influences, and the writer's craft in a philosophical and political context. Children who are encouraged to focus on craft and to reflect on their own responses (on how a book was written and how it affected them) develop active, critical, metacognitive reading strategies.

Cueing systems: four types of cues that organize language and make oral and written communication possible. The four cueing systems are the phonological (or sound) system of language, the syntactic (or structural) system of language, the semantic (or meaning) system of language, and the pragmatic (or social and cultural use) system of language.

Cursive writing: joining letters together to form a word in one continuous movement. Some controversy exists over the best time to lead children from manuscript to cursive writing.

Drop Everything and Read (DEAR): daily (silent) reading practice, in addition to regular reading instruction, in which students read self-selected library books. See also *sustained silent reading (SSR).*

Dialect: nonstandard, informal forms of a spoken language (in this case, Standard English) used by different social classes, cultural, ethnic, or regional groups. The style, or register, of Standard English is formal, and is used in textbooks, newspapers, most media, and schools. Each dialect is distinctive; it differs from Standard English in its phonology, syntax, and semantics, but is neither inferior nor substandard.

Dialogue: an interactive written or spoken conversation between or among any number of people. A dialogue is not a forum for "winning" (like a debate). Participants build on mutual trust and respect, acknowledge and support one another, offer ideas, encourage questioning, and create an opportunity for real communication.

Direct instruction: instruction that offers systematic, planned lessons with explicit information. Not necessarily confined to skill-and-drill activities, direct instruction provides information and opportunities for students to apply what they are learning with guidance from the teacher. See also *indirect instruction.*

Discourse: a linguistics term that describes a continuous spoken or written discussion. It is also used to denote a topic area or thought system shaped by commonly held assumptions and aims (e.g., feminist discourse, capitalist discourse, patriarchal discourse, post-structural discourse).

Directed Listening–Thinking Approach (DLTA): an approach by which the teacher prepares the student(s) for active listening habits. The teacher prepares students for reading (provides necessary background information to stimulate interest, and encourages predictions and focus) and reads aloud, stopping periodically to discuss student perceptions and predictions. On completion, the teacher encourages students' reflection and expression of response to the literature, and connection to their own experience.

D'Nealian handwriting: an innovative manuscript and cursive handwriting program designed to increase legibility and to ease the transition from manuscript to cursive handwriting.

Drama, as context for learning: a learning medium that offers a powerful form of communication, and can have a positive effect on students' oral language development and literacy learning. The experience of drama activities and role-playing can evoke an aesthetic response to literature, and build a deeper understanding of the lived experience of what others might have experienced, encouraging risk-taking, empathy, and creativity. Often divergent in nature, drama often results in an emergent curriculum with multiple meanings. Dramatic forms in the language arts include storytelling, puppetry, choral speech, choric drama, readers theatre, dramatization, and story theatre. All of these dramatic forms require students to create or interpret meaning within the "as if" world of drama. The forms described in this text require language to express this meaning. Scripts, props, and movement are also used.

Efferent listening: see *efferent reading.*

Efferent reading: reading to take information away; the information to be acquired, the solution to a problem, or the action to be carried out. *Efferent response* occurs as the student reads to locate, observe, and remember information, and reads directions and explanations. Rosenblatt (1978) suggests a continuum of efferent and aesthetic responses to literature. Although readers often use both purposes simultaneously, one approach generally predominates.

Elizabeth Mrazik-Cleaver Canadian Picture Book Award: presented annually to a Canadian children's book illustrator whose work on a new book is deemed both original and worthy.

Elkonin boxes: an aid to word segmentation, a difficult phonemic awareness activity for learners. The teacher shows an object, or picture of the object, and draws a series of boxes corresponding to the number of sounds heard in the word. Teacher or child moves a marker into each box as the sound is pronounced.

Emergent literacy: the concept that young children begin to learn to read and write very early in life through participating in real-life settings in which reading and writing are used, and through active involvement with literacy materials: for example, social and cultural language learning such as children's readiness to listen to stories read aloud, to notice labels and signs, and to experiment with pencils. It has replaced the traditional reading readiness approach.

English language learners (ELL): students whose native language is not English and who are in a course of study to learn English. The needs of linguistically diverse students are best met if teachers value and support the students' proficiency in their native languages while they acquire English.

Expository text: nonfiction, informational writing that invites both efferent (fact-finding) and aesthetic (personally pleasurable and expressive) reading, as children learn about their world. Expository texts of quality demonstrate accuracy (current and complete information) and organization (clear, logical, and readable). They are well designed (visually and aesthetically enhancing) and written in a lively, stimulating style that engages the reader's wonder and curiosity.

Family literacy programs: programs designed for families whose parents are nonfluent readers. Parents develop their own reading and writing competencies, learn how to support their children's reading, and participate with their children in reading and writing activities. Cultural differences are considered strengths to be built upon, not weaknesses (unlike the older "deficit" model).

Fantasy: a genre rooted in myth, legend, dreams, and subconscious archetypes. Well-written fantasy creates an imagined world (in which, e.g., time travel, or extraterrestrial beings, or talking animals occur) that is made psychologically credible to the reader through its richly detailed setting, inner logic, and internal consistency, and because, like all good fiction, it poses important questions about the human condition. Fantasy includes such subgenres as high fantasy (Ursula Le Guin's *A Wizard of Earthsea*, 1984), science fiction (Monica Hughes's *Keeper of the Isis Light*, 2000), time fantasy, (Kit Pearson's *Awake and Dreaming*, 1996; Julie Lawson's *White Jade Tiger*, 1993), and fantastic animal stories (E. B. White's *Charlotte's Web*, 1980).

Figurative language: language, conveyed by idioms and figures of speech, that is metaphorical, symbolic, and open to multiple interpretations. Children need to move beyond explicit, literal, dictionary meanings to understand how flexible, subtle, and expressive language can be.

Genre: the distinctive form of a category of literature (e.g., novel, poem, science fiction, biography) by which it is identified and classified (e.g., the form and function of an expository text differs from that of a folktale).

Governor General's Literary Awards: an award that recognizes literary excellence in French and English in annual prizes for fiction, poetry, drama, nonfiction, children's literature text, children's literature illustration, and translation. The prizes are highly prestigious, accompanied by elaborate presentation ceremonies, and timed to coincide with the major book-buying season.

Grammar: the structural organization of English; the rules governing how words are combined into sentences. The term often replaces *syntax*. Where grammar has traditionally been taught prescriptively (dealing with "correct" and "incorrect" usage), it is more usually taught today in a functional and descriptive manner.

Grand conversations: book discussions and literature circles in which students explore interpretations and reflect on their feelings. The teacher serves primarily as a facilitator-participant, and the focus is on clarifying and deepening students' understanding.

Guided reading: reading where the teacher and students (usually in small groups) read and talk their way through a text in a cycle of questioning, reading (aloud or silently), and discussion. This scaffolding enables students to develop and use reading strategies. Selections used for guided reading should be at the students' zone of proximal development.

Historical fiction: fiction set within a specific past time and place, and written with attention to authenticity of setting and accurate representation of what is known to be factual. Events are shown not in isolation, but as part of a historical continuity that gives meaning to the present time. Through understanding issues of the past, the reader is often given insight into contemporary problems.

Hypermedia: computer software that organizes and links multimedia information (sound, graphics, text, video, animation) so that the user can retrieve and modify information in various forms, and move from one medium to another in a nonlinear manner.

Hypertext: writing that is nonlinear. Reading hypertext is an associative rather than a sequential act. Readers can control what they read and the sequence in which they read it, by selecting at random, or by choosing options or pathways.

Indirect instruction: instruction that occurs as teachers respond to students' on-the-spot needs, questions, and teachable moments, and by the skills and behaviours that teachers themselves are modelling. See also *direct instruction*.

Inquiry-based units: units for which students and teacher develop their own questions to read about, write about, and study. Inquiry-based units are often interdisciplinary; used in conjunction with science, social studies, and/or fine arts.

Instructional reading level: the reading level at which the student can read successfully with regular classroom support. Teachers use the percentage of words students can read correctly to determine if the reading material is too difficult, too easy, or appropriate for the student at this time. If the student reads 95 percent of the words correctly, the book is easy, at the independent reading level for that child. If the student reads 90–94 percent correctly, the book is at the instructional reading level. If the student reads fewer than 90 percent of the words correctly, the book is too difficult, at the student's frustration level.

Integration: learning language in a way that is not separated from other subjects or fields of knowledge, but integrated with them and integral to them. Language teachers promote authentic communication about issues active in their students' experience, whether from their homes, communities, or other subjects.

Invented spelling: unique, invented spellings created by young children as they begin to write, based on their knowledge of the phonological system. Young children use ingenious strategies (like letter names to spell words, e.g., *U* for *you*) that differ at each stage of their way to becoming conventional spellers. Teacher analysis of a child's invented spelling provides information about the individual's level of spelling development and suggests the appropriate type of instruction.

Listening centre: a listening centre is an arrangement of listening devices, usually with individual headphones, that facilitates two or more students listening to the same source at the same time.

Literacy: having once meant *knowing how to read*, it has expanded to connote the competence to carry out the complex tasks of reading and writing related to the work world and life outside school. Other kinds of literacy (computer literacy, visual literacy, critical literacy, cultural literacy) indicate other crucial modes of making meaning. Literacy, then, is not a prescription, or reading list, but rather a way to come to learn about the world and to participate more fully in society.

Literacy centres: learning stations in primary classrooms where students can work in small groups to practise skills and explore literacy concepts. Students might, for example, manipulate literacy materials, write group poems, compile charts, watch a video, or experiment with artistic techniques. Teachers use many kinds of centres such as listening centres that allow students opportunities to hear stories/music and follow along with the text.

Manuscript handwriting: similar to the type style of primary-level textbooks. It is assumed to facilitate young children's introduction to reading and writing, the letters being easier to form and more legible than those of the cursive form.

Metacognition: the knowledge children acquire about their own cognitive processes. As children are able, for example, to reflect on their own literacy processes, and to understand which learning strategies are most effective for them, they become increasingly aware of what they know and don't know, and are able to regulate this knowledge to maximize learning.

Metalinguistics: language about language. *Metalinguistic awareness* is the capacity to use language to think and talk of language; to understand language as a formal code, that is, a system of communication. For example, two individuals in conversation discuss whether they understand one another's meaning. With children, metalinguistic awareness may refer to comprehension of such terms as *letter, word, sentence,* and *sound*.

Minilessons: brief direct-instruction lessons designed (within the larger context of the class process) to introduce, practise, or review a particular skill, concept, or strategy.

Miscues: reading errors. Teachers can categorize students' miscues according to the semantic, graphophonic, and syntactic cueing systems in order to examine what word-identification strategies students are using.

Morpheme: the smallest meaningful unit in language (e.g., *dog; play*). Word parts that change the meanings of words are also morphemes (*-s; -ing*). *Dog* is a free morpheme because it conveys meaning while standing alone; *-s* is a bound morpheme because it must be attached to a free morpheme to convey meaning.

Morphology: in linguistics, the study of the structure of words (as opposed to *syntax,* the study of the arrangement of words in the higher units of phrases, sentences, etc.). See also *morpheme.*

Multicultural literature: literature that meets criteria for good literature while also enriching and expanding the reader's cultural consciousness. Through access to diverse cultural contexts, mainstream students develop sensitivity to and appreciation for people of cultural groups other than their own; they expand their understanding of historical perspectives, often challenging traditional assumptions about the history of the dominant (especially North American) culture; and they raise issues of social justice, and are able to challenge racial and ethnic stereotypes. Non-mainstream students benefit from multicultural literature that makes the "insider" point of view visible in the social fabric. These students' reading is enriched when they find their own cultural experience and values acknowledged and respected; and when they find characters and events with whom they can identify.

Narrative: (1) the general term for a story or account of any event or experience, fact or fiction, long or short, detailed or simplified; and (2) the form that story takes. Narratives are frequently arranged according to cause and effect or chronology. The way people choose to tell a story often reveals their values and assumptions, and the way they make meaning. Teachers seek strategies to evoke and empower student narrative competency and expressiveness in all the language arts.

Native speakers ability: persons with the ability to use language in various situations and for various purposes. In order to meet the needs of linguistically diverse students, teachers try to help students to develop a high level of proficiency in their native language as well as to add English as a second language.

Newbery Medal: a medal named in honour of John Newbery (1713–1767), the first English publisher of children's books, that has been given annually (since 1922) by the American Library Association's Association for Library Service to Children. The recipient is recognized as the author of the most distinguished book in children's literature published in the United States in the preceding year. The winning book receives the Newbery Medal, and one or more runners-up are also recognized as "Honor" books.

Persuasive writing: writing with a purpose. The writer supports, develops, and consistently maintains a position, with the intention of persuading the reader by logic, or through an appeal to the reader's character or emotions.

Phonemic awareness: children's basic understanding that speech is composed of a series of individual sounds, provides the foundation for phonics. The emphasis is on the sounds of spoken words, not on reading letters or pronouncing letter names. Developing phonemic awareness enables children to use sound–symbol correspondences to read and spell words. Phonemic awareness is a powerful predictor of later reading achievement.

Phonetic spelling: spelling by choosing letters on the basis of sound alone (e.g., *LIV* for *live*; *NE* for *knee*). Phonetic spelling is decipherable because it represents all the essential sound features in a word. Phonetic spellers are typically about six years old. See also *invented spelling.*

Phonics: the set of relationships between *phonology* (the sounds in speech) and *orthography* (the spelling patterns of written language). Phonics is a controversial topic; current thinking is that reading is a complex process, and that the phonological system works in conjunction with the semantic, syntactic, and pragmatic systems, not in isolation. Adams (1990) recommends that phonics instruction (sound–symbol correspondences, how to blend sounds to decode words, how to segment sounds to spell, useful phonics generalizations or "rules") should be systematic, intensive, and completed by the end of third grade.

Phonological system: the system of sound patterns in language, and how they combine to create words and meaning.

Picture book: a short book (usually 32 pages, sometimes 24 or 48) with pictures on every page or double-page set (*spread*). Unlike in illustrated books (in which the illustrations are subordinate to the text), the art and text of picture books are equally important and function like an interdependent double text to convey the book's content, theme, and meaning.

Portfolios: systematic and meaningful collections of artifacts documenting students' language arts learning and development over a period of time, and reflecting their day-to-day learning in the language arts and across the curriculum. Students usually choose the items to place in their portfolios, within guidelines provided by the teacher; portfolios are therefore a useful vehicle for encouraging self-reflection, self-evaluation, and goal setting.

Pragmatic system: one of the four cueing systems that make oral and written communication possible. Pragmatics deals with the social and cultural contexts of language use. People make meaning with different intentions and for different audiences, and their language varies accordingly (e.g., in regional or cultural dialects and in peer-group speech communities).

Predictable books: books whose texts are characterized and structured by (1) repetition (of words, sentences, rhymes); (2) cumulative sequence (elements are repeated and expanded in each episode); (3) rhyme and rhythm; and/or (4) sequential patterns (like the alphabet or days of the week). Predictable books are often used in shared reading with young children and offer a valuable tool to emergent readers because their repetition enables children to predict the next sentence or episode.

Quickwrites: a writing strategy used to brainstorm ideas, to focus on content rather than mechanics, and to encourage the student's natural writing voice. Students write on a topic continuously for 5 to 10 minutes, letting their thoughts flow from mind to pen without focusing on mechanics or revision.

Reader response: both a critical and a pedagogical approach to literature. Reader response focuses on the reader's unadulterated, felt response to the text, based on the reader's own prior experience, cultural history, knowledge of life, and experience of other texts. The focus is on the reader, not on the literary tradition, and the teacher's role is to provide instruction that can arouse, challenge, refine, and enlarge the reader's response to literature.

Readers theatre: a formal dramatic presentation of a script by a group of readers. In readers theatre, children approach literature through performance rather than discussion. Students usually prepare scripts from books they have read, rehearsing, interpreting, and performing them through voice and gesture, rather than through action.

Readers workshop: an alternative to traditional reading instruction that provides students with choices, time to read and write, and opportunities for response through conversation and writing. Students read books that they choose themselves, and respond to books through writing in reading logs and conferencing. Readers workshop usually includes reading, sharing, minilessons, and reading aloud to students.

Reading logs: logs in which students respond to stories and books that they are reading or that are being read to them. As they gain experience reading and responding to literature, students frequently move from retellings and summaries to personal and interpretive comments.

Reading process: reading process is a five-stage conceptualization of making meaning from text: prereading, reading, responding, exploring, and applying.

Reading readiness: a former approach to literacy instruction that assumed that there is a point in children's development when it is time to begin teaching them to read and write. Kindergarten children were "readied" for formal reading and writing instruction, which would begin in the first grade. This approach has now been largely replaced by the concept of *emergent literacy*.

Resource-based units: units centred on a featured selection or several related books. Students work as a group (becoming a community of readers); read (independently, with a partner, or with the teacher); respond in reading logs and grand conversations; participate in minilessons on the unit's concept, strategy, or skill; and create projects to extend their reading. See also *grand conversations* and *minilessons*.

Rubrics: scoring guides to assess students' growth as writers. Rubrics may have several levels of assessment, with coherent and clearly articulated descriptors related to the domains of ideas, organization, language, and mechanics at each level. Clear criteria and specific expectations help students view writing less as a mystery, and more as a task that they can perform, and at which they can improve.

Scaffolding: support mechanisms that teachers, parents, or other more competent individuals provide to help children successfully perform a task within their zone of proximal development (Bruner, 1986; Vygotsky, 1978). Also see *zone of proximal development*.

Schemata (singular: schema): the cognitive structure's conceptual filing system. Schemata are mental frameworks in which children and adults organize and store the information derived from their experiences. Learners invent new categories and personalize them according to their values, interests, and cultural history. See also *accommodation* and *assimilation*.

Semantic map (or web): a diagram showing relationships among concepts; used to organize ideas, topics, and units of study. See also *clustering*.

Semantic system: one of the four cueing systems that make communication possible, *semantics* is the meaning system of language. Vocabulary is the key component; children acquire vocabulary, not only learning new words, but also, through a process of refinement, learning that words have both connotations and denotations (i.e., shades of meaning, several meanings, contextual meanings).

Skills: specific, automatic, or unconscious information-processing techniques, such as decoding and spelling, or reference and study skills. See also *strategy*.

SQ4R study strategy: a six-step technique in which students survey, question, read, recite, review, and reflect in order to read and remember information in a content-area reading assignment.

Standardized achievement tests: tests generally used to assess the achievement of individual students, and (like those used for university admission) to predict future performance and likelihood of success. Their value lies in offering teachers insight into their students within a wider context than the isolated classroom. However, their use is problematic for purposes other than individual assessment: for example, in certifying completion of a grade, evaluating teachers, accrediting schools, or validating the excellence of school systems.

Story map: a diagram or chart that helps students visualize structures and relationships in stories. Students add information, illustrations, and text from the story they are reading to enrich the story map, which may take the form of beginning–middle–end plot diagrams, character clusters (or theme, setting, genre clusters, etc.), Venn diagrams, plot profiles to chart tensions, and sociograms.

Storyboard: a sequential series of components used for ordering and other stage activities. A storyboard with picture book text and illustrations cut out and individually affixed to cards can be examined in terms of illustrations and/or arranged sequentially. A more sophisticated video storyboard might have dialogue, setting, and shooting directions, each organized sequentially.

Strategy: an overall method, behaviour, plan, or scheme to enable task performance or problem solving. One strategy can be used in various learning situations. Some thinking strategies that readers and writers use include the following: tapping prior knowledge, predicting, organizing ideas, visualizing, making connections, generalizing, and revising meaning. (*Skills*, on the other hand, are more specific automatic or unconscious information-processing techniques, such as decoding and spelling, or reference and study skills.)

Sustained silent reading (SSR): a daily period of silent reading in the classroom when children read self-selected books. See also *DEAR (Drop Everything and Read)* and *uninterrupted sustained silent reading (USSR)*.

Syntactic system: the structural organization of English; the grammar that regulates how words are combined into sentences. Also see *grammar*.

Theme study units: interdisciplinary units that integrate the language arts with social studies, science, math, and other curricular areas. Topics are broad and encompass many possibilities (e.g., civilization, inventions). Students use all the language arts as they investigate, solve problems, learn, and demonstrate their new learning.

Trade books: books published for readers as literature (stories, informational books, poems), and not as educational texts. Books published as part of an educational program, and used in schools, are referred to as *textbooks*.

Uninterrupted sustained silent reading (USSR): see *SSR* and *DEAR*.

Unit: a series of lessons planned around a curriculum text or theme, so that individual lessons work in consort with other lessons on a shared topic.

Visual literacy: the capacity to "read" and visually decode the artifacts of society (not just the art of high culture), moving from close observation and concrete description, to inferences and generalizations, to creative reflection and insight.

Word walls: large sheets of paper, initially blank, hung on a classroom wall, on which students and teacher write down accumulative lists of interesting, confusing, and important words from books they are reading and from thematic unit concepts.

Writers workshop: similar to readers workshop, but with a writing focus, writers workshop includes writing, sharing, and minilessons. Students write on topics they choose themselves, and assume ownership of their writing and learning. The teacher's role is that of facilitator to a community of writers.

Writing process: what students do as they think and write. The stages of the writing process are prewriting (gathering and organizing ideas); drafting (getting the ideas down on paper); revising (refining and clarifying ideas); editing (putting the writing in its final form, including mechanics and proofreading); and publishing (sharing with an appropriate audience). The stages are not necessarily linear, and in fact more frequently merge and recur cyclically.

Zone of proximal development: the range of tasks a child can perform with guidance from others but cannot yet perform independently. Vygotsky (1978) believed that children learn best when what they are attempting to learn is within this zone.

References

Professional References

Adams, M. J. (1990). *Beginning to read: Thinking and learning about print* (Executive Summary). Cambridge, MA: MIT Press.

Afflerbach, P., Pearson, P. D., & Paris, S. (2008). Clarifying differences between reading skills and reading strategies. *The Reading Teacher, 61*(5), 364–373.

Alberta Teachers Association. (2010). *Here comes everyone: Teaching in the intercultural classroom*. Edmonton, AB: Alberta Teachers Association.

Akhondi, M., Malayeri, F., & Samad, A. (2011). How to teach expository text structure to facilitate reading comprehension. *The Reading Teacher, 64*(5), 368–372.

Allen, J. (1999). *Words, words, words: Teaching vocabulary in grades 4–12*. Portland, ME: Stenhouse.

Allen, J. (2004). *Tools for teaching content literacy*. Markham, ON: Pembroke Publishers.

Altwerger, B., & Flores, B. (1994). Theme cycles: Creating communities of learners. *Primary Voices K–6, 2*, 2–6.

Alvermann, D. (2002). Preface. In D. Alvermann (Ed.), *Adolescents and literacies in a digital world*. New York: Peter Lang.

Alvermann, D., & Boothby, P. (1986). Children's transfer of graphic organizer instruction. *Reading Psychology, 7*(2), 87–100.

Anderson, I. W., & Krathwohl, D. R. (Eds.). (2001). *A taxonomy for learning, teaching, and assessing: A revision of Bloom's taxonomy of educational objectives* (complete ed.). New York: Longman.

Anderson, R. C., & Nagy, W. E. (1992). The vocabulary conundrum. *American Educator, 16*(4), 44–47.

Andrews, J., & Lupart, J. (1993). *The inclusive classroom: Educating exceptional children*. Scarborough, ON: Nelson.

Applebee, A. N. (1978). *The child's concept of story: Ages 2 to 17*. Chicago: University of Chicago Press.

Armbruster, B., Anderson, T., & Osterag, J. (1987). Does text structure/summarization instruction facilitate learning from expository text? *Reading Research Quarterly, 22*, 331–346.

Ashton-Warner, S. (1965). *Teacher*. New York: Simon & Schuster.

Askov, E., & Greff, K. N. (1975). Handwriting: Copying versus tracing as the most effective type of practice. *Journal of Educational Research, 69*, 96–98.

Asselin, M. (2002). Literacy links: Vocabulary instruction. *Teacher Librarian, 29*(3), 57–59.

Atwell, N. (1987). *In the middle: Writing, reading, and learning with adolescents*. Portsmouth, NH: Heinemann.

Atwell, N. (1998). *In the middle: New understandings about writing, reading, and literature* (2nd ed.). Toronto: Irwin Publishing.

Au, K. (1997). Literacy for all students: Ten steps toward making a difference. *The Reading Teacher, 51*(3), 186–194.

Avalos, M., Plasencia, A., Chavez, C., & Rascon, J. (2007). Modified guided reading: Gateway to English as a second language and literacy learning. *The Reading Teacher, 61*(4), 318–329.

Bainbridge, J., & Malicky, G. (2004). *Constructing meaning: Balancing elementary language arts* (2nd ed.). Toronto: Harcourt Canada.

Bainbridge, J., & Pantaleo, S. (1999). *Learning with literature in the Canadian elementary classroom*. Edmonton: University of Alberta Press.

Baker, D. (2013). Art integration and cognitive development. *Journal for Learning Through the Arts, 9*(1), 1–15.

Baker, D. and Setterington, K. (2004). *A guide to Canadian children's books*. Toronto, ON: McClelland & Stewart.

Ball, E., & Blachman, B. (1991). Does phoneme segmentation training in kindergarten make a difference in early word recognition and developmental spelling? *Reading Research Quarterly, 26*, 49–86.

Barber, K. (2006). *Six words you never knew had something to do with pigs and other fascinating facts about the language from Canada's word lady*. Toronto: Oxford University Press.

Barber, K. (Ed.). (2008). *Oxford Canadian spelling bee dictionary*. Don Mills, ON: Oxford University Press.

Barone, D. (1990). The written responses of young children: Beyond comprehension to story understanding. *The New Advocate, 3*, 49–56.

Bartel, M. (2005). Some ideas about composition and design elements, principles, and visual effects. Retrieved April 27, 2006, from www.goshen.edu/art/ed/compose.htm.

Bear, D. R., Invernizzi, M., Templeton, S., & Johnston, F. (2008). *Words their way: Word study for phonics, vocabulary, and spelling instruction* (4th ed.). Upper Saddle River, NJ: Merrill/Prentice Hall.

Bear, D. R., Invernizzi, M., Templeton, S., & Johnston, F. (2011). *Words their way: Word study for phonics, vocabulary, and spelling instruction* (5th ed.). Upper Saddle River, NJ: Pearson.

Beck, I., McKeown, M., & Kucan, L. (2002). *Bringing words to life: Robust vocabulary instruction*. New York: The Guilford Press.

Beech, J. (2004). Using a dictionary: Its influence on children's reading, spelling, and phonology. *Reading Psychology, 25*, 19–36.

Berthoff, A. E. (1981). *The making of meaning*. Montclair, NJ: Boynton/Cook.

Bielaczyc, K., Kapur, M., and Collins, A. (2013). Cultivating a community of learners in K–12 classrooms. In C. Hmelo-Silver, C. Chinn, C. Chan, & A. O'Donnell (Eds.), *The international handbook of collaborative learning* (pp. 233–249). New York, NY: Routledge.

Bishop, R. S. (Ed.). (1994). *Kaleidoscope: A multicultural booklist for grades K–8*. Urbana, IL: National Council of Teachers of English.

Blachowicz, C., & Fisher, P. (2000). Vocabulary instruction. In M. L. Kamil, P. B. Mosenthal, P. D. Pearson, & R. Barr (Eds.), *Handbook of Reading Research*, Vol. 3 (pp. 503–523). Mahwah, NJ: Lawrence Erlbaum Associates.

Blachowicz, C., & Fisher, P. (2006). *Teaching vocabulary in all classrooms* (3rd ed.). Columbus, OH: Pearson/Merrill-Prentice Hall.

Blachowicz, C. L. Z., & Lee, J. J. (1991). Vocabulary development in the whole literacy classroom. *The Reading Teacher, 45*, 188–195.

Black, S. E. (1989). *Improving the written communication skills of upper elementary alternative education students by using a word processor*. ERIC document ED321256.

Blackburn, E. (1985). Stories never end. In J. Hansen, J. Newkirk, & D. Graves (Eds.), *Breaking ground: Teachers relate reading and writing in the elementary school* (pp. 3–13). Portsmouth, NH: Heinemann.

Blair-Larsen, S., & Held Williams, K. (Eds.). (1999). *The balanced reading program: Helping all students achieve success*. Newark, DE: International Reading Association.

Blythe, T., & Gardner, H. (1990). A school for all intelligences. *Educational Leadership, 47*(7), 33–36.

Bodrova, E., & Leong, D. (2001). *Tools of the mind: A case study of implementing the Vygotskian approach in American early childhood and primary classrooms*. Geneva, Switzerland: UNESCO.

Bonin, S. (1988). Beyond storyland: Young writers can tell it other ways. In T. Newkirk & N. Atwell (Eds.), *Understanding writing* (2nd ed., pp. 47–51). Portsmouth, NH: Heinemann.

Books in Canada: The Canadian review of books. http://www.booksincanada.com/.

Booth, D., and Schwartz, L. (2004). *Literacy techniques for building successful readers and writers.* Markham, ON: Pembroke Publishers.

Borich, G. D. (2010). *Effective teaching methods* (7th ed.). Upper Saddle River, NJ: Pearson Prentice Hall.

Boushey, G., & Moser, J. (2006). *The daily five.* Portland, ME: Stenhouse Publishers.

Bowers, F. (1996). *The classic tradition of haiku: An anthology.* New York: Dover Publications.

Bowman, B., Donovan, S., & Burns, M. (Eds.). (2000). *Eager to learn: Educating our preschoolers.* Washington, DC: National Academy Press.

Bowser, J. (1993). Structuring the middle-school classroom for spoken language. *English Journal, 82,* 38–41.

Bradley, B., & Jones, J. (2007). Sharing alphabet books in early childhood classrooms. *The Reading Teacher, 60*(5), 452–463.

Brailsford, A., & Coles, J. (2004). *Balanced literacy in action.* Markham, ON: Scholastic.

Brenneman Eno, K. (2004). *Children's video stories: Using digital video to empower young children's imaginative play.* Ed.M. thesis. New York: Teachers College of Columbia University (unpublished).

Bright, R. (2002). *Write from the start: Writers workshop for the primary grades.* Winnipeg: Portage & Main Publishers.

Bright, R. and Smith, B. (2014). Critical thinking and writing informational texts in a grade three classroom. In L. Shedkestsky & J. Beaudry (Eds.), *Cases on teaching critical thinking through visual representation strategies.* Hershey, PA: IGI Global.

Bromley, K. D. (1996). *Webbing with literature: Creating story maps with children's books* (2nd ed.). Boston: Allyn & Bacon.

Bruce, B. (2002). Diversity and critical social engagement: How changing technologies enable new modes of literacy in changing circumstances. In D. Alvermann (Ed.), *Adolescents and literacies in a digital world.* (pp. 147–163). New York: Peter Lang.

Bruner, J. (1986). *Actual minds, possible worlds.* Cambridge, MA: Harvard University Press.

Buckingham, D., & Sefton-Green, J. (1998). In S. Howard (Ed.), *Wired up: Young people and the electronic media* (pp. vii–ix). London: UCL Press.

Burbules, N., & Bruce, B. (1995, November). This is not a paper. *Educational Researcher, 24*(8), 12–18.

Burmark, L. (2002). *Visual literacy: Learn to see, see to learn.* Alexandria, VA: Association for Supervision and Curriculum Development.

Burns, M. S., Griffin, P., & Snow, C. E. (Eds.). (1999). *Starting out right: A guide to promoting children's reading success.* Washington, DC: National Academy Press.

Businik, R. (1997). Reading and phonological awareness: What we have learned and how we can use it. *Reading Research and Instruction, 36,* 199–215.

Butler, A., & Turbill, J. (1984). *Towards a reading-writing classroom.* Portsmouth, NH: Heinemann.

Cairney, T. (1990). Intertextuality: Infectious echoes from the past. *The Reading Teacher, 43,* 478–484.

Cairney, T. (1992). Fostering and building students' intertextual histories. *Language Arts, 69,* 502–507.

Calfee, R., & Patrick, C. (1995). *Teach our children well: Bringing K–12 education into the 21st century.* Stanford, CA: Stanford Alumni Association.

Calkins, L. M. (1980). When children want to punctuate: Basic skills belong in context. *Language Arts, 57,* 567–573.

Calkins, L. M. (1994). *The art of teaching writing* (2nd ed.). Portsmouth, NH: Heinemann.

Calkins, L. M. (2010). *Launch an intermediate writing workshop.* Portsmouth, NH: Heinemann.

Calkins, L. M., Hartman, A., & White, Z. (2005). *One to one: The art of conferencing with young writers.* Portsmouth, NH: Heinemann.

Cameron, L. (1998). A practitioner's reflections. *Orbit: Phonics in the Literacy Program, 28*(4), 10–15.

Cammack, D. (2002). Literacy, technology, and room of her own: Analyzing adolescent girls' online conversations from historical and technological perspectives. *Yearbook of the National Reading Conference, 51,* 129–141.

Canadian Children's Book Centre. (1994). *Writing stories, making pictures: Biographies of 150 Canadian children's authors and illustrators.* Toronto: Canadian Children's Book Centre.

Carlson, A. (1991). *The preschooler and the library.* Metuchen, NJ: Scarecrow.

Carnine, D. W., Silbert, J., Kame'enui, E. J., & Tarver, S. G. (2004). *Direct instruction reading* (5th ed.). Upper Saddle River, NJ: Pearson.

Caserta-Henry, C. (1996). Reading buddies: A first-grade intervention program. *The Reading Teacher, 49,* 500–503.

Chandler-Olcott, K., & Mahar, D. (2003). "Tech-savviness" meets multiliteracies: Exploring adolescent girls' technology-related literacy practices. *Reading Research Quarterly, 38,* 356–385.

Chapman, M. (2002). Phonemic awareness in perspective. *Canadian Children, 27*(2), 18–25.

Chapman, V., & Sopko, D. (2003). Developing strategic use of combined-text trade books. *The Reading Teacher, 57,* 236–239.

Christensen, C. (2004). Relationship between orthographic-motor integration and computer use for the production of creative and well-structured written text. *British Journal of Educational Psychology, 74,* 551–564.

Cintorino, M. A. (1993). Getting together, getting along, getting to the business of teaching and learning. *English Journal, 82,* 23–32.

Clay, M. M. (1985). *The early detection of reading difficulties* (3rd ed.). Portsmouth, NH: Heinemann.

Clay, M. M. (2001). *Change over time in children's literacy development.* Portsmouth, NH: Heinemann.

Clymer, T. (1996). The utility of phonic generalizations in the primary grades. *The Reading Teacher, 50,* 182–187.

Coiro, J. (2003). Reading comprehension on the Internet: Expanding our understanding of reading comprehension to encompass new literacies. *The Reading Teacher, 56*(6). Retrieved June 3, 2013, from http://www.readingonline.org/electronic/elec_index.asp?HREF=/electronic/RT/2-03_column/index.html.

Cole, N. (1997). *The ETS gender study: How females and males perform in educational settings.* Princeton, NJ: Educational Testing Service.

Collins, V., Dickson, S., Simmons, D., & Kame'enui, E. (2006). *Metacognition and its relationship to reading comprehension: A synthesis of the research.* NCITE Research Synthesis. Portland: University of Oregon.

Comber, B. (1999). "Coming, ready or not!": What counts as early literacy? *Language and Literacy, 1*(1). Retrieved May 29, 2013, from http://www.langandlit.ualberta.ca/archives/vol11papers/coming.htm.

Comber, B., & Simpson, A. (2001). *Negotiating critical literacies in classrooms.* Mahwah, NJ: Erlbaum.

Connelly, V., Gee, D., & Walsh, E. (2007). A comparison of keyboarded and handwritten compositions and the relationship with transcription speed. *British Journal of Educational Psychology, 77,* 479–492.

Cooper, D. (2006). *Literacy: Helping children construct meaning*. Boston, MA: Houghton Mifflin.

Copeland, J. S. (1993). *Speaking of poets: Interviews with poets who write for children and young adults*. Urbana, IL: National Council of Teachers of English.

Copeland, J. S., & Copeland, V. L. (1994). *Speaking of poets 2: Interviews with poets who write for children and young adults*. Urbana, IL: National Council of Teachers of English.

Cornett, C., & Smithrim, K. (2001). *The arts as meaning makers: Integrating literature and the arts throughout the curriculum* (Canadian ed.). Don Mills, ON: Prentice Hall.

Cramer, R. (2004). *Language arts: A balanced approach to teaching reading, writing, listening, talking, and thinking*. Boston: Allyn and Bacon.

Crystal, D. (2001). *Language and the Internet*. Cambridge: Cambridge University Press.

Culham, R. (2003). *6 + 1 traits of writing: The complete guide, grades 3 and up*. New York: Scholastic.

Cullinan, B. E., Jaggar, A., & Strickland, D. (1974). Oral language expansion in the primary grades. In B. Cullinan (Ed.), *Black dialects and reading*. Urbana, IL: National Council of Teachers of English.

Cunningham, P. M. (2012). *Phonics they use: Words for reading and writing* (6th ed.). Boston: Pearson.

Cunningham, P. M., & Cunningham, J. W. (1992). Making words: Enhancing the invented spelling-decoding connection. *The Reading Teacher, 46*, 106–115.

Curry-Tash, M. (1998). The politics of teleliteracy and adbusting in the classroom. *English Journal, 87*(1), 43–48.

Dagenais, D., & Day, E. (1998). Classroom language experiences of trilingual children in French immersion. *The Canadian Modern Language Review/La Revue canadienne des langues vivantes, 54*(3), 376–393.

Daniels, H. (1994). *Literature circles: Voice and choice in the student-centered classroom*. York, ME: Stenhouse.

D'Aoust, C. (1992). Portfolios: Process for students and teachers. In K. B. Yancy (Ed.), *Portfolios in the writing classroom* (pp. 39–48). Urbana, IL: National Council of Teachers of English.

De Fina, A. A. (1992). *Portfolio assessment: Getting started*. New York: Scholastic.

Delacruz, E. (2009). Art education aims in the age of new media: Moving toward global civil society. *Art Education, 62*(5), 13–18.

Delacruz, S., & An, S. (2014). Lights, camera, iPads, action! How a fourth grade class learned 21st century literacies through various arts projects. *New Waves Educational Research & Development, 17*(2), 12–24.

Devers, W., & Cipielewski, J. (1993). *Every teacher's thematic booklist*. Toronto: Scholastic.

Dickinson, D. K., & Neuman, S. (Eds.). *Handbook of early literacy research* (2nd ed.). New York: Guilford Press.

D'Odorico, L., & Zammuner, V. (1993). The influence of using a word processor on children's story writing. *European Journal of Psychology of Education, 8*(1), 51–64.

Doll, E. (1941). The essentials of an inclusive concept of mental deficiency. *American Journal of Mental Deficiency, 46*, 214–219.

Donohue, L. (2007). *Guided listening: A framework for using read-aloud and other oral language experiences to build comprehension skills and help students record, share, value and interpret ideas*. Markham, ON: Pembroke Publishers.

Dudley-Marling, C., & Paugh, P. (2009). *A classroom teacher's guide to struggling writers*. Portsmouth, NH: Heinemann.

Duffelmeyer, F. (2002). Alphabet activities on the Internet. *The Reading Teacher, 55*(7), 631–635.

Duke, N. K. (2005). Comprehension of what for what: Comprehension as a non-unitary construct. In S. Paris & S. Stahl (Eds.), *Current issues in reading comprehension and assessment* (pp. 93–104). Mahwah, NJ: Erlbaum.

Duke, N. K., & Pearson, P. D. (2002). Effective practices for developing reading comprehension. In A. E. Farstrup & S. J. Samuels (Eds.), *What research has to say about reading instruction* (3rd ed., pp. 205–242). Newark, DE: International Reading Association.

Duke, N., & Pearson, P. D. (2008/2009). Effective practices for developing reading comprehension. *The Journal of Education, Vol. 189 (1/2)*, 107–122.

Dunning, S., & Stafford, W. (1992). *Getting the knack: 20 poetry writing exercises*. Urbana, IL: National Council of Teachers of English.

Dymock, S., & Nicholson, T. (2010). "High 5!" Strategies to enhance comprehension of expository text. *The Reading Teacher, 64*(3), 166–178.

Edwards, G., & Saltman, J. (2010). *Picturing Canada: A history of Canadian children's illustrated books and publishing*. Toronto, ON: University of Toronto Press.

Ehri, L., Nunes, S., Willows, D., Schuster, B., Yaghoub-Zadeh, Z., & Shannahan, T. (2001). Phonemic awareness instruction helps children learn to read: Evidence from the National Reading Panel's meta-analysis. *Reading Research Quarterly, 36*(3), 250–287.

Ehri, L., & Roberts, T. (2006). The roots of learning to read and write: Acquisition of letters and phonemic awareness. In D. K. Dickinson & S. Neuman (Eds.), *Handbook of early literacy research*, Vol. 2 (pp. 113–131). New York: Guildford Press.

Egawa, K. (1990). Harnessing the power of language: First graders' literature engagement with "Owl moon." *Language Arts, 67*(6), 582–588.

Eisner, E. (2002). *The arts and the creation of mind*. New Haven, CT: Yale University Press.

English Live, 2014. http://englishlive.ef.com/blog/many-words-english-language/.

Ewald, W. (2002). *The best part of me: Children talk about their bodies in pictures and words*. New York, NY: Little Brown Books for Young Readers.

Faigley, L., & Witte, S. (1981). Analyzing revision. *College Composition and Communication, 32*, 400–410.

Faltis, C. J. (1993). *Joinfostering: Adapting teaching strategies for the multilingual classroom*. Upper Saddle River, NJ: Prentice Hall/Merrill.

Farrell, T. (2006). *Succeeding with English language learners: A guide for beginning teachers*. Thousand Oaks, CA: Corwin.

Farris, P. J. (1997). *Language arts process, product, and assessment* (2nd ed.). Madison, WI: Brown & Benchmark Publishers.

Feng, S., & Powers, K. (2005). The short-and long-term effect of explicit grammar instruction on fifth graders' writing. *Reading Improvement, 42*(2), 67–72.

Fennessey, S. (1995). Living history through drama and literature. *The Reading Teacher, 49*, 16–19.

Ferris, S. (2014). Revoicing: A tool to engage all learners in academic conversation. *The Reading Teacher, 67*(5), 353–357.

Fisher, D., Lapp, D., & Wood, K. (2011). Reading for details in online and printed text: A prerequisite for deep reading. *Middle School Journal, 42*(3), 58–63.

Five, C. L. (1986). Fifth graders respond to a changed reading program. *Harvard Educational Review, 56*, 395–405.

Fitch, S. (2000). *Writing maniac: How I grew up to be a writer and you can too*. Markham, ON: Pembrooke Publishers.

Fleischman, P. (2008). *Big talk: Poems for four voices*. Cambridge, MA: Candlewick.

Fletcher, R. (2002). *Poetry matters: Writing a poem from the inside out.* New York, NY: HarperCollins.

Fletcher, R. (2005). *A writing kind of day: Poems for young poets.* Honesdale, PA: WordSong.

Flower, L., & Hayes, J. R. (1994). The cognition of discovery: Defining a rhetorical problem. In S. Perl (Ed.), *Landmark essays on writing process* (pp. 63–74). Davis, CA: Heragoras Press.

Flynt, E., & Brozo, W. G. (2009). It's all about the teacher. *The Reading Teacher, 62*(6), 536–538.

Fountas, I. C., & Pinnell, G. S. (1996). *Guided reading: Good first teaching for all children.* Portsmouth, NH: Heinemann.

Fountas, I., & Pinnell, G. (2008). *Benchmark assessment system* (2nd ed.). Portsmouth, NH: Heinemann.

Fraser, I. S., & Hodson, L. M. (1978). Twenty-one kicks at the grammar horse. *English Journal, 67,* 49–53.

Frasher, K. (2014). Music and literacy: Strategies using comprehension connections. *General Music Today, 27*(3), 6–9.

Freeman, D. E., & Freeman, Y. S. (1993). Strategies for promoting the primary languages of all students. *The Reading Teacher, 46,* 552–558.

Freeman, E. B., & Person, D. G. (Eds.). (1992). *Using nonfiction trade books in the elementary classroom: From ants to Zeppelins.* Urbana, IL: National Council of Teachers of English.

Freire, P. (1970). *Pedagogy of the oppressed.* New York: Continuum.

Freire, P., & Macedo, D. (1987). *Literacy: Reading the word and the world.* South Hadley, MA: Bergin & Garvey Publishers.

Funston, S., & Ingram, J. (1994). *A kid's guide to the brain.* Toronto: Greey de Pencier Books.

Furner, B. A. (1969). Recommended instructional procedures in a method emphasizing the perceptual-motor nature of learning in handwriting. *Elementary English, 46,* 1021–1030.

Gambrell, L. B. (2009). Creating opportunities to read more so that students read better. In E. H. Hiebert (Ed.), *Read more, read better* (pp. 251–266). New York: Guilford.

Gambrell, L. B. (2011). Seven rules of engagement: What's most important to know about motivation to read. *The Reading Teacher, 65*(3), 172–178.

Gambrell, L., Malloy, J., Marinak, B., & Mazzoni, A. (2015). Evidence-based best practices for comprehensive literacy in the age of the Common Core Standards. In L. B. Gambrell & L. M. Morrow (Eds.), *Best practices in literacy instruction* (5th ed., pp. 3–36). New York, NY: Guildford Press.

Gambrell, L. B., Malloy, J., & Mazzoni, S. (2007). Evidence based best practices for comprehensive literacy instruction. In L. B. Gambrell, L. Morrow., & S. Mazzoni (Eds.), *Best practices in literacy instruction* (3rd ed., pp. 11–36), New York: Guildford Press.

Gardner, H. (1993). *Multiple intelligences: The theory in practice.* New York: HarperCollins.

Gertridge, A. (2004). *Meet Canadian authors and illustrators.* Richmond Hill, ON: Scholastic.

Gentry, J. R. (1982). Developmental spelling: Assessment. *Diagnostique, 8,* 52–61.

Gentry, J. R., & Gillet, J. W. (1993). *Teaching kids to spell.* Portsmouth, NH: Heinemann.

Gere, A. R., & Abbott, R. D. (1985). Talking about writing: The language of writing groups. *Research in the Teaching of English, 19,* 362–381.

Gibbons, P. (1991). *Learning to learn in a second language.* Portsmouth, NH: Heinemann.

Gill, S. R. (2007). The forgotten genre of children's poetry. *The Reading Teacher, 60*(7), 622–625.

Giorgis, C., & Glazer, J. (2012). *Literature for young children: Supporting emergent literacy ages 0–8* (7th ed.). Upper Saddle River, NJ: Pearson.

Giroir, S., Romero Grimaldo, L., Vaughn, S., & Roberts, G. (2015). Interactive read-alouds for English learners in the elementary grades. *The Reading Teacher, 68*(8), 639–648.

Golden, J. M. (2001). *Reading in the dark: Using film as a tool in the English classroom.* Urbana, IL: National Council of Teachers of English.

Gonzalez, J., & Gonzalez, M. (1993). Phonological awareness in learning literacy. *Cognitive, 5,* 153–170.

Goodman, K. S. (1969). Analysis of oral reading miscues: Applied psycholinguistics. *Reading Research Quarterly, 4*(1), 9–30.

Goodman, K. S. (1993). *Phonics phacts.* Portsmouth, NH: Heinemann.

Graham, S. (1992). Issues in handwriting instruction. *Focus on Exceptional Children, 25*(2), 1–14.

Graves, D. H. (1983). *Writing: Teachers and children at work.* Portsmouth, NH: Heinemann.

Graves, D. H. (1992). *Explore poetry.* Portsmouth, NH: Heinemann.

Graves, D. H. (1994). *A fresh look at writing.* Portsmouth, NH: Heinemann.

Graves, D. H., & Hansen, J. (1983). The author's chair. *Language Arts, 60,* 176–183.

Graves, D. H., & Kittle, P. (2005). *My quick writes for inside writing.* Portsmouth, NH: Heinemann.

Graves, D. H., & Sunstein, B. S. (Eds.). (1992). *Portfolio portraits.* Portsmouth, NH: Heinemann.

Graves, M. (2006). *The vocabulary book: Learning and instruction.* New York: Teachers College Press.

Graves, M. F., & Watts-Taffe, S. (2008). For the love of words: Fostering word consciousness in young readers. *The Reading Teacher, 62*(3), 185–193.

Graves, M. F., & Watts-Taffe, S. M. (2002). The place of word consciousness in a research-based vocabulary program. In A. E. Farstrup & S. J. Samuels (Eds.), *What research has to say about reading instruction* (3rd ed., pp. 140–165). Newark, DE: International Reading Association.

Greenwood, B. (Ed.). (1994). *The CANSCAIP companion: A biographical record of Canadian children's authors, illustrators and performers.* Markham, ON: Pembroke.

Grierson, S. T., Anson, A., & Baird, J. (2002). Exploring the past through multigenre writing. *Language Arts, 80*(1), 51–59.

Griffith, F., & Olson, M. (1992). Phonemic awareness helps beginning readers break the code. *The Reading Teacher, 45,* 516–523.

Groff, P. J. (1963). Who writes faster? *Education, 83,* 367–369.

Gurak, L. (2001). *Cyberliteracy: Navigating the Internet with awareness.* New Haven, CT: Yale University Press.

Hackney, C. (1993). *Handwriting: A way to self-expression.* Columbus, OH: Zaner-Bloser.

Hagood, M. C., Stevens, L. P., & Reinking, D. (2002). What do THEY have to teach us? Talkin' 'cross generations! In D. Alvermann (Ed.), *Adolescents and literacies in a digital world* (pp. 68–83). New York: Peter Lang.

Hall, A. (2014). Beyond the author's chair: Expanding sharing opportunities in writing. *The Reading Teacher, 68*(1), 27–31. DOI:10.1002/trtr1297.

Hall, N. (1998). Real literacy in a school setting: Five-year-olds take on the world. *The Reading Teacher, 52*(1), 8–17.

Halliday, M. A. K. (2006). *Language as social semiotic: The social interpretation of language and meaning* (2nd ed.). New York: Continuum.

Hallows, J. (2002). *Proven techniques for teaching QWERTY keyboarding.* Retrieved September 6, 2013, from www.cwu.edu/~setc/ldtech/docs/keyboarding_techniques.pdf.

Hammerberg, D. (2001). Reading and writing "hypertextually": Children's literature, technology, and early writing instruction. *Language Arts, 78*(3), 207–216.

Hancock, M. R. (1992). Literature response journals: Insights beyond the printed page. *Language Arts, 61,* 141–150.

Hanna, P. R., Hanna, J. S., Hodges, R. E., & Rudorf, E. H. (1966). *Phoneme-grapheme correspondences as cues to spelling improvement.* Washington, DC: U.S. Department of Health, Education, and Welfare, Office of Education.

Hanrahan, M. (1999). Rethinking science literacy: Enhancing communication and participation in school science through affirmational journal writing. *Journal of Research in Science Teaching, 36*(6), 699–717.

Hansen, J. (2003). The language arts interact. In J. Flood (Ed.), *Handbook of research on teaching the English language arts* (2nd ed., pp. 1026–1034). Mahwah, NJ: Lawrence Erlbaum Associates.

Harris, V. J. (1992a). Multiethnic children's literature. In K. D. Wood & A. Moss (Eds.), *Exploring literature in the classroom: Content and methods* (pp. 169–201). Norwood, MA: Christopher-Gordon.

Harris, V. J. (Ed.). (1992b). *Teaching multicultural literature in grades K–8.* Norwood, MA: Christopher-Gordon.

Harrison, S. (1981). Open letter from a left-handed teacher: Some sinistral ideas on the teaching of handwriting. *Teaching Exceptional Children, 13,* 116–120.

Harste, J. C., Woodward, V. A., & Burke, C. L. (1984b). *Language stories and literacy lessons.* Portsmouth, NH: Heinemann.

Hartman, D. (1995). Eight readers reading: The intertextual links of proficient readers reading multiple passages. *Reading Research Quarterly, 30,* 520–561.

Hayden, R., & Kendrick, M. (2002). Understanding emergent literacy. In *Foundational training in family literacy: Trainers' guide* Edmonton: National Literacy Secretariat and Centre for Family Literacy Publication.

Head, M. H., & Readence, J. E. (1992). Anticipation guides: Using prediction to promote learning from text. In E. K. Dishner, T. W. Bean, J. E. Readence, & D. W. Moore (Eds.), *Reading in the content areas* (3rd ed., pp. 227–233). Dubuque, IA: Kendall/Hunt.

Heald-Taylor, G. (1987). How to use predictable books for K–2 language arts instruction. *The Reading Teacher, 40,* 656–661.

Heard, G. (1989). *For the good of the earth and sun: Teaching poetry.* Portsmouth, NH: Heinemann.

Heath, S. B. (1983a). Research currents: A lot of talk about nothing. *Language Arts, 60,* 999–1007.

Heath, S. B. (1983b). *Ways with words: Language, life, and work in communities and classrooms.* Cambridge: Cambridge University Press.

Hepler, S. (1991). Talking our way to literacy in the classroom community. *The New Advocate, 4,* 179–191.

Hiebert, E. (1989). *A research-based writing program for students with high access to computers.* ACOT Report #2. Cupertino, CA: Apple Computer, Inc.

Hilden, K., & Jones, J. (2013). Effective interactive read-alouds build stronger comprehension. *Reading Today, 30*(5), 17–19.

Hildreth, G. (1960). Manuscript writing after sixty years. *Elementary English, 37,* 3–13.

Hillerich, R. L. (1977). Let's teach spelling—not phonetic misspelling. *Language Arts, 54,* 301–307.

Hillocks, G. (1995). *Teaching writing as reflective practice.* New York: Teachers College Press.

Hirsch, E., & Niedermeyer, F. C. (1973). The effects of tracing prompts and discrimination training on kindergarten handwriting performance. *Journal of Educational Research, 67,* 81–83.

Hobbs, R., & Frost, R. (2003). Measuring the acquisition of media literacy skills. *Reading Research Quarterly, 38*(3), 330–355.

Holdaway, D. (1979). *The foundations of literacy.* Portsmouth, NH: Heinemann.

Holloway, J. (2010). Is that all you want me to do? In *Here comes everyone: Teaching in the intercultural classroom.* Edmonton, AB: Alberta Teachers Association.

Hopkins, L. B. (1987). *Pass the poetry, please!* New York: Harper & Row.

Horn, E. (1926). *A basic writing vocabulary.* Iowa City: University of Iowa Press.

Horn, E. (1957). Phonetics and spelling. *Elementary School Journal, 57,* 425–432.

Howell, H. (1978). Write on, you sinistrals! *Language Arts, 55,* 852–856.

Hughes, J. (2007). Poetry: A powerful medium for literacy and technology development. *What works? Research into practice,* Research Monograph #7. Toronto: The Literacy and Numeracy Secretariat.

Hunt, L. C., Jr. (1970). The effect of self-selection, interest and motivation upon independent, instructional, and frustration levels. *The Reading Teacher, 24,* 416.

Hurst, B., Scales, K. B., Frecks, E., & Lewis, K. (2011). Sign up for reading: Students read aloud to the class. *The Reading Teacher, 64*(6), 439–443.

International Reading Association. (2003). *Integrating literacy and technology in the curriculum: A position statement of the International Reading Association.* Retrieved May 1, 2006, from www.reading.org/downloads/positions/ps1048_technology.pdf.

International Reading Association. (2009). *New literacies and the 21st century technologies: A position statement of the International Reading Association* (now International Literacy Association). Newark, DE: International Reading Association.

Invernizzi, M. (2003). Concepts, sounds, and the ABCs: A diet for every young reader. In D. M. Barone & L. M. Morrow (Eds.), *Literacy and young children: Research-based practices* (pp. 140–156). New York: Guilford Press.

Jackson, A. D. (1971). A comparison of speed of legibility of manuscript and cursive handwriting of intermediate grade pupils. Unpublished doctoral dissertation, University of Arizona. *Dissertation Abstracts, 31,* 4384A.

Jobe, R., & Dayton-Sakari, M. (1999). *Reluctant readers: Connecting students and books for successful reading experiences.* Markham, ON: Pembroke Publishers.

Jobe, R., & Hart, P. (1991). *Canadian connection: Experiencing literature with children.* Markham, ON: Pembroke Publishers.

Johnson, A., Rezak, A., Hodges, G., Lawrence, M., Tippins, D., & Bongkotphet, T. (2008). Textual encounters of three kinds: Engaging in reading through community astronomy night. *The Reading Teacher, 62*(1), 54–63.

Jones, R., and Stott, J. (2000). *Canadian children's books: A critical guide to authors and illustrators.* Don Mills, ON: Oxford University Press.

Juel, C. (1991). Beginning reading. In R. Barr, M. L. Kamil, P. Mosenthal, & P. D. Pearson (Eds.), *Handbook of reading research* (Vol. 2, pp. 759–788). New York: Longman.

Karchmer, R. (2001). The journey ahead: Thirteen teachers report how the Internet influences literacy and literacy instruction in their K–12 classrooms. *Reading Research Quarterly, 36*(4), 442–466.

Kendrick, M. (2003). *Converging worlds: Play, literacy, and culture in early childhood.* Bern: Peter Lang.

Ketch, A. (2005). Conversation: The comprehension connection. *The Reading Teacher, 59*(1), 8–13.

Kiefer, B. (2009). *Charlotte Huck's children's literature* (10th ed.). Boston: McGraw-Hill.

Kiefer, B., & Tyson, C. (2010). *Charlotte Huck's children's literature: A brief guide.* New York, NY: McGraw-Hill.

Kintsch, W., & van Dijk, T. A. (1978). Toward a model of text comprehension and production. *Psychological Review, 85*(5), 363–394.

King, L., & Stovall, D. (1992). *Classroom publishing.* Hillsboro, OR: Blue Heron.

Kist, W. (2005). *New literacies in action: Teaching and learning in multiple media.* New York: Teachers College Press.

Klein, M. L. (1988). *Teaching reading comprehension and vocabulary: A guide for teachers.* Upper Saddle River, NJ: Prentice Hall/Merrill.

Knobel, M., & Lankshear, C. (2007). *A new literacies sampler.* New York: Peter Lang.

Krashen, S. (1982). *Principles and practices of second language acquisition.* Oxford: Pergamon Press.

Kuhl, D., & Dewitz, P. (1994). *The effect of handwriting style on alphabet recognition.* Paper presented at the Annual Meeting of the American Educational Research Association, New Orleans, LA.

Kutiper, K., & Wilson, P. (1993). Updating poetry preferences: A look at the poetry children really like. *The Reading Teacher, 47,* 28–35.

Laminack, L. L., & Wood, K. (1996). *Spelling in use: Looking closely at spelling in whole language classrooms.* Urbana, IL: National Council of Teachers of English.

Lane, B. (1993). *After the end: Teaching and learning creative revision.* Portsmouth, NH: Heinemann.

Lane, B. (2008). *But how do you teach writing? A simple guide for all teachers.* New York, NY: Scholastic Teaching Resources.

Langer, J. A. (1995). *Envisioning literature: Literary understanding and literature instruction.* New York: Teachers College Press.

Langhorne, M., Dunham, J., Gross, J., & Rehmke, D. (1989). *Teaching with computers: A new menu for the '90s.* Phoenix, AZ: Oryx Press.

Larson, L. (2008). Electronic reading workshop: Beyond books with new literacies and instructional technologies. *Journal of Adolescent & Adult Literacy, 52*(2), 121–131.

Law, B., & Eckes, M. (1990). *The more than just surviving handbook: ESL for every classroom teacher.* Winnipeg: Peguis.

Lehr, S. S. (1991). *The child's developing sense of theme: Responses to literature.* New York: Teachers College Press.

Leu, D. J., Jr. (2000). Literacy and technology: Deictic consequences for literacy education in an information age. In M. K. Kamil, P. Mosenthal, P. D. Pearson, & R. Barr (Eds.), *Handbook of reading research* (Vol. 3, pp. 743–770). Mahwah, NJ: Erlbaum.

Leu, D. J., Jr., Kinzer, C. K., Coiro, J., & Cammack, D. W. (2004). Toward a theory of new literacies emerging from the Internet and other information and communicating technologies. In B. Ruddell & N. Unrau (Eds.), *Theoretical models and processes of reading* (5th ed., pp. 1570–1613). Newark, DE: International Reading Association.

Lewis, R. B., Ashton, T. M., Haapa, B., Kieley, C. L., & Fielden, C. (1999). Improving the writing skills of students with learning disabilities: Are word processors with spelling and grammar checkers useful? *Learning Disabilities: A Multidisciplinary Journal, 9*(3), 87–98. ERIC Document Reproduction Service No. EJ594984.

Lindsay, G. A., & McLennan, D. (1983). Lined paper: Its effects on the legibility and creativity of young children's writing. *British Journal of Educational Psychology, 53,* 364–368.

Lipson, M. Y. (2007). *Teaching reading beyond the primary grades.* New York: Scholastic.

Luce-Kapler, R., & Dobson, T. (2005). In search of a story: Reading and writing e-literature. *Reading Online, 8*(6). Retrieved January 12, 2013, from www.readingonline.org/articles/art_index.asp?HREF=luce-kapler/index.html.

Lukens, R. (2006). *A critical handbook of children's literature* (8th ed.). New York: Allyn & Bacon.

Lundsteen, S. W. (1979). *Listening: Its impact on reading and the other language arts* (Rev. ed.). Urbana, IL: National Council of Teachers of English.

Lutz, W. (1989). *Doublespeak.* New York: HarperCollins.

Lutz, W. (1991). Notes toward a description of doublespeak (Rev. ed.). In W. Gibson & W. Lutz (Eds.), *Doublespeak: A brief history, definition, and bibliography, with a list of award winners, 1974–1990* (Concept Paper No. 2). Urbana, IL: National Council of Teachers of English.

Mackay, M. (2006). *Readers theatre and story vines.* Winnipeg: Portage & Main Press.

Macon, J. M., Bewell, D., & Vogt, M. E. (1991). *Responses to literature, Grades K–8.* Newark, DE: International Reading Association.

Marques, E. (1997). *100 jobs for kids and young adults: A self-improvement tool.* Toronto: WiseChild Press.

Marzano, R. J., Pickering, D., & McTighe, J. (1993). *Assessing student outcomes: Performance assessment using the dimensions of learning model.* Alexandria, VA: Association for Supervision and Curriculum Development.

Maslin, J. E., & Nelson, M. E. (2002). Peering into the future: Students using technology to create literacy products. *The Reading Teacher, 55*(7), 628–631.

Mason, J. (1984). Early reading from a developmental perspective. In P. D. Pearson, R. Barr, M. L. Kamil, & P. Mosenthal (Eds.), *Handbook of Reading Research* (pp. 505–543). New York: Longman.

McCarrier, A., Pinnell, G. S., & Fountas, I. (2000). *Interactive writing: How language and literacy come together, K–2.* Portsmouth, NH: Heinemann.

McCarthy, B. (1987). *The 4MAT system: Teaching to learning styles.* Barrington, IL: EXCEL, Inc.

McCarthy, P. (2008). Using sound boxes systematically to develop phonemic awareness. *The Reading Teacher, 62*(4), 346–349.

McCracken, R. A., & McCracken, M. J. (1972). *Reading is only the tiger's tail.* San Rafael, CA: Leswing Press.

McGee, L., & Richgels, D. (2012). *Literacy beginnings: Supporting young readers and writers* (6th ed.). Boston: Allyn & Bacon.

McGrath, J. (1991). Making friends: Books that transcend the barrier of strangeness. *Canadian Magazine, 19*(3), 153–160.

McKay, R., & Kendrick, M. (2001). Images of literacy: Youth children's drawing about reading and writing. *Canadian Journal of Research in Early Childhood Education, 8*(4), 7–22.

McKenna, M., Conradi, K., Young, C., & Jang, B. (2013). Technology and the common core standards. In L. M. Morrow, T. Shanahan, & K. Wixson (Eds.), *Teaching with the common core standards for English language arts, pre-K–2* (pp. 152–169). New York, NY: Guildford Press.

McKeon, C. (2001). The nature of children's e-mail in one classroom. *The Reading Teacher, 52*(7), 698–706.

McNabb, M. (2006). *Literacy learning in networked classrooms: Using the Internet with middle-level students.* Newark, DE: International Reading Association.

McTeague, F. (1992). *Shared reading in the middle and high school years.* Markham, ON: Pembroke.

MediaSmarts. (2012). *Media education in Canada: Digital and media literacy fundamentals.* Retrieved January 20, 2013, from http://mediasmarts.ca/digital-media-literacy-fundamentals.

Miller, D. (2010). *The book whisperer: Awakening the inner reader in every child.* San Francisco, CA: John Wiley & Sons.

Miller, D. (2013). *Reading in the wild: The book whisperer's keys to cultivating lifelong reading habits.* San Francisco, CA: Jossey-Bass Books.

Moffitt, A. S., & Wartella, E. (1992). A survey of leisure reading pursuits of female and male adolescents. *Reading Research and Instruction, 31*(2), 1–17.

Montgomery, D., Karlan, G., & Coutinho, M. (2001). The effectiveness of word processor spell checker programs to produce target words for misspellings generated by students with learning disabilities. *Journal of Special Education, 16*(2), 27–41.

Morrow, L. (2015). *Literacy development in the early years: Helping children read and write* (8th ed.). Upper Saddle River, NJ: Pearson.

Morrow, L. M. (1996). *Motivating reading and writing in diverse classrooms* (NCTE Research Report No. 28). Urbana, IL: National Council of Teachers of English.

Morrow, L. M. (2003). Motivating lifelong voluntary readers. In J. Flood, D. Lapp, J. R. Squire, & J. M. Jensen (Eds.), *Handbook of research on teaching the English language arts* (pp. 857–867). Mahwah, NJ: Erlbaum.

Morrow, L. M. (2005). *Literacy development in the early years: Helping children read and write* (5th ed.). Upper Saddle River, NJ: Pearson.

Nagy, W. E. (1988). *Teaching vocabulary to improve reading comprehension.* Urbana, IL: ERIC Clearinghouse on Reading and Communication Skills and the National Council of Teachers of English and the International Reading Association.

Nagy, W. E., & Herman, P. (1985). Incidental vs. instructional approaches to increasing reading vocabulary. *Educational Perspectives, 23*, 16–21.

National Council of Teachers of English. (1996). *Standards for the English language arts.* Urbana, IL: National Council of Teachers of English and the International Reading Association.

NCTE Elementary Section Steering Committee. (1996). Exploring language arts standards within a cycle of learning. *Language Arts, 73*, 10–13.

Neufeld, P. (2005/2006). Comprehension instruction in content area classes. *The Reading Teacher, 59*(4), 302–312.

Newfoundland and Labrador Department of Education. (2011). *English language arts: Kindergarten: Interim edition.* Curriculum Guide. St. John's: Newfoundland and Labrador Department of Education.

Newkirk, T. (2000). Misreading masculinity: speculations on the great gender gap in writing. *Language Arts, 77*(4), 177–184.

New London Group. (1996). A pedagogy of multiliteracies: Designing social futures. *Harvard Educational Review, 66*(1), 60–92.

Noguchi, R. R. (1991). *Grammar and the teaching of writing: Limits and possibilities.* Urbana, IL: National Council of Teachers of English.

Noyce, R. M., & Christie, J. F. (1983). Effects of an integrated approach to grammar instruction on third graders' reading and writing. *Elementary School Journal, 84*, 63–69.

Nystrand, M., Gamoran, A., & Heck, M. J. (1993). Using small groups for response to and thinking about literature. *English Journal, 82*, 14–22.

Oczkus, L. (2009). *Interactive think-aloud lessons: 25 surefire ways to engage students and improve comprehension.* Scarborough, ON: Scholastic.

Oczkus, L. D. (2003). *Reciprocal teaching at work: Strategies for improving reading comprehension.* Newark, DE: International Reading Association.

Ogle, D. M. (1986). K-W-L: A teaching model that develops active reading of expository text. *The Reading Teacher, 39*, 564–570.

Ohlhausen, M. M., & Jepsen, M. (1992). Lessons from Goldilocks: "Somebody's been choosing my books but I can make my own choices now!" *The New Advocate, 5*, 31–46.

Owocki, G., & Goodman, Y. (2002). *Kidwatching: Documenting children's literacy development.* Portsmouth, NH: Heinemann.

Pahl, K., & Rowsell, J. (2005). *Literacy & education: Understanding the new literacies in the classroom.* London: Paul Chapman Publishing.

Palinscar, A. (1985). *The unpacking of a multi-component, metacognitive training package.* Paper presented at the Annual Meeting of the American Educational Research Association, Chicago.

Palincsar, A. S., & Brown, A. L. (1986). Interactive teaching to promote independent learning from text. *The Reading Teacher, 39* (8), 771–777.

Papandropoulou, I., & Sinclair, H. (1974). What is a word? Experimental study of children's ideas on grammar. *Human Development, 17*, 241–258.

Paratore, J. (2006). Approaches to family literacy: Exploring the possibilities. *The Reading Teacher, 59*(4), 394–396.

Paris, S. G., & Jacobs, J. E. (1984). The benefits of informed instruction for children's reading awareness and comprehension skills. *Child Development, 55*, 2083–2093.

Paris, S. G., Wasik, B. A., & Turner, J. C. (1991). The development of strategic readers. In R. Barr, M. L. Kamil, P. B. Mosenthal, & P. D. Pearson (Eds.), *Handbook of reading research, Vol. 2,* (pp. 609–640). New York: Longman.

Parsons, L. (2001). *Response journals revisited: Maximizing learning through reading, writing, viewing, discussing, and thinking.* Markham, ON: Pembroke.

Pearman, C. (2008). Independent reading of CD-ROM storybooks: Measuring comprehension with oral retellings. *The Reading Teacher, 61*(8), 594–602.

Perfetti, C., Beck, I., Bell, L., & Hughes, C. (1987). Phonemic knowledge and learning to read are reciprocal: A longitudinal study of first grade children. *Merrill-Palmer Quarterly, 33*, 283–319.

Peterson, R., & Eeds, M. (1990). *Grand conversations: Literature groups in action.* New York: Scholastic.

Peterson, S. (2001). Teachers' perceptions of gender equity in writing assessment. *English Quarterly, 33*(1&2), 22–30.

Piaget, J. (1969). *The psychology of intelligence.* Totowa, NJ: Littlefield, Adams.

Piaget, J. (1975). *The development of thought: Equilibration of cognitive structures.* New York: Viking.

Piccolo, J. A. (1987). Expository text structures: Teaching and learning strategies. *The Reading Teacher, 40*, 838–847.

Piper, D. (1993). Students in the mainstream who face linguistic and cultural challenges. In J. Andrews & J. Lupart (Eds.), *The inclusive classroom: Educating exceptional children.* Scarborough, ON: Nelson.

Pitler, H., Hubbell, E.R., Kuhn, M., & Malenoski, K. (2007). *Using technology with classroom instruction that works.* Alexandria, VA: Association for Supervision and Curriculum Development.

Pollock, N., & Missiuna, C. (2005). *To write or to type—that is the question!* Hamilton, ON: McMaster University, CanChild Centre for Childhood Disability Research. Retrieved from http://dcd.canchild.ca/en/EducationalMaterials/resources/DCD_Typing.pdf.

Porter, C., & Cleland, J. (1995). *The portfolio as a learning strategy.* Portsmouth, NH: Heinemann.

Postman, N. (1992). The disappearance of childhood. In N. Postman (Ed.), *Conscientious objections: Stirring up trouble about language, technology and education* (pp. 147–161). New York: Vintage.

Prelutsky, J. (2005). *Read a rhyme, write a rhyme.* New York, NY: Dragonfly Books.

Prelutsky, J. (2008). *Pizza, pigs, & poetry: How to write a poem.* New York, NY: Greenwillow Books.

Pressley, M. (1992). Encouraging mindful use of prior knowledge: Attempting to construct explanatory answers facilitates learning. *Educational Psychologist, 27*, 91–109.

Pressley, M. (2000). What should comprehension instruction be the instruction of? In M. Kamil, P. Mosenthal, P. D. Pearson, & R. Barr (Eds.), *Handbook of reading research, Vol. 3* (pp. 545–562). Mahwah, NJ: Erlbaum.

Pressley, M., & Allington, R. (2015). *Reading instruction that works: The case for balanced teaching* (4th ed.). New York, NY: Guildford Press.

Purcell-Gates, V. (1996). Stories, coupons, and the TV Guide: Relationships between home literacy experiences and emergent literacy knowledge. *Reading Research Quarterly, 31*, 406–428.

Quill & Quire. http://www.quillandquire.com.

Rasinski, T. (2004). Creating fluent readers. *Educational Leadership, 61*(6), 46–51.

Rasinski, T. V., & Padak, N. D. (1990). Multicultural learning through children's literature. *Language Arts, 67*, 576–580.

Read, C. (1975). *Children's categorization of speech sounds in English* (NCTE Research Report No. 17). Urbana, IL: National Council of Teachers of English.

Read, C. (1986). *Children's creative spelling*. London: Routledge & Kegan Paul.

Read, S. (2005). First and second graders write informational text. *The Reading Teacher, 59*(1), 36–44.

Reed, B. (1992). Review of J. Lunn, *Canadian history from cows to catalogues*. *Canadian Review, 20*(6).

Reimer, K. M. (1992). Multiethnic literature: Holding fast to dreams. *Language Arts, 69*, 14–21.

Reinking, D. (1997). Me and my hypertext: A multiple digression analysis of technology and literacy [sic]. *The Reading Teacher, 50*(8), 626–643.

Reutzel, R. (2015). Early literacy research: Findings primary-grade teachers will want to know. *The Reading Teacher, 69*(1), 14–24.

Reyes, M. de la Luz. (1991). A process approach to literacy using dialogue journals and literature logs with second language learners. *Research in the Teaching of English, 25*, 291–313.

Rhodes, L. K., & Nathenson-Mejia, S. (1992). Anecdotal records: A powerful tool for ongoing literacy assessment. *The Reading Teacher, 45*, 502–511.

Roberts, S. (2002). Taking a technological path to poetry writing. *The Reading Teacher, 55*(7), 678–687.

Robinson, F. P. (1946). *Effective study* (2nd ed.). New York: Harper & Row.

Rog, L. (2003). *Guided reading basics*. Markham, ON: Pembroke Publishers.

Romano, T. (1995). *Writing with passion: Life stories, multiple genres*. Portsmouth, NH: Heinemann.

Roop, P. (1992). Nonfiction books in the primary classroom: Soaring with the swans. In E. B. Freeman & D. G. Person (Eds.), *Using nonfiction tradebooks in the elementary classroom: From ants to Zeppelins* (pp. 106–112). Urbana, IL: National Council of Teachers of English.

Roop, P. (1995). Keep the reading lights burning. In M. Sorensen & B. Lehman (Eds.), *Teaching with children's books: Paths to literature-based instruction* (pp. 197–202). Urbana, IL: National Council of Teachers of English.

Rosenblatt, L. M. (1978). *The reader, the text, the poem: The transactional theory of the literary work*. Carbondale: Southern Illinois University Press.

Rosenblatt, L. M. (1983). *Literature as exploration* (4th ed.). New York: Modern Language Association.

Rosenblatt, L. M. (1985). Viewpoints: Transaction versus interaction—A terminological rescue operation. *Research in the Teaching of English, 19*, 98–107.

Rosenblatt, L. M. (1991). Literature—S.O.S.! *Language Arts, 68*, 444–448.

Rosenblatt, L. M. (2005). *Making meaning with texts: Selected essays*. Portsmouth, NH: Heinemann.

Routman, R. (1996). *Literacy at the crossroads: Crucial talk about reading, writing, and other teaching dilemmas*. Portsmouth, NH: Heinemann.

Rowsell, J. (2005). Literacy revisited. *Orbit, 36*(1). Retrieved September 20, 2006, from http://www.oise.utoronto.ca/orbit/rowsell_editorial.html.

Ruddell, M. R. (2001). *Teaching content reading and writing* (3rd ed.). New York: John Wiley & Sons.

Rupley, W., Logan, J., & Nichols, W. (1998/1999). Vocabulary instruction in a balanced reading program. *The Reading Teacher, 52*(4), 336–346.

Sample Gosse, H., & Phillips, L. (2007). No gain in blame: Fostering collaborations between home and school. In Y. Goodman and P. Martens (Eds.), *Critical issues in early literacy* (pp. 191–201). Mahwah, NJ: Erlbaum.

Sampson, M., Rasinski, T., & Sampson, M. (2003). *Total literacy: Reading, writing and learning*. Belmont, CA: Wadsworth/Thomson Learning.

Scarcella, R. (1990). *Teaching language minority students in the multicultural classroom*. Upper Saddle River, NJ: Prentice Hall/Merrill.

Schmar-Dobler, E. (2003). Reading on the Internet: Linking literacy and technology. *Journal of Adolescent and Adult Literacy, 47*(1), 80–87.

Schmitt, M. C. (1990). A questionnaire to measure children's awareness of strategic reading processes. *The Reading Teacher, 43*, 454–461.

Scott, J., & Nagy, W. E. (2004). Developing word consciousness. In J. Baumann and E. Kame'enui (Eds.), *Vocabulary instruction: Research to practice* (pp. 201–217). New York: Guilford Press.

Sejnost, R., & Thiese, S. (2010). *Building content literacy: Strategies for the adolescent learner*. New York: Sage.

Serafini, F. (2004). *Lessons in comprehension: Explicit instruction in the reading workshop*. Portsmouth, NH: Heinemann.

Shafer, K. (1993). Talk in the middle: Two conversational skills for friendship. *English Journal, 82*, 53–55.

Shefelbine, J. (1995). *Learning and using phonics in beginning reading* (Literacy Research Paper no. 10). New York: Scholastic.

Shor, I. (1999). What is critical literacy? *Journal for Pedagogy, Pluralism & Practice, 1*(4). Retrieved September 6, 2013, from www.lesley.edu/journal-pedagogy-pluralism-practice/ira-shor/critical-literacy.

Short, K. G., Kauffman, G., & Kahn, L. H. (2003). "I just *need* to draw": Responding to literature across multiple sign systems. *The Reading Teacher, 54*(2), 160–171.

Silver, D. (2012). *Fall down 7 times, get up 8: Teaching kids to succeed*. Thousand Oaks, CA: Corwin Press.

Sims, R. (1982). *Shadow and substance: Afro-American experience in contemporary children's fiction*. Urbana, IL: National Council of Teachers of English.

Sippola, A. E. (1995). K-W-L-S. *The Reading Teacher, 48*(1), 542–543.

Skillings, M., & Ferrell, R. (2000). Student-generated rubrics: Bringing students into the assessment process. *The Reading Teacher, 53*, 452–455.

Slaughter, J. P. (1993). *Beyond storybooks: Young children and the shared book experience*. Newark, DE: International Reading Association.

Slavin, R. (1997). *Educational psychology* (5th ed.). Boston: Allyn & Bacon.

Smith, F. (1982). *Writing and the writer*. New York: Holt, Rinehart & Winston.

Smith, F. (1988). *Joining the literacy club: Further essays into education*. Portsmouth, NH: Heinemann.

Smith, J., & Read, S. (2005). *Early literacy instruction: A comprehensive framework for teaching reading and writing, K–3*. Columbus, OH: Pearson Education.

Snow, C., Burns, S., & Griffin, P. (1998). *Preventing reading difficulties in young children*. Washington, DC: National Academies Press.

Snow, C., Griffin, P., & Tabors, P. (2002). *The home-school study of language and literacy development*. Retrieved September 6, 2013, from http://www.gse.harvard.edu/~pild/homeschoolstudy.htm.

Snowball, D., & Bolton, F. (1999). *Spelling K–8: Planning and teaching*. Portland, ME: Stenhouse.

Sommers, N. (1994). Revision strategies of student writers and experienced adult writers. In S. Perl (Ed.), *Landmark essays on writing process* (pp. 75–84). Davis, CA: Heragoras Press.

Sorenson, M. (1993). Teach each other: Connecting talking and writing. *English Journal, 82*, 42–47.

Sowers, S. (1985). The story and the "all about" book. In J. Hansen, T. Newkirk, & D. Graves (Eds.), *Breaking ground: Teachers relate reading and writing in the elementary school* (pp. 73–82). Portsmouth, NH: Heinemann.

Spandel, V. (2005). *Creating young writers through 6-trait writing assessment and instruction* (4th ed.). Boston: Allyn & Bacon.

Spandel, V. (2008). *Creating young writers: Using the six traits to enrich writing process in primary classrooms* (2nd ed.). Boston: Allyn & Bacon.

Spandel, V. (2013). *Creating writers: 6 traits, process, workshops, and literature* (6th ed.). Boston, MA: Pearson.

Speaker, R. B., Jr., & Speaker, P. R. (1991). Sentence collecting: Authentic literacy events in the classroom. *Journal of Reading, 35*, 92–95.

Spires, H. A., & Estes, T. H. (2002). Reading in web-based learning environments. In C. C. Block & M. Pressley (Eds.), *Comprehension instruction: Research-based best practices* (pp. 115–125). New York: Guilford.

Stahl, S., & Nagy, W. (2006). *Teaching word meanings*. Mahwah, NJ: Lawrence Erlbaum.

Stanovich, K. (1980). Toward an interactive-compensatory model of individual differences in the development of reading fluency. *Reading Research Quarterly, 16*, 37–71.

Stanovich, P. (1998). Shaping practice to fit the evidence. *Orbit, 28*(4), 37–42.

Statistics Canada. (2012). 2011 census of population: Linguistic characteristics of Canadians. *The Daily* (Oct. 24). Retrieved April 3, 2013, from www.statcan.gc.ca/daily-quotidien/121024/dq121024a-eng.htm.

Stauffer, R. G. (1970). *The language experience approach to the teaching of reading*. New York: Harper & Row.

Steinbergh, J. W. (1993). Chandra: "To live a life of no secrecy." In S. Hudson-Ross, L. M. Cleary, & M. Casey (Eds.), *Children's voices: Children talk about literacy* (pp. 202–214). Portsmouth, NH: Heinemann.

Stewig, J. W. (1981). Choral speaking: Who has the time? Why take the time? *Childhood Education, 57*, 25–29.

Strong, W. (1996). *Writer's toolbox: A sentence-combining workshop*. New York: McGraw-Hill.

Sulzby, E. (1985). Kindergartners as readers and writers. In M. Farr (Ed.), *Advances in writing research, Vol. 1: Children's early writing development* (pp. 127–199). Norwood, NJ: Ablex.

Sumara, D., & Walker, L. (1991). The teacher's role in whole language. *Language Arts, 68*, 276–285.

Sweet, A., & Snow, C. (2003). Reading for comprehension. In A. P. Sweet & C. E. Snow (Eds.), *Rethinking reading comprehension* (pp. 1–11). New York: Guilford Press.

Tapscott, D. (1998). *Growing up digital: The rise of the net generation*. New York: McGraw-Hill.

Teale, W. H., Leu, D. J., Jr., Labbo, L. D., & Kinzer, C. (2002). The CTELL project: New ways technology can help educate tomorrow's reading teachers. *The Reading Teacher, 55*(7), 654–659.

Teale, W. H., & Sulzby, E. (1989). Emerging literacy: New perspectives. In D. S. Strickland & L. M. Morrow (Eds.), *Emerging literacy: Young children learn to read and write* (pp. 1–15). Newark, DE: International Reading Association.

Templeton, S., & Spivey, E. (1980). The concept of word in young children as a function of level of cognitive development. *Research in the Teaching of English, 14*, 265–278.

Thurber, D. N. (1987). *D'Nealian handwriting (Grades K–8)*. Glenview, IL: Scott, Foresman.

Tiedt, I. (1970). Exploring poetry patterns. *Elementary English, 45*, 1082–1084.

Tierney, R. J., & Pearson, P. D. (1992). Learning to learn from text: A framework for improving classroom practice. In E. K. Dishner, T. W. Bean, J. E. Readence, & D. W. Moore (Eds.), *Reading in the content areas: Improving classroom instruction* (pp. 85–99). Dubuque, IA: Kendall-Hunt.

Tompkins, G. E. (1994). *Teaching writing: Balancing process and product* (2nd ed.). Upper Saddle River, NJ: Prentice Hall/Merrill.

Tompkins, G. E. (1995). Hear ye, hear ye, and learn the lesson well: Fifth graders read and write about the American Revolution. In M. Sorensen & B. Lehman (Eds.), *Teaching with children's books: Paths to literature-based instruction* (pp. 171–187). Urbana, IL: National Council of Teachers of English.

Tompkins, G. E. (2013). *50 literacy strategies: Step by step* (4th Ed.). Boston: Pearson.

Tompkins, G. E., & McGee, L. M. (1983). Launching nonstandard speakers into Standard English. *Language Arts, 60*, 463–469.

Tompkins, G. E., & McGee, L. M. (1993). *Teaching reading with literature: Case studies to action plans*. Upper Saddle River, NJ: Prentice Hall/Merrill.

Tompkins, G. E., & Webeler, M. B. (1983). What will happen next? Using predictable books with young children. *The Reading Teacher, 36*, 498–502.

Treiman, R. (1985). Phonemic analysis, spelling, and reading. In T. H. Carr (Ed.), *The development of reading skills* (pp. 5–18). San Francisco: Jossey-Bass.

Trelease, J. (2013). *The new read-aloud handbook* (4th ed.). New York: Penguin.

Tunmer, W., & Nesdale, A. (1985). Phonemic segmentation skill and beginning reading. *Journal of Educational Psychology, 77*, 417–427.

Tunnell, M. O., & Ammon, R. (Eds.). (1993). *The story of ourselves: Teaching history through children's literature*. Portsmouth, NH: Heinemann.

Tunnell, M., Jacobs, J., Young, T., & Bryan, G. (2012). *Children's literature briefly*. Boston: Pearson.

Urzua, C. (1980). Doing what comes naturally: Recent research in second language acquisition. In G. S. Pinnell (Ed.), *Discovering language with children* (pp. 33–38). Urbana, IL: National Council of Teachers of English.

Vacca, R., Vacca, J., & Bogoray, D. (2005). *Content area reading: Literacy and learning across the curriculum* (Canadian ed.). Toronto: Pearson Canada.

Valencia, S. W., Hiebert, E. H., & Afflerbach, P. P. (1994). *Authentic reading assessment: Practices and possibilities.* Newark, DE: International Reading Association.

Venezky, R. L. (1970). *The structure of English orthography.* The Hague: Mouton.

Vygotsky, L. S. (1978). *Mind in society.* Cambridge, MA: Harvard University Press.

Vygotsky, L. S. (1986). *Thought and language.* Cambridge, MA: MIT Press.

Walker-Dalhouse, D. (1992). Using African-American literature to increase ethnic understanding. *The Reading Teacher, 45,* 416–422.

Walsh, M. (2003). "Reading" pictures: What do they reveal? Young children's reading of visual texts. *Reading: Literacy and language, 37*(3), 123–130.

Watts Pailliotet, A. (2000). Welcome to the new literacies department. *Reading Online, 4*(1). Retrieved from www.readingonline.org/newliteracies/wattspailliotet1.

Watts-Taffe, S., Gwinn, C., Johnson, J., & Horn, M. (2003). Preparing preservice teachers to integrate technology with the elementary literacy program. *The Reading Teacher, 57*(2), 130–138.

Weaver, C. (Ed.). (1994). *Success at last! Helping students with AD(H)D achieve their potential.* Portsmouth, NH: Heinemann.

Weaver, C. (1996). *Teaching grammar in context.* Portsmouth, NH: Heinemann.

Weaver, C. (1998). Teaching grammar in the context of writing. In C. Weaver (Ed.), *Lessons to share: On teaching grammar in context* (pp. 18–38). Portsmouth, NH: Heinemann.

Weaver, C., McNally, C., & Moerman, S. (2001). To grammar or not to grammar: That is not the question! *Voices from the Middle, 8,* 17–33.

Wepner, S., Valmont, W. & Thurlow, K. (Eds.). (2000). *Linking literacy and technology: A guide for K–8 classrooms.* Newark, DE: International Reading Association.

White, T. G., Sowell, J., & Yanagihara, A. (1989). Teaching elementary students to use word-part clues. *The Reading Teacher, 42,* 302–308.

Whitin, P. E. (1994). Opening potential: Visual response to literature. *Language Arts, 71,* 101–107.

Whitin, P. E. (1996). Exploring visual response to literature. *Research in the Teaching of English, 30,* 114–140.

Wiggins, G., & McTighe, J. (2006). *Understanding by design* (2nd ed.). Alexandria, WA: Association for Supervision and Curriculum Development.

Wilde, S. (1993). *You kan red this! Spelling and punctuation for whole language classrooms, K–6.* Portsmouth, NH: Heinemann.

Wilen, W. W. (1986). *Questioning skills for teachers* (2nd ed.). Washington, DC: National Education Association.

Wilfong, L. (2008). Building fluency, word-recognition ability, and confidence in struggling readers: The poetry academy. *The Reading Teacher, 62*(1), 4–13.

Winsor, P. J., & Pearson, P. D. (1992). *Children at risk: Their phonemic awareness development in holistic instruction.* Technical Report No. 556. Champaign, IL: Center for the Study of Reading.

Wittrock, M. C., & Alesandrini, K. (1990). Generation of summaries and analogies and analytic and holistic abilities. *American Research Journal, 27,* 489–502.

Wohlwend, K. (2010). A is for avatar: Young children in literacy 2.0 worlds and literacy 1.0 schools. *Language Arts, 88,* 144–152.

Wollman-Bonilla, J. E. (1989). Reading journals: Invitations to participate in literature. *The Reading Teacher, 43,* 112–120.

Wolvin, A. D., & Coakley, C. G. (1996). *Listening* (5th ed.). New York: McGraw-Hill.

Wong-Fillmore, L. (1985). When does teacher talk work as input? In S. M. Gass & C. G. Madden (Eds.), *Input in second language acquisition* (pp. 17–50). Rowley, MA: Newbury House.

Wormeli, R. (2001). *Meet me in the middle: Becoming an accomplished middle-level teacher.* Portland, ME: Stenhouse.

Wright, C. D., & Wright, J. P. (1980). Handwriting: The effectiveness of copying from moving versus still models. *Journal of Educational Research, 74,* 95–98.

Wu, X., & Newman, M. (2008). *Engage and excite all learners through a visual literacy curriculum.* Paper presented at the Annual Meeting of the American Educational Research Association, New York City, March 24–28. ERIC Number: ED502353.

Wylie, R. E., & Durrell, D. D. (1970). Teaching vowels through phonograms. *Elementary English, 47,* 787–791.

Xu, S. H. (2010). *Teaching English language learners: Literacy strategies and resources for K–6.* New York: Guilford Press.

Yaden, D. B., Jr. (1988). Understanding stories through repeated readalouds: How many does it take? *The Reading Teacher, 41,* 556–560.

Yokota, J. (1993). Issues in selecting multicultural children's literature. *Language Arts, 70,* 156–167.

Yopp, H. K. (1992). Developing phonemic awareness in young children. *The Reading Teacher, 45,* 696–703.

Yopp, H. K. (1995). Read-aloud books for developing phonemic awareness: An annotated bibliography. *The Reading Teacher, 48,* 538–542.

Yopp, H. K., & Yopp, R. H. (2006). *Literature-based reading activities* (4th ed.). Boston: Allyn & Bacon.

Yopp, H. K., & Yopp, R. H. (2009). Phonological awareness is child's play! *Young Children, 64*(1), 12–18, 21.

Yopp, H., & Yopp, R. (2000). Supporting phonemic awareness development in the classroom. *The Reading Teacher, 54*(2), 130–143. doi: 10.1598/RT.54.2.2.

Young, J., & Brozo, W. (2001). Boys will be boys, or will they? Literacy & masculinities. *Reading Research Quarterly, 36*(3), 316–325.

Zipke, M. (2008). Teaching metalinguistic awareness and reading comprehension with riddles. *The Reading Teacher, 62*(2), 128–137.

Children's Resources

Ablett, B. (2007). *Dear polar bear.* New York: Scholastic.

Abramson, B. (2006). *Off we go!* Toronto: Tundra Books.

Acer, D. (2008). *Gotcha! Mystery hunters: 18 amazing ways to freak out your friends.* Toronto: Kids Can Press.

Ada, A. (1998). *Yours truly, Goldilocks.* New York: Atheneum.

Adelson-Goldstein, J. (2009). *Oxford picture dictionary* (2nd Canadian English ed.). Toronto: Oxford University Press.

Adler, D. A. (1990). *A picture book of Helen Keller.* New York: Holiday House.

Ahenakew, F. (1999). *Wisahkechk flies to the moon.* Winnipeg: Pemmican Publications.

Ahlberg, A. (2000). *The bravest ever bear.* Cambridge, MA: Candlewick.

Ahlberg, J., & Ahlberg, A. (1986). *The jolly postman, or other people's letters.* Boston: Little, Brown.

Ahlberg, J., & Ahlberg, A. (2007). *The jolly postman, or other people's letters* (20th anniversary ed.). Boston: Little, Brown.

Ahlberg, J., & Ahlberg, A. (2012). *The jolly Christmas postman.* London: Puffin.

Aker, D. (2005). *One on one.* Toronto: HarperCollins.

Alderson, S. (2007). *The eco-diary of Kiran Singer.* Toronto: Tradewind Books.

Alborough, J. (2005). *Duck in the truck*. LaJolla, CA: Kane/Miller Book Publishers.

Alda, A. (2006). *Did you say pears?* Toronto: Tundra Books.

Ali, D., & Cho, M. (2005). *Media madness: An insider's guide to media*. Toronto: Kids Can Press.

Aliki. (1995). *Tabby: A story in pictures*. New York: HarperCollins.

Amosky, J. (2002). *All about frogs*. New York: Scholastic.

Ancona, G. (1993). *Powwow*. Orlando, FL: Harcourt Brace.

Andrae, G. (1999). *Giraffes can't dance*. New York, NY: Orchard Books. (P)

Andrews, J. (1985). *The very last first time*. Vancouver: Douglas & McIntyre.

Andrews, J. (1990). *The auction*. Toronto: Groundwood/Douglas & McIntyre.

Andrews, J. (1996). *Keri*. Toronto: Groundwood Books.

Andrews, J. (2011). *When apples grew noses and white horses flew: Tales of Ti-Jean*. Toronto: Groundwood Books.

Andrews, W. (1995). Understanding global warming. Toronto: Health Canada Ltd.

Anno, M. (1982). *Anno's Britain*. New York: Philomel.

Appelt, K. (2008). *The underneath*. New York: Atheneum.

Appelt, K. (2010). *Keeper*. New York: Antheneum.

Applegate, K. (2012). *The one and only Ivan*. New York: HarperCollins Childrens' Books.

Archibald, J., Friesen, V., & Smith, J. (1993). *Courageous spirits: Aboriginal heroes of our children*. Penticton, BC: Theytus Books.

Arnosky, J. (1995). *I see animals hiding*. New York: Scholastic.

Arsenault, G. (2002). *Acadian legends, folktales, and songs from Prince Edward Island* (S. Ross, Trans.). Charlottetown, PEI: Acorn Press.

Asch, F. (2007). *Mrs. Marlowe's mice*. Toronto: Kids Can Press.

Avi. (2004). *City of light, city of dark*. New York: Scholastic.

Awa, S., Akeeagok, S., Ziegler, A., & McDonald, S. (2011). *Uumajut, volume two: Learn more about arctic wildlife!* Toronto: Inhabit Media.

Azore, B. (2007). *Wanda and the frogs*. Toronto: Tundra Books.

Babbitt, N. (1975). Tuck everlasting. New York: Farrar, Straus & Giroux.

Badami, R. A. (2000). *The hero's walk*. Toronto: Vintage.

Bagdasarian, A. (2000). *Forgotten fire*. New York: Dorling Kindersley.

Baird, A. (2001). The witches of Willowmere. Toronto: Penguin.

Ballantyne, A. (1991). *Wisakyjak and the new world*. Waterloo, ON: Penumbra Press.

Ballantyne, E. (2001). *The Aboriginal alphabet for children*. Winnipeg, MB: Pemmican Publications.

Bang-Campbell, M. (2008). *Little rat makes music*. New York, NY: Houghton Mifflin. (P)

Bannatyne-Cugnet, J. (1992). *A prairie alphabet*. Illus. Y. Moore. Montreal: Tundra Books.

Bannatyne-Cugnet, J. (1993). *Grandpa's alkali*. Red Deer, AB: Red Deer College Press.

Barber, K. (2006). *Six words you never knew had something to do with pigs and other fascinating facts about the langauge from Canada's word lady*. Toronto: Oxford University Press.

Bar-el, D. (2011). *Pussycat, pussycat, where have you been?* Vancouver: Simply Read Books.

Barclay, J. (1998). *How cold was it?* Montreal: Lobster Press.

Barretta, G. (2007). *Dear deer: A book of homophones*. New York: Henry Holt.

Barnes, L. (1995). *Goldilocks and the three bears*. Toronto: Somerville House.

Barnette, M. (2003). *Dog days and dandelions*. New York: St. Martin's Press.

Barretta, G. (2006). *Now & Ben: The modern inventions of Benjamin Franklin*. New York: Holt.

Barton, R. (2003). *The bear says north: Tales from northern lands*. Toronto: Groundwood Books.

Base, G. (1988). *Animalia*. Don Mills, ON: Stoddart.

Bateman, R. (2005). *Backyard birds: An introduction*. Toronto: Scholastic Canada/Madison Press.

Bateman, R. (2010). *Vanishing habitats*. Toronto: Scholastic Canada.

Bates, C. (2001). *Shooting star*. Halifax, NS: James Lorimer & Co.

Baxter, J. R. (2007). *The way lies north*. Vancouver: Ronsdale Press.

Beck, A. (2002). *Elliot gets stuck*. Toronto: Kids Can Press.

Becker, H. (2012). *Alphabest*. Toronto: Kids Can Press.

Bedard, M. (2001). *Stained glass*. Toronto: Tundra Books.

Bell, W. (1999). *Forbidden city*. Toronto: Doubleday.

Bell, W. (2006). *The blue helmet*. Toronto: Doubleday.

Bell-Rehwoldt, S. (2009). *The kids' guide to building cool stuff*. Mankato, MN: Capstone Press.

Bellingham, B. (2005). *Lilly's special gift*. Halifax: Formac.

Bennett, J. (2000). *Jason Mason Middleton-Tap*. Vancouver: Raincoast.

Berenstain, S., & Berenstain, J. (1968). *Inside, outside, upside down*. New York: Random House.

Berkowitz, J. (2009). *Out of this world*. Toronto: Kids Can Press.

Beveridge, C. (2003). *Shadows of disaster*. Vancouver: Ronsdale Press.

Bial, R. (1996). With needle and thread. Boston, MA: Houghton Mifflin.

Birney, B. (2005). *The world according to Humphrey*. New York: Puffin.

Bishop, M. H. (2005). *Tunnels of tyranny*. Regina, SK: Coteau Books.

Black, S. (2001). *Follow the polar bears*. New York: Scholastic.

Blades, A. (1985). *By the sea: An alphabet book*. Toronto: Kids Can Press.

Blake, W. (1970). *Song of Innocence and of Experience*. Oxford: Oxford University Press. Originally published 1789–1794.

Bogart, J. E. (1999). *Jeremiah learns to read*. Toronto: Scholastic Canada.

Bogart, J. E. (2001). *The night the stars flew*. Toronto: North Winds Press.

Bogart, J. E. (2002). *Capturing joy: The story of Maud Lewis*. Toronto: Tundra Books.

Bollard, J. (2006). *Scholastic children's thesaurus*. Richmond Hill, ON: Scholastic.

Bondar, B., & Bondar, R. (1993). On the shuttle: Eight days in space. Toronto: Greey de Pencier Books.

Bondar, R. (1994). *Touching the earth*. Willowdale, ON: Firefly Books.

Booth, D. (Ed.). (1989). *Til all the stars have fallen: Canadian poems for children*. Illus. K. MacDonald Denton. Toronto: Kids Can Press.

Booth, D. (Ed.). (1990). *Voices on the wind: Poems for all seasons*. Illus. M. Lemieux. Toronto: Kids Can Press.

Booth, D., & Kovalski, M. (1993). *Doctor Knickerbocker and other rhymes: A Canadian collection*. Toronto: Kids Can Press.

Booth, D., & Reczuch, K. (1996). *The dust bowl*. Toronto: Kids Can Press.

Boraks-Nemetz, L. (1994). *The old brown suitcase*. Brentwood Bay, BC: Ben-Simon.

Bosak, S. V. (2004). *Dream: A tale of wonder, wisdom & wishes*. Toronto: TCP Press.

Bossley, M. M. (1996). *The perfect gymnast*. Toronto: James Lorimer.

Bouchard, D. (1990). *The elders are watching.* Tofino, BC: Eagle Dancer Enterprises.

Bouchard, D. (1994). *The colours of British Columbia.* Vancouver: Raincoast Books.

Bouchard, D. (1995). *If you're not from the prairie …* New York: Atheneum.

Bouchard, D. (1996a). *The dust bowl.* Toronto: Kids Can Press.

Bouchard, D. (1996b). *Voices from the wild: An animal sensgoria.* Vancouver: Raincoast Books.

Bouchard, D. (1997). *If Sarah will take me.* Victoria, BC: Orca Books.

Bouchard, D. (2006). *Nokum is my teacher.* Calgary: Red Deer Press.

Bouchard, D., & Willier, S. (2008). *The drum calls softly.* Calgary: Red Deer Press.

Bourgeois, P. (1990). *The amazing dirt book.* Toronto: Kids Can Press.

Bourgeois, P. (2000). *Franklin helps out.* Toronto: Kids Can Press.

Bourgeois, P. (2001a). *Franklin says I love you.* Toronto: Kids Can Press.

Bourgeois, P. (2001b). *Oma's quilt.* Toronto: Kids Can Press.

Bourgeois, P. (2002). *Franklin plays hockey.* Toronto: Kids Can Press.

Bourgeois, P. (2003). *Franklin's reading club.* Toronto: Kids Can Press.

Bourgeois, P. (2004). *Franklin forgives.* Toronto: Kids Can Press.

Bourgeois, P. (2005a). *Canadian fire fighters.* Toronto: Kids Can Press.

Bourgeois, P. (2005b). Canadian garbage collectors. Toronto: Kids Can Press.

Bourgeois, P. (2005c). Canadian police officers. Illus. K. LaFave. Toronto: Kids Can Press.

Bourgeois, P. (2005d). Canadian postal workers. Toronto: Kids Can Press.

Bourgeois, P. (2005b). *Franklin celebrates.* Toronto: Kids Can Press.

Bourgeois, P. (2007). *The jumbo book of space.* Toronto: Kids Can Press.

Bourgeois, P. (2008). *The dirt on dirt.* Toronto: Kids Can Press.

Bourgeois, P. (2012). *Franklin's partner.* Toronto: Kids Can Press.

Boynton, S. (1983). *A is for angry: An animal and adjective alphabet.* New York: Workman.

Boynton, S. (1987). *Pajama time!* New York: Workman.

Bradford, K. (2005). *Ghost wolf.* Victoria, BC: Orca Books.

Brallier, T. (2009). *Tess's tree.* Toronto: HarperCollins Canada.

Brand, D. (2006). *Earth magic.* Toronto: Kids Can Press.

Brandis, M. (2003). *The quarter-pie window.* Toronto: Tundra Books. Originally published 1985.

Brennan-Nelson, D. (2004). My teacher likes to say. Chelsea, MI: Sleeping Bear Press.

Brenner, B. (2000). *The earth is painted green: A garden of poems about our planet.* Toronto: Scholastic.

Brett, J. (1985). *Annie and the wild animals.* Boston: Houghton Mifflin.

Brett, J. (1989). *The mitten.* New York: Putnam.

Brett, J. (1991). *Berlioz the bear.* New York: Putnam.

Brett, J. (1992). *Trouble with trolls.* New York: Putnam.

Brett, J. (1995). *Armadillo rodeo.* New York: Putnam.

Brett, J. (2004). *The umbrella.* New York: G. P. Putnam's Sons.

Brett, J. (2006). *Hedgie blasts off.* New York: G. P. Putnam's Sons.

Brett, J. (2008). *Gingerbread friends.* New York: G. P. Putnam's Sons.

Brett, J. (2009). *Jan Brett's snow treasury.* New York: G. P. Putnam's Sons.

Brewster, H. (2011). *Deadly Voyage: RMS* Titanic. Toronto: Scholastic Canada.

Briggs, R. (1980). *The snowman.* Harmondsworth, UK: Puffin Books.

Bright, A. (2012). *Before we go.* Markham, ON: Red Deer Press.

Brighton, C. (1987). *Galileo's treasure box.* New York: Walker.

Brooker, M. F. (2011). *Hold the Oxo! A teenage soldier writes home.* Toronto: Dundurn Press.

Brooks, K. (2002). Lucas. Frome, UK: Chicken House.

Brooks, M. (1997). *The bone dance.* Toronto: Groundwood Books.

Brooks, M. (1999). *Being with Henry.* Toronto: Douglas & McIntyre.

Brosgol, V. (2011). *Anya's ghost.* New York: First Second.

Brouwer, S. (2007). *Titan clash.* Victoria, BC: Orca Books.

Browne, A. (2000). *Voices in the park.* New York: DK Children.

Browne, P. (1996). *A gaggle of geese: The collective names of the animal kingdom.* New York: Atheneum.

Browning, R. (1993). *The pied piper of Hamelin.* New York: Random House. Originally published 1842.

Brumbeau, J. (2001). *The quiltmaker's gift.* Toronto: Scholastic.

Bryan, L. (2005). *It's about me, it's about you.* Toronto: Pearson.

Bucholz, D. (2010). *The unofficial Harry Potter cookbook.* Avon, MA: Adams Media.

Buehner, C., & Buehner, M. (2007). *Goldilocks and the three bears.* New York: Dial.

Buffie, M. (1998). *Angels turn their backs.* Toronto: Kids Can Press.

Bunting, E. (1991). *Fly away home.* New York: Clarion.

Bunting, E. (1995). *Dandelions.* New York: Harcourt Brace.

Bunting, E. (2006). *One green apple.* New York: Clarion Books.

Burdett, L. (1997). *A midsummer night's dream for kids.* Willowdale, ON: Firefly Books.

Burnett, F. H. (1911). *The secret garden.* Toronto: Copp Clark.

Burton, K. (1995). One grey mouse. Toronto: Kids Can Press.

Butler, G. (1995). The Killik: A Newfoundland story. Montreal: Tundra Books.

Cabot, M. (2009). *Princess Mia.* Toronto: HarperCollins Canada.

Cameron, A. (1991). *Raven and snipe.* Madeira Park, NL: Harbour Publishing.

Campbell, E. (2003). *Goldilocks returns.* New York: Simon & Schuster.

Campbell, N. (2008). *Shin-chi's canoe.* Toronto: Groundwood Books.

Canadian Oxford dictionary (2nd ed.). (2004). Toronto: Oxford University Press.

Cardinal, P. (1997). *The Cree people.* Edmonton: Duval House.

Carle, E. (1969). *The very hungry caterpillar.* Cleveland, OH: World.

Carle, E. (1987). *A house for hermit crab.* Saxonville, MA: Picture Book Studio.

Carle, E. (1990). *The very quiet cricket.* New York: Philomel.

Carle, E. (1993). *Eric Carle: Picture writer.* MARC Records: Library video.com.

Carle, E. (1995). *The very lonely firefly.* New York: Philomel.

Carle, E. (1998). *Hello, red fox.* New York: Simon & Schuster.

Carle, E. (2007). *My very first book of animal sounds.* New York: Philomel.

Carle, E. (2011). *The artist who painted a blue horse.* New York: Philomel Books. (P)

Carney, E. (2009). *Frog!* New York: National Geographic Society.

Carney, M. (1997). At Grandpa's sugar bush. Toronto: Kids Can Press.

Carney, M. (2002). *Where does a tiger-heron spend the night?* Toronto: Kids Can Press.

Carroll, L. (2004). *Jabberwocky.* Illus. S. Jorisch. Toronto: Kids Can Press. Originally published 1872.

Carroll, L. (2008). Alice's Adventures in Wonderland. Illus. O. Lipchencko. Toronto: Tundra Books. Originally published 1865.

Carter, A. L. (2002). *Under a prairie sky*. Victoria, BC: Orca Books.

Carter, A. L. (2003). *My home bay*. Red Deer, AB: Red Deer Press.

Casselman, B. (2007). *Canadian words and sayings*. Toronto: McArthur & Company.

Cassidy, S. (2002). It's good to be small. Markham, ON: Fitzhenry & Whiteside.

Cassidy, S. (2004). Gummytoes. Markham, ON: Fitzhenry & Whiteside.

Celenza, A. (2006). *Gershwin's rhapsody in blue*. Watertown, MA: Charlesbridge. (P-M)

Cha, D. (1998). *Dia's story cloth*. New York: Lee & Low Books.

Chaconas, D. (2006). *Cord & Fuzz: Short and tall*. New York: Viking.

Chambers, C. (2007). *School days around the world*. London, UK: DK Publishing.

Chan, G. (2004). *An ocean apart*. Toronto: Scholastic.

Chase, E. (1996). *Secret dawn*. Richmond Hill, ON: North Winds Press.

Chataway, C. (2002). *The perfect pet*. Toronto: Kids Can Press.

Ciardi, J. (1992). *The hopeful trout and other limericks*. New York: Houghton Mifflin.

Citra, B. (1999). *Ellie's new home*. Victoria, BC: Orca Books.

Clark, J. (1995). *The dream carvers*. Toronto: Viking.

Clark, J., & Denton, K. M. (2006). Snow. Toronto: Groundwood Books.

Classical Kids. (1993). *Beethoven lives upstairs* [CD]. Pickering, ON: Classical Kids.

Classical Kids. (2000). *Tchaikovsky discovers America* [CD]. Pickering, ON: Classical Kids.

Cleary, B. (1999). *A mink, a fink, a skating rink: What is a noun?* Minneapolis, MN: Cariorhoda Books.

Cleary, B. (2001b). *Hairy, scary, ordinary: What is an adjective?* Minneapolis, MN: Cariorhoda Books.

Cleary, B. (2001a). *To root, to toot, to parachute: What is a verb?* Minneapolis, MN: Cariorhoda Books.

Cleary, B. (2002). *Under, over, by the clover: What is a preposition?* Minneapolis, MN: Cariorhoda Books.

Cleary, B. (2005). *Dearly, nearly, insincerely: What is an adverb?* New York: First Avenue Editions.

Cleary, B. (2009). *Skin like milk, hair of silk: What are similes and metaphors?* Minneapolis, MN: Millbrook Press.

Cleaver, E. (1969). How summer came to Canada. Toronto: Oxford University Press.

Climo, S. (1989). *The Egyptian Cinderella*. New York: Crowell.

Coates, J. (2010). *A hare in the elephant's trunk*. Markham, ON: Red Deer Press.

Cobb, M. (1995). *The quilt-block history of pioneer days*. Riverside, NJ: Millbrook Press.

Coerr, E. (1977). *Sadako and the thousand paper cranes*. New York: Putnam.

Coerr, E. (1993). Sadako. New York: Putnam.

Coffey, M. (1998). A cat in a kayak. Toronto: Annick Press.

Cohen, C. L. (1996). *Where's the fly?* New York: Greenwillow.

Cohen, L. (1995). *Dance me to the end of love*. New York: Welcome Enterprises.

Cole, J. (1981). *A snake's body*. New York: Morrow.

Cole, J. (1995). *The magic school bus inside a hurricane*. New York: Scholastic.

Cole, J. (2010). *The magic school bus and the climate challenge*. New York: Scholastic.

Coles, R. (1995). *The story of Ruby Bridges*. New York: Scholastic.

Collins, S. (2008). *The hunger games*. New York: Scholastic.

Collins Gage Canadian Intermediate Dictionary. (2005). Toronto: Nelson Education.

Collins Gage Canadian Intermediate Thesaurus. (2006). Scarborough, ON: Nelson Canada.

Collins primary thesaurus. (2004). New York: HarperCollins.

Coren, M. (1994). *The man who created Narnia: The story of C. S. Lewis*. Toronto: Lester Publishing.

Coren, S. (2006). *Why do dogs have wet noses?* Toronto: Kids Can Press.

Coulter, L. (2001). *Secrets in stone: All about Maya heiroglyphs*. Markham, ON: Scholastic Canada.

Craig, P. (2013). *A quilt for Jenna*. Eugene, OR: Harvest House Publishers.

Creech, S. (1995). *Walk two moons*. London: Macmillan Children's Books.

Creech, S. (2000). *The wanderer*. New York: HarperCollins.

Creech, S. (2001). *Love that dog*. New York: HarperCollins.

Creech, S. (2005). *Heartbeat*. New York: HarperCollins.

Creech, S. (2012). *The Great Unexpected*. New York: HarperCollins.

Cronin, D. (2000). *Click, clack, moo*. Toronto: Simon & Schuster Children's Publishing.

Cronin, D. (2002). *Giggle, giggle, quack*. Toronto: Simon & Schuster Children's Publishing.

Cullinan, B. E. (Ed.). (1996). *A jar of tiny stars: Poems by NCTE award-winning poets*. Honesdale, PA: Boyds Mills Press.

Cummer, D. (2013). *Brothers at war*. Toronto, ON: Scholastic Canada.

Cumyn, A. (2002). *The secret life of Owen Skye*. Toronto: Groundwood Books.

Curry, D. (2003). *How does your brain work?* New York, NY: Scholastic.

Cushman, K. (1994). Catherine, called Birdy. New York: HarperCollins.

Dahl, M. (2001). *The everything kids' joke book*. Avon, MA: Adams Media.

Dahl, M. (2006a). *If you were an adjective*. Minneapolis, MN: Picture Window Books.

Dahl, M. (2006b). *If you were an adverb*. Minneapolis, MN: Picture Window Books.

Dahl, M. (2006c). *If you were a noun*. Minneapolis, MN: Picture Window Books.

Danziger, P. (1994). *Amber Brown is not a crayon*. New York: Putnam.

Davidge, B. (1990). *Mummer's song*. Toronto: Douglas & McIntyre.

Davies, H. (2009). *The games book: How to play the games of yesteryear*. New York: Scholastic.

Davis, W. (2001). *Light at the edge of the world: A journey through vanishing cultures*. Vancouver: Douglas & McIntyre.

Daywalt, D. (2013). *The day the crayons quit*. New York, NY: Philomel Books. (P-M)

Delaunois, A. (2008). La clé. Illus. C. Delezenne. Montreal: Éditions de L'Isatis.

Demers, J. (1989). One more dinosaur. St. Petersburg, FL: Pages Publishing Group-Willowisp Press.

dePaola, T. (1985). Hey diddle diddle and other Mother Goose rhymes. New York: Putnam.

dePaola, T. (1988). *The legend of the Indian paintbrush*. New York: Putnam.

Dewar, T. (1993). Inside dinosaurs and other prehistoric creatures. Richmond Hill, ON: Scholastic Canada.

Dewey, A. (1995a). *Naming colors*. New York: HarperCollins.

Dewey, A. (1995b). *The sky*. Seattle, WA: Green Tiger Press.

Dickinson, E. (1978). *I'm nobody! Who are you? Poems of Emily Dickinson for children*. Owing Mills, MD: Stemmer House.

Dickinson, E. (1990). *A brighter garden: Poetry*. Illus. by Tasha Tudor. New York: Philomel Books.

Dillon, L., & Dillon, D. (2002). *Rap a tap tap: Here's Bojangles—think of that*. New York: Scholastic.

Domm, K. (2005). *Atlantic puffin: Brother of the north*. Halifax: Nimbus.

Donaldson, C. (2006). *Canada's wetland animals*. Toronto: Scholastic Canada.

Donaldson, J. (2000). *Monkey puzzle*. London: Macmillan Children's Books.

Dowd, O. (2002). *A young dancer's apprenticeship: On tour with the Moscow City Ballet*. Vancouver: Raincoast Books.

Downey, R. (2001). *Love is a family*. New York: HarperCollins.

Downie, M. A., & Rawlyk, G. (1980). A proper Acadian. Toronto: Kids Can Press.

Downie, M. A., & Robertson, B. (Comp.). (1987). *The new wind has wings: Poems from Canada*. Toronto: Oxford University Press.

Doyen, D., & Moser, B. (2009). *Once upon a twice*. New York, NY: Random House.

Doyle, B. (2001). *Mary Ann Alice*. Vancouver: Douglas & McIntyre.

Drake, J., & Love, A. (2009). *Kids book of the far north*. Toronto: Kids Can Press.

Duchesne, C., & Kunigis, P. (2012). *W is for wapiti! An alphabet songbook*. Montreal: The Secret Mountain.

Dunklee, A. (2011). My name is Elizabeth! Illus. M. Forsythe. Toronto: Kids Can Press.

DuPrau, J. (2003). *City of ember*. New York: Random House.

Durant, A. (2007). *Dear Santa Claus*. Somerville, MA: Candlewick Press.

Dyer, H. (2010). *Watch this space: Designing, defending, and sharing public spaces*. Toronto: Kids Can Press.

Ebbitt-Cutler, M. (2002). *Breaking free: The story of William Kurelek*. Toronto: Tundra Books.

Edwards, F. (1997). Downtown lost and found. Toronto: Firefly Books.

Edwards, W. (2004). *Monkey business*. Toronto: Kids Can Press.

Eger, D. (2006). *Who's in Maxine's tree?* Victoria, BC: Orca Book Publishers.

Ehlert, L. (1990). *Feathers for lunch*. Orlando, FL: Harcourt Brace.

Ehrlich, A. (2009). *The girl who wanted to dance*. Somerville, MA: Candlewick Press. (M)

Eliot, T. S. (1940). *Old Possum's books of practical cats*. London: Faber & Faber.

Ellis, D. (2000). *The breadwinner*. Vancouver: Douglas & McIntryre.

Ellis, D. (2002a). *A company of fools*. Markham, ON: Fitzhenry & Whiteside.

Ellis, D. (2002b). *Looking for X*. Toronto: Groundwood Books.

Ellis, D. (2002c). *Parvana's journey*. Toronto: Groundwood Books.

Ellis, D. (2003). *Mud city*. Toronto: Groundwood Books.

Ellis, D. (2004a). *The heaven shop*. Markham, ON: Fitzhenry & Whiteside.

Ellis, D. (2004b). Keeley: Book one: The girl from Turtle Mountain. Toronto: Penguin Canada.

Ellis, D. (2004b). *Three wishes: Palestinian and Israeli children speak*. Toronto: Groundwood Books.

Ellis, D. (2005a). Keeley: Book two: Keeley's big story. Toronto: Penguin Canada.

Ellis, D. (2005b). Our stories, our songs: African children talk about AIDS. Markham, ON. Fitzhenry & Whiteside.

Ellis, D. (2006a). *I am a taxi*. Toronto: House of Anansi Press.

Ellis, D. (2006b). *Keeley: Book three: Keeley and the mountain*. Toronto: Penguin Canada.

Ellis, D. (2007a). *Bifocal*. Markham, ON: Fitzhenry & Whiteside.

Ellis, D. (2007b). *Jakeman*. Markham, ON: Fitzhenry & Whiteside.

Ellis, D. (2007b). *Sacred leaf*. Toronto: House of Anansi Press.

Ellis, D. (2011). *No ordinary day*. Toronto, ON: Groundwood Books.

Ellis, D. (2012a). *Kids from Kabul*. Toronto, ON: Groundwood Books.

Ellis, D. (2012b). *My name is Parvana*. Toronto: Groundwood Books.

Ellis, D. (2013). *Looks like daylight: Voices of indigenous kids*. Toronto, ON: Groundwood Books.

Ellis, D. (2014). *Moon at nine*. Toronto, ON: Pajama Press.

Ellis, D. (2015). *My name is Parvana*. Toronto, ON: Groundwood Books.

Ellis, S. (2011). *That fatal night: The* Titanic *diary of Dorothy Wilton*. Toronto: Scholastic Canada.

Engle, M. (2015). *Drum dream girl: How one girl's courage changed music*. New York, NY: Houghton Miifflin Harcourt. (P-M)

Ernst, L. C. (1983). *Sam Johnson and the blue ribbon quilt*. New York: Mulberry Books.

Ernst, L. C. (2005). *Little Red Riding Hood: A newfangled prairie tale*. Toronto: Aladdin.

Fagan, C. (2007). *Ten old men and a mouse*. Toronto: Tundra Books.

Fagan, C. (2011). *Banjo of destiny*. Toronto: Groundwood Books.

Fauchon, J. (2005). *The Métis alphabet book*. Saskatoon: The Gabriel Dumont Institute.

Faulkner, M. (2004). *A day at the sugar bush: Making maple syrup*. Toronto: Scholastic Canada.

Feder, J. (1995). *Table, chair, bear: A book in many languages*. New York: Ticknor.

Fernandes, E. (2002). *Busy little mouse*. Toronto: Kids Can Press.

Filopovic, Z. (2006). *Zlata's diary: A child's life in wartime Sarajevo*. New York: Penguin.

Fine, E. H., & Josephson, J. P. (2007). *Armando and the blue tarp school*. New York, NY: Lee & Low Books.

Fitch, S. (1992). *There were monkeys in my kitchen*. Toronto: Doubleday.

Fitch, S. (1994). *I am small*. Toronto: Doubleday.

Fitch, S. (1995). *Mabel Murple*. Toronto: Doubleday.

Fitch, S. (1997a). *If you could wear my sneakers*. Toronto: Doubleday.

Fitch, S. (1997b). There's a mouse in my house. Illus. L. Watts. Toronto: Doubleday.

Fitch, S. (1999). *If I were the moon*. Toronto: Doubleday.

Fitch, S. (2002). *Writing maniac: How I grew up to be a writer and you can too*. Portland, ME: Stenhouse Publishers.

Fitch, S. (2005a). *If I had a million onions*. Vancouver, BC: Tradewind Books.

Fitch, S. (2005b). *The gravesavers*. Toronto: Doubleday.

Fitch, S. (2013). *Night sky wheel ride*. Vancouver, BC: Tradewind Books.

Fitch, S. (2014). *Singily skipping along*. Halifax, NS: Nimbus.

Flatt, L. (2012). *Counting on fall*. Toronto: OwlKids Books.

Flatt, L. (2013). *Sorting through spring*. Toronto: OwlKids Books.

Fleischman, P. (1988). *Joyful noise: Poems for two voices*. New York: Harper & Row.

Fleming, D. (1994). *Barnyard banter*. New York: Henry Holt.

Fleming, D. (2002). *Alphabet under construction*. New York: Henry Holt.

Flett, J. (2010). Owls see clearly at night: A Michif alphabet. Vancouver: Simple Read Books.

Florian, D. (1999). *Winter eyes*. New York: Greenwillow Books.

Flournoy, V. (1985). The patchwork quilt. New York: Dial.

Foggo, C. (1997). *One thing that's true*. Toronto: Kids Can Press.

Fonteyn, M. (1989). *Swan Lake*. San Diego, CA: Harcourt, Brace, Jovanovich.

Fowler, A. (1993). *Woolly sheep and hungry goats*. Chicago: Children's Press.

Fox, M. (1996). *Wilfrid Gordon McDonald Partridge*. Norwood, South Australia: Omnibus Books.

Fowler, J. (2010). *What's the point? A book about multiple meaning words*. Fort Worth, TX: AuthorHouse.

Frasier, D. (2000). *Miss Alaineus. A vocabulary disaster*. New York: Harcourt.

Friedrich, M. (2004). *You're not my real mother*. New York, NY: Little Brown.

Friesen, G. (2000). *Men of stone*. Toronto: Kids Can Press.

Fritz, J. (1992). *Surprising myself*. Katonah, NY: Richard C. Owen.

Fromer, L., & Gerstein, F. (2012). *My itchy body*. Toronto: Tundra Books.

Frost, R. (1978). *Stopping by woods on a snowy evening*. Illus. S. Jeffers. New York: Dutton.

Frost, R. (1982). *A swinger of birches: Poems of Robert Frost for young people*. Owing Mills, MD: Stemmer House.

Frost, R. (1988). *Birches*. Illus. E. Young. New York: Henry Holt.

Fullerton, A. (2008). *Libertad*. Markham, ON: Fitzhenry & Whiteside.

Gabbitas, C., & Barritt, L. (Eds.) (2015). *Poems and pictures children's poems–exercise and healthy food: An invitation that captured the primary school nation* (Vol. 3). Selby, UK: Poems and Pictures Ltd.

Gage Canadian beginner's dictionary. (2004). Scarborough, ON: Nelson Education Canada.

Gage Canadian first book of words. (2002). Toronto: Nelson Education Canada.

Gage Canadian junior dictionary. (2000). Toronto: Nelson Education Canada.

Gaiman, N. (2008). The graveyard book. New York: HarperCollins.

Gaiman, N. (2009). *Odd and the frost giants*. Illus. B. Helquist. New York: HarperCollins.

Galdone, P. (1970). *The three little pigs*. New York: Seabury.

Galdone, P. (1975). *The gingerbread boy*. New York: Seabury.

Galdone, P. (1978). *Cinderella*. New York: McGraw-Hill.

Galdone, P. (1986). Over in the meadow. New York: Simon & Schuster.

Gantos, J. (1998). Joey Pigza swallowed the key. New York: Farrar, Straus & Giroux.

Gantos, J. (2000). Joey Pigza loses control. New York: Farrar, Straus & Giroux.

Garg, A. (2002). *A word a day*. London: Wiley.

Garriel, B. (2004). *I know a shy fellow who swallowed a cello*. Honesdale, PA: Boyds Mills. (P-M)

Gavin, J. (2001). *Coram boy*. London: Egmont.

Gay, M.-L. (2002). *Stella, fairy of the forest*. Vancouver: Groundwood Books/Douglas & McIntyre.

Gay, M.-L. (2010). Roslyn Rutabaga and the biggest hole on earth! Toronto: Groundwood Books.

George, D. (1974). *My heart soars*. Saanichton, BC: Hancock House.

George, J. (2011). *Princess of the midnight ball*. New York, NY: Bloomsbury. (M-U)

George, J. C. (1972). *Julie of the wolves*. New York: Harper & Row.

George, J. C. (1997). *Arctic son*. New York: Hyperion.

Geraghty, P. (1995). *Solo*. London, UK: Red Fox (Random House).

Gerhard, A. (2013). *Listen to the birds: An introduction to classical music*. Montreal, QC: The Secret Mountain. (U)

Gerszak, R. (2011). *Beyond bullets: A photo journal of Afghanistan*. Toronto: Annick Press.

Ghent, N. (2003). *No small thing*. Toronto: HarperCollins.

Gibbons, G. (1990). *Weather words and what they mean*. New York: Holiday House.

Gilman, P. (1992). *Something from nothing*. Toronto: North Winds Press.

Gilman, P. (1994). *Jillian Jiggs to the rescue*. Richmond Hill, ON: Scholastic Canada.

Gilman, P. (1999). *Jillian Jiggs and the secret surprise*. Markham, ON: Scholastic Canada.

Gilmore, R. (2000). Mina's spring of colors. Markham, ON: Fitzhenry & Whiteside.

Givner, J. (2004). *Ellen Fremedon*. Toronto: Groundwood Books.

Glasser, R. (2006). *Fancy Nancy*. New York: HarperCollins Children's Books.

Goble, P. (1988). *Iktomi and the boulder*. New York: Orchard.

Goble, P. (1994). *Hau kola/Hello friend*. Katonah, NY: Richard C. Owen.

Goble, P. (2003). *Mystic horse*. New York: HarperCollins.

Godfrey, M. (1992). *Is it OK if this monster stays for lunch?* Toronto: Oxford University Press.

Godkin, C. (2002). *When the giant stirred: Legend of a volcanic island*. Markham, ON: Fitzhenry & Whiteside.

Godkin, C. (2006). *Fire! The renewal of a forest*. Markham, ON: Fitzhenry & Whiteside.

Golick, M. (1995). Wacky word games. Markham, ON: Pembroke Publishers.

Goodall, I. (2007). *Photographing greatness: The story of Karsh*. New York: Napoleon & Company.

Goodall, J. S. (1986). *The story of a castle*. New York: Macmillan.

Got, Y. (2001). *Sam's little sister*. San Francisco: Chronicle.

Graham, J. B. (1994). *Splish splash: Poems*. New York: Ticknor.

Graham-Barber, L. (1995). *A chartreuse leotard in a magenta limousine: And other words named after people and places*. New York: Hyperion.

Grandits, J. (2007). *Blue lipstick: Concrete poems*. Port Orange, FL: Sandpiper.

Granfield, L. (1995). *In Flanders fields: The story of the poem by John McCrae*. Illus. J. Wilson. Toronto: Lester Publishing.

Grant, A. (1995). *James McKay: A Métis builder of Canada*. Winnipeg: Pemmican.

Gravett, E. (2006a). *Meerkat mail*. New York: Simon and Shuster Books for Young Readers.

Gravett, E. (2006b). *Wolves*. London: Macmillan Children's Books.

Greenwod, B. (1999). *Pioneer Thanksgiving*. Toronto: Kids Can Press.

Greenwood, B. (2001). *Gold rush fever: A story of Klondike, 1898*. Toronto: Kids Can Press.

Greenwood, B. (2007). *Factory girl*. Toronto: Kids Can Press.

Gregory, N., & Lightburn, R. (1995). *How Smudge came*. Red Deer, AB: Red Deer College Press/Northern Lights Books.

Gryski, C. (1993). Boondoggle: Making bracelets with plastic lace. Toronto: Kids Can Press.

Gryski, C. (1995). Favourite string games. Toronto: Kids Can Press.

Guarino, D. (1989). Is your mama a llama? New York: Scholastic.

Guback, G. (1994). Luka's quilt. New York: Greenwillow.

Gutiérrez, E. (2005). *Picturescape*. Toronto: Simply Read Books.

Haddix, M. P. (1998). Among the hidden. New York: Simon & Schuster Books for Young Readers.

Hague, M. (1985). *Aesop's fables*. New York: Holt, Rinehart & Winston.

Hall, L. (1985). Just one friend. New York: Charles Scribner's Sons.

Hamill, S. (1995). *The sound of water*. Boston: Shambhala.

Hamilton, J. (Ed.). (2005). *Canadian poems for Canadian kids*. Vancouver: Subway Books.

Hamilton, V. (2000). *The girl who spun gold*. New York: Scholastic.

Hampton, W. (2001). *Meltdown: A race against nuclear disaster at Three Mile Island: A reporter's story*. Cambridge, MA: Candlewick.

Harley, A. (2009). *African acrostics: A word in edgeways*. Somerville, MA: Candlewick Press.

Harlow, J. H. (2004). *Thunder from the sea*. New York: McElderberry Books.

Harper, P. (2002). *Snow bear*. New York: Scholastic.

Harrison, M., & Stuart-Clark, Christopher (Eds.). (2007). *The Oxford book of children's poetry*. Oxford: Oxford University Press.

Harrison, T. (1982). *A northern alphabet*. Montreal: Tundra Books.

Harrison, T. (1997). Don't dig so deep, Nicholas! Toronto: Owl Books.

Harrison, T. (2002). *O Canada*. Toronto: Kids Can Press.

Harter, P. (1994). *Shadow play: Night haiku*. New York: Simon & Schuster.

Hartry, N. (1997). *Hold on, McGinty!* Toronto: Doubleday Canada.

Hass, R. (1995). *The essential haiku: Versions of Basho, Buson, & Issa*. New York: Ecco.

Hearn, E., & Milne, M. (Eds.) 2007. *Our new home: Immigrant children speak*. Toronto: Second Story Press.

Hedderwick, M. (2010). *Katie Morag delivers the mail*. New York: Red Fox Picture Books.

Hegerat, B. J. (2006). *Running toward home*. Edmonton: NeWest Press.

Heidbreder, R. (2003). *Eenie meenie Manitoba: Playful poems and rollicking rhymes*. Toronto: Kids Can Press.

Heidbreder, R. (2003). *See saw Saskatchewan: More playful poems from coast to coast*. Toronto: Kids Can Press.

Heidbreder, R. (2004). *Drumheller dinosaur dance*. Toronto: Kids Can Press.

Heidbreder, R. (2006). *Drumheller dinosaur dance*. Toronto, ON: Kids Can Press. (P–M)

Heidbreder, R. (2007). *Lickety-split*. Toronto: Kids Can Press.

Heidbreder, R. (2012). *Noisy poems for a busy day*. Toronto: Kids Can Press.

Heller, R. (1983). *The reason for a flower*. New York: Grosset & Dunlap.

Heller, R. (1987). *A cache of jewels and other collective nouns*. New York: Grosset & Dunlap.

Heller, R. (1988). *Kites sail high: A book about verbs*. New York: Grosset & Dunlap.

Heller, R. (1989). *Many luscious lollipops: A book about adjectives*. New York: Grosset & Dunlap.

Heller, R. (1990). *Merry-go-round: A book about nouns*. New York: Grosset & Dunlap.

Heller, R. (1991). *Up, up and away: A book about adverbs*. New York: Puffin.

Heller, R. (1995). *Behind the mask: A book of prepositions*. New York: Grosset & Dunlap.

Heller, R. (1998). *Fantastic! Wow! and Unreal! A book about interjections and conjuctions*. New York: Puffin Books.

Heller, R. (1999). *Mine all mine: A book about pronouns*. New York: Putnam.

Helmer, M. (2002). Three barnyard tales: The little red hen; The ugly duckling; Chicken little. Toronto: Kids Can Press.

Helmer, M. (2004a). *Funtime riddles*. Toronto: Kids Can Press.

Helmer, M. (2004b). *Recess riddles*. Toronto: Kids Can Press.

Henkes, K. (1991). *Chrysanthemum*. New York: Greenwillow.

Henkes, K. (1993). Owen. New York: Greenwillow.

Henkes, K. (1996). *Lilly's purple plastic purse*. New York: Greenwillow.

Hepworth, C. (1992). *Antics! An alphabetical anthology*. New York: Putnam.

Hesse, K. (1992). *Letters from Rifka*. New York: Holt.

Hesse, K. (2001). *Out of the dust*. Toronto: Scholastic.

Hiassan, C. (2004). *Hoot*. New York: Yearling.

Hickman, P. (1985). Bugwise. Toronto: Kids Can Press.

Hickman, P. (1996). *The Kids Canadian tree book*. Illus. H. Collins. Toronto: Kids Can Press.

Higgs, S. (2006). *Best friends, no matter what*. Toronto: Scholastic Canada.

Highway, T. (2001). *Caribou song*. Illus. B. Deines. Toronto: HarperCollins.

Highway, T. (2002). *Dragonfly kites*. Illus. B. Deines. Toronto: HarperCollins.

Highway, T. (2003a). *Fox on the ice*. Toronto: HarperCollins Canada.

Highway, T. (2003b). Interview. Retrieved March 10, 2004, from www.playwrightsworkshop.org/tomsonint.html.

Hill, E. (2007). *Spot's playtime pop-up*. New York: Putnam.

Hills, T. (2008). *What's up, duck? A book of opposites*. New York: Schwartz & Wade Books.

Hoban, T. (1973). *Over, under, and through and other spatial concepts*. New York: Macmillan.

Hoban, T. (1991). *All about where*. New York: Greenwillow.

Hoban, T. (2000). *Cubes, cones, cylinders, spheres*. New York: Greenwillow.

Hodge, D. (2008). *Who lives here? Wetlands*. Toronto: Kids Can Press.

Holtz, T. (2007). *Dinosaurs: The most complete, up to date encyclopedia for dinosaur lovers of all ages*. New York, NY: Random House.

Hood, S. (2005). *Pup and Hound in trouble*. Toronto: Kids Can Press.

Hood, S. (2012). *The tooth mouse*. Toronto: Kids Can Press.

Hooper, M. (2006). *Celebrity cat: With paintings from art galleries around the world*. London, UK: Frances Lincoln. (P–M)

Hopkins, L. B. (1984). *Surprises*. New York: Harper & Row.

Hopkins, L. B. (2004). *Wonderful words*. New York: Simon & Schuster.

Hopkins, L. B. (2011). *I am the book*. New York: Holiday House.

Hopkinson, D. (1993). *Sweet Clara and the freedom quilt*. New York: Knopf.

Horne, C. (1989). *Nykola and Granny*. Agincourt, ON: Gage Educational Publishing.

Horrocks, A. (2000). Topher. Don Mills, ON: Stoddart Kids.

Horrocks, A. (2010). *Silas's seven grandparents*. Victoria, BC: Orca.

Horton, C. (2000). *The French*. New York: Crabtree.

Horvath, P. (2002). *Everything on a waffle*. Toronto: Groundwood Books.

Horvath, P. (2012). One year in Coal Harbour. Toronto: Groundwood Books.

Howe, D., & Howe, J. (1979). *Bunnicula: A rabbit-tale of mystery.* New York: Atheneum.

Howe, J. (1982). *Howliday Inn.* New York: Atheneum.

Howe, J. (1983). *The celery stalks at midnight.* New York: Atheneum.

Howe, J. (1987). *Nighty-nightmare.* New York: Atheneum.

Howe, J. (1989a). *The fright before Christmas.* New York: Atheneum.

Howe, J. (1989b). *Scared silly.* New York: Atheneum.

Howe, J. (1990). *Hot fudge.* New York: Atheneum.

Howe, J. (1992). *Return to Howliday Inn.* New York: Atheneum.

Hoyt-Goldsmith, D. (1990). *Totem pole.* New York: Holiday House.

Hubbard, W. (1990). *C is for curious: An ABC book of feelings.* San Francisco: Chronicle Books.

Hudson, J. (1984). *Sweetgrass.* Edmonton: Tree Frog Press.

Hughes, L. (1994). *The dream keeper and other poems.* New York: Knopf.

Hughes, L. (1995). *The book of rhythms.* New York: Oxford University Press.

Hughes, M. (2001). *Jan's awesome party.* Halifax, NS: Formac Publishing.

Hughes, S. (2003). *Bobcat rescue.* Toronto: Scholastic Canada.

Hughes, S. (2010). *Case closed? Nine mysteries unlocked by modern science.* Toronto: Kids Can Press.

Hughes, S. (2011). *Off to class: Incredible and unusual schools around the world.* Toronto: Owlkids Books.

Hunt, L. (2015). *Fish in a tree.* New York, NY: Nancy Paulsen Books.

Husband, A. (2009). *Dear miss.* London: Meadowside Children's Books.

Huser, G. (2003). Stitches. Toronto: Groundwood Books.

Hutchins, H. (2009). *A second is a hiccup: A child's book of time.* Toronto: Scholastic Canada.

Hutchins, H. (2012). *Think again, Robyn.* Halifax, NS: Formac Publishing.

Hutchins, H., & Herbert, G. (2008). Mattland. Illus. D. Petričić. Toronto: Annick Press.

Hutchins, P. (1968). *Rosie's walk.* New York: Macmillan.

Hutchins, P. (1976). *Don't forget the bacon!* New York: Mulberry.

Hutchins, P. (1986). *The doorbell rang.* New York: Morrow.

Hutchins, P. (2002). *We're going on a picnic.* New York: HarperCollins.

Hyde, N. (2011). *Saving Armpit.* Markham, ON: Fitzhenry & Whiteside.

Hyde, N. (2012). *Hockey girl.* Markham, ON: Fitzhenry & Whiteside.

Hyman, T. S. (1983). *Little Red Riding Hood.* New York: Holiday House.

Ipellie, A., & MacDonald, D. (2007). *The Inuit thought of it: Amazing arctic innovations.* Toronto: Annick Press.

Jacobson, D. (2011). *My life with the salmon.* Penticton, BC: Theytus Books.

James, S. (2002). *Dear Greenpeace.* Somerville, MA: Candlewick Press.

Janni, R. (2012). *Jammy dance.* New York: FSG Kids.

Jardine-Stoddart, H. (2009) *Back to the beach.* Halifax, NS: Nimbus.

Javaherbin, M. (2014). *Soccer star.* S.l.: Cambridge, MA: Candlewick Press.

Jeffers, O. (2004). *How to catch a star.* New York: Philomel Books.

Jenkins, S. (2004). *Actual size.* Boston: Houghton Mifflin.

Jenkins, S. (2005). *Prehistoric actual size.* Boston: Houghton Mifflin.

Jenkins, S., & Page, R. (2006). *Move!* Boston: Houghton Mifflin.

Jocelyn, M. (2000). *Hannah's collections.* New York: Dutton Children's Books.

Jocelyn, M. (2005). *ABC 3.* Toronto: Tundra Books.

Joe, R. (2009). *For the children.* Sydney, NS: Breton Books.

Johnson, C. (1955; 2015). *Harold and the purple crayon.* New York, NY: Harper Collins. (P)

Johnston, J. (2001). *In spite of killer bees.* Toronto: Tundra Books.

Johnston, S. (1995). Alphabet city. Toronto: Penguin.

Jones, H. (1993). *The trees stand shining: Poetry of the North American Indians.* New York: Dial.

Jordan-Fenton, C., & Pokiak-Fenton, M. (2010). *Fatty legs: A true story.* Toronto: Annick Press.

Jordan-Fenton, C., & Pokiak-Fenton, M. (2011). *A stranger at home.* Toronto: Annick Press.

Jordan-Fenton, C., & Pokiak-Fenton, M. (2013). *When I was eight.* Toronto: Annick Press.

Jordon-Fenton, C., & Pokiak-Fenton, M. (2014). *Not my girl.* Toronto, ON: Annick Press.

Jorisch, S. (2001). *As for the princess? A folktale from Quebec.* Toronto: Annick Press.

Joyce, W. (2012). *The fantastic flying books of Mr. Morris Lessmore.* New York: Atheneum Books for Young Readers.

Juby, S. (2000). *Alice, I think.* Saskatoon, SK: Thistledown Press.

Juby, S. (2006). *Alice, realist at last.* Toronto, ON: HarperTrophy.

Juby, S. (2007). *Another kind of cowboy.* New York, NY: HarperCollins.

Juby, S. (2010). *Getting the girl.* New York, NY: HarperCollins.

Juby, S. (2015). *The truth commission.* Toronto, ON: Penguin Canada.

K'naan & Guy, S. (2012). *When I get older: The story behind "Wavin' Flag."* Toronto, ON: Tundra Books.

Kain, K. (2005). *The nutcracker.* Toronto, ON: Tundra Books. (P-M)

Kalan, R. (1995). Jump, frog, jump! New York: HarperTrophy.

Kalman, B. (1997). *Celebrating the pow-wow.* New York, NY: Crabtree Publishing.

Kalman, B. (2001). *Japan: The people.* New York; St. Catharines, ON: Crabtree.

Kalman, B., & Crossingham, J. (2006). *Insect homes.* New York: Crabtree.

Kaner, E. (1995). Towers and tunnels. Toronto: Kids Can Press.

Karas, G. (1994). *I know an old lady.* New York: Scholastic.

Keats, E. J. (1968). *A letter to Amy.* New York: Harper & Row.

Keeler, P., & Julio, L. (2006). *Drumbeat in our feet.* New York: Lee and Low Books.

Kelsey, E. (2012). You are stardust. Illus. S. Kim. Toronto: Owlkids Books.

Kennedy, C. (2013). *Poems to learn by heart.* New York, NY: Hyperion Books.

Kennedy, X. J., & Kennedy, D. M. (1982). *Knock at a star: A child's introduction to poetry.* Boston: Little, Brown.

Kernaghan, E. (1995). *Dance of the snow dragon.* Saskatoon: Thistledown Press.

Kew, T. (2011). *Breakaway.* Toronto: James Lorimer.

Khan, R. (1999). *Dahling, if you luv me, would you please, please smile.* Don Mills, ON: Stoddart Kids.

Kielburger, M., & Kielburger, C. (2002). *Take action! A guide to active citizenship.* New York: John Wiley & Sons.

King, D. (2014). *I see the sun in Russia.* S.l.: Hardwick, MA: Satya House Publications.

King, T. (1995). *Medicine River.* Toronto: Penguin.

King, T. (1998). *Coyote sings to the moon.* Toronto: Groundwood Books.

Kingsley, C. (2001). *Ten little puppies.* Toronto: Fitzhenry & Whiteside.

Kitagawa, M. (1986). *This is my own: Letter to Wes and other writings on Japanese Canadians, 1941–1948.* Vancouver: Talonbooks.

Kusugak, M. A. (1998). *Arctic stories.* Willowdale, ON: Annick Press.

Lach, W. (2006). *Can you hear it?* New York, NY: Harry N. Abrams. (P-M)

Langen, A., & Droop, C. (1994). *Letters from Felix: A little rabbit on a world tour.* New York: Abbeville Press.

Langlois, A. (2011). *Mia, Matt and the lazy gator.* Halifax, NS: Formac Publishing.

Langstaff, J. (1974). *Oh, a-hunting we will go.* New York: Atheneum.

Langston, L. (2003). *Lesia's dream.* Toronto: HarperTrophy.

Langston, L. (2006). *Exit point.* Victoria, BC: Orca Books.

Larsen, A. (2013). *In the tree house.* Toronto, ON: Kids Can Press.

Lauber, P. (1995). *Who eats what? Food chains and food webs.* New York: HarperCollins.

Lawrence, I. (2006). *Gemini summer.* New York: Yearling.

Lawson, J. (1992). A morning to polish and keep. Red Deer, AB: Red Deer College Press.

Lawson, J. (1996). *Whatever you do, don't go near that canoe.* Richmond Hill, ON: Scholastic Canada.

Lawson, J. (2003). *Arizona Charlie and the Klondike Kid.* Victoria, BC: Orca Books.

Lawson, J. (2010). *Think again.* Toronto: Kids Can Press.

Lawson, J. (2012). *Old MacDonald had her farm.* Toronto, ON: Annick Press.

Layne, S., & Layne, D. (2005). *T is for teachers: A school alphabet.* Chelsea, MI: Sleeping Bear Press.

Lear, E. (1995a). *Daffy-down-dillies: Silly limericks by Edward Lear.* Honesdale, PA: Wordsong.

Lear, E. (1995b). *There was an old man … A collection of limericks.* Illus. M. Lemieux. Toronto: Kids Can Press.

Lear, E. (2006). The owl and the pussycat. Illus. S. Jorisch. Toronto: Kids Can Press.

Lebox, A. (2002). *Salmon Creek.* Toronto: Groundwood Books.

Lee, D. (1974). *Alligator pie.* Toronto: Macmillan.

Lee, D. (1977). *Garbage delight.* Toronto: Macmillan.

Lee, D. (1983). *Jelly belly.* Toronto: Macmillan.

Lee, D. (2000). *Bubblegum delicious: Poems.* Toronto: Key Porter Books.

Lee, D. (2011). *Biomimcry: Inventions inspired by nature.* Toronto: Kids Can Press.

Leedy, L. (2003). *There's a frog in my throat! 440 animal sayings a little bird told me.* New York: Holiday House.

Leedy, L. (2009). *Crazy like a fox: A simile story.* New York: Holiday House.

Leedy, L. (2010). *My teacher is a dinosaur and other prehistoric poems, jokes, and amazing facts.* Tarrytown, NY: Marshall Cavendish Children.

LeFord, B. (1995). A blue butterfly: A story about Claude Monet. New York: Doubleday.

Lesynski, L. (1999). *Dirty dog boogie.* Toronto: Annick Press.

Lesynski, L. (2001). *Nothing beats a pizza.* Toronto: Annick Press.

Lesynski, L. (2004). *Zigzag: Zoems for zindergarten.* Toronto: Annick Press.

Lesynski, L. (2006). *"I did it because …": How a poem happens.* Toronto: Annick Press.

Lesynski, L. (2007). *Shoe shakes.* Toronto: Annick Press.

Levine, K. (2002). *Hana's suitcase: A true story.* Toronto: Second Story Press.

Levine, R. (2000). *Story of the orchestra: Listen while you learn about the instruments, the music, and the composers who wrote the music.* New York, NY: Black Dog & Leventhal. (M)

Levy, C. (2002). *Splash! Poems of our watery world.* New York, NY: Orchard Books.

Lewis, C. S. (2005). *The lion, the witch and the wardrobe.* New York: HarperFestival. Originally published 1950.

Lewis, J. P. (1995). *Black swan/white crow.* New York: Atheneum.

Lewis, J. P. (1996). *Riddle-icious.* New York: Knopf.

Lewis, W. (2000). Graveyard girl: Stories. Red Deer, AB: Red Deer Press.

Lewis, W. (2003). *In Abby's hands.* Calgary: Red Deer Press.

Lewison, W. C. (1992). *"Buzz," said the bee.* New York: Scholastic.

Lied, K. (2002). *Potato: A tale from the Great Depression.* Des Moines, IA: National Geographic Children's Books.

Lightfoot, G. (2010). *Canadian railroad trilogy.* Toronto, ON: Groundwood Books.

Lillie, P. (1993). *Everything has a place.* New York: Greenwillow.

Lindstrom, C. (2013). *Girls dance, boys fiddle.* Winnipeg, MB: Pemmican.

Lionni, L. (1961). On my beach there are many pebbles. London: Mulberry Books.

Lionni, L. (1969). *Alexander and the wind-up mouse.* New York: Pantheon.

Little, J. (1987). *Little by little: A writer's education.* New York: Viking Kestrel.

Little, J. (1991). *From Anna.* New York: HarperCollins Juvenile Books.

Little, J. (2001). Orphan at my door: The home child diary of Victoria Cape. Toronto: Scholastic Canada.

Little, J. (2002). *Birdie, for now.* Vancouver: Orca Books.

Little, J. (2003). *I gave my mom a castle.* Vancouver: Orca Books.

Little, J. (2007). *Dancing through the snow.* Toronto: Scholastic.

Litzinger, R. (1993). *The old woman and her pig.* New York: Harcourt, Brace, Jovanovich.

Livingston, M. C. (Sel.). (1991). *Lots of limericks.* New York: McElderry Books.

Lobel, A. (1970). *Frog and Toad are friends.* New York: Harper & Row.

Lobel, A. (1980). *Fables.* New York: Harper & Row.

Lobel, A. (1983). *The book of pigericks: Pig limericks.* New York: Harper & Row.

Lobel, A. (1990). *Alison's zinnia.* New York: Greenwillow.

Loewen, N., & Wu, D. (2011). *You're toast and other metaphors we adore.* Mankato, MN: Picture Window Books.

Lohnes, M. (2007). *F is for fiddlehead: A New Brunswick alphabet.* Chelsea, MI: Sleeping Bear Press.

Louie, A. (1982). *Yeh-Shen: A Cinderella story from China.* New York: Philomel.

Lowell, S. (1992). *The three little javelinas.* Flagstaff, AZ: Northland.

Lowell, S. (2008). *The elephant quilt: Stitch by stitch to California.* New York, NY: Farrar, Straus & Giroux.

Lowry, L. (1989). *Number the stars.* Boston: Houghton Mifflin.

Lowry, L. (1993). *The giver.* Boston: Houghton Mifflin.

Loxton, D. (2010). *Evolution: How we and all living things came to be.* Toronto: Kids Can Press.

Loyie, L. (2005). *As long as the river flows.* Toronto: HarperCollins.

Luenn, N. (1990). *Nessa's fish.* New York: Atheneum.

Lunn, J., & Gál, L. (1979). *Twelve dancing princesses.* Toronto: Methuen.

Lunn, J., & Moore, C. (1992). The story of Canada. Illus. A. Daniel. Toronto: Key Porter Books.

Luxbacher, I. (2003). The jumbo book of art. Toronto: Kids Can Press.

Luxbacker, I. (2006). *The jumbo book of outdoor art*. Toronto: Kids Can Press.

Macaulay, D. (1977). *Castle*. Boston: Houghton Mifflin.

Macaulay, D. (1998). *The new way things work*. Boston: Houghton Mifflin.

MacCarthy, P. (1991). *Herds of words*. New York: Dial.

MacLachlan, P. (1985). *Sarah, plain and tall*. New York: Harper & Row.

MacLachlan, P. (1994). *Skylark*. New York: HarperCollins.

Maclear, K. (2012). *Virginia Wolf*. Illus. I. Arsenault. Toronto: Kids Can Press.

Maes, N. (2011). *Crescent star*. Toronto: Dundurn Press.

Maggi, M. E., & Calderón, G. (2001). *The great canoe: A Karina legend*. Trans. E. Amado. Toronto: Douglas & McIntyre.

Major, K. (2000). *Eh? to zed: A Canadian abecedarium*. Red Deer, AB: Red Deer Press.

Major, K. (2003). *Ann and Seamus*. Toronto: Groundwood Books.

Maracle, L. (2008). *Will's garden*. Penticton, BC: Theytus Books.

Marineau, M. (1995). *Road to Chlifa*. Red Deer, AB: Red Deer College Press.

Markle, S. (1993). *Outside and inside trees*. New York: Bradbury Press.

Martin, A. (2014). *Rain reign*. New York, NY: Macmillan (Feiwel & Friends).

Martin, B., Jr. (1983). *Brown bear, brown bear, what do you see?* New York: Holt, Rinehart & Winston.

Martin, B., Jr. (1992). *Polar bear, polar bear, what do you hear?* New York: Holt, Rinehart & Winston.

Martin, B., Jr., & Archambault, J. (1989). *Chicka chicka boom boom*. New York: Simon & Schuster Books for Young Readers.

Martin, J. B. (1998). *Snowflake Bentley*. Boston: Houghton Mifflin.

Martin, J. B. (2001). *The lamp, the ice, and the boat called* Fish. Boston: Houghton Mifflin.

Martin, F. (1992). *The rough face girl*. New York: Putnam.

Masessa, E. (2007). *The time traveler's journal*. London: Tangerine Press.

Mason, A. (2004). *Owls*. Toronto: Kids Can Press.

Mason, A. (2005). *Move it! Motion, forces, and you*. Toronto: Kids Can Press.

Mason, A. (2006). *Change it! Solids, liquids, gases, and you*. Toronto: Kids Can Press.

Mastnak, R. (2011). *Dancing with Grandma*. Australia: Hardie Grant Books.

Matas, C. (1987). *Lisa*. Toronto: Lester & Orpen Dennys.

Matas, C. (1989). *Jesper*. Toronto: Lester & Orpen Dennys.

Matas, C. (1993). *Daniel's story*. Markham, ON: Scholastic Canada.

Matas, C. (1995). *The primrose path*. Winnipeg: Blizzard Publishing.

Matas, C. (2012). *Behind enemy lines: World War II: Sam Frederiksen, Nazi-occupied Europe, 1944* (I Am Canada series). Toronto: Scholastic Canada.

Matas, C. (2013a). *Greater than angels*. Toronto, ON: Scholastic Canada.

Matas, C. (2013b). *In my enemy's house*. Toronto, ON: Scholastic Canada.

Matas, C. (2013c). *Pieces of the past: The Holocaust diary of Rose Rabinowitz* (Dear Canada series). Toronto: Scholastic Canada.

McCormick, R. (2002). *Plants and art activities*. St. Catharines, ON: Crabtree Publishing.

McDonnell, P. (2006). *Art*. New York, NY: Little Brown. (P)

McFarlane, L. (2005). *Hockey stories*. Toronto: Key Porter Books.

McFarlane, S. (1995). *Tides of change*. Victoria, BC: Orca Books.

McFarlane, S., & Lightburn, R. (1998). *Waiting for the whales*. Victoria, BC: Orca Books.

McGowan, M. (2003). *Newton and the giant*. Toronto: HarperCollins.

McGugan, J. (2003). *Josepha: A prairie boy's story*. Red Deer, AB: Red Deer Press.

McIlwain, J. (2003). *Children's illustrated dictionary* (Canadian ed.). Toronto: Dorling Kindersley.

McLellan, J. (1991). *Nanabosho, Soaring Eagle and the great sturgeon*. Winnipeg: Pemmican Publications.

McLellan, J. (1993). *Nanabosho dances*. Winnipeg: Pemmican Publications.

McLellan, S. (2000). The chicken cat. Markham, ON: Fitzhenry & Whiteside.

McLeod, E. (2002). *Lessons from Mother Earth*. Toronto: Groundwood/Douglas & McIntyre.

McLeod, H. (2011). *Kiss me! (I'm a prince)*. Markham, ON: Fitzhenry & Whiteside.

McNaughton, L. (2006). *The Raintree rebellion*. Toronto: HarperTrophy Canada.

McNicoll, S. (2006). *Beauty returns*. Markham, ON: Fitzhenry & Whiteside.

McTighe, C. (2007). The sakura tree. Calgary: Red Deer Press.

Meyrick, J. (2007). *Gracie, the public gardens duck*. Halifax: Nimbus.

Mills, L. (1991). *The rag coat*. Boston: Little, Brown.

Milway, K. S. (2008). *One hen: How one small loan can make a big difference*. Toronto: Kids Can Press.

Milway, K. S. (2012). *Mimi's village: And how basic health care transformed it*. Toronto: Kids Can Press.

Mitgutsch, A. (1975). *From sheep to scarf*. Minneapolis, MN: Carolrhoda.

Moak, A. (2002). *A big city ABC*. Toronto: Tundra Books.

Mollel, T. (1990). The orphan boy. Toronto: Oxford University Press.

Mollel, T. (1991). *Rhinos for lunch and elephants for supper! A Maasai tale*. Toronto: Oxford University Press.

Mollel, T. (1992). *A promise to the sun*. Toronto: Little, Brown.

Montgomery, L. M. (1999). *Anne of Green Gables*. New York: HarperFestival. Originally published 1908.

Moore, C. (1995). *The night before Christmas*. New York: North-South. Originally published 1823.

Moses, W. (2008). *Raining cats and dogs*. New York: Philomel Books.

Moss, L. (1995). Zin! Zin! Zin! A violin. New York: Simon & Schuster.

Moss, L. (2000). *Zin zin a violin*. New York, NY: Alladin Picture Books. (P)

Moss, M. (2007). *Amelia writes again*. New York: Simon & Schuster Children's Books.

Moss, M. (2011). *Amelia's BFF: Amelia's notebook*. New York: Simon & Schuster Children's Books.

Most, B. (1991). *A dinosaur named after me*. Orlando, FL: Harcourt Brace.

Most, B. (1996). *Cock-a-doodle-moo*. New York: Harcourt Brace.

Mott, A. S. (2005). Reality television. In *Haunting fireside stories: Ghostly tales of the paranormal*. Edmonton, AB: Ghost House Books.

Mowat, F. (1995). *Born naked*. (n.p.): Mariner Books.

Munsch, R. (1980). *The paper bag princess*. Willowdale, ON: Annick Press.

Munsch, R. (1992). *Purple, green and yellow*. Toronto: Annick Press.

Munsch, R. (2000). *We share everything*. Toronto: Cartwheel Books.

Munsch, R. (2003). *Lighthouse: A story of remembrance*. Toronto: Scholastic Canada.

Munsch, R., & Kusugak, M. (1988). *A promise is a promise*. Toronto: Annick Press.

My first Canadian Oxford dictionary. (2009). Don Mills, ON: Oxford University Press.

My first Canadian Oxford thesaurus. (2003). Don Mills, ON: Oxford University Press.

National Geographic. (1996). *Creatures of long ago: Dinosaurs.* Los Angeles: The National Geographic Society.

Napier, M. (2007). *Z is for Zamboni: A hockey alphabet.* Chelsea, MI: Sleeping Bear Press.

Napoli, D. (2004). *Bound.* New York: Atheneum.

Naylor, P. R. (1991). *Shiloh.* New York: Atheneum.

Neering, R. (1990). *Pioneers.* Markham, ON: Fitzhenry & Whiteside.

New, W. (1998). *Vanilla gorilla: Poems.* Vancouver: Ronsdale Press.

Newman, F. (1980). *Round slice of moon and other poems for Canadian kids.* Toronto: Scholastic.

Nicolson, C. P. (2011). *Totally human: Why we look and act the way we do.* Toronto: Kids Can Press.

Nicholson, S. (2005). *Against the boards.* Toronto: James Lorimer.

Nielsen, S. (2010). *Dear George Clooney, please marry my mom.* Toronto: Tundra Books.

Niner, H. (2005). *I can't stop! A story about Tourette Syndrome.* New York, NY: Albert Whitman.

Northey, L. (2002). *I'm a hop hop hoppity frog.* Don Mills, ON: Stoddart Kids.

Novak, B. (2014). *The book with no pictures.* New York, NY: Dial Books. (P-M)

Noyes, A. (1981). *The highwayman.* Illus. C. Keeping. Oxford: Oxford University Press.

Numeroff, L. J. (1985). *If you give a mouse a cookie.* New York: Harper & Row.

Numeroff, L. J. (1991). *If you give a moose a muffin.* New York: HarperCollins.

Numeroff, L. J. (1993). *Dogs don't wear sneakers.* New York: Simon & Schuster.

Numeroff, L. J. (1995). *Chimps don't wear glasses.* New York: Simon & Schuster.

Numeroff, L. J. (1998). *If you give a pig a pancake.* New York: HarperCollins.

Numeroff, L. J. (2000). *If you take a mouse to the movies.* New York: HarperCollins.

Numeroff, L. J. (2002). *If you take a mouse to school.* New York: HarperCollins.

Numeroff, L. (2005). *If you give a pig a party.* New York: HarperCollins.

Numeroff, L. (2011). *If you give a dog a donut.* New York: HarperCollins.

Oberman, S. (1994). *The always prayer shawl.* Honesdale, PA: Boyd Mills Press.

O'Connor, J. (2005). *Fancy Nancy.* New York, NY: Harper Collins.

O'Connor, J. (2008). *Fancy Nancy's favorite fancy words: From accessories to zany.* New York: HarperCollins.

O'Dell, S., & Hall, E. (1992). *Thunder rolling in the mountains.* Boston: Houghton Mifflin.

Ohi, R. (2007). *A trip with Grandma.* Toronto: Annick Press.

O'Huigan, S. (1983a). *Scary poems for rotten kids.* Windsor, ON: Black Moss Press.

O'Huigan, S. (1983b). *Well, you can imagine.* Windsor, ON: Black Moss Press.

Oldland, N. (2011). *The busy beaver.* Toronto: Kids Can Press.

Onyefulu, I. (1993). *A is for Africa.* New York: Cobblehill Books.

Oppel, K. (2004). *Airborn.* Toronto: HarperCollins.

Oppenheim, J. (1996). *Have you seen bugs?* Richmond Hill, ON: Scholastic Canada.

Orloff, K. (2004). *I wanna iguana.* New York: Putnam.

Osborne, M. P. (1992). Dinosaurs before dark. New York: Scholastic.

Ostlere, C. (2011). *Karma.* Toronto: Puffin Canada.

Oxford learner's thesaurus. (2008). London: Oxford University Press.

Palacio, R. J. (2012). *Wonder.* New York, NY: Knopf Books for Young Readers.

Palatini, M. (2006). *Oink?* New York: Simon & Schuster for Young Readers.

Pallotta, J. (1990). *The frog alphabet book: And other awesome amphibians.* Watertown, MA: Charlesbridge.

Pallotta, J. (1994). *The desert alphabet book.* Watertown, MA: Charlesbridge.

Palmer, S. (2000). *A little alphabet book.* London: Oxford University Press.

Papineau, L., & Poulin, S. (2004). Un chant de Noël. Saint-Lambert, QC: Dominique et compagnie.

Parish, P. (1963). *Amelia Bedelia.* New York: Harper & Row.

Parish, P. (2004). *Teach us, Amelia Bedelia.* New York: HarperCollins.

Parish, P. (2012). *Amelia Bedelia 50th anniversary library.* New York, NY: Greenwillow Books.

Park, B. (2003). *Junie B., first grader: Toothless wonder.* New York: Random House Children's Books.

Park, L. S. (2005). *Yum! Yuck! A fold-out books of people sounds.* Watertown, MA: Charlesbridge.

Parnwell, E., & Grennan, M. (1996). *The Canadian Oxford picture dictionary: Monolingual.* Toronto: Oxford University Press.

Parrish, T. (2002). *The grouchy grammarian.* London: Wiley.

Partridge, E. (2005). *John Lennon: All I want is the truth.* New York: Viking.

Paterson, K. (1987). *Bridge to Terabithia.* New York: Crowell.

Paterson, K. (1994). *Flip-flop girl.* New York: Lodestar.

Paul, A. (1996). *Eight hands round: A patchwork alphabet.* New York: HarperTrophy.

Paulsen, G. (1987). *Hatchet.* New York: Bradbury Press.

Paulsen, G. (1988). *Dogsong.* New York: Bradbury Press.

Paulsen, G. (1993). *Harris and me: A summer remembered.* San Diego, CA: Harcourt Brace.

Paulsen, G. (1996). *Brian's winter.* New York: Delacourte Press.

Paulsen, G. (1999). *Brian's return.* New York: Delacourte Press.

Paulsen, G. (2000). *The beet fields: Memories of a sixteenth summer.* New York: Random House.

Peacock, S. (2012). Becoming Holmes: The boy Sherlock Holmes, his final case. Toronto: Tundra Books.

Pearson, D. (2005). *Kids do, animals too: A book pf playground opposites.* Toronto: Annick Press.

Pearson, K. (1991). Looking at the moon. Toronto: Viking.

Pearson, K. (2003). *The guests of war trilogy.* Toronto: Puffin Books.

Pearson, K. (2011). *The whole truth.* Toronto: HarperCollins Canada.

Pearson, K. (2012). *And nothing but the truth.* Toronto: HarperCollins Canada.

Perlman, J. (1993). *The tender tale of Cinderella Penguin: A classic tale retold.* Montreal: National Film Board of Canada.

Perlman, J. (2009). *The delicious bug.* Toronto: Kids Can Press.

Perry, S. (1995). *If . . .* Malibu, CA: J. P. Getty Museum and Children's Library Press.

Petronis, P., & Lisle, A. (2010). *Sewing school: Handsewing projects children will love to make.* North Adams, MA: Storey Publishing.

Philbrick, R. (1993). Freak the mighty. Toronto: Scholastic.

Phillips, W. (2010). Fishtailing. Toronto: Coteau Books.

Pitt, S. (2004). *Rain tonight: A story of Hurricane Hazel.* Toronto: Tundra Books.

Plain, F. (1994). *Grandfather drum.* Winnipeg: Pemmican.

Poe, E. (2009). *The raven: Complete tales and poems.* New York: Castle Books.

Polacco, P. (1990). *Thunder cake.* New York: Philomel.

Polacco, P. (1994a). *Firetalking.* Katonah, NY: Richard C. Owen.

Polacco, P. (1994b). *Pink and Say.* New York: Philomel.

Polacco, P. (2011). *The keeping quilt.* New York: Simon & Schuster.

Porter, P. (2004). *Sky.* Toronto: Groundwood Books.

Porter, P. (2005). *The crazy man.* Toronto, ON: Groundwood Books.

Porter, P. (2008). *Yellow moon, apple moon.* Toronto: Groundwood Books.

Potter, B. (1995). *Dear Peter Rabbit.* New York: Warne.

Poulsen, D. (1996). *Billy and the bearman.* Toronto: Napoleon Publishing.

Prelutsky, J. (Sel.). (1983). *The Random House book of poetry for children.* New York: Random House.

Prelutsky, J. (1984). *The new kid on the block.* New York: Greenwillow Books.

Prelutsky, J. (2000). *It's raining pigs and noodles.* New York: Greenwillow Books.

Prelutsky, J. (2007). *Good sports: Rhymes about running, jumping, throwing and more.* New York: Knopf Books for Young Readers.

Prince, B. (2004). *I came as a stranger: The Underground Railroad.* Toronto: Tundra Books.

Pulver, R. (2007). *Nouns and verbs have a field day.* New York: Holiday House.

Qitsualik-Tinsley, R., & Qitsualik, S. (2014). *Skraelings.* Toronto, ON: Inhabit Media Inc.

Raczka, B. (2006). *Here's looking at me: How artists see themselves.* Minneapolis, MN: Millbrook Press. (M–U)

Rae, J. (1998). Dog tales. Vancouver: Whitecap Books.

Rand, A. (2006). *Sparkle & spin: A book about words.* San Francisco, CA: Chronicle Books.

Rappaport, D. (2001). *Martin's big words: The life of Dr. Martin Luther King, Jr.* New York: Jump at the Sun.

Rathmann, P. (1995). Officer Buckle and Gloria. New York: Putnam.

Reczuch, K., & Manson, A. (1995). *Just like new.* Toronto: Groundwood Books.

Reid, B. (1991a). Zoe's snowy day. Toronto: HarperCollins.

Reid, B. (1991b). Zoe's sunny day. Toronto: HarperCollins.

Reid, B. (1991c). Zoe's windy day. Toronto: HarperCollins.

Reid, B. (1997). *The party.* Richmond Hill, ON: North Winds Press.

Reid, B. (2003). *The subway mouse.* Toronto: Scholastic Canada.

Reid, B. (2006). *Fox walked alone.* Toronto: Scholastic Canada.

Reid, B. (2009). Perfect snow. Richmond Hill, ON: North Winds Press.

Reid, B. (2011). Picture a tree. Toronto: North Winds Press.

Reid, B. (2012a). *Picture a tree.* Toronto, ON: North Winds Press.

Reid, B. (2012b). *The party.* Toronto: Scholastic Canada.

Reid, B. (2012c). *Zoe's year.* Toronto: Scholastic Canada.

Reid, B. (2015). *Two by two.* Toronto, ON: Scholastic Canada.

Renaud, A. (2008). *Missuk's snow geese.* Toronto: Simply Read Books.

Resau, L. (2007). *Red glass.* New York: Delacourte Press.

Richards, D. (1993). Soldier boys. Saskatoon: Thistledown Press.

Richardson, B. (2007). *The aunts came marching.* Vancouver: Raincoast Books.

Ringgold, F. (1996). *Tar Beach.* New York: Crown.

Ripley, C. (1991). *Two dozen dinosaurs: A first book of dinosaurs facts, mysteries, games and fun.* Toronto: Greey de Pencier Books.

Ritchie, S. (2009). *Follow that map! A first book of mapping skills.* Toronto: Kids Can Press.

Robertson, D. A. (2010). *Stone* (7 Generations, vol. 1). Illus. S. B. Henderson. Winnipeg: Highwater Press/Portage & Main Press.

Rodriguez, R. (2007). *Through Georgia's eyes.* New York, NY: Henry Holt. (P–M)

Roget's student thesaurus (Rev. ed.). (2001). Toronto: Pearson Scott Foresman.

Rondina, C. (2012). *Lighting our world.* Toronto: Kids Can Press.

Root, P. (2003). *The name quilt.* New York: Farrar, Straus, & Giroux.

Rose, C. (2012). *May B.* New York, NY: Schwartz & Wade.

Rosenstock, B. (2014). *The noisy paint box: The colours and sounds of Kandinsky's abstract art.* New York, NY: Knopf. (P)

Roth, V. (2011). *Divergent.* New York: Katherine Tegen Books/HarperCollins.

Rotner, S. (1996). *Action alphabet.* New York: Atheneum.

Rowland, D. (1991). *Little Red Riding Hood/The wolf's tale.* New York: Birch Lane Press.

Rowling, J. K. (1997). *Harry Potter and the philosopher's stone.* London: Bloomsbury.

Rowling, J. K. (2007). *Harry Potter and the deathly hallows.* London: Bloomsbury.

Roy, P. (2011). *Ghost of the Pacific.* Vancouver: Ronsdale Press.

Roy, P. (2013). *Me and Mr. Bell.* Sydney, NS: Cape Breton University Press.

Rubin, S. (2001). *Steven Spielberg: Crazy for movies.* New York: Abrams.

Rumford, J. (2010). *Rain school.* Boston, MA: HMH Books for Young Readers.

Ruurs, M. (2001). *A Pacific alphabet.* Vancouver: Whitecap Books.

Ruurs, M. (2006). *Wake up, Henry Rooster.* Markham, ON: Fitzhenry & Whiteside.

Ruurs, M. (2007). *In my backyard.* Toronto: Tundra Books.

Ruurs, M. (2009). *My school in the rainforest: How children attend school around the world.* New York, NY: M. Boyd's Mills Press.

Rylant, C. (1985). *The relatives came.* New York: Bradbury Press.

Rylant, C. (1988). *All I see.* New York: Orchard.

Sabuda, R. (1997). *Cookie count: A tasty pop-up.* New York: Little Simon.

Salas, L. (2011). *Bookspeak! Poems about books.* New York: Clarion Books.

San Souci, R. (1998). *Cendrillon: A Caribbean Cinderella.* New York: Simon and Schuster Books for Young Readers.

Savan, B. (1991). *Earthcycles and ecosystems.* Toronto: Kids Can Press.

Sayre, A. (2010). *Turtle, turtle: Watch out!* Watertown, MA: Charlesbridge.

Schendlinger, M. (2005). *Prepare to be amazed: The geniuses of modern magic.* Toronto: Annick Press.

Schlosser, E., & Wilson, C. (2006). *Chew on this: Everything you don't want to know about fast food.* New York: Houghton Mifflin.

Schneider, R. M. (1995). *Add it, dip it, fix it: A book of verbs*. Boston: Houghton Mifflin.

Schotter, R. (2006). *The boy who loved words*. New York: Schwartz & Wade Books.

Schulman, J. (2004). *Sergei Prokofiev's* Peter and the Wolf: *With a fully orchestrated and narrated CD*. New York, NY: Knopf. (P-M)

Schwartz, C. R. (2012). *The three ninja pigs*. New York: Putnam Juvenile.

Schwartz, E. (2011). *The case of the missing deed*. Toronto: Tundra Books.

Schwartz, V. F. (2003). *Initiation*. Toronto: Fitzhenry & Whiteside.

Scieszka, J. (1989). *The true story of the 3 little pigs!* New York: Viking.

Scieszka, J. (1998). *Squids will be squids: Fresh morals, beastly fables*. Toronto: Viking (Penguin Books).

Scillian, D. (2010). *D is for down under: An Australian alphabet*. Ann Arbour, MI: Sleeping Bear Press.

Scowen, K. (2006). *My kind of sad: What it's like to be young and depressed*. Toronto: Annick Press.

Scrimger, R. (1998). *The nose from Jupiter*. Toronto: Tundra Books.

Scrimger, R. (2002a). *Noses are red*. Toronto: Tundra Books.

Scrimger, R. (2002b). *Princess Bun Bun*. Toronto: Tundra Books.

Scrivener, L. (2000). *Terry Fox: His story*. Toronto: McClelland & Stewart.

Seattle, C. (1991). *Brother Eagle, Sister Sky*. New York: Dial.

Selznick, B. (2007). *The invention of Hugo Cabret*. New York: Scholastic.

Sendak, M. (1963). *Where the wild things are*. New York: Harper & Row.

Serafini, F. (2008). *Looking closely inside the garden*. Toronto: Kids Can Press.

Service, R. (1986). *The cremation of Sam McGee*. Illus. T. Harrison. Toronto: Kids Can Press. Originally published 1907.

Service, R. (1988). *The shooting of Dan McGrew*. Illus. T. Harrison. Toronto: Kids Can Press. Originally published 1907.

Seuss, Dr. (1957). *The cat in the hat*. New York: Random House.

Seuss, Dr. (1963). Hop on Pop. New York: Random House.

Shannon, C. (1996). *Spring: A haiku story*. New York: Greenwillow.

Shannon, R. (2004). *Franklin's picture dictionary*. Toronto: Kids Can Press.

Shapiro, S., & Shapiro, S. (2011). *Better together*. Toronto: Annick Press.

Sharmat, M. W. (1972). *Nate the Great*. New York: Dell.

Shaw, N. (1992). Sheep out to eat. Boston: Houghton Mifflin.

Shea, P. D. (1995). *The whispering cloth: A refugee's story*. Honesdale, PA: Boyds Mills Press.

Sheidlower, J. (1998). *Jesse's word of the day*. New York: Random House.

Shlasko, R. (2011). *Molly and the sword*. New York, NY: Jane & Street Publishers. (P-M)

Shoveller, H. (2006). *Ryan and Jimmy and the well in Africa that brought them together*. Toronto: Kids Can Press.

Sidman, J. (2005). *Song of the water boatman and other pond poems*. Boston: Houghton Mifflin.

Siegel, S. (2006). *To dance: A ballerina's graphic novel*. New York, NY: Simon and Schuster. (M-U)

Sierra, J. (2000). *The gift of the crocodile: A Cinderella story*. New York: Simon and Schuster Books for Young Readers.

Sierra, J. (2006). *Thelonius Monster's sky high fly pie*. New York: Random House.

Silsbe, B. (2001). *A tree is just a tree?* Vancouver: Raincoast.

Silverstein, S. (1974). *Where the sidewalk ends*. New York: Harper & Row.

Silverstein, S. (1981). *A light in the attic*. New York: Harper & Row.

Silverstein, S. (2005). *Runny babbit: A billy sook*. New York: HarperCollins.

Simmie, L. (1986). *An armadillo is not a pillow*. Saskatoon: Western Producer Prairie Books.

Singer, M. (1995). *A wasp is not a bee*. New York: Holt.

Singer, M. (2002). *Footprints on the roof: Poems about the earth*. New York, NY: Knopf.

Singer, M. (2010). *Mirror, mirror*. Boston, MA: Dutton.

Singer, M. (2012). *A stick is an excellent thing: Poems celebrating outdoor play*. New York, NY: Clarion.

Sís, P. (1998). *Tibet: Through the red box*. New York: Farrar, Straus & Giroux.

Sisulu, E. (1996). *The day Gogo went to vote*. Boston: Little, Brown.

Skreslet, L., & MacLeod, E. (2001). *To the top of Everest*. Toronto: Kids Can Press.

Skuy, D. (2011). *Undergrounders*. Toronto: Scholastic Canada.

Skrypuch, M. F. (1996). *Silver threads*. Toronto: Viking.

Skrypuch, M. F. (2001). *Hope's war*. Toronto: Boardwalk Books.

Skrypuch, M. F. (2003). *Nobody's child*. Toronto: Dundurn Press.

Slade, A. (2001). *Dust*. Toronto: HarperCollins.

Slade, A. (2012). Island of doom (The Hunchback Assignments IV). New York: HarperCollins.

Slavin, B. (2007). *Transformed*. Toronto: Kids Can Press.

Smith, C. (2000). *Jingle dancer*. New York, NY: Morrow Junior Books.

Smith, D. (2014). *If: A mind-bending new way of looking at big ideas and numbers*. Toronto, ON: Kids Can Press.

Smith, D. J. (2011). *This child, every child: A book about the world's children*. Toronto: Kids Can Press.

Smith, J. (1995). *Out from Boneville* (Bone vol. 1). Columbus, OH: Cartoon Books.

Smith, L. (2011). *Grandpa Green*. New York: Roaring Brook Press.

Smith, P., & Shalev, Z. (2007). *A school like mine: A unique celebration of schools around the world*. London, UK: DK Publishing.

Smith, R. (2007). *Peak*. Orlando, FL: Harcourt Children's Books.

Smith, S. (2004). *Goldilocks and the three Martians*. New York: Dutton.

Smucker, B. (1977). Underground to Canada. New York: Irwin and Co. Ltd.

Smucker, B. (1995). *Selina and the bear paw quilt*. Illus. J. Wilson. Toronto: Lester Publishing.

Soule, J. (1964). *Never tease a weasel*. New York, NY: Dragonfly Books.

Souza, D. M. (1994). Northern lights. Minneapolis, MN: Carolrhoda.

Spalding, A. (2006). *Secret of the dance*. Victoria, BC: Orca. (P-M)

Spier, P. (1971). *Gobble growl grunt*. New York: Doubleday.

Spinelli, J. (2000). *Stargirl*. New York: Knopf.

Spires, A. (2011). *Small Saul*. Toronto: Kids Can Press.

Spring, D. (2005). *The righteous smuggler*. Toronto: Second Story Press.

Stanley, D. (1990). *The conversation club*. New York: Macmillan.

Staunton, T. (2012). *Morgan gets cracking*. Halifax, NS: Formac Publishing.

Steer, D. (2005). *Thank you, little mouse*. Toronto: Scholastic Canada.

Steig, W. (1969). *Sylvester and the magic pebble*. New York: Simon & Schuster.

Steltzer, U. (1995). *Building an igloo*. New York: Holt.

Stemp, H. (2013). *Amelia and me*. St. John's, NL: Flanker Press.

Stenhouse, T. (2001). *Across the steel river*. Toronto: Kids Can Press.

Steptoe, J. (1987). *Mufaro's beautiful daughters: An African tale*. New York: Lothrop, Lee & Shepard.

Steptoe, J. (1989). *The story of Jumping Mouse*. New York: HarperCollins.

Stevenson, R. L. (1985). *Happy thought: Poems for children*. Illus. V. Gad. Toronto: Midway Publications.

Steward, S. (2003). *Raven quest*. Toronto: Scholastic.

Stinson, K. (1982). *Red is best*. Toronto: Annick Press.

Stinson, K. (2007). *Mom and Dad don't live together anymore*. Toronto: Annick Press.

Stinson, K. (2009). *Love every leaf: The life of landscape architect Cornelia Hahn Oberlander*. Toronto: Tundra Books.

Stinson, K. (2010). *Highway of heroes*. Markham, ON: Fitzhenry & Whiteside.

Stinson, K. (2013). *The man with the violin*. Toronto, ON: Annick Press. (P-M)

Stoll, E. (2000). *Mouse paint*. New York, NY: Harcourt. (P)

Stone, T., Winters, K., & Sherritt-Fleming, L. (2009). *aRTHYTHMetic*. Toronto: Gumboot Books.

Stratton, A. (2008). *Leslie's journal* (Rev. ed.). Toronto: Annick Press.

Student's Oxford Canadian dictionary (2nd ed.). (2007). Toronto: Oxford University Press.

Swanson, D. (2001). *Burp! The most intersting book you'll ever read about eating*. Toronto: Kids Can Press.

Swanson, D. (2007). *Bugs up Close*. Toronto: Kids Can Press.

Szpirglas, J. (2005). *They did what?! Your guide to weird & wacky things people do*. Vancouver: Maple Tree Press.

Tambert, U. (2012). *The darkest corner of the world*. Toronto: Dancing Cat Books.

Tanaka, S. (1996). *I was there: On board the* Titanic. Toronto: Scholastic.

Tanaka, S. (1999). *Secrets of the mummies: Uncovering the bodies of ancient Egyptians*. Richmond Hill, ON: Scholastic Canada.

Tanaka, S. (2000). *The buried city of Pompeii: What it was like when Vesuvius exploded*. New York: Hyperion Press.

Tanaka, S. (2006). *Wings*. New York: Purple Bear Books.

Tanaka, S. (2008). *Amelia Earhart: The legend of the lost aviator*. New York: Madison Press/Abrams Books for Young Readers.

Tanaka, S. (2012). *Climate change* (Rev. ed.). Toronto: Groundwood Books.

Tankard, J. (2007). *Grumpy bird*. Toronto: Scholastic Canada.

Taylor, C. (1994). *Summer of the mad monk*. Vancouver: Greystone Books.

Taylor, C. (1997). Vanishing act. Red Deer, AB: Red Deer College Press.

Taylor, C. (2002). *Buffalo hunt*. Toronto: Penguin Books.

Taylor, C. (2005). *Angelique, book two: The long way home*. Toronto: Penguin Canada.

Taylor, C. J. (1994). *Bones in the basket*. Montreal: Tundra Books.

Taylor, C. J. (2004). *Peace walker: The legend of Hiawatha and Tekanawita*. Toronto: Tundra Books.

Taylor, H. *When Bear stole the chinook: A Siksika tale*. New York: Farrar Straus and Giroux.

Taylor, J. Making room. Toronto: Tundra Books.

Taylor, M. D. (1976). *Roll of thunder, hear my cry*. New York: Dial.

Teague, M. (2002). *Dear Mrs. Larue: Letters from obedience school*. Toronto: Scholastic.

Teague, M. (2008). *LaRue for mayor: Letters from the campaign trail*. New York: Blue Sky Press.

Telgemeier, R. (2012). *Smile*. Toronto: Graphix/Scholastic Canada.

Tennyson, A., & Côté, G. (2005). The lady of Shallot. Toronto: Kids Can Press.

Terban, M. (1984). *I think I thought and other tricky verbs*. New York: Clarion.

Terban, M. (1986). *Your foot's on my feet! And other tricky nouns*. New York: Clarion.

Terban, M. (1988). *Guppies in tuxedos: Funny eponyms*. New York: Clarion.

Terban, M. (1989). *Superdupers! Really funny real words*. New York: Clarion.

Terban, M. (1990). *Punching the clock: Funny action idioms*. New York: Clarion Books.

Terban, M. (1992). *Funny you should ask: How to make up jokes and riddles with wordplay*. New York: Clarion.

Terban, M. (1993). *It figures! Fun figures of speech*. New York: Clarion.

Terban, M. (2007). *In a pickle and other funny idioms*. New York: Sandpiper.

Thayer, E. (2006). *Casey at the bat*. Toronto: Kids Can Press. Originally published 1888.

Thien, M. (2001). *The Chinese violin*. Vancouver, BC: Whitecap Books. (P)

Thisdale, F. (2011). Nini. Toronto: Tundra Books.

Thomas, L. (2008). *Ha, ha! Ha! And much more: The ultimate round-up of jokes, riddles, facts, and puzzles*. Toronto: Maple Tree Press.

Thomas, P. (2007). *Nature's paintbox*. Minneapolis, MN: Millbrook Press. (M-U)

Thompson, L. (2015). *Emmanuel's dream: The true story of Emmuel Ofosu Yeboah*. New York, NY: Schwartz & Wade.

Thornhill, J. (2006). *I found a dead bird: The kids' guide to the cycle of life & death*. Toronto: Maple Tree Press.

Tolhurst, M. (1990). *Somebody and the three Blairs*. New York: Orchard Books.

Tolowa, M. (1995). The orphan boy. Don Mills, ON: Stoddart.

Toten, T. (2001). The game. Calgary: Red Deer Press.

Toten, T. (2006). *Me and the blondes*. Toronto: Penguin.

Tougas, C. (2008). *Art supplies*. Victoria, BC: Orca. (M)

Tresselt, A. (1964). *The mitten*. New York: Lothrop, Lee & Shepard.

Trottier, M. (2006). *Three songs for courage*. Toronto: Tundra Books.

Trottier, M. (2011). Migrant. Toronto: Groundwood Books.

Tullet, H. (2014). *Mix it up*. Toronto, ON: Chronicle Books. (P)

Tullson, D. (2005). *Red sea*. Victoria, BC: Orca Books.

Uchida, Y. (1993). *The bracelet*. New York: Philomel.

Uegaki, C. (2005). *Suki's kimono*. Toronto, ON: Kids Can Press.

Ulmer, M. (2006). *Loonies and toonies: A Canadian number book*. Chelsea, MI: Sleeping Bear Press.

Ulmer, M. (2007). *M is for maple*. Chelsea, MI: Sleeping Bear Press.

Uluadluak, D. (2013). *Kamik: An Inuit puppy story*. Iqualuit, Nunavut: Inhabit Media.

Underwood, D. (2010). *The quiet book*. Boston: Houghton Mifflin Books for Children.

Unobagha, U. (2000). *Off to the sweet shores of Africa*. San Francisco: Chronicle Books.

Vaage, C. (1995). *Bibi and the bull*. Red Deer, AB: Red Deer College Press.

Van Allsburg, C. (1981). *Jumanji*. Boston: Houghton Mifflin.

Van Allsburg, C. (1985). *The Polar Express*. Boston: Houghton Mifflin.

Van Allsburg, C. (1987). *The Z was zapped*. Boston: Houghton Mifflin.

Van Allsburg, C. (1993). *The sweetest fig*. Boston: Houghton Mifflin.

Van Allsburg, C. (1996). *The mysteries of Harris Burdick* (Portfolio ed.). Boston: Houghton Mifflin.

Van Allsburg, C. (2011). *Just a dream*. Boston: HMH Books for Young Readers. Originally published 1990.

Vande Griek, S. (2002). *The art room*. Toronto, ON: Douglas & McIntyre. (U)

Vande Griek, S. (2011). *Loon*. Toronto: Groundwood Books.

Vande Griek, S., & Milelli, P. (2002). *The art room*. Toronto: Groundwood Books.

Vernon, C. (2011). *Nowhere else on Earth: Standing tall for the Great Bear Rainforest*. Victoria, BC: Orca Books.

Villeneuve, A. (2013). *Loula is leaving for Africa*. Toronto, ON: Kids Can Press.

Viorst, J. (1972). *Alexander and the terrible, horrible, no good, very bad day*. New York: Atheneum.

Volponi, P. (2009). *Response*. Toronto: Viking.

Waboose, J. B., & Deines, B. (2000). *SkySisters*. Toronto: Kids Can Press.

Wakan, N. (1993). *Haiku—one breath poetry*. Vancouver: Pacific Rim Publishers.

Waldman, D. (2009). *Clever Rachel*. Victoria, BC: Orca Books.

Wallace, I. (2000). *Duncan's way*. Toronto: Douglas & McIntyre.

Walsh, A. (1994). *Shabash!* Victoria, BC: Beach Holme Publishers.

Walsh, A. (2001). *Heroes of Isle aux Morts*. Toronto: Tundra Books.

Walsh, E. S. (1993). *Hop jump*. New York: Harcourt Brace.

Walters, E. (1997). *Trapped in ice*. Toronto: Puffin Books.

Walters, E. (1998). *The war of the eagles*. Vancouver: Orca Books.

Walters, E. (2003). *Run*. Toronto: Viking.

Walters, E. (2006). *Stuffed*. Victoria, BC: Orca Books.

Walters, E. (2013). *My name is Blessing*. Toronto, ON: Tundra Books.

Walton, R. (2011). *Around the house the fox chased the mouse: Adventures in prepositions*. Layton, UT: Gibbs Smith.

Ward, D. (2008). *Archipelago*. Red Deer, AB: Red Deer Press.

Waters, K. (1989). *Sarah Morton's day: A day in the life of a pilgrim girl*. New York: Scholastic.

Waterton, B. (1978). A salmon for Simon. Vancouver: Douglas & McIntyre.

Watt, M. (2006). Scaredy squirrel. Toronto: Kids Can Press.

Watt, M. (2008). Chester. Toronto: Kids Can Press.

Watts, I. (2000). *Remember me*. Toronto: Tundra Books.

Watts, L. E. (2005). The baabaasheep quartet. Markham, ON: Fitzhenry & Whiteside.

Weale, D. (2004). *Three tall trees*. Charlottetown, PEI: Acorn Press.

Weir, R., & Routhier, A. (2003). *O Canada: Our national anthem*. Toronto: North Winds Press.

Weisner, D. (1990). *Hurricane*. New York: Clarion.

Weisner, D. (1991). *Tuesday*. New York: Clarion.

West, C. (1996). *"I don't care!" said the bear*. Cambridge, MA: Candlewick.

Whamond, D. (2012). *Oddrey*. Toronto: OwlKids Books.

Whelan, G. (1992). Bringing the farmhouse home. Riverside, NJ: Simon & Schuster.

White, E. B. (1980). *Charlotte's web*. New York: HarperCollins. Originally published 1952.

Whitman, W. (1988). *Voyages: Poems*. Ed. L. B. Hopkins; illus. C. Mikolaycak. San Diego, CA: Harcourt Brace Jovanovich.

Whitman, W. (1991). *I hear America singing*. Illus. R. Sabuda. New York: Philomel.

Wiebe, R. (1992). *Chinook Christmas*. Red Deer, AB: Red Deer College Press.

Wilder, L. I. (1953). *Little house on the prairie*. Illus. G. Williams. New York: Scholastic.

Willard, N. (1981). *A visit to William Blake's inn: Poems for innocent and experienced travelers*. New York: Harcourt Brace Jovanovich.

Willems, M. (2005). *Leonardo the terrible monster*. New York: Hyperion.

Willems, M. (2009). *Elephants cannot dance*. New York, NY: Hyperion. (P)

Williams, K. L., Mohammed, K., & Chayka, D. (2007). *Four feet, two sandals*. Grand Rapids, MI: Eerdmans Books for Young Readers.

Williams, S. (1989). *I went walking*. San Diego: Harcourt Brace Jovanovich.

Wilson, B. (2005). Izzie: Book two: Trongate fury. Toronto: Penguin Books.

Wilson, K. (2002). *Bear snores on*. New York: Simon & Schuster.

Wilson, K. (2003). *A frog in the bog*. New York: Margaret K. McElderry Books.

Wilson, K. (2011). *Bear feels scared*. New York: Little Simon.

Winstanley, N. (2011). *Cinnamon baby*. Toronto: Kids Can Press.

Winter, J. (2013). *Henri's scissors*. New York, NY: Beach Lane Books. (P)

Wise Brown, M. (1949). *The important book*. New York: Harper & Row.

Wolff, V. E. (1988). Probably still Nick Swansen. New York: Holt.

Wood, A. (2006). *Alphabet rescue*. New York, NY: Scholastic.

Woods, F. (2007). *The green book of poetry: An anthology of children's poetry about the environment*. Oswestry, UK: Schemes.

Wyn Klunder, B. (2007). *Other goose: Recycled rhymes for our fragile times*. Toronto: Groundwood Books.

Wynne-Jones, T. (1992). Zoom upstream. Toronto: Groundwood Books.

Wynne-Jones, T. (1995). *The maestro*. Toronto: Groundwood Books.

Wynne-Jones, T. (2000). The boy in the burning house. Toronto: Groundwood Books.

Wynne-Jones, T. (2003). *Ned Mouse breaks away*. Toronto: Groundwood.

Wynne-Jones, T. (2006). *Rex Zero and the end of the world*. Toronto: Groundwood Books.

Yamada, K. (2013). *What do you do with an idea?* Seattle, WA: Compendium, Inc.

Yarrow, P., & Lipton, L. (2007). *Puff the magic dragon*. New York, NY: Sterling. (P)

Ye, T.-X. (2002). *White lily*. Toronto: Doubleday Canada.

Ye, T.-X., & Bell, W. (2003). *Throwaway daughter*. Toronto: Doubleday Canada.

Yee, P. (1989). *Tales from Gold Mountain: Stories of the Chinese in the new world*. Toronto: Groundwood Books.

Yee, P. (1996a). Ghost train. Toronto: Groundwood Books.

Yee, P. (1996b). *Struggle and hope: The story of Chinese Canadians*. Toronto: Umbrella Press.

Yee, P. (2006). *What happened this summer*. Vancouver: Tradewind Books.

Yee, P. (2009). *Shu-Li and Diego*. Vancouver: Tradewind Books.

Yerxa, L. (1993). *Last leaf, first snowflake to fall*. Toronto, ON: Douglas & McIntyre.

Yerxa, L. (1993). Last leaf first snowflake to fall. Vancouver: Douglas & McIntyre.

Yolen, J. (1987). *Owl moon*. New York: Philomel.

Yolen, J. (1993). *Welcome to the green house*. New York: Putnam.

Yolen, J. (1995). *The three bears rhyme book*. New York: Harcourt.

Yolen, J. (1996). *Sacred places*. New York: Harcourt Brace.

Yolen, J. (2000). *Color me a rhyme: Nature poems for young people*. Honesdale, PA: Boyds Mills Press.

Yolen, J. (2006). *How do dinosaurs learn their colors?* New York: Blue Sky Press.

Young, A. (2006). *Belinda and the glass slipper*. New York, NY: Penguin Young Readers.

Young, B. (2012). *Charlie: A home child's life in Canada*. Vancouver: Ronsdale Press.

Young, C. (2011a). A few blocks. Toronto: Groundwood Books.

Young, C. (2011b). *Ten birds*. Toronto: Kids Can Press.

Young, E. (1997). *Mouse match: A Chinese folktale*. San Diego, CA: Silver Whistle.

Zeman, L. (1999). *Sinbad: From the tales of the thousand and one nights*. Montreal: Tundra Books.

Zelinsky, P. O. (1986). *Rumpelstiltskin*. New York: Dutton.

Zemach, M. (1983). *The little red hen*. New York: Farrar, Straus & Giroux.

Zoehfeld, K. W. (1995). How mountains are made. New York: HarperCollins.

Zoehfeld, K. W. (2010). *Where did dinosaurs come from?* New York, NY: Harper Collins.

Zweibel, A. (2005). *Our tree named Steve*. New York: G. P. Putnam's Sons.

Name Index

A

Adler, D. A., 47
Afflerbach, P., 35
Ahenakew, F., 48
Ahlberg, A., 278
Ahlberg, J., 278
Akeeagok, S., 152
Aker, D., 152
Alborough, J., 204
Ali, D., 252
Aliki, 45
Altwerger, B., 54
Alvermann, D., 16
Anderson, R. C., 70
Andrews, J., 61, 62, 213, 367
Anno, M., 45
Appelt, K., 198, 205
Applegate, K., 368
Archambault, J., 84
Atwell, N., 53, 56, 57, 164, 389, 391
Avalos, M., 86
Avi, 46
Awa, S., 152

B

Babbitt, N., 362
Bainbridge, J., 8, 48, 50
Baker, D., 106, 358
Ball, E., 74
Bannatyne-Cugnet, J., 212
Barber, K., 296, 298, 321
Barclay, J., 292
Bar-el, D., 154
Barone, D., 222
Barretta, G., 290
Bartel, M., 336
Base, G., 45
Bear, D. R., 154, 311, 312, 320
Beech, J., 316
Berthoff, A. E., 222
Bewell, D., 223
Bielaczyc, K., 33
Bishop, R. S., 106
Blachman, B., 74
Blachowicz, C., 154, 293
Black, S., 85
Blackburn, E., 214
Blair-Larsen, S., 179
Bogart, J. E., 29, 102, 252
Bondar, R., 142, 254
Booth, D., 47, 152, 212, 230, 232
Borich, G. D., 60
Bosak, S., 348
Bossley, M. M., 253
Bouchard, D., 212
Bourgeois, P., 269
Bowers, F., 239
Boynton, S., 45
Brailsford, A., 53
Brandis, M., 201
Brennan-Nelson, D., 290
Brenneman Eno, K., 210
Brett, J., 382
Briggs, R., 45
Bright, A., 152
Bright, R., 92
Brooker, M. F., 221
Brooks, M., 152
Browne, A., 205
Browning, R., 228–229
Bruce, B., 16
Bruner, J., 43
Bryan, G., 48
Bryan, L., 85
Buckingham, D., 19

Bunting, E., 212
Burdett, L., 303
Burke, C. L., 71
Burnett, F. H., 21
Butler, A., 177

C

Cabot, M., 198
Cairney, T., 212, 213, 214
Calderón, G., 52
Calkins, L. M., 56, 57, 160, 166, 167, 170
Campbell, N., 152
Carle, E., 45, 84, 146, 255, 308
Carney, M., 103
Carnine, D. W., 60
Carroll, L., 292
Casselman, B., 290
Chan, G., 195
Chandler-Olcott, K., 16
Chapman, V., 251
Chavez, C., 86
Cho, M., 252
Ciardi, J., 228, 241
Cintorino, M. A., 119, 120
Cipielewski, J., 106
Climo, S., 48
Clymer, T., 80
Coakley, C. G., 101
Cole, J., 47, 221, 251, 253
Cole, N., 179
Coles, J., 53
Coles, R., 29
Collins, A., 33
Collins, S., 152, 283
Collins, V., 222
Comber, B., 21, 70
Cooper, D., 222
Copeland, J. S., 230
Copeland, V. L., 230
Coren, M., 47
Cornett, C., 336, 361, 363, 364, 366, 370
Coulter, L., 261
Creech, S., 102, 153, 204
Cronin, D., 367
Crossingham, J., 158
Crystal, D., 306
Culham, R., 174, 175
Cullinan, B. E., 230
Cummer, D., 103
Curry, D., 359

D

Daniels, H., 56, 152
Davidge, B., 253
Davis, W., 224
Dayton-Sakari, M., 106
Deines, B., 22
dePaola, T., 51
Devers, W., 106
Dickinson, D. K., 69
Dickson, S., 222
Dillon, D., 370
Dillon, L., 370
Dobson, T., 18
Donaldson, J., 54
Donohue, L., 103
Dowd, O., 253
Downie, M. A., 47
Dudley-Marling, C., 64
Duffelmeyer, F., 19
Duke, N. K., 211
Dunning, S., 308
DuPrau, J., 283

E

Ebbitt-Cutler, M., 252
Eckes, M., 17
Edwards, G., 106
Eeds, M., 152
Egawa, K., 304
Eikhart, Shirley, 359
Ellis, Deborah, 21, 22, 23, 60, 135, 198, 384
Ellis, S., 145
Ernst, L. C., 204
Ewald, W., 2

F

Faltis, C. J., 17
Farrell, T., 122
Ferris, S., 121
Filopovic, Z., 254
Fine, 372
Fisher, P., 154, 293
Fitch, Sheree, 47, 49, 75, 173, 229, 230, 232, 245
Flatt, L., 253
Fleischman, P., 47, 230, 232
Fleming, D., 253
Fletcher, R., 245
Flores, B., 54
Foggo, C., 152
Fountas, I. C., 149, 186
Fox, M., 359
Fraser, I. S., 300
Freeman, D. E., 14
Freeman, Y. S., 14
Freire, P., 21
Frost, R., 342
Fullerton, A., 60

G

Gaiman, N., 203, 222
Galdone, P., 84, 204, 228
Gamoran, A., 119
Gavin, J., 204
Gentry, J. R., 311
George, D., 54, 152
Gertridge, A., 106
Gibbons, P., 17
Gill, S. R., 224
Gillet, J. W., 311
Gilman, P., 296
Gilmore, R., 49
Giorgis, C., 44
Giroir, S., 15
Glazer, J., 44
Goble, P., 51
Golden, J. M., 339
Goodall, J. S., 45
Goodall, Lian, 252
Goodman, K. S., 8, 77
Graham, J. B., 238
Grandits, J., 238
Granfield, L., 252
Grant, A., 49
Graves, D. H., 57, 95, 162, 167, 224
Gravett, E., 152, 278
Greenwood, B., 202, 348, 377
Gutiérrez, E., 361
Guy, S., 102
Gwinn, C., 18

H

Hagood, M. C., 19
Hall, A., 95
Hall, N., 336
Halliday, M. A. K., 8

Hamill, S., 239
Hamilton, J., 49
Hamilton, V., 45
Hammerberg, D., 267
Harper, P., 351
Harris, V. J., 50
Harrison, M., 47
Harrison, T., 324, 356, 361, 362
Harste, J. C., 71
Harter, P., 239
Hartman, A., 166
Hartman, D., 211
Hass, R., 239
Hayden, R., 96
Heard, G., 224
Heath, S. B., 4, 70, 118
Heck, M. J., 119
Heidbreder, R., 228
Held Williams, K., 179
Heller, R., 47, 296, 305
Henkes, K., 303, 304
Hesse, K., 213
Highway, Tomson, 22, 51
Hilden, K., 81
Hill, E., 44
Hillerich, R. L., 317
Hobbs, R., 342
Hodson, L. M., 300
Holloway, J., 12
Hopkins, L. B., 230, 232, 233
Horn, M., 18
Horne, C., 49
Horton, C., 49
Howe, D., 157, 158
Howe, J., 157, 158
Hughes, L., 229, 231
Hunt, L., 396
Hunt, L. C., 396
Hurst, B., 95
Hutchins, P., 45, 84
Hyde, N., 144, 204
Hyman, T. S., 204, 364

I

Invernizzi, M., 70, 154, 311, 312

J

Jackson, A. D., 324
Jacobs, J. E., 33, 48
Jacobson, D., 102
Janeczko, P. B., 238
Jang, B., 90
Jardine-Stoddart, H., 361
Jeffers, O., 29
Jenkins, Steve, 44, 252
Jepsen, M., 143
Jobe, R., 106
Joe, R., 51
Johnson, J., 18
Johnston, F., 154, 311, 312
Jones, H., 49
Jones, R., 106
Jordan-Fenton, Christy, 16, 50
Josephson, 372
Joyce, W., 339
Juel, C., 79
Julio, L., 370

K

Kacer, Kathy, 135
Kain, K., 370
Kalman, B., 49, 158
Kame'enui, E. J., 60, 222
Kapur, M., 33

Subject Index

Note: Entries for figures are indicated by "*f*."